Frommer's

Denmark

5th Edition

by Darwin Porter & Danforth Prince

Here's what the critics say about Frommer's:

"Amazingly easy to use. Very portable, very complete."
—*Booklist*

"Detailed, accurate, and easy-to-read information for all price ranges."
—*Glamour Magazine*

"Hotel information is close to encyclopedic."
—*Des Moines Sunday Register*

"Frommer's Guides have a way of giving you a real feel for a place."
—*Knight Ridder Newspapers*

Wiley Publishing, Inc.

Published by:

Wiley Publishing, Inc.

111 River St.
Hoboken, NJ 07030-5774

ISBN: 978-0-470-10058-5

Editor: Billy Fox
Production Editor: Ian Skinnari
Cartographer: Andrew Dolan
Photo Editor: Richard Fox
Anniversary Logo Design: Richard Pacifico
Production by Wiley Indianapolis Composition Services

Front cover photo: Copenhagen: Shadow of street lamp on building at Nyboder
Back cover photo: Copenhagen: Old Harbor scenic, boats moored in foreground

For information on our other products and services or to obtain technical support, please contact our Customer Care Department within the U.S. at 800/762-2974, outside the U.S. at 317/572-3993 or fax 317/572-4002.

Wiley also publishes its books in a variety of electronic formats. Some content that appears in print may not be available in electronic formats.

Manufactured in the United States of America

5   4   3   2   1

Contents

List of Maps

An Invitation to the Reader

In researching this book, we discovered many wonderful places—hotels, restaurants, shops, and more. We're sure you'll find others. Please tell us about them, so we can share the information with your fellow travelers in upcoming editions. If you were disappointed with a recommendation, we'd love to know that, too. Please write to:

Frommer's Denmark, 5th Edition
Wiley Publishing, Inc. • 111 River St. • Hoboken, NJ 07030-5774

An Additional Note

Please be advised that travel information is subject to change at any time—and this is especially true of prices. We therefore suggest that you write or call ahead for confirmation when making your travel plans. The authors, editors, and publisher cannot be held responsible for the experiences of readers while traveling. Your safety is important to us, however, so we encourage you to stay alert and be aware of your surroundings. Keep a close eye on cameras, purses, and wallets, all favorite targets of thieves and pickpockets.

About the Authors

As a team of veteran travel writers, **Darwin Porter** and **Danforth Prince** have produced numerous titles for Frommer's, including best-selling guides to Italy, France, the Caribbean, England, and Germany. Porter, a former bureau chief of *The Miami Herald*, is also a Hollywood biographer, his most recent releases entitled *Katharine the Great*, the latter a close-up of the private life of the late Katharine Hepburn, and *Howard Hughes: Hell's Angel*. Prince was formerly employed by the Paris bureau of the *New York Times*, and is today the president of Blood Moon Productions and other media-related firms.

Frommer's Star Ratings, Icons & Abbreviations

Every hotel, restaurant, and attraction listing in this guide has been ranked for quality, value, service, amenities, and special features using a **star-rating system.** In country, state, and regional guides, we also rate towns and regions to help you narrow down your choices and budget your time accordingly. Hotels and restaurants are rated on a scale of zero (recommended) to three stars (exceptional). Attractions, shopping, nightlife, towns, and regions are rated according to the following scale: zero stars (recommended), one star (highly recommended), two stars (very highly recommended), and three stars (must-see).

In addition to the star-rating system, we also use **seven feature icons** that point you to the great deals, in-the-know advice, and unique experiences that separate travelers from tourists. Throughout the book, look for:

Finds	Special finds—those places only insiders know about
Fun Fact	Fun facts—details that make travelers more informed and their trips more fun
Kids	Best bets for kids and advice for the whole family
Moments	Special moments—those experiences that memories are made of
Overrated	Places or experiences not worth your time or money
Tips	Insider tips—great ways to save time and money
Value	Great values—where to get the best deals

The following **abbreviations** are used for credit cards:

AE	American Express	DISC	Discover	V	Visa
DC	Diners Club	MC	MasterCard		

Frommers.com

Now that you have the guidebook to a great trip, visit our website at **www.frommers.com** for travel information on more than 3,000 destinations. With features updated regularly, we give you instant access to the most current trip-planning information available. At Frommers.com, you'll also find the best prices on airfares, accommodations, and car rentals—and you can even book travel online through our travel booking partners. At Frommers.com, you'll also find the following:

- Online updates to our most popular guidebooks
- Vacation sweepstakes and contest giveaways
- Newsletter highlighting the hottest travel trends
- Online travel message boards with featured travel discussions

What's New in Denmark

Many of the old towns and villages remain relatively the same year after year, but we've noted some updates and changes below. Of course, in cosmopolitan Copenhagen the pulse always beats faster, so there's lots to report. Here are some of the newest developments in various categories.

COPENHAGEN   Accommodations In the past year or so, Copenhagen has seen the opening of more hotels than in its entire history. Old "dragons" are being spruced up to meet the competition, hotels are opening in completely new buildings, and former hotels are being recycled into something better.

That virtual landmark, the Sophie Amalie, has shed its skin and emerged as the new **Front Hotel Copenhagen** (© 33-13-34-00), one of the finest addresses in the capital, the epitome of Danish modern with chic furnishings such as trendy black leather. See p. 68.

On the Esplanaden, near the Danish Resistance Museum, **Comfort Hotel Esplanaden** (© 33-48-10-00) is a new hotel in the moderately priced field. A building from the 1800s has been considerably upgraded, its interior gutted, and turned into this bastion of comfort with a functionally modern interior. See p. 69.

During the life of this edition, the staid old **Palace** (© 33-14-40-50) is being vastly restored and redesigned, beginning with the opening of the chic "The Night Wing." More changes are in the air, although this 1910 hotel will remain open during its conversion into a more exciting choice for the postmillennium. See p. 72.

Set within a very short walk of the Tivoli, **Hotel 27** (© 70-27-56-27) is in the middle of a wholesale transformation into something far more glamorous than it was under a different name. By the time that this edition appears, all the work should be complete, and the rooms will have a chic Danish modern design, often in blacks and reds. See p. 77.

After a major overhaul and many changes, the Park Hotel has become **Hotel Fox** (© 33-13-30-00). The owners hired 21 separate designers from all over Europe to strut their stuff—and so they did, turning the Fox into one of the most avant-garde of all Danish modern hotels in Copenhagen. Each room is a highly idiosyncratic work of art. See p. 77.

Opening in the summer of 2006, **Copenhagen Island Hotel** (© 33-38-96-00) rose up on the southern harbor. With its daringly avant-garde architecture, it lies in a rapidly developing section that is becoming one of the trendiest in Copenhagen. The bedrooms, for many visitors, evoke cabins in a cruise ship. See p. 82 for more information. In the same area, **Marriott Copenhagen** (© 88-33-99-00) is elegant, opening onto panoramic views of the harbor. The interior is a combination of traditional and hypermodern. See p. 83.

Not all the hotels are expensive, certainly not **Danhostel Copenhagen City** (© 33-11-85-85). Rising 16 floors over the southern harbor, unprecedented for a youth hostel in Europe, it's been called "The Mother of all Youth Hostels," housing more than 1,000 occupants at the same time. See p. 83.

Dining The new choice for visiting celebrities and others is **M.R. (Mads Reflund)** (✆ **33-91-09-49**), a posh and trendy enclave of modern continental cuisine. Creative, imaginative cooking goes into a series of fixed-price menus of three to seven courses, each based on market-fresh ingredients deftly handled by the kitchen staff. See p. 88 for more information. Also enjoying a love affair with the press is that bastion of Nordic cuisine, **NOMA** (✆ **32-96-32-97**). Many of its specialties are plucked from the chilling waters of the North Atlantic. Fish, the house specialty, is poached, grilled, pickled, smoked, or salted according to old Nordic traditions. See p. 88.

Another new restaurant very much in vogue is **Olsen** (✆ **33-14-64-00**), which showcases the finest of Danish cuisine but offers an array of finely honed Italian and French dishes as well. Trend-conscious locals and visitors enjoy the good times, the grand cuisine, and the chic atmosphere. See p. 88.

You'll find not just visiting Japanese businessmen but devotees of Japanese cuisine from around the world at **Umami** (✆ **33-38-75-00**), which has been installed in the former headquarters of a bank from the 19th century. A fashionable address for dining, Umami is permeated with an aura of Japanese minimalism, offering an imaginative cuisine and the town's best sushi. See p. 91.

Attractions Danish modern is showcased at the **Danish Design Center** (✆ **33-69-33-69**), which features "classic" modern designers of yesterday as well as emerging stars. The five-story center features contemporary exhibitions of design as well. See p. 127.

FREDENSBORG This town is the site of Fredensborg Slot, the castle where the royal family takes up residence in the summer. For years, it's been known for its family-style restaurant, Prinsessen. The site of that restaurant is still here, lying a short walk from the castle, but now it's **Da Oscar** (✆ **48-48-01-25**), serving the best Italian cuisine in the area, especially succulent pastas and freshly caught fish. See p. 171.

ROSKILDE In a move that made headlines around the world, the remains of the czarina, Maria Feodorovna, the mother of the last emperor of Russia, were removed from **Roskilde Cathedral** in 2006 and returned to St, Petersburg. She married Alexander and bore him six children, one of whom, Nicholas II, was executed at the time of the Russian revolution, The remains of her body were taken out of the Danish cathedral and returned to Russia, where she was reburied with her relatives. See p. 187.

ODENSE In the birthplace of Hans Christian Andersen, **Le Brasserie** (✆ **66-14-11-00**) is the hot new dining ticket. Its French menu today owes a culinary debt to Asia, a sort of fusion cuisine. Its bistro fare is based on market-fresh ingredients and features such specialties as a "duet" of Danish veal and French duck with anise-poached fennel. See p. 272.

SKAGEN On the North coast of Jutland, there is no more acclaimed place to stay or dine than the new **Ruth's Hotel** (✆ **98-44-11-24**), which lies among the sand dunes of this artists' colony and summer resort. The on-site spa is the best in Jutland, and the restaurant, Ruth's Gourmet, is acclaimed as one of the top five in the country outside Copenhagen. See p. 405.

The Best of Denmark

Denmark presents visitors with everything from a world-class city in Copenhagen to historic castles, wind-swept offshore islands, quaint villages, and more. To help you decide how best to spend your time in Denmark, we compiled a list of our favorite experiences and discoveries. In the following pages you'll find the kind of candid advice we'd give our close friends.

1 The Best Danish Experiences

- **A Day (and Night) at Tivoli Gardens:** These 150-year-old pleasure gardens are almost worth the trip to Copenhagen by themselves. They offer a little bit of everything: open-air dancing, restaurants, theaters, concert halls, an amusement park . . . and, oh yes, gardens. From the first bloom of spring until the autumn leaves start to fall (*note:* Tivoli's closed in the winter), they're devoted to lighthearted fun. The gardens are worth a visit any time but are especially pleasant at twilight when the lights begin to glint among the trees. See p. 112.

- **A Week Down on the Farm:** The best way to see the heart of Denmark and meet the Danes is to spend a week on one of their farms. Nearly 400 farms, all over the country, take in paying guests. Stick a pin anywhere on a map of Denmark away from the cities and seacoast, and you'll find a thatched and timbered farm, or perhaps a more modern homestead. Almost anyplace makes a good base from which to explore the rest of the country on day trips. You join the host family and other guests for

meals. You can learn about the farm, and help with the chores if you like. Activities range from bonfires and folk dancing to riding lessons or horse-and-buggy rides. Although there's no official agency to arrange such holidays, many visitors seeking this kind of accommodation surf the Internet for farms that advertise their willingness to receive guests. Another way to hook up is to decide what part of Denmark you'd like to visit, then contact the tourist office for a list of farms willing to accept paying guests.

- **On the Trail of the Vikings:** Renowned for centuries of fantastic exploits, the Vikings explored Greenland to the north, North America to the west, and the Caspian Sea to the south and east from roughly A.D. 750 to 1050. Their legacy lives on in Denmark. Relive the age of Vikings at the **Nationalmuseet** in Copenhagen, which displays burial grounds of the Viking period, along with the largest and richest hoards of treasure, including relics from the "Silver Age." Even Viking costumes are exhibited. See p. 124. At Roskilde, explore the **Viking Ship Museum,** containing five vessels found in a fjord nearby, the largest of which was built in Ireland around 1060 and manned by 60 to 100 warriors. See p. 191. If you're in Ribe, check out the **Museum of the Viking Age,** where a multimedia room, "Odin's Eye," introduces the visitor to the world of the Vikings through a vivid sound and vision experience. See p. 321. And, at Jelling, see two **enormous mounds** (the largest in Denmark), one of which was the burial ground of King Gorm. See "Jelling," in chapter 11.

- **In the Footsteps of H. C. Andersen:** To some visitors, this storyteller is the symbol of Denmark itself. The fairy tale lives on in Odense, on the island of Funen, where Andersen was born the son of a shoemaker in 1805. His childhood home, a small half-timbered house on Munkemøllestræde, where he lived from 1807 to 1817, has been turned into a museum. You can also visit **H. C. Andersen's Hus,** where much of his memorabilia is stored (including his walking stick and top hat), and take a few moments to listen to his tales on tape. But mostly you can wander the cobblestone streets that he knew, marveling at the life of this man—and his works—that, in the words of his obituary, struck "chords that reverberated in every human heart," as they still do today. See "Odense: Birthplace of Hans Christian Andersen," in chapter 9.

- **Cycling Around Ærø:** Regardless of how busy our schedule, we always like to devote at least one sunny day to what we view as the greatest cycling trip in Denmark: a slow, scenic ride around the island of Ærø, lying off the coast of Funen. Relatively flat, its countryside dotted with windmills, the island evokes the fields of Holland, but is unique unto itself. Country roads will take you across fertile fields and into villages of cobbled streets and half-timbered houses. This is small-town Denmark at its best. Yes, you'll even pass a whistling postman in red jacket and gold-and-black cap looking like an extra in one of those Technicolor MGM movies from the '40s. See p. 289.

2 The Best Hotels

- **Phoenix Copenhagen** (Copenhagen; ✆ **33-95-95-00;** www.phoenix copenhagen.com): The Danish Communist Party used to have its headquarters here, but the "Reds" of the Cold War era wouldn't recognize this pocket of posh today. It reeks of capitalistic excess and splendor, from its dazzling public rooms with French antiques to its rooms with Louis XVI styling. See p. 65.

- **Hotel d'Angleterre** (Copenhagen; ✆ **800/448-8355** in the U.S., or 33-12-00-95; www.remmen.dk): Some critics rate this as the finest hotel in Denmark. As it drifted toward mediocrity a few years back, a massive investment was made to save it. Now the hotel is better than ever—housing a swimming pool and a nightclub. Behind its Georgian facade, much of the ambience is in the traditional English mode. Service is perhaps the finest in Copenhagen. See p. 65.

- **Falsled Kro** (Falsled; ✆ **62-68-11-11;** www.falsledkro.dk): Not only is this Funen Island's finest accommodation, but it's the quintessential Danish inn, with origins going back to the 1400s. This Relais & Châteaux property is now a stellar inn with elegant furnishings as well as a top-quality restaurant, rivaling the best in Copenhagen. See p. 287.

- **Hotel Hesselet** (Nyborg; ✆ **65-31-30-29;** www.hesselet.dk): This stylish modern hotel on Funen Island occupies a woodland setting in a beech forest. The spacious rooms are artfully decorated, often with traditional furnishings. A library, Oriental carpets, and an open fireplace add graceful touches to the public areas. Many Copenhagen residents come here for a retreat, patronizing the hotel's gourmet restaurant at night. See p. 258.

- **Hotel Dagmar** (Ribe; ℭ 75-42-00-33; www.hoteldagmar.dk): Jutland's most glamorous hotel was converted from a private home in 1850, although the building itself dates back to 1581. This half-timbered hotel encapsulates the charm of the 16th century, with such adornments as carved chairs, sloping wooden floors, and stained-glass windows. Many bedrooms are furnished with antique canopy beds. A fine restaurant, serving both Danish and international dishes, completes the picture. See p. 323.

3 The Best Restaurants

- **Era Ora** (Copenhagen; ℭ 32-54-06-93): This is the best Italian restaurant in Denmark. This 20-year-old restaurant is the domain of two Tuscan-born partners who have delighted some of the most discerning palates in Copenhagen. Denmark's superb array of fresh seafood, among other produce, is given a decidedly Mediterranean twist at this citadel of refined cuisine. See p. 84.
- **Godt** (Copenhagen; ℭ 33-15-21-22): Even the Queen of Denmark dines at this superb restaurant, celebrated for its international cuisine. The best and freshest produce and various ingredients at the market are fashioned into the most pleasing and quintessential dishes. See p. 84.
- **The Paul** (Copenhagen; ℭ 33-75-07-75): Winning a coveted Michelin star, this is the best restaurant among the deluxe dining rooms of the Tivoli Gardens. Drawing gourmet diners with its carefully crafted international menu, it offers an inspired cuisine in these pleasure gardens. There is a daring and innovation here found in no other Tivoli restaurant. See p. 107.
- **Marie Louise** (Odense; ℭ 66-17-92-95): Glittering with crystal and silver, this dining room on a pedestrian street is one of the finest on the island of Funen. In an antique house, this Danish/Franco alliance offers a cuisine that's the epitome of taste, preparation, and service. Seafood and fish are the favored dishes. See p. 272.
- **Falsled Kro** (Falsled; ℭ 62-68-11-11): Even if you don't stay at the hotel, consider stopping for a meal. A favorite among well-heeled Europeans, this restaurant produces a stellar French-inspired cuisine and uses seasonal produce from its own gardens. The succulent salmon is smoked in one of the outbuildings, and the owners breed quail locally. Such care and attention to detail make this one of Denmark's top restaurants. See p. 287.

4 The Best Buys

- **Danish Design:** It's worth making a shopping trip to Denmark. The simple but elegant style that became fashionable in the 1950s has made a comeback. Danish modern chairs, glassware, and even buildings have returned. Collectors celebrate "old masters" such as Arne Jacobsen, Hans

Wegner, and Poul Kjærholm, whose designs from the 1940s and 1950s are sold in antiques stores. Wegner, noted for his sculptured teak chairs, for example, is now viewed as the grand old man of Danish design. Younger designers have followed in the old masters' footsteps, producing carefully crafted items for the home—everything from chairs, desks, and furnishings to table settings and silverware. For the best display of Danish design today, walk along the pedestrians-only Strøget, the major shopping street in Copenhagen. The best single showcase for modern Danish design may be **Illums Bolighus,** Amagertorv 10 (© **33-14-19-41**). See p. 146.

- **Crystal & Porcelain:** Holmegaard crystal and Royal Copenhagen porcelain are household names, known for their beauty and craftsmanship. These items cost less in Denmark than in the

United States, although signed art glass is costly everywhere. To avoid high prices, you can shop for seconds, which are discounted by 20% to 50% (sometimes the imperfection can be detected only by an expert). The best center for these collectors' items in Copenhagen is **Royal Copenhagen Porcelain,** Amagertorv 6 (© **33-13-71-81**).

- **Silver:** Danish designers have made a name for themselves in this field. Even with taxes and shipping charges, you can still save about 50% when purchasing silver in Denmark as compared with in the United States. If you're willing to consider "used" silver, you can get some remarkable discounts. The big name in international silver—and you can buy it at the source—is **Georg Jensen,** Amagertorv 6, Copenhagen (© **33-11-40-80**). See p. 147.

5 The Most Scenic Towns & Villages

- **Dragør:** At the doorstep of Copenhagen, this old seafaring town once flourished as a bustling herring port on the Baltic. Time, however, has passed it by, and for that we can be grateful, because it looks much as it used to, with half-timbered ocher and pink 18th-century cottages topped with thatch or red-tile roofs. The entire village is under the protection of the National Trust of Denmark. A 35-minute ride from the Danish capital will take you back 2 centuries. See "Side Trips from Copenhagen," in chapter 5.

- **Ærøskøbing:** This little village on the country's most charming island (Ærø) is storybook Denmark. A 13th-century market town, Ærøskøbing is a Lilliputian souvenir of the past, complete with gingerbread houses. You

expect Hansel and Gretel to arrive at any moment. See "Ærø," in chapter 9.

- **Odense:** The birthplace of Hans Christian Andersen is Denmark's third-largest city, and still has a medieval core. You can walk its cobblestone streets and admire its half-timbered houses. Other than its associations with the writer, Odense is a worthwhile destination in its own right, filled with attractions (including **St. Canute's Cathedral**). On the outskirts, you can explore the 1554 Renaissance castle, Egeskov, as well as a 10th-century Viking ship at Ladby. See "Odense: Birthplace of Hans Christian Andersen," in chapter 9.

- **Ribe:** On the Jutland peninsula (the European mainland), this is the best-preserved medieval town in Denmark, and is known for its narrow cobblestone lanes and crooked, half-timbered houses. An important trading center during the Viking era, today it's known as the town where the endangered stork—the subject of European myth and legend—nests every April. The National Trust protects the medieval center. From April to mid-September a night watchman circles Ribe, spinning tales of the town's legendary days and singing traditional songs. See "Ribe" in chapter 10.

- **Ebeltoft:** On Jutland, this well-preserved town of half-timbered buildings is the capital of the Mols hill country. It's a town of sloping row houses, crooked streets, and local handicraft shops. The Town Hall looks as if it had been erected for kindergarten children; in Ebeltoft you can also visit the 1860 frigate *Jylland,* the oldest man-of-war in Denmark. See "Ebeltoft" in chapter 11.

6 The Best Active Vacations

- **Fishing:** For centuries, much of Denmark relied on the sea and whatever the country's fishermen could pull out of it for its diet. Since then, no *smørrebrød* (open-faced sandwich) buffet has been complete without a selection of shrimp, herring, and salmon. The preparations of plaice, cod, eel, perch, and trout are culinary art forms. The seas off Funen, especially within the Great Belt, have yielded countless tons of seafood, and that tradition has encouraged anglers and sports enthusiasts to test their luck in the rich waters of the Baltic. Many outfitters can introduce you to the mysteries of fresh- and saltwater fishing.

- **Biking:** A nation of bikers, Denmark has organized the roads to suit the national sport. A network of bike routes and paths is protected from heavy traffic, and much of the terrain is flat. Bicycling vacations are available as inclusive tours that cover bike rental, ferry tickets, and accommodations en route. Some deluxe tours transport your luggage from one hotel to the next. For more information, contact the **Danish Cycling Federation,** Rømersgade 7, DK-1362 Copenhagen (℃ **33-32-31-21;** www.dcf.dk).

- **Camping:** With about 550 officially sanctioned campgrounds, Denmark has one of the highest numbers, per capita, of campgrounds of any nation in the world, and living in a tent or a pop-up trailer in the great outdoors is something of a national obsession. There are plenty of campsites near the city limits of Copenhagen, and many more are located around the country in areas of scenic or historic interest, some near the sea. The official website and address of the **Danish Camping Federation** is www.campingraadet.dk. Either via their website, or by calling or writing them at Campingrådet, Mosedalsvej 15, DK-2500 Valby (℃ **39-27-88-44**), you can request that the staff send you information about the nation's campsites. Other sources of information about camping are available at www.visitdenmark.com (the official website of the Danish Tourist Board), or an equivalent site, www.dk-camp.dk, which lists more than 300 campsites that are privately owned. You can obtain a free *DK Camping Danmark* catalog at all DK-CAMPing grounds, tourist offices, and many service stations.

- **Golf:** There are about 130 golf courses scattered across the flat, sandy, and sometimes windy landscapes of Denmark, many of them landscaped around the sand dunes, ponds, forests, and rocky outcroppings for which the country is well-known. Most clubs welcome visitors, although in some cases you might be asked to present a membership card from your club at home. Local tourism offices are usually well versed in steering golfers to worthwhile courses, but for some insight into what's available, visit **www.golfonline.dk**.

7 The Best Castles & Palaces

- **Christiansborg Palace** (Copenhagen): The queen receives official guests here in the Royal Reception Chamber, where you must don slippers to protect the floors. The complex also holds the Parliament House and the Supreme Court. From 1441 until the fire of 1795, this was the official residence of Denmark's monarchy. You can tour the richly decorated rooms, including the Throne Room and banqueting hall. Below you can see the well-preserved ruins of the 1167 castle of Bishop Absalon, founder of Copenhagen. See p. 123.

- **Rosenborg Castle** (Copenhagen): Built by Christian IV in the 17th century, this red-brick Renaissance castle remained a royal residence until the early 19th century, when the building was converted into a museum. It still houses the crown jewels, and its collection of costumes and royal memorabilia is unequaled in Denmark. See p. 121.

- **Kronborg Slot** (Helsingør): Shakespeare never saw this castle, and Hamlet (if he existed at all) lived centuries before it was built. But Shakespeare did set his immortal play here. Intriguing secret passages fill its cannon-studded bastions, and it often serves as the backdrop for modern productions of *Hamlet*. The brooding statue of Holger Danske sleeps in the dungeon, but according to legend, this Viking chief will rise again to defend Denmark if the country is endangered. See p. 172.

- **Frederiksborg Castle** (Hillerød): Known as the Danish Versailles, this moated *slot* (castle) is the most elaborate in Scandinavia. It was built in the Dutch Renaissance style of red brick with a copper roof, and its oldest parts date from 1560. Much of the castle was constructed under the direction of the "master builder," Christian IV, from 1600 to 1620. Fire ravaged the castle in 1859, and the structure had to be completely restored. It is now a national history museum. See p. 164.

- **Egeskov Castle** (Kværndrup): On the island of Funen, this 1554 Renaissance "water castle" is set amid splendid gardens. The most romantic example of Denmark's fortified manors, the castle was built in the middle of a moat, surrounded by a park. The best-preserved Renaissance castle of its type in Europe, it has many attractions on its grounds, including airplane and vintage-automobile museums. See p. 266.

8 The Best Offbeat Experiences

- **Journeying Back to the 1960s:** If you're nostalgic for the counterculture of the 1960s, it lives on in Christiania, a Copenhagen community located at the corner of Prinsessegade and Badsmandsstræde on Christianshavn. Founded in 1972, this anarchists' commune occupies former army barracks; its current residents preach a gospel of drugs and peace. Christiania's residents have even organized their own government and passed laws, for example, to legalize drugs. They're not complete anarchists, however, since they venture into the city at least once a month to pick up their social welfare checks. Today you can wander about their community, which is complete with a theater, cafes, grocery stores, and even a local radio station. See chapter 5.

- **Exploring Erotica:** Denmark was the first country to "liberate" pornography, in 1968, and today there's a museum in Copenhagen devoted to the subject. In the **Erotica Museum** (at Købmagergade 24; © **33-12-03-11**), you can learn about the sex lives of such famous figures as Nietzsche, Freud, and even Duke Ellington. Founded by a photographer of nudes, the museum has exhibits ranging from the tame to the tempestuous—starting from Etruscan drawings and progressing to the further reaches of the erotic and sexual. See p. 125.

- **Calling on Artists & Craftspeople:** West Jutland has many open workshops where you can see craftspeople in action; you can meet the potter, the glass blower, the painter, the textile designer, and even the candlestick maker. Local tourist offices can tell you which studios are open to receive guests in such centers as Ærø, Tønder, and Ribe.

2

Planning Your Trip to Denmark

In the following pages, we've compiled all of the practical information you'll need to plan your trip in advance—airline information, what things cost, a calendar of events, and more.

1 The Regions in Brief

ZEALAND

Home to Denmark's capital, **Copenhagen,** the island of Zealand draws more visitors than any other region. The largest island in Denmark, Zealand is also the wealthiest and most densely populated. Other cities include **Roskilde,** about 30km (19 miles) west of Copenhagen, which is home to a landmark cathedral (burial place of many kings) and a collection of Viking vessels discovered in a fjord. In the medieval town of **Køge,** witches were burned in the Middle Ages. One of the most popular attractions on the island is **Helsingør** ("Elsinore" in English), about 40km (25 miles) north of Copenhagen, where visitors flock to see "Hamlet's castle." Off the southeast corner of the island lies the island of **Møn,** home to Møns Klint, an expanse of white cliffs that rises sharply out of the Baltic.

JUTLAND

The peninsula of Jutland links the mostly island nation of Denmark with Germany. It is the only part of Denmark on the European continent. Jutland has miles of coastline, with some of northern Europe's finest sandy beaches. Giant dunes and moors abound on the west coast, whereas the interior has rolling pastures and beech forests. Jutland's more interesting towns and villages include **Jelling,** heralded as

the birthplace of Denmark and the ancient seat of the Danish kings; here you can see an extensive collection of Viking artifacts excavated from ancient burial mounds. The Viking port of **Ribe** is the oldest town in Denmark. It's known throughout the world as the preferred nesting ground for numerous endangered storks. The resort of **Fanø,** with its giant dunes, heather-covered moors, and forests, is an excellent place to bird-watch or view Denmark's varied wildlife. The university city of **Århus** is Jutland's capital and second only to Copenhagen in size. **Aalborg,** founded by Vikings more than 1,000 years ago, is a thriving commercial center in northern Jutland. It lies close to Rebild National Park and the Rold Forest.

FUNEN

With an area of 2,980 sq. km (1,150 sq. miles), Funen is Denmark's second-largest island. Called the "garden of Denmark," Funen is known to the world as the birthplace of Hans Christian Andersen. Orchards, stately manors, and castles dot its rolling countryside. **Odense,** Andersen's birthplace, is a mecca for fairy-tale writers and fans from around the world. Nearby stands Egeskov Castle, resting on oak columns in the middle of a small lake. It's Europe's best-preserved Renaissance castle. Funen has a number of

Denmark

bustling ports, including **Nyborg** in the east and **Svendborg** at the southern end of the island. **Ærøskøbing** is a medieval market town that's a showplace of Scandinavian heritage.

BORNHOLM

In the Baltic Sea, southeast of Zealand and close to Sweden, lies the island of Bornholm. Prehistoric monuments and runic stones pepper the countryside, and numerous fishing villages dot the shoreline. On the northern coast, near **Hammerhus,** the Bornholm Animal and Nature Park is home to many native species as well as some that have been introduced from other parts of Scandinavia. Some of Europe's largest castle ruins dot this region of the island. The town of **Rønne** is the site of Denmark's oldest regional theater; it stages numerous concerts and shows year-round. The island of **Christiansø**, off the coast of Bornholm, was the site of Denmark's penal colony. Criminals sentenced to life imprisonment were deported to the island, where they spent their lives in slavery.

2 Visitor Information

VISITOR INFORMATION

TOURIST OFFICES In the **United States,** contact the **Scandinavian Tourist Board,** 655 Third Ave., 18th Floor, New York, NY 10017 (© 212/885-9700; www. goscandinavia.com), for maps, sightseeing information, ferry schedules, or whatever other travel information you need. You can also try the **Danish Tourist Board,** 655 Third Ave., 18th Floor, New York, NY 10017 (© 212/885-9700; www. visitdenmark.com).

In the **United Kingdom**, contact the **Danish Tourist Board,** 55 Sloane St., London SW1X 9SY (© 020/7259-5959).

WEBSITES To begin your exploration of Denmark, visit the **Scandinavian Tourist Board** (www.goscandinavia.com), the **Danish Tourist Board** (www.visit denmark.com), and **Wonderful Copenhagen** (www.woco.dk), all of which offer extensive links to other organizations, accommodations, attractions, and other information. Get information on Danish culture, tour suggestions, and events at **CultureNet Denmark** (www.kulturnet.dk).

3 Entry Requirements & Customs

ENTRY REQUIREMENTS

U.S., Canadian, U.K., Irish, Australian, and New Zealand citizens with a **valid passport** don't need a visa to enter Denmark if they don't expect to stay more than 90 days and don't expect to work there. If after entering Denmark you want to stay more than 90 days, you can apply for a permit for an extra 90 days at your home country's consulate, which as a rule is granted immediately. If your passport is lost or stolen, head to your consulate as soon as possible for a replacement.

CUSTOMS
WHAT YOU CAN BRING INTO DENMARK

Foreign visitors can bring along most items for personal use duty-free, including fishing tackle, a pair of skis, two tennis rackets, a baby carriage, two hand cameras with 10 rolls of film, and 400 cigarettes or a quantity of cigars or pipe tobacco not exceeding 500 grams (1.1 lb.). There are strict limits on importing alcoholic beverages. However, for alcohol bought tax-paid, limits are much more liberal than in other countries of the European Union.

WHAT YOU CAN TAKE HOME

Returning **U.S. citizens** who have been away for at least 48 hours are allowed to bring back, once every 30 days, $800 worth of merchandise duty-free. You'll be charged a flat-rate of duty on the next $1,000 worth of purchases. Any dollar amount beyond that is dutiable at whatever rates apply. On mailed gifts, the duty-free limit is $200. Be sure to have your receipts or purchases handy to expedite the declaration process.

With some exceptions, you cannot bring fresh fruits and vegetables into the United States. For specifics on what you can bring back, download the invaluable free pamphlet *Know Before You Go* online at **www.cbp.gov.** (Click on "Travel" and then click on "Know Before You Go.") Or contact the **U.S. Customs & Border Protection (CBP),** 1300 Pennsylvania Ave. NW, Washington, DC 20229 (© **877/ 287-8667**), and request the pamphlet.

For a clear summary of **Canadian** rules, write for the booklet *I Declare,* issued by the **Canada Border Services Agency** (© **800/461-9999** in Canada, or 204/ 983-3500; www.cbsa-asfc.gc.ca). Canada allows its citizens a C$750 exemption, and you're allowed to bring back duty-free one carton of cigarettes, 1 can of tobacco, 40 imperial ounces of liquor, and 50 cigars. In addition, you're allowed to mail gifts to Canada valued at less than C$60 a day, if they're unsolicited and don't contain alcohol or tobacco (write on the package UNSOLICITED GIFT, UNDER $60 VALUE). All valuables should be declared on the Y-38 form before departure from Canada, including serial numbers of valuables you own, such as foreign cameras. *Note:* The $750 exemption can be used only once a year and only after an absence of 7 days.

Citizens of the U.K. who are **returning from a European Union (EU) country** will go through a separate Customs Exit (called the "Blue Exit") for EU travelers. In essence, there is no limit on what you can bring back from an EU country, as long as the items are for personal use (this includes gifts), and you have already paid the necessary duty and tax. However, customs law sets out guidance levels. If you bring in more than these levels, you may be asked to prove that the goods are for your own use. Guidance levels on goods bought in the EU for your own use are 3,200 cigarettes, 200 cigars, 400 cigarillos, 3 kilograms of smoking tobacco, 10 liters of spirits, 90 liters of wine, 20 liters of fortified wine (such as port or sherry), and 110 liters of beer.

The duty-free allowance in **Australia** is A$900 or, for those under 18, A$450. Citizens can bring in 250 cigarettes or 250 grams of loose tobacco, and 2.25 liters of alcohol. If you're returning with valuables you already own, such as foreign-made cameras, you should file form B263. A helpful brochure available from Australian consulates or Customs offices is *Know Before You Go.* For more information, call the **Australian Customs Service** at © **1300/363-263,** or log on to www.customs.gov.au.

The duty-free allowance for **New Zealand** is NZ$700. Citizens over 17 can bring in 200 cigarettes, 50 cigars, or 250 grams of tobacco (or a mixture of all three if their combined weight doesn't exceed 250g), plus 4.5 liters of wine and beer, and 1.125 liters of liquor. New Zealand currency does not carry import or export restrictions. Fill out a certificate of export, listing the valuables you are taking out of the country; that way, you can bring them back without paying duty. Most questions are answered in a free pamphlet available at New Zealand consulates and Customs offices: *New Zealand Customs Guide for Travellers, Notice no. 4.* For more information, contact **New Zealand Customs Service,** The Customhouse, 17–21 Whitmore St., Box 2218, Wellington (© **0800/428-786** or 04/ 473-6099; www.customs.govt.nz).

4 Money

CURRENCY

Although Denmark is a member of the European Union, the Danes rejected the euro as their form of currency. They continue to use the **krone** (crown), which breaks down into 100 **øre**. The plural is **kroner**. The international monetary designation for the Danish kroner is "DKK." (The Swedish currency is the kronor, but note the different spelling.)

It's a good idea to exchange at least some money—just enough to cover airport incidentals and transportation to your hotel—before you leave home (though don't expect the exchange rate to be ideal), so you can avoid lines at airport ATMs. You can exchange money at your local American Express or Thomas Cook office or at your bank. American Express also dispenses traveler's checks and foreign currency via **www.americanexpress. com** or © **800/807-6233,** but they'll charge a $15 order fee and additional shipping costs. American Express cardholders should dial © **800/221-7282;** this number accepts collect calls, offers service in several foreign languages, and exempts Amex gold and platinum cardholders from the 1% fee.

ATMs

Plus, Cirrus, and other networks connecting automated-teller machines operate throughout Denmark. If your credit card has a PIN (personal identification number), you can probably use your card at Danish ATMs to withdraw money from your bank account and credit card. Always determine the frequency limits for withdrawals, and check to see if your PIN must be reprogrammed for use abroad. Discover cards are not accepted in Denmark.

For **Cirrus** locations abroad, call © **800/424-7787** or go to www.master card.com. For **PLUS** usage abroad, check www.visa.com or call © **800/843-7587.**

Also keep in mind that many banks impose a fee every time a card is used at a different bank's ATM, and that fee can be higher for international transactions (up to $5 or more). On top of this, the bank from which you withdraw cash may charge its own fee. For international withdrawal fees, ask your bank.

You can also get cash advances on your **credit card** at an ATM. Keep in mind that credit card companies try to protect themselves from theft by limiting the funds someone can withdraw outside their home country, so call your credit card company before you leave home. And keep in mind that you'll pay interest from the moment of your withdrawal, even if you pay your monthly bills on time.

CURRENCY EXCHANGE

Many hotels in Denmark will not accept a dollar- or pound-denominated personal check; those that do will certainly charge for making the conversion. In some cases, a hotel may accept countersigned traveler's checks or a credit or charge card.

If you're making a deposit on a hotel reservation that doesn't take credit cards, it's cheaper and easier to pay with a check drawn on a Norwegian bank. This can be arranged by a large commercial bank or by a specialist like **Ruesch International,** 700 11th St. NW, 4th Floor, Washington, DC 20001 (© **800/424-2923** or 202/ 408-1200; www.ruesch.com). It performs a wide variety of conversion-related tasks, usually for about $15 per transaction.

If you need a check payable in a Danish currency, call Ruesch's toll-free number, describe what you need, and write down the transaction number. Mail your dollar-denominated personal check (payable to Ruesch International) to the Washington, D.C., office. When it's received, the company will mail you a

The Danish Krone

For American Readers   At this writing, $1 = approximately 5.9 kroner. (Danish kroner are identified throughout this guidebook as DKK.) Stated differently, 1DKK = approximately 17¢. This was the rate of exchange used to calculate the dollar values given throughout this edition. Bear in mind that throughout the context of this book, dollar amounts less than $10 are rounded to the nearest nickel, and dollar amounts greater than $10 are rounded to the nearest dollar.

For British Readers   At this writing, £1 = approximately 11DKK, or, stated differently, 1DKK = approximately 9 pence. This was the rate of exchange used to calculate the pound values in the table below.

Regarding the Euro   At the time of this writing, one Danish kroner = .134€. Stated differently, 1€ = approximately 7.46DKK.

These rates can and probably will change during the lifetime of this edition. For updates on these currency conversions, check an up-to-date source at the time of your arrival in Denmark.

DKK	US$	UK£	Euro €	DKK	US$	UK£	Euro €
1	0.17	0.09	0.13	75	12.75	6.75	10.05
2	0.34	0.18	0.27	100	17.00	9.00	13.40
3	0.51	0.27	0.40	125	21.25	11.25	16.75
4	0.68	0.36	0.54	150	25.50	13.50	20.10
5	0.85	0.45	0.67	175	29.75	15.75	23.45
6	1.02	0.54	0.80	200	34.00	18.00	26.80
7	1.19	0.63	0.94	225	38.25	20.25	30.15
8	1.36	0.72	1.07	250	42.50	22.50	33.50
9	1.53	0.81	1.21	275	46.75	24.75	36.85
10	1.70	0.90	1.34	300	51.00	27.00	40.20
15	2.55	1.35	2.01	350	59.50	31.50	46.90
20	3.40	1.80	2.68	400	68.00	36.00	53.60
25	4.25	2.25	3.35	500	85.00	45.00	67.00
50	8.50	4.50	6.70	1,000	170.00	90.00	134.00

check denominated in the requested currency for the specified amount, minus the $3 charge. The company can also help you with wire transfers, as well as the conversion of VAT (value-added tax) refund checks. Information is mailed upon request.

In England, contact **Ruesch International Ltd.,** Lower Cookham Road, Maidenhead Berkshire SL6 8XY (© **0845/880-0400**).

TRAVELER'S CHECKS

Traveler's checks are something of an anachronism from the days before the ATM made cash accessible at any time. Traveler's checks used to be the only sound alternative to traveling with dangerously large amounts of cash. They were as reliable as currency but, unlike cash, could be replaced if lost or stolen.

These days, traveler's checks are less necessary because most cities have 24-hour

What Things Cost in Copenhagen	US$	UK£	DKK
Train from the airport to the city center	4.60	2.45	27.00
Subway from the Central Station to outlying suburbs	3.05	1.60	18.00
Double room at the Hotel d'Angleterre (very expensive)	417.00	221.00	2,452.00
Double room, with bathroom, at the Kong Arthur (moderate)	258.00	137.00	1,517.00
Double room, without private bathroom, at the Hotel Nebo (inexpensive)	117.00	62.00	688.00
Lunch for one at the Restaurant Els (moderate)	34.00	18.00	200.00
Lunch for one at Café Zeze (inexpensive)	26.00	14.00	153.00
Dinner for one, without wine, at Kommandanten (very expensive)	112.00	59.00	659.00
Dinner for one, without wine, at Copenhagen Corner (moderate)	44.00	23.00	259.00
Dinner for one, without wine, at Nyhavns Færgekro (inexpensive)	32.00	17.00	188.00
Pint of beer (draft Pilsner or lager)	8.50	4.50	50.00
Cup of coffee in a cafe or bar	4.70–6.50	2.50–3.40	28.00–38.00
Coca-Cola in a cafe or bar	5.10	2.70	30.00
Admission to the Tivoli Gardens	13.00	6.75	76.00
Movie ticket	11.00	5.85	65.00
Ticket to the Royal Theater	12.00–114.00	6.30–60.00	71.00–670.00

ATMs that allow you to withdraw small amounts of cash as needed. However, keep in mind that you will likely be charged an ATM withdrawal fee if the bank is not your own, so if you're withdrawing money every day, you might be better off with traveler's checks—provided that you don't mind showing identification every time you want to cash one.

You can get traveler's checks at almost any bank. **American Express** offers denominations of $20, $50, $100, $500, and (for cardholders only) $1,000. You'll pay a service charge ranging from 1% to 4%. You can also get American Express traveler's checks over the phone by calling ⓒ **800/221-7282;** Amex gold and platinum cardholders who use this number are exempt from the 1% fee.

Visa offers traveler's checks at banking locations nationwide. The service charge ranges between 1.5% and 2%; checks come in denominations of $20, $50, $100, $500, and $1,000. Call ⓒ **800/732-1322** for information. AAA members can obtain Visa checks for a fee of $9.95 (for checks up to $1,500) at most AAA offices or by calling ⓒ **866/339-3378. MasterCard** also offers traveler's checks. Call ⓒ **800/223-9920** for a location near you.

Foreign-currency traveler's checks are useful if you're traveling to one country, or to the Euro zone; they're accepted at locations such as bed-and-breakfasts where dollar checks may not be, and they minimize the amount of math you have to do at your destination. **American Express, Thomas Cook, Visa,** and **MasterCard** offer foreign-currency traveler's checks. You'll pay the rate of exchange at the time of your purchase (so it's a good idea to monitor the rate before you take the plunge), and most companies charge a transaction fee per order (and a shipping fee if you order online).

If you choose to carry traveler's checks, be sure to keep a record of their serial numbers separate from your checks in the event that they are stolen or lost. You'll get a refund faster if you know the numbers.

5 When to Go

CLIMATE

Denmark's climate is mild for a Scandinavian country—New England farmers experience harsher winters. Summer temperatures average between 61°F and 77°F (16°C–25°C). Winter temperatures seldom go below 30°F (–1°C), thanks to the warming waters of the Gulf Stream. From the weather perspective, mid-April to November is a good time to visit.

Denmark's Average Daytime Temperatures

	Jan	Feb	Mar	Apr	May	June	July	Aug	Sept	Oct	Nov	Dec
°F	32	32	35	44	53	60	64	63	57	49	42	37
°C	0	0	2	7	12	16	18	17	14	9	6	3

HOLIDAYS

Danish public holidays are New Year's Day, Maundy Thursday, Good Friday, Easter Sunday, Easter Monday, Labor Day (May 1), Common Prayers Day (fourth Fri after Easter), Ascension Day (mid-May), Whitsunday (late May), Whitmonday, Constitution Day (June 5), Christmas Day, and Boxing Day (December 26).

DENMARK CALENDAR OF EVENTS

Note: Exact dates below apply for 2007. Should you be using this guide in 2008, check with local tourist boards for exact dates.

May

Carnival in Copenhagen. A great citywide event. There's also a children's carnival. For information, call ✆ **35-38-85-04;** www.karneval.dk. Mid-May.

Ballet and Opera Festival ✮✮✮ (Copenhagen). Classical and modern dance and two operatic masterpieces are presented at the Old Stage of the Royal Theater in Copenhagen. For tickets, contact the Royal Theater, Box 2185, DK-1017 Copenhagen (✆ **33-69-69-69-33;** www.kgl-teater.dk). Mid-May to June.

Aalborg Carnival ✮. This is one of the country's great spring events. The streets fill with people in colorful costumes. Thousands take part in the celebration, which honors the victory of spring over winter. For information, call ✆ **98-13-72-11;** www.karneval aalborg.dk. Late May.

June

Viking Festival ✮✮✮ (Frederikssund, 8 miles southwest of Hillerød). For two weeks every summer, "bearded Vikings" present old Nordic sagas in an open-air setting. After each performance, a traditional Viking meal is served. Call ✆ **47-31-06-85** or visit www.vikingespil.dk for more information. Late June to early July.

Midsummer's Night (countrywide). This age-old event is celebrated throughout Denmark. It is the longest day of the year. Festivities throughout the nation begin at around 10pm with bonfires and celebrations along the myriad coasts. June 21.

July

Roskilde Festival ⋆. Europe's biggest rock festival has been going strong for 30 years, now bringing about 90,000 revelers each year to the central Zealand town. Besides major rock concerts, which often draw big names, scheduled activities include theater and film presentations. For more information, call ✆ **46-36-66-13;** www. roskilde-festival.dk. Early July.

Copenhagen Jazz Festival. International jazz musicians play in the streets, squares, and theaters. Pick up a copy of *Copenhagen This Week* to find the venues. For information, call ✆ **33-93-20-13;** www.jazzfestival.dk. Early July.

July 4th (Rebild). Rebild National Park, near Aalborg, is one of the few places outside the United States to honor American Independence Day. For more information, contact the Aalborg Tourist Bureau, Østerågade 8, DK-9000 Aalborg (✆ **99-30-60-90;** www.visitaalborg.com). July 4th.

Funen Festival. This annual musical extravaganza draws big, international headliners. The festival's music is often hard-core rock, but gentler, classical melodies are presented as well. It takes place in the city of Odense, on the island of Funen. For more information, call the Odense tourist bureau (✆ **66-12-75-20;** www.visitodense.com). Early July.

August

Fire Festival Regatta (Silkeborg). Denmark's oldest and biggest festival features nightly cruises on the lakes, with thousands of candles illuminating the shores. The fireworks display on the last night is the largest and most spectacular in northern Europe. Popular Danish artists provide entertainment at a large, fun fair. For more information, contact the Turistbureau, Godthåbsuej 4, DK-8600 Silkeborg (✆ **86-85-31-55;** www.ildregatta.dk). Mid-August.

Fall Ballet Festival ⋆⋆⋆ (Copenhagen). The internationally acclaimed Royal Danish Ballet returns home to perform at the Old Stage of the Royal Theater just before the tourist season ends. For tickets, contact the Royal Theater, Box 2185, DK-1017 Copenhagen (✆ **33-69-69-69;** www.kgl-teater.dk). Mid-August to September.

Århus Festival Week ⋆. A wide range of cultural activities—including opera, jazz, classical and folk music, ballet, and theater—is presented. It's the largest cultural festival in Scandinavia. Sporting activities and street parties abound as well. For more information, contact ✆ **89-40-91-85;** www.aarhusfestival. dk. Late August to early September.

6 The Active Vacation Planner

BEACHES

With some 8,000km (5,000 miles) of coastline, Denmark has many long strips of sandy beaches. In many cases, dunes protect the beaches from sea winds. Most of these beaches are relatively unspoiled, and the Danes like to keep them that way (any polluted beaches are clearly marked). Many Danes like to go nude at the beach. Nudist beaches aren't clearly identified; often you'll see bathers with and without clothing using the same beach. The best beach resorts are those on the north coast of Zealand and the southern tip of the island of Bornholm. Beaches on the east coast of Jutland are also good, often attracting Germans from the south. Funen also has a number of good beaches, especially in the south.

BIKING

A nation of bikers, the Danes have organized their roads to suit this national sport. Bikers can pedal along a network of biking routes and paths protected from heavy traffic. The Danish landscape is made for this type of vacation. Most tourist offices publish biking-tour suggestions for their own district; it's a great way to see the sights and get in shape at the same time. The **Dansk Cyklist Forbund** (Danish Cycling Federation), Rømersgade 5, DK-1362 Copenhagen (© 33-32-31-21; www.dcf.dk), publishes excellent guides covering the whole country. They can also provide information about a number of prepackaged biking vacations that are available.

FISHING

Since no place in Denmark is more than 56km (35 miles) from the sea, fishing is a major pastime. Denmark also has well-stocked rivers and lakes, including fjord waters around the Limfjord. Anglers between the ages of 18 and 67 must obtain a fishing permit from the Danish Directorate of Fisheries for 30DKK ($5.35/£2.70) for 1 day, 90DKK ($16/ £8.10) for 1 week; these are available at any post office. Jutland is known for its good trout fishing; salmon is also available, but it is found more readily in Norway. Anglers who fish from the beach can catch eel, mackerel, turbot, sea trout, plaice, and flounder. For more information about fishing in Denmark, contact **Sportsfiskerforbund,** Worsåesgade 1,

DK-7100 Vejle (© **75-82-06-99;** www. sportsfiskeren.dk).

GOLF

Denmark's undulating landscape is ideal for the construction of golf courses. Prospective golfers should bring with them a valid golf club membership card from home. For information on the best courses near where you're staying, contact local tourist offices.

HANG GLIDING & PARAGLIDING

Although Denmark is a relatively flat country, good possibilities for paragliding do exist. **The Danish Union of Windgliders** provides information about suitable locations. As a rule, the union has arranged with local landowners that a slope or some other suitable place may be used. Since equipment cannot be rented in Denmark, clients must bring their own. More information is available from **Dansk Drageflyver Union** (© **46-14-15-09;** www.danskdrageflyverunion.dk).

SAILING

Denmark has about 600 harbors, both large and small, including the island of Bornholm. Those who like to sail have many opportunities to do so, especially in the open waters of the Baltic or in the more sheltered waters of the South Funen Sea between Lolland/Falster and Zealand. The Limfjord in North Jutland is also ideal for sailing. Many sailing boats are available for rent, as are cruisers. For information, contact the tourist offices.

WALKING

About 20 pamphlets describing walks of short or long duration in Danish forests are printed in English and are available from local tourist offices.

7 Travel Insurance

Check your existing insurance policies and credit card coverage before you buy travel insurance. You may already be covered for lost luggage, cancelled tickets, or medical expenses.

The cost of travel insurance varies widely, depending on the cost and length of your trip, your age and health, and the type of trip you're taking, but expect to pay between 5% and 8% of the vacation itself.

You can get estimates from various providers through **InsureMyTrip.com.** Enter your trip cost and dates, your age, and other information, for prices from more than a dozen companies.

TRIP-CANCELLATION INSURANCE

Trip-cancellation insurance helps you get your money back if you have to back out of a trip, if you have to go home early, or if your travel supplier goes bankrupt. Allowed reasons for cancellation can range from sickness to natural disasters to the State Department declaring your destination unsafe for travel.

For more information, contact one of the following recommended insurers: **Access America** (© 866/807-3982; www.accessamerica.com); **Travel Guard International** (© 800/826-4919; www.travelguard.com); **Travel Insured International** (© 800/243-3174; www.travelinsured.com); and **Travelex Insurance Services** (© 888/457-4602; www.travelexinsurance.com).

MEDICAL INSURANCE
Excellent medical facilities are widely available in Denmark, and almost all doctors are fluent in English. Emergency medical treatment is free in Denmark for non-Danes, however, the patient will be charged for follow-up care. Tourists do no qualify for treatment under the Danish National Health Services, except in the case of an emergency as mentioned. If, however, the local medical facility determines that the emergency occurred as a result of a pre-existing medical condition, the visitor must be prepared to pay for all services received. As a safety net, you may want to buy travel medical insurance. If you require additional medical insurance, try **MEDEX Assistance** (© 410/453-6300; www.medexassist.com) or **Travel Assistance International** (© 800/821-2828; www.travelassistance.com; for general information on services, call the company's Worldwide Assistance Services, Inc., at © **800/777-8710;** www.worldwideassistance.com).

LOST-LUGGAGE INSURANCE
On domestic flights, checked baggage is covered up to $2,500 per ticketed passenger. On international flights (including U.S. portions of international trips), baggage coverage is limited to approximately $9.07 per pound, up to approximately $635 per checked bag. If you plan to check items more valuable than the standard liability, see if your valuables are covered by your homeowner's policy, or get baggage insurance as part of your comprehensive travel-insurance package. Don't buy insurance at the airport, as it's usually overpriced. Be sure to take any valuables or irreplaceable items with you

---

Tips Quick ID

Tie a colorful ribbon or piece of yarn around your luggage handle, or slap a distinctive sticker on the side of your bag. This makes it less likely that someone will mistakenly appropriate it. And if your luggage gets lost, it will be easier to find.

in your carry-on luggage, as many valuables (including books, money, and electronics) aren't covered by airline policies.

If your luggage is lost, immediately file a lost-luggage claim at the airport, detailing the luggage contents. For most airlines, you must report delayed, damaged, or lost baggage within 4 hours of arrival. The airlines are required to deliver luggage, once found, directly to your house or destination free of charge.

8 Health & Safety

STAYING HEALTHY

Denmark is viewed as a "safe" destination, although problems, of course, can and do occur anywhere. You don't need to get shots, most foodstuff is safe, and the water in cities and towns is potable. If you're concerned, order bottled water. It is easy to get a prescription filled in towns and cities, and nearly all places throughout Denmark contain hospitals with English-speaking doctors and well-trained medical staffs.

Denmark is part of the civilized world. In fact, it's one of the most advanced countries on the planet.

WHAT TO DO IF YOU GET SICK AWAY FROM HOME

Any foreign consulate can provide a list of area doctors who speak English. If you get sick, consider asking your hotel concierge to recommend a local doctor—even his or her own. You can also try the emergency room at a local hospital. Many hospitals also have walk-in clinics for emergency cases that are not life threatening; you may not get immediate attention, but you won't pay the high price of an emergency room visit. We list hospitals and emergency numbers under "Fast Facts," p. 41.

If you worry about getting sick away from home, consider purchasing **medical travel insurance** and carry your ID card in your purse or wallet. In most cases, your existing health plan will provide the coverage you need. See the section on insurance, above, for more information.

If you suffer from a chronic illness, consult your doctor before your departure.

For conditions like epilepsy, diabetes, or heart problems, wear a **MedicAlert identification tag** (© 888/633-4298; www.medicalert.org), which will immediately alert doctors to your condition and give them access to your records through MedicAlert's 24-hour hot line. In addition to the classic MedicAlert bracelet or emblem, you can now also purchase a MedicAlert E-HealthKEY, a flashdrive with all your medical information that attaches to your keychain. For more information, visit the MedicAlert website.

Pack **prescription medications** in your carry-on luggage, and carry prescription medications in their original containers. Also bring along copies of your prescriptions in case you lose or run out of your pills. Carry the generic name of prescription medicines, in case a local pharmacist is unfamiliar with the brand name.

And don't forget sunglasses and an extra pair of contact lenses or prescription glasses.

Contact the **International Association for Medical Assistance to Travellers (IAMAT)** (© 716/754-4883 or in Canada 416/652-0137; www.iamat.org) for tips on travel and health concerns in Scandinavia and lists of local, English-speaking doctors. The United States **Centers for Disease Control and Prevention** (© 800/311-3435; www.cdc.gov) provides up-to-date information on necessary vaccines and health hazards by region or country.

STAYING SAFE

Denmark has a relatively low crime rate with rare, but increasing, instances of

Healthy Travels to You

The following government websites offer up-to-date health-related travel advice:

- **Australia:** www.smartraveller.gov.au
- **Canada:** www.hc-sc.gc.ca/index_e.html
- **U.K.:** www.dh.gov.uk/PolicyAndGuidance/HealthAdviceForTravellers/fs/en
- **U.S.:** www.cdc.gov/travel

violent crime. Most crimes involve the theft of personal property from cars or residences or in public areas. Pickpockets and purse snatchers often work in pairs or groups, with one distracting the victim while another grabs valuables. Often they operate in or near the major rail stations in Copenhagen. Hotel breakfast rooms and lobbies attract professional, well-dressed thieves who blend in with guests and target purses and briefcases left unguarded by unsuspecting tourists and business travelers. Valuables should not be left unguarded in parked vehicles.

The loss or theft abroad of a U.S. passport should be reported immediately to the local police and the nearest U.S. Embassy or Consulate. If you are the victim of a crime while overseas, in addition to reporting to local police, contact the nearest U.S. Embassy or Consulate for assistance. The Embassy/Consulate staff can, for example, assist you in finding appropriate medical care and contacting family members or friends, and explain how funds can be transferred. Although the investigation and prosecution of the crime is solely the responsibility of local authorities, consular officers can help you to understand the local criminal justice process and to find an attorney if needed.

U.S. citizens may refer to the Department of State's pamphlet *A Safe Trip Abroad* for ways to promote a trouble-free journey. The pamphlet is available by mail from the **Superintendent of Documents, U.S. Government Printing Office,** Washington, DC 20402; via the Internet at www.gpoaccess.gov; or via the Bureau of Consular Affairs home page at http://travel.state.gov.

9 Specialized Travel Resources

TRAVELERS WITH DISABILITIES

Most disabilities shouldn't stop anyone from traveling. There are more options and resources out there than ever before.

In general, Denmark's trains, airlines, ferries, department stores, and malls are accessible. For information about wheelchair access, ferry and air travel, parking, and other matters, contact the **Danish Tourist Board** (see "Visitor Information," earlier in this chapter).

Useful information for people with disabilities is provided by *De Samvirkende Invalideorganisationer* (**Danish Disability Council,** abbreviated in Denmark as DSI), Bredgade 25, 1260 Copenhagen, Denmark (© **33-11-10-44;** www.dch.dk). Established in 1934, it organizes 29 smaller organizations, each involved with issues of concern to physically challenged people, into one coherent grouping that represents the estimated 300,000 persons with disabilities living in Denmark today.

Many travel agencies offer customized tours and itineraries for travelers with disabilities. **Flying Wheels Travel** (© **507/451-5005;** www.flyingwheelstravel.com) offers escorted tours and cruises that emphasize sports, and private tours in minivans with lifts. **Access-Able Travel**

Source (© 303/232-2979; www.access-able.com) offers extensive access information and advice for traveling around the world with disabilities. **Accessible Journeys** (© 800/846-4537 or 610/521-0339; www.disabilitytravel.com) caters specifically to slow walkers and wheelchair travelers and their families and friends.

Organizations that offer assistance to travelers with disabilities include **Moss-Rehab** (www.mossresourcenet.org), which provides a library of accessible-travel resources online; the **Society for Accessible Travel & Hospitality (SATH)** (© 212/447-7284; www.sath.org; annual membership fees: $45 adults, $30 seniors and students), which offers a wealth of travel resources for all types of disabilities and informed recommendations on destinations, access guides, travel agents, tour operators, vehicle rentals, and companion services; and the **American Foundation for the Blind (AFB)** (© 800/232-5463; www.afb.org), a referral resource for those who are blind or visually impaired that includes information on traveling with Seeing Eye dogs.

For more information specifically targeted to travelers with disabilities, the community website **iCan** (www.icanonline.net) has destination guides and several regular columns on accessible travel. Also check out the quarterly magazine *Emerging Horizons* (www.emerginghorizons.com) and *Open World* magazine, published by SATH.

FOR BRITISH TRAVELERS

The **Royal Association for Disability and Rehabilitation (RADAR),** Unit 12, City Forum, 250 City Rd., London EC1V 8AF (© 020/7250-3222; www.radar.org.uk), publishes three holiday "fact packs." The first provides general information, including tips for planning and booking a holiday, obtaining insurance, and handling finances; the second outlines transportation available when going abroad and equipment for rent; and the third deals with specialized accommodations. Another good resource is **Holiday Care Service,** 7th Floor, Sunley House, 4 Bedford Park, Croydon, Surrey CR0 2AP (© 0845/124-9971; www.holidaycare.org.uk), a national charity advising on accessible accommodations for the elderly and persons with disabilities.

GAY & LESBIAN TRAVELERS

In general, Denmark is one of the most gay-friendly countries in Europe and was one of the first to embrace same-sex marriages. Antidiscrimination laws have been in effect since 1987. Most Danes are exceptionally friendly and tolerant of lifestyles of either sexual preference. Obviously, an urban center such as Copenhagen will have a more openly gay life than rural areas. In many ways, the Erotic Museum in Copenhagen illustrates the city's attitudes toward sex—both heterosexual and homosexual. The history of both forms of sexual pleasure is presented in an unprejudiced manner.

The **Danish National Association for Gays and Lesbians** (Landsforeningen for Bøsser og Lesbiske, abbreviated as LBL) maintains its headquarters at Teglgaardstræde 13, 1007 Copenhagen (© 33-13-19-48; www.lbl.dk), with branches in at least four of the larger cities of Denmark. You might find it hard to reach a live person on their telephone line (their hours of operation are limited), but they maintain one of the most informative and user-friendly websites of any gay organization in Europe, complete with maps on how to reach the gay and lesbian venues they describe on their site.

The **International Gay and Lesbian Travel Association (IGLTA)** (© 800/448-8550 or 954/776-2626; www.iglta.org) is the trade association for the gay and lesbian travel industry, and offers an online directory of gay- and lesbian-friendly travel businesses; go to their website and click on "Members."

Many agencies offer tours and travel itineraries specifically for gay and lesbian travelers. **Above and Beyond Tours** (© 800/397-2681; www.abovebeyond tours.com) is the exclusive gay and lesbian tour operator for United Airlines. **Now, Voyager** (© 800/255-6951; www. nowvoyager.com) is a well-known San Francisco–based gay-owned and -operated travel service.

Olivia Cruises & Resorts (© 800/631-6277; www.olivia.com) charters entire resorts and ships for exclusive lesbian vacations and offers smaller group experiences for both gay and lesbian travelers.

The following travel guides are available at most travel bookstores and gay and lesbian bookstores, or you can order them online: *Frommer's Gay & Lesbian Europe,* an excellent travel resource, which offers a chapter on Copenhagen; *Spartacus International Gay Guide* (Bruno Gmünder Verlag; www.spartacus world.com/gayguide) and *Odysseus: The International Gay Travel Planner* (Odysseus Enterprises Ltd.), both good, annual English-language guidebooks focused on gay men; the **Damron** guides (www.damron.com), with separate, annual books for gay men and lesbians.

Gay.com Travel (© 800/929-2268 or 415/644-8044; www.gay.com/travel or www.outandabout.com), is an excellent online successor to the popular *Out & About* print magazine. It provides regularly updated information about gay-owned, gay-oriented, and gay-friendly lodging, dining, sightseeing, nightlife, and shopping establishments in every important destination worldwide. British travelers should click on the "Travel" link at **www.uk.gay.com** for advice and gay-friendly trip ideas.

The Canadian website **GayTraveler** (**gaytraveler.ca**) offers ideas and advice for gay travel all over the world.

SENIOR TRAVEL

Mention the fact that you're a senior citizen when you make your travel reservations. Although all of the major U.S. airlines except America West have cancelled their senior-discount and coupon-book programs, many hotels in Scandinavia still offer discounts for seniors. In most cities, people over the age of 60 may qualify for reduced admission to theaters, museums, and other attractions, as well as discounted fares on public transportation.

Members of **AARP** (formerly known as the American Association of Retired Persons), 601 E St. NW, Washington, DC 20049 (© **888/687-2277**; www.aarp. org), get discounts on hotels, airfares, and car rentals. AARP offers members a wide range of benefits, including *AARP: The Magazine* and a monthly newsletter. Anyone over 50 can join.

Many reliable agencies and organizations target the 50-plus market. **Elderhostel** (© 877/426-8056; www.elder hostel.org) arranges study programs for those 55 and over (and a spouse or companion of any age) in the U.S. and in more than 80 countries around the world. Most courses last 5 to 7 days in the U.S. (2–4 weeks abroad), and many include airfare, accommodations in university dormitories or modest inns, meals, and tuition. **ElderTreks** (© 800/741-7956; www.eldertreks.com) offers small-group tours to off-the-beaten-path or adventure-travel locations, restricted to travelers 50 and older.

INTRAV (© 800/456-8100; www. intrav.com) is a high-end tour operator that caters to the mature, discerning traveler, not specifically seniors, with trips around the world that include guided safaris, polar expeditions, private-jet adventures, and small-boat cruises down jungle rivers.

Recommended publications offering travel resources and discounts for seniors

Traveling with Minors

It's always wise to have plenty of documentation when traveling in today's world with children. For changing details on entry requirements for children traveling abroad, keep up-to-date by going to the U.S. State Department website: **http://travel.state.gov.** To prevent international child abduction, EU governments have initiated procedures at entry and exit points. These often (but not always) include requiring documentary evidence of relationship and permission for the child's travel from the parent or legal guardian not present. Having such documentation on hand, even if not required, facilitates entries and exits. All children must have their own passport. To obtain a passport, the child *must* be present—that is, in person—at the center issuing the passport. Both parents must be present as well. If not, then a notarized statement from the parents is required. Any questions parents or guardians might have can be answered by calling the **National Passport Information Center** at ✆ **877/487-2778** Monday to Friday 8am to 8pm Eastern Standard Time.

---

include the quarterly magazine *Travel 50 & Beyond* (www.travel50andbeyond.com); *Travel Unlimited: Uncommon Adventures for the Mature Traveler* (Avalon); *101 Tips for Mature Travelers,* available from Grand Circle Travel (✆ **800/221-2610** or 617/350-7500; www.gct.com); and *Unbelievably Good Deals and Great Adventures That You Absolutely Can't Get Unless You're Over 50* (McGraw-Hill), by Joann Rattner Heilman.

FAMILY TRAVEL

The family vacation is a rite of passage for many households, one that in a split second can devolve into a *National Lampoon* farce. But as any veteran family vacationer will assure you, a family trip can be among the most pleasurable and rewarding times of your life.

Most Danish hoteliers let children 12 and under stay in a room with their parents free; others do not. Sometimes this requires a little negotiation at the reception desk.

Danes like kids but don't offer a lot of special amenities for them. For example, a kiddies' menu in a restaurant is a rarity. You can, however, order a half portion, and most waiters will oblige.

At attractions—even if it isn't specifically posted—inquire if a kids' discount is available. European Community citizens under 18 are admitted free to all state-run museums.

To locate those accommodations, restaurants, and attractions that are particularly kid-friendly, refer to the "Kids" icon throughout this guide.

Recommended family travel Internet sites include **Family Travel Forum** (www.familytravelforum.com), a comprehensive site that offers customized trip planning; **Family Travel Network** (www.familytravelnetwork.com), an award-winning site that offers travel features, deals, and tips; **Traveling Internationally with Your Kids** (www.travelwithyourkids.com), a comprehensive site offering sound advice for long-distance and international travel with children; and **Family Travel Files** (www.thefamilytravelfiles.com), which offers an online magazine and a directory of off-the-beaten-path tours and tour operators for families.

STUDENT TRAVEL

If you're planning to travel outside the U.S., you'd be wise to arm yourself with an **International Student Identity Card (ISIC),** which offers substantial savings on rail passes, plane tickets, and entrance fees. It also provides you with basic health and life insurance and a 24-hour help line. The card is available for $22 from **STA Travel** (© **800/781-4040** in North America; www.sta.com), the biggest student travel agency in the world. If you're no longer a student but are still under 26, you can get an **International Youth Travel Card (IYTC)** for the same price from the same people, which entitles you to some discounts. **Travel CUTS** (© **800/667-2887** or 416/614-2887; www.travelcuts.com) offers similar services for both Canadians and U.S. residents. Irish students may prefer to turn to **USIT** (© **01/602-1600;** www.usitnow.ie), a specialist in student, youth, and independent travel.

SINGLE TRAVELERS

Single travelers are often hit with a "single supplement" to the base price of accommodations. To avoid it, you can agree to room with other single travelers on the trip, or you can find a compatible roommate before you go from one of the many roommate-locator agencies.

Travel Buddies Singles Travel Club (© **800/998-9099;** www.travelbuddies worldwide.com), based in Canada, runs intimate, single-friendly group trips and

will match you with a roommate free of charge. **TravelChums** (© **212/787-2621;** www.travelchums.com) is an Internet-only travel-companion matching service with elements of an online personals-type site, hosted by the respected New York–based Shaw Guides travel service. **The Single Gourmet Club** (www.singlegourmet.com/chapters.php) is an international social, dining, and travel club for singles of all ages, with club chapters in 21 cities in the U.S. and Canada. Annual membership fees vary from city to city.

Many reputable tour companies offer singles-only trips. **Singles Travel International** (© **877/765-6874;** www.singlestravelintl.com) offers singles-only trips to places like Scandinavia. **Backroads** (© **800/462-2848;** www.backroads.com) offers more than 160 active-travel trips to 30 destinations worldwide, including Denmark.

For more information, check out Eleanor Berman's latest edition of *Traveling Solo: Advice and Ideas for More Than 250 Great Vacations* (Globe Pequot), a guide with advice on traveling alone, whether on your own or on a group tour.

10 Planning Your Trip Online

SURFING FOR AIRFARES

The most popular online travel agencies are **Travelocity** (www.travelocity.com or www.travelocity.co.uk); **Expedia** (www.expedia.com, www.expedia.co.uk, or www.expedia.ca); and **Orbitz** (www.orbitz.com).

In addition, most airlines now offer online-only fares that even their phone agents know nothing about. For the websites of airlines that fly to and from your destination, go to "Getting There," p. 29.

Other helpful websites for booking airline tickets online include:

- www.biddingfortravel.com
- www.cheapflights.com

- www.hotwire.com
- www.kayak.com
- www.lastminutetravel.com
- www.opodo.co.uk
- www.priceline.com
- www.sidestep.com
- www.site59.com
- www.smartertravel.com

For much more about airfares and savvy air-travel tips and advice, pick up a copy of *Frommer's Fly Safe, Fly Smart* (Wiley Publishing, Inc.).

SURFING FOR HOTELS

In addition to **Travelocity, Expedia, Orbitz, Priceline,** and **Hotwire** (see

Frommers.com: The Complete Travel Resource

For an excellent travel-planning resource, we highly recommend **Frommers.com** (www.frommers.com), voted Best Travel Site by *PC Magazine*. We're a little biased, of course, but we guarantee that you'll find the travel tips, reviews, monthly vacation giveaways, bookstore, and online-booking capabilities thoroughly indispensable. Among the special features are our popular **Destinations** section, where you'll get expert travel tips, hotel and dining recommendations, and advice on the sights to see for more than 3,500 destinations around the globe; the **Frommers.com Newsletter,** with the latest deals, travel trends, and money-saving secrets; our **Community** area featuring **Message Boards,** where Frommer's readers post queries and share advice (sometimes even our authors show up to answer questions); and our **Photo Center,** where you can post and share vacation tips. When your research is done, the **Online Reservations System** (www.frommers.com/book_a_trip) takes you to Frommer's preferred online partners for booking your vacation at affordable prices.

above), the following websites will help you with booking hotel rooms online:

- www.hotels.com
- www.quickbook.com
- www.travelaxe.net
- www.travelweb.com
- www.tripadvisor.com

It's a good idea to **get a confirmation number** and **make a printout** of any online booking transaction.

SURFING FOR RENTAL CARS

For booking rental cars online, the best deals are usually found at rental-car company websites, although all the major online travel agencies also offer rental-car reservations services. Priceline and Hotwire work well for rental cars, too; the only "mystery" is which major rental company you get, and for most travelers the difference between Hertz, Avis, and Budget is negligible.

TRAVEL BLOGS AND TRAVELOGUES

To read a few blogs about Denmark, try these:

- www.travelblog.com
- www.travelblog.org
- www.worldhum.com
- www.writtenroad.com

11 The 21st-Century Traveler

INTERNET ACCESS AWAY FROM HOME

Travelers have any number of ways to check their e-mail and access the Internet on the road. Of course, using your own laptop—or even a PDA (personal digital assistant) or electronic organizer with a modem—gives you the most flexibility. But even if you don't have a computer, you can still access your e-mail and even your office computer from cybercafes.

WITHOUT YOUR OWN COMPUTER

It's hard nowadays to find a city that *doesn't* have a few cybercafes. Although there's no definitive directory for cybercafes—these are independent businesses, after all—

Online Traveler's Toolbox

Veteran travelers usually carry some essential items to make their trips easier. Following is a selection of handy online tools to bookmark and use.

- **Airplane Seating and Food.** Find out which seats to reserve and which to avoid (and more) on all major domestic airlines at www.seatguru.com. And check out the type of meal (with photos) you'll likely be served on airlines around the world at www.airlinemeals.com.
- **Foreign Languages for Travelers** (www.travlang.com). Learn basic terms in more than 70 languages and click on any underlined phrase to hear what it sounds like.
- **Intellicast** (www.intellicast.com) and **Weather.com** (www.weather.com). Get weather forecasts for all 50 states and for cities around the world.
- **Mapquest** (www.mapquest.com). This best of the mapping sites lets you choose a specific address or destination, and in seconds, it will return a map and detailed directions.
- **Subway Navigator** (www.subwaynavigator.com). Download subway maps and get savvy advice on using subway systems in dozens of major cities around the world.
- **Time and Date** (www.timeanddate.com). See what time (and day) it is anywhere in the world.
- **Universal Currency Converter** (www.xe.com/ucc). See what your dollar or pound is worth in more than 100 other countries.
- **Visa ATM Locator** (www.visa.com), for locations of PLUS ATMs worldwide, or **MasterCard ATM Locator** (www.mastercard.com), for locations of Cirrus ATMs worldwide.

three places to start looking are at **www.cybercaptive.com**, **netcafes.com**, and **www.cybercafe.com**.

Aside from formal cybercafes, most **youth hostels** nowadays have at least one computer with Internet access. And most **public libraries** across the world offer Internet access free or for a small charge. Avoid **hotel business centers,** unless you're willing to pay exorbitant rates.

Most major airports now have **Internet kiosks** scattered throughout their gates. These kiosks, which you'll also see in shopping malls, hotel lobbies, and tourist information offices around the world, give you basic Web access for a per-minute fee that's usually higher than cybercafe prices. The kiosks' clunkiness and high price means they should be avoided whenever possible.

WITH YOUR OWN COMPUTER

More and more hotels, cafes, and retailers are signing on as Wi-Fi (wireless fidelity) "hotspots." Mac owners have their own networking technology: Apple AirPort. **Boingo** (www.boingo.com) and **Wayport** (www.wayport.com) have set up networks in airports and high-class hotel lobbies. IPass providers (see below) also give you access to a few hundred wireless hotel lobby setups. To locate other hotspots that provide **free wireless networks** in cities around the world, go to **www.personaltelco.net/index.cgi/Wireless Communities**.

For dial-up access, most business-class hotels throughout the world offer dataports for laptop modems, and a few thousand hotels in the U.S. and Europe now offer free high-speed Internet access. In addition, major Internet service providers (ISPs) have **local access numbers** around the world, allowing you to go online by placing a local call. The **iPass** network also has dial-up numbers around the world. You'll have to sign up with an iPass provider, who will then tell you how to set up your computer for your destination(s). For a list of iPass providers, go to www.ipass.com and click on "Individuals Buy Now." One solid provider is **i2roam** (www.i2roam.com; © **866/811-6209** or 920/235-0475).

Wherever you go, bring a **connection kit** of the right power and phone adapters, a spare phone cord, and a spare Ethernet network cable—or find out whether your hotel supplies them to guests.

USING A CELLPHONE
OUTSIDE THE U.S.

The three letters that define much of the world's **wireless capabilities** are GSM (Global System for Mobiles), a big, seamless network that makes for easy cross-border cellphone use throughout Europe and dozens of other countries worldwide. In the U.S., T-Mobile, AT&T Wireless, and Cingular use this quasi-universal system; in Canada, Microcell and some Rogers customers are GSM, and all Europeans and most Australians use GSM.

If your cellphone is on a GSM system, and you have a world-capable multiband phone such as many (but not all) Sony Ericsson, Motorola, or Samsung models, you can make and receive calls across civilized areas on much of the globe. Just call your wireless operator and ask for "international roaming" to be activated on your account. Unfortunately, per-minute charges can be high—usually $1 to $1.50 in Western Europe.

While you can rent a phone from any number of overseas sites, including kiosks at airports and at car-rental agencies, we suggest renting the phone before you leave home. North Americans can rent one before leaving home from **InTouch USA** (© **800/872-7626;** www.intouch global.com) or **RoadPost** (© **888/290-1606** or 905/272-5665; www.roadpost. com). InTouch will also, for free, advise you on whether your existing phone will work overseas; simply call © **703/222-7161** between 9am and 4pm EST, or go to **http://intouchglobal.com/travel.htm**.

12 Getting There

BY PLANE

Flying in winter—Scandinavia's off season—is cheapest; summer is the most expensive. Spring and fall are in between. In any season, midweek fares (Mon–Thurs) are the lowest.

THE MAJOR AIRLINES
FROM NORTH AMERICA SAS (Scandinavian Airlines Systems; © **800/ 221-2350** in the U.S., or 0870/6072- 7727 in the U.K.; www.scandinavian.net) has more nonstop flights to Scandinavia from more North American cities than any other airline, and it has more flights to and from Denmark and within Scandinavia than any other airline in the world. From Seattle and Chicago, SAS offers nonstop flights to Copenhagen daily in midsummer and almost every day in winter; from Newark, New Jersey, there are

---

Baggage, Weight Allowance

Effective September 2006, SAS imposed a maximum weight allowance of 70 pounds per bag. If any piece of baggage exceeds this weight, it must be repacked or sent as cargo.

daily flights year-round to Copenhagen. SAS's agreement with United Airlines, the "Star Alliance," connects the gateway cities of Seattle, Chicago, New York, and Washington, D.C. to other U.S. cities (such as Dallas/Fort Worth, Denver, Houston, Los Angeles, Minneapolis/St. Paul, and San Francisco).

Nonstop flights to Copenhagen from the greater New York area take about 7½ hours; from Chicago, around 8½ hours; from Seattle, 9½ hours.

FROM THE U.K. British Airways (© **800/AIRWAYS,** or 0870/850-9850 in the U.K.; www.britishairways.com) offers convenient connections through Heathrow and Gatwick to Copenhagen. The price structure (and discounted prices on hotel packages) sometimes makes a stopover in Britain less expensive than you might have thought. **SAS** offers five daily nonstop flights to Copenhagen from Heathrow (1¾ hr.), two daily nonstops from Glasgow (2 hr.), and three daily nonstops from Manchester (2 hr., 20 min.). Other European airlines with connections through their home countries to Copenhagen include **Icelandair**

(© **800/223-5500** in the U.S., or 0870/787-4020 in the U.K.; www.icelandair.com); **KLM** (© **800/225-2525** in the U.S., or 0870/507-4074 in the U.K.; www.klm.com); and **Lufthansa** (© **800/645-3880** in the U.S., or 0870/8377-747 in the U.K.; www.lufthansa.com). Be aware, however, that unless you make all your flight arrangements in North America before you go, you might find some of these flights prohibitively expensive.

FLYING FOR LESS: TIPS FOR GETTING THE BEST AIRFARE

Passengers sharing the same airplane cabin rarely pay the same fare. Travelers who need to purchase tickets at the last minute, change their itinerary at a moment's notice, or fly one-way often get stuck paying the premium rate. Here are some ways to keep your airfare costs down:

- Passengers who can book their ticket **long in advance,** who can **stay over Saturday night,** or who **fly midweek** or **at less-trafficked hours** may pay a fraction of the full fare. If your schedule is flexible, say so, and ask if you

---

Tips Getting Through the Airport

- Arrive at the airport 1 hour before a domestic flight and 2 hours before an international flight; if you show up late, tell an airline employee and he or she will probably whisk you to the front of the line.
- Beat the ticket-counter lines by using airport electronic kiosks or even online check-in from your home computer, which allows you to print out boarding passes in advance. Curbside check-in is also a good way to avoid lines.
- Bring a current, government-issued photo ID such as a driver's license or passport. Children under 18 do not need government-issued photo IDs for flights within the U.S., but they do for international flights.
- Speed up security by removing your jacket and shoes before you're screened. In addition, remove metal objects such as big belt buckles. If you've got metallic body parts, a note from your doctor can prevent a long chat with the security screeners.
- Use a TSA-approved lock for your checked luggage. Look for Travel Sentry certified locks at luggage or travel shops and Brookstone stores (or online at www.brookstone.com).

Tips New Security Measures

Because of increased security measures, Transportation Security Administration has made changes to the prohibited items list. At press time, all liquids and gels—including shampoo, toothpaste, perfume, hair gel, suntan lotion, and all other items with similar consistency—**are prohibited** from carry-on baggage and the security checkpoint. Pack these items in your checked baggage. Carrying liquids of any sort to the screening checkpoint will cause you delays, and will most likely result in the item being confiscated.

With the ever-changing security measures, we recommend that you check the **Transportation Security Administration's** website, www.tsa.gov, as near to your departure date as possible to make sure that no other restrictions have been imposed.

---

can secure a cheaper fare by changing your flight plans.

- You can also save on airfares by keeping an eye out in local newspapers for **promotional specials** or **fare wars,** when airlines lower prices on their most popular routes. You rarely see fare wars offered for peak travel times, but if you can travel in the off months, you may snag a bargain.
- Search **the Internet** for cheap fares (see "Planning Your Trip Online").
- **Consolidators,** also known as bucket shops, are great sources for international tickets, although they usually can't beat the Internet on fares within North America. Start by looking in Sunday newspaper travel sections; U.S. travelers should focus on the *New York Times, Los Angeles Times,* and *Miami Herald.* For less-developed destinations, small travel agents who cater to immigrant communities in large cities often have the best deals. *Beware:* Bucket shop tickets are usually nonrefundable or rigged with stiff cancellation penalties, often as high as 50% to 75% of the ticket price, and some put you on charter airlines, which may leave at inconvenient times and experience delays.

Several reliable consolidators are worldwide and available on the Net.

STA Travel (© 800/781-4040; www.sta.com) is now the world's leader in student travel. **ELTExpress (Flights.com)** (© 800/872-8800; www.eltexpress.com) started in Europe and has excellent fares worldwide, but particularly to that continent. It also has "local" websites in 12 countries. **FlyCheap** (© 800/359-2427; www.1800flycheap.com) is owned by package-holiday megalith MyTravel. **Air Tickets Direct** (© 800/778-3447; www.airticketsdirect.com) is based in Montreal and leverages the currently weak Canadian dollar for low fares.

- Join **frequent-flier clubs.** Accrue enough miles, and you'll be rewarded with free flights and elite status. It's free, and you'll get the best choice of seats, faster response to phone inquiries, and prompter service if your luggage is stolen, if your flight is canceled or delayed, or if you want to change your seat. You don't need to fly to build frequent-flier miles—**frequent-flier credit cards** can provide thousands of miles for doing your everyday shopping.

BY CAR

You can easily drive to Denmark from Germany. Many people drive to Jutland from Hamburg, Bremerhaven, and Lübeck. A bridge links Jutland and the central island of Funen. In 1998 a bridge opened that goes across the Great Belt from Funen to the island of Zealand, site of the city of Copenhagen. The bridge lies near Nyborg, Denmark. Once in West Zealand, you'll still have to drive east across the island to Copenhagen.

Car-ferry service to Denmark from the United Kingdom generally leaves passengers at Esbjerg, where they must cross from Jutland to Copenhagen. From Germany, it's possible to take a car ferry from Travemünde, northeast of Lübeck, which will deposit you at Gedser, Denmark. From here, connect with the E55, an express highway north to Copenhagen.

BY TRAIN

If you're in Europe, it's easy to get to Denmark by train. Copenhagen is the main rail hub between Scandinavia and the rest of Europe. For example, the London–Copenhagen train—through Ostende, Belgium, or Hook, Holland—leaves four times daily and takes 22 hours. About 10 daily express trains run from Hamburg to Copenhagen (5½ hr.). There are also intercity trains on the Merkur route from Karlsruhe, Germany, to Cologne to Hamburg to Copenhagen. The Berlin-Ostbahnhof-Copenhagen train (8½ hr.) connects with Eastern European trains. Two daily express trains make this run.

Thousands of trains run from Britain to the Continent, and at least some of them go directly across or under the Channel, through France or Belgium and Germany into Denmark. For example, a train leaves London's Victoria Station daily at 9am and arrives in Copenhagen the next day at 8:25am. Another train leaves London's Victoria Station at 8:45pm and arrives in Copenhagen the next day at 8:20pm. Both go through Dover–Ostende, or with a connection at Brussels. Once you're in Copenhagen, you can make rail connections to Norway,

Finland, and Sweden. Because of the time and distances involved, many passengers rent a couchette (sleeping berth), which costs around £18 ($34) per person. Designed like padded benches stacked bunk-style, they're usually clustered six to a compartment.

If you plan to travel extensively on European and/or British railroads, it would be worthwhile for you to get a copy of the latest edition of the *Thomas Cook European Timetable of Railroads.* It's available online at www.thomascooktimetables.com.

RAIL PASSES FOR NORTH AMERICAN TRAVELERS

EURAILPASS If you plan to travel extensively in Europe, the **Eurailpass** might be a good bet. It's valid for first-class rail travel in 18 European countries. With one ticket, you travel whenever and wherever you please; more than 100,000 rail miles are at your disposal. The pass is sold only in North America.

The **Eurail Global Pass** allows you unlimited travel in 18 Eurail-affiliated countries. You can travel on any of the days within the validity period which is available for 15 days, 21 days, 1 month, 2 months, 3 months, and some other possibilities as well. Prices for first class adult travel are $635 for 15 days, $829 for 21 days, $1,025 for 1 month, $1,449 for 2 months, and $1,789 for 3 months. Children 4 to 11 pay half fare; those 3 and under travel for free.

A **Eurail Global Pass Saver,** also valid for first-class travel in 18 countries, offers a special deal for two or more people traveling together. This pass costs $539 for 15 days, $699 for 21 days, $869 for 1 month, $1,229 for 2 months, and $1,519 for 3 months.

A **Eurail Global Youth Pass** for those 12 to 25 allows second-class travel in 18 countries. This pass costs $415 for 15 days, $539 for 21 days, $669 for 1 month, $945 for 2 months, and $1,165 for 3 months.

SCANRAIL PASS If your visit to Europe will be primarily in Scandinavia, the Scanrail pass may be better and cheaper than the Eurailpass. This pass allows its owner a designated number of days of free rail travel within a larger time block. (Presumably, this allows for days devoted to sightseeing scattered among days of rail transfers between cities or sites of interest.) You can choose a total of any 5 days of unlimited rail travel during a 2-month period, 10 days of rail travel within a 2-month period, or 21 days of unlimited rail travel. The pass, which is valid on all lines of the state railways of Denmark, Finland, Norway, and Sweden, also offers discounts or free travel on some (but not all) of the region's ferry lines as well. The pass can be purchased only in North America. It's available from any office of **RailEurope** (© **800/848-7245** in the U.S., or 800/361-7245 in Canada) or **ScanAm World Tours,** 108 N. Main St., Cranbury, NJ 08512 (© **800/545-2204;** www.scandinaviantravel.com).

Depending on whether you choose first- or second-class rail transport, 5 days out of 2 months costs $149 to $298; 8 days out of 2 months costs $180 to $360, 10 days out of 2 months costs $200 to $400, and 21 consecutive days of unlimited travel costs $232 to $463. Seniors get an 11% discount, and students receive a 30% discount.

EURAIL DENMARK PASS For those who plan to travel only in Denmark, a series of cost-cutting passes are offered. The major one is the **Eurail Denmark Pass,** offering both first- and second-class unlimited travel on Denmark's national rail network. For travel any 3 or 7 days within a 1-month period, the 3-day pass costs $77 to $166 for adults (first and second class), or $39 to $58 for children ages 4 to 11. The 7-day pass goes for $116 to $181 for adults or $58 to $91 for children.

Two or more passengers traveling together can take advantage of the **Eurail**
Denmark Saverpass,** offering unlimited travel in first and second class. On this deal, you get 3 days of travel in 1 month for $64 to $103 for adults or $32 to $52 for children 4 to 11. For 7 days in 1 month, the cost ranges from $103 to $155 for adults or $52 to $78 for children.

A better deal for passengers under 26 is the **Eurail Denmark Youthpass,** costing $51 for 3 days in 1 month or $90 for 7 days.

RAIL PASSES FOR BRITISH TRAVELERS

If you plan to do a lot of exploring, you may prefer one of the three rail passes designed for unlimited train travel within a designated region during a predetermined number of days. These passes are sold in Britain and several other European countries.

An **InterRail Pass** is available to passengers of any nationality, with some restrictions—they must be under age 26 and able to prove residency in a European or North African country (Morocco, Algeria, and Tunisia) for at least 6 months before buying the pass. It allows unlimited travel through Europe, except Albania and the republics of the former Soviet Union. Prices are complicated and vary depending on the countries you want to include. For pricing purposes, Europe is divided into eight zones; the cost depends on the number of zones you include. For ages 25 and under, the most expensive option (3,135DKK/$556/£285) allows 1 month of unlimited travel in all eight zones and is known to the staff as a "global." The least expensive option (1,595DKK/$283/£145) allows 16 days of travel within only one zone.

Passengers age 26 and older can buy an **InterRail 26-Plus Pass.** The cost varies from 2,266DKK ($402/£206) for 16 days to 4,323DKK ($766/£393) for 1 month. Passengers must meet the same residency requirements that apply to the InterRail Pass.

By Package, the Easiest Way to Go

For travelers who feel more comfortable if everything is prearranged—hotels, transportation, sightseeing excursions, luggage handling, tips, taxes, and even meals—a package tour is the obvious choice, and it may even help save money. A reliable tour operator is **Scantours, Inc.**, 3439 Wade St., Los Angeles, CA 90006 (© **800/223-7226** or 310/636-4656; www.scantours.com).

For information on buying individual rail tickets or any of the just-mentioned passes, contact **National Rail Inquiries,** Victoria Station, London (© **08705/ 848-848**). Tickets and passes also are available at any of the larger railway stations as well as selected travel agencies throughout Britain and the rest of Europe.

BY SHIP & FERRY

It's easy to travel by water from several ports to Denmark. Liners carrying cars and passengers operate from England, Germany, Poland, Norway, and Sweden. Check with your travel agent about these cruises.

FROM BRITAIN DFDS Seaways (© **0870/252-0524**; www.dfdsseaways. com) runs vessels year-round between Harwich, England, and Esbjerg in West Jutland. The crossing takes 16 to 20 hours. The same line also sails from Newcastle upon Tyne to Esbjerg, but only in the summer, as part of a 22-hour passage. Overnight cabins and space for cars are available on both routes.

FROM NORWAY & SWEDEN Norwegian Coastal Voyage Inc. (© **800/ 323-7436** or 212/319-1300 in the U.S.; www.coastalvoyage.com) operates vessels from Oslo to Hirtshals in North Jutland.

Stena Line runs popular sea links from Oslo to Frederikshavn, North Jutland (11½ hr.), and from Gothenburg, Sweden, to Frederikshavn (3 hr.). For information, schedules, and fares, contact **Stena Line UK, Ltd.** (© **08705/70-70-70**; www.stenaline.co.uk). For 24-hour updates on sailing, call © **08705/755-755.**

13 Special-Interest Tours

BUS TOURS ScanAm World Tours (© **800/545-2204**; www.scanamtours. com) offers a tour through the "Heart of Fairy Tale Denmark." You can choose a 5-day, 4-night trip through Hans Christian Andersen country, including a visit to Odense (his birthplace) and an excursion to Legoland. Tours begin at $485 per person.

SELF-DRIVE TOURS Several companies offer self-drive tours, which usually include accommodations, rental cars, and customized itineraries. **Scantours Inc.** (© **800/545-2204**; www.scantours.net) features the 5-day "Taste of Danish Castles & Manor Houses" tour, which is available year-round. Prices begin at $1,395 per person. The company also sponsors a tour of Danish inns. The 4-day self-drive tour includes accommodations, breakfast, car rental, and an itinerary. Prices start at $435 per person.

BICYCLE TOURS An excellent way to explore the flat, rolling Danish countryside is on a bicycle. Numerous organizations (including Scantours Inc. and ScanAm Tours) sponsor bike tours through various regions of the country. You can choose one that covers the castles, beaches, and fjords of northern Denmark; the southern Funen islands; the beaches and marshland of western Jutland; or the lake country in eastern Jutland. **Blue Marble Travel** (℡ 215/923-3788; www.bluemarble.org) offers 7-day excursions to Hans Christian Andersen country and several small islands in the Baltic for $1,850 per person. **Dansk Cyklist Forbund,** Rømersgade 7, DK-1362 Copenhagen K (℡ 33-32-31-21; www.dcf.dk), can provide the latest information on cycling tours in Denmark.

ADVENTURE TRAVEL OPERATORS

In North America, a few companies offer adventure trips to Denmark. **Crossing Latitudes,** 420 W. Koch St., Bozeman, MT 59715 (℡ 800/572-8747 or fax 406/585-5356; www.crossinglatitudes.com), offers sea kayaking and backpacking expeditions throughout the region; and **Blue Marble Travel,** 211 South St., Philadelphia, PA 19147 (℡ 215/923-3788; www.bluemarble.org), features reasonably priced biking and hiking trips in Denmark and Norway.

IN THE U.K.

The oldest travel agency in Britain, **Cox & Kings,** Gordon House 10, Greencoat Place, London SW1P 1PH (℡ 020/7873-5000; www.coxandkings.co.uk), was established in 1758. Today the company specializes in unusual, if pricey, holidays. Its offerings in Scandinavia include cruises through the spectacular fjords and waterways, bus and rail tours through sites of historic and aesthetic interest, and visits to the region's best-known handicraft centers, Viking burial sites, and historic churches. The company's staff is noted for its focus on tours of ecological and environmental interest.

To cycle through the splendors of Scandinavia, you can join Britain's oldest and largest association of bicycle riders, the **Cyclists' Touring Club,** Cotterell House, 69 Meadrow, Godalming, Surrey GU7 3HS (℡ 0870/873-0060; www.ctc.org.uk). Founded in 1878, it charges £33

($59) a year for membership, which includes information, maps, a subscription to a newsletter packed with practical information and morale boosters, plus recommended cycling routes through virtually every country in Europe. The organization's information bank on scenic routes through Scandinavia is especially comprehensive. Membership can be arranged over the phone with a credit card (such as MasterCard, Visa, Access, or Barclaycard).

LEARNING VACATIONS

Danish Cultural Institute (Det Danske Kultur Institutu), Farvergade 27L, DK-1463 Copenhagen (℡ 33-13-54-48; fax 33-15-10-91; www.dankultur.dk), offers summer seminars in English, including a course in Danish culture. Credit programs are available, but many courses are geared toward professional groups from abroad. An especially interesting course for those with some knowledge of Danish is "Danmark, Danskerne, Dansk," which includes language instruction.

An international series of programs for persons over 50 who are interested in combining travel and learning is offered by **Interhostel,** developed by the University of New Hampshire. Each program lasts 2 weeks, is led by a university faculty or staff member, and is arranged in conjunction with a host college, university, or cultural institution. Participants may stay longer if they want. Interhostel offers programs consisting of cultural and intellectual activities, with field trips to museums and other centers of interest. For information, contact the University of New Hampshire, Division of Continuing Education, 6 Garrison Ave., Durham, NH 03824 (℡ 800/313-5327 or 603/862-2015; www.learn.unh.edu).

Another good source of information about courses in Denmark is the **American Institute for Foreign Study (AIFS),** River Plaza, 9 W. Broad St., Stamford,

Heritage—The Search for Roots

More than 12 million North Americans have Scandinavian roots, many in Denmark. To help you trace your ancestry, Danish consulates can furnish fact sheets. Many original Danish records are available on microfilm from **The Family History Library**, 35 N. West Temple, Salt Lake City, UT 84150 (© **801/240-2331**).

Established in 1992, the **Danish Immigrant Museum**, Elk Horn, Iowa (© **712/764-7001**; www.dkmuseum.org), is devoted to telling the story of migration to the United States.

In Denmark itself, the major archives concerning immigration are held at **Det Danske Udvandrerarkiv** (Danes' Worldwide Archives), Arkivstræde 1, P.O. Box 1731, DK-9100 Aalborg (© **99-31-42-20**; fax 98-10-22-48; www. emiarch.dk).

CT 06902 (© **866/906-2437**; www.aifs. org). This organization can set up transportation and arrange for summer courses, with bed and board included.

The largest organization dealing with higher education in Europe is the **Institute of International Education (IIE)**, 809 United Nations Plaza, New York, NY 10017 (© **212/883-8200**; www.iie.org). A few of its booklets are free, but for $47, plus $6 for postage, you can buy the more definitive *Vacation Study Abroad*. The Information Center in New York is open to the public Tuesday through Thursday from 11am to 4pm. The institute is closed on major holidays.

One well-recommended clearinghouse for academic programs throughout the world is the **National Registration Center for Study Abroad (NRCSA)**, 823 N. 2nd St., P.O. Box 1393, Milwaukee, WI 53203 (© **414/278-0631**; www.nrcsa. com). The organization maintains language study programs throughout Europe.

HOME STAYS

Friendship Force International (FFI), 34 Peachtree St. NW, Suite 900, Atlanta, GA 30303 (© **404/522-9490**; www. friendshipforce.org), is a nonprofit organization that encourages friendship among people worldwide. Dozens of branch offices throughout North America arrange visits, usually once a year. Because of group bookings, the airfare to the host country is usually less than the cost of individual tickets. Each participant spends 2 weeks in the host country, one as a guest in the home of a family and the second traveling in the host country.

Servas, 1125 16th St., Suite 201, Arcata, CA 95521 (© **707/825-1714**; www.usservas.org), is an international nonprofit, nongovernmental, interfaith network of travelers and hosts whose goal is to help promote world peace, goodwill, and understanding. (Its name means "to serve" in Esperanto.) Servas hosts offer travelers hospitality for 2 days. Travelers pay an $85 annual fee and a $25 deposit after filling out an application and being approved by an interviewer (interviewers are located across the United States). They then receive Servas directories listing the names and addresses of Servas hosts.

HOME EXCHANGES

One of the most exciting breakthroughs in modern tourism is the home exchange. Sometimes the family automobile is included. Of course, you must be comfortable with the idea of having strangers in your home, and you must be content to spend your vacation in one place.

Home exchanges cut costs. You don't pay hotel bills, and you can also save money by shopping in markets and eating in. One potential problem, though, is that you may not get a home in the area you request.

Intervac, U.S., 30 Corte San Fernando, Tiburon, CA 94920 (© **800/756-4663;** www.intervacus.com), is part of the largest worldwide exchange network. It publishes four catalogs a year, containing more than 10,000 homes in more than 52 countries. Members contact each other directly. The cost is $86 plus postage, which includes the purchase of three of the company's catalogs (which will be mailed to you), plus the inclusion of your own listing in whichever one of the three catalogs you select.

The Invented City, 41 Sutter St., Suite 1090, San Francisco, CA 94104 (© **415/846-7588;** www.invented-city.com), publishes home-exchange listings three times a year. For the $50 membership fee, you can list your home with your own written descriptive summary.

HomeLink (© **800/638-3841;** www.homelink.org) will send you five directories a year—in one of which you're listed—for $80.

14 Getting Around Denmark

BY PLANE
The best way to get around Denmark is by private car on the excellent road network. In lieu of that, nearly all major towns, and certainly most Danish cities, are serviced by trains, except certain offshore islands, which can be reached only by ferryboat. If you're traveling extensively in Europe, special European passes are also available.

SAS'S VISIT SCANDINAVIA FARE
The vast distances of greater Scandinavia encourage air travel between various far-flung points. One of the most worthwhile promotions is SAS's **Visit Scandinavia Pass.** Available only to travelers who fly SAS across the Atlantic, it includes up to six coupons, each of which is valid for any SAS flight within or between Denmark, Norway, and Sweden. Each coupon costs $80, a price that's especially appealing when you consider that an economy-class ticket between Stockholm and Copenhagen can cost as much as $250 each way. The pass is especially valuable if you plan to travel to the northern frontiers of Sweden or Norway; in that case, the savings over the price of an economy-class ticket can be substantial. For information on buying the pass, call **SAS** (© **800/221-2350;** www.scandinavian.net).

WITHIN DENMARK   For those in a hurry, **SAS** (© **32-32-00-00** in Denmark) operates daily service between Copenhagen and points on Jutland's mainland. From Copenhagen it takes about 40 minutes to fly to Aalborg, 35 minutes to Århus, and 30 minutes to Odense.

Fares to other Danish cities are sometimes included in a transatlantic ticket at no extra charge, as long as the additional cities are specified when the ticket is written.

BY TRAIN
Flat, low-lying Denmark, with its hundreds of bridges and absence of mountains, has a large network of railway lines that connect virtually every hamlet with the largest city, Copenhagen. For **information, schedules, and fares** anywhere in Denmark, call © **70-13-14-15.** Waiting times for a live person on this telephone line range from long to very long. Alternatively, you can check the Danish National Railways website, **www.dsb.dk**, for schedules and prices, and to reserve seats.

A word you're likely to see and hear frequently is *Lyntog* ("Express Trains"), which are the fastest trains presently operational in Denmark. Be warned in advance that the most crowded times on Danish trains are Fridays, Sundays, and national holidays, so plan your reservations accordingly.

On any train in Denmark, children between the ages of 4 and 15 are charged half-price if they're accompanied by an adult, and up to two children under 4 can travel free with an adult on any train in Denmark. Seniors 65 or older receive a discount of 20% for travel on Fridays, Sundays, and holidays, and a discount of 45% every other day of the week. No identification is needed when you buy your ticket, but the conductor who checks your ticket might ask for proof of age.

The Danish government offers dozens of discounts on the country's rail networks—depending on the type of traveler, days or hours traveled, and destination. Because discounts change often, it's best to ask for a discount based on your age and the number of days (or hours) you intend to travel.

BY BUS

By far the best way to visit rural Denmark is by car, but if you want or need to travel by bus, be aware that you'll probably get your bus at the railway station. (In much of Scandinavia, buses take passengers to destinations not served by the train; therefore, the bus route often originates at the railway station.) The arrival of trains and departure of buses are usually closely timed.

For seniors 65 and over, round-trip bus tickets are sometimes offered at one-way prices (excluding Sat, Sun, and peak travel periods around Christmas and Easter). Most discounts are granted only to seniors who are traveling beyond the city limits of their point of origin.

BY CAR

RENTALS Avis, Budget, and Hertz offer well-serviced, well-maintained fleets of cars. You may have to reserve and pay for your rental car in advance (usually 2 weeks, but occasionally as little as 48 hr.) to get the lowest rates. Unfortunately, if your trip is canceled or your arrival date changes, you might have to fill out a lot of forms for a refund. All three companies may charge slightly higher rates to clients who reserve less than 48 hours in advance and pay at pickup. The highest rates are charged to walk-in customers who arrange their rentals after they arrive in Denmark. **If at all possible you should reserve a car before you leave North America.**

The Danish government imposes a whopping **25% tax on all car rentals.** Agencies that encourage prepaid rates almost never collect this tax in advance—instead, it's imposed as part of a separate transaction when you pick up the car. Furthermore, any car retrieved at a Danish airport is subject to a one-time supplemental tax of 255DKK ($45/£23), so you might prefer to pick up your car at a downtown location. Membership in certain travel clubs or organizations (such as AAA or AARP) might qualify you for a modest discount.

Avis (© **800/331-1212** in the U.S. and Canada; www.avis.com) maintains four offices in Copenhagen: two at the arrivals hall of the airport, one at Landgreven 10 (© **70-24-77-64**), and another at Kampmannsgade 1 (© **70-24-77-07**).

Budget (© **800/527-0700** in the U.S.; © **800/472-3325** in Canada; www.budget.com) has two rental locations in Copenhagen. The larger branch is at the Copenhagen airport (© **35-53-39-00**), and the other office is at Vesterfarimagsgade 7 (© **33-55-70-00**).

Hertz (© **800/654-3001** in the U.S. and Canada; www.hertz.com) has two offices in Copenhagen, one at the airport (℅ **33-17-90-20**) and the other at Ved Vesterport 3 (℅ **33-17-90-20**).

Also consider using a small company. **Kemwel** (℅ **800/678-0678** in the U.S.; www.kemwel.com) is the North American representative for two Denmark-based car companies, Van Wijk and Hertz. It may be able to offer attractive rental prices to North Americans who pay in full at least 10 days before their departure. Seniors and members of AAA get a 5% discount.

15 Tips on Accommodations

There are other alternatives, but most visitors to Denmark check into a hotel. Accommodations range from the most basic, perhaps lacking private bathrooms, to the most deluxe. Outside of Copenhagen, you are likely to encounter first class in the top category instead of luxe accommodations. The one thing you'll not find is a truly cheap hotel. Even the most inexpensive hotels might be considered a bit pricey in some parts of the world. To compensate, many hotels, especially chain members, offer discounted rates on weekends when hotels lose their most reliable client—the commercial traveler.

Our accommodation listings include service charges and taxes so you won't be shocked when the time comes to pay the bill and a lot of extras are added on, as is the situation in many European countries.

Denmark classifies its hotels by stars ranging from one (the most basic) to five (deluxe). A hotel without a restaurant is called Hotel *Garni*. One-star hotel rooms have a hand basin with hot and cold running water and at least one bathroom per 10 rooms for communal use; two-star hotels have at least 30% of the units with private bathrooms; three-star hotels offer rooms with their own private bathroom (such hotels also have an elevator if there are more than two floors). Moving up, four-star hotels offer round-the-clock reception, an a la carte restaurant, room service, minibars, laundry service, and a bar. The best hotels in Denmark are five-stars, with luxuriously appointed rooms, often indoor pools, professionally staffed fitness centers, air-conditioning, safes in the rooms, and round-the-clock room service, among other luxuries.

If you have not booked a room prior to your arrival in Copenhagen, you may call personally at **Wonderful Copenhagen Tourist Information** at Bernstorffsgade 1, opposite the Central Station next to Tivoli. A handling fee of $9 is charged. There is also a booking desk, charging the same handling fee, at the **Copenhagen Airport Arrival Hall.**

Advance booking online is possible through **Wonderful Copenhagen Tourist Information & Booking Center,** Gammel Kongevej 1, DK 1610 Copenhagen (℅ **70-22-24-42;** www.visitcopenhagen. dk). Outside Copenhagen, bookings can be made online at www.visitdenmark. com, through local tourist offices, or directly with the hotel.

ALTERNATIVE ACCOMMODATIONS

If you'd like to avoid a stay in a hotel, consider these other options:

Bed & Breakfast   Dansk Bed & Breakfast publishes a catalogue of guesthouses throughout Denmark that receive visitors for overnight stays, fortifying them the next morning with a hearty Danish breakfast. A typical B&B might be an 18th-century farmhouse built of granite and half-timbering. Contact **Dansk Bed & Breakfast** at Sankt Peders Stræde 41, DK-1453 Copenhagen (℅ **39-61-04-05;** www.bedandbreakfast.dk).

The densest concentration of B&Bs is found on the Hans Christian Andersen island of Funen. There is a separate organization handling these bookings: **Nyborg Tourist Office,** Torvey 9, DK-5800 Nyborg (✆ **65-31-02-80;** www.bed-breakfast-fyn.dk). A typical overnight price for a double room in a B&B is 170DKK ($30/£15).

Castles & Manor Houses   Denmark is riddled with old manor houses and even a few small castles that receive paying guests all year. In our view, this type of lodging is the most exciting way to stay in Denmark, because of the grandeur of the buildings. You get to feel like a king (or queen), or at least a prince or princess for the night. Some of the establishments in this category are more like country homes than castles or manors. By taking in boarders, many of the owners of these privately owned estates are preserving Denmark's cultural heritage. For more information, contact **Danish Castles & Manor Houses,** Sankt Leonis Stræde 1A, DK-8800 Viborg (✆ **86-60-38-44;** www.slotte-herregaarde.dk).

Danish Inns   Nearly 100 atmospheric, old-world accommodations spread across the country have formed an association, offering rooms in *kros* (inns) that often date back hundreds of years. The bedrooms, however, are mostly renovated in the modern style. You get atmosphere and comfort, and most often good, solid food, both regional dishes and in many cases French specialties as well. For this type of accommodation, book through **Danska Kroer og Hoteller,** Vejlevej 16, DK- 8700 Horsens (✆ **75-64-87-00;** www.krohotel.dk).

Farm Holidays   As previously mentioned, farms all over Denmark receive paying guests. To get close to the heart of the country and to meet the Danes, there is no better way than spending a week on one of these farms. In addition to an atmospheric stay, you can enjoy good country cooking with fresh vegetables, newly laid eggs, and rich butter. You stay on a farm as the guest of the family, joining members and other guests for meals. Often lodgings are in a small apartment on the grounds or even a cottage near the main building. In many cases you do your own housekeeping. Prices average around $30 per person, including a full Danish breakfast. You can book with the farm directly or else go through **Landsforeningen for Landboturisme,** Lerbakken 7, DK-8410 Rønde (✆ **87-37-39-00;** www.bondegaardsferie.dk).

Holiday Homes   Yes, it's possible to rent your own house—most often a seaside cottage—throughout Denmark. The house may be a snug retreat for two or spacious enough to accommodate 10 to 12 guests. Some of these holiday homes are within a 30-minute drive of Copenhagen. They are available all year, and prices begin at around 2,950DKK ($500/£266) per week, the rates depending on the season, size, and location. Naturally, seaside holiday homes are the most sought after and most expensive in July and August. Many of the best homes are found on the west coast of Jutland, often with an indoor swimming pool and sauna. To book one of these homes contact one of the following organizations: **Dansommer** (✆ **86-17-61-22;** www.dansommer.com); **Novasol AS** (✆ **73-75-66-11;** www.novasol.com); and **Sol og Strand** (✆ **99-44-44-44;** www.sologstrand.com).

Chain Hotels & Discounts: The most prevalent chain hotel in Denmark is **Best Western** (✆ **800/937-8376;** www.bestwestern.com). It offers a Best Western Advance Card that allows you to take advantage of special "summer low" or "winter special promotion" rates, and grants such privileges as allowing one child under the age of 12 to stay free in a room shared with parents.

16 Recommended Books

HISTORY & PHILOSOPHY *A Kierkegaard Anthology,* edited by Robert Bretall (Princeton University Press), explores the work of the Copenhagen-born philosopher who developed an almost-pathological sense of involvement in theology. A representative selection of some of his more significant works is included.

Copenhagen, A Historical Guide, by Torben Ejlersen (published by Høst & Søn in Denmark, and available at most bookstores there), an 88-page guide, takes you on a brief tour of the city that began as a ferry landing and became one of the most important capitals of Europe.

Of Danish Ways, written by two Danish-Americans, Ingeborg S. MacHiffic and Margaret A. Nielsen (Harper & Row, 1984), is a delightful account of this land and its people. It has a little bit of everything: history, social consciousness, customs, food, handicrafts, art, music, and theater.

BIOGRAPHY & LITERATURE *Andersen's Fairy Tales,* by H. C. Andersen (New American Library), and *The Complete Hans Christian Andersen Fairy Tales* (Crown) are anthologies that include all of his most important works, such as *The Little Mermaid, The Tinderbox,* and *The Princess and the Pea.*

Danish Literature: A Short Critical Guide, by Paul Borum (Nordic Books), is a well-written review that explores Danish literature from the Middle Ages to the 1970s.

Out of Africa (Modern Library), *Letters from Africa* (University of Chicago Press), and *Seven Gothic Tales* (Random House) are all by Karen Blixen (who wrote under the name Isak Dinesen), one of the major authors of the 20th century, who gained renewed fame with the release of the 1985 movie *Out of Africa,* with Meryl Streep and Robert Redford. *Isak Dinesen,* by Judith Thurman (St. Martin's Press), chronicles Blixen's amazing life from an unhappy childhood in Denmark to marriage to Baron Blixen to immigration to Kenya to her passionate love affair with Denys Finch Hatton.

FAST FACTS: Denmark

Business Hours Most **banks** are open Monday through Friday from 9:30am to 4pm (Thurs to 6pm), but outside Copenhagen, banking hours vary. **Stores** are generally open Monday through Thursday from 9am to 5:30pm, Friday 9am to 7 or 8pm, and Saturday noon to 2pm; most are closed Sunday.

Drug Laws Penalties for the possession, use, purchase, sale, or manufacturing of drugs are severe. The quantity of the controlled substance is more important than the type of substance. Danish police are particularly strict with cases involving the sale of drugs to children.

Electricity Voltage is generally 220 volts AC, 50 to 60 cycles. In many camping sites, 110-volt power plugs are also available. Adapters and transformers may be purchased in Denmark. It's always best to check at your hotel desk before using an electrical outlet.

Embassies All embassies are in Copenhagen. The embassy of the **United States** is at Dag Hammärskjölds Allé 24, DK-2100 Copenhagen (© 33-41-71-00). Other embassies are the **United Kingdom,** Kastelsvej 40, DK-2100 Copenhagen (ⓒ 35-44-52-00); **Canada,** Kristen Berniskows Gade 1, DK-1105 Copenhagen K (ⓒ 33-48-32-00); **Australia,** Dampfærgevej 26, DK-2100 Copenhagen (ⓒ 70-26-36-76); and **Ireland,** Østbanegade 21, DK-2100 Copenhagen (ⓒ 35-42-32-33).

Emergencies Dial ⓒ **112** for the fire department, the police, or an ambulance, or to report a sea or air accident. Emergency calls from public telephone kiosks are free (no coins needed).

Holidays See "When to Go," earlier in this chapter.

Language Danish is the national tongue. English is commonly spoken, especially among young people. You should have few, if any, language barriers. The best phrase book is *Danish for Travellers* (Berlitz).

Liquor Laws To consume alcohol in Danish bars, restaurants, or cafes, customers must be 18 or older. There are no restrictions on children under 18 who drink at home or, for example, from a bottle in a public park. Danish police tend to be lenient unless drinkers become raucous or uncontrollable. There is no leniency, however, in the matter of driving while intoxicated. It's illegal to drive with a blood-alcohol level of 0.8 or more, which could be produced by two drinks. If the level is 1.5, motorists pay a serious fine. If it's more than 1.5, drivers can lose their license. If the level is 2.0 or more (usually produced by six or seven drinks), a prison term of at least 14 days might follow. Liquor stores in Denmark are closed on Sunday.

Mail Most post offices are open Monday through Friday from 9 or 10am to 5 or 6pm and Saturday from 9am to noon; they're closed Sunday. All mail to North America is sent airmail without extra charge. Mailboxes are painted red and display the embossed crown and trumpet of the Danish Postal Society.

Maps The best map for touring Denmark is part of the series published by Hallwag. It's for sale at all major bookstores in Copenhagen, including the most centrally located one, **Boghallen,** Rådhuspladsen 37 (ⓒ **33-47-25-60**), in the Town Hall Square.

Newspapers & Magazines English-language newspapers are sold at all major news kiosks in Copenhagen but are much harder to find in the provinces. London papers are flown in for early-morning delivery, but you may find the *International Herald Tribune* or *USA Today* more interesting. Pick up a copy of *Copenhagen This Week,* printed in English, which contains useful information.

Passports **For Residents of the United States:** Whether you're applying in person or by mail, you can download passport applications from the U.S. State Department website at **http://travel.state.gov**. For general information, call the **National Passport Agency** (ⓒ 202/647-0518). To find your regional passport office, either check the U.S. State Department website or call the **National Passport Information Center** toll-free number (ⓒ **877/487-2778**) for automated information.

 For Residents of Canada: Passport applications are available at travel agencies throughout Canada or from the central **Passport Office,** Department of Foreign Affairs and International Trade, Ottawa, ON K1A 0G3 (ⓒ **800/567-6868**; www.ppt.gc.ca).

For Residents of the United Kingdom: To pick up an application for a standard 10-year passport (5-yr. passport for children under 16), visit your nearest passport office, major post office, or travel agency or contact the **United Kingdom Passport Service** at ℂ **0870/521-0410** or search its website at www.ukpa.gov.uk.

For Residents of Ireland: You can apply for a 10-year passport at the **Passport Office,** Setanta Centre, Molesworth Street, Dublin 2 (ℂ **01/671-1633;** www.citizensinformation.ie). Those under age 18 and over 65 must apply for a €12 3-year passport. You can also apply at 1A South Mall, Cork (ℂ **021/272-525**), or at most main post offices.

For Residents of Australia: You can pick up an application from your local post office or any branch of Passports Australia, but you must schedule an interview at the passport office to present your application materials. Call the **Australian Passport Information Service** at ℂ **131-232,** or visit the government website at www.passports.gov.au.

For Residents of New Zealand: You can pick up a passport application at any New Zealand Passports Office or download it from their website. Contact the **Passports Office** at ℂ **0800/225-050** in New Zealand or 04/474-8100, or log on to www.passports.govt.nz.

Pharmacies They're known as *apoteker* in Danish and are open Monday through Thursday from 9am to 5:30pm, Friday 9am to 7pm, and Saturday 9am to 1pm.

Police Dial ℂ **112** for police assistance.

Radio & TV No English-language radio or TV stations broadcast from Denmark. Only radios and TVs with satellite reception can receive signals from countries such as Britain. News programs in English are broadcast Monday through Saturday at 8:30am on Radio Denmark, 93.85 MHz. Radio 1 (90.8 MHz VHF) features news and classical music. Channels 2 and 3 (96.5/93.9 MHz) include some entertainment, broadcast light news items, and offer light music. Most TV stations transmit from 7:30am to 11:30pm. Most films (many of which are American) are shown in their original languages, with Danish subtitles.

Restrooms All big plazas, such as Town Hall Square in Copenhagen, have public lavatories. In small towns and villages, head for the marketplace. Hygienic standards are usually adequate. Sometimes men and women patronize the same toilets (signs read TOILETTER or WC). Otherwise, men's rooms are marked HERRER or H, and women's rooms are marked DAMER or D.

Safety Denmark is one of the safest European countries for travelers. Copenhagen, the major population center, naturally experiences the most crime. Muggings have been reported in the vicinity of the railway station, especially late at night, but crimes of extreme violence are exceedingly rare. Exercise the usual precautions you would when traveling anywhere.

Taxes The 25% VAT (value-added tax) on goods and services is known in Denmark as *moms* (pronounced "mumps"). Special tax-free exports are possible, and many stores will mail goods home to you, circumventing *moms.* If you want to take your purchases with you, look for shops displaying Danish tax-free shopping notices. Such shops offer tourists tax refunds for personal export. This refund applies to purchases of at least 300DKK (US$54/£27/C$62) for U.S. and Canadian visitors. Danish Customs must stamp your tax-free invoice when you leave the country. You can receive your refund at Copenhagen's Kastrup International Airport when you depart. If you go by land or sea, you can receive your refund by mail. Mail requests for refunds to Danish Tax-Free Shopping A/S, H. J. Holstvej 5A, DK-2605 Brøndby, Denmark. You'll be reimbursed by check, cash, or credit- or charge-card credit in the currency you want.

For the refund to apply, the 300DKK must be spent in one store, but not necessarily at the same time. Some major department stores allow purchases to be made over several days or even weeks, at the end of which receipts will be tallied. Service and handling fees are deducted from the total, so actual refunds come up to about 19%. Information on this program is available from the Danish Tourist Board (see "Visitor Information," earlier in this chapter).

A 25% *moms* is included in hotel and restaurant bills, service charges, entrance fees, and repair bills for foreign-registered cars. No refunds are possible on these items.

Telephone The country code for Denmark is **45**. It should precede any call made to Denmark from another country.

Danish phones are fully automatic. Dial the eight-digit number; there are no city area codes. Don't insert any coins until your party answers. At public telephone booths, use two 50-øre coins or a 1-krone or 5-krone coin only. You can make more than one call on the same payment if your time hasn't run out. Emergency calls are free.

Time Denmark operates on Central European Time—1 hour ahead of Greenwich Mean Time and 6 hours ahead of Eastern Standard Time. Daylight saving time is from the end of March to the end of September.

Tipping Tips are seldom expected, but when they are, you should give only 1DKK to 2DKK (15¢–35¢/9p–18p). Porters charge fixed prices, and tipping is not customary for hairdressers or barbers. Service is built into the system, and hotels, restaurants, and even taxis include a 15% service charge in their rates. Because of the service charge, plus the 25% *moms,* you'll probably have to pay an additional 40% for some services!

Consider tipping only for special services—some Danes would feel insulted if you offered them a tip.

Water Tap water is safe to drink throughout Denmark.

3

Suggested Itineraries
for Denmark

Vacations are getting shorter, and a "lean-and-mean" schedule is called for if you want to experience the best of Denmark in a relatively small amount of time. Fortunately, the country is small and enjoys a good road system or else an efficient network of ferryboats to take you to its offshore islands in all weather conditions.

If you're a time-pressed traveler, as most of us are, you may find the first two itineraries helpful in organizing your time and picking and choosing among the many tempting destinations.

1 Denmark in 1 Week

Use the following itinerary to make the most out of a week in Denmark, but feel free to drop a place or two to save a day to relax. One week provides just enough time to take in the major attractions of **Zealand** (an island dominated by Copenhagen) and the neighboring island of **Funen,** centering around the birthplace of Hans Christian Andersen at Odense.

On the first day you can see both **Louisiana,** the most acclaimed modern art museum outside of Copenhagen, and also the so-called Hamlet's Castle at **Helsingør.** The following day you can head for **Roskilde** to see both its famous cathedral and its **Viking Ship Museum.** After a 2-night stopover, you can motor south to the yachting port of **Svendborg,** your launch pad for the island of **Ærø** for a 2-night visit. This tiny island is the most enchanting in all of the Scandinavian countries—and almost no one disputes that.

Day ❶: Louisiana Museum ✫✫✫ & Helsingør ✫

On **Day 1** of our driving tour, after wrapping up your visit to Copenhagen and renting a car, head north in the morning to the town of Humlebæk, 30km (19 miles) north of Copenhagen for a morning visit to the **Louisiana Museum of Modern Art** (p. 158), which opens at 10am. This is one of the greatest art museums of Scandinavia and you'll want to give it at least an hour or two.

From Copenhagen follow coastal road 152, known as Strandvej. Depending on traffic, the scenic drive takes some 45 minutes. After a visit, continue north from Humlebæk into Helsingør, a distance of 14km (8⅓ miles), following the same Strandvej route. Once in Helsingør, you can check into a hotel for the night, but if you don't want to change hotels so often, you can use Copenhagen as your base and return there for the night.

There are many attractions in Helsingør, but the one magnet for most visitors is **Kronborg Slot** (p. 121), fabled as "Hamlet's Castle," even though Shakespeare presumably never visited it and Hamlet may never have existed. Allow at least an hour for an afternoon visit here after lunch in Helsingør.

Day ❷: The Cathedral City of Roskilde ☆☆

On the morning of **Day 2,** leave Helsingør (or Copenhagen if you spent the night there) for a drive west to **Roskilde.** The distance is 30km (19 miles) west of Copenhagen, but a distance of 72km (45 miles) southwest of Helsingør. From Copenhagen head west on the E21 express highway; from Helsingør follow Route 6 southwest.

If you're on Route 6 from Helsingør, you can stop off for a morning visit to **Hillerød,** a distance of 25km (16 miles) southwest of Helsingør, or a jaunt of 35km (22 miles) north of Copenhagen. This town possesses one of the great treasures of Denmark and is well worth a detour regardless of where you spent the night. Hillerød is the home of **Frederiksborg Castle** (p. 164), which has been called "the Danish Versailles." Surrounded by a moat, it is the most beautiful royal residence in Denmark and the setting for the Museum of National History, with one of Denmark's greatest collections of historical paintings. Allow at least 1½ hours for a visit.

From Hillerød, continue along Route 6 southwest into **Roskilde,** where you can check into a hotel for the night. In the afternoon, visit the **Roskilde Domkirke** (p. 188) and try to take a 90-minute boat tour of the **Roskilde Fjord** (p. 193). If you can't schedule a visit to the fjord, then call on the **Lejre Research Center** (p. 192), which in spite of its dull name is actually a reconstructed Iron Age village.

Days ❸ & ❹: Odense ☆☆ & H. C. Andersen

On the morning of **Day 3,** leave Zealand altogether and drive west to the neighboring island of Funen, whose capital is **Odense,** lying 134km (83 miles) to the west of Roskilde. From Roskilde, take Route 14 southwest to the express highway E20, continuing west to the port of Korsør, where you cross the Great Belt Bridge into Funen, entering the island through its gateway city of Nyborg. Once on land in Funen, continue west along E20 until you see the cutoff arteries leading north into the center of Odense. Once here, book into a hotel for a 2-night stay.

After lunch you can take in some of the major sights of the city, including the **H. C. Andersen's Childhood Home** (p. 265). If it's summer you might even hook up with a 2-hour walking tour, taking in all the highlights. Check with the tourist office.

On the morning of **Day 4,** visit **Funen Village** (p. 264), an open-air regional museum depicting life in Denmark in the 1700s and 1800s. In a busy afternoon you can visit both **Egeskov Castle** (p. 266), one of the grandest in Denmark, as well as **Ladbyskibet** (p. 267), 19km (12 miles) northeast of Odense to see the ruins of a 10th-century Viking ship.

Day ❺: Svendborg ☆: Favorite Port for Yachties

On the morning of **Day 5,** check out of your hotel in Odense and drive 43km (27 miles) south to the port city of **Svendborg,** following Route 9. Once in Svendborg, check into a hotel for the night and set out to see the rather minor sights in town, including **Anne Hvides Gård** (p. 276), **St. Jorgen's Church** (p. 276), and **St. Nicolaj Church** (p. 276). After lunch you can explore nearby islands, each linked to Svendborg by bridge. These include the horseshoe-shaped **Thurø** (p. 281), called

0 50 mi
0 50 km

Skagerrak

NORTH SEA

JUTLAND

Kattegat

Zealand (Sjælland)

Funen (Fyn)

Skagen   Gothenburg (Göteborg)   Borås
Hirtshals
Hjørring   Frederikshavn
Brønderslev   Læsø
                               Varberg
Thisted   **Aalborg** (Ålborg)
Nykøbing Mors
Lemvig   Skive   Hobro   Anholt   Halmstad
Struer   Viborg   Randers
Holstebro
Ringkøbing   Silkeborg   **Århus**   Helsingør ③ Helsingborg
Skjern   Hillerød ⑤
         Herning   Horsens   Samsø   Frederikssund ② Øresund
Grindsted   Vejle   Holbæk   **COPENHAGEN**
Varde   Fredericia   Kalundborg   Roskilde ④ ① (København)
Esbjerg   Kolding   Ringsted   Køge   **Malmö**
Fanø   Ribe   **Odense** ⑥   Slagelse
Rømø   Haderslev   Nyborg   Store   Næstved
         Åbenrå   Fåborg   Bælt
Westerland   Tønder   **Svendborg** ⑦   Møn
Sylt   Sønderborg   Ærø ⑧   Nakskov   Lolland   Nykøbing
Flensburg   Langeland   Rødbyhavn   Falster
Amrum   **GERMANY**

DAY 1: LOUISIANA MUSEUM & HELSINGØR

1 Copenhagen
2 Humlebæk
3 Helsingør

DAY 2: THE CATHEDRAL CITY OF ROSKILDE

4 Roskilde
5 Hillerød

DAYS 3 & 4: ODENSE & H.C. ANDERSEN

6 Odense

*DAY 5: SVENDBORG, FAVORITE PORT
    FOR YACHTIES*

7 Svendborg

*DAYS 6 & 7: ÆRØ, DENMARK'S MOST
    BEAUTIFUL ISLAND*

8 Ærø

"The Garden of Denmark," and **Tåsinge** (p. 281), where you can visit several attractions such as the church tower at **Bregninge Kirkebakke** (p. 282) for its panoramic views. After a call on the 17th-century **Valdemars Slot** (p. 283), you can spend the rest of the afternoon just exploring at random. Since the island is so small, it's almost impossible to get lost. Return to Svendborg for the night.

Days ⑥ & ⑦: Ærø ★★: Denmark's Most Beautiful Island

On the morning of **Day 6**, leave Svendborg by driving to the port, where you can board a car ferry heading for the island of **Ærø**, lying 29km (18 miles) across the water south of Svendborg. Check into a hotel in the little picture-postcard capital of **Ærøskøbing** for 2 nights and set out to explore the island.

Begin first on foot by walking the cobblestone streets of this most enchanting of Danish villages, saving the driving tour of the island for the following day. The main attraction of the town is Ærøskøbing itself, although there are specific sights of minor interest, including the **Ærø Museum** (p. 292) and an 18th-century church, **Ærøskøbing Kirke** (p. 292). Dine in an old *kro* (inn) and later walk down by the water to watch the yachts and other boats bobbing in the harbor at night.

On the morning of **Day 7,** while still based in Ærøskøbing, set out on a leisurely motor tour of the island, stopping at random to enjoy anything that fascinates you. We'd head east to the "second city" on **Marstal,** really just a modest port town. After a 2-hour visit here you can take the southern road all the way to the little port of **Søby** in the northwest. From Søby you can drive southeast back to Ærøskøbing for the night.

The following morning you can take the ferryboat back to Svendborg, where you can drive north once again toward Odense, linking with the E20 to carry you east across the Great Belt Bridge to Zealand and back to Copenhagen, where you can make air or rail connections to your next destination.

2 Denmark in 2 Weeks

After having driven through the highlights of the islands of Zealand and Funen, we tackle the largest landmass of Denmark, the peninsula of **Jutland** linking Denmark with the continent of Europe—Germany in this case. In just 1 week you can skim the highlights of this history-rich part of Denmark.

Our tour continues in the marshlands of South Jutland in the area's capital, **Tønder,** and proceeds north to **Ribe,** which for most visitors is the sightseeing highlight of the entire peninsula. This is followed by a trip to **Fanø,** the most beautiful island off the coast of Jutland.

We'll follow that with a trip to **Silkeborg** to call on the Tollund Man (who is 2,400 years old). Both of the two leading cities of Jutland, **Århus** and **Aalborg,** can be visited before we head for the northernmost point of Jutland, the artists' colony and summer resort of **Skagen.**

Day ❽: Tønder ⟨F⟩: Capital of the Marshlands

Our tour begins in South Jutland in one of Denmark's oldest towns, **Tønder,** lying on the banks of the River Vidå in the center of the southern marshlands, a section of Denmark that once belonged to Germany. Tønder lies at a distance of 277km (172 miles) southwest of Copenhagen. To arrive in Jutland, you can use the port of Kolding as your gateway. Driving distance from Copenhagen to Kolding is 208km (129 miles). You can cross the bridge from Funen in the east, then follow Route 161 into Kolding. The final trip from Kolding to Tønder is a distance of 85km (53 miles). From Kolding take Route 25 southwest to the junction with Route 11, which will carry you to the turnoff for Tønder, reached along Route 419 heading west.

Once in Tønder, check into a hotel for the night and set out to explore the area, whose highlight will be the little village of **Møgeltønder,** lying 4km (2½ miles) west from Tønder via Route 419.

This charming old-world village is one of the highlights of South Jutland (our coverage begins on p. 312). Back in Tønder, you can wander up and down its old

Denmark in 2 Weeks

town, taking in its quaintness. Specific visits aren't necessary as it is the antique homes of Tønder that form its appeal, although you might drop into the 16th-century church of **Kristkirken** (p. 309).

Day ➒: Ribe ✿✿: Nesting Place for Storks

On the morning of **Day 2**, leave Tønder and head north for 47km (29 miles) to **Ribe,** which, like Tønder itself, is one of Denmark's oldest towns. From Tønder follow Route 11 north all the way. You should arrive in Ribe in time to see all its highlights in 1 day, after checking into a hotel for the night.

Spend 2 or 3 hours exploring its **Gamle Stan** (Old Town), centered around the Torvet, the town's ancient market square. Our full coverage of the sightseeing highlights of **Ribe** begins on p. 318. Its chief attractions include **Ribe Domkirke,** site of Denmark's earliest wooden church, and the **Ribe VikingeCenter** 2km (1¼ miles) south of the center, a re-creation of Ribe in the early Middle Ages.

Day ⑩: Fanø ★★: Beautiful Island in the North Sea

On the morning of **Day 3,** leave Ribe and drive to the island of **Fanø,** 47km (29 miles) northwest of Ribe. From Ribe, head north on Route 11 to Route 24, which you follow northwest into the city of Esbjerg, where you can board a car ferry to Fanø. Once on the island, check into a hotel for the night, then set out to explore. Our coverage of the attractions of Fanø begins on p. 327. But most motorists will want to skip any of the man-made attractions and devote the rest of the day to exploring this most beautiful of North Sea islands itself. If the weather's fair, try to get in some beach time.

Day ⑪: Silkeborg & the Oldest Man in the World

On the morning of **Day 4,** leave Fanø and return by car ferry to the port of Esbjerg. Head northeast to the city of **Silkeborg,** a distance of 139km (86 miles). From Esbjerg follow Route 12 north. Near the town of Varde it becomes Route 11, which you follow all the way to the junction of Route 15, which takes you due east into Silkeborg.

Once here, check into a hotel for the night. Call first at the **Silkeborg Museum** (p. 353), where you can see the 2,400-year-old "Tollund Man," who was discovered in an amazing state of preservation in a peat bog in 1950. Other attractions include the **Silkeborg Kunstmuseum** (p. 352), one of the finest provincial art museums in Scandinavia, and **AQUA Ferskvands Akvarium** (p. 352), North Europe's largest freshwater aquarium.

Day ⑫ Århus ★★★: "World's Smallest City"

On the morning of **Day 5,** leave Silkeborg and drive 43km (27 miles) to the west, following Route 15. Once at **Århus,** check into a hotel for the night and set about to spend 1 busy day. Since Århus is hard to cover in just 1 day, as it's so much larger than the previous destinations, we suggest you take a 2-hour tour, leaving in summer at 10am and covering all the major highlights. After lunch you can spend another 2 hours wandering **Den Gamle** (p. 361), an open-air museum of historic buildings. If time remains, pay a visit to the **Århus Kunstmuseum** (p. 361) and the **Århus Domkirke** (p. 360), the cathedral honoring St. Clemens.

Day ⑬ Aalborg ★: Capital of North Jutland

On the morning of **Day 6,** leave Århus heading for **Aalborg,** the largest city in Jutland, a distance of 112km (70 miles) north of Århus. From Århus take the express highway, E45, north into Aalborg, where you can check into a hotel for the night. For the best overview, head for the lookout tower, **Aalborg Tårnet** (p. 384), for a panoramic view of this vast (in Denmark's terms) city. The **Aalborg Zoologiske Have** (p. 384) is usually a must on many a visitor's itinerary, as are stopovers at **Jens Bang's Stenhus** (p. 385) and **Nordjyllands Kunstmuseet** (p. 385), the best museum of modern art in North Jutland. Cap your day with an evening visit to the major amusement park in the north of Jutland, **Tivoliland** (p. 386). Okay, so it's not as great as Copenhagen's Tivoli Gardens (but, what is?).

Day ⑭ Skagen ★★: An Artists' Colony

On the morning of **Day 7,** leave Aalborg and drive northeast for about 100km (60 miles) to **Skagen** at the tip of Jutland, where you can check into a hotel for your final night. While enjoying the bracing air of the North Sea, you can set about to explore **Skagen Havn** (p. 402), the colorful harbor, followed by visits to **Den Tilsandede Kirke** (p. 403), an old church mostly buried in the sand dunes. You'll definitely want to visit the **Skagens Museum** (p. 404), the best showcase for the Skagen School of painting that was launched here between the 1870s and the 1900s. If you've finished in time, you can also drive 50km (31 miles) to Hirtshals, a neighboring town, to see the spectacular

Nordsømuseet (p. 404), an aquarium of North Sea marine life. From Aalborg, you can drive back to Copenhagen, or else return your car in Aalborg if you made arrangements in advance. You can also take a plane or train ride back to the Danish capital for transportation links to the rest of the world.

3 The Islands of Denmark in 1 Week

We've already visited the two major islands of Denmark, both Funen and Zealand, even the peninsula of Jutland. The two tours above have covered all the highlights of the island, even the offshore islands of **Fanø** and **Ærø**. There are many other offshore islands, some of little interest to visitors. But Denmark has some major vacation islands not documented, notably **Bornholm, Møn,** and **Rømø.** We'll visit all of them in this nutshell tour. Except for the longer passage to Bornholm, all of these islands can be quickly reached by causeway or else car ferries.

Days ❶ & ❷: Bornholm 𝒜𝒜:
Pearl of the Baltic

On the morning of **Day 1,** assuming you've wrapped up your visit to Copenhagen, you can sail over to the island of Bornholm in the Baltic. This is where Copenhageners themselves go for their vacations. From Copenhagen you can take a 7-hour car ferry to **Bornholm,** where you can check into a hotel for 2 nights, since you will have spent most of Day 1 getting to the island.

On the morning of **Day 2,** you can set out to explore most of the island, which can be easily accomplished in 1 day. Highlights of a visit to the island include the capital of **Rønne,** where you can visit **Erickssons Gård,** (p. 235), a well-preserved 19th-century farmhouse. Other major stopovers include **Svaneke** (p. 245) and **Gudhjem** (p. 248). Pick up a map from the tourist office and plot a day tour to see how much ground you can cover. Complete coverage of Bornholm's highlights is found in chapter 8.

Day ❸: Møn 𝒜𝒜 & Its Chalk Cliffs

On the morning of **Day 3,** return to Copenhagen by the 7-hour car ferry.

Once in the capital, head south to **Møn,** an island lying off the eastern coast of Zealand, a drive of 130km (81 miles) south of Copenhagen. From Copenhagen follow the express highway E20 south (it becomes the E47/E55). At the junction with Route 59, follow it east, crossing the Dronning Alexandrines Bridge, which will take you into **Stege,** the capital of Møn. You can overnight here.

Since you won't have time until the following day, you can save the sights of Møn until the following morning of Day 4.

Days ❹ & ❺: Ærø 𝒜𝒜𝒜: The
Most Beautiful Island

Plan an early-morning visit to **Møns Klint** (p. 221), the famous chalk cliffs on Møn. After a drive around the scenic highlights of the island (our coverage begins on p. 289), you can cross the bridge back onto the island of Zealand. From here you can drive to our next destination, **Ærø,** an island off the southern coast of Funen.

From Stege, drive west along Route 59 to the express highway, E47/E65. Follow it north to E20, cutting west toward the port of Korsør. Once here you can drive

The Islands of Denmark in 1 Week

DAYS 1 & 2: BORNHOLM, PEARL OF THE BALTIC	**6** Svendborg
	7 Ærøskøbing
1 Bornholm	
2 Ronne	*DAY 6: RØMØ, THE GEM OF THE NORTH FRISIAN ISLANDS*
DAY 3: MØN & ITS CHALK CLIFFS	**8** Rømø
3 Møn	
4 Stege	*DAY 7: FANØ, NORTH SEA HAVEN FOR BEACH LOVERS*
DAYS 4 & 5: ÆRØ, THE MOST BEAUTIFUL ISLAND	**9** Fanø
5 Ærø	

across the Great Belt Bridge. In Funen continue along the E20 to the junction of Route 9 going south to **Svendborg.** At Svendborg you'll be at a point 146km (91 miles) west of Copenhagen. Because the distances are so short, you can hop across the country, going from island to island easily in just 1 day.

From Svendborg take a car ferry to the island of **Ærø,** where you can book into a hotel for 2 nights. You'll need the second

night here because you will have spent a good part of 1 day reaching **Ærø** itself. The best bet for a hotel stay is in the little capital of **Ærøskøbing,** which can easily be explored on foot in the late afternoon of your arrival on the island.

On the morning of **Day 5,** while still based in Ærøskøbing, follow the suggestion for Day 7, as outlined earlier in this chapter, in "Denmark in 1 Week."

Day ⑥: Rømø ⚲: The Gem of North Frisian Islands

On the morning of **Day 6,** leave Ærø, taking the car ferry back to the port of Svendborg. Follow Route 9 north to the junction with express highway E20 heading west to the peninsula of Jutland. Stay on E20 all the way to the city of Esbjerg on the west coast of Jutland, where you take Route 11 continuing south, cutting west across the causeway leading to the island of **Rømø.** The stone causeway from the mainland is a 10km (6¼-mile) drive. Once at Rømø, you will have come a total distance of 288km (179 miles) southwest from Copenhagen.

Check into a hotel on Rømø and set out for a wild romp on the beach if the weather's warm and sunny. Like most offshore islands of Denmark, the man-made attractions here hardly compete with the beauty of the island itself. The best sandy beaches are found on the west side of the island.

Day ⑦: Fanø ⚲⚲: North Sea Haven for Beach Lovers

On the morning of **Day 7,** leave Fanø and cross back over the causeway to the mainland of Jutland. Once here, return to Route 11 heading north toward Ribe. Bypass Ribe, taking Route 24 to the port of Esbjerg. From Esbjerg a car ferry transports motorists to **Fanø,** where you can check into a hotel for your final night. For more details, see Day 3 for Fanø under "Denmark in 2 Weeks," above.

4 Denmark for Families in 1 Week

Denmark offers many attractions that kids enjoy, none more notable than the Tivoli Gardens in Copenhagen. Perhaps your main concern with having children along is pacing yourself with museum time. Our suggestion is to explore **Copenhagen** for 2 days with family in tow, then spend Day 3 visiting "Hamlet's Castle" in the north before heading over to the island of Funen, centering at its capital, **Odense,** birthplace of Hans Christian Andersen, whose work is known to children around the world because of his massive number of foreign translations. Finally, we go to Jutland, which is Denmark's mainland link to the continent (via Germany). Here we visit its two major attractions, **Århus** and **Aalborg,** both containing Tivoli-like amusement parks of their own, plus numerous other attractions.

Days ❶ & ❷: Arrival in Copenhagen ⚲⚲⚲

Before renting a car to explore the countryside, you can take in the glories of Copenhagen itself, the most kid-friendly of all Scandinavia capitals. After your arrival and after you've checked into a hotel for 2 nights, take one of the bus and boat tours for orientation purposes. See "Organized Tours" (p. 140). Follow this up with a guided tour of **Amalienborg Palace** (p. 116), where Queen Margrethe II lives with her royal family. After lunch, descend on the **Tivoli Gardens** (p. 112), where you and your kids can wander for hours and also eat dinner.

On the morning of **Day 2,** pay a call on **Den Little Havfrue** (p. 118), "The Little Mermaid," the most photographed statue in Scandinavia. After that, explore **Ny Carlsberg Glyptotek** (p. 112), one of the greatest art museums in Europe. If your child is older, he or she will find much art to fascinate here, perhaps a pre-historic sculpture of a hippopotamus. In the afternoon visit **Frilandsmuseet** (p. 130), an open-air museum and reconstructed village that evokes life in the

Denmark for Families in 1 Week

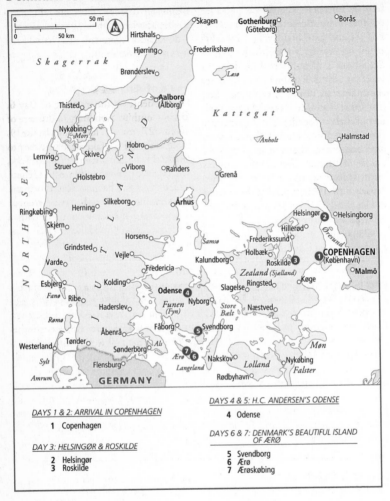

19th century, lying at Lyngby on the fringe of Copenhagen.

When you return to Copenhagen, you can do as many families do and pay a final visit to **Tivoli Gardens,** or else you can visit another amusement park, **Bakken** (p. 132), on the northern fringe of the city. If you like merry-go-rounds and roller coasters, Bakken is even more fun for some families than the more carefully manicured Tivoli.

Day ③: Helsingør 🎀 & Roskilde 🎀🎀
On the morning of **Day 3,** check out of your hotel and drive 40km (25 miles) north of Copenhagen, taking the E4 express highway. Once at Helsingør you can pay a morning visit to the Dutch-Renaissance–style **Kronborg Castle,** legendary home of Shakespeare's fictional Hamlet. Kids may think that Walt Disney created this dank, spooky place, which is surrounded by a deep moat.

After a 1-hour visit, you can head for our final destination of the day, the cathedral city of **Roskilde,** lying 72km (45 miles) southwest. It's reached by following Route 6 all the way. Check into a hotel in Roskilde for the day and set about to explore this ancient city. Call first at the **Roskilde Domkirke** (p. 188). Kids delight in seeing the 16th-century clock where a tiny sculpted St. George on horseback marks the hour by charging a dragon. Afterward, drive 20km (12 miles) north of Roskilde to see the **Viking Ship Museum** (p. 191), displaying the remains of five wrecked Viking-era ships. Return to Roskilde for the night.

Days ④ & ⑤: H. C. Andersen's Odense ⌒⌒

On the morning of **Day 4,** drive west from Roskilde for 134km (83 miles) until you reach Odense. To do so, you have to cross the Great Belt Bridge into Nyborg, lying west on the Funen side. From Nyborg, E20 will carry you to Odense, where you can check into a hotel for 2 nights. In Odense follow the same family-friendly itinerary as outlined in Days 3 & 4 under "Denmark in 1 Week" (earlier in this chapter).

Days ⑥ & ⑦: Denmark's Beautiful Island of Ærø ⌒⌒⌒

Leave Odense on the morning of **Day 6,** driving south to Svendborg, a distance of 43km (27 miles), following Route 9. Once at Svendborg take a car ferry over to the island of Ærø, a distance of 29km (18 miles) from Svendborg. Once here, check into a hotel in the tiny island's capital, **Ærøskøbing,** for 2 nights and set about to explore this Lilliputian town with a driving tour of the island to follow on Day 7.

Use the same family-friendly itinerary as outlined under **Days 6 & 7** under "Denmark in 1 Week" (earlier in this chapter).

After a visit to Ærø, you can easily return to Copenhagen the following day, using a bridge and a ferryboat. Copenhagen lies 176km (109 miles) to the east of Ærø.

4

Settling into Copenhagen

Like Mighty Mouse, Denmark may be small but it packs a powerful punch. Its capital, Copenhagen, seems to be the seat of everything Danish—artistic, financial, and political.

The Frommer guides have long maintained their loyalty to promoting the glories of Copenhagen, and we continue that long-ago commitment. In his first guide, *Europe on $5 a Day*, Arthur Frommer wrote, "After Copenhagen, the rest of Europe will become a footnote." An exaggeration, of course, but Copenhagen after all these decades remains the "fun" capital of Scandinavia—and also the most affordable—and the Danes continue to practice their own *joie de vivre*. There is an enthusiasm for life here that always sweeps us up in its spell.

The city continues to change. Middle Eastern restaurants now compete with old-fashioned eateries serving food that Grandmother Denmark used to cook. Internet cafes have become the rendezvous point of choice for young Danes instead of the traditional sudsy taverns beloved by their parents. The city isn't as safe as it used to be: Crime and drugs are on the rise. In other words, welcome to the modern world.

But some things never change. Many Copenhageners still bike to work along the city's canals. We still join the locals who follow their noses to the cafes where the smell of freshly baked bread lures us in for a morning Danish and a cup of freshly brewed coffee. Along the way, we still pass that little old shopkeeper out soaping down his glass windows.

"We are a bit unconventional but affable," a former mayor told us. "We have big hearts and can accommodate all lifestyles and persuasions. There's also a rebellious streak of independence in us. Our cartoonists will even dare depict Mohammed as a physical person, which can get us into a bit of trouble in less tolerant societies. But we wouldn't be Danes if we didn't exercise our freedoms."

Copenhagen, the capital of Denmark, got its name from the word *køben-havn,* which means "merchants' harbor." It grew in size and importance because of its position on the Øresund (the Sound), the body of water between Denmark and Sweden, guarding the strategic passage of all maritime traffic heading into or out of the Baltic.

From its humble beginnings, Copenhagen has become the largest city in Scandinavia, home to 1.8 million people, the seat of one of the oldest kingdoms in the world.

Over the centuries Copenhagen has suffered more than its share of invasions and disasters. In the 17th century, the Swedes repeatedly besieged it, and in the 18th century, it endured the plague and two devastating fires. The British attacked twice during the Napoleonic wars in the early 1800s. In 1940, the Nazis invaded Denmark and held onto Copenhagen until 1945, when the British army moved in again, this time as liberators.

Copenhagen is a city with much charm, as reflected in its canals, narrow streets, and old houses. Its most famous resident was Hans Christian Andersen, whose memory lives on. Another of Copenhagen's world-renowned inhabitants was Søren Kierkegaard, who used to take long morning strolls in the city, planning his next addition to the collection of essays that eventually earned him the title "father of existentialism."

In 2000, the Øresund Bridge was officially opened, physically linking Sweden and Denmark for the first time. Today there's a 15km (9⅓-mile) car and train link between Zealand (the eastern part of Denmark, the island on which Copenhagen sits) and Skane (the southern part of Sweden). If you'd like to link a visit with Copenhagen to Malmö, Copenhagen's fast-growing counterpart across the border in Sweden, or perhaps visit some of the châteaux of southern Sweden, just drive across the bridge.

Copenhagen still retains some of the characteristics of a village. If you ignore the suburbs, you can cover most of the central belt on foot. It's almost as if the city were designed for strolling, as reflected by its Strøget, the longest and oldest pedestrians-only street in Europe.

1 Orientation

GETTING THERE

BY PLANE   You arrive at **Kastrup Airport** (℃ 32-31-32-31; www.cph.dk), 12km (7½ miles) from the center of Copenhagen. Air-rail trains link the airport with the Central Railway Station in the center of Copenhagen. The ride takes 13 minutes, and costs 27DKK ($4.80/£2.45). Located right under the airport's arrivals and departures halls, the Air Rail Terminal is a short escalator ride from the gates. You can also take a SAS bus to the city terminal; the fare is 26DKK ($4.55/£2.30) A taxi to the city center costs between 150DKK and 200DKK ($27–$36/£14–£18).

BY TRAIN   Trains arrive at the **HovedBanegården** (Central Railroad Station; ℃ 70-13-14-15 for rail information), in the center of Copenhagen, near Tivoli Gardens and the Rådhuspladsen. The station operates a luggage-checking service, but room bookings are available only at the tourist office (see "Visitor Information," below).

From the Central Railroad Station, you can connect with the **S-tog,** a local train; trains depart from platforms in the terminal itself. The information desk is near tracks 5 and 6.

BY BUS   Buses from Zealand and elsewhere pull into the Central Railroad Station. For bus information, call ℃ **36-13-14-15** daily 7am to 9:30pm.

BY CAR   If you're driving from Germany, a car ferry will take you from Travemünde to Gedser in southern Denmark. From Gedser, get on E55 north, an express highway that will deliver you to the southern outskirts of Copenhagen. If you're coming from Sweden via the Øresund Bridge, it will deposit you on the city's eastern outskirts, close to Kastrup airport. From here, it's a short drive into the center.

VISITOR INFORMATION

The **Copenhagen Tourist Information Center,** Vesterbrogade 4A (℃ **70-22-24-42;** www.visitcopenhagen.com), adjacent to the main entrance of Tivoli, dispenses information. It's open in July and August Monday to Saturday 9am to 8pm; May and June Monday to Saturday 9am to 6pm; September to April Monday to Friday 9am to 4pm and Saturday 9am to 2pm.

CITY LAYOUT

MAIN ARTERIES & STREETS   The heart of Old Copenhagen is a warren of pedestrian streets, bounded by Nørreport Station to the north, Rådhuspladsen (Town

Hall Square) to the west, and Kongens Nytorv, a busy square that's positioned at the top of the Nyhavn Canal, to the east. **Strøget,** the longest continuous pedestrians-only route in Europe, goes east from Town Hall Square to Kongens Nytorv, and is made up of five interconnected streets: Frederiksberggade, Nygade, Vimmelskaftet, Amagertorv, and Østergade. Strøget is lined with shops, bars, restaurants, pizza parlors, and, in summer, sidewalk cafes. **Pistolstræde** contains a maze of galleries, restaurants, and boutiques, housed in restored 18th-century buildings.

Fiolstræde (Violet St.), a dignified street with antiques shops and bookshops, cuts through the university (Latin Quarter). If you turn into Rosengaarden at the top of Fiolstræde, you'll come to **Kultorvet** (Coal Square), just before you reach Nørreport Station. Here you join the third main pedestrian street, **Købmagergade** (Butcher St.), which winds around and finally meets Strøget at Amagertorv.

At the end of Strøget you approach **Kongens Nytorv** (King's Square). This is the site of the Royal Theater and Magasin, the largest department store in Copenhagen. This will put you at the beginning of **Nyhavn,** the former seamen's quarter that has been gentrified into an upmarket area of expensive restaurants, apartments, cafes, and boutiques.

The government of Denmark has been centered for the past 800 years on the small and very central downtown island of **Slotsholmen,** which is connected to the center by eight different bridges. The island's most immediately visible attraction is the imperial-looking granite mass of Christiansborg Castle, home of the Danish Parliament, the Prime Minister's offices, the country's Supreme Court, and several museums.

The center of Copenhagen is **Rådhuspladsen** (Town Hall Square). From here it's a short walk to the Tivoli Gardens, the major attraction of Copenhagen, the Central Railroad Station, and the Bus Station terminus. **Vesterbrogade,** a wide, densely trafficked boulevard, passes by Tivoli en route to the Central Railroad Station. **H. C. Andersens Boulevard,** a major avenue named after Denmark's most famous writer, runs beside the Rådhuspladsen and Tivoli Gardens.

FINDING AN ADDRESS   All even numbers are on one side of the street, all odd numbers on the other. Buildings are listed in numerical order. A, B, or C is often inserted after the street number.

NEIGHBORHOODS IN BRIEF
For a map of Copenhagen, see p. 155.

Tivoli Gardens Steeped in nostalgia, these amusement gardens were built in 1843 on the site of former fortifications in the heart of Copenhagen, on the south side of Rådhuspladsen. Some 160,000 flowers and 110,000 electric lights set the tone, and a collection of restaurants, dance halls, theaters, beer gardens, and lakes attract many thousands of visitors every year.

Strøget This pedestrians-only urban walkway stretches between Rådhuspladsen and Kongens Nytorv, two of the city's most visible and busiest plazas. En route along its trajectory are two spectacular, although smaller, squares, Gammeltorv and Nytorv, "old" and "new" squares, which seem to blossom during the warm-weather months with outdoor seating—extensions of the many restaurants which line its edges. The word "Strøget" usually doesn't appear on any maps. Instead, Strøget encompasses five interconnected streets: Frederiksberggade, Nygade, Villelskaftet, Amagertorv, and Østergade.

Nyhavn/Kongens Nytorv Nyhavn ("New Harbor") was originally conceived in the 1670s by the Danish king as a shelter from the storms of the North and Baltic Sea, and as a means of hauling building supplies into central Copenhagen, Nyhavn today is the site of a denser concentration of restaurants than any other neighborhood in Copenhagen. Moored beside its granite embankments, you'll see old or even antique fishing boats, some of which remain in place to preserve the sense of old-fashioned nostalgia. For many generations, Nyhavn was the haunt of sailors looking for tattoos, cheap drinks, and other diversions. Nowadays it's one of the most obviously gentrified sections of the city, with outdoor terraces which are mobbed during warm-weather months with chattering, sometimes hard-drinking Danes on holiday. At the top or western terminus of the Nyhavn canal is the five-sided Kongens Nytorv (King's New Market), site of the deluxe Hotel d'Angleterre and the Royal Theater.

Indre By This is the Old Town, the heart of Copenhagen. Once filled with monasteries, it's a maze of streets, alleyways, and squares. The neighborhood around Gammeltorv and Nørregade, sometimes called "The Latin Quarter," contains many buildings linked with the university. The **Vor Frue Kirke** (cathedral of Copenhagen) is here, as is the **Rundetårn** (Round Tower).

Slotsholmen This island, site of Christiansborg Palace, was where Bishop Absalon built Copenhagen's first fortress in 1167. Today it's the seat of the Danish parliament and home of Thorvaldsen's Museum. Bridges link Slotsholmen to Indre By. You can also visit the Royal Library (site of a recent hypermodern new wing described as the "Black Diamond"), the Theater Museum, and the Royal Stables. The 17th-century Børsen (stock exchange) is also here.

Christianshavn Set on the opposite side of Copenhagen's harbor from the rest of the city, this was the "new town" ordered by master builder King Christian IV in the early 1500s. The town was originally constructed in the Dutch Renaissance style to house workers in the shipbuilding industry. Visitors come today mainly to see the Danish Film Museum on Store Søndervoldstræde, and **Vors Frelsers Kirke,** on the corner of Prinsessegade and Skt. Annægade. Sightseers can climb the spire of the old church for a panoramic view. Within the Christianshavn district is the offbeat community of **Christiania.** In 1971 many young and homeless people moved in, without the city's permission, proclaiming Christiania a "free city" (that is, partially exempt from the rules and regulations of the Danish government) within the orbit of Greater Copenhagen. It has been a freewheeling and controversial place ever since.

Once filled with barracks for soldiers, Christiania is within walking distance of Vor Frelsers Kirke at Christianshavn. You can enter the area on Prinsessegade. The craft shops and restaurants here are fairly cheap because the residents refuse to pay Denmark's crippling 25% sales tax.

Vesterbro Once a hotbed slum loaded with junkies and prostitutes, Vesterbro would be comparable to the East Village or Williamsburg in New York City. Its main street, **Istedgade,** runs west from the Central Railway Station. Don't come here for monuments or museums, but for hip cafes, bars, music, and ethnic restaurants. No longer a slum, Vesterbro's sense of newfound hipness centers on the cafes and bars around the Halmtorvet, Vesterbro's main square. Expect gentrification but also cultural diversity such as Turkish-Kurdish gift shops, food markets loaded with fruits you might not immediately recognize, barbers from Istanbul, and from time to time, a sex shop like those that proliferated here during the '70s and '80s.

Nørrebro Adjacent to Vesterbro (see above), Nørrebro takes the immigrant overflow, and is also rich in artisan shops and ethnic restaurants, especially Turkish and Pakistani. This area has been a blue-collar neighborhood since the middle of the 19th century. The original Danish settlers have long since departed, replaced by immigrants who are not always greeted with a friendly reception in Copenhagen. The area also abounds with trend-conscious artists, students, and musicians who can't afford the high rents elsewhere. Numerous secondhand clothing stores—especially around Sankt Hans Torv—give Nørrebro the flavor of a Middle Eastern bazaar. Antiques shops (believe us, many of the furnishings and objets d'art aren't authentic) also fill the area. Most of these "antiques" stores lie along Ravnsborgade. The district is also home to a historic cemetery, Assistens Kirkegård, burial ground

of both Hans Christian Andersen and Søren Kirkegaard, just to the west of Nørrebrogade. If you're looking for the densest concentrations of the nightlife for which the district has become famous, head for either **Sankt Hans Torv** or **Blågårdsgade.**

Frederiksberg Heading west of the inner city along Vesterbrogade, you will reach the residential and business district of Frederiksberg. It grew up around **Frederiksberg Palace,** constructed in the Italianate style with an ocher facade. A park, Frederiksberg Have, surrounds the palace. To the west of the palace is the **Zoologisk Have,** one of the largest zoos in Europe.

Dragør Dragør is a fishing village south of the city that dates from the 16th century. Along with Tivoli, this seems to be everybody's favorite leisure spot. It's especially recommended for its aura of an 18th-century Danish village if you only have time to see the Copenhagen area. Walk its cobblestone streets and enjoy its 65 old red-roofed houses, designated as national landmarks.

2 Getting Around

Copenhagen is a walker's paradise, neat and compact. Many of the major sightseeing attractions are close to one another.

BY PUBLIC TRANSPORTATION

A joint zone fare system includes Copenhagen Transport buses; State Railway, Metro, and S-tog trains in Copenhagen and North Zealand; plus some private railway routes within a 40km (25-mile) radius of the capital, enabling you to transfer from train to bus and vice versa with the same ticket.

BASIC FARES A *grundbillet* (basic ticket) for both buses and trains costs 18DKK ($3.20/£1.60). Up to two children age 11 and under ride for half fare when accompanied by an adult. For 105DKK ($19/£9.45) you can purchase a ticket allowing 24-hour bus and train travel through nearly half of Zealand; it's half-price for children 7 to 11, and free for children 6 and under.

DISCOUNT PASSES The **Copenhagen Card** entitles you to free and unlimited travel by bus and rail throughout the metropolitan area (including North Zealand), 25% to 50% discounts on crossings to and from Sweden, and free admission to many sights and museums. The card is available for 1 or 3 days and costs 199DKK ($35/ £18) and 429DKK ($77/£39), respectively. Up to two children under the age of 10 are allowed to go free with each adult card. If you have three or more children, a 50% discount is granted. Buy the card at tourist offices, at the airport, at train stations, and at most hotels. For more information, contact the Copenhagen Tourist Information Center (see the previous section, "Orientation") or click on www.cphcard.com.

For information about low-cost train, ferry, and plane trips, go to **Wasteels**, Skoubogade 6 (© **33-14-46-33**), in Copenhagen. It's open Monday to Friday 9am to 5pm and Saturday 10am to 3pm.

Eurailpasses (which must be purchased in the U.S.) and **Nordturist Pass** tickets (which can be purchased at any train station in Scandinavia) can be used on local trains in Copenhagen. (For a more complete discussion of the cost/use of these passes, see p. 32.)

BY BUS Copenhagen's well-maintained buses are the least expensive method of getting around, and most buses leave from Rådhuspladsen in the heart of the city. A basic ticket allows 1 hour of travel and unlimited transfers within the zone where you started your trip. For information, call © **36-13-14-15.**

BY METRO In 2002, Copenhagen launched its first Metro line, taking passengers from east to west across the city or vice versa. Operating 24 hours, the metro links the western and eastern sections of Copenhagen to the center. Eventually, when completed, the metro will run all the way to the airport. Nørreport is the transfer station to the **S-tog** system, the commuter rail link to the suburbs. Metro trains run every 2 minutes during rush hours and every 15 minutes at night. Fares are integrated into the existing zonal systems (see "Basic Fares," above).

BY S-TOG The S-tog connects the heart of Copenhagen, most notably the Central Station, with the city's suburbs. Use of the tickets is the same as on buses (see "Basic Fares," above). You can transfer from a bus line to an S-tog train on the same ticket. Eurailpass holders generally ride free. For more information, call © **70-13-14-15.**

BY CAR

Because of the widespread availability of traffic-free walkways in Copenhagen, and its many parks, gardens, and canalside promenades, the Danish capital is well suited to pedestrian promenades. It's best to park your car in any of the dozens of city parking lots, then retrieve it when you're ready to explore the suburbs or countryside. Many parking lots are open 24 hours, but a few close between 1 and 7am; some close on Saturday afternoon and on Sunday when traffic is generally lighter. The cost ranges from 23DKK to 25DKK ($3.90–$4.25/£2.10–£2.25)per hour or 240DKK ($41/£22) for 24 hours. Two centrally located parking lots are **Industriens Hus,** H. C. Andersens Blvd. 18 (© **33-91-21-75**), open Monday to Friday 7am to midnight, Saturday 9am to 1am, Sunday 9am to midnight; and **Park City,** Israels Plads (© **70-22-92-20**), open daily from 6am to midnight for entry. (You can exit from this facility any time, 24 hr. a day.)

BY TAXI

Watch for the FRI (free) sign or green light to hail a taxi, and be sure the taxis are metered. **Taxa 4x35** (© **35-35-35-35**) operates the largest fleet of cabs. Tips are included in the meter price: 19DKK to 32DKK ($3.25–$5.45/£1.70–£2.90) at the drop of the flag and 12DKK ($2.15/£1.10) per kilometer (about ⅔ mile) thereafter, Monday to Friday 7am to 4pm. From 6pm to 6am, and all day Saturday and Sunday, the cost is 15DKK ($2.70/£1.35) per kilometer. Many drivers speak English.

BY BICYCLE

To reduce pollution from cars (among other reasons), many Copenhageners ride bicycles. In her younger days, even the queen of Denmark could be seen cycling around just like her subjects. You can rent a bike at **Københavns Cyklebors,** Gothersgade 157 (© **33-14-07-17**). Depending on the bike, daily rates range from 60DKK to 150DKK ($10–$26/£5.40–£14), with deposits from 200DKK to 300DKK ($34–$51/£18–£27). Hours are Monday to Friday 8:30am to 5:30pm and Saturday 10am to 1:30pm.

FAST FACTS: Copenhagen

American Express Amex is represented throughout Denmark by **Nyman & Schultz,** Nørregade 7A (© **33-13-11-81;** bus: 34 or 35), with a branch in Terminal 3 of the Copenhagen Airport. Fulfilling all the functions of American Express except for foreign exchange services, the main office is open Monday to Thursday 8:30am to 4:30pm, and Friday 8:30am to 4pm. The airport office remains open until 8:30pm Monday to Friday. On weekends, and overnight on weekdays, a recorded message, in English, will deliver the phone number of a 24-hour AMEX service in Stockholm. This is useful for anyone who has lost a card or traveler's checks.

Bookstores One of the best and most centrally located is **Politikens Boghallen,** Rådhuspladsen 37 (© **33-47-25-60;** bus: 2, 8, or 30), offering more English titles than its competitors. Hours are Monday to Friday 10am to 7pm, and Saturday 10am to 4pm.

Business Hours Most **banks** are open Monday to Friday 10am to 4pm (to 6pm Thurs). **Stores** are generally open Monday to Thursday 9am to 6pm, Friday 9am to 7 or 8pm, and Saturday 9am to 2pm; most are closed Sunday. **Offices** are open Monday to Friday 9 or 10am to 4 or 5pm.

Currency Exchange Banks give better rates than currency kiosks. The main branch of Den Danske Bank (The Danish Bank), Holmens Kanal, 2-12 (© **33-44-00-00**), is open Monday to Friday from 10am to 4pm (to 5:30pm Thurs). When banks are closed, you can exchange money at **Forex** (© **33-11-29-05**) in the Central Railroad Station, daily 8am to 10pm, or at the **Change Group,** Østergade 61 (© **33-93-04-55;** bus: 9 or 10), daily 8:30am to 8:15pm.

Dentists During regular business hours, ask your hotel to call the nearest English-speaking dentist. For emergencies, go to **Tandlægevagten,** Oslo Plads 14 (© **35-38-02-51;** bus: 6 or 9), near Østerport Station and the U.S. Embassy. It's open Monday to Friday 8am to 9:30pm and Saturday, Sunday, and holidays 10am to noon. Be prepared to pay in cash.

Doctors To reach a doctor, dial ℰ **38-11-40-00** 24 hours a day (www.copenhagen doctors.dk). The doctor's fee is payable in cash and visits cost 120DKK ($21/£11) per visit from Monday to Friday 8am to 4pm and 160DKK ($29/£14) all other times. The doctor will arrive within 45 minutes and provide most medication. Language is hardly a problem in Denmark, where virtually all doctors speak English.

Emergencies Dial ℰ **112** to report a fire or to call the police or an ambulance. State your phone number and address. Emergency calls from public telephones are free (no coins needed).

Hospitals In cases of illness or accident, even foreigners are entitled to free medical treatment in Denmark. One of the most centrally located hospitals is **Rigshospitalet,** Blegdamsvej 9 (ℰ **35-45-35-45;** bus: 10).

Internet Access To check your e-mail or to send messages, go to **Copenhagen Hovebibliotek,** Krystalgade 15 (ℰ **33-73-60-60;** bus: 5, 14, or 16), open Monday to Friday 10am to 7pm, Saturday 10am to 2pm.

Lost Property The Lost and Found Property office at Slotsherrensvej 113, 2720 Vanløse (ℰ **38-74-88-22;** bus: 12 or 22), is open Monday, Wednesday, and Friday 9am to 2pm, Tuesday and Thursday 9am to 5:30pm.

Luggage Storage & Lockers Luggage can be stored in lockers at Central Railroad Station. Lockers are accessible Monday to Saturday 5:30am to 1am and Sunday 6am to 1am. The cost is between 25DKK and 35DKK ($4.25–$6.25/ £2.25–£3.15) for 24 hours, depending on the size of your luggage.

Newspapers Foreign newspapers, particularly the *International Herald Tribune* and *USA Today,* are available at the Central Railroad Station in front of the Palladium movie theater on Vesterbrogade, at many newspaper kiosks on Strøget, and at the newsstands of big hotels. Foreign fashion and lifestyle magazines are also widely sold.

Pharmacies An *apotek* (pharmacy) open 24 hours a day is **Steno Apotek,** Vesterbrogade 6C (ℰ **33-14-82-66;** bus: 6), lying opposite the Central Railroad Station.

Police In an emergency, dial ℰ **112.** For other matters, go to the police station at Halmtorvet 20 (ℰ **33-25-14-48**).

Post Office For information about the Copenhagen post office, phone ℰ **80-20-70-30.** The main post office, where your *poste restante* (general delivery) letters can be picked up, is located at Tietgensgade 37, DK-1704 København (ℰ **80-20-70-30;** bus: 10 or 46). It's open Monday to Friday 11am to 6pm and Saturday 10am to 1pm. The post office at the Central Railroad Station is open Monday to Friday 8am to 9pm, Saturday 9am to 4pm, and Sunday 10am to 4pm.

Restrooms Public toilets are at Rådhuspladsen (Town Hall Square), at the Central Railroad Station, and at all terminals. Look for the signs TOILETTER, WC, DAMER (women), or HERRER (men). There is no charge.

Safety Compared with other European capital cities, Copenhagen is relatively safe. However, since the early 1990s, with the increase of homelessness and unemployment, crime has risen. Guard your wallet, purse, and other valuables as you would when traveling in any big city.

Taxes Throughout Denmark you'll come across MOMS on your bills, a government-imposed value-added tax of 25%. It's included in hotel and restaurant bills, service charges, entrance fees, and repair of foreign-registered cars. No refunds are given on these items. For more information, see "Shopping," in chapter 5.

Transit Information Day or night, phone ℂ **70-13-14-15** for bus, Metro, and S-tog information.

3 Where to Stay

High season in Denmark is May to September, which pretty much coincides with the schedule at Tivoli Gardens. Once Tivoli closes for the winter, lots of rooms become available. Make sure to ask about winter discounts, and ask if breakfast is included (usually it isn't).

Nearly all doubles come with a private bathroom. Find out, though, whether this means a shower or a tub. At moderate and inexpensive hotels, you can save money by requesting a room without a bathroom. Keep in mind that in most moderate and nearly all of the inexpensive hotels, bathrooms are cramped, and there's never enough room to spread out all of your stuff. Many were added to older buildings that weren't designed for bathrooms. Also, get used to towels that are much thinner than you might like—not the thick, fluffy types always demanded by Frank Sinatra when he checked into a hotel anywhere in the world.

Several moderately priced hotels in Copenhagen are known as **mission hotels;** they were originally founded by a temperance society, but now about half of them are fully licensed to serve alcohol. They tend to cater to middle-class families.

RESERVATIONS SERVICE　At Bernstorffsgade 1, across from the Tivoli's main entrance, the Tourist Information Center maintains a useful hotel-booking service, **Værelsænvisningen** (ℂ **70-22-24-42**). In person, the charge, whether you book into a private home, a hostel, or a luxury hotel, is 100DKK ($17/£9) per person. This fee is waived when booking by telephone or Internet. You'll also be given a city map and bus directions. This particular office doesn't accept advance reservations; it can arrange private accommodations if the hotels in your price range are already full. The office is open April 19 to September 30, daily 9am to 9pm, and October to April 18, Monday to Friday 9am to 5pm and Saturday 9am to 2pm.

In the same building is another service—the **Hotel Booking Service** (ℂ **70-22-24-42**)—that will reserve hotel rooms in advance.

NEAR KONGENS NYTORV & NYHAVN

Once the home of sailor bars and tattoo parlors, Nyhavn is now a chic, up-and-coming section of Copenhagen. The central canal, filled with 19th-century boats and the 18th-century facades of the buildings around it, contributes to the area's evocative ambience.

VERY EXPENSIVE

Hotel d'Angleterre ★★★ *Kids*   If hotels were crowned like the queen of Denmark, the coronation would surely place the gem-studded crown on this bastion of elegance, deluxe comfort, and sophistication. "Don't even consider any other choice—they're all dumps," Marlene Dietrich, appearing at the Tivoli Gardens, once wrote in a note to her companion, Noël Coward. The world of politicians, rock stars, and even crowned heads must have taken the advice of The Blue Angel. Although they weren't exactly seen strolling through the lobby arm in arm, both the Baroness Margaret Thatcher and Madonna (called a "transvestite" by that Kazakh TV reporter "Borat") have also checked in.

With 250 years of history, the d'Angleterre is one of the oldest deluxe bastions in the world, although it's kept abreast of the times with modern comforts. Its royal suite is— guess what?—fit for a king (or queen as the case may be). The seven-story property at the top of Nyhavn is a member of the Leading Hotels of the World. It was built as a private club for English merchants before its transformation into a hotel in 1805. Hans Christian Andersen was among the first celebrity guests. One of the most recent "big name" residents to check in was Michael Jackson. When the staff refused to sell him a suit of armor in the public rooms, he threatened to buy the entire hotel. And you believe all those headlines that he was broke? The midsize-to-spacious bedrooms are beautifully furnished in a medley of styles. We prefer the Empire and Louis XVI rooms, though you may opt for the conservatively modern. Each high-ceilinged bedroom comes with a private marble bathroom with robes, phone, and a tub/shower combo. The deluxe rooms are in front; those facing the courtyard are smaller but more tranquil.

Kongens Nytorv 34, DK-1050 København. ⓒ 800/448-8355 in the U.S., or 33-12-00-95. Fax 33-12-11-18. www. remmen.dk. 123 units. 2,450DKK–2,950DKK ($417–$502/£221–£266) double; from 5,000DKK ($850/£450) suite. AE, DC, MC, V. Parking 175DKK ($30/£16). Bus: 1, 6, or 9. **Amenities:** Restaurant; bar; indoor heated pool; fitness center; spa; sauna; 24-hr. room service; babysitting; laundry service; dry cleaning; nonsmoking rooms. *In room:* A/C, TV, dataport, Wi-Fi, minibar, hair dryer, safe.

Phoenix Copenhagen ★★   Though it falls a bit short of its goal, this government-rated four-star hotel poses a serious challenge to the discreet grandeur of the d'Angleterre. It saw the light of day in the 1680s when it was constructed to accommodate the aristocratic courtiers of Amalienborg Palace, which is visible from the rear of the hotel. In 1847 the guesthouse was torn down and rebuilt as a luxury Victorian-style hotel, attracting the English nobility. It was compared to the mythical phoenix rising from the ashes—hence, its name.

Tons of white and colored marble were imported to create a modern version of the Louis XVI style. Beautiful wool carpeting and chandeliers add glamour to the standard guest rooms, but many are a bit too small for our tastes. If you're willing to pay more, opt for one of the business-class rooms or perhaps a suite. Each accommodation comes with an Italian marble bathroom with robes and a tub/shower combo. You'll catch us hanging out with Danish publishers in the English-style pub, Murdock's Books & Ale, devouring beer and *smørrebrød* (open-faced sandwiches) against a backdrop of mahogany and brass, later dining from an international menu in the Restaurant Von Plessen, named to honor the original owner of the hotel.

Bredgade 37, DK-1260 København. ⓒ **33-95-95-00.** Fax 33-33-98-33. www.phoenixcopenhagen.com. 213 units. 1,850DKK–2,890DKK ($315–$491/£166–£260) double; 2,190DKK–3,600DKK ($372–$612/£197–£324) suite. AE, DC, MC, V. Parking 113DKK ($19/£10). Bus: 1, 6, 9, or 10. **Amenities:** Restaurant; bar; car rental; 24-hr. room service; babysitting; laundry service; dry cleaning; nonsmoking rooms. *In room:* A/C, TV, dataport, Wi-Fi, minibar, hair dryer, trouser press (in some), iron, safe.

Copenhagen Accommodations

Absalon Hotel og
  Absalon Annex **12**
Ascot Hotel **27**
Bertram Hotel Guldsmeden **6**
Carlton Hotel Guldsmeden **7**
City Hotel Nebo **16**
Clarion Collection
  Hotel Neptun **35**
Clarion Collection Mayfair **11**
Comfort Hotel Esplanaden **38**
Copenhagen Admiral
  Hotel **37**
Copenhagen Island Hotel **21**
Copenhagen Strand **30**
Danhostel Copenhagen
  City **23**
DGI-byen's Hotel **19**
First Hotel Vesterbro **10**
Front Hotel Copenhagen **36**
Grand Hotel **13**
Hotel Ansgar **18**
Hotel d'Angleterre **33**
Hotel Fox **4**
Hotel Jørgensen **3**
Hotel Opera **32**
Hotel Selandia **9**
Hotel Skt. Petri **28**
Hotel 27 **24**
Ibis Copenhagen
  Crown Hotel **8**
Ibsens Hotel **2**
Kong Arthur **1**
Kong Frederik **26**
Le Meridien Palace Hotel **25**
Maritime **29**
Marriott Copenhagen **20**
Phoenix Copenhagen **34**
Radisson SAS Royal **14**
Radisson SAS Scandinavian
  Hotel **22**
Saga Hotel **17**
Scandic Copenhagen **5**
71 Nyhavn **31**
Sofitel Plaza Copenhagen **15**

EXPENSIVE

Clarion Collection Hotel Neptun ✮   The dream of this place never quite came true. Founded in 1854, the hotel was meant to be the gathering place for the bohemian and literati set. These days, commercial clients, a scattering of tourists, and even tour groups dominate the client list, but the main lounge still 'evokes an upper-crust living room in an English country house, with its traditional furnishings and even a chess table.

Many of the bedrooms open onto two covered interior courtyards, adding a little glamour to the joint. Ask for one of the bedrooms that open onto a courtyard, as they are the brightest during the day and the most tranquil in the evening. Bedrooms are tastefully furnished in a modern style, and most of them are either small or midsize. The tiled bathrooms, though modest in size, are well equipped and maintained, each with a tub/shower combo. Another feature of the hotel is an outdoor terrace on the sixth floor where you can order drinks in the summer. Some bright young chefs operate the hotel's restaurant, lying next door. **The Gendarmen** offers a seasonally adjusted menu that respects traditional Danish recipes but prepares many of them with a lighter touch. Check it out.

Skt. Annæ Plads 18–20, DK-1250 København. ✆ **800/654-6200** in the U.S., or 33-96-20-00. Fax 33-96-20-66. www.choicehotels.dk. 133 units. 1,290DKK–1,925DKK ($219–$327/£116–£173) double; 2,095DKK–2,595DKK ($356–$441/£189–£234) suite. Breakfast 125DKK ($23/£11). AE, DC, MC, V. Parking 125DKK ($21/£11). Bus: 1, 6, 9, or 19. **Amenities:** Restaurant; bar; room service (noon–9pm); babysitting; laundry service; dry cleaning; nonsmoking rooms. *In room:* A/C, TV, dataport (in some), minibar, hair dryer, safe.

Front Hotel Copenhagen ✮   From the outside, this boxy-looking building might remind you of the rash of angular modern construction that blossomed throughout Central Europe during the Cold War. On the inside, however, it's one of the hottest and most appealing recently opened hotels in town. It originated in 1964 as a hotel. After several different configurations, most recently a radical upgrade in 2005, it now enjoys a link with the nearby Hotel d'Angleterre, one of the most elegant and most expensive in town, and a location close to the very central Nyhavn Canal. Throughout, the decor is minimalist and somewhat self-consciously linked to the Spartan-looking heyday of Denmark's modern design movement. In fact, it's so minimalist that some parts of it, including the lobby area, might remind you of a college dormitory, except for the snazzily uniformed and endearingly cheerful staff. Bedrooms benefit from very large windows, high-quality Danish modern furniture, lots of sunlight, and panoramic views, and are accessible via the hotel's only really visible drawback—small, awkwardly configured elevators that are simply too cramped for the amount of use they get. Bedrooms contain furniture, some of it upholstered with black leather, that evoke the best in postmillennium design.

Skt. Annæ Plads 21, P.O. Box 9076, DK-1022 København. ✆ **33-13-34-00.** Fax 33-11-77-07. www.front.dk. 31 units. 1,590DKK–2,790DKK ($284–$497/£143–£251) double. AE, DC, MC, V. Metro: Kongens Nytorv. **Amenities:** Restaurant; bar; health club and exercise area; laundry service; dry cleaning. *In room:* A/C, TV, Wi-Fi, minibar.

Hotel Skt. Petri ✮✮✮   If your name is Johnny Depp (traveling incognito) or if you're the playboy-columnist Taki Theodoracopulos, perhaps the notorious Claus von Bulow, and the d'Angleterre is just too staid for you, slip in through the back door here to avoid the paparazzi. Karl Rove is too square to be accepted, but for the world's fashionistas and interior designers, this is a mandatory stopover for the chic flying into Copenhagen. Since the 1930s the site of this hotel was the much-loved department store, Dalle Valle. Today, in an amazing reincarnation, it's become one of the grandest hotels in Copenhagen—and our personal favorite. Modern Danish design, as interpreted by interior designer Per Arnoldi, is showcased here. Rooms are individually done in a minimalist yet elegant style, with bright, cheerful colors and such touches as Mondrian-inspired headboards. The beds are among the most comfortable we've encountered in the Danish capital, with down mattress pads, soft pillows, Angora blankets, and comfy duvets. Opt for a double with terrace on the fifth or sixth floors. The ceilings in most rooms are a bit low, but the lobby rises three floors, embracing an atrium garden. Musicians, artists, and designers are among those we've seen in the fashionable **Bar Rouge** or in **Brasserie Bleu.** If you won't believe us when we tell you how fabulous this place is, perhaps you'll listen to the "talking elevator" (you heard that right).

Krystalgade 22, DK-1172 København. © 33-45-91-00. Fax 33-45-91-10. www.hotelsktpetri.com. 268 units. 998DKK–2,695DKK ($178–$480/£90–£243) double; from 3,395DKK ($605/£306) suite. AE, DC, MC, V. Parking 195DKK ($35/£18). S-tog: Nørreport. **Amenities:** Restaurant; bar; fitness room; 24-hr. room service; laundry service; dry cleaning; nonsmoking rooms; rooms for those w/limited mobility. *In room:* A/C, TV, dataport, Wi-Fi, minibar, hair dryer, safe.

71 Nyhavn ✦✦ Few people dream of sleeping in a warehouse until they check in here. Back in 1804 this building on the corner between the harbor and Nyhavn Canal housed everything from bales of cotton from America to live chickens from the Danish countryside. Today the massively restored red-brick structure, converted into a hotel in 1971, is one of the most successful examples of recycling in the Danish capital. The smell of spices from the Far East has long faded, but the architects wisely kept the Pomeranian fir beams for atmosphere. That the building is standing at all today is something of a miracle because an 1807 British bombardment destroyed most of the surrounding structures.

We like to wake up in the morning here, pulling back the draperies for a view of the old ships anchored at Nyhavn. If there's a downside, it's the smallness of most of the bedrooms, though each comes with a tiled bathroom with a tub/shower combo. "Don't say that our rooms are tiny," the assistant manager told us. "We prefer the word *cozy.*" He's right: They are that, all right, with crisscrossing timbers, soft leather furniture, and dark wood accents. Gastronomic evenings are a daily event in the on-site Pakhuskælderen, where the menu is seasonally adjusted.

Nyhavn 71, DK-1051 København. © 33-43-62-00. Fax 33-43-62-01. www.71nyhavnhotel.com. 150 units. Mon–Thurs 1,885DKK–2,500DKK ($336–$446/£170–£225) double, 3,135DKK–5,235DKK ($559–$934/£282–£471) suite; Fri–Sun 1,430DKK–1,840DKK ($255–$328/£129–£166) double, 3,900DKK–5,200DKK ($695–$927/£351–£468) suite. Rates include breakfast (weekends only). AE, DC, MC, V. Free parking. S-tog: Kongensnytorv. **Amenities:** Restaurant; bar; car rental; room service (7am–10:30pm); babysitting; laundry service; dry cleaning; nonsmoking rooms. *In room:* A/C, TV, dataport, Wi-Fi, minibar, hair dryer, trouser press, iron, safe.

MODERATE

Comfort Hotel Esplanaden This hotel is a bit dull but comfortable, and moderately priced—reason enough to recommend it. It occupies a much-upgraded mid-19th-century building with a pair of long-suffering caryatids, human figures supposedly bearing the weight of the building's facade, flanking the front entrance. Inside, you'll find a functionally modern interior with very few antique touches, a roster of much-used but well-maintained bedrooms, and a simple decor that's efficient, and aggressively unpretentious. Don't expect frills or very many grace notes, as everything is fast paced with frequent turnover. But the location is on the stylish Bredgade (albeit at its less stylish end), close to the museum of the Danish Resistance and the northern end of Copenhagen's harborfront.

Bredgate 78, DK-1260 København. (✆) **33-48-10-00.** Fax 33-48-10-66. www.choicehotels.dk. 116 units. 950DKK–1,595DKK ($169–$284/£86–£144) double; 1,150DKK–1,795DKK ($205–$320/£104–£162) suite. AE, DC, MC, V. **Amenities:** Restaurant; bar; limited room service; free Internet use in lobby. *In room:* TV, minibar.

Copenhagen Admiral Hotel   In 1787 the building housing this hotel put bread on the table of many Copenhageners. The former grain warehouse was turned into a hotel in 1988, and in terms of its physical plant, is the most serious rival of 71 Nyhavn, which has a slight edge. Its location is 2 blocks from the Nyhavn Canal, where sailors of yore went for tattoos and prostitutes. Today many rooms with French balconies open onto harbor views. But thousands of tourists have replaced those sailors of yesterday. Huge timber ceiling beams and roof supports evoke the warehouse; otherwise, the hotel is completely modern, carrying a four-star rating from the government.

Should the queen invite you by for tea, you are only a couple of hundred yards from Amalienborg. No two of the midsize rooms here are identical, but each comes with rustic wooden beams and tasteful Danish furniture from classic designers. All the furniture is custom made of solid teak, and each unit is equipped with a small bathroom with bidet and tub/shower combo. The split-level sixth-floor suites—actually studios—are the best accommodations, with large sitting areas and upgraded furnishing. On-site is the **SALT Restaurant & Bar,** with exposed beams and whitewashed walls, and a superb French and Mediterranean cuisine using Danish raw materials whenever possible.

Toldbodgade 24–28, DK-1253 København. (✆) **33-74-14-14.** Fax 33-74-14-16. www.admiralhotel.dk. 366 units. 1,540DKK–1,565DKK ($275–$279/£139–£141) double; 1,625DKK–2,500DKK ($290–$446/£146–£225) suite. AE, MC, V. Free parking. Bus: 1, 9, 10, 28, or 41. **Amenities:** Restaurant; bar; nightclub; sauna; 24-hr. room service; laundry service; dry cleaning; nonsmoking rooms; solarium. *In room:* TV, dataport, minibar, hair dryer.

Copenhagen Strand 🏵 *(Value*   This hotel is rated only three stars by the government, but, frankly, we think that only its lack of a restaurant keeps it from four-star status. In 2002 two 18th-century brick-and-timber warehouses were recycled into a hotel at a site only a 5-minute walk from Nyhavn. Because of its harborfront location, the snug lobby has a maritime theme with pictures of ships on the walls and chic brown leather sofas. Many of the old-fashioned architectural details of the building have been retained, and there is a certain nautical gloss here, with varnished wood, brass hardware, and marine artifacts. We like to drop in at the bar in the lobby, where the reception staff works double time mixing drinks and pulling pints.

The medium-size rooms are cozy but predictably less richly decorated than the lobby. For the most part, they are small, cozy, and both tastefully and comfortably furnished with Danish modern. Each unit comes with a sparkling bathroom with tub/shower combo. The best accommodations, if you can afford them, are 16 double executive rooms, plus junior suites and deluxe suites, each of which opens onto a panoramic view of the harbor.

Havnegade 37, DK-1058 København K. (✆) **33-48-99-00.** Fax 33-48-99-01. www.copenhagenstrand.dk. 174 units. Mon–Thurs 1,670DKK–2,360DKK ($284–$401/£150–£212) double, 2,875DKK–3,290DKK ($489–$559/£259–£296) suite; Fri–Sun 1,330DKK–1,875DKK ($226–$319/£120–£169) double, 2,085DKK–3,115DKK ($354–$530/£188–£280) suite. Rates include buffet breakfast. AE, DC, MC, V. Parking 210DKK ($36/£19). Tram: 1 or 6. **Amenities:** Breakfast room; bar; car rental; business center; 24-hr. room service; babysitting; laundry service; dry cleaning; nonsmoking rooms. *In room:* TV, dataport (in most), Wi-Fi, minibar, hair dryer, trouser press, iron.

Hotel Opera (★ *Finds*) Discreet, traditional, and inviting, this five-story member of a well-respected Danish chain lies on a tranquil, old-fashioned street just behind what used to be the opera house. All those opera stars who used to stay here now lodge elsewhere and perform at the new opera house. Despite the change in the opera's venue, this hotel retains its original name, along with an elegant wood-paneled lobby that evokes a sense of Britannic charm. In the lobby, directly in front of you as you enter, is an exact copy of the most famous statue in Denmark, *The Little Mermaid*. According to the staff, it was cast as one of three identical statues, one of which is the famous version sitting on the rocks near the entrance to the city's harbor. The midsize bedrooms are conservatively and traditionally furnished and comfortable—appropriate refuges from the madding crowds at the nearby Nyhavn. Only breakfast is served within this hotel, but there are many good restaurants nearby.

Tordenskjoldsgade 15, DK-1055 København. (℃) **33-47-83-00.** Fax 33-47-83-01. www.operahotelcopenhagen.com. 92 units. Mon–Thurs 1,535DKK–1,840DKK ($261–$313/£139–£166) double; 2,565DKK–3,080DKK ($436–$524/£231–£277) suite. Fri–Sun 1,025DKK–1,435DKK ($174–$244/£92–£129) double; 2,055DKK–2,465DKK ($349–$419/£185–£222) suite. AE, DC, MC, V. **Amenities:** Bar; laundry service; dry cleaning. *In room:* TV, Wi-Fi.

Maritime This hotel on a tranquil street near the waterfront has some expensive neighbors, such as the d'Angleterre, but it keeps its prices more affordable. For its location alone, near Nyhavn Canal, it's a recommendable choice. We used to be put off by a certain rigid staff attitude, although on our last visit we found the staff far more helpful and cooperative. The hotel has benefited from some refurbishing and updating, while keeping to its maritime theme. Even though the building itself is a century old—maybe older—all the well-furnished, midsize bedrooms are up-to-date, both comfortably and tastefully furnished, each unit coming with a well-kept private bathroom with a shower. Even if you want a sandwich at 4 o'clock in the morning, one is available, along with a choice of drinks, in the lobby 24 hours.

Peder Skrams Gade 19, DK-1054 København. (℃) **33-13-48-82.** Fax 33-15-03-45. www.hotel-maritime.dk. 64 units. 925DKK–1,700DKK ($157–$289/£83–£153) double; 1,350DKK–2,200DKK ($230–$374/£122–£198) triple. Rates include breakfast. AE, DC, DISC, MC, V. Bus: 1, 6, or 9. **Amenities:** Restaurant; bar; lounge; laundry service; dry cleaning; nonsmoking rooms. *In room:* TV, dataport, hair dryer.

NEAR RÅDHUSPLADSEN & TIVOLI GARDENS

Some of the most expensive hotels in Copenhagen are here. In the heart of the city, around Rådhuspladsen (Town Hall Square), Tivoli Gardens, and the Central Railroad Station, you'll be near all public transportation and many attractions.

VERY EXPENSIVE

Bertram Hotel Guldsmeden (★) This is the newer and more elegant twin of the also-recommended Carlton Hotel Guldsmeden. Both lie within about 300 yards of one another, on a wide and busy boulevard that runs into the rear of Copenhagen's Central Railway station, within about a 10-minute walk. Rising six stories, the hotel originated in 2006, after a 19th-century town house was radically restored, with special emphasis on the landscaping within the building's central courtyard. Rooms overlook the courtyard, the noisy Vesterbrogade, or the quieter neighborhood in back. Furniture in the bedrooms was imported from Indonesia, and includes four-poster beds and the heavy, artfully simple lines in natural wood that go well with the concepts of Danish modern design and the bright pastel colors in which the rooms are painted. We are especially delighted with the organic breakfast buffet, with excellent grainy breads, homemade yogurt, charcuterie, and French cheese—all served on hand-decorated Mexican crockery. Staff is friendly and accommodating, and overall, the hotel is viewed as a well-chosen, well-conceived middle-bracket choice within a rapidly gentrifying neighborhood loaded with bars, cafes, and increasingly distant memories of the porno shops and sex-industry staples that used to flourish here.

Vesterbrogade 107, 1620 København V. (C) **33-25-04-05.** Fax 33-25-04-02. www.hotelguldsmeden.dk. 47 units. 1,497DKK ($254/£135) double; 1,695DKK ($288/£153) suite. Rates include breakfast buffet. AE, DC, MC, V. Parking 75DKK ($13/£6.75). Bus: 6A. **Amenities:** Restaurant; bar; limited room service; babysitting; laundry service; dry cleaning; nonsmoking rooms. *In room:* TV, Wi-Fi, minibar, hair dryer, safe.

Le Meridien Palace Hotel 🐓🐓
Changes are in the air, so what we say here is not written in stone. Opened in 1910 and declared a historic landmark in 1985, the Palace Hotel has been a respite for countless camera-shy celebrities. Although the hotel has tried to keep abreast of the times, it's no longer the front-runner it once was (that distinction now belongs to other recommended hotels, including the Kong Frederik and the Angleterre). That will change, however, during the lifetime of this edition, thanks to an ongoing renovation that will soon bring the hotel from government-rated four- to five-star status. The transformation of the accommodations had already begun in the fall of 2006, with the opening of "The Night Wing," with all new interiors, carpets, draperies, and plumbing. The decor in this wing is individually designed, and, as its name suggests, inspired by the "mystical hues of night." The other contemporary-looking rooms are attractively furnished in an updated version of the Danish modern style—elegant, simple, and comfortable. Most bathrooms are cramped, but they do have tub/shower combos. The best rooms are on the top floor, away from street noise. If you're assigned a room on floors two or three, you are still in luck—they have high ceilings and tasteful furnishings and appointments. Notice the soaring tower associated with this hotel—it rivals that of Town Hall, which lies almost immediately next door. The reception-desk staff is especially helpful in arranging for theater tickets, tours, and transportation. Be careful not to confuse this hotel, by the way, with the Sofitel Plaza Hotel, which is a radically different entity somewhat closer to the railway station. It's an easy error to make, and one with which the desk staff is all too familiar.

Rådhuspladsen 57, DK-1550 København. (C) **800/448-8355** in the U.S., or 33-14-40-50. Fax 33-14-52-79. www.palace-hotel.dk. 162 units. 2,150DKK ($366/£194) double; 3,300DKK ($561/£297) suite. 20% discount may be available on weekends and in midwinter, depending on occupancy. AE, DC, MC, V. Parking 250DKK ($43/£23). Bus: 2, 30, 32, 33, 34, or 35. **Amenities:** Restaurant; bar; 24-hour room service; massage; babysitting; laundry service; dry cleaning; nonsmoking rooms. *In room:* TV, minibar, hair dryer, trouser press, safe.

Radisson SAS Royal 🐓🐓🐓
There are two Radisson SAS hotels in Copenhagen, but we infinitely prefer this one because of its pedigree, although its competitor, the Radisson SAS Scandinavia, attracts those with more modern tastes. The Royal, Copenhagen's first skyscraper, in the city center near Tivoli and Town Hall Square, is famous within the orbit of the Danish design world because of the role of Arne Jacobsen, one of the patriarchs of Danish design. Between 1958 and 1960, he designed not only the hotel but most of the furnishings within it. These included chairs, including the blue-and-white egg chair and the swan chair, whose lines and premises were then copied and distributed around the world as examples of the best of modern Danish design. Today the building is classified as a historic monument that retains most if not all of Arne Jacobsen's original mandates. Rooms are beautifully furnished and well maintained with light maple furnishings and the world-famous Jacobsen chairs and

lamps. The porter who carried our baggage even pointed out the large and rather heavy door handles that were also the creation of the fabled designer. The most requested chamber is no. 606, which is kept just as it was in 1960, except for paint and repairs. All the Jacobsen furnishings in this room are original, including the radiators. Several of the units open onto views over the Tivoli Gardens and the rooftops of Copenhagen. Bathrooms have tub/shower combos and are spacious, except for those in the single rooms, which are small and often lack tubs. At the Business Club on the top floors, guests can take advantage of a lounge with complimentary refreshments, speedier check-ins, and such amenities as free cable and Internet connections. The hotel is among the most kid-friendly in the capital, with a children's menu in the Café Royal, crib and bedding facilities, and a kiddie playroom.

The hotel has the prestigious Italian restaurant **Alberto K** on the top floor. There are also the **Café Royal,** a lobby bar, and the **Royal Lounge Bar,** featuring live jazz on weekends.

Hammerichsgade 1, DK-1611 København. (ℭ) **800/333-3333** in the U.S., or 33-42-60-00. Fax 33-42-63-00. www. radissonsas.com. 260 units. 1,595DKK–2,600DKK ($271–$442/£144–£234) standard double; 2,145DKK–2,845DKK ($365–$484/£193–£256) executive double; 2,600DKK–9,000DKK ($442–$1,530/£234–£810) suite. AE, DC, MC, V. Parking 180DKK ($31/£16). Bus: 14 or 16. **Amenities:** Restaurant; bar; fitness room; sauna; kids' playroom; 24-hr. room service; massage; babysitting; laundry service; dry cleaning; nonsmoking rooms; solarium. *In room:* A/C, TV, dataport, minibar, coffeemaker, hair dryer, iron, safe.

EXPENSIVE

First Hotel Vesterbro 🏵🏵   Just a 5-minute walk from the Tivoli Gardens, this luxury hotel is the third largest in Denmark. Of course, big doesn't always mean best, but in this case Vesterbro is a standout in a city where the competition is rough. When this hotel opened in 1999, it was the first newly built hotel in the center of Copenhagen in more than 15 years. Rooms are midsize to spacious and as modern as tomorrow. In the so-called "Lady Rooms," we were impressed with the robes laid out, the makeup mirror, the beauty products from Clarins, the dress hangers, even an assortment of women's magazines. We would have thought Martha Stewart had just checked out if we didn't know otherwise. The sun-flooded lobby sets the high sense of style and fashion, with windows going from floor to ceiling. The furnishings are like a showcase of Danish design with much use of blond wood. We loved the style, comfort, and taste of the bedrooms, with their pastel-colored walls that brighten a dull gray day in Copenhagen, along with the Spanish cherrywood furniture and the modern lithographs. Our favorite spot here is the atrium garden, lined in brick, and a suntrap on a fair day, ideal for its hanging baskets. You sit at marble tables on wicker chairs. No need to leave the hotel at night for dinner. On-site is the highly professional **Restaurant & Bar Idun,** offering a superb contemporary Danish cuisine with a selection of international specialties as well. Since it's just a short walk to the Central Station, the hotel is convenient to most buses. Guests can use for free a fitness center nearby.

Vesterbrogade 23–29, DK-1620 København. (ℭ) **33-78-80-00.** Fax 33-78-80-80. www.firsthotels.com. 403 units. 1,400DKK–2,050DKK ($238–$349/£126–£185) double. AE, DC, MC, V. Parking 200DKK ($34/£18). **Amenities:** Restaurant; bar; room service (6:30am–11pm); laundry service; dry cleaning; nonsmoking rooms; rooms for those w/limited mobility. *In room:* A/C, TV, dataport, minibar, hair dryer, trouser press, iron, safe.

Grand Hotel 🏵   This 1880 landmark hotel near the Central Station was growing a bit stale but a major postmillennium overhaul has given it a new lease on life. It should be around for at least another 100 years if it keeps having those periodic face-lifts. The charm of the old structure, where celebrities—the "Who's Who of Yesterday"—used to stay, was preserved and respected. But all the midsize-to-spacious bedrooms were tastefully and comfortably updated with modern amenities installed. Bathrooms are quite superior, generous in size, and furnished with tub/shower combos. Singles opening onto the courtyard are more tranquil but don't have views, and the corner rooms are the best and most expensive because they have been the most recently renovated and are larger.

The **Frascati Bar** overflows in summer onto a sidewalk cafe, and the **Restaurant Frascati** serves freshly prepared Italian specialties. We like the Grand a lot and nostalgically recall that it was our first-ever choice for a hotel on our inaugural visit to Copenhagen years ago.

Vesterbrogade 9A, DK-1620 København. (℃ 33-27-69-00. Fax 33-27-69-01. www.grandhotelcopenhagen.com. 161 units. 1,295DKK–2,050DKK ($220–$349/£117–£185) double; 2,050DKK–3,090DKK ($349–$525/£185–£278) suite. Rates include buffet breakfast. AE, DC, MC, V. Bus: 1, 6, 16, 27, 28, or 29. **Amenities:** Restaurant; bar; car rental; business center; room service (7am–11pm); laundry service; dry cleaning; nonsmoking rooms. *In room:* A/C, TV, dataport, minibar, hair dryer, trouser press.

Kong Frederik ★★ *Finds*   There are two "Kongs" among the hotels of Copenhagen, both Kong Frederik and Kong Arthur. Of the two, we think Frederik is "King Kong." The smallest of the ultrachic hotels in Copenhagen, Kong Frederik has the feeling of an unpretentious but elegant private club thanks to discreet service, dark paneling, and a labyrinth of antiques-filled lounges. Many guests, and we agree, feel that it's much cozier than the Hotel d'Angleterre. Originally built around 1850 as two separate hotels, and then combined around a central courtyard about 1990, it has always appealed to glamorous showbiz types. The midsize rooms are conservatively decorated in a wide array of styles with striped fabrics, overstuffed chairs, and antique prints. The hotel has some of the best bathrooms in town, with good lighting, top-brand toiletries, and tub/shower combinations. One Frommer reader from Los Angeles found these bathrooms "sexy," but offered no reason.

The separately recommended restaurant, **Brasserie Le Coq Rouge** (p. 91), is recognized for its fine cuisine and excellent service.

Vester Voldgade 25, DK-1552 København. (℃ 800/448-8355 in the U.S., or 33-12-59-02. Fax 33-93-59-01. www. remmen.dk. 110 units. 1,240DKK–1,840DKK ($211–$313/£112–£166) double; from 3,240DKK ($551/£292) suite. AE, DC, MC, V. Parking 220DKK ($37/£20). Bus: 1, 6, or 28. **Amenities:** Restaurant; bar; fitness center; spa; room service (7am–10pm); laundry service; dry cleaning; nonsmoking rooms. *In room:* TV, minibar, hair dryer, safe.

Radisson SAS Scandinavia Hotel ★★   Talk about keeping up with the times: This hotel has been in constant renovation between 2005 and 2007, and we find it looking better than the day it opened in 1975. Our hearts still belong to the Radisson SAS Royal, however. But for a sleek, modern, skyscraper look, this hotel, a 15-minute walk east of Tivoli, reigns supreme. It is in the predictable Radisson SAS chain style, and could be standing in almost any city—not just Copenhagen. The hotel's most winning feature is that it is run in a rather personal way, filled with an enthusiastic, professional staff who will ease your adjustment into the Danish capital. First-class, midsize rooms are attractive and comfortable, with many luxuries including beautifully kept bathrooms with tub/shower combos. Greater comfort is found on the top floors at the Business Club, where guests also have such complimentary amenities as free cable and Internet connections.

There are four restaurants in this mammoth hotel, each attracting a clientele of locals as well as hotel guests. The two most elegant are the **Blue Elephant,** which serves Thai food, and **The Dining Room,** a panoramic and formal eatery set on the building's 25th floor. On the lobby level are a pair of less expensive restaurants: **Mama's and Papa's**, serving Italian food, grilled steaks, and fresh seafood, much of it from the nearby North Sea; and **Kyoto**, a Japanese restaurant with a full complement of sushi. Gamblers enjoy the **Casino Copenhagen.**

Amager Blvd. 70, DK-2300 København. ℂ **800/333-3333** in the U.S., or 33-96-50-00. Fax 33-96-55-00. www.radisson sas.com. 542 units. Mon–Thurs 1,700DKK–2,000DKK ($289–$340/£153–£180) double, from 2,350DKK ($400/£212) suite; Fri–Sun 1,300DKK–1,600DKK ($221–$272/£117–£144) double, suites same as above. Rates in suites include breakfast. 1 child stays free in parent's room. AE, DC, MC, V. Parking 130DKK ($22/£12). Bus: 15. **Amenities:** 4 restaurants; 2 bars; indoor heated pool; squash court; fitness center; sauna; boutiques; room service (6:30am–11:30pm); massage; babysitting; laundry service; dry cleaning; nonsmoking rooms; rooms for those w/limited mobility; casino; solarium. *In room:* TV, dataport, coffeemaker, iron.

Scandic Copenhagen 𝄞𝄞
The Radisson SAS Scandinavia does it better and more dramatically, but this 18-story steel-and-glass member of a chain is serious competition. Built near the Tivoli Gardens in 1972, and much renovated and improved since then, it rises over the city's lakes near the Tycho Brahe Planetarium. In winter businesspeople fill up the hotel, where the concierge staff can arrange for typists, translators, and other services. In summer most of the clients are here for the sights and attractions.

As in all hotels in these high-rises, the higher up you go, the more panoramic the view, of course. The so-called "cozy" economy singles are just too tiny unless you're shorter than Tom Cruise and don't need much leg space. The superior rooms are among the best of the modern hotel rooms in Copenhagen, and the top-floor superior plus units approach a luxury standard. Opening onto panoramic views, the suites are spacious and luxurious. In the standard rooms, bathrooms tend to be small with showers—no tubs.

The Blue Garden is the hotel's most prestigious dining room, while simple pub grub can be ordered in the **Red Lion Pub.**

Vester Søgade 6 (Box 337), DK-1601 København. ℂ **33-14-35-35**. Fax 33-32-12-23. www.scandic-hotels.com. 486 units. 1,290DKK–2,100DKK ($219–$357/£116–£189) double; 1,190DKK–2,400DKK ($202–$408/£107–£216) suite. Rates include continental breakfast. AE, DC, MC, V. Parking 120DKK ($20/£11). Bus: 1 or 14. **Amenities:** Restaurant; bar; exercise room; sauna; concierge; room service (6am–10pm); massage; laundry service; dry cleaning; nonsmoking rooms; rooms for those w/limited mobility. *In room:* A/C, TV, dataport, minibar, hair dryer, trouser press, iron.

Sofitel Plaza Copenhagen 𝄞𝄞
If we told you that the likes of Keith Richards and Tina Turner have checked in, would that be a plus or a minus? Perhaps a plus for Turner, a minus for the poor, beaten-up Richards. The hotel is still going strong, but actually it is past its heyday. Commissioned by King Frederik VIII in 1913, it once hosted its share of big-name celebrities to Copenhagen, even royalty. Today queens and kings stay elsewhere, although rock stars find it suits them just fine, especially its location opposite the Tivoli Gardens and close to the Central Railway Station.

Still imbued with a turn-of-the-20th-century atmosphere, it has been successfully overhauled for first-class comfort without losing its ambience, such as antique furnishings. As befits the age and era of this hotel, guest rooms come in various sizes and configurations, many evoking an English country house. Antiques, double-glazed windows, and views of the cityscape make this a winning choice. For a kind of Paris garret atmosphere, book one of the top-floor rooms with dormered windows, among the coziest in Copenhagen, especially if you're a romantic duo on an off-the-record weekend. Bathrooms are generous in size, are completely tiled, and contain tub/shower combos and makeup mirrors. Its Library Bar is our favorite place for a drink in town.

Bernstorffsgade 4, DK-1577 København. © **800/221-4542** in the U.S., or 33-14-92-62. Fax 33-93-93-62. www.sofitel. com. 93 units. 2,150DKK ($366/£194) double; 6,695DKK ($1,138/£603) suite. 1 child stays free in parent's room. AE, DC, MC, V. Parking 165DKK ($28/£15). Bus: 1 or 6. **Amenities:** Restaurant; bar; fitness center; car rental; 24-hr. room service; babysitting; laundry service; dry cleaning; nonsmoking rooms. *In room:* A/C, TV, dataport, minibar, hair dryer, safe.

MODERATE

Ascot Hotel 🏵 (*Value*)   The word "ascot," because of its British associations, usually suggests elegance—but not so here. This is one of the best small hotels in Copenhagen, despite the perception that it's in need of some sprucing up. On a side street about a 2-minute walk from Town Hall Square, the inn of personality and charm was built in 1902 (on 492 wooden pilings rescued from a medieval fortification that had previously stood on the site). In 1994, the hotel annexed an adjacent building designed in the 19th century as a bath house; its black-marble columns and interior bas-reliefs are historically notable. Martin Nyrop, who designed the landmark Town Hall, also was the architect for the bathhouse. The furniture is rather standard, but the finest units open onto the street. Nevertheless, the units in the rear get better air circulation and more light. The tiled bathrooms are generous in size and equipped with tub/shower combos.

Studiestræde 61, DK-1554 København. © **33-12-60-00.** Fax 33-14-60-40. www.ascothotel.dk. 120 units. 1,090DKK– 1,480DKK ($185–$252/£98–£133) double; 1,695DKK–2,560DKK ($288–$435/£153–£230) suite. Rates include buffet breakfast. Winter discounts available. AE, DC, MC, V. Parking 85DKK ($14/£7.65). Bus: 14 or 16. **Amenities:** Restaurant; bar; fitness center; room service (7am–11pm); laundry service; dry cleaning; nonsmoking rooms. *In room:* TV, dataport, hair dryer.

Carlton Hotel Guldsmeden 🏵 (*Finds*)   Housed in a much-renovated 19th-century townhouse in the heart of the rapidly gentrifying Vesterbro neighborhood, within a 15-minute walk west from Tivoli and the Central Railway Station, this is a government-rated three-star hotel offering good value and occasional doses of genuine charm. The structure might be old, but the bedrooms are contemporary-looking and up-to-date, ranging from small to midsize. Each is handsomely decorated in a vaguely French colonial style with high ceilings, wood paneling, and four-poster beds imported from Indonesia. The best rooms contain such luxuries as fireplaces, balconies with summer furniture, and claw-foot bathtubs instead of showers. The place is made more homelike and inviting by the original art decorating the walls and a judicious use of elegant teak furnishings, along with carpets from Pakistan and pottery from Mexico. Its newer sister hotel, Bertram's Hotel Guldsmeden, is more charming and a bit more plush, and, unlike the Carlton, contains its own restaurant.

Vesterbrogade 66, DK-1620 København. © **33-22-15-00.** Fax 33-22-15-55. www.hotelguldsmeden.dk. 64 units. 1,375DKK ($234/£124) double; 1,695DKK ($288/£153) junior suite. Rates include buffet breakfast. AE, DC, MC, V. Bus: 6A. Parking 75DKK ($13/£6.75). **Amenities:** Breakfast room; bar; bike rental; limited room service; laundry service; nonsmoking rooms. *In room:* TV, dataport, Wi-Fi, minibar, hair dryer, safe.

DGI-byen's Hotel 🏵 (*Kids*) (*Finds*)   There's no hotel like this one in all Copenhagen. Right behind the Central Station and convenient to most public transportation, this government-rated three-star hotel attracts sports lovers to its precincts, which contain a bowling alley, a gigantic swim center, a spa, a "climbing wall," a shooting range, and, oh yes, a hotel. (The "DGI" within its name translates as "Danish Gymnastics Association.") This is a dynamic, flexible so-called multicenter attracting schoolchildren, sports clubs, company executives, and regular visitors. Bedrooms, midsize to large, reflect the presuppositions and tenets of Danish modern design. Interiors are simple yet tasteful and comfortable with dark wood furnishings and blond wood floors.

Swimming is free to hotel guests within the public indoor pool, located a short distance from the hotel, but access to the spa costs extra. The on-site **restaurant,** serving good and reasonably priced food, was created from an old cattle market that stood here in 1870.

Tietgensgade 65, DK-1704 København. ℭ **33-29-80-70.** Fax 33-29-80-59. www.dgi-byen.dk. 104 units. 925DKK–1,595DKK ($157–$271/£83–£144) double. AE, DC, MC, V. Parking 130DKK ($22/£12). **Amenities:** Restaurant; bar; lounge; 5 indoor heated pools; sports center; spa; Jacuzzi; sauna; babysitting; laundry service; dry cleaning; nonsmoking rooms; rooms for those w/limited mobility; solarium. *In room:* TV, dataport, hair dryer.

Hotel Fox 🎯 *Kids*   In 2005, one of Copenhagen's most unusual and trend-conscious hotels opened within the premises of what until then had been a staid and predictable staple (the Park Hotel) on the Copenhagen hotel scene. The new owners solicited the talents of 21 separate designers from throughout Europe, each of whom submitted plans for new interior decors which reflected their individual whims and priorities. The result is a small-scale hotel that really appreciates the concept of "design" and which, in the opinion of some detractors, has carried it to levels that are almost overwhelming. Its white-painted facade carries renditions of street graffiti that might be almost too artful or too "carefully rehearsed." Each room is a highly idiosyncratic work of art, ranging from tongue-in-cheek enclaves of camp to rigorously streamlined case studies for postindustrial minimalism. Unless you've already requested a particular theme in advance, a computer at the reception desk will show you the visuals of where you're about to sleep. Choices, among many others, include a room dominated by a theme related to boxing, a unit filled with taurine (bull-inspired) souvenirs, an accommodation with syrupy reminders of Heidi, and one devoted to an all-American theme that features extrawide beds for fullbacks and their Brunhildes. **The Fox Kitchen and Bar** (p. 96) on-site is self-consciously trendy, and is recommended separately in "Where to Dine."

Jarmers Plads 3, DK-1551 København. ℭ **33-13-30-00.** Fax 33-14-30-33. www.hotelfox.dk. 61 units. Doubles 920DKK–1,620DKK ($156–$275/£83–£146). Rates include breakfast. AE, DC, MC, V. Parking 150DKK ($26/£14) nearby, 12DKK ($2.05/£1.10) per hour on street. Bus: 14 or 16. **Amenities:** Restaurant; bar; laundry service; dry cleaning. *In room:* TV, hair dryer, safe.

Hotel 27 🎯   This is the most recent incarnation of a large and highly visible hotel that has been owned and operated by a series of owners, most recently the well-recommended Palace Hotel, which lies nearby. Set within a very short walk from Tivoli, and now operating independently of any other partners, it's a large, six-story hotel which opened in 2006 with only 50 rooms operational, the rest coming into use in early 2007. Rooms feature Danish modern design in color schemes of white, black, and soft reds, each with a modestly sized but serviceable bathroom trimmed in slabs of polished stone. At press time for this edition, many aspects of the completed hotel were still being defined, but we fully expect this to be a well-managed, up-to-date member of Copenhagen's middle-bracket hotel scene for many years to come.

Løngangstræde 27, DK-1468 København. ℭ **70-27-56-27.** Fax 70-27-96-27. www.hotel27.dk. 203 units. 790DKK–990DKK ($134–$168/£71–£89) double. Rates include buffet breakfast. AE, DC, MC, V. Bus: 1, 5, or 6. **Amenities:** Bar; laundry service; dry cleaning; nonsmoking rooms. *In room:* TV, hair dryer.

Kong Arthur 🎯 *Kids*   Most guests checking in here think this hotel was named after England's legendary King Arthur. Actually, the Arthur in its name comes from Arthur Frommer, one of the early owners of this hotel and the founding father of the Frommer guides. Right by the Copenhagen lakes and close to Rosenborg Palace, Kong Arthur is a government-rated four-star hotel lying a 15-minute walk from the Tivoli

Kids Family-Friendly Accommodations

DGI-byen's Hotel (p. 76). For many kids, staying here is like being in a deluxe playground, with a multicenter designed especially for children, plus five indoor heated swimming pools. If your kid is athletic, this hotel has more sporting facilities than any other in Denmark.

Hotel d'Angleterre (p. 65). This elegant hotel contains a swimming pool and in-house video; both help keep children entertained. The hotel provides an appropriate setting for the Danish equivalent of Eloise's adventures at New York's old Plaza Hotel.

Hotel Fox (p. 77). Each room has its own decor, with some that appeal directly to children, including the whimsical if surreal room devoted to Heidi and a few of the pastures in Switzerland's high Alps.

Ibsens Hotel (p. 61). This hotel caters to families on a budget, since many of its triple rooms are large enough to house mom, dad, and one or two kids. There are no other special features for kids, however.

Kong Arthur (p. 77). Once a home for Danish orphans, this is a safe haven in a residential section near tree-lined Peblinge Lake.

Gardens. Charm, high-quality comfort, and a welcoming atmosphere greet you today, but back in 1882, things were a bit more rawboned here. The building was once a home for Danish orphans leading a Dickensian existence. We like to go down to breakfast since it's served in a large greenhouse-like room that's flooded with light on sunny days. Bedrooms range from midsize to spacious, and each is tastefully and comfortably furnished with carpets and spacious, tiled bathrooms with tub/shower combos.

Nørre Søgade 11, DK-1370 København. ℰ 33-11-12-12. Fax 33-32-61-30. www.kongarthur.dk. 117 units. 1,520DKK–1,720DKK ($258–$292/£137–£155) double; from 3,020DKK ($513/£272) suite. Rates include buffet breakfast. AE, DC, MC, V. Free parking. Bus: 5, 7, or 16. **Amenities:** 4 restaurants; bar; sauna; car rental; 24-hr. room service; massage; babysitting; laundry service; dry cleaning; nonsmoking rooms. *In room:* TV, dataport, minibar, hair dryer, trouser press, safe.

INEXPENSIVE

City Hotel Nebo (Value) The neighborhood that surrounds this hotel, alas, is still the heart of Copenhagen's "red light" district, but families have been checking in and out of the hotel for generations, finding it perfectly adequate in spite of the surreal quality of a seedy neighborhood that is slowly but inexorably becoming more respectable. In the vicinity of the train station, the hotel opened back in the 1930s as an alcohol-free mission hotel. Its owners are still a Christian foundation whose philosophy is that "everyone should be able to afford an accommodation in Copenhagen." Backpackers often rent the "low economy" rooms sharing the adequate hallway facilities. For more money you can rent small but tastefully decorated doubles, or even some family rooms sleeping up to four guests.

Istedgade 6, DK-1650 København. ℰ 33-21-12-17. Fax 33-23-47-74. www.nebo.dk. 128 units, 88 with bathroom. 690DKK ($117/£62) double without bathroom, 860DKK ($146/£77) double with bathroom; 840DKK ($143/£76) family room for 3, 990DKK ($168/£89) family room for 4. Additional bed 150DKK ($26/£14) extra. Rates include buffet breakfast. AE, DC, MC, V. Parking 40DKK ($6.80/£3.60). Bus: 1, 6, 16, 28, or 41. **Amenities:** Breakfast room; lounge. *In room:* TV.

Ibis Copenhagen Crown Hotel *Value*   When you see the name Ibis at some 650 hotels on the continent or in Scandinavia, you'll know that the price is right. In business for more than a century, this welcoming hotel lies only a short walk from the Tivoli Gardens and the main train station. You enter through a tranquil, beautiful courtyard, evoking Copenhagen of long ago. The traffic-clogged Vesterbrogade is a short distance away but you feel that this is a well-maintained, safe, and quiet haven once you enter. The midsize bedrooms are classically and tastefully decorated, some of them opening onto Vesterbrogade, the rest onto the courtyard. Each accommodation comes with a full bathroom with tub/shower combo. The most attractive feature of this hotel is its rooftop **restaurant,** where a varied Scandinavian breakfast buffet is served overlooking the rooftops of the city.

Vesterbrogade 41, DK-1620 København. ✆ **33-21-21-66.** Fax 33-21-00-66. www.accorhotels.com. 80 units. 625DKK–850DKK ($106–$145/£56–£77) double. Rates include breakfast. AE, DC, MC, V. Bus: 6. **Amenities:** Restaurant; bar; laundry service; dry cleaning; nonsmoking rooms. *In room:* TV, dataport, minibar, hair dryer.

ON HELGOLANDSGADE & COLBJØRNSENSGADE

In the 1970s this area behind the railroad station became one of the major pornography districts of Europe, but subsequent hotel renovations, much-publicized civic efforts, and the gradual decline of the porno shops have led to a continuing gentrification. Today, with the original 19th-century facades mostly still intact and often gracefully restored, the district is safer than you might think and offers some of the best hotel values in Copenhagen.

MODERATE

Clarion Collection Mayfair *☆*   Those Clarion Collection people, a hotel chain known for creating havens of charm and comfort, have moved in on the long-established Mayfair 2 blocks west of the Central Station to give it a new zest for life. Rated three stars by the government, the hotel isn't as well known as it should be, but has enjoyed refurbishing and redecorating, making it a choice address in Copenhagen. In some of its furnishings and decor, it evokes a well-heeled private home in England. Bedrooms come in a wide range of sizes, but each is tastefully furnished and comfortable, with full marble bathrooms with tub/shower combos. The best accommodations here have small sitting areas, so you don't feel you're living in a box. The district around the hotel is becoming increasingly trendy, with the opening of new shops, cocktail lounges, and restaurants.

Helgolandsgade 3, DK-1653 København. ✆ **877/424-6423** in the U.S., or 70-12-17-00. Fax 33-23-96-86. www.choice hotels.com. 105 units. 1,095DKK ($186/£99) double; from 2,330DKK ($396/£210) suite. AE, DC, MC, V. Bus: 6, 16, 28, 29, or 41. **Amenities:** Breakfast room; bar; lounge; bike rental; babysitting; laundry service; dry cleaning; nonsmoking rooms. *In room:* TV, fax, dataport, hair dryer, trouser press, iron, safe.

INEXPENSIVE

★**Absalon Hotel og Absalon Annex** *☆* *Value*   In the increasingly gentrified Vesterbro area, the Absalon traces its origins to a love story that unfolded at the nearby railroad station. Shortly after the yet-to-be father of the present owners began his first job as a porter at a neighboring hotel, he was asked to go to the station to pick up a new babysitter who had just arrived from Jutland. They fell in love, married, and bought the first of the buildings that became the hotel. Two of their children were born in

Room 108. This family-run lodging, one of the best-managed hotels in the neighborhood, consists of four townhouses that were joined into one building and became a hotel in 1938. It has a spacious blue-and-white breakfast room, and an attentive staff directed by third-generation owners. The first generation was on hand to welcome first-time tourists carrying a dog-eared book called *Europe on $5 a Day*. The guest rooms are simple and modern, and come in various sizes ranging from cramped to spacious. We find that those on the fifth floor have the most character. These rooms get the most light and are elegantly furnished in a modified Louis XIV style or in a classical English style, with marble bathrooms with tubs. Overflow guests are housed in one of the rather functional rooms in the Absalon Annex. Bathrooms are equipped with tub/shower combos. For years we have been impressed with the thoughtful extras provided by this hotel—for example, they set aside a luggage room where they will store your bags free if you'd like to travel lighter into the Danish countryside.

Helgolandsgade 15, DK-1653 København. ℭ 33-24-22-11. Fax 33-24-34-11. www.absalon-hotel.dk. 262 units. 900DKK–1,150DKK ($153–$196/£81–£104) double; 1,100DKK–1,300DKK ($187–$221/£99–£117) triple; 1,260DKK–1,810DKK ($214–$308/£113–£163) suite. Rates include buffet breakfast. AE, DC, MC, V. Bus: 6, 10, 16, 27, or 28. **Amenities:** Breakfast room; lounge; laundry service; dry cleaning; nonsmoking rooms. *In room:* TV, dataport (in some), hair dryer (in some), trouser press.

Hotel Ansgar   Just when we were about to drop this tired old workhorse from the guide, it burst into bloom again, with renovated and modernized bedrooms. Decorating magazines may not be too impressed but you get tasteful rooms which are comfortable but plain in Danish modern—no clutter here. Although its prices have risen, the hotel is still a good value and has been ever since it opened in 1885 in a five-story structure. Think of the rooms as cozy instead of small—it's better that way. Two dozen large rooms can accommodate up to six (that's a bit crowded) and are suitable for Brady Bunch–style families. The bedrooms contain well-kept bathrooms with Danish modern shower units (no great compliment). Guests arriving at Kastrup Airport can take the SAS bus to the Air Terminal at the Central Railroad Station, walk through the station, and be inside the hotel in less than 4 minutes.

Colbjørnsensgade 29, DK-1652 København. ℭ 33-21-21-96. Fax 33-21-61-91. www.ansgar-hotel.dk. 81 units. 850DKK–1,250DKK ($145–$213/£77–£113) double. Rates include buffet breakfast. Extra bed 200DKK ($34/£18). AE, DC, MC, V. Bus: 6, 10, 28, or 41. **Amenities:** Breakfast room; lounge; room service (7am–10pm); laundry service; dry cleaning; nonsmoking rooms. *In room:* TV.

★ **Hotel Selandia**   Thousands upon thousands of budget-conscious visitors have been making their way from the railway station to the doors of this hotel ever since it opened in 1928. "We're not glamorous and we attract no movie gods or rock stars," a member of the staff told us, "but we do get budget-conscious visitors from abroad plus regular clients and their families who journey to Copenhagen from the countryside of Denmark." The hotel has kept abreast of the times, now offering free Internet access at the reception. An elevator carries visitors to all floors, one of which features superior units decorated in the style of Louis XVI (before he was beheaded, of course). Such extras in these upgraded rooms include a Bang & Olufsen TV, a minibar, and a beverage maker. In a ground-floor room, an impressive Danish buffet breakfast is laid out each morning, and hot and cold drinks are available throughout the day.

Helgolandsgade 12, DK-1653 København. ℭ 33-31-46-10. Fax 33-31-46-09. www.hotel-selandia.dk. 87 units, 57 with bathroom. 450DKK–695DKK ($77–$118/£41–£63) double without bathroom; 690DKK–995DKK ($117–$169/£62–£90) double with bathroom. Extra bed 200DKK ($34/£18). Rates include breakfast. AE, DC, MC, V.

Closed Dec 20–Jan 2. Bus: 1, 6, 10, 14, 16, 27, or 28. **Amenities:** Breakfast room; lounge. *In room:* TV, minibar (in some), fridge, beverage maker (in some), hair dryer, trouser press (in some).

Saga Hotel   In 1947 two developers purchased two late-19th-century apartment buildings that had survived the Nazi occupation and set out to gut them and turn them into hotel rooms. One of the owners told the press at the time, "We predicted that many tourists would return to Denmark after the war years and many of them would need a clean, respectable, but affordable place to stay." Those long-ago words still ring true today. As trendy, boutique hotels rise up almost yearly, the Saga is rather like it was when it was created, although it has kept up with the times with improvements such as Internet access. The five-story building still has no elevator and some of its rooms are still without a private bathroom. As such, it attracts groups of international visitors in summer and Danish student and convention groups in winter. The rooms are small to midsize, each furnished in Danish modern, and most are equipped with a private bathroom with tub/shower combo. The hotel is especially attractive to families in that it offers some very spacious units with three, four, or even five beds. A generous Scandinavian buffet breakfast is another temptation, and the hotel will also allow you to use its storage facilities at no extra charge.

Colbjørnsensgade 18–20, DK-1652 København. ⓒ **33-24-49-44.** Fax 33-24-60-33. www.sagahotel.dk. 79 units, 31 with bathroom. 480DKK–750DKK ($82–$128/£43–£68) double without bathroom; 600DKK–950DKK ($102–$162/£54–£86) double with bathroom. Rates include breakfast. Extra bed 150DKK ($26/£14). Modest winter discounts. AE, DC, MC, V. Bus: 6, 10, 16, 28, or 41. **Amenities:** Breakfast room; lounge; nonsmoking rooms. *In room:* TV, Wi-Fi.

AT NANSENSGADE
MODERATE

Ibsens Hotel 🄵 🄺 The Brøchner-Mortensen family succeeds in combining an old-fashioned nostalgia with all the modern amenities today's traveler demands. A charming, government-rated three-star hotel in the Nansensgade area, right by the lakes, it is convenient for trips to both Rosenborg Palace and the Tivoli Gardens. In an area filled with cafes and trendy restaurants, the hotel first opened its doors in 1906, surviving wars, occupation, and changing tastes, and somehow keeping abreast of it all. The guest rooms are comfortably and tastefully furnished, each well maintained and containing private bathrooms that are a bit cramped but have tub/shower combos. These cozy rooms open onto a beautiful courtyard. We like the way the hotel offers you a choice of decor on each floor. One floor, for example, showcases Danish modern, whereas another floor has more of a bohemian aura and is filled with antiques. "If you're a modernist and your tastes are minimalist, we have a bed awaiting you," said a member of the reception staff. "But if you're the more exuberant type—wildly romantic—we can also provide a nest for your poetic soul."

Vendersgade 23, DK-1363 København. ⓒ **33-13-19-13.** Fax 33-13-19-16. www.ibsenshotel.dk. 118 units. 1,220DKK–1,420DKK ($207–$241/£110–£128) double; 2,200DKK ($374/£198) suite. Rates include buffet breakfast. AE, DC, MC, V. Bus: 5, 14, or 16. **Amenities:** 2 restaurants; bar; car rentals; babysitting; laundry service; dry cleaning; nonsmoking rooms. *In room:* TV, Wi-Fi.

INEXPENSIVE

Hotel Jørgensen   When this hotel first opened in 1984, it became Denmark's first gay hotel, and many of its foreign guests thought it'd been named in honor of a former American GI, George, who later, after a little surgery, became famous as the transgendered Christine Jorgensen, making headlines around the world with her sex change. In a stucco-fronted building that opened in 1906 as the headquarters of a publishing house, the hotel has changed over the decades. Located on a busy boulevard in central Copenhagen, it now caters to a conventional mix of clients of all sexual persuasions. Many of its guests are backpackers drawn to its cheap lodgings in dormitory rooms segregated by genders and holding between 6 and 12 beds. Although clients over 35 are aggressively discouraged from renting any of the dormitory rooms, they're welcome within the conventional bedrooms. The hotel is reasonably well-maintained, prices are more or less affordable, and the small rooms are conventional and well organized. Bathrooms, in those units that have them, are well kept and contain tub/shower combos.

Rømersgade 11, DK-1362 København. ℂ **33-13-81-86.** Fax 33-15-51-05. www.hoteljoergensen.dk. 24 units; 13 dorm rooms (150 beds). 700DKK ($119/£63) double; 140DKK ($24/£13) per person in dorm. Rates include breakfast. MC, V. Parking 120DKK ($20/£11). Bus: 14 or 16. **Amenities:** Breakfast room; lounge. *In room:* TV.

THE SOUTHERN HARBORFRONT

Much of Copenhagen is expanding westward onto the harborfront of Copenhagen. This expansion of the city includes such hot new hotels as the Marriott and the Copenhagen Island Hotel, both of which are recommended below. City planners for this new district have insisted that pedestrians be granted unrestricted access to the harborfront promenade, allowing them to stroll between *Den Lille Havfruen* (Little Mermaid) near the northern entrance to the harbor, as far south as the Copenhagen Island Hotel and the immediately adjacent Tyske Shopping Plaza. En route, across the harbor, rise hypermodern structures of international renown, among them the new Opera House.

EXPENSIVE

Copenhagen Island Hotel ℝ̂   The Danes are cursed with the belief that any new construction they inaugurate must be more innovative and cutting edge than anything built previously. And as you approach this wildly innovative new hotel, opened in the summer of 2006, you might get the idea that Danish architecture for once went just a wee bit too far. It rises from a position that's immediately adjacent to the waterfront of Copenhagen's south harbor, a neighborhood that's the trendiest in Denmark. It all began in 1999 with the filling in of marshy lowlands, then proceeded with the dredging of a canal that now surrounds it, like a medieval moat, on three sides. The result is literally an "island" ringed with boardwalks, out of which rises a sparkling glass cube that's linked to another cube made from concrete and—you guessed it—more glass. Once you're inside, you'll find the place either fascinating or terrifying—or perhaps a combination of both—thanks to vertigo-inducing catwalks that crisscross the soaring glass-enclosed lobby. And if you're afraid of heights or harbor repressed thoughts of suicide, don't even think about looking down onto the stone floor of the lobby from the dizzying, glass-sided parapets and translucent stair treads that traverse its open, echoing volumes.

In contrast to the dramatic minimalism of the lobby area, bedrooms are compact, even claustrophobic, much akin to white-walled cabins within a cruise ship. Each contains some jazzy decorative touches and fancy-schmancy lighting tricks, but nothing that really masks the cramped dimensions and the sense of cookie-cutter regularity. "Executive" status will get you a balcony that juts out above the cobblestones of the harborfront promenade, but not a lot more. Breakfast buffets here are copious and well-orchestrated, served to a clientele that includes lots of tour groups from Asia, North America, and Slavic Europe. The architect of this place, incidentally, is a big name in Danish design: Kim Utzon, the son of the architect who designed the famous

Opera House in Sydney's harbor. Overall, this is a deliberately nonconformist newcomer to the Hansen Hotel group, a chain that includes 17% of the hotel beds of Copenhagen.

Kalvebod Brygg 53, DK-1560 København. © **33-38-96-00**. Fax 33-38-96-01. www.copenhagenisland.dk. 326 units. 1,500DKK–2,500DKK ($255–$425/£135–£225) double; 3,500DKK ($595/£315) suite. AE, DC, MC, V. S-tog: Dybbøls-bro. **Amenities:** Restaurant; bar; business center; laundry service; dry cleaning. *In room:* A/C, Wi-Fi, minibar.

Marriott Copenhagen 𝒦   One of the capital's newest blockbuster hotels rises like a glassy, postmodern cube from a position a few feet from the pedestrian promenade facing Copenhagen's southern harborfront. The lobby is pleasing, plush, and upscale, with carpets, elegant upholstery, and deep sofas, providing a dramatic contrast to the Spartan angularity of such nearby competitors as the also-recommended Copenhagen Island Hotel. Most of the public areas, and half of the accommodations, open onto sweeping views of the harbor and its dramatic combination of antique and hypermodern architecture, just across the channel. The midsize bedrooms are comfortably and tastefully furnished with sleek Danish modern styling, coming with tiled bathrooms that are well equipped and provided with tub/shower combos. Expect a clientele of upscale tour groups, such as those associated with Seabourn cruises, and international business travelers. It manages to combine upscale international corporate chain mentality with a thoughtful staff. During clement weather, tables are set out on flowering terraces beside the harbor; the rest of the year, the action moves inside into the hermetically sealed, mostly glass-lined interior.

Kalvebod Brygge 5, DK-1560 København. © **88-33-99-00**. Fax 88-33-99-99. www.marriott.com/cphdk. 395 units. 1,595DKK–1,895DKK ($271–$322/£144–£171) double; 2,395DKK–2,895DKK ($407–$492/£216–£261) suite. S-tog: Dybbølsbro. **Amenities:** Restaurant; bar; health club; business center; 24-hour room service; massage; babysitting; laundry service; dry cleaning. *In-room:* A/C, TV, Wi-Fi, minibar, safe.

INEXPENSIVE

Danhostel Copenhagen City 𝒱𝒶𝓁𝓊𝑒   Budget travel, often in hostels, is something like a religion in Denmark. The country is home to hundreds of youth hostels which are widely scattered throughout each of the country's regions. This newest addition to the country's roster of youth hostels opened in 2005 in a white-sided high-rise venue that's one of the most visible buildings along the harborfront, and within a 15-minute walk from Tivoli and the Central Railroad Station. Rising 16 floors (highly unusual for a youth hostel), and hailed by some hostelers as "The Mother of all Youth Hostels," it contains room for more than 1,000 occupants at a time, making it the largest youth hostel in Europe. The hostel used to be an office building. It does a roaring business throughout the year, welcoming individual travelers of any age over 18. Each of the accommodations contains between 4 and 12 beds; a bathroom with toilet, sink, and shower; and virtually no other amenities. Don't expect luxury: You'll pay a one-time 60DKK ($10/£5.40) supplement for sheets and towels, which you can keep until they're too dirty to use. Other than breakfast, no meals are served on-site, but there are many restaurants and bars nearby, and the views (which face either the old town and the Town Hall or Copenhagen's harbor and Christianshavn) are sweepingly spectacular. If you don't already have a youth hostel card, the front desk at this place will sell you one. It costs 35DKK ($5.95/£3.15) for a one-time stay within this particular hostel, or 160DKK ($27/£14) for a card that's universally accepted and valid for a full year.

H. C. Andersens Blvd. 50, DK-1553 København. © **33-11-85-85**. Fax 33-11-85-88. www.danhostel.dk/copenhagen city. 1,020 beds. 520DKK–600DKK ($88–$102/£47–£54) double, triple, or quad. Rental of bed linen 60DKK ($10/£5.40) extra. Breakfast 50DKK ($8.50/£4.50) extra per person. AE, DC, MC, V. Bus 5A. **Amenities:** Breakfast room. *In room:* No phone.

4 Where to Dine

It's estimated that Copenhagen has more than 2,000 cafes, snack bars, and restaurants, and a higher number of Michelin-starred restaurants than any other city in Europe in 2006 (10 with at least one Michelin star), each within an area measuring 4 sq. km (about 1½ sq. miles) on each side. The most convenient restaurants are either in Tivoli Gardens or around Rådhuspladsen (Town Hall Square), around the Central Railroad Station, or in Nyhavn. Others are in the shopping district, on streets off of Strøget.

You pay for the privilege of dining in Tivoli; prices are always higher. Reservations are not usually important, but it's best to call in advance. Nearly everyone who answers the phone at restaurants speaks English.

NEAR KONGENS NYTORV & NYHAVN
VERY EXPENSIVE

Era Ora ✸✸✸ ITALIAN A Danish friend confided that whenever his wife discovers he'd been cheating on her, he always takes her for dinner here—"and all is forgiven." This reminder of the "Golden Age" is on virtually everyone's list as the very best Italian restaurant in Denmark and is one of the best restaurants in Copenhagen. Established in 1982 by Tuscan-born partners Edelvita Santos and Elvio Milleri, it offers an antique-looking dining room, with additional seating for parties of up to 12 in the wine cellar. You're likely to find some chic people dining here, including members of Denmark's royal family, lots of politicians, and well-known Danish writers and artists. The cuisine is based on Tuscan and Umbrian models, with sophisticated variations inspired by Denmark's superb array of fresh seafood and produce. Time plays a key role in the success of this restaurant, whose chefs believe that quality food takes dedication, so nothing is rushed—neither the food nor the guests. Traditional favorites include a platter of 10 types of antipasti, arguably the best version of these Italian hors d'oeuvres in the country. The menu offers a mouthwatering array of classics combined with more imaginative dishes created by the produce of the season and the inspiration of the highly skilled chefs. Dishes have subtle flavorings and "sing" in harmony when ingredients are mixed. The chefs continue to invent and reinvent flavor combinations with a wizardry that's nothing short of staggering.

Their homemade pastas with the town's most savory Italian sauces are freshly made each day—and are succulent. In autumn the rack of venison is justifiably praised by food critics, and the veal dishes are the best we've sampled in Copenhagen. The chefs also do wonders with the fresh fish and shellfish caught off Danish coasts. Desserts are dreamy concoctions, and the clever sommelier guides diners through an impressive cellar with some of the continent's greatest vintages.

Overgaden Neden Vandet 33B. ⓒ **32-54-06-93.** Reservations required. Fixed-price menus 700DKK–2,300DKK ($119–$391/£63–£207). AE, DC, MC, V. Mon–Sat 7pm–1am. Bus: 2 or 8.

Godt ✸✸✸ INTERNATIONAL Its cuisine is as haute as ever, but Godt's reputation has been eclipsed by trendier and more newsworthy restaurants just as good. Nonetheless, it still remains a favorite of ours. A consistent small-scale choice that's known to everyone in the neighborhood, including the Queen, this very formal restaurant offers two floors of minimalist and modern decor that never exceeds more than 20 diners at a time. Food is prepared fresh every day, based on what's best at the market. The chefs have prodigious talent and imagination, and the dishes are constantly changing. The sauces are sublime, as are the herbs and seasonings. Certain dishes appear frequently on the menu—perhaps the sautéed Norwegian redfish with a purée of celery and watercress sauce which is an example of the chef's prowess. Using hand-picked ingredients, the chef turns out a perfectly roasted rack of hare with fresh cranberries and roasted chanterelles. Desserts are a high-flying trip to Valhalla, especially the fresh figs marinated with black currant liqueur, wrapped in phyllo pastry and served with a coulis of pears and a velvety chocolate mousse.

Gothersgade 38. ℭ **33-15-21-22.** Reservations required. Fixed-price menus 480DKK–600DKK ($82–$102/£43–£54). AE, MC, V. Tues–Sat 6pm–midnight. Closed July and Dec 23–Jan 3. Bus: 6, 10, or 14.

Kommandanten ✮✮✮ INTERNATIONAL   Some of our most savvy food-wise friends in Copenhagen insist that this is the country's best restaurant, and we always like to argue the point over a bottle of wine, citing our other recommendations that also richly earn their three stars. Praise has included, "If God were to visit Denmark, this is where he'd dine." Other critics, such as *Time Out,* have attacked not the cuisine but the patrons, citing "stern, fat men with equally fat cigars and even fatter expense accounts." On our latest rounds, the Armani-clad patrons didn't seem especially fat but they did carry American Express platinum cards, as they gazed at the menu when not taking in a trio of Andy Warhol originals of Margrethe II in the downstairs dining room.

To date, this is the only Michelin restaurant in Copenhagen to have received two coveted stars, a rating it has held since 1997. Although a restaurant has stood on this historic street for 75 years, it only reached levels of haute cuisine in 1990. The 1698 burger's house, in which the restaurant is encased, contains numerous small rooms on several levels, evocative of Copenhagen at the time of the author Ludvig Holberg.

The cuisine reflects the seasons and features the very finest products and high-quality ingredients that the country offers. The aim of the chefs is simplicity in which natural flavors are never subdued, as when a misguided cook within a less illustrious restaurant might pour licorice sauce over halibut. The menu, changed every 2 weeks, offers both classical dishes and innovative selections, such as spring chicken with rhubarb set off zestily with an orange and lemon verbena sauce. The luminously fresh halibut comes with smoked eel, fresh peas, and elderflower, a first-rate taste sensation. At last we learned the secret of cooking lobster *à la nage.* The secret ingredient is anise seed.

Ny Adelgade 7. ℭ **33-12-09-90.** Reservations required. Main courses 330DKK–400DKK ($56–$68/£30–£36); fixed-price 5-course menu 790DKK ($134/£71). AE, DC, MC, V. Mon–Sat 5:30–10pm. Bus: 1 or 6.

● **Kong Hans Kælder** ✮✮✮ FRENCH/DANISH/ASIAN   This vaulted Gothic cellar, once owned by King Hans (1455–1513), not only lies in the oldest building in Copenhagen, but also is the site of the best restaurant. Only Kommandanten (see above) gives it serious competition. Five centuries ago the site of the restaurant was a vineyard, a tradition still honored by the name of the street—Vingårdsstræde. Grapes were an ingredient in many of the dishes of the time.

Hans Christian Andersen once lived upstairs, writing *Love in the Nicola Tower.* In *Only a Minstrel,* he wrote of his little garret, claiming that even though the rich folks who lived on the floors below had "the whole of the merry street to themselves," he had "the great vista of the heavens where the stars shone in the clear evening."

Chef Thomas Rode Andersen has turned the cellar into a *Relais Gourmands* (a member of the exclusive society of gourmet restaurants), and he creates dishes whose arrangement on a platter might have been done by an inspired impressionist painter. They are not only delectable but also artistically arranged on your platter.

Copenhagen Dining

86

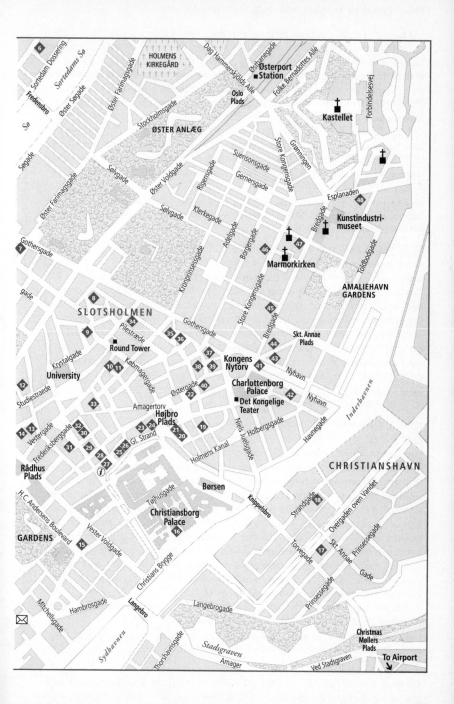

The chef is mainly inspired by the classic traditions of French gastronomy, though he feels free to draw upon the cuisines and raw materials of other countries. He doesn't believe in drowning a dish, and allows its natural flavor to shine through. In autumn fresh partridge and pigeon arrive from the fields, the same place where the mushrooms are gathered. He even smokes his own salmon on-site for 36 hours in an antique oven. Blue lobsters are yanked from a tank, and other freshly caught fish and shellfish come from harbors nearby. The menu is inventive, delicious, sublime, and full of flavor, with market-fresh ingredients decisively seasoned and appearing in combinations perhaps unknown to you. Take, for example, foie gras with dried wild goose breast and beet root stalks, followed by breast of duck with *bigarade* sauce (a classic duck sauce made with oranges and wine). For dessert, what can beat plum ice cream with Armagnac?

Vingårdsstræde 6. ✆ **33-11-68-68.** Reservations required. Main courses 260DKK–390DKK ($44–$66/£23–£35); fixed-price menu 735DKK–925DKK ($125–$157/£66–£83). AE, DC, DISC, MC, V. Mon–Sat 6–10pm. Closed July 20–Aug 10 and Dec 24–26. Bus: 1, 6, or 9.

M.R. (Mads Reflund) ✷✷✷ MODERN CONTINENTAL   It's posh, it's trendy, and if you're a visiting celebrity, this would be a discreet address. The decor is bright and cheerful with contrasting textures in a theme that evokes a Danish fairy tale. Not that he's ego crazed, but the owner and head chef, Mads Reflund, chose his own initials for this swank rendezvous for discerning palates. All menu items are configured as a series of set-price menus based on between three and seven courses. Expect creative, imaginative combinations of scallops, lobster, vanilla, cardamom seed, and truffles, and many more delights, each configured into novel concoctions that you might not have thought of without the superb intervention of MR himself. Everything is calm, hushed, impeccably decorated, and in all ways social and culinary, very savvy.

5 Kultorvet. ✆ **33-91-09-49.** Reservations recommended. Set-price menus 500DKK–700DKK ($85–$119/£45–£63). AE, DC, MC, V. Mon–Sat 6–9pm. Metro: Nørreport.

NOMA ✷✷✷ NORDIC   With a certain testosterone-driven enthusiasm, the chefs here celebrate the cuisine of the cold North Atlantic. In fact, the name of the restaurant is short for *nordatlantiskl mad,* or North Atlantic food. During its relatively short life, this showcase of Nordic cuisine has received greater amounts of favorable press than virtually any other restaurant in Denmark. Positioned within an antique, stone-sided warehouse in Christianshavn, it makes it an almost religious duty to import ultrafresh fish and shellfish three times a week from Greenland, Iceland, and the Faroe Islands. Chef Rene Redzepi concocts platters where fish is poached, grilled, pickled, smoked, or salted according to old Nordic traditions, then served in ways that are sometimes more elaborately decorated, and more visually flamboyant by far, than the decor of the white, rather Spartan setting in which they are served. Come here for crayfish, lobster, halibut in a foamy wasabi-flavored cream sauce, and practically any other creature that thrives in the cold waters of Nordic Europe. You expect to see, within the simple, stripped-down decor of this place, celebrities from throughout Northern Europe, including members of the Danish royal family.

Strandgade 93. ✆ **32-96-32-97.** Reservations recommended. Main courses 295DKK–350DKK ($50–$60/£27–£32); set-price menus 550DKK–650DKK ($94–$111/£50–£59). AE, DC, MC, V. Mon–Fri noon–2pm and Mon–Sat 6–10pm. Bus: 2 or 8.

Olsen ✷ *Finds* FRENCH/DANISH/ITALIAN   Is it a stylish lounge or a *bistro moderne,* as it proclaims? Perhaps a fusion of both. How fitting for a menu that is aggressively continental/fusion, not sticking just to recipes from the Danish kitchen but freely borrowing from two of the most-favored vacation lands for Copenhageners—France and Italy. Join trend-conscious locals and enter a world of low-slung banquettes, dark colors, and avant-garde photographs that share space with whimsical mosaics. Our waiter promised us, "You'll have a good time, and the food is great."

The good times are always guaranteed, and, if the food is not great, it's very good indeed, with a menu that the chefs adjust every 5 weeks. The sea bay shrimp won us over with its fragrance of a lime-flavored mousseline sauce. To beguile jaded palates, the chefs offer Skagen or Serrano ham with lusciously ripe avocados and crisp fresh greens. The pan-fried filet of zander is a classic, coming with a tarragon-flavored cream sauce. The old Austrian emperor, Franz Josef, would surely approve of the plate-size Wiener schnitzel with fresh green peas and bacon. For dessert, the rhubarb tart with clotted cream may be an acquired taste, but it captivated us.

Ved Stranden. ℂ **33-14-64-00.** Reservations recommended. Lunch main courses 48DKK–115DKK ($8.15–$20/£4.30–£10); dinner main courses 175DKK–215DKK ($30–$37/£16–£19), set-price menu 345DKK ($59/£31). AE, DC, MC, V. Mon–Sat noon–4pm and 6–10pm. Bus: 8; Metro: Kongens Nytorv.

Pierre André ⊀⊀⊀ FRENCH   The fickle local media have deserted this place and moved on to other grazing fields. Pierre André is viewed as "no longer on the cutting edge." To some extent, that is true. There is a stiffness and formality here, but we think it's a bit much to compare the atmosphere to the parlor of a funeral home. What is overlooked is that Pierre André chefs are still among the finest in Copenhagen, if you're lured by their take on a classic French cuisine. Named after the two sons of the Danish/French couple who own the place, this restaurant is painted a warm shade of terra cotta and is close to Nyhavn and the Hotel d'Angleterre. Menu items are elegant and stylish, as shown by a house specialty of carpaccio of foie gras "Emilia-Romagna," served with shaved Parmesan and truffles. Other winning starters include a salad of curried lobster with broccoli; braised filet of turbot with mushrooms, leeks, and—a surprise and a delight—mango sauce; wild venison with a bitter chocolate sauce, corn, and cranberries; and a dessert specialty of chocolate cake wherein the innards are partially liquefied in a gooey but delectable concoction that runs onto your plate. Everything we've sampled has been a burst of flavor, ranking with the top restaurants of Paris or London. The chefs have considerable talent to create imaginative dishes packed with robust flavors, but nothing that's overpowering.

Ny Østergade 21. ℂ **33-16-17-19.** Reservations required. Main courses 275DKK–395DKK ($47–$67/£25–£36); fixed-price menus 400DKK–755DKK ($68–$128/£36–£68). AE, DC, MC, V. Tues–Sat noon–2pm and 6–10pm. Closed 3 weeks July–Aug. Bus: 6, 10, or 14.

EXPENSIVE

Café Lumskebugten ⊀ *finds* DANISH   This spic-and-span, well-managed bastion of Danish charm has an unpretentious elegance that's admired throughout the capital. A now-legendary matriarch named Karen Marguerita Krog established it in 1854 as a tavern for sailors. As the tavern's reputation grew, aristocrats, artists, and members of the Danish royal family came to dine. Today a tastefully gentrified version of the original beef hash is still served.

Antique ship models decorate two glistening white dining rooms, and in summer, service spills onto the tables on the outdoor terraces. The food is excellent, but be prepared for a long experience here, as the staff tends to move politely but slowly through the service rituals, sometimes making meals here more lengthy and drawn out than you might have wanted. The selection of dishes takes you back to the way Danes ate in the 1950s, and that's not meant as a put-down by us. Danes like their own version of soul food. In this case it means fried platters of herring or Danish fish cakes with mustard sauce and minced beet root. The sugar-marinated salmon with a mustard cream sauce remains one of the delights of the Danish kitchen, as does a "symphony" of fish with saffron sauce and new potatoes. You might order as a starter another classic: herb-flavored tartare of salmon.

Esplanaden 21. ⓒ **33-15-60-29.** Reservations recommended. Main courses 175DKK–275DKK ($30–$47/£16–£25); 5-course fixed-price dinner 545DKK ($93/£49). AE, DC, MC, V. Mon–Fri 11:30am–10pm; Sat 5–10pm. Bus: 1, 6, or 9.

Le Sommelier ⚑ FRENCH   With a name like Sommelier, you expect some of Copenhagen's finest wine to be served here, and you're not disappointed. The good news is that many of the best selections are sold by the glass. The restaurant, which opened in 1997, offers more than 850 different bottles, and, as might be predicted, the sommelier here is one of the sharpest in the business. Chef Francis Cardenau's cuisine is inspired, especially his luncheon and dinner set menus, which are created fresh every day depending "on whatever inspiration the market provides." His cooking is characterized by virtuoso presentations such as foie gras poached in consommé with Sauternes *gelée* as a starter. Habitués find his main courses "seductive," and we agree, especially when we sample such dishes as a filet and loin of roast suckling pig with a velouté of fresh morels.

The chef never overextends himself or prepares dishes too elaborate. A savory stuffed rabbit appears frequently on the menu, or else you may want to sample the *poisson du jour,* or fish of the day. For our kroner, the chef still makes the best crème brûlée in town. Perhaps it's putting gilt on the lily, but he also serves it with marinated melon and a velvety vanilla ice cream.

Bredgade 63. ⓒ **33-11-45-15.** Reservation recommended. Main courses 185DKK–245DKK ($31–$42/£17–£22); fixed-price menus 260DKK–365DKK ($44–$62/£24–£33). AE, DC, MC, V. Mon–Thurs noon–2pm and 6–10pm; Fri noon–2pm and 6–11pm; Sat 6–11pm; Sun 6–10pm. Bus: 1A, 2A, 3A, or 4A.

Restaurant Els DANISH/FRENCH   This former coffeehouse is one of the most charming and upscale restaurants in Nyhavn, and certainly the one with the best decor. Meticulously preserved since it was installed in 1854, it's lined with murals which feature maidens in diaphanous dresses cavorting beneath trellises in a mythical garden. Dripping with Art Nouveau grace notes, they're believed to be the work of 19th-century muralist Christian Hitsch, who adorned parts of the interior of the Danish Royal Theater. Hans Christian Andersen was a regular here, and just before our arrival, novelist John Irving dropped in for lunch with a Danish journalist, discussing the European marketing for one of his novels.

Each day there's a different fixed-price menu, as well as a la carte offerings. Most dishes are perfectly prepared, including pepper-pickled salmon served with fresh herbs and watercress; lobster soup; grilled scallops with chestnuts and a confit of tomatoes; grilled calf's liver with onion marmalade, tomatoes, and thyme; breast of chicken roasted with honey and ginger, and served with vermouth sauce; and saddle of lamb with a compote of plums and red onions. You might follow all this with black-currant sorbet with cassis. The restaurant was named, incidentally, after the nickname of the wife ("Elsa") of its founder.

Store Strandstræde 3 (off Kongens Nytorv). ⓒ **33-14-13-41.** Reservations recommended. Main courses 158DKK–265DKK ($27–$45/£14–£24); sandwiches (lunch only) 50DKK–85DKK ($8.50–$14/£4.50–£7.65); fixed-price

2-course lunch 200DKK ($34/£18); fixed-price 3-course lunch 225DKK ($38/£20); fixed-price 5-course dinner 495DKK ($84/£45). AE, DC, MC, V. Mon–Sat noon–3pm; daily 5:30–10pm. Closed July. Bus: 1, 6, or 10.

Umami ⭐⭐ JAPANESE   One dinner at the übertrendy restaurant Nobu in Manhattan did it all for the owners of this restaurant. Returning to Copenhagen, they created their own version of a gastronomic sushi temple luring the power players and major celebs who come to Copenhagen. The setting is beneath the high ceilings of what was originally built as a bank during the 19th century. Permeated with a sense of Japanese minimalism, within sightlines of the kind of clientele who knows precisely how fashionable this place is, you can enjoy creative cuisine that's been written about almost as a matter of course within the Danish press. Don't overlook the place as a potential lounge and club, especially on Friday and Saturday nights, when a DJ spins tunes from a spot near the bar. Drink suggestion? Try sake infused with lemon grass, or any of several kinds of hallucinogenic martini. The street level is the site of the cocktail bar; upstairs is the restaurant, and sushi is available virtually anywhere. *Note:* One of the most whimsical corners of the place is within the former vault, site of today's men's and ladies' toilets.

If you're not quite sure what Japanese cooking is with a French touch, try the seared foie gras with eel, Nashi pear, and seafood salad, or the sake-steamed mussels with chili and cilantro, even the grilled scallops with Yuzu-chili. Ingredients are fresh, flavor combinations are novel, and presentation is elegant and stylish, as evoked by such dishes as Wagyu beef with three sauces or rabbit loin stuffed with shiitake mushrooms and served with pickled eggplant. Minimal cooking makes for a superb texture, as represented by the breast of guinea fowl teriyaki.

The restaurant has even claimed to have discovered five tastes to add to already accepted sour, sweet, salty, and bitter that can be distinguished by the human tongue. Chefs used *kombu,* a special type of seaweed made into crystals of amino acid glutamine and monosodium glutamate to produce a flavor enhancer for many of their more inspired dishes.

59 Store Kongensgade. © 33-38-75-00. Reservations recommended. Main courses 150DKK–175DKK ($26–$30/£14–£16); set-price menus 485DKK–850DKK ($82–$145/£44–£77). AE, DC, MC, V. Daily noon–3pm and 6pm–1am. No lunch during July. Metro: Kongens Nytorv.

MODERATE

Brasserie Le Coq Rouge DANISH/FRENCH   In 2005, when one of the most elegant hotels in Copenhagen reconfigured what had been a rather staid and doddering old bar and grill, diners took notice. Today, this snappy and stylish replica of a Parisian brasserie attracts busy crowds at both lunch and dinner. The food is as good as it should be, but that is good enough for most of the savvy foodies seen ordering here. The terrine of foie gras is sublime, but we also go for the charcuterie platters, especially at lunch. The seafood platter has an assortment of some of the best fish caught off Danish waters, and the confit of duckling with lentils takes us back on a journey to southwest France. One of us more discreetly ended our meal with a divine cheese platter, our invited guest opting for pure sin—chocolate cake topped with chocolate mousse and Grand Marnier.

In the Kong Frederick Hotel, Vester Voldgade 25. © 33-12-59-02. Lunch main courses 85DKK–165DKK ($14–$28/£7.65–£15); dinner main courses 159DKK–175DKK ($27–$30/£14–£16); set-price menus 295DKK ($50/£27). AE, DC, MC, V. Daily 11:30am–10pm. Bus: 1, 6, or 28.

Café à Porta ⭐ DANISH/ENGLISH Hans Christian Andersen used to come here for takeout, but he'd have to peddle a lot of fairy tales to be able to afford this place today. This is Copenhagen's version of a high-ceilinged, congenially battered grand cafe. Set directly on Copenhagen's most central square, close to the posh dining terrace of Hotel d'Angleterre, it's a comforting and generously proportioned lineup of rooms from the Belle Epoque, with some add-on layers of decor from the *La Dolce Vita* era of the '50s. It was established nearly 200 years ago by a Portuguese merchant, Señor à Porta, who gave it his name. Old-fashioned accents include zinc-topped bars, evoking Emile Zola's Paris, marble and wood parquet floors, and some of the most intricate ceiling decors in town. Menu items range from the straightforward and simple, such as freshly made, crisp salads, to well-stuffed sandwiches. As the day goes on, more complicated dishes appear at the tables, including grilled lobster and a tender, plate-sized Wiener schnitzel. That all these same dishes were being served at the turn of the 20th century doesn't bother the chefs at all, as they prepare old favorites such as flank steak with french fries or a tournedos Rossini like Hemingway ate at the liberation of Paris in 1944. Copenhagen's trendy young things are rediscovering this favorite watering hole of their grandparents, delighting in its lavish sense of kitsch which was fashionable "between the wars."

Kongens Nytorv 17. ℃ **33-11-05-00.** Salads and sandwiches 85DKK–115DKK ($14–$20/£7.65–£10); main courses 185DKK–245DKK ($31–$42/£17–£22); 3-course fixed-price dinner 495DKK ($84/£45). AE, DC, MC, V. Aug–June daily 8am–midnight; July daily 11am–10pm. Kitchen closed daily 4–5pm. Bus: 1, 6, 9, or 10.

Café Victor DANISH/FRENCH Since 1981 this cafe/restaurant has been a Copenhagen tradition, and its cappuccino machine is hard at work all day long. Hip, artsy, and boasting Parisian decor and service, this is a Danish version of a bustling French bistro, replete with zinc bar tops, a staff clad in black and white, and row upon row of expensive whiskeys and cognacs lined up on the bar like religious icons on an altar. The arts-oriented crowd sits at the curved, illuminated bar or at tables, contributing to a "see-and-be-seen" ethic that manages to be both fun and stylish at the same time—sort of a hip, Scandinavian interpretation of *La Dolce Vita*. At lunchtime, menu items include meal-size servings that focus on, among others, club sandwiches; a platter piled high with five different kinds of herring; smoked eel with scrambled eggs and chive; steamed paupiette of fish; terrine of foie gras; and filet of pork with cream sauce. At dinner, look for Victor's "Crazy" Caesar salad; mussels in white wine; seared tuna with fennel, spinach, and lime-flavored salsa; grilled rib-eye steak; and asparagus-studded risotto.

Ny Østergade 8. ℃ **33-13-36-13.** Reservations recommended. Lunch platters, salads, and sandwiches 60DKK–155DKK ($10–$26/£5.40–£14); dinner main courses 95DKK–175DKK ($16–$30/£8.55–£16). AE, DC, MC, V. Mon–Wed 8am–1am; Thurs–Sat 8am–2am; Sun 11am–11pm. Bus: 1, 6, or 9.

Cap Horn ⭐ ORGANIC/INTERNATIONAL "We've chased out the whores and the drunken sailors, and now serve fine food to respectable people," our waiter assured us with a tongue-in-cheek smile. Actually, she wasn't too far off the mark. Originally built in the 1600s during the reign of Christian IV, these premises used to be one of Europe's most notorious brothels, with a sign in its lobby that warned, SPANKING COSTS EXTRA. This is one of the best of the restaurants along the Nyhavn waterfront, thanks to a solid and sustained concentration on high-quality food and organic ingredients, and a decor lifted directly from the seafaring days before Nyhavn began attracting so many tourists. It has an outdoor terrace where, during warm weather, competition is fierce for a table. Otherwise you can retreat from the outside melee to three cozy inside dining rooms. The decor was inspired by the interior of a late-19th-century ship: polished brass, mahogany, teak, nautical accessories, a blazing fireplace that's strategically positioned to be visible from throughout most of the interior, and even a skylight removed intact from an antique fishing craft. There's yet another dining area at the top of a steep flight of steps that manages to be both minimalist and severely antique at the same time. It's rumored to shelter an angry ghost—supposedly the spirit of a local woman (Isabella) whose favorite sailor (Peter) scorned her, leading to her suicide. She's occasionally seen around midnight, shattering a plate or upsetting a vase in a fit of pique.

Salads, when configured as a lunch in their own right, can be glorious—crisp and fresh with a wide choice of dressings. Lunches also focus on some of the area's best *smørrebrød*, those open-faced sandwiches. It may seem a strange marriage, but many locals prefer the combination platter of herring and steak. "Cap burgers," made from chopped organic sirloin of beef, are a justifiably popular dish. The fare grows more elaborate at dinner, allowing you to dip into nostalgia as you order a classic Andalusian-style gazpacho, followed by a leg of venison with potatoes in a parsley-flavored butter sauce. When the waiter delivered a tantalizing grilled daurade, he warned, "Never let it get cold." There is always a focus on whatever fresh produce is available at the time of your visit. We hit it lucky: fresh chanterelles and just-harvested asparagus.

Nyhavn 21. © **33-12-85-04.** Reservations recommended. Lunch platters 149DKK–165DKK ($25–$28/£13–£15); dinner main courses 165DKK–179DKK ($28–$30/£15–£16). AE, DC, MC, V. Daily 9am–5pm and 7–11pm. Bus: 1, 6, 9, or 10.

L'Alsace ☆ CONTINENTAL   We have only one "beef" about this place. It's so intimate you can hear personal conversations at the next table. One night Elton John told his table that religion is such an evil force in the world that it should be done away with. Queen Margrethe was overheard speaking about Queen Elizabeth II, but the Danish queen was discreet and made only flattering references. It is not known if Pope John Paul II uttered any indiscreet remarks while dining here. He spoke in such a soft whisper he could not be overheard. Most diners come not to eavesdrop but to partake in some of the best recipes from the continental kitchen. In summer, weather permitting, meals are served in a cobblestone-studded courtyard that's directly accessible from the all-pedestrian Strøget. In an 18th-century building, an Austrian established the restaurant in 1978, and it's been a durable fixture on the Copenhagen dining scene ever since, providing a welcome change from too constant a diet of Danish food. Amid a striking collection of modern paintings, many of them by an artist named Wilhelm Fredy, you can order dishes from across the culinary divides of Europe. Many derive from Alsace, including sauerkraut studded with pork knuckles and pork sausages, and a terrine of foie gras. There are also succulent oysters from the Atlantic coast of France, plate-sized Wiener schnitzels, *tafelspitz* (Habsburg-style boiled beef with horseradish), carpaccio from Italy, bouillabaisse inspired by the traditions of Provence, savory Spain-derived tapas, Austrian-style roulades of beef, pepper steaks, roasted duck with orange sauce, Chilean sea bass with Pernod sauce, and other items that change according to the whim of the chef and the availability of ingredients. Dessert brings pastries inspired by France and Austria as well as a sublime version of rhubarb pie.

Ny Østerg 9. © **33-14-57-43.** Reservations recommended. Lunch main courses 127DKK–208DKK ($22–$35/£11–£19); dinner main courses 172DK–260DKK ($29–$44/£15–£23); rice menus 351DKK–505DKK ($60–$86/£32–£45). AE, DC, MC, V. Mon–Sat 11:30am–midnight. Bus: 5.

(Kids) **Family-Friendly Restaurants**

Copenhagen Corner (p. 98)   A special children's menu features such dishes as shrimp cocktail and grilled rump steak.

Fregatten (p. 109)   This is the preferred choice for the whole family visiting the summertime Tivoli Gardens. Danish and international food is served in a replica of an 18th-century ship.

Kobenhavner Cafeen (p. 100)   Sturdy and reliable, this has long been a family favorite in Copenhagen with both locals and foreigners, who dig into old-fashioned Danish fare. Kids go for the *frikadeller,* or ping-pong-size meatballs.

Restaurant/Café Nytorv (p. 95)   One of the best children's menus in town is a regular feature at this landmark cafe/restaurant on Copenhagen's most elegant square.

INEXPENSIVE

Café Zeze CONTINENTAL   On some days, if you have an ambitious sightseeing agenda, only a cafe will do to get you in and out quick. Set in a neighborhood with a dense collection of shops and offices, this hip bistro and cafe has a reputation for good food and brisk service. You'll find a cheerful-looking setup with a high ceiling, mirrors, and a mostly yellow interior. Noise levels can get a bit high, especially late at night when more folk seem to be drinking than eating, but overall the place can be a lot of fun. Menu items change frequently, but expect a well-prepared medley of dishes. The menu is better than some fast-food joint, and the cooks use market-fresh ingredients to create old favorites such as grilled chicken breast with fresh mushrooms or filet of lamb with shiitake mushrooms. Sometimes they even use their imaginations, dressing up a sautéed turkey breast with coconut and chile sauce or else roasted guinea fowl with fresh shrimp and braised arugula.

Ny Østergade 20. (✆) **33-14-23-90.** Reservations recommended. Lunch main courses 75DKK–92DKK ($13–$16/ £6.75–£8.30); dinner main courses 100DKK–175DKK ($17–$30/£9–£16). AE, DC, MC, V. Mon–Sat 11:30am–4:30pm and 5:30–10pm (last order). Bar and cafe Mon–Thurs 9am–midnight; Fri–Sat 9am–3am. Bus: 350 F.

Nyhavns Færgekro ⟨ *finds* DANISH/FRENCH   The "Nyhavn Ferry Inn" near the harbor has a long tradition and many loyal fans, of which we include ourselves. The house is old, dating from the final years of the 18th century. Diners enjoy not only their food but also a view of the surrounding 18th-century houses and the canal from the popular summer terrace. Inside, the decor is unusual, with a spiral stairway from an antique tram and a black-and-white "checkerboard" marble floor. Lights serve as call buttons to summon the staff when you want service.

The kitchen prepares a daily homemade buffet of 10 types of herring in different styles and sauces, including fried, *rollmops* (rolled or curled herring), and smoked. Some people make a full meal of the herring. You can also order *smørrebrød*—everything from smoked eel with scrambled eggs to chicken salad with bacon. A true Dane, in the tradition of Nyhavn, orders a schnapps or *akvavit* at lunch. Denmark has a tradition of making spicy *akvavit* from the herbs and plants of the land—Saint-John's-wort from

Tisvilde Hegn, sloe-leaf from the wild moors, green walnuts from the south of Funen, and many other varieties. Dinners here are relatively limited, usually configured as a fixed-price menu, with main courses including a choice of either grilled salmon or grilled entrecôte—nothing particularly imaginative but perfectly adequate and well-prepared.

Nyhavn 5. ⓒ **33-15-15-88.** Reservations required. Lunch herring buffet 89DKK ($15/£8); fixed-price dinner 189DKK ($32/£17). DC, MC, V. Daily 11:30am–4pm and 5–11:30pm. Closed Jan 1 and Dec 24–25. Bus: 1, 6, or 9.

Parnas DANISH   This is the best place in Copenhagen for late-night refugees to satisfy their munchies. The food may not be the best, but where else can you order a grilled steak and a beer at 3 o'clock in the morning? Opposite the city's largest department store, Magasin, this late-night refuge is decorated like a warm, rustic, old-fashioned Danish *kro* (inn). Begin with three different kinds of herring or marinated salmon, followed by fried sliced pork with parsley sauce, several different preparations of sole and salmon, or the house specialty—*Parnas Gryde,* which combines grilled sirloin with bacon, marrow, and mushrooms, with béarnaise sauce on the side. This platter has been on the menu since the restaurant opened in the 1930s. After midnight a limited menu is available, and live music begins at 8:30pm.

Lille Kongensgade 16. ⓒ **33-11-49-10.** Reservations required. Main courses 98DKK–168DKK ($17–$29/£8.80–£15). AE, DC, MC, V. Mon–Thurs noon–3am; Fri–Sat noon–5am. Bus: 1 or 6.

Restaurant/Café Nytorv *(Kids)* DANISH   It occupies a building at the most distant end of the most elegant square in central Copenhagen, a baroque perimeter that's particularly charming on warm summer nights. Inside, you'll find a warren of cozy dining areas, each low-ceilinged, each evoking 19th-century Copenhagen, and each a bastion of uncompromising Danish nationalism in all things cultural and culinary. The place, like so many others in the area, used to shelter drunks, sailors, and prostitutes. Don't come here expecting cutting-edge cuisine or decor, as very little has changed since the early 1960s in terms of decor—and since the early 1920s in terms of cuisine. But prices are relatively affordable for this part of town; *smørrebrød* are suitably thick; and the *Københavner platte,* a platter piled high with Danish herring, cheese, meatballs, and more, is filling. If you happen to have children in tow, there's a kids' menu, and it's otherwise hard to turn down for diners of any age. Menu items include Danish pork sausage with potatoes, beef sirloin with béarnaise, *frikadeller* with potatoes, *biksemal* (Danish hash), and Madagascar-style pepper steak.

Nytorv 15. ⓒ **33-11-77-06.** Reservations recommended. Sandwiches 45DKK–79DKK ($7.65–$13/£4.05–£7.10); main courses 99DKK–119DKK ($17–$20/£8.90–£11); set menus 199DKK–265DKK ($34–$45/£18–£24); children's menu 49DKK ($8.35/£4.40). AE, DC, MC, V. Mon–Fri 11:30am–10pm; Sat noon–9pm. Bus: 1, 6, or 10.

Skindbuksen *(Moments)* DANISH   Call this a local favorite. This place is more Danish than the queen, and probably a lot more fun. Although it's in an expensive neighborhood, it not only is reasonable in price but is a down-home type of place (that is, down-home Danish style). This atmospheric landmark has long drawn beer drinkers in the neighborhood. Many locals, often old sailors, swear by its *skipperlabskovs,* the Danish version of a meat-and-potato hash that has kept many a mariner from starvation over the years. This popular dish is often sold out at noon. A good variety of *smørrebrød* is always a luncheon favorite. You can order other dishes too, including homemade soups, pâtés, fresh shrimp, and a local favorite, tender beef served with a béarnaise sauce. There is live piano music Monday to Saturday from 8pm to 12:30am.

Lille Kongensgade 4 (off Kongens Nytorv). ⓒ **33-12-90-37.** Reservations recommended. Main courses 85DKK–149DKK ($14–$25/£7.65–£13). MC, V. Daily 11:30am–midnight (kitchen closes at 10pm). Bus: 1, 6, 15, or 26.

NEAR ØSTERBRO

MODERATE

Le Saint-Jacques 🍴 FRENCH   Rather bizarrely, this place designed its interior to look like a small church in the heart of Østerbro. Set in a single dignified dining room, in a building that's at least a century old, this well-respected French restaurant has a talent for defining itself as an unofficial embassy of Gallic goodwill. During mild weather, you can escape from the somewhat cramped interior in favor of a table on the street outside, adding a flavor that might remind you of something in the south of France. Menu items change frequently, based on the inspiration of the chef and the availability of ingredients. A steady hand in the kitchen admirably presents dishes to diners who usually have traditional tastes. Excellent ingredients also go into this skillful cuisine, and the wide-ranging wine list includes vintages from around the world. The waiters promise you they will deliver good food, and they do, as exemplified by the North Atlantic scallops with salmon roe and leeks in a beurre blanc sauce. One couldn't hope to do better than order one of the free-range chickens with a cream-flavored morel sauce. Finally, you also can't go wrong with the filet of sole enlivened with a slight balsamic glaze.

Skt. Jacobs Pladsen 1. 🕐 **35-42-77-07.** Reservations recommended. Lunch main courses 78DKK–135DKK ($13–$23/ £7–£12); dinner main courses 198DKK ($34/£18); 3-course menu 315DKK ($54/£28); 4-course menu 395DKK ($67/£36); 5-course menu 455DKK ($77/£41). AE, DC, MC, V. Daily noon–midnight. Bus: 1A or 14.

NEAR RÅDHUSPLADSEN & TIVOLI

EXPENSIVE

Fox Kitchen and Bar 🍴 SCANDINAVIAN   This is the fashionable and trend-conscious restaurant that's associated with the also-recommended hotel—the one where each room is the often-eccentric decorative statement of an individual artist. They don't serve lunch, but every afternoon, the bar area of this restaurant is filled to capacity with the young, the restless, the bored, and, sometimes, the beautiful. Expect earth tones, wood chairs, and a judicious use of plastic mixed with fine hardwoods. Menu items are competently prepared, often with flair, and might include marinated hake with nasturtium flowers and mildly smoked rapeseed oil. We still recall with great fondness the pan-seared filet of plaice, with celeriac, cauliflower, and two real delights—a parsley-flavored sorbet and a foamy dill sauce. Innovation combined with carefully crafted dishes is the house style, as exemplified by the anise- and chervil-marinated tenderloin of lamb with tender green lentils and cold yogurt. Flavors are blended beautifully in the spinach lasagna with savory goat cheese and a rich vegetable bouillon. After the dishes are tucked away, the bar area here continues on till at least midnight.

In the Hotel Fox, 3 Jarmers Plad. 🕐 **33-13-30-00.** Reservations recommended. Main courses 140DKK–175DKK ($24–$30/£13–£16); fixed-price menu 285DKK ($48/£26). AE, DC, MC, V. Daily 5–11pm. Bus: 5A, 14, or 16.

TyvenKokkenHansKoneog-HendesElsker 🍴 *Finds* 🍴🍴 INTERNATIONAL/ FRENCH   In olden days these headquarters were the seat of the most famous brothel in Copenhagen, advertising that there was no lust that could not be satisfied here. Today the demands of most customers can be satisfied just by offering a finely honed cuisine. The restored 18th-century townhouse near Rådhuspladsen (Town Hall Square) is one of the city's most unusual and one of its best restaurants. Its bizarre name comes from Peter Greenaway's cannibalistic *The Cook, The Thief, His Wife and*

> **Tips** **Quick Bites in Copenhagen**
>
> Copenhagen has many hot dog stands, chicken and fish grills, and *smørre-brød* counters that serve good, fast, inexpensive meals.
>
> **Hot dog stands,** especially those around Rådhuspladsen, offer *polser* (steamed or grilled hot dogs) with shredded onions on top and *pommes frites* (french fries) on the side.
>
> The *bageri* or *konditori* (bakery), found on almost every block, sells fresh bread, rolls, and Danish pastries.
>
> **Viktualiehandler** (small food shops), found throughout the city, are the closest thing to a New York deli. You can buy roast beef with free *log* (fried onions). The best buy is smoked fish. Ask for a Bornholmer, a large, bone-less sardine from the Danish island of Bornholm, or for *røgost,* a popular and inexpensive smoked cheese. Yogurt fans will be delighted to know that the Danish variety is cheap and tasty. It's available in small containers—just peel off the cover and drink it right out of the cup as the Danes do. *Hytte ret* (cottage cheese) is also good and cheap.
>
> The favorite lunch of Scandinavians, particularly Danes, is the open-faced sandwich called **smørrebrød.** The purest form is made with dark rye bread, called *rugbrød.* Most taverns and cafes offer *smørrebrød,* and many places serve it as takeout food.
>
> You can picnic in any of the city parks in the town center. Try Kongs-garten near Kongens Nytorv; the Kastellet area near *Den Lille Havfrue;* Botanisk Have (site of the Botanical Gardens); the lakeside promenades in southeastern Copenhagen; and the old moat at Christianshavn. Remember not to litter!

Her Lover, a brilliant film with macabre feast scenes. The two-story restaurant offers tables with a view over old Copenhagen upstairs. The chefs here are inspired in their selection of an innovative fixed-price menu, which we find to be among the best in Copenhagen. The menu changes weekly, but we enjoy the "Lobstermenu" with cham-pagne. It begins with grilled lobster's claw and turbot with green peas and pearl onions, proceeds to encompass risotto with lobster fragments and fresh chanterelles, and follows with lobster tail with seared foie gras. Everything is good here, even some-thing simple but sublime like entrecôte with fresh vegetables. Finish off with a luscious dessert or a platter of various European farm cheeses.

Magstræde 16. ② **33-16-12-92.** Reservations recommended. Main courses 180DKK–375DKK ($31–$64/£16–£34); 6-course fixed-price menu 600DKK ($102/£54). AE, DC, MC, V. Wed–Sat 6pm–2am.

MODERATE

Atlas Bar/Restaurant Flyvefisken DANISH/THAI/INTERNATIONAL   This joint has always been a darling of local hipsters, and you may want to join them for a slice of Copenhagen life often not seen by the casual visitor. The cuisine at these two restaurants (prepared in the same kitchen) includes lots of vegetarian food inspired by the fare of Thailand, Mexico, and India, with a Danish overview toward tidiness and coziness. On the street level, the cramped, cozy Atlas Bar serves a busy lunchtime crowd, but slackens off a bit at night, when the wood-sheathed Flyvefisken (Flying Fish) opens for dinner upstairs. Upstairs, expect a bit more emphasis on Thai cuisine and its fiery flavors, including lemongrass, curries, and several of the hot, spicy fish soups native to Bangkok. Although the authenticity of the Thai cuisine has lost a bit of its zest in the long jump from Thailand, it's still a change of pace from typical Danish fare. Expect crowds here, especially at lunch, when the place is likely to be full.

Lars Bjørnstræde 18. ℂ **33-14-95-15.** Reservations recommended. Lunch main courses 75DKK–140DKK ($13–$24/£6.75–£13); dinner main courses 110DKK–200DKK ($19–$34/£9.90–£18). AE, DC, MC, V. Atlas Bar Mon–Sat noon–10pm. Restaurant Flyvefisken Mon–Sat 5:30–10pm. Bus: 5 or 6A.

Copenhagen Corner *(Kids* INTERNATIONAL/FRENCH   This is no doubt the most convenient place for a good meal in the heart of Copenhagen. It's an especially good choice if you're going to the Tivoli Gardens nearby and don't want to pay the inflated food prices charged there. Set amid some of the heaviest pedestrian traffic in Copenhagen, this deeply entrenched landmark restaurant opens onto Rådhuspladsen, around the corner from the Tivoli Gardens. Outfitted with some of the accessories of a greenhouse-style conservatory for plants, it offers well-prepared, unpretentious meals to dozens of city residents throughout the day and evening. The menu, which offers many Danish favorites, will place you deep in the heart of Denmark, beginning with three kinds of herring or freshly peeled shrimp with dill and lemon. There's even a carpaccio of filet of deer for the most adventurous palates. The soups are excellent, such as the consommé of white asparagus flavored with chicken and fresh herbs. The fish is fresh and beautifully prepared, especially the steamed Norwegian salmon with a "lasagna" of potatoes, or the baked halibut with artichokes. Meat and poultry courses, although not always equal to the fish, are tasty and tender, especially the veal liver Provençal.

H. C. Andersens Blvd. 1A. ℂ **33-91-45-45.** Reservations recommended. Main courses 128DKK–255DKK ($22–$43/£12–£23); 3-course fixed-price menu 375DKK ($64/£34). AE, DC, MC, V. Daily 11:30am–11pm. Bus: 1, 6, or 8.

Søren K *(★* INTERNATIONAL/FRENCH   Named after Denmark's most celebrated philosopher, this is an artfully minimalist dining room that's on the ground floor of the Black Diamond (the ultramodern, intensely angular addition to the Royal Library). It has the kind of monochromatic gray and flesh–toned decor you might find in Milan, and glassy, big-windowed views that stretch out over the nearby canal. Menu items change frequently, but the chef never cooks with butter, cream, or high-cholesterol cheese, making a meal here a low-cholesterol as well as a savory experience. In a land known for its "butter-and-egg men," this type of cooking is heresy. Some Danes boycott it but foreign visitors, especially those watching their waistlines, flock here for a superb meal. Your taste buds will love you if you order such dishes as a velvety foie gras, a carpaccio of veal, and a truly superb oyster soup. Attention to detail and a proud professionalism distinguish such main dishes as veal chops served with lobster sauce and a half-lobster or else roasted venison with nuts and seasonal berries with a marinade of green tomatoes, the latter providing a wonderful savory taste that we enjoy. To reach this place, you'll have to enter the library, and pass through the lobby of the new Black Diamond Wing.

On the ground floor of the Royal Library's Black Diamond Wing, Søren Kierkegaards Plads 1. ℂ **33-47-49-50.** Reservations recommended. Lunch main courses 92DKK–145DKK ($16–$25/£8.30–£13); dinner main courses 195DKK–225DKK ($33–$38/£18–£20); fixed-price 3-course dinner 395DKK ($67/£36); 6-course tasting menu 495DKK ($84/£45). AE, DC, MC, V. Mon–Sat 11am–10:30pm. Bus: 1, 2, 5, 8, or 9.

Sult ⚘ DANISH/FRENCH   If you, like us, were turned on by the novel *Sult,* by Norwegian author Knut Hamsun, you might want to try out the restaurant whose moniker pays homage to the book. This fashionable, trendy eatery is inside the Danish Film Institute's center and is both a cultural and a gourmet experience. The setting is like a modern museum with wood floors, towering windows, and lofty ceilings. Chef Fredrik Ohlsson has traveled the continent for his culinary inspiration, although he specializes in French cuisine. Using market-fresh ingredients, he often elevates his food to the sublime. Just describing the rather simple dishes does not suggest their artfulness in seasonings and natural flavors. The chef will take a grilled tuna or a filet of lamb, even oven-baked lemon sole, and make something special out of it. If you don't want to make decisions, opt for one of the fixed-price menus, which are innovative and engaging to the palate. The wine list is impressive but rather high priced.

Vognmagergade 8B. © **33-74-34-17.** Reservations recommended. Main courses 185DKK ($31/£17). Fixed-price menus 240DKK–425DKK ($41–$72/£22–£38). AE, DC, MC, V. Tues–Sat noon–midnight; Sun 11am–10pm. S-tog: Nørreport.

INEXPENSIVE

Axelborg Bodega DANISH   Since 1912 down-home cooking Danish style has been served in this cafe across from Benneweis Circus and near Scala and the Tivoli. In fair weather you can sit out enjoying a brisk Copenhagen evening and people-watching. Most regulars here opt for the *dagens ret* (daily special), which is the equivalent of the old blue-plate special served at diners throughout America in the 1940s. Typical Danish dishes are featured on those specials, invariably *frikadeller* and the inevitable pork chops, which was the favorite dish of the Nazi occupation forces in the early '40s. A wide selection of *smørrebrød* is also available, costing 52DKK to 76DKK ($8.85–$13/£4.70–£6.85) each. Although the atmosphere is somewhat impersonal, this is a local favorite; diners enjoy the recipes from grandma's attic.

Axeltorv 1. © **33-11-06-38.** Reservations recommended. Main courses 95DKK–148DKK ($16–$25/£8.55–£13). AE, DC, MC, V. Restaurant daily 11am–9pm. Bar daily 11am–2am. Bus: 1 or 6.

Café Sorgenfri *(Value* SANDWICHES   The English translation for this place means "without sorrows." Should you have any sorrows, you can drown them in your beer here in a cafe sheltered in a house from 1796. The draught beer flows freely throughout the day in the cafe's antique interior with its subdued lighting and fresh flowers. Don't come here expecting grand cuisine, or even a menu with any particular variety. This place has thrived for 150 years selling beer, schnapps, and a medley of *smørrebrød* that appeal to virtually everyone's sense of workaday thrift and frugality. With only about 50 seats, the joint is likely to be crowded around the lunch hour, with somewhat more space during the midafternoon. Everything inside reeks of old-time Denmark, from the potted shrubs that adorn the facade to the well-oiled paneling that has witnessed many generations of Copenhageners selecting and enjoying sandwiches. Between two and four of them might compose a reasonable lunch (sandwiches, not Copenhageners!), depending on your appetite. You'll find it in the all-pedestrian shopping zone, in the commercial heart of town.

Brolæggerstræde 8. © **33-11-58-80.** Reservations recommended for groups of 4 or more. Smørrebrød 45DKK–75DKK ($7.65–$13/£4.05–£6.75). AE, DC, MC, V. Daily 11am–9pm. Bus: 5 or 6.

Chili AMERICAN   Boisterous, informal, and with an American theme, this is the most recent incarnation of a once-famous 19th-century establishment known to many generations of Danes as Tokanten and our favorite hangout from long ago. Today, lacking its former bohemian atmosphere, Chili serves at least 17 versions of burgers, available in quarter- and half-pound sizes, whose descriptions read like a map of the world. Choices include Hawaii burgers (with pineapple and curry), English burgers (with bacon and fried eggs), French burgers (with mushrooms in cream sauce), Danish burgers (with fried onions), and all the Texas burgers and chili burgers you could want. Also available are well-stuffed sandwiches and grilled steak platters. Service is fast, and the ambience is unpretentious.

Vandkunsten 1. ⓒ **33-91-19-18.** Main courses 42DKK–165DKK ($7.15–$28/£3.80–£15); burgers and sandwiches 65DKK–98DKK ($11–$17/£5.85–£8.80). No credit cards. Mon–Sat 11am–midnight; Sun 11am–11pm. Bus: 6A.

Domhus Kælderen DANISH/INTERNATIONAL   For some reason this eatery seems to attract a lot of foreign visitors, especially English hipsters. To understand some of the dialogue, you may need a translator, unless you understand: "Did you see that bird kick that bloke in the huevos?" Its good food, and a location across the square from City Hall also guarantees a large number of lawyers and their clients. This is a bustling and old-fashioned emporium of Danish cuisine. The setting is a half-cellar room illuminated with high lace-draped windows that shine light down on wooden tables and 50 years of memorabilia. Menu items at lunch might include *frikadeller,* and heaping platters of herring, Danish cheeses, smoked meats and fish, salads, and a worthy assortment of *smørrebrød.* The dinner menu is more ambitious, calling for a harder effort on the part of the kitchen staff, who turn out pickled salmon and several fine cuts of beef—our favorite choices—served with either a béarnaise or pepper sauce. Also look for the catch of the day, prepared in virtually any way you like. The food is typically Danish and well prepared, and you get no culinary surprises here; but then, you are rarely disappointed.

Nytorv 5. ⓒ **33-14-84-55.** Reservations recommended. Lunch main courses 68DKK–148DKK ($12–$25/£6–£13); dinner main courses 128DKK–198DKK ($22–$34/£12–£18); set menus 225DKK–275DKK ($38–$47/£20–£25). AE, DC, MC, V. Daily 11am–4pm and 5–10pm. Bus: 5.

Husmann Vinstue (Value) SANDWICHES   Would you believe that when we worked on an earlier version of this guide prior to 1980 a single woman wasn't allowed in this joint without a male escort? Now that women are allowed, one might ask why they fought to gain entrance in the first place. It's not that special but we love it for its old-time atmosphere. It was founded back in 1888 as an all-male tavern, and the decor hasn't changed much since then in this two-fisted, bustling luncheon stopover. In spite of the somewhat seedy atmosphere, we find that the cooks make some of the most satisfying *smørrebrød* in town. The fresh raw materials and the homemade cooking are first-rate, as you devour ping-pong-ball-size meatballs, several varieties of herring, and small cuts of tender Danish beef. Surely you will agree with us that Danish cheese is among the finest in the world.

Larsbjørnsstræde 2. ⓒ **33-11-58-86.** Reservations recommended. Main courses 61DKK–98DKK ($10–$17/£5.50–£7.85). AE, DC, MC, V. Daily 11:30am–4pm (last order). Bus: 5.

Kobenhavner Cafeen DANISH (Kids)   Danes go here for their comfort-food fix, and we like to join them. One of the smallest (about 45 seats) restaurants in this pedestrians-only zone, the Kobenhavner works hard to convey a sense of old-time Denmark. There's been an inn on this site since the 12th century, but the current structure dates from the 19th century. The setting is cozy, and you can enjoy authentically old-fashioned food items whose preparation adheres to methods practiced by many Danish grandmothers. Expect a roster of open-faced sandwiches at both lunch and dinner; *frikadeller;* grilled filets of plaice with butter sauce and fresh asparagus; roasted pork with braised red cabbage; and *biksemal,* a type of seafood hash that was served several times a week in many Danish homes throughout World War II. One of the most appealing items, a specialty of the house, is the *Københavner platte,* which features several preparations of herring, marinated salmon, shrimp, meatballs, fresh vegetables, and fresh-baked, roughly textured bread with butter. Be warned that Santa impersonators might be entertaining the children in the crowd during your visit, even if your visit happens to fall during the month of August.

Badstuestæde 10. ⓒ **33-32-80-81.** Reservations recommended. *Smørrebrød* 45DKK–89DKK ($7.65–$15/£4.05–£8); main courses 89DKK–159DKK ($15–$27/£8–£14). AE, DC, MC, V. Daily 11am–midnight. Bus: 5 or 6.

Puk's Restaurant DANISH   We admire this eatery for never pretending to be more than what it is, which is a place to go for real Danish cooking. Without any particular flair, it dispenses hearty and filling meals based on market-fresh ingredients. Solid and reliable, this restaurant is housed inside the thick stone walls of a former 18th-century brewery. You can enjoy a drink or two in the atmospheric pub next door. Most serious diners head down a flight of stairs from the street into the cellar-level restaurant. Menu selections include Danish meatballs, platters of *smørrebrød* or several kinds of smoked fish, herring offered either cold and marinated or fried and served with dill and new potatoes, and tournedos of beef with a sauce made from fresh tomatoes and herbs. The cooks prepare these dishes like your mother does—assuming she's Danish.

Vandkunsten 8. ⓒ **33-11-14-17.** Reservations required in summer and Dec only. Main courses 108DKK–168DKK ($18–$29/£9.75–£15). AE, DC, MC, V. Daily 11:30am–10pm. Bus: 1A, 2A, or 6A.

Riz Raz (*Value* MIDDLE EASTERN/VEGETARIAN   If you're ravenous, this is the best food deal we can find in Copenhagen. Imagine an all-you-can-eat Mediterranean buffet at a very decent price in high-priced Denmark. Bustling and unpretentious, this decidedly un-Danish hideaway offers the best all-vegetarian buffet in Copenhagen. There's additional seating outdoors during mild weather. Expect a medley of virtually every vegetable known to humankind, prepared either au naturel or as part of a marinated fantasy that might include the antipasti of Italy, the hummus of Lebanon, or an array of long-simmered casseroles inspired by the cuisine of the Moroccan highlands. There's also a selection of pastas, some of them redolent with garlic, oil, and Mediterranean spices, as well as a limited array of meat and fish dishes. Service staff is composed mostly of students from countries around the world. Beer and wine are served, which means that the staff doesn't take any hair shirt, holier-than-thou attitude as they do in so many other vegetarian restaurants.

Kompagnistræde 20 (at Knabrostræde). ⓒ **33-15-05-75.** Vegetarian buffet 59DKK ($10/£5.30) per person; main courses 100DKK–179DKK ($17–$30/£9–£16). AE, DC, MC, V. Daily 11:30am–midnight. Bus: 5 or 6.

Slotskælderen DANISH   A star on the *smørrebrød* circuit, this landmark opened in 1797 but since 1910 has been owned by the same family. Habitués call the place "Gitte Kik," the name of the owner and granddaughter of the founder, and a woman who's often identified, along with her arch rival, Ida Davidsen, as "*smørrebrød* queen" of Copenhagen. We have long grown bored with Ida's sandwiches, and her joint is far too touristy for our tastes; so we've passed the crown of "sandwich queen" along to Gitte Kik. Everything—the Danish wood trim, the old photographs, and the gold walls—adds up to *hygge*, a coziness that has attracted such notables as the prince of Denmark, the king and queen of Sweden, and the late Victor Borge, one of the most famous entertainers to ever emerge from Denmark, and once adored by American TV audiences—and still remembered by those of a certain age. Try the marinated salmon, fresh tiny shrimp, or hot *frikadeller*. The smoked-eel and scrambled-egg sandwich is the best of its kind, although we admit that this is an acquired taste—an eel sandwich is not everybody's idea of a good time.

Fortunstræde 4. © **33-11-15-37.** Reservations recommended. Smørrebrød 39DKK–75DKK ($6.65–$13/£3.50–£6.75). AE, DC, MC, V. Tues–Sat 11am–3pm. Bus: 1A, 15, or 19.

NEAR ROSENBORG SLOT
VERY EXPENSIVE
St. Gertruds Kloster ★★★ *Finds* INTERNATIONAL   Surely this is how the medieval kings of Denmark must have dined, with Hamlet pondering the question in the background. It is the most romantic restaurant in Denmark, a great place to pop the question or tell your spouse you want a divorce. There's no electricity in the labyrinth of 14th-century underground vaults, and the 1,500 flickering candles, open grill, iron sconces, and rough-hewn furniture create an elegant ambience. Enjoy an aperitif in the darkly paneled library. The chefs display talent and integrity, their cuisine reflecting precision and sensitivity. Every flavor is fully focused, each dish balanced to perfection. Try the fresh, homemade foie gras with black truffles, lobster served in a turbot bouillon, venison (year-round) with green asparagus and truffle sauce, or a fish-and-shellfish terrine studded with chunks of lobster and salmon. These dishes range from being merely good to being sublime. Because of the high prices, you're likely to find a higher-than-usual percentage of foreign visitors, and not too many native Copenhageners.

Hauser Plads 32. © **33-14-66-30.** Reservations required. Main courses 250DKK–320DKK ($43–$54/£23–£29); fixed-price menu 488DKK–528DKK ($83–$90/£44–£48). AE, DC, MC, V. Daily 5–11pm. Closed Dec 25–Jan 1. Bus: 4E, 7E, 14, or 16.

AT GRÅBRØDRETORV

Gråbrødretorv (Grey Friars Square), in the heart of Copenhagen's medieval core, is named after the monks who used to wander through its premises in medieval times. Now viewed as charming and hip, the area is a late-night destination that's not unlike what you'd find in the Latin Quarter of Paris. The setting is low-key, unpretentious, and representative of the brown-brick architecture that fills most of the rest of historic Copenhagen.

MODERATE
Bøf & Ost DANISH/FRENCH   Even if the food weren't good, we'd like to come here on a summer evening to occupy a cafe-style table overlooking Grey Friars Square. We consider this eatery the best people-watching place in Copenhagen. This neighborhood favorite created a bit of a buzz when it first opened in a 1728 building constructed over cellars from a medieval monastery. But that buzz has long died down as fickle foodies have found newer places other than "Beef & Cheese" to pamper their stomachs. But, even though abandoned by the media in search of something new, the place still turns out food as good as it was the day it opened. The lobster soup wins us over, and we often follow with some of the best beef tenderloin steaks in town. After all, Bøf & Ost has to live up to its namesake. The cheese in its name is justified when

a platter with six different selections of the best cheese in the country arrives for you to devour with crusty and freshly baked bread. One local diner confided in us: "The food is not worthy of God's own table but it's so good for me I come here once a week."

Gråbrødretorv 13. ℂ **33-11-99-11.** Reservations required. Main courses 149DKK–199DKK ($25–$34/£13–£18); fixed-price lunch menu 118DKK ($20/£11). DC, MC, V. Mon–Sat 11:30am–10:30pm. Closed Jan 1. Bus: 5.

Peder Oxe's Restaurant/Vinkælder Wine Bar ✮ DANISH   The setting alone has a certain romance, as in the Middle Ages it was the site of a monastery for gray-robed friars who couldn't own anything and were forced to beg for a living. Selections from the salad bar cost 35DKK ($5.95/£3.15) when accompanied by a main course, but the offerings are so tempting that many prefer to enjoy salad alone for 79DKK ($13/£7.10) per person. Although fresh salad buffets now stretch from the New York islands to the Pacific coastline, the idea had never been introduced into Denmark until Peder Oxe pioneered the concept. It was an immediate success. The restaurant continues to this day to select its mesclun, arugula, escarole, watercress, iceberg, spinach, and other popular lettuce greens, and it also uses fine raw materials for its classic dishes, turning to the entire world kitchen for inspiration.

The cooks serve only beef from free-range cattle, along with freshly caught fish and shellfish. Game from the Danish countryside appears on the menu in autumn, and Danish lamb, among the best in Europe, is a standard feature. Other dishes include a tantalizing lobster soup and those tiny Danish bay shrimp we like to devour. You can also drop in for lunch at any time of the day to order lighter fare, such as open-faced sandwiches or even a Danish hamburger. ("Do you want chili mayonnaise with that?")

We have found that the chefs cook the best fried herring in all of Copenhagen here, and we'll let you in on their secret. They coat filleted fish with Dijon mustard, grated fresh horseradish, and even caviar before rolling them in rye flour and pan-frying them in Danish country butter. When we were neophytes here, we once ordered smoked eel, hearing it was smoked on the premises. Assuming we were eel aficionados, the waiter asked, "Sir, do you want silver eel, broad-headed eel, or point-headed eel?" All are smoked with juniper berries and are delicious, but that silver eel wins our Frommer hearts.

Gråbrødretorv 11. ℂ **33-11-00-77.** Reservations recommended. Main courses 89DKK–189DKK ($15–$32/£8–£17); fixed-price lunch menu 67DKK–118DKK ($11–$20/£6–£11). DC, MC, V. Daily 11:30am–midnight. Bus: 5.

INEXPENSIVE

Murdoch's Books & Ale DANISH   Many of the patrons of this relatively inexpensive old-fashioned pub realize only belatedly that it's associated with the very upscale Phoenix Hotel, which occupies the upper floors of the same building, immediately across the Bredgade from the baroque grandeur of the rear side of Amalienborg Palace. Inside, you'll find a long and narrow room with a prominent and very accommodating mahogany bar, an entire wall of purely decorative books (they're not actually intended for reading); leather banquettes, and a menu that's devoted to the kind of platter that usually suffices as a meal in its own right. Menu items include, among others, a lunch plate loaded with three oft-changing Danish delicacies and cheese; vitello tonnato, the Italian version of thin-sliced veal with liquefied tuna; small-scale sirloin steaks with butter-fried onions and a cucumber salad; and "Murdoch's burger" with pecorino cheese, tomatoes, bacon, and fried potatoes. There's also a platter devoted exclusively to walnuts and a selection of Danish cheeses.

In the Phoenix Hotel, 37 Bredgade. (© **33-95-92-00.** Daily noon–1am. Main courses 95DKK–165DKK ($16–$28/ £8.55–£15). AE, DC, MC, V. Bus: 1.

Pasta Basta *(Value)* ITALIAN   When the kroner in your pocket becomes the jangle of coins—not the rustle of paper—head here for a great deal on dining. This restaurant's main attraction is a table loaded with cold antipasti and salads, one of the best deals in town. With more than nine selections on the enormous buffet, it's sometimes called the "Pasta Basta Table." For 79DKK ($13/£7.10) you can partake of all that you can eat, plus unlimited bread. The restaurant itself is divided into half a dozen cozy dining rooms, each decorated in the style of ancient Pompeii, and is located on a historic cobblestone street off the main shopping boulevard, Strøget. Its fans and devotees praise it for its policy of staying open late—usually several hours later than most of the other restaurants in town—something that might come in useful on one of those long midsummer nights when you've miscalculated how late it really is, and suddenly can't find a restaurant that's still serving dinner.

Every day the chefs prepare 15 different homemade pastas. How to choose? You can, if you wish, go with our favorite—saffron-flavored fettuccine in a white-wine sauce with grilled salmon strips and a garnish of salmon caviar. Other menu choices include carpaccio served with olive oil and basil, a platter with three kinds of Danish caviar (whitefish, speckled trout, and vendace), thin-sliced salmon with a cream-based sauce of salmon roe, and Danish suckling lamb with fried spring onions and tarragon. Dessert offerings include an assortment of Danish, French, and Italian cheeses, crème brûlée, and *tartufo,* an Italian ice-cream treat.

Valkendorfsgade 22. (© **33-11-21-31.** Reservations recommended. Main courses 98DKK–169DKK ($17–$29/£8.80– £15). DC, MC, V. Daily 11:30am–2am. Bus: 5.

NEAR CHRISTIANSBORG
VERY EXPENSIVE
Krogs Fiskerestaurant ✯✯✯ SEAFOOD   Orson Welles claimed that this fish restaurant was the only place north of the Riviera that knew how to make a bouillabaisse. The great actor/director and gourmet/gourmand was just one of the celebrities who has praised this seafood restaurant, one of the oldest in Copenhagen, dating from 1910. Only a short walk from Christiansborg Castle, the restaurant stands in a historic district of 19th-century houses, and its building dates from 1789 when it opened as a fish shop. The canal-side plaza where fishermen moored their boats is now the site of the restaurant's outdoor terrace. The walls of the high-ceilinged restaurant are covered with gold-plated mirrors and paintings from the 1800s, the work of a Danish artist, Valdemar Andersen.

Even for inveterate quibblers like us, it is hard to find something to fault in the fish dishes served here, as they are among the freshest in Copenhagen. The chefs strike a studied balance between modernized traditional dishes and updated haute cuisine classics—all at celestial prices. The caviar is the city's finest, even if it is from the terrorist state of Iran. With the main courses, "nouvelle" cuisine here is something served at the turn of the 20th century, including a divine plaice meunière with lemon, parsley, and brown butter. The Dover sole is even prepared at the table, and the shellfish selection, served hot or cold, is without equal in Copenhagen. This is a most engaging restaurant, especially if you're over 50—the "sweet young things" of Copenhagen dine at trendier joints. Before the waiter arrives with the bill, make sure you've taken your heart medication.

Gammel Strand 38. ⓒ **33-15-89-15.** Reservations required. Main courses 328DKK–585DKK ($56–$99/£30–£53); fixed-price 5-course menu 750DKK ($128/£68). AE, DC, MC, V. Mon–Sat 6–11pm. Bus: 1 or 2.

INEXPENSIVE

Thorvaldsen DANISH   For some odd reason, with seemingly no connection, this affordable eatery is named for Bertel Thorvaldsen, Denmark's greatest sculptor, who was born in Copenhagen on November 19, 1768. This restaurant is hardly a citadel of grand cuisine, but it offers some of the best tasting and least expensive *smørrebrød* in town, along with a changing daily array of old-fashioned Danish cookery. Against a backdrop of walls covered with old tapestries, you can partake of this hearty and very filling cuisine. Locals begin with various versions of herring or smoked salmon. You can go on to the typical dishes of the day, which almost invariably include fried plaice. An occasional special appears with flair and flavor, including, for example, free-range Danish roasted chicken with a saffron sauce and accompanied by a helping of risotto. For dessert, opt for the fresh fruit with vanilla ice cream. Tables are placed outside in a courtyard if the weather allows.

Gammel Strand 34. ⓒ **33-32-04-00.** Reservations recommended. Main courses 89DKK–259DKK ($15–$44/£8–£23). MC, V. Mon–Thurs 11am–10pm; Fri–Sat 11am–10:30pm. Bus: 1A.

IN NØRREBRO
MODERATE

Nørrebro Bryghus ⚑ *Finds* DANISH   This is the best and most appealing restaurant in the Nørrebro district, a big-time, big-city brewery restaurant that dwarfs almost every other restaurant in the neighborhood. Occupying two floors of what was originally built in 1857 as a metal foundry, it brews between 10,000 and 20,000 liters of beer per month, as many as 10 different kinds, all of which are dispensed in copious amounts within the restaurant. In addition, many of the dishes served here are braised, fried, or stewed in beer. And if you're interested in how the fruit of the hops is actually concocted, you can sign up for any of the free brewery tours conducted here every Monday to Thursday from 5 to 6pm (Danish-language versions) and from 6 to 7pm (English-language versions). Menu items change with the season and with whatever beer happens to have been brewed within the previous week or so. Examples include crisp-fried whitefish served with roasted and glazed fennel in Pacific Pale Ale in a coriander beurre blanc and tarragon sauce; cold tomato consommé flavored with Çeske Böhmer beer, smoked shrimps, scallops, and shellfish oil; poached filet of beef served with mangetout peas, new carrots, and haricots verts, served with sage sauce flavored with La Granja Stout; Parmesan (aged 36 months) with flower honey flavored with lemon zest and Skt. Hans Dubbel; and raspberry *feuilleté* with milk foam, raspberry sorbet with Stuykman Wit beer, and sugar cookies. One of the genuinely sought-after facets of this place involves reserving the "brewmaster's table" for a specially composed seven- or eight-course meal, each course liberally soused with a different beer, with a minimum of eight diners needed for the full-fledged experience.

Ryesgade 3. ⓒ **35-30-05-30.** Reservations not necessary, except for brewmaster's table. Lunch platters 78DKK–155DKK ($13–$26/£7–£14); dinner main courses 189DKK–198DKK ($32–$34/£17–£18); fixed-price menus 235DKK–398DKK ($40–$68/£21–£36). AE, DC, MC, V. Sun–Wed 11:30am–3pm and 5:30–10pm, with bar open till midnight; Thurs–Sat 11:30am–3pm and 5:30–10:30pm, with bar open till 2am. Bus: 3A.

Pussy Galore's Flying Circus ⚑ INTERNATIONAL   No restaurant in Copenhagen has such an amusing name. Named after the James Bond character, this trendy eatery is in a trendy neighborhood. From inexpensive fresh salads to some of the juiciest burgers in town, it's a great place to eat, drink, and make the scene. The location is a bit away from the center but that doesn't seem to bother one of its patrons, Prince Frederik, the playboy heir to the throne. Media types also flock here.

In summer, tables overflow onto the sidewalk. Many books that review the world's best bars, including one by "Black Bush Whiskey," list this place among the globe's best watering holes. As an attractive waiter confided to us, "Café Ketchup gets the young and beautiful; we get the younger and more beautiful." Against a 1990s minimalist decor, with Arne Jacobsen chairs, partake of great cocktails (especially those mojitos). Many regulars drop in every morning for eggs and bacon, returning in the evening for, perhaps, a wok-fried delight.

Sankt Hans Torv 30. ℂ **35-24-53-00.** Reservations not accepted. Main courses 70DKK–115DKK ($12–$20/£6.30–£10). AE, DC, MC, V. Mon–Fri 8am–2am; Sat–Sun 9am–2am. Bus: 3A.

IN FREDERIKSBERG
VERY EXPENSIVE
Formel B. ★★★ DANISH/FRENCH   Should you be forced to invite the Queen out to dinner, take her here. She'll be impressed. This is the most misnamed restaurant in Copenhagen. Its English translation is "basic formula." It's not basic nor does it indulge in formula cookery. On the border between the Frederiksberg and Vesterbro neighborhoods, the formal and ultrastylish restaurant is the culinary showcase of two local geniuses, Kristian Møller and Rune Jochumsen, who justifiably are having a torrid romance with the Danish press.

No chefs in Copenhagen are as fanatical about serving fresh ingredients as this pair, who take the best of Danish raw materials and transform them into classical French dishes. They believe that dining should be a "total experience which speaks to all the senses." A lofty ambition indeed, but they more or less succeed in their stated goal.

On a daily basis their specially picked suppliers arrive—fresh vegetables from their own farm in Lammefjorden, dairy products from Grambogård. They even have their own mushroom grower who brings them fresh cèpes and chanterelles. Their menu is seasonally adjusted and changes every 2 weeks. The moment a terrine of foie gras with truffles and gooseberries arrived at the table, we knew we were in for a grand gastronomic experience—and so we were as we proceeded through the monkfish with lemon chutney and the slightly salted and glazed quail with those fresh chanterelles. When the tender rack of veal with foie gras and fresh cherries arrived at the table, our night had been made. But there was more to come. Fresh raspberries with a licorice sherbet proved a grand finale.

Vesterbrogade 182, Frederiksberg. ℂ **33-25-10-66.** Reservations required. Fixed-price menu 700DKK ($119/£63). AE, DC, MC, V. Mon–Sat 6–10pm. Bus: 6A.

IN TIVOLI
Food prices in the Tivoli Gardens restaurants are about 30% higher than elsewhere. To compensate for this, skip dessert and buy something less expensive (perhaps ice cream or pastry) later at one of the many stands in the park. Take bus nos. 1, 6, 8, 16, 29, 30, 32, or 33 to reach the park and any of the following restaurants. *Note:* These restaurants are open only May to mid-September.

VERY EXPENSIVE

The Paul ✿✿✿ INTERNATIONAL   Winning a coveted Michelin star, the first for a restaurant in the Tivoli Gardens, this is one of the three or four most sought-after culinary landmarks in town. Enough Danish and European journalists have written about this place to have almost guaranteed its fame, a fame that's supplemented by its location within one of the most famous architectural experiments in Tivoli: The Glassalen is a greenhouse-style building once used as a concert hall and designed by Poul Henningsen as a statement of Danish Pride immediately after World War II. The mastermind behind this sophisticated venue is British-born Chef Paul Cunningham, whose stated desire is to provide Tivoli revelers "with an intense gourmet experience." The experience you'll have might strike you because of its originality and, according to some diners, its amused sense of eccentricity. Cocktails are served in a bar area that evokes the very best of Danish design during the 1950s—a kind of oversized, unpretentious, and airy celebration of furniture which later graced airport lounges around the world, accented with one of the horses from Tivoli's original carrousels, pegged high on an otherwise-all-white wall.

The staff might not even bring table settings to your table until they (or Paul himself) engage you in a dialogue about what the kitchen can offer on any given night—a selection which will invariably be spectacular. And if you chafe at the idea of spending too much time at any particular table, no one will mind if you ask for the third, or fifth course, for example, to be served at a table with, say, a different view. Come here for superb food, a sense of international and very hip whimsy, and a creative and upbeat sense of fun. ("I was raped and pillaged and imported into Denmark when I married my Danish wife.") And how does Paul describe the historically important "Gubi Chairs" that line the edges of his bar area? "Like a combination between a tongue and a toilet seat." Paul, more than any other chef in Copenhagen, brings fresh, new, and exciting ideas to his cuisine, spending his winters when the restaurant is closed "traveling, tasting, experiencing, and absorbing new inspirations." When we last visited, we asked Paul to serve us what Bill Clinton had tasted on his visit. What arrived was hardly Bubba food but a divine free-range chicken from the island of Bornholm served with a confit of veal sweetbreads. We also tasted a perfect butter-roasted Dover sole with corn, capers, and chanterelles. The rhubarb-and-vanilla terrine for dessert brought an enchantment to the already enchanted setting of the Tivoli.

Tivoli. © **33-75-07-75.** Reservations recommended. Fixed-price menu with wine 700DKK–800DKK ($119–$136/£63–£72). AE, DC, MC, V. Mon–Sat noon–2pm and 6–8pm. Closed Oct–Mar.

EXPENSIVE

Divan II ✿✿ DANISH/FRENCH   This landmark restaurant in a garden setting is one of the finest in Tivoli, and certainly one of the most expensive, though not the rival of Paul. It was established in 1843, the same year as Tivoli itself, and long ago witnessed the demise of its less-expensive associate, Divan I. Expect garden terraces that seem forever flowering, splashing fountains, and an interior decor, renovated in 2006, that was inspired by a lattice-ringed greenhouse. The service is uniformly impeccable, a fact that's appreciated by such recent clients as, among others, retired U.S. General and former Secretary of State Colin Powell. The cuisine is among the most sophisticated in Copenhagen. The credo of the chefs is to create excellent meals using the best ingredients, but without audacious inventions. Try the breast of free-range cockerel from Bornholm, which is braised in white wine and served with morels and fresh shallots. Roasted rack of Danish veal with new peas and morels, or tournedos Rossini, are always appealing. An ongoing staple, served successfully many hundreds of times here, is the "Madame Waleska," steamed filets of sole which are elaborately presented with truffles and a lobster-studded Mornay sauce. Strawberries Romanoff finishes off the meal delightfully.

Tivoli. ℂ **33-75-07-50.** Reservations recommended. Main courses 230DKK–365DKK ($39–$62/£21–£33); fixed-price menus 495DKK–595DKK ($84–$101/£45–£54). AE, DC, MC, V. Daily, during opening dates of Tivoli, noon–4:30pm and 7–10:30pm. It's closed whenever Tivoli is closed.

La Crevette ✸ SEAFOOD/DANISH   This restaurant has been around for so long that it's a cliché of Tivoli dining, but as the manager rightly protests, "You shouldn't ignore us just because we're not new and trendy like Paul. Our food is as good or better than it always was, and you don't have to rob a bank to dine with us—only a mere convenience store." This exclusive restaurant offers more varied seafood dishes than any of its Tivoli competitors. Housed in a 1909 pavilion, it has an outdoor terrace, a modern dining room, and a well-trained staff. The seafood is fresh, flavorful, and prepared in innovative ways—pickled slices of salmon come with oyster flan and egg cream with chives, and a bisque of turbot is served with veal bacon and quail's eggs. Meat and poultry courses are extremely skimpy on the menu, but you don't come here for that. Finish your repast with a selection of cheese from France, Denmark, and Italy (served with marinated prunes, a nice touch), or the fresh pastries of the day. The restaurant has its own confectionery.

Tivoli. ℂ **33-14-60-03.** Reservations recommended. Main courses 255DKK–315DKK ($43–$54/£23–£28); 4-course fixed-price dinner 455DKK ($77/£41). AE, DC, MC, V. Daily noon–midnight.

MODERATE

Café Ketchup INTERNATIONAL   Set within the direct sightline of Tivoli's biggest stage, and loaded with contented or animated drinkers during concerts, this is the most consistently popular middle-bracket restaurant in Tivoli, the grounds of which are loaded with worthy competitors. It radiates outward like the spokes of a wheel from a central Beaux Arts core, a glass-ceilinged pavilion ringed with covered terraces, a boon whenever it rains. If there's a trendy lounge-bar within Tivoli that's favored by the young, the beautiful, and the restless, this is it. Some paparazzi hang out here in summer, hoping to catch a visiting celebrity picking his (or her) nose. In fact, it might remind you of the postmodern hip of a secluded bar in such newly fashionable outlying districts as Nørrebro, but with more flowers and an enhanced sense of whimsy. There's a nearly hallucinogenic collection of cocktails offered (martinis, sours, juleps, and more). The cuisine is competent without being great. The best food items include Brittany oysters with lemon and shallot-flavored vinegar; mussels in a Pernod-flavored cream sauce with fennel and summer onions; miso-baked halibut with spinach and garlic-flavored potatoes; venison with sautéed foie gras; and pear-flavored sorbet with Danish raspberries and cream.

Tivoli. ℂ **33-75-07-57.** Main courses 150DKK–355DKK ($26–$60/£14–£32). AE, DC, MC, V. Daily noon–4pm and 5–10pm. Bar open till midnight.

Færgekroen DANISH   If you like honest, straightforward fare, without a lot of trimmings, and don't like to spend "Tivoli prices," a mug of cold beer is waiting for you here. Nestled in a cluster of trees at the edge of the lake, this restaurant resembles a pink half-timbered Danish cottage. In warm weather, try to sit on the outside dining terrace.

The menu offers drinks, snacks, and full meals. The latter might include an array of omelets, beef with horseradish, fried plaice with melted butter, pork chops with red cabbage, curried chicken, and fried meatballs. The food, prepared according to old recipes, is like what you might get down on a Danish farm. If you like honest, straight-forward fare, without a lot of trimmings, and don't like to spend a lot of money, this might be the place for you. A pianist provides singalong music from Tuesday to Satur-day starting at 8pm. The owners of this place recently invested in their own on-site microbrewery, which produces two kinds of beer, both of which taste wonderful.

Tivoli. © **33-12-94-12.** Main courses 110DKK–205DKK ($19–$35/£9.90–£18). AE, DC, MC, V. Daily 11am–midnight (hot food until 9:45pm).

Fregatten (St. George III) *Kids* DANISH/INTERNATIONAL The setting is one of the most charming and whimsical in Tivoli. Officially, at least, it's a kid's favorite, but that doesn't stop lots of adults from being beguiled by it too. Floating atop a fresh-water lake in the middle of Tivoli, it's a miniature replica of a ship that was built in the 1740s for the Danish king, replete with undersize cannons, sails, glistening brass, and all the military regalia that you'd expect to be associated with the pride of the 18th-century Danish navy. In the 1860s, the miniature ship was donated by the Dan-ish king to the founder of Tivoli, who displayed it like one of the treasures of the park. It evokes the kind of prop that Michael Jackson might have added to his arsenal of kid-friendly toys on his estate at Neverland. Pirate madness combines with flights of "Lost Boys who never grow up" in the form of a poop deck; rope ladders; a bronze cannon; and, below decks, a combination of teak, mahogany, copper, and cozily posi-tioned dining tables. Even the Queen of Denmark has dined here, with her young grandchildren in tow. Lunches are less formal, and less expensive, than dinners. Plat-ters include roasted chicken stuffed with chervil and ginger-pickled carrots; smoked salmon platters with dill-flavored cream sauce; and herring in curry sauce. More elab-orate dinners might include foie gras with elderberry jelly and new apples; grilled cat-fish with crab cakes; steaks of beef tenderloin with chili sauce; and chocolate milkshakes with mint-marinated strawberries.

Tivoli. © **33-15-92-04.** Lunch main courses 65DKK–155DKK ($11–$26/£5.85–£14); fixed-price lunches 145DKK–235DKK ($25–$40/£13–£21); dinner main courses 235DKK ($40/£21); fixed-price dinners 375DKK ($64/£34). AE, DC, MC, V. Daily noon–3pm and 5–10pm.

KLAMPENBORG

The suburb of Klampenborg is a residential community known as "The White City," lying 12km (7½ miles) north of Copenhagen's center. Take the S-tog train C+KLAMP-ENBORG to reach it from the Central Railroad Station.

Restaurant Jacobsen *Finds* DANISH/FRENCH No other restaurant in Europe can claim so undiluted a link to one of the great designers of the 1930s. But that is exactly the theme of this angular, glass-sided restaurant. The building was erected in 1937 and has functioned as a restaurant ever since. But it wasn't until 1999 that the crew here really began selling Danish design superstar Arne Jacobsen as the site's aesthetic focus. Within a medium-gray color scheme that overlooks the sea, you'll find examples of Jacobsen's designs for tables and chairs whose rectilinear lines have been overused in modern airports and doctors' waiting rooms ever since. However, here the allure and the craftsmanship are much higher. Even the design of the carpet was by Jacobsen, and someone might let you know that the chair you'll sit on is the

"No. 7," of which more than five million copies were manufactured since their premiere. No one will mind if you ignore the Jacobsen mystique and quietly consume your elegant dinner. But if you're a glutton or fanatic for Danish design, most members of the staff here are deeply versed in the Arne opus, and will sometimes relate personalized tales of the master designer and his eccentricities. If we bestowed toques and culinary laurels, instead of stars, we'd be generous in awarding the highly skilled chefs plenty of them. They frequently change their menus based on the best produce of the season, so we can't recommend any specialties. Impeccable ingredients and beautiful sauces distinguish such dishes as tender filet of beef with fresh chanterelles and a tantalizing red-wine sauce. A classic like filet of hake with a truffle-flavored cream sauce is given a modern twist by a dash of wasabi. Sometimes a chef is judged by how good he can make a simple dish. If that is so, we take delight in recommending the sublime fresh scallops, which are sautéed and come with a lemon-flavored butter sauce.

Strandvejen 449, Klampenborg. © **39-63-43-22.** Reservations required. Main courses 170DKK–198DKK ($29–$34/ £15–£18). Fixed-price menus 335DKK–435DKK ($57–$74/£30–£39). AE, DC, MC, V. Mon–Sat noon–10pm; Sun 11am–10pm. S-tog from Central Station to Klampenborg.

Exploring Copenhagen

There is talk of a Renaissance in Copenhagen, as Denmark moves deeper into the 21st century. Much of the city, with its copper-domed landmarks, is cutting edge. A sea of change is sweeping across Copenhagen as tired, seedy old buildings are restored—many turned into boutique hotels. At trendy restaurants, young Danes are reinventing the cuisine of their ancestors, too long dominated by the Danish pig.

Museums are becoming more user-friendly, and even the Queen is appearing on the streets in scarlet red. The culture and charm of old Copenhagen is still here, but in a word the city has become "cool."

A dynamic new life, spurred in part by the young and the changes brought by newly arriving immigrants, has made this venerable old city more vibrant than it's ever been in its history.

"You couldn't be bored here if you tried," a visiting dancer from London told us. He was referring to the around-the-clock summer fun offered in the Danish capital, everything from a free-love-and-drug commune to beer breweries, baroque palaces, art-filled museums, and even an erotica museum.

On a summer evening, there is no greater man-made attraction in all of Scandinavia than a stroll through the Tivoli pleasure gardens, which seems to have emerged intact from the days when the world was young . . . and so were we. The Danes love childhood too much to abandon it forever, no matter how old they get—so Tivoli keeps alive the magic of fairy lights and the wonder of yesteryear.

Although many visitors arrive in Copenhagen just to attend the Tivoli, there's a lot more going on here. The city is proud of its vast storehouse of antiquities and holds its own with most other capitals of Europe, although dwarfed, of course, by London, Paris, and Rome.

People come to Copenhagen for various reasons—some to absorb the city's art, others merely to have fun. Copenhagen hasn't become another Hamburg yet, but it still peddles miles of porno and sex toys, for which it became infamous in the 1970s. Several annual summer festivals take place here, and live bands—some of the best in Europe—appear in parks to keep Copenhagen rocking around the clock when the sun shines. One actor who settled into Copenhagen found it an "orgy" of boats, bikes, joggers, rollerbladers, and beer.

Shopping is another reason visitors show up here, as the city is world famous for its beautifully designed wares for the home, including porcelain by Bing & Grøndahl and Royal Copenhagen and sterling silver by Georg Jensen, among other big names. Strøget remains one of the most fabled shopping streets of Europe.

Some Danes endorse all that "Wonderful, Wonderful Copenhagen" tourist propaganda. "Tell your readers we have everything," said a tourist official. "We even attract transsexual wannabes who want to change their gender. As you know, we became famous for that way back in the '50s."

Other disgruntled "natives" resent those tourist brochures, and some cynical individual, every now and then, goes and chops off the head of The Little Mermaid in protest.

"We don't think Copenhagen is so wonderful," said a squatter at the commune of Christiania. "In fact, we think it sucks." That's why she and others created an illegal, self-governed, and "free living" community called Christiania back in 1971. In spite of police interference, it's still going strong right in the heart of Copenhagen. On the community's "pusher street," vendors sell their hard drugs.

The summer sun may not set until 11pm, but in winter expect cold, cloudy, dark, rainy weather. "We brood like Hamlet then," said a local. "But winter or summer, we're super friendly and welcoming . . . and in English too."

After years of traveling to Denmark, we heartily agree with that assessment.

1 Seeing the Sights

IN & AROUND THE TIVOLI GARDENS

Tivoli Gardens ★★★ *Moments*   Created in 1843, the Tivoli Gardens gave Walt Disney an idea, and look what he did with it. The original is still here, standing in an 8-hectare (20-acre) garden in the center of Copenhagen. Its greatest admirers call it a pleasure park or flower garden, its critics suggesting that it's one giant beer garden. Michael Jackson, after appearing here, tried to buy the entire complex but was turned down, as were the Disney interests as well. The Tivoli is the virtual symbol of Denmark, and no Dane wants to see it go to foreigners.

Let's face it: The Tivoli is filled with schmaltz but somehow with its glitz, glamour, and gaiety it manages to win over hardened cynics. Children prefer it during the day but adults tend to like it better at night, when more than 100,000 specially made soft-glow light bulbs and at least a million regular bulbs are turned on—what an electric bill.

It features thousands of flowers, a merry-go-round of tiny Viking ships, games of chance and skill (pinball arcades, slot machines, shooting galleries), and a Ferris wheel of hot-air balloons and cabin seats. The latest attraction at Tivoli, "The Demon," is the biggest roller coaster in Denmark. Passengers whiz through three loops on the thrill ride, reaching a top speed of 80kmph (50 mph). There's also a playground for children.

An Arabian-style fantasy palace, with towers and arches, houses more than two dozen expensive restaurants, from a lakeside inn to a beer garden. Take a walk around the edge of the tiny lake with its ducks, swans, and boats.

A parade of the red-uniformed Tivoli Boys Guard takes place on weekends at 5:20 and 7:20pm (also on Wed at 5pm), and their regimental band gives concerts on Saturday at 3pm on the open-air stage. The oldest building at Tivoli, the Chinese-style Pantomime Theater with its peacock curtain, offers pantomimes in the evening.

For more on the nighttime happenings in Tivoli—fireworks, bands, orchestras, dance clubs, variety acts—see "Copenhagen After Dark," later in this chapter.

Vesterbrogade 3. ⊙ **33-15-10-01.** www.tivoligardens.com. Admission 75DKK ($13/£6.75) adults, 40DKK ($6.80/ £3.60) children 3–11; combination ticket including admission and all rides 200DKK ($34/£18) adults, 115DKK ($19/£10) children 3–11. Closed mid-Sept to mid-Apr. Bus: 1, 16, or 29.

Ny Carlsberg Glyptotek ★★★   Talk about putting sudsy beer money to good use. The Glyptotek, behind Tivoli, is one of the great art museums of Europe. Founded by the 19th-century art collector Carl Jacobsen, Mr. Carlsberg himself, the museum includes modern art and antiquities. It reopened in June of 2006 after a 3-year closing and the expenditure of 100 million DKK ($17 million/£9 million), part of which was spent for the construction of a ..ing that celebrates the ancient Mediterranean world.

The modern section has both French and Danish art, mainly from the 19th century. Sculpture, including works by Rodin, is on the ground floor, and works of the Impressionists and related artists, including van Gogh's *Landscape from St. Rémy* ✿, are on the upper floors. Egyptian, Greek, and Roman antiquities are on the main floor; Etruscan, Greek, and Cypriot on the lower floor. The Egyptian collection ✿✿ is outstanding; the most notable piece is a prehistoric rendering of a hippopotamus. Fine Greek originals (headless Apollo, Niobe's tragic children) and Roman copies of Greek bronzes (4th-c. Hercules) are also displayed, as are some of the noblest Roman busts—Pompey, Virgil, Augustus, and Trajan. The Etruscan collection ✿✿✿—sarcophagi, a winged lion, bronzes, and pottery—is a favorite of ours and the best such collection outside Italy.

In 1996 the Ny Glyptotek added a French masters' wing. Constructed of white marble and granite, it's in the inner courtyard, which can be reached only through the Conservatory. In a climate- and light-controlled environment, you'll find an extensive collection of French masterpieces, including works by Manet, Monet, Degas, and Renoir, as well as an impressive collection of French sculpture, such as Rodin's *The Burghers of Calais,* plus 30 of his other works. The display features Cézanne's famous *Portrait of the Artist* ✿✿, as well as about 35 paintings ✿✿ by former Copenhagen resident Paul Gauguin. Consider dropping into the museum's restaurant, Café Glyptoteket, which some locals find so appealing that they come here for its sake alone, with no intention of visiting the museum.

Dantes Plads 7. ⓒ 33-41-81-41. www.glyptoteket.dk. Admission 50DKK ($8.50/£4.50) adults, free for children under 12, free for everyone Wed and Sun. Tues–Sun 10am–4pm. Bus: 1, 2, 5, 6, 8, or 10.

Rådhus (Town Hall) and World Clock

We have never been able to work up much enthusiasm for this towering monument, the City Hall of Copenhagen. It was said to have been inspired by the main tower at the Piazza del Campo in Siena. The original is magnificent, the one in Copenhagen a bit dull. The architect, Martin Nyrop, wanted to create a building that would "give gaiety to everyday life and spontaneous pleasure to all." We're not so sure he succeeded but check it out anyway. Statues of Hans Christian Andersen and Niels Bohr (the Nobel Prize–winning physicist) are worth a look. Jens Olsen's **World Clock** is open for viewing Monday to Friday 10am to 4pm and Saturday at 1pm. Frederik IX set the clock on December 15, 1955. The clockwork is so exact that it's accurate to within half a second every 300 years. Climb the tower for an impressive view, but it's not for the faint of heart—300 steps with no elevator.

To the east of the Rådhus is one of Copenhagen's most famous landmarks, the **Lurblæserne** (Lur Blower Column), topped by two Vikings blowing an ancient trumpet called a *lur.* There's a bit of artistic license taken here. The *lur* actually dates from the Bronze Age (ca. 1500 B.C.), while the Vikings lived some 1,000 years ago. But it's a fascinating sight anyway.

Rådhuspladsen. ⓒ 33-66-25-82. Admission to Rådhus 30DKK ($5.10/£2.70); 5DKK (85¢/45p) children 5–12, free for children under 5. Guided tour of Rådhus 30DKK ($5.10/£2.70) Mon–Sat 3pm. Guided tour of tower Oct–May Mon–Sat noon; June–Sept Mon–Fri 10am, noon, and 2pm, Sat noon. Bus: 1, 6, or 8.

Copenhagen Attractions

AMALIENBORG PALACE & ENVIRONS

Amalienborg Palace 🏰🏰 If the beloved *Dronning* is in residence, a swallowtail flies from the roof of this palace. The Dronning is the Queen, Margrethe II, who became the ruler of Denmark in 1953 only after the laws of succession were changed to allow a woman to ascend to the throne. The daughter of King Frederik IX and Queen Ingrid was born in 1940 during one of her country's darkest hours, the Nazi takeover of Denmark.

She studied at universities in London and the Sorbonne in Paris before becoming a member of the Women's Flying Corps and the Women's Auxiliary Air Force in England. After her marriage to a French diplomat, Henri Comte de Laborade de Monpezat, in 1967, she had two sons, Frederik, born in 1968, and Joachim, born in 1969.

She has turned out to be a hardworking, progressively modern royal who is more accessible and beloved by her subjects than her counterpart, the Queen of England. Although not true monarchists and a very liberal people with a tradition of democratic equality, the Danes love their queen. A survey revealed one of the reasons why. "She puffs cigars like a smokestack," claim her admirers. Come with us as we visit where she lives, and don't forget to bring along a package of cigarettes in case you run into Her Majesty.

These four 18th-century French-style rococo mansions—opening onto one of the most attractive squares in Europe—have been the home of the Danish royal family since 1794, when Christiansborg burned. Visitors flock to see the changing of the guard at noon when the royal family is in residence. This has been called Copenhagen's greatest photo op but it doesn't impress us as much as the changing of the guard at London's Buckingham Palace.

The Royal Life Guard in black bearskin busbies (like the hussars) leaves Rosenborg Castle at noon and marches along Gothersgade, Nørre Voldgade, Frederiksberggade, Købmagergade, Østergade, Kongens Nytorv, Bredgade, Skt. Annæ Plads, and Amaliegade, to Amalienborg. After the event, the Guard, still accompanied by the band, returns to Rosenborg Castle via Frederiksgade, Store Kongensgade, and Gothersgade.

In 1994, some of the official and private rooms in Amalienborg were opened to the public. The rooms, reconstructed to reflect the period 1863 to 1947, all belonged to members of the royal family, the Glücksborgs, who ascended the throne in 1863. The highlight is the period devoted to the long reign (1863–1906) of Christian IX (1818–1906) and Queen Louise (1817–98). The items in his study and her drawing room—gifts from their far-flung children—reflect their unofficial status as "parents-in-law to Europe." Indeed, the story of their lives has been called "the Making of a Dynasty." Both came from distant sides of the then-heirless royal family to create a "love match." The verses for their 1842 wedding song (a Danish tradition) were written by Hans Christian Andersen.

Christian and Louise gave their six children a simple (by royal standards) but internationally oriented upbringing. One daughter, Alexandra, married Edward VII of England; another, Dagmar, wed Czar Alexander III of Russia. The crown prince, later Frederik VIII, married Louise of Sweden-Norway; another son became king of Greece, and yet another declined the throne of Bulgaria. In 1905 a grandson became king of Norway.

In the 1880s, members of the Danish royal family, numbering more than 50, got together regularly each summer at the Fredensborg Palace, north of Copenhagen. The children, now monarchs in their own right, brought Christian IX and Louise

Frommer's Favorite Copenhagen Experiences

Sitting at an Outdoor Cafe Because of Copenhagen's long gray winters, sitting at an outdoor cafe in the summer and drinking beer or eating is always a favorite pastime. The best spot is at Nyhavn (New Harbor), beginning at Kongens Nytorv, where you can enjoy ice cream while admiring the tall rigged ships with bowsprits moored in the canal.

Going to Tivoli This is the quintessential summer adventure in Copenhagen, a tradition since 1843. It's an amusement park with a difference—even the merry-go-rounds are special, using a fleet of Viking ships instead of the usual horses.

Strolling Strøget In Danish, the word *strøget* means "to stroll"—and that's exactly what all born-to-shop addicts do along this nearly 1.2km (¾-mile) stretch, from Rådhuspladsen to Kongens Nytorv. For a change of pace, midway along the Strøget's length, consider a detour onto the Vestergade, which runs parallel to the Strøget. It's lined with historic buildings and a roster of cozy bars.

Exploring Alternative Lifestyles Not for everybody, but worth a look, is a trip to the Free City of Christiania, on the island of Christianshavn (bus: 8 from Rådhuspladsen). Since 1971 some 1,000 squatters have illegally taken over 130 former army barracks (spread across 8 hectares/20 acres) and declared the area a free city. You can shop, dine, and talk to the natives about this community with its own doctors, clubs, stores, and even its own flag. Exercise caution here, however; there are pickpockets about.

Charting the Development of Modern Danish Design Two museums offer an overview of furniture designs that changed the look of the post–World War II universe. They include the **Danish Design Center** (www.ddc.dk), opened in 2001, and the older, more extensive, and more eclectic exhibits within the always-fascinating **Copenhagen Museum of Decorative and Applied Art.** Hungry for more? The comprehensive collections at **Louisiana,** in Humlebæk, almost always focus on some aspect of the "structural vigor" of top-notch Danish design, in permutations that are wide and broad enough to keep you absorbed and fascinated for at least a day.

presents—works of art from the imperial workshops and from jewelers such as Fabergé—as well as souvenirs, embroideries, and handicrafts made by the grandchildren. All became treasures for the aging king and queen, and many are exhibited in the museum rooms today.

Also open to the public are the studies of Frederik VIII and Christian X. Thanks to his marriage to Louise of Sweden-Norway, the liberal-minded Frederik VIII (1843–1912), who reigned from 1906 to 1912, had considerable wealth, and he furnished Amalienborg Palace sumptuously. The king's large study, decorated in lavish neo-Renaissance style, testifies to this.

The final period room in the museum is the study of Christian X (1870–1947), the grandfather of current queen Margrethe II, who was king from 1912 to 1947. He

---

(Fun Fact   Danish Design

While there's been a massive postwar output of modern furniture in Norway and Sweden, and architectural innovations by such Finnish designers as Alvar Aalto, the streamlined, uncluttered look of modern Scandinavian design is most associated with Denmark. That's because innovations were made during the 1950s by such local luminaries as Hans Wegner, Poul Kjærholm, and Arne Jacobsen, who were trained as architects. Connoisseurs who appreciate their radical departures from previous styles avidly showcase their mid-century furniture and tableware designs.

The original inspiration for Danish design is believed to be the organic curves of Art Nouveau, wherein critics have defined sinuousness and an uncluttered elegance as "the curved line in love with itself." Danish modern managed to transform Art Nouveau from a decorative, nonessential adornment into an aesthetically pleasing, utilitarian stylistic approach that coincided with the industrial boom in Europe after World War II.

What makes a desirable and sought-after piece of Danish design? Some critics have referred to it as "structural vigor," others as "the visual expression of a socially just society" or "aesthetic functionalism," through simple and straightforward materials, including wood (usually oak, maple, ash, and, to a lesser degree, walnut and teak), steel, aluminum, silver, and copper. The best pieces of Danish modern stress flawless craftsmanship, a design that suits the ergonomics of the object's intended use, and subservience of form to function. Respect for the beauty of the components of a piece demands use of the finest materials. The artful simplicity of each piece is achieved only after laborious hours of lathing, polishing, mortise-and-tenoning, and fitting the components into a simple whole.

As the postwar years progressed, new industrial processes developed experimental materials (which later became mainstream): Bakelite, high-grade

---

became a symbol of national resistance during the German occupation of Denmark during World War II. Along with the period rooms, a costume gallery and a jewelry room are open to the public. The Amalienborg Museum rooms compose one of two divisions of the Royal Danish Collections; the other is at Rosenborg Palace in Copenhagen.

Christian VIII's Palace. ✆ **33-40-10-10.** www.rosenborgslot.dk. Admission 50DKK ($8.50/£4.50) adults, 30DKK ($5.10/£2.70) students, 15DKK ($2.55/£1.35) children 5–12, free for children 4 and under. May–Oct daily 10am–4pm; Nov–Apr daily 11am–4pm. Closed Mon. Bus: 1, 6, 9, or 10.

***Den Lille Havfrue* (The Little Mermaid)** ✶ *Moments*   The statue *everybody* wants to see in Copenhagen is the slightly smaller than life-size bronze of *Den Lille Havfrue,* inspired by Andersen's famous fairy tale *The Little Mermaid.* Edvard Eriksen sculpted the statue, unveiled in 1913. It rests on rocks right off the shoreline of the seagoing entrance to Copenhagen's harbor, close to Castellet and the Langelinie cruise piers.

In spite of its small size, the statue is as important a symbol to Copenhageners as the Statue of Liberty is to New Yorkers. Tragedy struck on January 6, 1998. An anonymous tipster called a freelance television cameraman in the middle of the night to plastics, spun aluminum, and spun steel. All these were carefully integrated into the growing canon of tenets associated with Danish modern, especially the integrity of design plus aesthetically pleasing functionalism.

Home design before World War II embodied clunky bourgeois ideals. Following the devastation of the war and its aftermath, the modern design movement emerged from the peculiar corner of the world that was Denmark, a land that during the 1950s found itself uncomfortably positioned between eastern and western Europe. Danish *joie de vivre* rose to the challenge. Within the streamlined designs, there's an implicit belief in the intelligence of the consumer as typified in the socialist idealism of the 1930s, and an implied rejection of the romantic ideals, arrogant nationalism, and imperialism that motivated some of the carnage of World War II. There's also an endearing (perhaps even quaint) sense of optimism that science and technology can alleviate many of society's problems and ills.

The style was unusual for what it was, and perhaps even more unusual for what it was not. There isn't a trace of kitsch about it—the very fact that the best examples of the style have endured for almost half a century (with few alterations or adaptations) attests to its timelessness. In contrast, the Naugahyde sofas and Eisenhower-era "moderne" accessories that swept across other parts of the world look hopelessly outdated today.

The allure of Danish modern hasn't been lost on art historians: Most visitors to Copenhagen's Museum of Decorative and Applied Art head straight for the Danish modern exhibits, featuring works that were purchased directly from the designers and artists in the 1950s. Hot objects on the auction circuit that fetch high prices today include mid-century cocktail shakers and the ergonomically balanced "egg chairs."

check out the 1.2m (4-ft.) bronze Mermaid. She'd lost her head. Most of the city responded with sadness. "She is part of our heritage, like Tivoli, the Queen, and stuff like that," said local sculptor Christian Moerk.

The Mermaid had also been decapitated in 1964. The culprits at that time were never discovered, and the head was never recovered. In the early 1900s some unknown party or parties cut off her arm. The original mold exists so it's possible to recast the bronze and weld back missing body parts. The arm was replaced.

Although not taking blame for the last attack in 1998, the Radical Feminist Faction sent flyers to newspapers to protest "the woman-hating, sexually fixated male dreams" allegedly conjured by the statue's bronze nudity. After the last decapitation, the head turned up at a TV station, delivered by a masked figure. In the spring, welders put her head back on, making the seam invisible. Today *The Little Mermaid*—head, fishy tail, and all—is back to being the most photographed nude woman in Copenhagen.

Because of all these attacks, the statue, seen by about one million visitors a year, may actually be moved out of the reach of both vandals and tourists to a safer, more secure place. City officials are considering such a proposal. At present, many visitors claim they can't see the statue because throughout the day other tourists are constantly climbing all over her to have their picture taken.

In 2006 another Little Mermaid sculpture was unveiled, a "genetically modified sister," lying 400m (1,312 ft.) from the original Little Maid. The new bronze is by Bjørn Nørgaard, a professor at the Royal Danish Academy of Fine Arts. Like the original, Nørgaard's mermaid also sits on a rock, but her features are twisted and her limbs exaggeratedly long and skeletal. Nørgaard created the sculpture for the Danish Pavilion at Expo 2002, the World's Fair held in Hanover, Germany.

Near *The Little Mermaid* statue is **Gefion Springvandet** (Gefion Fountain), sculpted by Anders Bundgaard. Gefion was a Scandinavian goddess who plowed Zealand away from Sweden by turning her sons into oxen.

Also in the area is **Kastellet** at Langelinie (✆ **33-11-22-33**), a pentagonal citadel, replete with moats, constructed by King Frederik III in the then-virtually-impregnable style of the 1660s. Some of Copenhagen's original ramparts still surround the structure. Although today, the site is brightened with beds of seasonal flowers and statues honoring prominent Danes, the Citadel functioned as the capital's first line of defense from seagoing invasion until the 18th century. During the Nazi occupation of Copenhagen, the Germans made it their headquarters. Today the Danish military occupies the buildings. You can, however, explore the beautiful grounds of Churchillparken surrounding Kastellet. At the entrance to the park stands St. Albans, the English church of Copenhagen. You can still see the double moats built as part of Copenhagen's defense in the wake of the Swedish siege of the capital on February 10, 1659. The ruined citadel can be explored daily from 6am to sunset.

Langelinie on the harbor. Free admission. Bus: 1, 6, or 9.

Frihedsmuseet (Museum of Danish Resistance, 1940–45) ✦

As World War II buffs, we always pay at least one visit here on every trip to Copenhagen. There's always some new piece of information to learn. In 1942 Hitler sent King Christian X a birthday greeting. The response was terse. In retaliation, Hitler sent Werner Best, one of the architects of the Gestapo, to rule Denmark. Hitler used Denmark mainly as a "larder" to feed his Nazi armies during the war. The Danes resisted at every turn, including spiriting away 7,000 Danish Jews to neutral Sweden before they could be deported to Germany. This museum also reveals the tools of espionage and sabotage that the Danes used to throw off the Nazi yoke in World War II. Beginning softly with peace marches in the early days of the war, the resistance movement grew from a fledgling organization into a highly polished and skilled underground that eventually electrified and excited the Allied world: "Danes Fighting Germans!" blared the headlines.

The museum highlights the workings of the outlaw press, the wireless communications equipment, and illegal films; relics of torture and concentration camps; British propaganda leaflets dropped in the country; satirical caricatures of Hitler; information about Danish Jews, and, conversely, about Danish Nazis; and material on paralyzing nationwide strikes. In all, this moment in history is graphically and dramatically preserved. An armed car, used against Danish Nazi informers and collaborators, is displayed on the grounds.

Churchillparken. ✆ **33-13-77-14**. www.frihedsmuseet.dk. Free admission. May–Sept 15 Tues–Sat 10am–4pm, Sun 10am–5pm; Sept 16–Apr Tues–Sat 11am–3pm, Sun 11am–4pm. Bus: 1, 6, or 9.

Kunstindustrimuseet (Museum of Decorative and Applied Art) ✦   Admittedly, this museum of decorative and applied art is for aficionados and is not everyone's "cuppa," but for what it is, it is the finest such museum in Scandinavia. With more than 300,000 decorative objects on view, it's a lot to digest but worth at least 2 hours of your time.

The rococo building itself is one of the historic landmarks of Copenhagen, containing four wings surrounding a garden. It was part of the Royal Frederik Hospital, built from 1752 to 1757 during the reign of King Frederik V, and it was here in a hospital bed that Søren Kierkegaard drew his last breath in 1855.

Allowed to rot and grow seedy, the building in the 1920s was taken over by the city, restored, and turned into a series of rooms, arranged in chronological order, that trace living rooms from the Middle Ages up to the 20th century.

Pride of place is given to furniture, tapestries, other textiles, pottery, porcelain, glass, and silver, and there are many exhibits focusing on the innovative role of Danish modern design—mostly furniture and fabrics—since the 1930s. There are also rare collections of Chinese and Japanese art and handicrafts. The library contains around 65,000 books and periodicals dealing with arts and crafts, architecture, costumes, advertising, photography, and industrial design. The gardens surrounding the museum are open during museum hours. In summer theatrical performances are staged here for both adults and children, and the museum restaurant offers alfresco cafe-style tables when the weather is fair. With its manicured grounds and beautiful old linden trees, as well as strategically placed sculptures, we find these gardens one of the most charming of the outdoor spaces of Copenhagen, an ideal place to take a break.

Bredgade 68. ℂ **33-18-56-56**. www.kunstindustrimuseet.dk. Admission to museum 40DKK ($6.80/£3.60) adults, free for children under 18. Free admission to library. Museum Tues–Fri 10am–4pm; Sat–Sun noon–4pm. Library Tues–Sat 10am–4pm. S-tog: Østerport. Bus: 1, 6, or 9.

Davids Samling ✦ *Finds*   When we first climbed the stairs to the top floor of this museum, we were astonished to discover an unheralded surprise—the Nordic world's greatest collection of art from the **World of Islam** ✦✦✦, dating from the 7th to the 19th century and looted from such distant points as Spain or West India. An astonishing array of pottery, weaponry, glassware, silverware, texts, and textiles, among other exhibits, awaits you.

Christian Ludvig David, a lawyer in the Danish High Court with wide-ranging tastes, began this collection. He died in 1960, leaving his carefully chosen treasure-trove to the city, and since that time the museum has added to his bequests.

It's true that most visitors ignore the barrister's collection as they rush to take in the wonders of Rosenborg Slot or the Statens Museum for Kunst, both of which are nearby, but the Samling collection deserves at least 1½ hours of your time. In addition to those Islamic treasures, the museum includes floors devoted to European fine and applied art from the 18th to the 20th century. Regrettably, the museum is closed for renovations until June of 2008.

David's other major bequest was his summer villa in the northern suburbs of Copenhagen at Marienborg, reserved for the Danish prime minister's use.

Kronprinsessegade 30. ℂ **33-13-55-64**. Free admission. Tues–Sun 1–4pm. Bus: 1, 6, 9, 10, 19, 29, 31, 42, or 43.

ROSENBORG CASTLE, THE BOTANICAL GARDENS & ENVIRONS
Rosenborg Slot (Rosenborg Castle) ✦✦✦   "It's cool in a Robin Leach kinda way," wrote an American student after viewing this palace, the greatest and purest

Renaissance structure in Denmark, since its facade hasn't changed since 1633. It has survived fires and wars and stands to delight us today, or at least those of us who have 2 hours to spare.

Christian IV conceived of the palace in 1606 but it began with **Kongens Have** ⭐, the King's Garden, which still surrounds the palace today, and is one of the more delightful places in Copenhagen for a stroll. The king liked the place so much he built a summer pavilion here, which eventually led to the creation of this monumental red-brick *slot* (castle), inspired by the Dutch Renaissance style, and today one of the most beautiful and evocative monuments of Denmark.

It houses everything from narwhal-tusked and ivory coronation chairs to Frederik VII's baby shoes—all artifacts from the Danish royal family, who for many generations relegated this elegant building to the role of a storage bin for royal artifacts. Officially, its biggest draws are the dazzling **crown jewels and regalia** ⭐⭐⭐ in the basement Treasury, which houses a lavishly decorated coronation saddle from 1596 and other treasures. Try to see the **Knights Hall** ⭐ in Room 21, with its coronation seat, three silver lions, and relics from the 1700s. Room 3 was used by founding father Christian IV (lucky in love, unlucky in war), who died in this bedroom decorated with Asian lacquer art and a stucco ceiling.

Øster Voldgade 4A. © **33-15-32-86.** www.rosenborgslot.dk. Admission 65DKK ($11/£5.85) adults, 40DKK ($6.80/£3.60) students and seniors, free for children under 17. Palace and treasury (royal jewels) Jan–Apr Tues–Sun 11am–2pm; May and Sept–Oct daily 10am–4pm; June–Aug daily 10am–5pm; Nov–Dec 17 Tues–Sun 11am–2pm. S-tog: Nørreport. Bus: 5, 10, 14, 16, 31, 42, 43, 184, or 185.

Botanisk Have (Botanical Gardens) ⭐

Cacti, orchids, and palm trees always draw us to the most splendid 10 hectares (25 acres) in all of Denmark. Planted from 1871 to 1874—and still around to thrill us to this day—these botanical gardens are on a lake that was once part of the city's defensive moat around Rosenborg Slot, which fronts the gardens. In fact, after a visit to Rosenborg, we always like to come here to wind down after devouring so many royal treasures. Greenhouses grow both tropical and subtropical plants, none finer than the **Palm House** ⭐⭐, which appears even more exotic this far north. Retreat here on a rainy day and imagine you're in the tropics. An alpine garden also contains mountain plants from all over the world.

Gothersgade 128. © **35-32-22-40.** www.botanic-garden.ku.dk. Free admission. May–Sept daily 8:30am–6pm; Oct–Apr Tues–Sun 8:30am–4pm. Closed Dec 24 and Jan 1. S-tog: Nørreport. Bus: 5A, 14, 40, 42, or 43.

Statens Museum for Kunst (Royal Museum of Fine Arts) ⭐⭐⭐ Kids

We could spend an entire day here and still find some new artistic discovery. If you can't afford so much time, give it at least 2 hours, or more if you can spare it. The largest museum in Denmark houses painting and sculpture from the 13th to the present century, the collection originally acquired by the kings of Denmark.

The old museum building dates back to 1896, the creation of architect Wilhelm Dahlerup, but it has been greatly extended with modern wings. In 1750 Frederik V launched the collection by purchasing vast art from the continent, especially Flemish and Dutch paintings, but also Italian and German works. Bruegel, Rubens, Rembrandt, and Memling are just some of the artists waiting to dazzle you. Of all these works, we are drawn to a masterpiece by Andrea Mantegna, *Christ as the Suffering Redeemer* ⭐⭐⭐.

The so-called Danish Golden Age of painting from the 19th century forms one of the greatest treasures of the museum. Except for Edvard Munch from Norway, most of these Scandinavian artists will not be known to the general public. One of the best treats here is a mighty symbolist work, *Christ in the Kingdom of Death* ✦✦, by P. C. Skovgaard, representing a milestone in Danish art. Nearly all the Danish masters of the era are exhibited, including the famous Skagen and Funen painters.

Generous donations or long-term loans have beefed up the former royal collection of paintings and sculptures. In 1928 Johannes Rump donated a huge collection of early French modernists. The predictable Braque and Picasso works are here, but there is a stunning collection of **25 paintings by Henri Matisse** ✦✦.

The **Italian school** ✦✦ is also a rich trove of art, with works by Filippino Lippi, Titian, and Tintoretto. The museum also contains one of the world's oldest collections of **European prints and drawings** ✦✦✦, including contributions from Giacometti, Rembrandt, Degas, and Toulouse-Lautrec. Some of these copper prints, drawings, etchings, watercolors, and lithographic works go back to the 1400s. The German painter Albrecht Dürer claimed that he gave the King "the best pieces of all my prints."

Also on-site is a **Children's Museum** on the ground floor, with hands-on displays. At a workshop held daily from 2 to 4pm, kids can draw and paint and, if a budding Rodin, sculpt. If you want to take a break, head for the stylish cafe decorated by artist Viera Collaro and offering a view of the greenery of Østre Anlæg, a park and a lake.

Sølvgade 48–50. ℭ **33-74-84-94.** www.smk.dk. Free admission. Tues and Thurs–Sun 10am–5pm; Wed 10am–8pm. Bus: 10, 14, 26, 40, 43, 184, or 185.

Den Hirschsprungske Samling (Hirschsprung Collection) ✦   The setting for the museum is romantic, as it's beautifully situated in the green parklands of Østre Anlæg on the old ramparts of Copenhagen. Never has the "dancing light and sparkling waters" of the Danish seashore and countryside been so evocatively captured as it is in this highly personal collection of art from Denmark's so-called "Golden Age" of painting (1800–50), when naturalism was not just in bloom, but flowering at its zenith.

You may not even recognize the names of any of the artists on display, but you can still have a visual treat for 1 to 1½ hours by wandering through, focusing on whatever captures your fancy. The collection was financed by the smoking of tobacco. Heinrich Hirschsprung (1836–1908), a tobacco manufacturer, bequeathed his treasures to the Danish state, which housed them in a neoclassical building constructed in 1911 in back of the Fine Arts Museum.

Just as long as the painters were Danish, Hirschsprung collected their art over a period of 40 years—paintings, drawings, and sculptures, including the Skagen artists, the Symbolists, and the *Fynboerne* (Natives of Funen). We feel a great intimacy was created here by the museum's wise decision to exhibit beautiful interiors featuring furniture from the homes and studios of many of the artists. Captivating us were such artists as Eckersberg, Købke, and Lundbye, and the Skagen painters P. S. Krøyer and Anna and Michael Ancher.

Stockholmsgade 20. ℭ **35-42-03-36.** www.hirschsprung.dk. Admission 35DKK ($5.95/£3.15) adults, free for children under 16, free to all Wed. Wed–Mon 11am–4pm. Bus: 6A, 14, 40, 42, or 43.

CHRISTIANSBORG PALACE & ENVIRONS

Christiansborg Slot (Christiansborg Palace) ✦✦✦   Over the centuries Christiansborg Castle has led a rough life ever since the founding father of Copenhagen, Bishop Absalon, completed the first castle here in 1167. That one burned down—and so did the next two palaces.

Christiansborg Slot was a royal residence beginning in 1416 when Erik of Pomerania moved in. The royals lived here until fleeing to more comfortable quarters at Amalienborg Slott in 1794. Christian VI ordered that the entire castle be torn down in 1732: He didn't like Frederik IV's aesthetic tastes, finding Christiansborg "an eyesore." But his new place burned down on the night of February 26, 1794.

What is left standing today is a granite-and-copper palace from 1928. It stands on Slotsholmen, a small island in the center of Copenhagen that has been the seat of political power in Denmark for 800 years. Today it houses the Danish Parliament, the Supreme Court, this prime minister's offices, and the Royal Reception Rooms. A guide will lead you through richly decorated rooms, including the Throne Room, Banqueting Hall, and the Queen's Library. Before entering, you'll be asked to put on soft overshoes to protect the floors.

Under the palace, visit the well-preserved ruins of the 1167 castle of Bishop Absalon.

You can also see **Kongelige Stalde & Kareter** 🅐, Christiansborg Ridebane 12 (🕐 **33-40-10-10**), the royal stables and coaches. Elegantly clad in riding breeches and jackets, riders exercise the royal horses. Vehicles include regal coaches and "fairy tale" carriages, along with a display of harnesses in use by the royal family since 1778. Admission is 10DKK ($1.70/90p) for adults, free for children under 12. The site can be visited May to October Saturday to Sunday 2 to 4pm.

Christiansborg Slotsplads. 🕐 **33-92-64-92.** Guided tour of Royal Reception Rooms 60DKK ($10/£5.40) adults, 25DKK ($4.25/£2.25) children 4–17. Admission to castle ruins 40DKK ($6.80/£3.60) adults, 15DKK ($2.55/£1.35) children 4–17. Free admission to parliament. Guided tours of Reception Rooms May–Sept daily 11am, 1pm, and 3pm; Oct–Apr Tues–Sun at 3pm. Ruins May–Sept daily 10am–4pm; Oct–Apr Tues–Sun 10am–4pm. English-language tours of parliament year-round daily 11am, 1pm, and 3pm. Bus: 1, 2, 5, 8, or 9.

Nationalmuseet (National Museum) 🅐🅐🅐 *(Kids)*   The nucleus of this museum started out as Frederik II's "Royal chamber of Curiosities" in 1650. It just grew and grew until it's now the Nordic world's greatest repository of anthropological artifacts. Housed in a sumptuous once-royal palace, the museum is "not just for students," as one bored critic noted.

There's something here for everyone, even for kids who gravitate to the on-site Children's Museum geared to ages 4 to 12. You never know what you'll come upon, including the *lur* horn, a Bronze Age instrument that is among the oldest of its kind in Europe. It still makes music. The world-famous *Sun Chariot* 🅐🅐🅐 is an elegant Bronze Age piece of pagan art. Dating from around 1,200 B.C., the rare find was unearthed by a farmer plowing his ground in 1902.

The museum is divided into five different departments, beginning with the Prehistoric Wing on the ground floor, with artifacts from the reindeer stalkers of the Ice Age to the Vikings, with runic stones, helmets, and fragments of battle gear. This department will reopen in May of 2008.

In the Runic Stone Hall, the **Hjortespring Boat** 🅐🅐 dates from around 300 B.C. This "war canoe" is the oldest plank-built boat unearthed in the north of Europe. One of the most stunning displays in this hall is the **Golden Age Room** 🅐🅐🅐, with its dazzling display of gold objects, some dating back to 1,000 B.C.

One of the richest sections of the museum lies upstairs in the Medieval and Renaissance Departments, covering both the pre- and post-Reformation eras. Naturally exhibits are strong in ecclesiastical art but also well represented in the decorative art accumulated by a trio of Danish Renaissance kings, including Christian III and IV as well as Frederik II. A rare treasure here are Frederik II's tapestries made for the Great Hall of Kronborg Slot.

The Peoples of the World Department is one of the oldest ethnographical collections in the world, with artifacts ranging from Papua New Guinea to Central America. This section also displays artifacts of the Eskimo culture that still flourishes in Greenland, which is under the control of Denmark. The **Royal Collection of Coins and Medals** 𝕬𝕬 lies in one of the loveliest rooms (no. 146) in Copenhagen, with views over Christiansborg Slot. The salon displays various coins from antiquity. The **Collection of Antiquities** 𝕬𝕬𝕬 has been called "the British Museum in miniature." It contains everything from two fragments from the Parthenon, stolen by a Danish naval officer in 1687, to Holy Roman cups depicting Homeric legends.

Ny Vestergade 10. ℭ 33-13-44-11. www.natmus.dk. Free admission. Tues–Sun 10am–5pm. Closed Dec 24–25 and Dec 31. Bus: 1, 2, 5, 6, 8, 10, or 41.

Erotica Museum Everything you ever wanted to know about sex will be revealed to you here, although we could skip those vivid depictions of venereal skin diseases. All age groups are represented here, from teenagers to octogenarians. This is perhaps the only museum in the world where you can go to learn about the sex lives of such famous people as Freud, Nietzsche, and Duke Ellington. Founded by Ole Ege, a well-known Danish photographer of nudes, it's within walking distance of Tivoli and the Central Railroad Station. In addition to providing a glimpse into the sex lives of the famous, the exhibits present a survey of erotica around the world as well as through the ages.

The exhibits range from the tame to the tempestuous—everything from Etruscan drawings and Chinese paintings to Greek vases depicting a lot of sexual activity. On display are remarkable lifelike tableaux created by craftspeople from Tussaud's Wax Museum, as well as a collection of those dirty little postcards Americans tried to sneak home through Customs back in the 1920s and 1930s.

As you ascend the floors of the museum, the more explicit the exhibits become. By the time you reach the fourth (top) floor, a dozen video monitors are showing erotic films, featuring everything from black-and-white films from the 1920s—all made underground—to today's triple X–rated releases.

Købmagergade 24. ℭ 33-12-03-11. www.museumerotica.dk. Admission 109DKK ($19/£9.80). Visitors under 15 must be accompanied by an adult. May–Sept daily 10am–11pm; Oct–Apr Sun–Thurs 11am–8pm, Fri–Sat 10am–10pm. S-tog: Nørreport.

Tøjhusmuseet (Royal Arsenal Museum) 𝕬 If in your darkest soul you have a bloody heart, and want to see the weapons that man has used to kill his fellow man over the centuries, you've come to the gruesome doorstep. Actually, the long Arsenal Hall on the ground floor is an architectural curiosity, the longest arched hall in Europe, with its cross vaults supported by 16 heavy center pillars. Displayed here is an armada of weapons, some 350 historical guns, mortars, and howitzers, with artillery equipment dating from 1500 up to the present day. The Armory Hall upstairs was once a storehouse for hand weapons, and today has 7,000 of these killers, some dating as far back as 1300. Christian IV's original arsenal building was constructed between 1589 and 1604 with the thickest walls in Copenhagen, measuring 4m (13 ft.). The most beautiful weapons—if such a word can be used in this context—are the ivory-inlaid pistols and muskets. The royal suits of armor are almost works of art unto themselves. Here is where we'll go out on a limb: This arsenal museum is the finest of its kind in the world.

Tøjhusgade 3. ✆ **33-11-60-37**. www.thm.dk. Admission 40DKK ($6.80/£3.60) adults, 20DKK ($3.40/£1.80) students and seniors, free for children under 18. Tues–Sun noon–4pm. Closed Jan 1, Dec 23–26, and Dec 31. Bus: 1, 2, 5, 8, and 9.

Thorvaldsens Museum   This is the oldest art gallery in Denmark, having opened on September 18, 1848. This museum on Slotsholmen, next door to Christiansborg, houses the greatest collection of the works of Bertel Thorvaldsen (1770–1844), the biggest name in neoclassical sculpture. Thorvaldsen's life represented the romanticism of the 18th and 19th centuries: He rose from semipoverty to the pinnacle of success in his day. He's famous for his most typical, classical, restrained works, taken from mythology: Cupid and Psyche, Adonis, Jason, Hercules, Ganymede, Mercury—all of which are displayed at the museum. His *Jason* was one of his first works and remains one of our favorites. It brought fame and success to him throughout Europe and set him off on a long career after its completion in 1803. In addition to the works of this latter-day exponent of Roman classicism, the museum also contains Thorvaldsen's personal, and quite extensive, collection—everything from the Egyptian relics of Ptolemy to the contemporary paintings he acquired during his lifetime (*Apollo Among the Thessalian Shepherds*). After many years of self-imposed exile in Italy, Thorvaldsen returned in triumph to his native Copenhagen, where he died a national figure and was buried here in the courtyard of his own personal museum.

Bertel Thorvaldsens Plads 2. ✆ **33-32-15-32**. www.thorvaldsensmuseum.dk. Admission 20DKK ($3.40/£1.80) adults, free for children under 18, free to all Wed. Tues–Sun 10am–5pm. Closed Jan 1, Dec 24–25 and Dec 31. Bus: 1A, 2, 15, 26, 29, or 650S.

IN THE OLD TOWN (INDRE BY)

Rundetårn (Round Tower)   For the most **panoramic view** of the city of Copenhagen, climb the spiral ramp (no steps) leading up to the top of this tower, which was built in 1642. The spiral walk to the top is unique in European architecture, measuring 268m (880 ft.) and winding itself seven times around the hollow core of the tower, forming the only link between the individual parts of the building complex. Obviously not wanting to walk, Peter the Great, in Denmark on a state visit, galloped up the ramp on horseback, preceded by his carriage-drawn czarina. Rundetårn is also the oldest functioning observatory in Europe, in use until 1861 by the University of Copenhagen. Now anyone can observe the night sky through the astronomical telescope in the winter months.

Købmagergade 52A. ✆ **33-73-03-73**. www.rundetaarn.dk. Admission 25DKK ($4.25/£2.25) adults, 5DKK (85¢/45p) children 5–15. Tower June–Aug Mon–Sat 10am–8pm, Sun noon–8pm; Sept–May Mon–Sat 10am–5pm, Sun noon–5pm. Observatory Oct 15–Mar 22 Tues–Wed 7–10pm; June 20–Aug 10 Sun 1–4pm. Bus: 5, 7E, 14, 16, or 42.

Vor Frue Kirke (Copenhagen Cathedral)   For such an important European capital as Copenhagen, the cathedral of the Danish capital is relatively modest. The reason that it's so lacking in art and treasures was because of a fanatical attack by Lutheran zealots during the darkest days of the Reformation. They came through here destroying precious treasures that should have been saved for future generations to appreciate.

The cathedral itself, designed by C. F. Hansen, was the third such building erected here. The original Gothic structure was destroyed by fire in 1728, and the second cathedral damaged by British bombardments in 1807.

The church is often used for funerals of the country's greatest men and women—the funeral of Hans Christian Andersen took place here in 1875, and that of Søren Kierkegaard in 1855.

We like to come here mainly to listen to certain musical events (ask at this tourist office for details) and to see several sculptures by the great Thorvaldsen, including his majestic *Christ and the Apostles* 🕏🕏.

Nørregade. 🕐 **33-14-41-28.** Free admission. Mon–Fri 8am–5pm. Bus: 5 or 6A.

MORE MUSEUMS

Arken Museum for Moderne Kunst (Arken Museum of Modern Art) 🕏 (Finds)

Of the major modern art museums of Copenhagen, this one is the most undiscovered because it lies in the dreary suburb of Ishøj, although just a 15-minute train ride from the center of Copenhagen. Constructed of white concrete and steel, and evoking the hull of a beached ship, the museum was built in 1996 to celebrate Copenhagen's designation as European City of Culture for that year. Architectural critics were appalled when 25-year-old Søren Robert Lund was selected to design the museum while still a student at the Royal Danish Academy of Fine Arts. But in time Lund has won over some of his attackers, especially when the building won a major award for the best design for a new gallery in Europe. But that wasn't until 1988.

Artists who show their works here remain almost universal in their condemnation of Lund, feeling that the frame with its curious "marine architecture" competes with the picture—that is, the art exhibited inside. The museum owns some 300 works of art (not all on exhibit at once), but it supplements this trove with temporary exhibitions devoted to, say, the works of Picasso. In addition to gallery space, the museum has a concert hall, sculpture courtyards, and a restaurant.

Ishøj Strandpark, Skovvej 100. 🕐 **43-54-02-22.** www.arken.dk. Admission 40DKK ($6.80/£3.60) adults, free for children under 18. Tues–Sun 10am–5pm; Wed until 9pm. Train: E or A to Ishøj Station, then bus 128.

Danish Design Center 🕏

According to the Danes—and we're inclined to agree with them—no people on earth are as quick to embrace modern design as the people of Copenhagen. Locals rarely find almost any design "over the top." They are more likely to say, in the words of one critic, "Too much? Hell! We'll take two for the living room and one for the bedroom." Architect Henning Larsen designed the five-story center, which hides behind a smoked-glass exterior although announcing that it's a "window to the world" as far as avant-garde design is concerned. Through "golden oldie" exhibits and contemporary shows, the center focuses not just on Danish designers but provides a showcase "for innovators from across the planet." This is the best place for not only looking at the work of classic designers, but seeing the "hotties" among the cream of young Danish designers as well. You can also enjoy soups, sandwiches, pastries, salads, and coffees in the on-site Café Dansk, which, naturally, has the most sophisticated design of any cafe in Copenhagen.

27 H. C. Andersens Blvd. 🕐 **33-69-33-69.** www.ddc.dk. Admission 40DKK ($6.80/£3.60) adults, 20DKK ($3.40/£1.80) children 12–18, free for children 11 and under. Mon–Tues and Thurs–Fri 10am–5pm; Wed 10am–9pm; Sat–Sun 11am–4pm. Bus: 5A, 6A, 10, or 12.

Dansk Jødisk Museum

Daniel Libeskind, the architect who submitted the winning design for the World Trade Center Memorial in New York, also designed this museum in a wing of the Royal Library. It's been turned into the national center for Jewish art and culture, with both secular and religious exhibits ranging from films to paintings. The most dramatic exhibits focus on the rescue of Danish Jews in 1943—despite Denmark's occupation by the Nazis. Unlike many societies, Danish Jews and "Danish Danes" successfully merged into a single culture, with little tension between them.

The first minority museum ever to open in Denmark, the museum also holds interest for people who aren't Jewish. In 1906, when the Royal Library was built, it enclosed the Royal Boat House, which was ordered constructed by Christian IV in 1622. The Jewish Museum is in a wing of the Royal Library which includes the Royal Boat House, making it "a building within a building within a building."

Proviantpassagen 6. ⓒ 33-11-22-18. Admission 40DKK ($6.80/£3.60) adults, 30DKK ($5.10/£2.70) students, free for children 15 and under. June–Aug Tues–Sun 10am–5pm; Sept–May Tues–Fri 1–4pm, Sat–Sun noon–5pm. Bus: 1, 2, 5, 6, 8, or 9.

Den Kongelige Afstøbningssamling (Royal Cast Collection)   On any afternoon, you might find a lonely would-be sculptor wandering about. This museum, founded in 1895 as a branch of the Statens Museum for Kunst, seems little known. But it's such a curiosity we had to recommend it; in fact, it contains one of the largest and oldest cast collections in the world, comprising some 2,000 plaster casts modeled from famous sculptures from the past 4,000 years of western culture. The best-known original works from antiquity and the Renaissance are scattered throughout the museums of the world, but this world of plaster unites many of them—Egyptian sphinxes, gold from Atreus's treasury, *Venus de Milo*, the Pergamon altar, and marble sculpture from the Acropolis. Most of the collection was made from 1870 to 1915 by leading European plaster workshops.

Vestindisk Pakhus, Toldbodgade 40. ⓒ 33-74-84-94. www.smk.dk. Free admission. Tues and Thurs–Sun 10am–5pm; Wed 10am–8pm. Bus: 1, 6, or 9.

Kongelige Bibliotek (Royal Library) ⋇   It's not London's British Library, but the Danish Royal Library, dating from the 1600s, is the largest and most impressive in the Norse countries. The classical building with its high-ceilinged reading rooms is a grand and impressive place. The library owns original manuscripts by such Danish writers as H. C. Andersen and Karen Blixen (Isak Dinesen). In 1998, sorely in need of more storage space for its many historically important records, the library was expanded with the addition of a gargantuan and sharply angular granite annex, the Black Diamond, which extended the venerable antique structure out and over the waterfront traffic artery, expanding it in a dazzling (and dizzying) study in architectural contrasts. If you have the time, don't suffer from any kind of vertigo, and aren't stopped by a security guard, consider taking the elevator to the highest floor of the echoing interior spaces of the Black Diamond. Because of locked doors and security codes on that level, you'll probably remain within the hallways, and not within any of the "Sanctum sanctorums"; but even from the catwalks and walkways of the top floor, the sense of height, the interplay of sunlight and shadows, and the perspectives from the topmost floor can be both terrifying and awe-inspiring. An irony? In keeping with the Black Diamond's role as a repository for books, its floors, as designated by the elevators inside, are labeled as Levels A, B, and C rather than the more conventional designations as 1, 2, and 3. Likened to Sydney's Opera House for its evocative and enigmatic appearance, the Black Diamond's progressive but boxy-looking design adds to the monumentality of the waterfront promenade—by the harbor between the bridges Langebro and Knippelsbro. A myriad of dazzling, reflective slabs of black granite from Zimbabwe cover the facade, and its exterior walls slant sharply at disconcerting angles. Along with space for 200,000 books, the Black Diamond features a bookshop, an upscale restaurant (Søren K, which is recommended in chapter 4 under "Where to Dine"), six reading rooms, a courtyard for exhibitions, and a 600-seat concert hall. After viewing the interiors of

both the old and new sections of the library, you can wander through its formal gardens, past the fishpond and statue of philosopher Søren Kierkegaard.

Søren Kierkegaards Plads 1. ⓒ 33-47-47-47. www.kb.dk. Free admission. Mon–Fri 10am–5pm. Bus: 1, 2, 5, 6, 8, or 9.

Orlogsmuseet (Royal Naval Museum)   Do you ever lie awake at night wondering what happened to the propeller from the German U-boat that sank the *Lusitania*? Look no further: It's here at this former naval hospital in Søkvasthuset, opening onto the Christianshavn Kanal. That's not all that's here, as you can follow the history of Denmark, a maritime nation, through the exhibits of its royal navy. Although there are a lot of artifacts that won't interest you, many will. More than 300 model ships, many based on designs that date from as early as 1500, are on view, and some of them were designed and constructed by naval engineers, serving as prototypes for the construction of actual ships that ventured into the cold, dark waters of the North Sea. The models are wide ranging—some are fully "dressed," with working sails, whereas others are cross-sectional with their frames outlined. You get a vast array of other naval artifacts too, including an intriguing collection of figureheads, some of which are artworks themselves. For us, nothing is as glamorous or splendid as an ornate state barge from 1780.

Overgaden Oven Vandet 58. ⓒ 33-11-60-37. www.orlogsmuseet.dk. Admission 40DKK ($6.80/£3.60) adults, free for children under 16. Tues–Sun noon–4pm. Bus: 2, 19, or 350S.

Teatermuseet   Hans Christian Andersen was once a ballet student here, although we can't imagine how this awkward "ugly duckling" looked onstage performing *Swan Lake*. Theater buffs flock to this museum in the Old Court Theater that was constructed by King Christian VII in 1767 as the first court theater in Copenhagen. In 1842 the theater was overhauled and given its present look, but the curtain went down for the last time in 1881. It made a "comeback" as a museum in 1992, tracing the history of the Danish theater from the 18th century to modern times. The public has access to the theater boxes, the stage, and the old dressing rooms. Some of the great theatrical performances of Europe, from Italian opera to pantomime, took place on this stage, and photographs, prints, theatrical costumes, and even old stage programs tell the story, from Ludvig Holberg to the present day.

Christiansborg Ridebane 18. ⓒ 33-11-51-76. Admission 30DKK ($5.10/£2.70) adults, free for children under 18. Tues and Thurs 11am–3pm; Wed 11am–5pm; Sat–Sun 1–4pm. Bus: 1, 2, 12, 15, 19, 26, 29, 33, or 650.

THE CHURCHES OF COPENHAGEN

For a visit to the Copenhagen Cathedral, see p. 126.

Frederikskirke (Marble Church) ✿   In many ways this landmark church is more richly decorated and impressive than Copenhagen's cathedral, Vor Frue Kirke. Instead of Frederikskirke, Danes often call this building *Marmorkirken* (Marble Church). Lying just a short walk from Amalienborg Palace, it began unsuccessfully in 1749. The original plan was to use "quarries" of expensive Norwegian marble. The treasury dried up in 1770, and work came to a halt. It wasn't resumed until late in the 19th century when an industrialist, C. F. Tietgen, put up the money for its completion. This time a cheaper Danish marble was used instead. The original design was for neoclassical revival, but in the end the church was constructed in the Roman baroque style, opening in 1894. Inspired by Michelangelo's dome for St. Peter's in Rome, the Danish church was crowned with a copper dome, measuring 46m (151 ft.) high, making it one of the largest in the world.

Frederiksgade 4. ℭ **33-15-01-44.** Free admission. Church Mon–Thurs 10am–5pm; Fri–Sun noon–5pm. Dome June 15–Aug 31 daily 1 and 3pm; Sept–June 14 Sat–Sun 1 and 3pm. Bus: 1, 6, or 9.

Holmens Kirke　This Lutheran church became world famous in 1967 when Queen Margrethe II married Prince Henrik here. Built in 1619, this royal chapel and naval church lies across the canal from Slotsholmen, next to the National Bank of Denmark. Although the structure was converted into a church for the Royal Navy in 1619, its nave was built in 1562 as an anchor forge. By 1641 the ever-changing church was renovated to its current, predominantly Dutch Renaissance style. The so-called "royal doorway" was brought from Roskilde Cathedral in the 19th century. Inside, the extraordinary feature of this church is its ostentatious **baroque altar** 𝕲𝕲 of unpainted oak, a carved pulpit by Abel Schrøder the Younger that extends right to the roof. In the burial chamber are the tombs of some of Denmark's most towering naval figures, including Admiral Niels Juel, who successfully fought off a naval attack by Swedes in 1677 in the Battle of Køge Bay. Peder Tordenskjold, who defeated Charles XII of Sweden during the Great Northern War in the early 1700s, is also entombed here.

Holmens Kanal. ℭ **33-13-61-78.** Free admission. Mon–Fri 9am–2pm; Sat 9am–noon. Bus: 1, 2, 6, 8, 9, 10, 31, 37, or 43.

Vor Frelsers Kirken　The architect of the 1752 staircase of the "Church of Our Savior" was Laurids de Thurah. A legend still persists about him. It is said that he constructed the staircase encircling the building the wrong way. Climbing to the top, and belatedly realizing what he'd done, he jumped to his death. A good story, but it's not true. According to more reliable reports, he died poverty-stricken in his sleep in his own bed in 1759. The green-and-gold tower of this Gothic structure is a Copenhagen landmark, dominating the Christianshavn area. Inside, view the splendid baroque altar, richly adorned with a romp of cherubs and other figures. There are also a lovely font and an immense three-story organ from 1698. Four hundred vertigo-inducing steps will take you to the top, where you'll see a gilded figure of Christ standing on a globe, and a **panoramic view** 𝕲𝕲𝕲 of the city. *Warning:* Those steps grow narrower as they reach the pinnacle.

Skt. Annægade 29. ℭ **32-57-27-98.** Free admission to church. Admission to tower 20DKK ($3.40/£1.80) adults, 10DKK ($1.70/90p) children 5–14, free for children under 5. Apr–Aug Mon–Sat 11am–4:30pm, Sun noon–4:30pm; Sept–Oct Mon–Sat 11am–3:30pm, Sun noon–3:30pm; Nov–Mar daily 11am–3:30pm. It is possible to visit the tower only Apr–Oct. Metro: Christianshavn.

A GLIMPSE INTO THE PAST RIGHT OUTSIDE COPENHAGEN
Frilandsmuseet (Open-Air Museum) 𝕲𝕲𝕲　Your schedule may allow you to visit only Copenhagen with no time for the Danish countryside. But there is a way out of that—call it a look at "Denmark in a Nutshell." At one of the largest and oldest (1897) open-air museums in the world, you can wander into a time capsule of long ago—a sort of Danish version of the Scottish Brigadoon—and return to a town that still lives on in the 19th century, when Hans Christian Andersen was writing all those fairy tales. This reconstructed village in Lyngby, on the fringe of Copenhagen, recaptures Denmark's one-time rural character. The "museum" is nearly 36 hectares (89 acres), a 3km (1¾-mile) walk around the compound, and includes more than 50 re-created buildings—farmsteads, windmills, and fishermen's cottages. Exhibits include a half-timbered 18th-century farmstead from one of the tiny windswept Danish islands, a primitive longhouse from the remote Faroe Islands, thatched fishermen's huts from Jutland, tower windmills, and a potter's workshop from the mid–19th century. Folk dancers in native costume perform, and there are demonstrations of lacemaking and loom weaving.

Adjacent to the open-air museum stands **Brede Værk** ☞, an intact industrial plant that gives a complete picture of a former factory community which closed in 1956. The Nationalmuseet moved to preserve it as a reminder of Denmark's past. Still intact are the cottages of the working-class families, even the houses of the foremen. Their former eating house has been turned into a restaurant today, and there are even an orphanage and a nursery garden. The old factory buildings house exhibitions illustrating "The Cradle of Industry." Our delight here is touring **Brede House** ☞☞, a neoclassical manor dating from 1795. The owner of the mill, Peter van Hemert, lived here with his family before he went bankrupt in 1805. He pictured himself a fanciful decorator, decking his halls like he was Louis XVI.

The park is about 14km (8⅔ miles) from the Central Railroad Station. There's an old-style restaurant at the entryway to the museum.

Kongevejen 100. ☎ **33-13-44-11.** www.natmus.dk. Free admission. Apr 4–Oct 22 Tues–Sun 10am–5pm. Closed Oct 23–Apr 3. S-tog: Sorgenfri (leaving every 20 min. from Central Station). Bus: 184 or 194.

LITERARY LANDMARKS

Fans of **Hans Christian Andersen** may want to seek out the various addresses where he lived in Copenhagen, including Nyhavn 18, Nyhavn 20, and Nyhavn 67. He also lived for a time at Vingårdsstræde 6.

Assistens Kirkegård (Assistens Cemetery) ☞ Dating from 1711, and the largest burial ground in Copenhagen, this is the liveliest cemetery we've ever encountered in Europe. Instead of a tranquil "rest in peace" kind of place, it's been turned into a public park. Families come here for picnics, and aspirant rock bands use it as an open-air venue to perform before a live, captive audience. Sunbathers don't seem to mind stripping down for a "bath" on the grave of the dear departed.

It also contains the graves of the two towering literary figures of Denmark, both Hans Christian Andersen and Søren Kierkegaard. Both of these men were rivals in life, but in this graveyard they are at peace with one another. Many critics today believe both men were latent homosexuals. Martin Andersen Nexø, a famous novelist of his time who depicted the struggles of the working class, is also buried here, as are many other famous Danes, a sort of "Who Was Who." Even the brewer who still keeps half of Denmark drunk at night, Carlsberg patriarch Christen Jacobsen, is interred here.

Nørrebrogade/Kapelvej 4. ☎ **35-37-19-17.** Free admission. Jan–Feb 8am–5pm; Mar–Apr and Sept–Oct 8am–6pm; May–Aug 8am–8pm; Nov–Dec 8am–4pm. Bus: 5, 7E, or 16.

Københavns Bymuseet & Søren Kierkegaard Samlingen We come here not to see the city museum exhibits so much, but to learn more about one of Denmark's most enigmatic authors, Søren Kierkegaard. A section of the museum is devoted to the "Father of Existentialism," his life illustrated by personal belongings, drawings, letters, books, and old photographs. Born in Copenhagen on May 3, 1813, he eventually died in his beloved city in October of 1855 when he collapsed on the street. He was only 42. As a hedonistic youth he indulged himself—not in liquor like some writers but in the consumption of pastry. His pastry bill in 1836 was said to equal the annual wage of a typical Danish family. His most famous work was created in 1843 when he wrote his philosophical novel, *Enten/Eller (Either/Or)*. From an early age Kierkegaard proclaimed himself a genius—and so he was.

If you hang around, you can check out some of the city museum collections. Unless you're interested in sewers and gas pipes, we'd suggest you skip the "Underground

Tips   **Special & Free Events**

Much of Copenhagen is a summer festival, especially at the **Tivoli Gardens** (p. 112). Although the gardens have an entrance fee, once you're inside, many of the concerts and other presentations are free. A total of 150 performances each summer are presented at the Concert Hall (which seats 1,500), or in the smaller Glassalen Hall (seats 700). Of these, more than 100 are free. Pantomime performances at the Pantomime Theater are also free. Performances on the open-air stage are free every night (closed Mon). Likewise, **Bakken Amusement Park** (p. 132), which by most yardsticks is the oldest amusement park in the world, offers many free events. And you don't have to pay an admission to enter—only if you patronize the various attractions.

The **birthday of Queen Margrethe** on April 16 is a celebration with the queen and the royal family driving through the pedestrian street, Strøget, in a stagecoach escorted by hussars in full regalia. People also gather in Amalienborg Slotsplads (the square that's the focal point of the Royal Family's residence in Copenhagen), usually cheering wildly in a style that some observers claim evokes star worship at a rock concert.

The **Copenhagen Jazz Festival** in early July is one of the greatest in the world, and many of the concerts are free. Squares, parks, and a wide range of cafes and clubs resound with the sound of jazz—in all, some 450 concerts are staged at this time. Visitors arrive for the festival from as far away as China and Australia, and over the years the festival has attracted such jazz greats as Ray Charles and Dizzy Gillespie. For more information, check out www.festival.jazz.dk.

Exhibition." The section on old shop fronts evoking Copenhagen of yesterday is intriguing if you'd like to see the city the way it was.

Vesterbrogade 59. ✆ 33-21-07-72. www.kbhbymuseum.dk. Admission 20DKK ($3.40/£1.80) adults, free for children under 18, free to all Fri. Thurs–Mon 10am–4pm; Wed 10am–9pm. Bus: 6, 16, 27, or 28.

ESPECIALLY FOR KIDS

Copenhagen is a wonderful place for children, and many so-called adult attractions except the Erotica Museum also appeal to kids. **Tivoli** is an obvious choice, as is the statue of *Den Lille Havfrue (The Little Mermaid)* at Langelinie. Try to see the changing of the Queen's Royal Life Guard at **Amalienborg Palace,** including the entire parade to and from the royal residence. Kids also enjoy **Frilandsmuseet,** the open-air museum. (For details on these sights, see listings earlier in this chapter.) Other attractions great for kids include the following.

Bakken Amusement Park   This is the Tivoli on a bad hair day but a lot of fun if you don't like your amusement parks too manicured. On the northern edge of Copenhagen, about 12km (7½ miles) from the city center, this amusement park was created 35 years before the Pilgrims landed at Plymouth Rock. It's a local favorite, featuring roller coasters, dancing, a tunnel of love, and a merry-go-round. Open-air restaurants are plentiful, as are snack bars and ice-cream booths. Some individual attractions—100 or so rides—charge a separate admission fee—proceeds support this unspoiled natural preserve. We like to visit to see the singing girls and cabaret at **Bakkens Hvile** 𝄐𝄐. They rival the Rockettes at New York City's Radio City Music Hall and remain the most popular revue in Denmark. There are no cars in the park—only bicycles and horse-drawn carriages are allowed.

Dyrehavevej 62, Klampenborg. 𝄏 **39-63-73-00**. www.bakken.dk. Free admission; rides cost 10DKK–50DKK ($1.70–$8.50/90p–£4.50) each. Summer daily noon–midnight. Closed mid-Sept to late Mar. S-tog: Klampenborg (about 20 min. from Central Railroad Station); then walk through the Deer Park or take a horse-drawn cab.

Danmarks Akvarium (Denmark's Aquarium) Opened in 1939, a year before the Nazi invasion of Denmark, this is not among the world-class aquariums such as the one that opened in Atlanta, Georgia. Give it a look only if you happen to be visiting the grounds of **Charlottenlund Slot** at Hellerup, a coastal suburb of Copenhagen. After walking through the grounds (the palace is not open), site of a royal residence since 1690, drop in at the zoo. Although it was enlarged in 1974, it still features only 90 or so tanks of the usual marine "suspects"—sharks, turtles, piranhas, and both the fish which can survive in the North Sea and those from more tropical waters.

Strandvejen, in Charlottenlund Fort Park, Charlottenlund. 𝄏 **39-62-32-83**. www.akvarium.dk. Admission 85DKK ($14/£7.65) adults, 45DKK ($7.65/£4.05) children 10–14, free for children under 10. May–Aug daily 10am–6pm; Sept–Oct and Feb–Apr daily 10am–5pm; Nov–Jan daily 10am–4pm. S-tog: Charlottenlund. Bus: 14 or 166.

Experimentarium (Hands-On Science Center) 𝄐𝄐 It is said that curators from all over the world come here to plan the science museums of the 21st century. This is the most interactive museum in the Nordic world. In the old mineral-water-bottling hall of Tuborg breweries 5km (3 miles) north of Copenhagen in Hellerup, this museum has a hands-on approach to science. Visitors use not only their hands but all five of their senses as they participate in some 300 interactive exhibitions and demonstrations divided into three themes: "Man," "Nature," and "The Interaction Between Man and Nature." Visitors hear what all the world's languages sound like, make a wind machine blow up to hurricane force, check their skin to test how much sun it can take, dance in an inverted disco, program a robot, gaze at an optical illusion, experience a human-size gyroscope, or visit a slimming machine. Families can work as a team to examine enzymes, make a camera from paper, or test perfume. Exhibitions change frequently and—from what we've seen—thrill adults almost more than the kids.

Tuborg Havnevej 7, Hellerup. 𝄏 **39-27-33-33**. www.experimentarium.dk. Admission 120DKK ($20/£11) adults, 75DKK ($13/£6.75) children 3–11, free for children under 3. Mon and Wed–Fri 9:30am–5pm; Tues 9:30am–9pm; Sat–Sun 11am–5pm. Closed Dec 23–25, Dec 31, and Jan 1. S-tog: Hellerup or Svanemøllen. Bus: 1, 14, or 21.

Louis Tussaud Wax Museum Now a part of Tivoli, the Louis Tussaud Wax Museum (he was the great-grandson of Madame Tussaud) offers a sense of kitschy fun, and the opportunity to get "scared witless" in the dungeon. As such, it's a campy but major attraction in Copenhagen, featuring more than 200 wax figures—everybody from Danish kings and queens to Leonardo da Vinci. Some of these wax effigies, frankly, are way off the mark, whereas other likenesses are right on target. We applaud the museum for including famous figures from Denmark instead of just concentrating on more fabled international stars and legends. Children can visit the Snow Queen's Castle, or watch Frankenstein and Dracula guard the monsters and vampires. We always head here thinking the attraction will be just too corny for us, but end up finding effigies that enthrall us.

H. C. Andersens Blvd. 22. 🕿 **33-11-89-00**. www.tussaud.dk. Admission 80DKK ($14/£7.20) adults, 59DKK ($10/£5.30) children 10–15, 35DKK ($5.95/£3.15) children 5–9. Apr 16–Sept 13 daily 10am–11pm; Sept 14–Apr 15 daily 10am–6pm. Last entry 1 hr. before closing. Bus: 1, 2, 16, 28, 29, or 41.

Tycho Brahe Planetarium   When ET makes his first real earth landing—that is, not in a film—he'll no doubt set down here first to honor the famed Danish astronomer Tycho Brahe (1546–1601). Of course, Brahe got a lot of things wrong—after all, he disagreed with Copernicus and still believed that the earth stood at the center of the universe. But he did some things right, including mapping the position of more than 1,000 fixed stars—and he did all this with the naked eye since Galileo didn't emerge with his telescope until 1610. Long before those stories about Michael Jackson's alleged faux nose surfaced, Brahe actually had a silver snout. The original fell to the ground after a duel in Rostock.

On a dome-shaped screen, IMAX films are shown, creating the marvel of the night sky, with its planets, galaxies, star clusters, and comets. If Brahe could have lived to see this enthralling film, he obviously would no longer believe the earth was the center of the universe. The permanent exhibition, "The Active Universe," doesn't quite answer all the questions of the mysteries of space, but it deals with a lot of them. Exhibitions on natural science and astronomy may leave you with a lingering feeling for space travel if the Tycho Brahe of tomorrow could only find more inhabitable planets than Mars and Jupiter.

Gammel Kongevej 10. 🕿 **33-12-12-24**. Admission 25DKK ($4.25/£2.25) adults, 15DKK ($2.55/£1.35) children 10–15, free for children under 10. OMNIMAX films 95DKK ($16/£8.55) adults, 65DKK ($11/£5.85) children 10–15, free for children under 10. Mon–Fri 9:30am–9pm; Sat–Sun 10:30am–9pm. Bus: 1 or 14.

Zoologisk Have (Copenhagen Zoo)   This zoo has come a long way, baby, since 1859 when it opened with stuffed birds, a seal in a bathtub, and a turtle in a bucket. Today at its location in Frederiksberg, west of the center of Copenhagen, it is home to 3,300 animals and 264 species. The zoo, in fact, is a window to the wilds of the world, with animals from the icy snowfields of Greenland to the hot, dusty savannas of Africa. You get to see everything from the musk oxen and reindeer of the far north to the hungry lions of Kenya. Expect the usual apes and elephants from a Tarzan movie, but thrill also to a close encounter with a polar bear. The world is filled with ragtag Children's Zoos, but the one here is exceptional. Kids can pet beasts who are "not too wild." The highlight for the kiddies is an Eiffel-like tower that rises 40m (131 ft.) dating from 1905. *Warning:* The zoo is mobbed on Sundays in summer.

Roskildevej 32, Frederiksberg. 🕿 **72-20-02-00**. www.zoo.dk. Admission 100DKK ($17/£9) adults, 60DKK ($10/£5.40) children 3–11, free for children under 3. Jan–Feb and Nov–Dec daily 9am–4pm; Mar Mon–Fri 9am–4pm, Sat–Sun 9am–5pm; Apr–May and Sept Mon–Fri 9am–5pm, Sat–Sun 9am–6pm; June–Aug daily 9am–6pm; Oct daily 9am–5pm. S-tog: Valby. Bus: 4A, 6A, 26, or 832.

WALKING TOUR 1	THE OLD CITY

Start:	Rådhuspladsen.
Finish:	Tivoli Gardens.
Time:	1½ hours.
Best Times:	Any sunny day.
Worst Times:	Rush hours (Mon–Fri 7:30–9am and 5–6:30pm).

COPENHAGEN
Area of detail

1 Rådhuspladsen
2 Lavendelstræde
3 Slutterigade
4 Nytorv
5 Strøget
6 Helligåndskirken
7 Kongens Nytorv
8 Nikolaj Kirke
9 Højbro Plads
10 Gammel Strand
11 Snaregade
12 Magstræde
13 Tivoli Gardens

Start in the center of Copenhagen at:

❶ Rådhuspladsen (Town Hall Square)

Pay a visit to the bronze statue of Hans Christian Andersen, the spinner of fairy tales, which stands near a boulevard bearing his name. Also on this square is a statue of two *lur* horn players that has stood here since 1914.

Bypassing the *lur* horn players, walk east along Vester Voldgade onto a narrow street on your left:

❷ Lavendelstræde

Many houses along here date from the late 18th century. At Lavendelstræde 1, Mozart's widow (Constanze) lived with her second husband, Georg Nikolaus von Nissen, a Danish diplomat, from 1812 to 1820.

The little street quickly becomes:

❸ Slutterigade

Courthouses rise on both sides of this short street, joined by elevated walkways. Built between 1805 and 1815, this was Copenhagen's fourth town hall, now the city's major law courts. The main courthouse entrance is on Nytorv.

Slutterigade will lead to:

❹ Nytorv

In this famous square, you can admire fine 19th-century houses. Philosopher Søren Kierkegaard (1813–55) lived in a house adjacent to the courthouse.

Cross Nytorv, and veer slightly west (to your left) until you reach Nygade, part of the:

❺ Strøget

At this point, this traffic-free shopping street has a different name. (It actually began at Rådhuspladsen and was called Frederiksberggade.) The major shopping street of Scandinavia, Strøget is a stroller's and a shopper's delight, following a 1km (⅔-mile) path through the heart of Copenhagen.

Nygade is one of the five streets that compose Strøget. Head northeast along this street, which becomes winding and narrow Vimmelskaftet, then turns into Amagertorv. Along Amagertorv, on your left, you'll come across the:

❻ Helligåndskirken (Church of the Holy Ghost)

Complete with an abbey, Helligåndshuset is the oldest church in Copenhagen, founded at the beginning of the 15th century. Partially destroyed in 1728, it was reconstructed in 1880 in a neoclassical style. Some of the buildings on this street date from 1616. The sales rooms of the Royal Porcelain Factory are at Amagertorv 6.

Next you'll come to Østergade, the last portion of Strøget. You'll see Illum's department store on your left. Østergade leads to the square:

❼ Kongens Nytorv

Surrounding Copenhagen's largest square, with an equestrian statue of Christian IV in the center, are many restored antique buildings. The statue is a bronze replica of a 1688 sculpture.

At Kongens Nytorv, head right until you come to Laksegade. Then go south along this street until you reach the intersection with Nikolajgade. Turn right. This street will lead to the:

❽ Nikolaj Kirke

The building dates from 1530 and was the scene of the thundering sermons of Hans Tausen, a father of the Danish Reformation.

TAKE A BREAK
A mellow spot for a pick-me-up, either a refreshing cool drink or an open-faced sandwich, **Cafeen Nikolaj**, Nikolaj Plads 12 (✆ 33-11-63-13), attracts both older shoppers and young people. You can sit and linger over a cup of coffee, and no one is likely to hurry you. You can visit anytime in the afternoon, perhaps making it your luncheon stopover. The setting is within the interior of (during cold weather), or in the shadow of (during warm weather), this charming antique red-brick church.

After seeing the church, head left down Fortunstræde to your next stop, a square off Gammel Strand:

❾ Højbro Plads

You'll have a good view of Christiansborg Palace and Thorvaldsens Museum on Slotsholmen. On Højbro Plads is an equestrian statue honoring Bishop Absalon, who founded Copenhagen in 1167. Several old buildings line the square.

Continue west along:

❿ Gammel Strand

From this waterfront promenade—the name means "old shore"—the former edge of Copenhagen, you'll have a panoramic look across to Christiansborg Palace. A number of antique buildings line this street, and at the end you'll come upon the Ministry of Cultural Affairs, occupying a former government pawnbroking establishment, dating from 1730.

To the right of this building, walk up:

⓫ Snaregade

This old-fashioned provincial street is one of the most evocative of the old city. Walk until you reach Knabrostræde. Both streets boast structures built just after the great fire of 1795. Where the streets intersect, you'll see the Church of Our Lady.

Make your way back to Snaregade, and turn right to one of Copenhagen's best-preserved streets:

⓬ Magstræde

Proceed along to Rådhusstræde. Just before you reach Rådhusstræde, notice the two buildings facing that street. These are the oldest structures in the city, dating from the 16th century.

Walk across Vandkunsten, a square at the end of Magstræde, then turn right down Gasegade, which doesn't go very far before you turn left along Farvergade. At this street's intersection with Vester Voldgade, you'll come to the Vartov Church. Continue west until you reach Rådhuspladsen. Across the square, you'll see the:

⓭ Tivoli Gardens

You'll find the entrance at Vesterbrogade 3. Attracting some 4.5 million visitors every summer, this amusement park has 25 different entertainment choices and attractions and just as many restaurants and beer gardens.

WALKING TOUR 2   KONGENS NYTORV TO LANGELINIE

Start:	Kongens Nytorv.
Finish:	*Den Lille Havfrue* (The Little Mermaid).
Time:	1½ hours.
Best Time:	Any sunny day.
Worst Times:	Rush hours (weekdays 7:30–9am and 5–6:30pm).

Although Nyhavn, once a boisterous sailors' quarter, has quieted down, it's still a charming part of old Copenhagen, with its 1673 canal and 18th-century houses.

Begin at:

❶ Kongens Nytorv

The "King's New Market" dates from 1680. It contains Magasin, the biggest department store in the capital, plus an equestrian statue of Christian IV.

On the northeast side of the square is:

❷ Thott's Mansion

Completed in 1685 for a Danish naval hero and restored in 1760, it now houses the French Embassy. Between Bredgade and Store Strandstræde, a little street angling to the right near Nyhavn, is Kanneworff House, a beautifully preserved private home that dates from 1782. On the west side of the square, at no. 34, is the landmark Hotel d'Angleterre. Also here is an old anchor memorializing the Danish seamen who died in World War II.

On the southeast side of the square is:

❸ The Royal Theater

Founded in 1748, the theater presents ballet, opera, and plays. Statues of famous Danish dramatists are out front. The present theater, constructed in 1874, has a neo-Renaissance style.

With your back to the Hotel d'Angleterre, walk toward the water along:

❹ Nyhavn

Once filled with maritime businesses and seamen's bars and lodgings, Nyhavn is now "restaurant row." First, walk along its north (left) side. In the summer, cafe tables border the canal, giving it a festive atmosphere. At the port end of the canal, you can see the Naval Dockyards, and Christianshavn across the harbor. Beautiful old homes, antiques shops, and more restaurants line the southern bank. Nyhavn was the home of Hans Christian Andersen at various times. He lived at no. 20, where he wrote his first fairy tales, in 1835, and at no. 67 from 1845 to 1864. He spent the last 2 years of his life at no. 18, where he died in 1875.

On the quieter (south) side of the canal, you can see:

❺ Charlottenborg Palace

The style of the building, now the Danish Academy of Fine Arts, is pure baroque. The name comes from Queen Charlotte Amalie, who moved there in 1700.

Walk back to the harbor end of Nyhavn and turn left onto Kvæsthusgade, which will take you to:

❻ Skt. Annæ Plads

Before the radical transformation of Copenhagen's harborfront, ferries used to depart from piers here for other destinations in Scandinavia, including Oslo. Now, however, the harborfront, and the back of this desirable long and narrow square, is the site of one of the biggest urban transformations in the city's history. The ferryboat terminals have moved to the commercial neighborhood of Nordhavn, and the city seems to be watching what will eventually emerge from this site, just a short walk from Nyhavn and its rows of restaurants. Many consulates, two hotels, and fine old buildings open onto it.

Walk inland along the plaza and turn right onto Amaliegade, which leads under a colonnade into symmetrical majesty of the cobble-covered Amalienborg Plads, site of:

❼ Amalienborg Palace

In the square's center is a statue of Frederik V. When the queen is in residence, the changing of the guard takes place here daily at noon. The palace is the official residence of the queen and her French prince, but sections of it are open to visitors. The palace is actually composed of a quartet of nearly identical baroque mansions, each interconnected with galleries or subterranean passages, and each positioned at cardinal points of the same octagon-shaped square. The queen lives in a wing that's adjacent to the neoclassical colonnade.

Between the square and the harbor are the gardens of:

❽ Amaliehavn

Among the most beautiful in Copenhagen, these gardens were laid out by Jean Delogne, who made lavish use of Danish granite and French limestone. The bronze pillars around the fountain were the work of Arnaldo Pomodoro, an Italian sculptor. From this point, look across the harbor at the most exciting and unusual recently constructed building in town, the **Danish Opera House.** With a soaring rooftop that evokes the reinforced concrete structures of Le Corbusier, and a design that evokes the outspread wings of a dove, it was created by Henning Larsen, "The House Architect of Copenhagen," with perfect acoustics and "chandeliers

Walking Tour 2: Kongens Nytorv to Langelinie

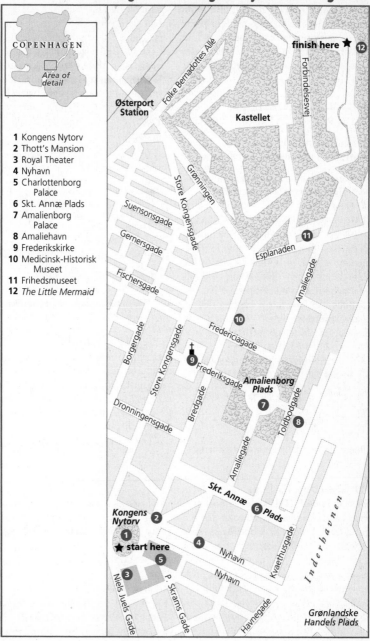

COPENHAGEN

Area of detail

1 Kongens Nytorv
2 Thott's Mansion
3 Royal Theater
4 Nyhavn
5 Charlottenborg
  Palace
6 Skt. Annæ Plads
7 Amalienborg
  Palace
8 Amaliehavn
9 Frederikskirke
10 Medicinsk-Historisk
   Museet
11 Frihedsmuseet
12 *The Little Mermaid*

Østerport Station

Kastellet

finish here ★ 12

Folke Bernadottes Allé

Forbindelsesvej

Grønningen

Store Kongensgade

Suensonsgade

Gernersgade

Fischersgade

Borgergade

Store Kongensgade

Dronningensgade

Niels Juels Gade

P. Skrams Gade

Esplanaden

11

Amaliegade

Fredericiagade

† 9 Frederiksgade

10

Bredgade

Amalienborg Plads

7

Toldbodgade

8

Skt. Annæ 6 Plads

Amaliegade

Kvæthusgade

Kongens Nytorv 2

1

★ start here

3

5

4

Nyhavn

Nyhavn

Havnegade

Inderhavnen

Grønlandske Handels Plads

that might have been inspired by a show palace in Las Vegas." From your waterfront vantage, notice the way that the location of the Opera House repeats the rectilinear layout of Amalienborg Palace and the nearby Marble Church; the buildings each line up along the same lines, a brilliant combination of baroque and postmodern architecture combined into a coherent whole.

After viewing the waterfront gardens, walk away from the water, crossing Amalienborg Plads and emerging onto Frederiksgade. Continue along this street until you reach:

❾ Frederikskirke

This church is often called the *Marmorkirken* (marble church). Construction began in 1740, but had to stop in 1770 because of the costs. The church wasn't completed until 1894—using Danish marble instead of more expensive Norwegian marble. The church was modeled on and intended to rival St. Peter's in Rome; indeed, it ended up with one of the largest church domes in Europe. Supported on a dozen towering piers, the dome has a diameter of 32m (105 ft.).

Facing the church, turn right and head north along Bredgade, passing at no. 22 the:

❿ Medicinsk-Historisk Museet (Medical History Museum)

The collection is gruesome, with fetuses, dissected heads, and the like.

TAKE A BREAK
Before you approach *Den Lille Havfrue*, consider tea and a snack at Café **Lumskebugten,** Esplanaden 21 (✆ **33-15-60-29;** see "Where to Dine," in chapter 4). Dating from 1854, and permeated with a sense of the cozy, old-fashioned Denmark of long ago, this cafe offers a cold plate served throughout the afternoon. There are five specialties: beef tartare, fish cakes with mustard sauce, marinated salmon, baked cod, and shrimp.

Bredgade ends at Esplanaden, which opens onto Churchillparken, a green belt bordering the water. Turn right and walk along Esplanaden until you come to Churchillparken and the:

⓫ Frihedsmuseet

The Danish Resistance museum commemorates the struggle against the Nazis from 1940 to 1945.

After leaving the museum, walk toward the water along Langelinie, where signs point the way to:

⓬ The Little Mermaid

Perched on rocks just off the harbor bank, *Den Lille Havfrue,* the most photographed statue in Scandinavia, dates from 1913. The bronze figure, by Edvard Eriksen, was modeled after the figure of prima ballerina Ellen Price. In time, this much-attacked and abused statue became the symbol of Copenhagen.

ORGANIZED TOURS

BUS & BOAT TOURS   The boat and bus sightseeing tours in Copenhagen range from get-acquainted jaunts to in-depth excursions. Either of the following tours can be arranged through **Copenhagen Excursions** (✆ **32-54-06-06**) or **Vikingbus** (✆ **32-66-00-00**). Inexpensive bus tours depart from the *lur* blowers' statue at Town Hall Square, and boat trips leave from Gammel Strand (the fish market) or Nyhavn. Visit **www.sightseeing.dk** for more information.

For orientation, hop on a bus for the 1½-hour **City Tour,** which covers scenic highlights like *The Little Mermaid,* Rosenborg Castle, and Amalienborg Palace. Tours depart from the City Hall Square daily at 9:30am, 11:30am, and 1:30pm May 15 to September 30. They cost 130DKK ($22/£12) for adults, 65DKK ($11/£5.85) for children under 12.

We heartily recommend the **City and Harbor Tour,** a 2½-hour trip by launch and bus that departs from Town Hall Square. The boat tours the city's main canals, passing

The Little Mermaid and the Old Fish Market. It operates May 15 to September 30, daily at 9:30am, 11:30am, and 1:30pm. It costs 175DKK ($30/£16) for adults, 90DKK ($15/£8.10) for children under 12.

Shakespeare buffs may be interested in an afternoon excursion to the castles of North Zealand. The 7-hour tour explores the area north of Copenhagen, including Kronborg (Hamlet's castle); briefly visits Fredensborg, the queen's residence; and makes a stopover at Frederiksborg Castle and the National Historical Museum. Tours depart from Town Hall Square, running February to April and October to December Wednesday and Sunday at 9:30am; May to September Wednesday, Saturday, and Sunday at 9:30am. The cost is 430DKK ($73/£39) for adults, 225DKK ($38/£20) for children under 12.

GUIDED WALKS THROUGH COPENHAGEN   Staff members of the Copenhagen Tourist Information Office conduct 2-hour guided walking tours of the city every Monday and Friday to Sunday at 10am, between May and September. The price is 80DKK ($13/£7.20) for adults, 25DKK ($4.20/£2.25) for children 10–15, free for children under 10. For information, contact the **Copenhagen Tourist Information Center,** Vesterbrogade 4A (© **70-22-24-42;** www.visitcopenhagen.com).

A VISIT TO COPENHAGEN'S MOST FAMOUS BREWERY   Carlsberg is the most famous beer in Denmark and the country's best-known brand internationally. Much of it is produced within an old-fashioned brewery constructed in 1847, which was enlarged in 2005 with the addition of a spanking-new microbrewery that's devoted to the production of at least four "affiliated" brews which are being marketed under the brand name of "Jacobsen." Jointly, the brewery turns out at least three million bottles of beer a day. Even Danny Kaye, in Denmark to film *Hans Christian Andersen* for Samuel Goldwyn, drank a beer here, although this gourmet later admitted, "I infinitely prefer French wine." From within the newly redesigned Visitors' Center, you can take a self-guided tour of both sides of the brewery, walking around an observation gallery whose English-language signs and flickering video screens will explain the brewing process. The factory is open for visits Tuesday to Sunday 10am to 4pm. Entrance (and access to the self-guided tours) costs 45DKK ($7.65/£4.05) per person (there's no discount for children), and each adult visitor is given a free beer at the end of the tour, with the option of buying more at the on-site pub. The entrance to the brewery is graced with a pair of sculpted elephants, each with armored regalia that includes a swastika. That doesn't mean the company was a Nazi sympathizer— Carlsberg used the symbol as part of its image long before Hitler. Take bus no. 26 from Copenhagen Central Station or from the Town Hall Square in Copenhagen to **Carlsberg Brewery,** Gamle Carlsberg Vej 11 (© **33-27-13-14**).

PLAYING OUTDOORS

BICYCLING   The absence of hills and the abundance of parks and wide avenues with bicycle lanes make cycling the best way to explore Copenhagen. Bike-rental shops and stands are scattered throughout the city. Two suggestions are **Københavns Cyker,** Reventlowsgade 11 (© **33-33-86-13;** bus: 6 or 10), and **Dan Wheel,** Colbjørnsensgade 3 (© **33-21-22-27;** bus: 28 or 41). A deposit of 500DKK ($85/£45) is required. Alternatively, **City Bike** is a great way to get around central Copenhagen. Bike racks are located throughout the city center; the service is free and you unlock your bike with a 20DKK ($3.40/£1.80) deposit. When you return the bike your deposit is returned. The bikes are available from May to December (www.bycyklen.dk).

FITNESS   **Form & Fitness,** Øster Allé 42E (© **35-55-00-78**; bus: 9 or 10), offers a day pass for 150DKK ($26/£14). Aerobics, weights, and fitness machines are available Monday to Thursday 6:30am to 11pm, Friday 6:30am to 9pm, Saturday and Sunday 8am to 6pm.

GOLF   Denmark's best-known golf course, and one of its most challenging to golfers around the world, is at the **Rungsted Golf Klub,** Vestre Stationsvej 16, Rungsted (© **45-76-85-82**; bus: 3, 16, or 45). It's in the heart of Denmark's "Whisky Trail," a string of homes and mansions known for their allure to retirees, about 21km (13 miles) north of Copenhagen. Some degree of competence is required, so beginners and intermediate golfers might want to hold off. If you're an advanced golfer, call for information and to arrange a tee time. Greens fees run 350DKK to 550DKK ($60–$94/£32–£50) for a full day's use of the club's 18 holes. To play, you must present evidence of a 21 handicap on Saturday and Sunday, or 25 on weekdays. With advance notice, you can rent clubs for 250DKK ($43/£23). No carts are allowed on the ecologically fragile course, which is open year-round, except when it is snowing.

JOGGING   The many parks (known to locals as "green lungs") of Copenhagen provide endless routes for joggers. Our favorite, just west of the city center, circles Lakes Sortedams, St. Jorgens, and Peblinge. The paths that wind through the Frederiksborg gardens are also well suited for joggers.

SWIMMING   In spite of an often bone-chilling climate, swimming is a favorite Danish pastime. The **Frederiksborg Svømmehal,** Helgesvej 29 (© **38-14-04-04**; bus: 6 or 18), is open to the public Monday to Friday 7am to 9pm, Saturday 9am to 4pm, Sunday 9am to 2:30pm. Tickets cost 30DKK ($5.10/£2.70). You can also try **Sundby Swimming-pool,** Sundbyvestervej 50 (© **32-58-55-68**; bus: 30 or 31); or **Kildeskovshallen,** Adolphsvej 25 (© **39-77-44-00**; bus: 165).

TENNIS   Visitors usually pay a large supplement to play tennis at hotels and clubs in Copenhagen. There's a high hourly rate, and courts must be reserved in advance. At the **Hotel Mercur,** Vester Farimagsgade 17 (© **33-12-57-11**; bus: 40 or 46), visitors pay 130DKK ($22/£12) for the first hour, 100DKK ($17/£9) for each additional hour. Another club is **Københavns Boldklub,** Peter Bangs Vej 147 (© **38-71-41-50**; bus: 1); this club is in Frederiksberg, a neighborhood west of central Copenhagen.

2 Shopping

Copenhagen is in the vanguard of shopping in Europe, and much of the action takes place on **Strøget,** the pedestrian street in the heart of the capital. Strøget begins as Frederiksberggade, north of Rådhuspladsen, and winds to Østergade, which opens onto Kongens Nytorv. The jam-packed street is lined with stores selling everything from porcelain statues of *Youthful Boldness* to open-faced sandwiches piled high with Greenland shrimp, pizza slices, all kinds of clothing, and some of the most elegant porcelain in Europe. There are also high-volume franchises of both McDonald's and Burger King.

Between stops, relax with a drink at an outdoor cafe, or just sit on a bench and people-watch.

In two nearby walking areas—**Gråbrødretorv** and **Fiolstræde**—you can browse through antiques shops and bookshops.

Bredgade, beginning at Kongens Nytorv, is the antiques district, where prices tend to be very high. **Læderstræde** is another shopping street that competes with Bredgade in antiques.

BEST BUYS   In a country famed for its designers and craftspeople, the best buys are in stainless steel, porcelain, china, glassware, toys, functionally designed furniture, textiles, and jewelry—especially silver jewelry set with semiprecious stones.

SHIPPING IT HOME & RECOVERING VAT   Denmark imposes a 25% tax on goods and services, a "value-added tax" known in Denmark as **MOMS** (pronounced "mumps" and every bit as painful). Tax-free exports are possible. Many stores will mail goods to your home so you can avoid paying the tax. If you want to take your purchases, look for shops displaying Danish tax-free shopping notices. Such shops offer tourists tax refunds for personal export. This refund applies to purchases of over 300DKK ($51/£27) for visitors from the United States and Canada—spent at the same store, but not necessarily all at once. For more information, see "Taxes" in "Fast Facts: Denmark," in chapter 2. For answers to tax refund questions, call **Global Refund** (② **32-52-55-66**).

STORE HOURS   In general, shopping hours are 9:30 or 10am to 5:30pm Monday to Thursday, to 7 or 8pm on Friday, and to 2pm on Saturday. Most shops are closed Sunday, except the kiosks and supermarket at the Central Railroad Station. Here you can purchase food until 10pm or midnight. The Central Railroad Station's bakery is open until 9pm, and one kiosk at Rådhuspladsen, which sells papers, film, and souvenirs, is open 24 hours.

SHOPPING A TO Z
AMBER
The Amber Specialist   The owners, known to customers as the "Amber Twins," will sell you "the gold of the north." This petrified resin originated in the large coniferous forests that covered Denmark some 35 million years ago. The forest disappeared, but the amber lasted, and is now used to create handsome jewelry. This shop carries a large collection of stunning amber set in 14-karat gold. Frederiksberggade 28. ② **33-11-88-03**. Bus: 28, 29, or 41.

ART GALLERIES & AUCTION HOUSES
Bruun Rasmussen   Established shortly after World War II, this is Denmark's leading auction house. July is usually quiet, although the premises remain open for appraisals and purchases. The season begins in August, with an auction of paintings and fine art. Viewing time is allowed before auctions, which are held about once a month. There are also auctions of art, wine, coins, books, and antique weapons. Bredgade 33. ② **33-13-69-11**. Bus: 1, 6, 9, or 10.

Galerie Asbæk   This modern-art gallery has a permanent exhibit of the best local artists, along with changing shows by Scandinavian and foreign artists. A bookshop and cafe serving French-inspired Danish food is on the premises. Graphics and posters are for sale. Bredgade 20. ② **33-15-40-04**. www.asbaek.dk. Bus: 1, 6, 9, 10, 28, 29, or 41.

BOOKS
Boghallen   This big store at Town Hall Square carries many books in English, as well as a wide selection of travel-related literature, including maps. It stocks books in English on Danish themes, such as the collected works of Hans Christian Andersen. Rådhuspladsen 37. ② **33-47-25-60**. Bus: 2, 8, or 30.

COFFEE & TEA

Specialkobmanden   It's the best-scented store in Copenhagen, thanks to hundreds of containers of exotic coffees, teas, and spices that would send any caffeine addict into orbit. Scattered within this cornucopia of abundance are coffee varieties from Jamaica, Cuba, and Kenya; teas from the slopes of Mount Kilimanjaro; olive oils from Italy and France; even a blend of tea named after (and presumably favored by) Princess Mary, the (relatively) new Australia-born bride of Denmark's crown prince. Established in 1972, the shop is a favorite of local residents, who seek out the place for the new, the unusual, and the esoteric. Hovedvagtsgade 6. © **33-15-12-88.** Bus: 1, 6, or 9.

DANISH DESIGN

DDC Shop ✦ *Finds*   On the premises of the Danish Design Centre (p. 127), this store is like a small exhibition of Danish design . . . except everything is for sale. The shop showcases products that evoke some of the best craftsmanship of modern Danish designers today. The assortment of items for sale is always changing and continuously expanding, but invariably only high-quality items are offered for sale. 27 H. C. Andersens Blvd. © **33-69-33-69.** Bus: 5A, 6A, 10, or 12.

Normann Copenhagen   In the Østerbro district, this is an international design firm installed in a long-deserted old movie house. Jan and Poul are the two Normanns, one with the last name of Andersen and the other called Madsen. Locals flock here to purchase ever-changing furniture and objects in Danish design, including avant-garde ceramics. Østerbrogade 70. © **35-27-05-40.** www.normann-copenhagen.com. Bus: 3.

Rosendahl ✦✦   It all started with a wine stopper when this company's founder, Erik Rosendahl, invented a cone-shaped object that would fit all wine bottles. It took Denmark by storm. Today Rosendahl is one of the country's leading producers of gifts for the home, each object from clear glass to bone china based on fine craftsmanship and practical design. The company is known for its innovative accessories for the table and its professional, easy-to-use kitchen utensils. Bremerholm 1. © **70-27-66-33.** www.rosendahl. dk. Bus: 1, 6, 8, 9, or 10.

DEPARTMENT STORES

Birger Christensen ✦✦   This spacious store is one of the most luxe in Copenhagen, filled with beautiful and expensive clothes, even seal and sable furs from the far north of Scandinavia. In addition to clothing from Danish designers, the store also carries all the big names such as Prada and Chanel, and it clothes both men and women rather glamorously. The 20th century in fashion is a distant memory. This store's clothing is as modern as tomorrow. Østergade 38. © **33-11-55-55.** www.birger-christensen.com. Bus: 1, 6, or 9.

Bruuns Bazaar ✦✦   Starting out small in 1995, two brothers, Teis and Bjørn Brunn, soon had fashionistas beating a path to their door. Their clothing is now seen on the catwalks of Paris and has, in fact, gone around the world. Today the "Bazaar" is an innovative and international design company, creating beautiful clothing for both men and women, as well as accessories. Somehow they manage to blend a classic style with cutting-edge designs. The shop also designs a trendy line for younger women and carries a collection of delicate footwear for women in the most "seductive" of colors. Krønprinsensgade 8 & 9. © **33-32-19-99.** www.bruunsbazaar.com. bus: 1, 6, or 9.

Illum ✿   One of Denmark's top department stores, Illum is on Strøget. Take time to browse through its vast store of Danish and Scandinavian design. There are a restaurant and a special export cash desk at street level. Østergade 52. © **33-14-40-02.** Bus: 1, 6, 9, or 10.

Mads Nørgaard   All the big names in international labels are sold here, but "Mads," lying along the Strøget, turns out some beautifully made clothing on its own label. The women's jeans look street-smart, and the menswear is fashionable and right up-to-date. The selection of elegant T-shirts—if a T-shirt can be elegant—is the best in town. Amagertorv 15. © **33-32-01-19.** Bus: 1, 6, 8, 9, or 10.

Magasin ✿✿   A classy department store, Magasin is the biggest in Scandinavia. It offers a complete assortment of Danish designer fashion, a large selection of glass and porcelain, and souvenirs. Goods are shipped abroad tax-free. Kongens Nytorv 13. © **33-11-44-33.** Bus: 1, 6, 9, or 10.

Munthe plus Simonsen ✿   This is where the Danish supermodel Helena Christensen, and even Crown Princess Mary, go to shop. The walls are lined with buffalo skin to create a warm, cozy mood for the fashion on parade. Designers Naja Munthe and Karen Simonsen founded this award-winning design company in 1994, and they still select the colors, individual designs, and fabrics used in their line of women's wear. Their line also includes mens' suit jackets and tailored outerwear jackets and coats in alpaca wool. Grønnegade 10. © **33-32-03-12.** www.muntheplussimonsen.dk. Bus: 1, 6, or 9.

Sneaky Fox   Although these designers turn out seductive, "foxy" party dresses, the owners earned their fame for their Sneaky Fox hosiery, which has swept Denmark and spilled over into Norway, Sweden, Germany, France, and Holland. Created in 1986 in a basement location, the company grew and grew with its unique "one size fits all" concept in hosiery. Studiestræde 25A. © **33-91-25-20.** www.sneakyfox.dk. Bus: 14 or 16.

FURS

Birger Christensen   This is one of Scandinavia's leading fur shops. It has its own designer line, two well-stocked floors of inventory, and furs and fashions by some of the world's leading designers, including Valentino and Oscar de la Renta. You can also purchase—cheaper than the furs—a selection of cashmere or wool blended coats with fur lining and fur trim, and conventional (nonfur) sportswear from Chanel, Yves St-Laurent, Marc Jacobs, and Prada. This is swank shopping and very, very expensive. Østergade 38. © **33-11-55-55.** Bus: 1, 6, 9, 10, 19, 29, 31, 42, or 43.

GLASSWARE, PORCELAIN & CRYSTAL

Rosenthal Studio-Haus ✿✿✿   You'll find an array of ceramic works here, especially by well-known Danish artist Bjørn Wiinblad, whose figures we find whimsical and delightful. You can also get some good buys on Orrefors crystal, including some stunning bowls. The sculptural reliefs, handmade in lead crystal, range from miniatures to giant animals in limited world editions of 199 pieces. They often depict the animals of the far north. Frederiksberggade 21. © **33-14-21-01.** Bus: 28, 29, or 41.

Royal Copenhagen Porcelain ✿✿✿   Royal Copenhagen's trademark, three wavy blue lines, has come to symbolize quality. Founded in 1775, the factory was a royal possession for a century before passing into private hands in 1868. Royal Copenhagen's Christmas plates are collectors' items. The factory has turned out a new plate each year since 1908, most of the designs depicting the Danish countryside in winter. There's a huge selection of seconds on the top floor, and unless you're an expert, you probably can't tell the difference. Visitors are welcome at the **factory** at Søndre Fasan-vej 5 (© **38-14-48-48**), where tours are given Monday to Friday from 9am to 3pm. (These tours, which occur at a location about 15km [9⅓ miles] west of Copenhagen, can be arranged, along with transportation from central Copenhagen, by contacting the Royal Copenhagen store at the phone number listed above.) Purchases cannot be made at the factory.

There are also various porcelain and silver retailers in this same location, as well as the Royal Copenhagen Antiques shop, which specializes in buying and selling antique Georg Jensen, Royal Copenhagen, Bing & Grøndahl porcelain, and Michelson Christmas spoons. In November of 2006 the showrooms of this place were radically renovated into a pale blue and white design that include plays of both natural and arti-ficial light, sound, and perfume. In the Royal Scandinavia retail center, Amagertorv 6 (Strøget). © **33-13-71-81**. www.royalcopenhagen.com. Bus: 1, 2, 6, 8, 28, 29, or 41 for the retail outlet; 1 or 14 for the factory.

HOME FURNISHINGS

Illums Bolighus ✦✦✦   A center for modern Scandinavian and Danish design, this is one of Europe's finest showcases for household furnishings and accessories. It stocks furniture, lamps, rugs, textiles, bedding, glassware, kitchenware, flatware, china, jew-elry, and ceramics. The store also sells women's and men's clothes and accessories, and there's even a gift shop. Amagertorv 10 (Strøget). © **33-14-19-41**. www.illumsbolighus.com. Bus: 28, 29, or 41.

Lysberg, Hansen & Therp   This major interior-decorating center offers fabrics, carpets, and furniture. The model apartments are furnished in impeccable taste. The company manufactures its own furniture in traditional design and imports fabrics, usually from Germany or France. The gift shop has many hard-to-find creations. Bredgade 77. © **33-14-47-87**. Bus: 1, 6, 9, or 10.

Paustian ✦✦✦   Copenhagen's leading furniture showroom, in the somewhat distant industrial Nordhavn section, will ship anywhere in the world. The finest of Scandina-vian design is on display, along with reproductions of the classics. There's a well-recom-mended adjoining restaurant. Kalkbrænderiløbskaj 2. © **39-16-65-65**. www.paustian. dk. S-tog: Nordhavn.

JEWELRY

Hartmann's Selected Estate Silver & Jewelry ✦ *Finds*   This shop buys silver and jewelry from old estates and sells it at reduced prices. Sometimes it's possible to purchase heirloom Georg Jensen estate silver. Ulrik Hartmann, the store's owner, launched his career as a 10-year-old trading at a local flea market, but went on to greater things. The shop is near Kongens Nytorv. While in the neighborhood, you can walk for hours, exploring the auction rooms, jewelry shops, and art galleries in the vicinity. Bredgade 4. © **33-33-09-63**. Bus: 1, 6, 9, or 10.

Kære Ven   One of the city's oldest diamond dealers, in business for more than 100 years, this outlet advertises itself as offering "prices from another century." That's a gross exaggeration, but you can often find bargains in antique jewelry, even old Georg Jensen silver. An array of rings, earrings, necklaces, and bracelets are sold, along with other items. A few items in the store are sold at 50% off competitive prices, but you have to shop carefully and know what you're buying. Star Kongens Gade 30. © **33-11-43-15**. www.kaereven.dk. Bus: 1, 6, 9, or 10.

MUSIC

Axel Musik   One of the best-stocked music stores in the Danish capital, Axel also has another branch in the city's main railway station. In Scala Center (ground floor), Axeltorv 2. ℂ **33-14-05-50.** Bus: 1, 6, or 8.

PEWTER & SILVER

Georg Jensen ✦✦✦   Georg Jensen is legendary for its silver. For the connoisseur, there's no better address. On display is the largest and best collection of Jensen Holloware in Europe. The store also features gold and silver jewelry in traditional and modern Danish designs. In the Royal Scandinavia retail center, Amagertorv 6 (Strøget). ℂ **33-11-40-80.** www.georgjensen.com. Bus: 1, 6, 8, 9, or 10.

SHOPPING CENTER

In addition to the centers described above, for excellent buys in Scandinavian merchandise, as well as tax-free goods, we recommend the **shopping center at the airport.** A VAT-refund office is located nearby.

3 Copenhagen After Dark

Danes know how to party. A good night means a late night, and on warm weekends, hundreds of rowdy revelers crowd Strøget until sunrise. Merrymaking in Copenhagen is not just for the younger crowd; jazz clubs, traditional beer houses, and wine cellars are routinely packed with people of all ages. Of course, the city has a more highbrow cultural side as well, exemplified by excellent theaters, operas, ballets, and one of the best circuses in Europe.

To find out what's happening at the time of your visit, pick up a free copy of *Copenhagen This Week* at the tourist information center. The section marked "Events Calendar" has a week-by-week roundup of the "hottest" entertainment and sightseeing events in the Danish capital.

TIVOLI GARDENS ✦✦✦

In the center of the gardens, the large **open-air stage** books vaudeville acts (tumbling clowns, acrobats, aerialists) who give performances every Friday night at 10pm, and on an arbitrary, oft-changing schedule that varies from week to week and summer to summer. Spectators must enter through the turnstiles for seats, but there's an unobstructed view from outside if you prefer to stand. Jazz and folkloric groups also perform here during the season. Admission is free.

The 150-year-old outdoor **Pantomime Theater,** with its Chinese stage and peacock curtain, is near the Tivoli's Vesterbrogade 3 entrance and presents shows Tuesday to Thursday at 6:15 and 8:15pm; Friday at 7:30 and 9pm; Saturday at 8:15 and 9:30pm; and Sunday at 4:30 and 6:30pm. The repertoire consists of 16 different commedia dell'arte productions featuring the entertaining trio Pierrot, Columbine, and Harlequin—these are authentic pantomimes that have been performed continuously in Copenhagen since 1844. Admission is free.

The modern **Tivolis Koncertsal** (concert hall) is a great place to hear top artists and orchestras, led by equally famous conductors. Opened in 1956, the concert hall can seat 2,000, and its season—which begins in late April and lasts for more than 5 months—has been called "the most extensive music festival in the world." Performances of everything from symphony to opera are presented Monday to Saturday at 7:30pm, and sometimes at 8pm, depending on the event. Good seats are available at prices ranging from 200DKK to 700DKK ($34–$119/£18–£63) when major artists are performing—but most performances are free. You can buy tickets at the main booking office on Vesterbrogade 3 (© **33-15-10-12** or 45-70-15-65) or on the web by clicking on www.billetnet.dk.

Tivoli Glassalen (© **33-15-10-12**) is housed in a century-old octagonal gazebo-like building with a glass, gilt-capped canopy. Shows are often comedic/satirical performances by Danish comedians in Danish, and these usually don't interest non-Danish audiences. A noteworthy exception to this are the annual Christmas programs, presented in November and December, in English. There are also musical reviews, with a minimum of any spoken language, presented throughout the year. Tickets range from 200DKK to 400DKK ($34 to $68/£18–£36).

THE PERFORMING ARTS

For tickets to most of the musical, cultural, and sports-themed entertainment venues of Denmark, check out **Billetnet,** a local branch of Ticketmaster. You can purchase tickets through www.billetnet.dk, or by calling © **45/70-15-65-65.**

For **discount seats** (sometimes as much as 50% off), go in person to a ticket kiosk at the corner of Fiolstræde and Nørre Voldgade, across from the Nørreport train station. Discount tickets are sold the day of the performance and may be purchased Monday to Friday noon to 5pm and Saturday noon to 3pm.

Copenhagen Opera House ★★★   Opened by Queen Margrethe, this $441-million, 1,700-seat opera house is the luxurious home of the Royal Danish Opera. The opera house is the gift of the A. P. Møller and Chastine McKinney Møller Foundation, which is headed by Mærsk McKinney-Møller, one of the wealthiest men in the country. Prior to his donation of the opera house, he had already received, directly from the Queen, Denmark's highest honor, the coveted and intensely prestigious Order of the Elephant. Designed by Danish architect Henning Larsen, the opera house uses precious stones and metals, including 105,000 sheets of gold leaf, and chandeliers which out-sparkle and outshine anything in Las Vegas. In addition to the international artists, the opera house also showcases the works of such Danish composers as Carl Nielsen and Poul Ruders. You can dine at the on-site **Restauranten** before curtain time, with a three-course menu costing 425DKK ($72/£38). In addition, there is an **Opera Café,** serving sandwiches, salads, and light Danish specialties. The season runs from mid-August until the beginning of June. During that period, tours of the building are offered daily on a frequently changing schedule, which usually requires a phone call as a means of hammering out the schedule. Ekuipagemesteruej 10. © **33-69-69-33.** Tickets standing-room space 70DKK ($12/£6.30); seats 200DKK–400DKK ($34–$68/ £18–£36). Box office © 33-69-69-69; Mon–Sat noon–6pm.

Det Kongelige Teater (Royal Theater)   Performances by the world-renowned **Royal Danish Ballet** ★★★ and **Royal Danish Opera** ★★★, dating from 1748, are major winter cultural events in Copenhagen. Because the arts are state-subsidized in Denmark, ticket prices are comparatively low, and some seats may be available at the box office the day before a performance. The season runs August to June. Kongens Nytorv. © **33-69-69-69.** www.kgl-teater.dk. Tickets 70DKK–670DKK ($12–$114/£6.30–£60), half-price for seniors over 66 and people under 26. Bus: 1, 6, 9, or 10.

THE CLUB & MUSIC SCENE

DANCE CLUBS

Den Røde Pimpernel   Throughout most of the day, this place functions as a lively dining and drinking emporium within the heart of Tivoli, whose walls are painted a vivid shade of red in honor of its gallant 17th-century namesake, *The Scarlet Pimpernel*. Every evening after 10pm, however, its tables are moved away to create a wide-open dance floor. The youngest clients, those in their 30s, tend to appear on Thursday and Sunday; other nights, the patrons are a bit more staid, aged anywhere from 30 to a youthful 50-ish. It's open daily noon to 4am. Bernstorffsgade 3, Tivoli. ✆ **33-75-07-60.** Cover 60DKK ($10/£5.40); free before 10pm. Bus: 2, 8, or 30.

NASA   Its name has changed several times in the past decade, but even so, this is the most posh and prestigious of three nightclubs that occupy three respective floors of the same building. The late-night crowd of 25- to 40-year-olds includes many avid fans of whatever musical innovation has just emerged in London or Los Angeles. The decorative theme includes lots of white, lots of mirrors, and lots of artfully directed spotlights. Don't be surprised to see a room full of expensively, albeit casually, dressed Danes chattering away in a cacophony of different languages. Technically, the site is a private club, but polite and presentable newcomers can usually gain access. It's open only Friday and Saturday midnight to 6am. Gothersgade 8F, Bolthensgaard. ✆ **33-93-74-15.** Cover 100DKK ($17/£9) for nonmembers. Bus: 1, 6, or 9.

The Rock   Thanks to an armada of designers who developed it, and thanks to its self-appointed role as a "Design Disco," its interior is more artfully outfitted than any other in Copenhagen. Expect lots of postmodern gloss, references to the California rave movement, an occasional emphasis on dance music of the 1980s, a small corner outfitted like a cozy beer hall, and a clientele that seems familiar with the music and ambience of some very hip clubs in Europe and the United States. Part of its interior was based on a waiting room of a 1970s Scandinavian airport, complete with then-innovative streamlined design that's been associated with Denmark ever since. It's open Friday and Saturday 11pm till at least 5:30am. Skindergade 45. ✆ **33-13-26-25.** Cover 60DKK ($10/£5.40). Bus: 1 or 6.

Rust   Rust sprawls over a single floor in the Nørrebro district where the clientele is international and high-energy. Since 1989 faithful patrons have been flocking to its restaurant, several bars, a dance floor, and a stage where live musicians perform every Thursday night beginning around 9pm. Meals are served Wednesday to Saturday 5:30pm to around midnight, and at least someone will begin to boogie on the dance floor after 9:30pm, as drinks flow. The setting is dark and shadowy, "a great place to feel up your partner—or someone else's," one of the patrons told us. There are places to sit, but none so comfortable that you'll stay in one spot for too long. No one under age 21 is admitted but you'll see very few over age 45. Open Wednesday to Saturday 9pm to at least 5am. Guldbergsgade 8. ✆ **35-24-52-00.** Cover 50DKK–110DKK ($8.50–$19/£4.50–£9.90) Wed–Sat. Bus: 5 or 6.

Vega   Consider this brick-built circular 19th-century monument as the closest thing in town to an old hippie be-in, where you'll enter a multifaceted, multipurpose environment with an open mind and then pick the site that best suits your mood of the minute. At least two of the venues inside are devoted to live concerts that begin, according to a baffling and oft-changing schedule, any time between 8 and 11pm, depending on the inclinations of the musicians, and for which entrance usually varies

Value Nighttime Experiences for Free (Well, Almost)

You don't have to go to clubs or attend cultural presentations to experience Copenhagen nightlife. If you want to have a good time and save money too, consider doing as the Danes do: Walk about and enjoy the city and its glittering lights for free, perhaps stopping at a lovely square to have a drink and watch the world pass by.

Copenhagen's elegant spires and tangle of cobbled one-way streets are best viewed at night, when they take on the aura of the Hans Christian Andersen era. The old buildings have been well preserved, and at night they're floodlit. The city's network of drawbridges and small bridges is also particularly charming at night.

One of the best places for a walk is **Nyhavn** (New Harbor), which until about 25 years ago was the haunt of sailors and some of the roughest dives in Copenhagen. Today it's gone upmarket and is the site of numerous restaurants and bars. In summer you can sit out at one of the cafe tables watching life along the canal and throngs of people from around the world passing by—all for the price of your Carlsberg. Along the quay you can also see a fleet of old-time sailing ships. Hans Christian Andersen lived at three different addresses along Nyhavn: nos. 18, 20, and 67.

Another neighborhood that takes on special magic at night is **Christianshavn,** whose principal landmark is **Christiansborg Slot** (castle), a massive granite pile surrounded by canals on three sides. The ramparts of Christianshavn are edged with walking paths, which are lit at light. This neighborhood, which glows under the soft, forgiving light of antique street lamps, is the closest Copenhagen comes to the charm of the Left Bank in Paris. You can wander for hours through its cobbled streets and 18th-century buildings. The area also abounds with cafes, bars, and restaurants. Originally the

from 100DKK to 180DKK ($17–$31/£9–£16). And when the concert ends, you'll still find at least three other dining and drinking emporiums inside, some with live music of their own, and each with a distinctly different ambience. And on nights when there happens not to be any live music, the smaller bars and dining areas inside are likely to be rocking and rolling the night away. Most venues inside require a minimum age of 20, and except for the concerts whose prices are noted above, entrance to each of the bars and restaurants is free. It lies in Vesterbrø, behind the railway station. Phones may or may not be answered, depending on the whim of whomever is tending house. Enghavevej 40. ② **33-26-09-51** or 33-25-70-11. For concert schedules, click on www. vega.dk. Bus: 1, 6, 9, or 19.

COPENHAGEN'S BIGGEST NIGHTCLUB

Cirkusbygningen Wallmans   In a former circus building near Town Hall Square, this is the best place for patrons who like a spectacular Las Vegas–style dinner show. It's a bit corny and very Scandinavian, but enjoys great success with both visitors and locals. Some 1,000 guests can be entertained here by 22 artists on nine stages while section was built by King Christian IV to provide housing for workers in the shipbuilding industry, but in the past decades real estate prices here have soared.

For a more offbeat adventure—although it's not the safest place at night—you can head for the commune of **Christiania,** a few blocks to the east of Vor Frelsers Kirke. This area once housed Danish soldiers in barracks. When the soldiers moved out, the free spirits of Copenhagen moved in, occupying the little village, even though—technically speaking—they are squatters and in violation of the law. They declared the area a "free city" on September 24, 1971. Copenhagen authorities have not moved in to oust them in all this time, fearing a full-scale riot. The area is a refuge for petty criminals and drug dealers. But there has been success in the community as well, evoking the communes of the 1960s. For example, the villagers have helped hundreds of addicts kick heroin habits.

At night, adventurous visitors enter Christiania to eat at one of the neighborhood's little restaurants, many of which are surprisingly good. Prices here are the cheapest in Copenhagen, because the restaurant managers refuse to pay taxes. You can also wander through some of the shops selling handmade crafts. Because most establishments are small and personal, you can also invite yourself in, perhaps to listen to innovative music or see some cultural presentation. Currently your best bet for dining is **Spiseloppen.** Later you can visit the jazz club **Loppen,** where you'll hear some of the best jazz in the city. If you're a vegetarian, as are many members of the commune, head for the vegetarian restaurant **Morgensted.** (These two restaurants and the club don't have addresses, but they're easy to spot.)

enjoying a four-course dinner. After the show, the interior is transformed into a gigantic nightclub with dancing. Incidentally, the artists also wait on your table.

Open Wednesday to Saturday only, except in November when it is also open on Tuesday. The bar opens at 6pm, and the restaurant serves until 6:45pm. Shows stretch out with breaks from 7 to 11:15pm, followed by dancing that goes on till around 2am, including dinner. Admission to the show is 575DKK ($98/£52) except on Friday and Saturday, when it rises to 695DKK ($118/£63). Jernbanegade 8. © **33-16-37-00.** www. wallmans.com. Bus: 1, 16, or 29.

JAZZ, ROCK & BLUES
Copenhagen JazzHouse ✦   The decor is modern and uncomplicated and serves as a consciously simple foil for the music and noise. This club hosts more performances by non-Danish jazz artists than any other jazz bar in town. Shows begin relatively early, at around 8:30pm, and usually finish early, too. Around midnight on Friday and Saturday, the club is transformed from a live concert hall into a dance club (open until 5am). It's closed Mondays; otherwise, it keeps a confusing schedule that

changes according to the demands of the current band. Niels Hemmingsensgade 10. © **33-15-26-00.** Cover charge 65DKK–280DKK ($11–$48/£5.85–£25) when live music is performed. Bus: 10.

La Fontaine This is a dive that hasn't changed much since the 1950s, but it's the kind of dive that—if you meet the right partner, or if you really groove with the music—can be a lot of fun. Small, and cozy to the point of being cramped, it functions mostly as a bar, every Tuesday to Saturday 8pm to 6am or even 8am. Sunday hours are 9pm to 1am. Live music is performed on Friday and Saturday, when free-jazz artists play starting around 11:30pm. Kompagnistræde 11. © **33-11-60-98.** Cover 50DKK ($8.50/£4.50) Fri–Sat. Bus: 5 or 10.

Mojo Blues Bar "Our clients come here for the booze and the blues," the manager rather accurately told us. Mojo is a candlelit drinking spot that offers blues music, 90% of which is performed by Scandinavian groups. This grubby but strangely appealing joint is open daily 8pm to 5am. Løngangstræde 21C. © **33-11-64-53.** Cover 50DKK ($8.50/£4.50) Fri–Sat. Bus: 2, 8, or 30.

THE BAR SCENE
PUBS
Café Zirup Set on a street that's packed with worthy competitors, this cafe and bar is loaded with people who seem fun, charming, and engaged with life and the well-being of their companions. Its name translates as "syrup." The venue is youthful and hip. Salads, sandwiches, and platters cost from 89DKK to 99DKK ($15–$17/£8–£8.90). Open Monday to Thursday 10am to midnight, Friday and Saturday 10am to 2am. Læderstræde 32. © **33-13-50-60.** Bus: 1, 6, 9, or 10.

Le Coq Rouge Cozy, traditional, and radically reconfigured in 2006 into a replica of a Parisian brasserie, this is the kind of bar where a businessperson could feel at home after a transatlantic flight. Recommended separately in "Where to Dine" (see chapter 4), it's on the ground floor of one of Copenhagen's most legendary (and discreet) hotels. Platters of French and Danish food go for 120DKK to 200DKK ($20–$34/£11–£18) each. Open Monday to Saturday from noon to midnight. Beer costs 45DKK ($7.65/£4.05); drinks begin at 52DKK ($8.85/£4.70). In the Kong Frederik Hotel, Vester Voldgade 25. © **33-12-48-48.** Bus: 5A, 6A, 26, and 250S.

Library Bar 🌟🌟🌟 Frequently visited by celebrities and royalty, the Library Bar was once rated by the late Malcolm Forbes as one of the top five bars in the world. In a setting of antique books and works of art, you can order everything from a cappuccino to a cocktail. The setting is the lobby level of the landmark Hotel Plaza, commissioned in 1913 by Frederik VIII. The bar was originally designed and built as the hotel's library; Oregon pine was used for the paneling, and hundreds of books line the walls. It's open daily from noon to midnight (till 2am on Fri and Sat). Beer costs 50DKK ($8.50/£4.50); drinks cost from 68DKK to 78DKK ($12–$13/£6.10–£7). In the Hotel Plaza, Bernstorffsgade 4. © **33-14-92-62.** Bus: 10, 15, or 26.

Nyhavn 17 This is the last of the honky-tonk pubs that used to make up the former sailors' quarter, and even this last bastion has seen a rapid gentrification in recent years. This cafe is a short walk from the patrician Kongens Nytorv. In summer you can sit outside. It's open Sunday to Thursday 10am to 2am and Friday and Saturday to 3am. Beer costs 46DKK ($7.80/£4.15), and drinks start at 60DKK ($10/£5.40). Nyhavn 17. © **33-12-54-19.** Bus: 1, 6, 27, or 29.

COPENHAGEN'S BEST WINE BAR

Hvids Vinstue ✿✿   Built in 1670, this old wine cellar is a dimly lit safe haven for an eclectic crowd, many patrons—including theatergoers, actors, and dancers—drawn from the Royal Theater across the way. In December only, a combination of red wine and cognac is served. It's open Monday to Saturday 10am to 1am; Sunday from 10am to 8pm. Beer costs 38DKK ($6.45/£3.40); wine costs 29DKK ($4.95/£2.60). Open-faced sandwiches are 55DKK ($9.35/£4.95), and include a free beer. Kongens Nytorv 19. ✆ **33-15-10-64.** Bus: 1, 6, 9, or 10.

GAY & LESBIAN CLUBS

Boiz Bar   Two hundred years ago, the antique and richly beamed interior of this place was used to shelter cattle. Today, in a much-sanitized format, it's a whimsically outfitted men's bar and restaurant contained within one large room with a cozy annex bar a few paces away. There are at least three separate bars/drinking areas within this establishment, a cluster of tables in the center of the larger of the two rooms, with leather upholstery and the kind of lighting that makes everyone look dramatic, especially the crowd of mostly gay men ages 20 to 50. Main courses in the restaurant cost from 129DKK to 169DKK ($22–$29/£12–£15), and a glass of beer costs 36DKK ($6.10/£3.25). Most of the time, this place functions as a flamboyant version of an old Danish *kro* (inn), but every Friday and Saturday beginning at 10pm, there's a drag show, with artists imported from London, followed by a high-energy scene on the dance floor that is active till around 5am. Hours are Sunday to Thursday 4pm to 2am, Friday and Saturday 4pm to 5am. Magstræde 12-14. ✆ **33-14-52-70.** Bus: 6A.

Centralhjornet   This is the oldest gay bar in Copenhagen, having attracted a clientele of self-styled "pederasts and queers" as far back as the early 20th century, when same-sex love was identified in terms very different from what it is today. Old-fashioned, wood-paneled, and cozy, it's absolutely mobbed with gay and, to a lesser extent, lesbian tourists during the Christmas holidays. It's open every day of the year from 2pm to midnight. Between October and May, there's a drag show presented here every Thursday night beginning around 10pm. Kattesundet 18. ✆ **33-11-85-49.** Bus: 14 or 16.

Cosy Bar   It runs a fine line between a crowd that favors leather, and what you'd expect from a working crew of men performing manual labor down by the harborfront. Popular and cruisy, it's open daily 11pm till 8am, dispensing ample amounts of schnapps and suds during the course of a working night. Studiestræde 24. ✆ **33-12-74-27.** Bus: 6 or 29.

Jailhouse Copenhagen   The name of this bar reminds us of Elvis's "Jailhouse Rock." It's set amid the densest concentration of gay men's bars in town, about a block from its nearest competitor (the also-recommended Men's Bar, which attracts a similar clientele). This is the bar most quickly cited as an amicable and amenable watering hole for the leather, bear, and S&M communities—or those who merely dream about them. The name of the place influences its decor: Imagine a large, shadowy space with a prominent, beer-soaked bar, battered walls and floors, and iron bars that subdivide the space into a series of simulated jail cells. If you're in the mood for a meal, there's a restaurant upstairs, where crisp white napery contrasts with simulations of cellblocks. Food is Danish and Scandinavian, with specialties that focus on old-fashioned, tried-and-true comfort food, with some modern and somewhat experimental twists. Overall, food is a lot better than what you might have expected in jail. The bar is open from 2pm to 2am (Thurs and Fri until 5am), and entrance is free, with a beer costing 35DKK ($5.95/£3.15). The restaurant is open only Thursday to Saturday 6 to 11pm, with a fixed-price, three-course meal going for 230DKK ($39/£21). Studiestræde 12. (✆ **33-15-22-55**. Bus: 2, 8, or 30.

The Men's Bar This is the only leather bar in town, filled with a bemused collection of uniforms, leather, Levi's, and gay-icon memorabilia. Amicable and fraternal, it showcases a framed portrait, in full military uniform, of "The cutest prince in Europe," crown Prince Frederik, happily and recently married to "that woman." Note that if it's a particularly hot day, someone might encourage you to take off your shirt, in exchange for which, if you're a newcomer, the bartender is likely to give you a free glass of schnapps. It's open daily 3pm to 2am. A beer will set you back 20DKK ($3.40/£1.80). Teglgaardstræde 3. (✆ **33-12-73-03**. Bus: 2, 8, or 30.

Pan Club This nationwide organization was established in 1948 for the protection and advancement of gay and lesbian rights in headquarters in a 19th-century yellow building off of the Strøget. A dance club occupies three of its floors, and a modern cafe is on the ground level. Every night is gay night, although a lot of straights come here for the music. The cafe is open Thursday 9pm to 4am; Friday and Saturday 10pm to 5am. The dance club is open Friday 10pm to 5am and Saturday 10pm to 6am. Knabrostræde 3. (✆ **33-11-19-50**. Cover 60DKK ($10/£5.40) for dance club. Bus: 28, 29, or 41.

XXX COPENHAGEN

The heady "boogie nights" of the '70s, when pornography aficionados flocked to Copenhagen to purchase X-rated materials, are long gone. Copenhagen is no longer the capital of sex, having long ago lost out to Hamburg and Amsterdam, but many city residents can quote the year when a landmark ruling from Denmark's supreme court made printed pornography legal (1967). Despite the fact that pornographic Copenhagen is not as cutting edge or raunchy as it was (and we're all somewhat more jaded these days), it's still possible to take a walk here on the wild side any night of the week. Two of the densest concentrations of porno and the sex industry still lie on **Istedgade** and **Helgolandsgade,** both of them near the rail terminus in the center of the city. Ironically, the sex shops peddling magazines and X-rated films stand virtually adjacent to decent and well-recommended family hotels. Mothers can often be seen hustling their sons past the window displays.

GAMBLING

Casino Copenhagen Let the dice roll. Danish authorities allowed the country's first fully licensed casino to open in the first-class SAS Scandinavia Hotel in 1990. Today gamblers play such popular games as roulette, baccarat, blackjack, slot machines, and the newly popular rage, poker. The whole operation is overseen by Casinos of Austria, the largest casino operator in Europe. It's open daily 2pm to 4am. Jackets (but not neckties) are required for men, and presentation of a valid ID (passport or driver's license) is necessary. In the SAS Scandinavia Hotel, Amager Blvd. 70. (✆ **33-96-59-65**. Cover 85DKK ($14/£7.65), but entrance is free every Wed 5–7pm. Bus: 5A or 250.

4 Side Trips from Copenhagen

BEACHES

Locals and visitors are flocking to a newly created beach, **Amager Beach Park** ⊛, which opened in 2006, lying only a 15-minute drive from the center of Copenhagen, a distance of 5km (3 miles). The beach lies on the Øresund coastline with a view of

Sweden and the Øresund Bridge that now links Denmark with Sweden. You can swim, sunbathe, scuba dive, race boats, or just admire the ships on the Øresund Sound while having a cup of coffee. Off the existing Amager Beach, a completely new island was created with wide, sandy beaches and bathing jetties. Tons of sand were brought in to create the island beach, which is about 2km (1¼ mile) long and 50m (164 ft.) wide. In a newly dug lagoon are paddling beaches for children. By the time you read this, three Metro stations should be open right by the beach, which will make it easy to zip over here from Copenhagen if the sun's out. For more information, visit www. amager-strand.dk.

The beach closest to Copenhagen is **Bellevue** (S-tog: Klampenborg), but the water is not recommended for swimming. (Klampenborg, the community that's adjacent to Bellevue Beach, can provide distractions in addition to a beach: It's the site of the "White City" or "White Town," a residential community designed in the 1930s by modernist master Arne Jacobsen, and revered by Danes as a prime example of the workability of Danish architecture and design. If you head out here, consider a meal at the Restaurant Jacobsen, which is separately recommended in "Where to Dine" in chapter 4.

If you don't mind traveling farther afield, take a trip (by train or car) to the beaches of North Zealand—**Gilleleje, Hornbæk, Liseleje,** and **Tisvildeleje** (see chapter 6). Although these are family beaches, minimal bathing attire is worn.

To reach any of these beaches, take the train to Helsingør and then continue by bus. Or you can make connections by train to Hillerød and switch to a local train; check at the railroad station for details. If you drive, you may want to stay for the evening dance clubs at the little beach resort towns dotting the north coast of Zealand.

DRAGØR 🎭🎭
5km (3 miles) S of Copenhagen's Kastrup Airport

Even if you have to skip the rest of Denmark, head to this little fishing port to see what an idyllic Danish village looks like. Though we don't mean to put it down, the Frilandsmuseet (p. 130) was an artificially created site—and a grand one at that—but Dragør is the real thing. Young professionals are flocking here from Copenhagen to purchase homes. They're within an easy commute of the city, but in the old-fashioned world of Dragør that goes back to the 19th century at night (albeit with modern conveniences).

This old seafaring town on the island of Amager is filled with well-preserved half-timbered ocher and pink 18th-century cottages with steep red-tile or thatched roofs, many of which are under the protection of the National Trust.

Dragør (pronounced *Drah*-wer) was a busy port on the herring-rich Baltic Sea in the early Middle Ages, and when fishing fell off, it became a sleepy little waterfront village. After 1520, Amager Island and its villages—Dragør and Store Magleby—were inhabited by the Dutch, who brought their own customs, Low-German language, and agricultural expertise to Amager, especially their love of bulb flowers. In Copenhagen you still see wooden-shoed Amager locals selling their hyacinths, tulips, daffodils, and lilies in the streets.

ESSENTIALS
GETTING THERE   By Bus   Take bus nos. 30, 33, or 73E from Rådhuspladsen (Town Hall Square) in Copenhagen (trip time: 35 min.).

SEEING THE SIGHTS

Amager Museum   This museum is only of passing interest and could be skipped in favor of spending more time walking the streets of Dragør. But if you do duck into it, you'll learn how strong the influence of the Dutch used to be here, ever since farmers from Holland settled Dragør in the 16th century. King Christian II ordered them to provide fresh flowers and produce for his court and so they did. The interiors of a Dutch house reveal how they decorated their homes and lived in modest comfort, and the Amager Dutch, as they were known, live again in the exhibits of their rich textiles, fine embroidery, and such artifacts as silver buckles and buttons.

Hovedgaden 4–12, Store Magleby. (©) **32-53-93-07.** www.amagermuseet.dk. Admission 30DKK ($5.10/£2.70) adults, 10DKK ($1.70/90p) children 5–14, free for children under 5. May–Sept Tues–Sun noon–4pm; Oct–Mar Wed and Sun noon–4pm. Closed in Apr. Bus: 30, 33, or 350S.

Dragør Museum   As you're wandering along Dragør's harborfront, you can spend 20 minutes or so looking inside the town's oldest fisherman's cottage, dating from 1682. The exhibits are modest but reveal how the Amager Dutch lived here when they settled Dragør. Pictures and artifacts reveal that their lives were devoted to farming, goose breeding, seafaring, fishing, ship piloting, and salvaging the cargo of ships wrecked off the coast.

Havnepladsen 2–4. (©) **32-53-41-06.** www.dragoermuseum.dk. Admission 20DKK ($3.40/£1.80) adults, 10DKK ($1.70/90p) children 10–15, free for children under 10. May–Sept Tues–Sun and holidays noon–4pm. Closed Oct–Apr. Bus: 30, 32, or 350S.

WHERE TO STAY

Dragør Badehotel   Back in 1907 a railway line was extended from Copenhagen to this fishing hamlet, and this government-rated three-star hotel opened that same year to greet visitors. The rail line is long gone but the much-improved and modernized hotel still remains. Restoration in recent years has brought much-needed change but the old style that prevailed around the turn of the 20th century was respected. The midsize bedrooms are furnished in Nordic modern with exceedingly comfortable beds, and maintenance is top rate around here. Most of the accommodations come with a view of the sea, and the most desirable units open onto their own private balconies. Traditional Danish cuisine is served in the main restaurant or else you can dine on the open-air terraces in summer. Nonguests are welcome to enjoy the hotel's restaurant. There are six different preparations of herring to get you going, followed by a "Dragør Plate" of mixed meats and pâtés, tender schnitzels, homemade soups, and a selection of *smørrebrød* (open-faced sandwiches) at lunch.

Drogdensvej 43, DK-2791 Dragør. (©) **32-53-05-00.** Fax 32-53-04-99. www.badehotellet.dk. 34 units. 795DKK–995DKK ($135–$169/£72–£90) double. AE, DC, MC, V. Bus: 30, 33, or 73E. **Amenities:** Restaurant; lounge; laundry service; nonsmoking rooms; rooms for those w/limited mobility. *In room:* TV, minibar.

WHERE TO DINE

The Dragør Badehotel (see above) also offers excellent cuisine.

Restaurant Beghuset DANISH   Even on the most rushed of visits, we like to schedule at least one meal at this old-fashioned dining room, which not only serves good, home-cooked food but also is a nostalgic reminder of Denmark of yesterday. This cafe and restaurant on a cobblestone street in the center of town looks like an idyllic cottage. To reach the restaurant section, you walk through the cafe. Although the menu changes every 2 to 3 months to accommodate seasonal items, a weary traveler in search of sustenance will be tempted by selections like fish soup, Swedish caviar, thinly sliced smoked lamb with a balsamic dressing on a bed of seasonal greens, and fresh oysters. Main courses include a divinely cooked guinea fowl braised in red wine served with bacon of veal (their own invention) and herbs, and Dragør plaice roasted in butter and served with either parsley sauce or a bacon-thyme sauce, just like grandmother used to bake.

Strandgade 14. © **32-53-01-36.** Reservations recommended. 1-course lunch 169DKK–198DKK ($29–$34/£15–£18); 2-course lunch 198DKK ($34/£18); 3-course lunch 225DKK–275DKK ($38–$47/£20–£25); dinner main courses 178DKK–218DKK ($30–$37/£16–£20); 3-course fixed-price dinner 358DKK ($61/£32); 4-course fixed-price dinner 398DKK ($68/£36). AE, DC, MC, V. Tues–Sun noon–3pm and 6–9pm. Bus: 30, 33, or 73E.

Strandhotel DANISH✦   In spite of its name, this establishment no longer accepts overnight guests but is one of the finest restaurants in Dragør, offering a more imaginative cuisine than the standard (yet good) Danish fare featured at the Beghuset (see above). Strandhotel is still going strong, but it's been a long time since Frederik III used to drop by for a bowl of the chef's eel soup. Even Søren Kierkegaard used to come here to brood.

At lunchtime an ample spread of *smørrebrød* is served, although other offerings include filet of pork in paprika sauce, a savory smoked filet of eel, fried or poached plaice, and a delectable trout with almonds. At dinner the chefs tempt you with such dishes as grilled tuna with raspberries or oven-baked whitefish served in a banana leaf, the flavor enhanced by a saffron cream sauce.

Strandlinbyn 9, Havnen. © **32-53-00-75.** Reservations recommended. Main courses 158DKK–196DKK ($27–$33/£14–£18); lunch *smørrebrød* 78DKK–188DKK ($13–$32/£7–£17); "quick lunch" 188DKK ($32/£17). AE, DC, MC, V. Daily 9am–9:30pm. Closed Nov–Mar. Bus: 350S.

HUMLEBÆK (LOUISIANA MUSEUM)
30km (19 miles) N of Copenhagen

The area running along the coast north of Copenhagen is called both the Danish Riviera and Millionaire's Row. Some of the wealthiest people in Denmark live in palatial homes between Copenhagen and the town of Humlebæk. But the only reason most visitors come to this former fishing village, unless they have a private invitation, is to visit the world-famous Louisiana Museum, our favorite art center in all of Denmark.

ESSENTIALS
GETTING THERE   By Train   Humlebæk is on the Copenhagen–Helsingør train line; there are two trains per hour that leave Copenhagen's main railway station heading toward Humlebæk (trip time: 40 min.). Once you reach Humlebæk, the Louisiana Museum is a 10-minute walk.

By Bus   Take the S-tog train, line A or B, to Lyngby station. From there, take bus no. 388 along the coast road. There's a bus stop at the museum.

By Car   Follow the Strandvej (coastal road no. 152) from Copenhagen. The scenic drive takes about 45 minutes.

SEEING THE SIGHTS
Louisiana Museum of Modern Art ✦✦✦ *Kids*   A lot of Americans think this museum for some odd reason was named for the state of Louisiana. Actually the museum's name came from the fact that the first owner of the estate here, Alexander Brun, had three wives. Bizarrely, each of his spouses was named Louise. In a spacious old park with a panoramic view across Øresund to Sweden, this is one of the greatest

museums of modern art in the Nordic world. The modest collection of Scandinavian art that opened here in 1954 has grown and grown with bequests and donations, and future architects have added more galleries onto the existing 19th-century villa.

The museum opened with works by the COBRA group, the name of artists from the cities of COpenhagen, BRussels, and Amsterdam. These original works are displayed along with some of the finest paintings and sculpture by international artists such as Calder, Dubuffet, Max Ernst, Giacometti, Picasso, and Warhol.

The museum has one of the largest exhibition spaces in Europe, and major exhibitions of contemporary art are staged here. There is also an extensive program of concerts, lectures, films, discussions with authors, and public debates. Children find their own haven here, especially at the **Børnehuset,** or children's house, and the **Søhaven,** or Sea Garden. The museum's cafe is on a terrace with Alexander Calder's sculptures.

Gl. Strandvej 13. ☎ **49-19-07-19.** www.louisiana.dk. Admission 80DKK ($14/£7.20) adults, 70DKK ($12/£6.30) students, free for children 18 and under. Wed 10am–10pm; Thurs–Tues 10am–5pm. Closed Dec 24–25 and Dec 31.

WHERE TO DINE
Louisiana Café DANISH   Since 1772 there has been an inn on this spot, feeding wayfarers of yore who took horse and carriage along the coast heading for Helsingør. Today much of yesterday has been swept away and what remains is this cafe-restaurant which is the best and also the most convenient place for lunch, lying only a short walk from the museum. If you're so enthralled with the museum that you're still around at dinnertime, you can also dine here before heading back to the heart of Copenhagen.

We've always found the food satisfying in an old-fashioned sort of way, although we never feel we have to call the editors of *Gourmet* magazine on our cellphones. At lunch most diners dig into a range of open-faced sandwiches—usually three will satisfy. At night you can partake of recipes based on tried-and-true dishes such as a platter-size Wiener schnitzel. Veal also comes in medallions with a rich morel sauce. Herring is dressed up with a sherry sauce, and deep-fried filet of plaice comes with shrimp just recently caught off the coast.

Gl. Strandvej 13. ☎ **49-19-07-19.** Reservations recommended. Main courses 178DKK–225DKK ($30–$38/£16–£20). AE, DC, MC, V. Daily 10am–9:30pm.

RUNGSTEDLUND: HOME OF KAREN BLIXEN
21km (13 miles) N of Copenhagen

Between Copenhagen in the south and Helsingør in the north, the second-most-important stopover is this elegant town where many Danes come in the summer to rent cottages, which they often surround with flower gardens. By all means, make the museum of Louisiana your first major stopover, but if time remains, you can pay your respects to one of the greatest of all Scandinavian writers (see below).

GETTING THERE   By Train   From Copenhagen's Central Railroad Station, trains run to Rungsted Kyst every 30 minutes. However, since this rail stop is still half a mile from the museum, it is better to take the train to Klampenborg, where you can board **bus** no. 388, which offers frequent service to a bus stop about a block from the entrance to the museum.

By Car   Head north from Copenhagen along the E4 to Helsingør until you reach the turnoff east marked RUNGSTED.

THE MUSEUM

Ever since we discovered the writings of Isak Dinesen in high school, we've been devoted fans. She remains our favorite Danish writer (forgive us, Hans). Since the 1985 release of *Out of Africa,* starring Robert Redford and Meryl Streep, thousands of fans have visited the former home of Baroness Karen Blixen, who wrote under her maiden name, Isak Dinesen. Her home, Rungstedlund, at Rungsted Strandvej III (© **45-57-10-57**), is midway between Copenhagen and Helsingør on the coastal road.

Karen's father, Wilhelm Dinesen, purchased the estate in 1879. She left in 1914 for Kenya when she married Sweden-born Bror van Blixen Finecke, but returned in 1931 and stayed until her death in 1962. It was at Rungstedlund that Blixen wrote her first major success, *Seven Gothic Tales,* which we consider more memorable than *Out of Africa.* She also wrote collections of stories, *Winter's Tales* and *Last Tales,* here. Before Blixen's father acquired the property, it was called Rungsted Kro, attracting travelers going north from Copenhagen to Helsingør.

Blixen wrote in Ewald's Room, named in honor of poet Johannes Ewald, who stayed at the place when it was an inn. Before her death, Blixen established the Rungstedlund Foundation, which owns the property and its 16-hectare (40-acre) garden and bird sanctuary. The gardens have long been open to the public, but in 1991 the foundation invited Queen Margrethe to open the museum.

In one part of the museum is a small gallery with exhibits in oil, pastel, and charcoal—all by Blixen. The museum is filled with photographs, manuscripts, and memorabilia that document Blixen's life in both Africa and Denmark.

Visitors pay 40DKK ($6.80/£3.60) to enter, although children under 12 go free. It's open May to September, Tuesday to Sunday 10am to 5pm; October to April, Wednesday to Friday 1 to 4pm and Saturday and Sunday 11am to 4pm.

Blixen is buried in the grave at the foot of Edwaldshøj, a hill on the estate.

WHERE TO DINE

Restaurant Nokken 𝒢𝒢 DANISH/SEAFOOD   On a summer night, we always like to sit out here enjoying a drink on the terrace overlooking the harbor of Øresund, taking in a picture-postcard vista of yachts and sailboats returning to shoreline under an amber-and-pink nighttime sky. Another reason for coming here is that the elegant restaurant serves some of the best food along the Danish Riviera. The setting is amid light-grained paneling and nautical accessories, a short walk downhill from Karen Blixen's house. You'll find it near the sea-battered piers next to the harbors, a fact that gives it a raffish feeling despite its reputation for well-prepared, savory fish and seafood. There's a bar near the entrance that's a hangout for boat owners and local millionaires, and when you eventually get hungry, head for the dining room. The specialty is a seafood platter piled high with mussels, shrimp, oysters, and lobster. There are also fresh fish dishes, including filets of lemon sole with hollandaise sauce, or you can try the roasted, herb-scented Danish lamb, or the scampi with sweet-and-sour sauce. The cuisine is generous, uncomplicated, and always market fresh.

Rungsted Havn 44. © **45-57-13-14**. Reservations recommended. Lunch platters 87DKK–210DKK ($15–$36/£7.85–£19); dinner main courses 190DKK–227DKK ($32–$39/£17–£20); fixed-price menu 295DKK ($50/£27). AE, DC, MC, V. Daily noon–4:30pm and 5:30–10:30pm.

6

North Zealand

Most visitors, with their clock ticking, dash north of Copenhagen to chase after "Hamlet's ghost" at Helsingør—and that's it for North Zealand. But as the famous author Isak Dinesen (aka Karen Blixen) might have said, "That would be a shame—stick around a bit and discover some wonder."

"But who is this Isak Dinesen?" you ask if you don't already know. If you are a Meryl Streep fan and were of moviegoing age in 1985, you saw that Oscar-winning actress as Karen Blixen in *Out of Africa.* Or else you can catch the movie on the late show or watch it on DVD.

We don't want to oversell North Zealand, because its charms are subtle and it might be a little too slow-paced and idyllic for those who want more excitement in their vacation. But the Queen of Denmark, who's rich enough to go anywhere, often comes here for a royal vacation. In fact, in July, like another Queen in London, she opens her summer palace at Fredensborg, inviting the public in to see how the other half lives. That's why the province is called "Royal North Zealand." And its overall allure is more posh, more stylish, and a lot more interesting (at least in terms of who comes here, and who owns the local real estate) than are the landscapes of the less densely populated, more agrarian, and less wealthy South Zealand.

Hamlet and the Queen aren't the only fun things. Just across the sound from Sweden, North Zealand is riddled with sandy seashores, studded with lakes, peppered with fishing villages, and layered with unspoiled woodlands. With mercury-like feet, you can see most of the goodies in only 2 days. Of course, you'll want to pay your respects to Isak Dinesen (or Karen) at Rungstedlund, even if you aren't so sure of who she was. The Louisiana Museum of Modern Art at Humlebæk is one of the most renowned modern-art museums in Denmark and one of our favorite bastions of contemporary art in all of Europe (trust us, we've seen them all). For information on the Dinesen abode and Louisiana, see "Side Trips from Copenhagen," in chapter 5.

We've read books on the famous arctic explorer, Knud Rasmussen, and a visit to his home near Hundested will give you a vicarious thrill if you're the adventurous type. Devotees of architecture head for the cathedral at Roskilde, the old capital of Denmark. And, once here, you can also take a look at the Viking Ship Museum, reliving the saga of those raping, pillaging boys who used to descend on England for some loot, some virgins, and an all-around good time, swilling down tankard after tankard of English brew before continuing with their dirty deeds.

Don't overlook the possibility of a beach outing, although you may at first think the water is better suited for polar bears. Wherever you stay in North Zealand, you are not far from a beach. A blue flag flying over the beach indicates that its waters are clean. Danes can be seen frolicking in the nude—they're a shameless bunch—on the beach during their too-short summer days. But they're not just fair-weather friends. Even on a blustery autumn afternoon, or when the Nordic winds of spring are still cold, you'll find them walking along the strands, smelling the fresh air, and listening to the crashing of waves. They even visit their beaches on crisp, fresh winter days for long walks. In fact, it was our Danish friends who taught us the glory of a beach stroll in winter, a custom we've been addicted to ever since.

If you can't make it to Norway, you can sample "Fjord Country" in Denmark. Around the fjords of Roskilde and Isefjord are charming towns such as Hundested, with its beautiful light (praised by artists) and its bustling harbor, and Frederiksværk, with its canal system. On the gentle banks of Isefjord you'll find such lively centers as Holbæk and the already-mentioned Roskilde itself ("the town of kings").

For North Zealand rail information, you can call the main station in Copenhagen (p. 57). For train and bus information within Denmark call ✆ **70-13-14-15.**

1 Hillerød

35km (22 miles) NW of Copenhagen

We don't expect you to fall in love with Hillerød. Unless you've consumed a lot of Danish beer, it can be a bit dull. We come here not only because it's a transport hub for North Zealand, especially for those connecting to trains heading for the north shore beaches, but to see its sprawling castle of Frederiksborg.

After a fire swept over it in 1859, even the royal family found the repairs too costly. They gave it up to the Carlsberg beer baron, J. C. Jacobsen, and he spearheaded the move to create the extravagant palace you see today.

You can spend at least an hour and a half here wandering through its chambers before falling in love with the baroque gardens out back and wishing, with a greedy eye, they were yours to romp in.

Even if you don't like palaces and gardens, the ideal time to arrive here is in summer for the Viking Festival (see below).

If you, like us, are into long walks, you've come to the right place. Hillerød, in the heart of North Zealand, is surrounded by some of the most beautiful and extensive woodlands in the country. Christian IV used to ride through here back in 1602, and you can follow his trails. Space is too cramped here for us to go into all the best walks and trails to follow, but the tourist office will give you a leaflet outlining "the best of the best." Even the dour philosopher Søren Kierkegaard reveled in the tranquility of these forests.

To the south sprawl the woodlands of **Store Dyrehave,** but we prefer the northern stretch of **Gribskov,** the second-largest forest in Denmark. The woodlands are still rich in game, and we take delight in spotting the pale, tailless roe deer. It's estimated there are some 800 fallow deer here, each distinguished by its white-speckled hide.

If you don't like to walk, you can also ask the tourist office for another leaflet, *Bicycle Routes in North Zealand.* Routes drawn on the map follow the most scenic paths, roads, and forest trails.

The forests of Gribskov front our favorite North Zealand lake, **Esrum Sø.** If you like bathing in admittedly chilly waters, sailing a boat, or fishing, you've come to the right place. The parklands of Fredensborg Slot (see below) lie on the eastern shore of the lake, where chances are good in summer that you can hook up with one of the concessions featuring sailing trips on this gorgeous lake.

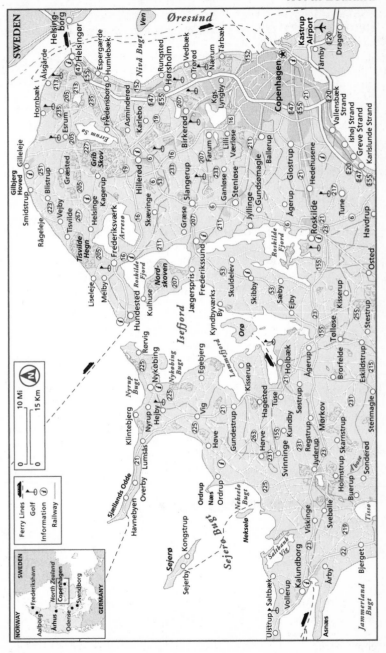

ESSENTIALS

GETTING THERE   The S-tog from Copenhagen arrives every 10 minutes throughout the day (trip time: 40 min.).

By Train   Trains link Hillerød with Helsingør in the east, and there are also rail links with Gilleleje and Tisvildeleje.

By Bus   Hillerød has good bus connections with the major towns of North Zealand: bus no. 305 from Gilleleje; bus nos. 306, 336, and 339 from Hornbæk; and bus nos. 336 and 339 from Fredensborg.

By Car   From Copenhagen, take Route 16 north.

VISITOR INFORMATION   The **tourist office,** Cristiansgade 1 (© **48-24-26-26;** www.hillerodturist.dk), is open Monday to Wednesday 10:30am to 5:30pm and Thursday to Friday 10:30am to 4:30pm.

SPECIAL EVENTS   Every summer some 250 men, women, and children revert to their wild past. They don their Viking costumes and go on a rampage, re-creating the drama of the Viking age when the mere expression "the Vikings are coming" sent terror throughout a land about to be conquered. **Frederikssund Vikingespil (Viking Festival)** ⊛⊛⊛ is the big event of the Danish summer. If possible, try to adjust your schedule to take in the fun. Visit **www.vikingespil.dk** for more information.

Frederikssund, a town 13km (8 miles) southwest of Hillerød and 48km (30 miles) northwest of Copenhagen, stages the 2-week Vikingespil in late June and early July. Nordic sagas are revived—and the record is set straight about who "discovered" America 5 centuries before Christopher Columbus. The festival features a series of plays, medieval and modern, about the Vikings.

The traditional play is performed nightly at 8pm, and a Viking banquet follows. Tickets for the festival are 125DKK ($21/£11) adults, 40DKK ($6.80/£3.60) children 5 to 12 (it's not suitable for children 4 and under). The dinner costs 159DKK ($27/£14) adults, 95DKK ($16/£8.55) children 5 to 12. Trains depart for Frederikssund at 20-minute intervals from Copenhagen's Central Railroad Station (trip time: 50 min.), and there are enough trains back to Copenhagen after the spectacle ends to allow commutes from the capital. From the station at Frederikssund, it's a 20-minute walk to the site of the pageant. For details, contact the tourist information office in Copenhagen or phone the Frederikssund Tourist Office (© **47-31-06-85**).

SEEING THE SIGHTS

Frederiksborg Slot (Frederiksborg Castle) ⊛⊛⊛   We don't like giving labels to places that are designed to mislead. Don't fall for that hype about Frederiksborg Castle being "the Danish Versailles." Versailles, it isn't. It *is* the most beautiful royal residence in Denmark. Surrounded by a moat, the *slot* (castle) was constructed on three islands in a lake. Like Kronborg, it was built in Dutch Renaissance style (red brick, copper roof, sandstone facade). The oldest parts date from 1560 and the reign of Frederik II. His more extravagant son, Christian IV, erected the main part of the castle from 1600 to 1620. Danish monarchs used it for some 2 centuries. From 1671 to 1840, Danish kings were crowned in Christian IV's chapel, which is still used as a parish church. Since 1693 it has been a chapel for the knights of the Order of the Elephant and of the Grand Cross of Danneborg. Standing in the gallery is an old organ built by Esaias Compenius in 1610. Every Thursday from 1:30 to 2pm, the chapel organist plays for museum visitors.

Since 1878 the castle has housed **Det Nationalhistoriske Museum (the Museum of National History).** Founded by the brewer J. C. Jacobsen as part of the Carlsberg Foundation, it encompasses the Great Hall and the former Audience Chamber of Danish monarchs. The museum contains the best collection of portraits and histori-cal paintings in the country, all the stiff-necked greats and the wannabes. You can explore 70 of its rooms, each with paintings, gilded ceilings, and tapestries covering entire walls. The 20th-century collection on the third floor is a bit livelier, with its chronologically arranged exhibits. There are portraits and paintings here, but some-how the photographs are even more intriguing.

The castle is a 15-minute walk or a short taxi ride from the train station.

In Frederiksborg Slot. ℂ **48-26-04-39.** www.frederiksborgmuseet.dk. Admission 60DKK ($10/£5.40) adults, 15DKK ($2.55/£1.35) children 6–15, free for children under 6. Nov–Mar daily 11am–3pm; Apr–Oct daily 10am–5pm. Bus: 701 from Hillerød Station.

Frederiksborg Castle Garden 🏵🏵   For decades these gardens were used by three kings of Denmark, including Frederik IV, Christian VI, and Frederik V. They were designed by Johan Cornelius Krieger in just 5 years, from 1720 to 1725. In a flight of fancy, he got carried away, creating a cascade with water canals and fountains, along with promenades, groves of trees, and even a parterre sporting royal monograms to flatter the egos of his patrons.

Sadly, during the reign of Christian VII (1766–1808), he wasn't in the mood for a baroque romp. The tightwad king, preoccupied with military matters, felt the gardens had grown out of style, and he also complained that they were too expensive for his royal purse to maintain. By 1933, the gardens had decayed. But in recent times, in just 3 years monies were found to re-create the gardens as they were in their baroque hey-day. As many as 65,000 box plants and 166 pyramid-shaped yews have been planted in the parterre, while 375 limes and 7,000 hornbeam plants create the avenues and groves. The cascade floor consists of nearly half a kilometer (¼ mile) of dressed gran-ite stones. During the summer, the Frederiksborg Castle Garden forms the venue for several recurring concerts, maypole celebrations, and other cultural events.

Rendelæggerbakken 3. ℂ **48-26-04-39.** Free admission. May–Aug daily 10am–9pm; Sept and Apr daily 10am–7pm; Oct and Mar daily 10am–5pm; Nov–Feb daily 10am–4pm. Bus: 701 from Hillerød Station.

Visiting a Medieval Monasery's Remains

The ruins of an Augustinian monastery, **Abelholt Klostermuseum**, Abelholt 4 (ℂ **48-24-34-48**), aren't everyone's cuppa, but if you're a doctor or a devotee of eerie medieval ruins, consider a visit. You reach the site of this monastery, founded in 1175, by driving west of Hillerød for 6km (3¾ miles)—it's sign-posted. If you got sick in North Zealand centuries ago, you tried to make your way here, as the local monks had various methods used in healing.

An on-site museum explains the primitive living conditions of the time, and archaeologists have dug up skeletons of the former monks that are now on dis-play and could be rented out for a horror flick. Healing methods used by these early monks are also exhibited. You can wander through a garden adjoining the museum to see the types of medicinal herbs grown. Admission is 15DKK ($2.55/£1.35), free for those 12 and under. Hours are from March to October Tuesday to Sunday 11am to 4pm.

SHOPPING

This is not a compelling reason to come to Hillerød, but you might be surprised at how many goods there are to buy. In the town center is the sprawling **SlotsArkaderne** 🖈 shopping center, close to Frederiksborg Castle, with an entrance on Nordstensvej. Opened in 1992, its distinctive interior design has been hailed throughout Denmark. It is definitely shopper-friendly. Within the center are some 50 specialty shops, in one of the most beautiful shopping malls in Europe. Open Monday to Friday 10am to 7pm and Saturday 10am to 4pm.

There are a number of specialty stores throughout the town. Right in front of the castle, **Sweater House,** Slangerupgade 1 (✆ **48-25-51-25**), offers the town's best selection of Scandinavian sweaters, often in blue-and-white patterns. Since Danish toys enjoy world renown, you might want to check out the selection at **Fætter BR,** Slots-Arkaderne 27 (✆ **48-26-07-55**).

WHERE TO STAY

The **Hillerød Tourist office** offers a wide range of excellent, yet inexpensive, B&Bs in and around town. These are mostly seasonal openings, and some owners open one year and not the other; but the list in the tourist office is always current.

Although the hotel recommended below is fine, many guests prefer the more glamorous Fredensborg Store Kro (see below).

Hotel Hillerød   With its smart, sleek Danish design, this is the town's best choice for overnighting. Okay, so its low-slung design and features might remind you of a motel on the outskirts of a large American city. Even so, the hotel is furnished both sensibly and comfortably, and all the bedrooms are well maintained with Danish modern pieces and neatly kept bathrooms with shower units. Most of the accommodations come with a small kitchenette, as well as a private terrace. Breakfast is the only meal served, and, even if there are any shortcomings here, the attentive staff makes up for it. The location is a 3-minute walk from the town's commercial center.

Milnersvej 41, DK-3400 Hillerød. ✆ **48-24-08-00.** Fax 48-24-08-74. www.hotelhillerod.dk. 74 units, 63 with kitchenette. 1,110DKK ($189/£100) double. Rates include breakfast. AE, DC, MC, V. **Amenities:** Breakfast room; lounge; laundry service; dry cleaning; nonsmoking rooms; rooms for those w/limited mobility. *In room:* TV, minibar, coffeemaker, hair dryer, trouser press, safe.

WHERE TO DINE

John F. Kennedy Pub-Café DANISH/INTERNATIONAL   Set on the main square of Hillerød, its name was selected in 1996 by the owner, an avid fan of virtually everything associated with the memory of JFK. During the day this place mainly functions as a cafe and restaurant, where good-tasting menu items include New Orleans–style barbecue, grilled shrimp, well-stuffed club sandwiches, and succulent pastas. However, when the food service winds down, beginning around 7pm, it transforms itself into a bar designed for drinking, talking, and flirting. We like it best then. Action spills over onto an outdoor terrace, and every Friday and Saturday an annex room is transformed into a dance club, **Club Annabell,** which can get quite rowdy. Entry is 50DKK ($8.50/£4.50); a bottle of Carlsberg goes for 25DKK ($4.25/£2.25). No one under age 21 is allowed inside.

Torvet 4. ✆ **48-26-04-05.** Fixed-price meals 52DKK–73DKK ($8.85–$12/£4.70–£6.60). AE, DC, MC, V. May–Sept Mon–Sat 2–11pm; Oct–Apr Tues–Sat noon–7pm. Bar until 2am year-round.

Slotskroen 🖈 DANISH   After calling on the Queen, we always like to pop in here for lunch. It's been going strong since it opened its doors in 1795 and is the oldest tavern in town. But it's also kept abreast of the times in both its menu selections and its decor. Nowadays, food is served only at lunchtime (although on rare occasions, dinner is offered). Within a trio of cozy and historic-looking dining rooms, some of whose windows open onto direct views of the nearby castle, you can enjoy access to a *smörgåsbord* that's laden with tasty hot and cold dishes, several kinds of open-faced Danish sandwiches, *frikadeller* (meatballs), and freshly made salads. There's also an outdoor terrace for use during warm weather.

Slotsgade 67. © **48-20-18-00**. *Smörgåsbord* buffet 169DKK ($29/£15). AE, DC, MC, V. Daily noon–5pm.

Spisestedet Leonora ⊛ DANISH   Since the 1970s this well-managed tavern has flourished in the former Frederiksborg Castle stables. Don't panic—the original smell is long gone. It's the most sought-after dining spot in town for anyone visiting the castle, partly because of its array of carefully crafted open-faced sandwiches. The place also serves succulent grilled meats, especially Danish lamb; homemade crisp, fresh salads; and platters of homemade, warm dishes, the kind your Danish grandmother used to make. These platters are big enough to make a meal unto themselves.

Frederiksborg Slot. © **48-26-75-16**. Main courses 55DKK–145DKK ($9.35–$25/£4.95–£13); lunch plate 98DKK ($17/£8.80); *smørrebrød* 42DKK–98DKK ($7.15–$17/£3.80–£8.80). DC, MC, V. Daily 10am–5pm. Closed 1 week at Christmas. Bus: 701 or 702.

HILLERØD AFTER DARK

The best place to go is the **John F. Kennedy Pub-Café** (see "Where to Dine," above), which transforms itself into **Club Annabell** on Friday and Saturday nights.

ON THE FRINGE: A RENAISSANCE CASTLE & MODERN ART

You're in for a treat if you've budgeted an hour or two to drive over to **Selsø Slot** ⊛, Selsøvej 30 at Hornsherred (© **47-52-01-71**), the first Renaissance-style castle built in 1575. Of course, all that baroque styling you see today is from 1733. The owners couldn't leave a good thing alone. Selsø is one of the few private manor houses in Zealand that can be thoroughly explored, yet it seems little publicized and most visitors pass it by without knowing it's there.

The Great Hall is still as it was in 1733 when those new decorators came through, adding touches such as ornate plaster ceilings, fine paintings, and 4-meter (13-ft.) marble panels. You can also wander down to the vaults from 1560, and even see the old manor kitchen and its open fireplace and scullery. A dungeon below the gatehouse is a bit spooky. Kids delight in a room devoted to them with its hundreds of tin soldiers. Before heading here, ask at the tourist office about orchestral concerts staged here. Hopefully, you'll get to see one for yourself. The setting's perfect. Hillerød makes a good center for exploring neighboring attractions.

From the center of Hillerød, take Route 6 south, following the signs to Copenhagen. At Route 53, turn west. Fifty-five kilometers (34 miles) from Hillerød you'll come to Selsø Slot. The location at Hornsherred is east of Skibby, south of Skuldelev, and 56km (35 miles) west of Copenhagen.

Admission is 40DKK ($6.80/£3.60) adults, 10DKK ($1.70/90p) children. The castle is open mid-June to mid-August, daily 11am to 4pm; and mid-August to late October, Saturday and Sunday 1 to 4pm (closed otherwise).

Frederikssund (see above) is usually visited at the time of its Viking pageant. But the opening of an art museum here in 1957 made the hamlet a year-round attraction. The **J. F. Willumsen's Museum,** Jenriksvej 4 (© **47-31-07-73**), is devoted to the paintings, drawings, engravings, sculpture, ceramics, and photographs of the well-known

Danish artist J. F. Willumsen (1863–1958), one of Denmark's leading symbolists, who spent most of his creative years in France. The museum also displays the works of other artists which were once part of Willumsen's private collection. Hours are year-round Tuesday to Sunday 10am to 5pm. Admission is 35DKK ($5.95/£3.15) adults, 15DKK ($2.55/£1.35) students, free for children under 15. From Hillerød, take Route 6 south, following the signs to Copenhagen. At Route 53 head west. The total distance from Hillerød is 40km (25 miles).

2 Fredensborg ★

9.5km (6 miles) W of Helsingør; 40km (25 miles) N of Copenhagen

The great time to visit is in July, when the Queen graciously opens the doors of Fredensborg Slot (palace) to visitors from around the world. Elizabeth II of England has a lot more money, a lot more paintings, and much more precious furnishings, but the Danish queen's summer abode is impressive as well, though not as grand as Frederiksborg Slot (see above), with which it is often confused.

On the southeast shore of Esrum Sø, the country's second-largest lake, Fredensborg is more than a royal palace. Many visitors rush through, visiting the palace and then departing immediately. However, you can stay and dine in the area and enjoy a number of other attractions as well (see below).

The first inhabitants of the town were people who helped serve the royal court. But over the years others moved in, and today the town is a lively little place even when the Queen isn't in residence. To Denmark, it occupies a position somewhat similar to Windsor in England. The town is home to some 40 specialty shops.

The palace is a major backdrop for events in the life of the royal family—weddings, birthday parties, and the like. Heads of states from many of the countries of the world are received here when they pay state visits. And foreign ambassadors present their credentials to the monarch here as well.

ESSENTIALS

GETTING THERE   By Train   From Copenhagen's Central Railroad Station, frequent trains run to Fredensborg, but there are no buses.

By Car   From Copenhagen, head north on the E55 toward Helsingør, turning west on Route 6.

VISITOR INFORMATION   Fredensborg Turistinformation, Slotsgade 2 (© 48-48-21-00), is open Monday to Friday noon to 4pm.

EXPLORING THE AREA

Esrum Sø ★ not only is the second-largest lake in Denmark, but also is exceptionally deep: 22m (72 ft.) in some places. Since 1949, the land around the lake has been protected by the government. It is a winter feeding ground for large numbers of waterfowl. You can enjoy a trip on the lake if for no other reason than to admire the flocks of noble swans—there's not an "Ugly Duckling" among them.

If the weather is good enough and there's enough business to warrant its departure, a local outfitter, **Færgefart Bådudlejning på Esrum Sø,** Skipperhuset, in the village of Sørup (© 48-48-01-07), leads tours in an open boat through the lake's shallow waters. The emphasis is on ecology, and the tour is conducted in Danish with halting English and German explanations added afterward. The duration of the tour is around 45 minutes, and the cost is 50DKK ($8.50/£4.50).

Esrum Kloster, Klostergade 11, Esrum (✆ **48-36-04-00**), was founded in 1151 and has a long and ancient history, especially when it was the most powerful Cistercian monastery in Scandinavia. Eleven monks arrived to lay the foundation stone of what later became the abbey, surrounded by forest, meadows, lake, and fields. The Middle Ages come alive here as you view the second-floor exhibit of the monastic period.

The mounted exhibition gives you an idea of the layout of the monastery and the everyday life of the monks. The exhibition on the main floor deals with Esrum Abbey after the Reformation. The cloisters underwent many changes, becoming a royal hunting lodge, a base for a regiment of dragoons, a stud farm for horses, even a post office and district tax office. As a result of King Frederik II's horse-breeding interests, the fabled Frederiksborg horse was produced, highly prized for its skill and stamina.

In addition to the exhibitions, regular concerts and theatrical performances are staged here, both inside and outside the monastery.

The abbey is open January 5 to May 8 Thursday to Sunday 10am to 4pm; May 9 to June 30 and August 1 to October 23 Tuesday to Sunday 10am to 4pm; July Tuesday to Sunday 10am to 5pm (Thursday until 9pm); October 24 to December 18 Thursday to Sunday 10am to 4pm. It's closed December 19 to January 4. Admission is 40DKK ($6.80/£3.60), 20DKK ($3.40/£1.80) for children 5–15, free for children under 5.

From Fredensborg, you can get to Esrum by bus (marked ESRUM), getting off at Hovedgaden. From here, walk for less than half a kilometer (¼ mile) along the Klostergade, which leads you to the entrance of the abbey. Motorists can take Route 205 north from Fredensborg.

From Hillerød to Esrum, you can catch bus nos. 305, 306, or 331, a 25-minute ride, for around 20DKK ($3.40/£1.80).

Fredensborg Slot ⚜ This is the summer residence of the Danish royal family. Once it was called the palace of "the parents-in-law" of Europe. King Christian IX and Queen Louise had sons and daughters sitting on thrones in many of the royal houses of Europe, and they would gather in the summer months to catch up on royal gossip and scandals.

Although the palace has been added on to many times, it still retains its baroque, rococo, and classic features.

When the queen is in residence today, visitors assemble at noon to watch the changing of the guard—but don't expect this ceremony to match that of Buckingham Palace in London. On Thursdays, except in July, the queen often appears to acknowledge a regimental band concert in her honor.

The Danish architect J. C. Krieger built the palace for King Frederik IV. Originally there was only the main building with a Cupola Hall. Over the years the palace was extended with such additions as the Chancellery House and the Cavaliers Wing. Though hardly one of the impressive royal palaces of Europe, it has its own charm, especially in the Domed Hall and the Garden Room.

The palace opens onto a 275-year-old **baroque garden** ⚜⚜. A public part of the palace garden is open year-round daily 1 to 5pm, but the private, reserved royal garden and Orangery are open only limited hours in July. These are some of the largest and best-preserved gardens in Denmark. Note how strictly symmetrical and geometrical the shapes are. Drawing on Italian designs for their inspiration, Frederik IV and J. C. Krieger laid out the palace gardens in the 1720s. In the 1760s Frederik V redesigned the garden, adding elements from French baroque horticulture.

Slottet. ℂ **33-40-31-87.** Admission 40DKK ($6.80/£3.60) adults, 15DKK ($2.55/£1.35) children 5–14, free for children under 5. Joint ticket for the Palace and the Orangery and Herb Garden 60DKK ($100/£5.40) adults, 25DKK ($5.30/£2.25) for children 5–14, free for children under 5. Palace July daily 1–5pm; public garden daily 1–5pm; private garden July Sun–Fri 9am–5pm; Orangery July daily 1–4:30pm.

WHERE TO STAY

Endruplund Country House 𝄞 *(Finds)*   This little hidden-away charmer was created from a farmhouse that stood here in the early part of the 20th century. It's been run by the same family since 1926, and is a comfortable little oasis for those seeking old-fashioned Danish ambience. It is set less than a kilometer (about ½ mile) northeast of Fredensborg's center. Today, you'll find comfortable, somewhat eccentric rooms, each personalized by the hardworking efforts of the inn's owner, Karen Windinge, whose critically acclaimed dried-flower arrangements are artfully scattered throughout her comfortable and eclectically decorated guesthouse. About half of the rooms share a bathroom with a shower unit. No meals are served other than breakfast.

Holmeskovvej 5, DK-3480 Fredensborg. ℂ **48-48-02-38.** Fax 48-48-35-17. www.countryhouse.dk. 17 units, 11 with bathroom. 380DKK ($65/£34) double without bathroom; 440DKK ($75/£40) double with bathroom. MC, V. From Fredensborg's center, follow the signs to Helsingør. **Amenities:** Breakfast room; lounge. *In room:* No phone.

Fredensborg Store Kro 𝄞𝄞   A 10-minute walk from the train station and 5 minutes from Esrum Lake, this is one of the most venerable old inns in Zealand, and a personal favorite of ours, lying a 10-minute walk from the train station or a 5-minute leisurely stroll from Esrum Lake. It was commissioned in 1723 by Frederik IV. Since it is right next door to Fredensborg Castle, many guests of the royal family once stayed here. No two rooms are alike, but all are equally charming, as taste and elegance rule throughout. Over the years such modern extras as private bathrooms with tub/shower combinations have been added. Ask for a room with a view of the palace—although only five are available, and they are of course the most requested. In 1997 President Clinton dropped in to the inn for a look when he was visiting the queen at Fredensborg. The hotel restaurant is the finest in the area (see "Where to Dine," below).

Slotsgade 6, DK-3480 Fredensborg. ℂ **48-40-01-11.** Fax 48-48-45-61. www.storekro.dk. 49 units. 1,280DKK–1,600DKK ($218–$272/£115–£144) double; 2,453DKK ($417/£221) suite. Rates include breakfast. AE, DC, MC, V. Bus: 336 or 733E. **Amenities:** Restaurant; bar; room service (7am–11pm); laundry service; dry cleaning; rooms for those w/limited mobility. *In room:* TV, dataport, minibar, hair dryer.

Pension Bondehuset 𝄞 *(Finds)*   For a romantic getaway, this compound of Dutch-roofed buildings at the edge of Esrum Lake was originally constructed in the 1700s by the local shipbuilder less than a kilometer (about ½ mile) south of the center of Fredensborg. For years, it functioned as a boatyard and repair site for watercraft on the lake, but since the Larsen family took over, it has been a cozy and sought-after hotel. Part of its allure derives from its brightly colored public areas with plush furnishings. Rooms are outfitted in sedate, eminently tasteful motifs similar to what you'd expect in a private manor house. All units have well-maintained bathrooms with tub/shower combinations.

Sørupvej 14, DK-3480 Fredensborg. ℂ **48-48-01-12.** Fax 48-48-03-01. www.bondehuset.dk. 15 units. 1,350DKK ($230/£122) double. Rates include half-board. DC, MC, V. **Amenities:** Dining room; bar; lounge. *In room:* Hair dryer.

WHERE TO DINE

Anna Sophie 𝄞𝄞 DANISH/FRENCH   Should the queen accept your invitation for a meal, take her here. Hopefully, the weather will be cooperative. That way, you can dine outside in the garden, idyllic on a summer night. Otherwise, you can retreat into the elegant dining room, which is also fit for a queen. The cooking is not only delectable—it's often inspired. The chef assumes that when it comes to lunch appetizers, everybody likes herring. We certainly do, especially the herring plate with three variations on this fish. At night the starters grow more elaborate, including a lightly smoked foie gras with dried goose breast and a rhubarb compote. The sautéed lamb is always perfectly prepared with baked plum tomatoes and a savory sauce. The chef always bakes a special cake of the day for dessert.

Slotsgade 6. ⓒ 48-40-01-50. Reservations recommended. Main courses 95DKK–208DKK ($16–$35/£8.55–£19). AE, DC, MC, V. Daily noon–3pm and 6–10pm.

Da Oscar ITALIAN   This small, family-run restaurant a short walk from Fredensborg Castle has a lot of panache, verve, and sensitivity. Originally built in the 1930s, the premises might remind you of a small-scale villa. Inside, you'll find a trio of cozy dining rooms, a cuisine that focuses on Italian dishes, and food items that include succulent pastas and freshly caught fish. The pastry chef makes a tempting array of goodies every day, big on calories and taste, horrible on your Kate Moss waistline. Grilled Danish lamb and savory pizzas are also offered. At any time, if the more substantial offerings don't appeal to you, you can order any of at least a dozen artfully contrived *smørrebrød* (open-faced sandwiches).

Slotsgade 3A. ⓒ 48-48-01-25. Reservations recommended. Main courses 149DKK–179DKK ($25–$30/£13–£16); fixed-price menu 239DKK–289DKK ($41–$49/£22–£26). MC, V. Daily 5–11pm.

Restaurant Skipperhuset ★★ *Finds* DANISH/FRENCH   Picture this: alfresco dining on Lake Estrum. Not only that, but you're actually on the grounds of the royal summer residence of the queen. In the 18th century, this site was the royal boathouse. Part of the experience of dining at this restaurant is the path you'll use to reach it—a long promenade lined with trees originally laid out as one of the decorative avenues associated with Fredensborg Slot. Today, this much-altered boathouse is a well-respected restaurant where cuisine manages to combine elements of the best of Danish and French traditions. The cooks here have experience and an expert sense of precise, clear flavors. Menu items we continue to enjoy include breast of chicken stewed with young vegetables and summer cabbage; fried mackerel with spinach, apples, olives, and lemon-thyme sauce; and a dessert specialty of stewed rhubarb with sugared biscuits.

Skipperallee 6. ⓒ 48-48-17-17. Reservations recommended. Main courses 38DKK–198DKK ($6.45–$34/£3.40–£18); fixed-price menus 268DKK ($46/£24). DC, MC, V. Tues–Sun noon–6pm.

3 Helsingør (Elsinore): In Search of Hamlet ★

40km (25 miles) N of Copenhagen; 24km (15 miles) NE of Hillerød; 72km (45 miles) NE of Roskilde

Does it really matter to the pilgrims flocking to this town that Hamlet never existed? Or that William Shakespeare never visited Helsingør? To the pilgrims wanting to see "Hamlet's Castle," the power of legend is what really matters.

Don't be disappointed if you arrive by train or bus. Make your way through the noisy, congested crowds and the fast-food stalls and move deeper into Helsingør. Once you do that, you'll find that it has a certain charm, with a market square, medieval lanes, and old half-timbered and brick buildings, many constructed by ships' captains in the heyday of the 19th-century shipping industry.

In 1429 King Erik of Pomerania ruled that ships passing Helsingør had to pay a toll for sailing within local waters. The town quickly developed into the focal point for international shipping, bringing in a lot of revenue. King Erik also constructed the Castle of Krogen, later rebuilt by Christian IV as the Castle of Kronborg. For a while Helsingør prospered and grew so much that it was the second-largest town in the country.

Today much of the town's prosperity depends on those free-spending Hamlet devotees and that sliver of water between Denmark and Sweden, with ferries leaving frequently for Helsingborg.

ESSENTIALS

GETTING THERE   By Train   There are frequent trains from Copenhagen (trip time: 50 min.).

By Car   Take E-4 north from Copenhagen.

By Ferry   Ferries ply the waters of the narrow channel separating Helsingør (Denmark) from Helsingborg (Sweden) in less than 25 minutes. They're operated around the clock by **Scandlines** (© **33-15-15-15;** www.scandlines.dk), which charges 21DKK ($3.55/£1.90) each way for a pedestrian without a car, and 254DKK ($43/£23) each way for a car with up to nine persons inside. Between 6am and 11pm, departures are every 20 minutes; 11pm to 6am, departures are timed at intervals of 40 to 80 minutes. The process is simple and straightforward: You simply drive your car onboard and wait in your car. Border formalities during the crossing between Denmark and Sweden are perfunctory, and although you should carry a passport, you might not even be asked for it.

VISITOR INFORMATION   The **tourist office,** at Havnepladsen 3 (© **49-21-13-33;** www.visithelsingor.dk), is open Monday to Friday 10am to 4pm and Saturday 10am to 1pm; June 20 to August 31 Monday to Friday 10am to 5pm, and Saturday 10am to 3pm.

SEEING THE SIGHTS

Kronborg Slot ★★★   There is no evidence that Shakespeare ever saw this sandstone-and-copper Dutch Renaissance–style castle, full of intriguing secret passages, but he made it famous in *Hamlet.* If Hamlet had really lived, it would have been centuries before Kronborg was built (1574–85). You're to be forgiven if you suddenly burst into Richard Burton's famous soliloquy of "to be or not to be." After all, *Hamlet* is the most frequently performed drama in the world, a historical challenge to all great actors such as Sir John Gielgud and Lord Laurence Olivier. Count yourself lucky if you missed Mel Gibson's pathetic attempt to play the Mad Dane in the 1990 movie directed by Franco Zeffirelli, who should have known better. Except for "Mad Mel," the film had a great cast, with Glenn Close as Gertrude, Alan Bates as Claudius, and Paul Scofield as "the Ghost."

The castle, on a peninsula jutting out into Øresund, was restored in 1629 by Christian IV after it had been gutted by fire. Other events in its history include looting, bombardment, occupation by Swedes, and use as a barracks (1785–1922). The facade is covered with sandstone, and the entire castle is surrounded by a deep moat—but no dragon. You approach the castle via a wooden bridge and by going through Mørkeport, a gate from the 16th century. This will lead you to the main courtyard of Kronborg.

Note: Instead of entering the castle at once, you can walk around the moat to the waterfront, where you can view a spectacular vista of the Swedish coast. At the platform—backed by massive bronze guns—Hamlet is said to have seen the ghost of his father, shrouded in pea-soup fog.

ATTRACTIONS ●
Danmarks Tekniske Museet
  (Technical Museum of Denmark) **2**
Helsingør Bymuseet **7**
Kronborg Slot **4**
Karmeliterklostret **5**
Marienlyst Slot **1**
Skt. Mariæ Church **6**
Skt. Olai Kirke **8**

ACCOMMODATIONS ■
Hotel Marienlyst **3**
Skandia Hotel **10**

DINING ◆
Kærgaarden (dining complex) **11**
Ophelia Restaurant **9**
San Remo **12**

The starkly furnished Great Hall is the largest in northern Europe. Originally 40 tapestries portraying 111 Danish kings were hung around this room on special occasions. They were commissioned by Frederik II and produced around 1585. Only seven remain at Kronborg; the rest have disappeared except for seven in the Nationalmuseet in Copenhagen. The church, with its original oak furnishings and the royal chambers, is worth exploring. The bleak and austere atmosphere adds to the drama. Holger Danske, a mythological hero who is believed to assist Denmark whenever the country is threatened, is said to live in the basement. That "hero" didn't emerge when Nazi storm troopers invaded Denmark on Hitler's orders, but the legend, like the legend of Hamlet, still persists. Also on the premises is the **Danish Maritime Museum** (© **49-21-06-85**), which explores the history of Danish shipping. Unless you're really nautical, you might skip this if you're rushed for time. However, that would mean you'd miss seeing the world's oldest surviving ship's biscuit, dating from 1852. There is also an impressive collection of model ships and other sailors' memorabilia. More intriguing are relics of Denmark's colonial past in the West Indies (Caribbean), West Africa, Greenland, and even India.

Guided tours are given every half-hour October to April. In summer you can walk around on your own. The castle is less than a kilometer (about ½ mile) from the rail station. On November 30, 2000, Kronborg was added to UNESCO's World Heritage List.

Kronborg. © **49-21-30-78**. www.kronborgcastle.com. Admission 60DKK ($10/£5.40) adults, 15DKK ($2.55/£1.35) children 6–14, free for children under 6. Joint ticket for the castle and the Danish Maritime Museum 75DKK ($13/£6.75) adults, 60DKK ($10/£5.40) children. May–Sept daily 10:30am–5pm; Apr and Oct Tues–Sun 11am–4pm; Nov–Mar Tues–Sun 11am–3pm. Closed Dec 25.

Skt. Mariæ Kirke 𝕗

Too often neglected by those Hamlet-crazed visitors, this former Carmelite monastery is one of the best preserved in the North of Europe. Rumor has it, the monks here used to flagellate themselves inside its walls like that albino monk did in the controversial film *The Da Vinci Code.*

The church was built between 1430 and 1500, and much of its original architecture remains. You can see the newly renovated organ that was used by the famous baroque composer, Dietrich Buxtehude, from 1660 to 1668. Murals dating from the 1480s have also been restored, and there is an impressive altarpiece from 1637. The interior contains two galleries, a royal gallery and a rococo gallery, dating from the 17th and 18th centuries. After the Reformation, the monastery was dissolved and converted into a retirement home.

Inside the walls of the ecclesiastical compound is the **Karmeliterklostret Monastery** 𝕗, which can be visited on a guided tour. After the monks were booted out, this building was turned into a hospital specializing in brain surgery. With so little known about brain surgery in those days, you can imagine how botched the operations were.

In case you get asked on some trivia TV quiz, the body of the notorious Dyveke, mistress of Christian II, was buried here upon her death in 1517. Local gossips claimed that the king "wore her out."

The monastery lies near the intersection of Havnegade and Kronborgvej.

Skt. Annagade 38. © **49-21-17-74**. Free admission. Mon–Sat 9am–noon, Thurs 4–6pm. Guided tours May 16–Sept 15 Mon–Fri at 2pm. 20DKK ($3.40/£1.80) adults, 5DKK (85¢/45p) children 10–15, free for children under 10.

Skt. Olai Kirke

After a visit to the monastery above, and only if time remains, you can walk nearby to see this church, which is actually the cathedral of Helsingør. It was named after the patron saint Olai, a Norwegian king (spelled "Olav" in Norwegian), who died in 1030. Throughout the church are illustrations of this saintly king slaying the dragon of paganism.

The present building dates from 1559, constructed on the site of a small Romanesque church from the 1200s.

At the dawn of the 21st century, restorers opened many of the burial chambers here, discovering very well-preserved mummies. Had Danish monks learned the secrets of the Egyptians? After studying these long-dead corpses, they were sealed away once more and buried beneath a floor of concrete and tile to "safeguard the peace of the dead now and forever."

Architecturally, the christening chapel and the baptistery of this spired church are worth a brief inspection. Also take in the ornately decorated altar. Sankt Olai takes up a city block between Stengade and Sankt Olai Gade.

Skt. Annagade 12. © **49-21-04-43**. Free admission. May–Aug Mon–Sat 10am–4pm; Sept–Apr daily 10am–2pm.

A Hamlet "Sommer" in the Courtyard of Kronborg

Some 4 centuries have gone by since the Bard wrote *Hamlet,* but the age-old drama is still performed here in August in the courtyard of the so-called Hamlet's Castle, Kronborg. That great theatrical couple Laurence Olivier and his wife Vivien Leigh performed *Hamlet* here, as have many other theatrical greats since 1816. After a 21-year pause, performances began anew in 2000. Tickets for this event cost 235DKK ($40/£21). For ticket information, contact **Helsingør Teaterkontor,** Havnepladsen 3 (© **49-20-08-11;** billet@helsingor-teater.dk). The box office is open Monday to Friday noon to 4pm.

Helsingør Bymuseet   This Renaissance townhouse was built in 1520 by Carmelite friars as a hospital for foreign sailors suffering from diseases; time has erased that sad history. Today it's the "attic" of Helsingør, a magnificent Renaissance townhouse filled with the city's relics. Children, or at least little girls, gravitate to the collection of 200 antique dolls. There is also a fine-scale model of Helsingør in 1801. The banquet hall on the main floor is filled with the chief goodies, artifacts left over from the golden age of Helsingør when it was a major shipping center. As for some of those portraits, they evoke the type you hide in your own family attic. In the basement are relics of the Middle Ages, best left undisturbed in our view.

Helsingørsgade 65. © **49-28-18-00.** www.helsingor.dk/museum/bymuseet.htm. Admission 15DKK ($2.55/£1.35) adults, free for children under 10. May–Oct Tues–Sun 11am–4pm.

Marienlyst Slot ⍟   Kronborg is all militant in its architecture and ghostly in its literary associations. But Marienlyst Slot, built by French architect N. H. Jardin from 1759 to 1763, is a place where you might actually live. In fact, up until 1953 it was a private residence before being turned into a museum. The location is 1km (⅔ mile) north of Helsingør. Allow 30 minutes or so to wander in the well-landscaped park surrounding the Slot. There's a panoramic view of the Sound from the top of a steep slope behind the palace.

In the 16th century, King Frederik II used this site for his summer gardens before the present palace was constructed. The interior is in the Louis XVI style, with a collection of lackluster paintings. One intrigued us as an oddity: the painting is half Venice, half Copenhagen. To lure English romantics in the 19th century, locals claimed that "Hamlet's grave" could be found in the garden out back. Thinking Hamlet was an actual prince, these visitors were instructed "to think melancholy thoughts."

Marienlyst Allé 32. © **49-28-18-30.** Admission 30DKK ($5.10/£2.70) adults, free for children under 16. Daily noon–4pm.

Danmarks Tekniske Museet (Technical Museum of Denmark) ⍟ *Finds*   Did you know that rich Danes were driving an automobile, the Hammelvognen, back in 1888? They were and it's on display here. Would you like to see what the world's first typewriter looked like? You can do so here. There's even the world's first electromagnetic sound recorder (tape recorder) on display. Steam engines, antique electric appliances, bicycles, vintage cars, and the oldest Danish airplanes are on display here. The location is in the southern part of town in a former iron foundry.

Although there are many exhibits, including a pewter workshop, we are most intrigued by the 30 or so airplanes, ranging from gyrocopters to helicopters. Our favorite is called the "Danish Edison," an invention of J. C. Ellhammer. Danes will tell you he made the first flight in Europe in 1906. Regrettably, if this is true, his feat was never recorded.

Fabriksvej 25. © **49-22-26-11.** Admission Jan 2–Apr and Oct 1–Dec 30 50DKK ($8.50/£4.50) adults, 25DKK ($4.25/ £2.25) children 10–15, free for children under 10. May–Sept 65DKK ($11/£5.85) adults, 25DKK ($4.25/£2.25) children. Tues–Sun 10am–5pm.

WHERE TO STAY

Hotel Marienlyst ★ On the western outskirts of town beyond the castle, this hotel is about as close to Las Vegas as you'll get in Denmark. Even if you don't like its flashy neon aggressiveness, it's the best and most comfortable place to stay in town. Composed of three buildings, its headquarters and oldest core were built around 1850, while the largest of its annexes went up in the mid-1970s. With a panoramic view over the gray sea toward Sweden, this hotel contains a glossy outbuilding with one of only six gambling casinos in Denmark. Rooms are a study in sleek Nordic styling—comfortable and beautifully maintained. The bathrooms are neatly kept, with tub/ shower combinations. Many rooms have balconies or terraces, and 86 have a view of the sound. The suites and apartments have a kitchen and dishwasher.

Nordre Strandvej 2, DK-3000 Helsingør. © **49-21-40-00.** Fax 49-21-49-00. www.marienlyst.dk. 222 units. 1,120DKK–1,825DKK ($190–$310/£101–£164) double; 2,175DKK–2,775DKK ($370–$472/£196–£250) suite. Rates include breakfast. AE, DC, MC, V. Bus: 340. **Amenities:** 2 restaurants; bar; indoor heated pool; children's pool and water slide; fitness center; spa; room service (7am–11pm); massage; babysitting; laundry service; dry cleaning; non-smoking rooms; rooms for those w/limited mobility; casino. *In room:* TV, dataport, hair dryer.

Skandia Hotel *Value* Attracting the economy-minded, this hotel provides simple but clean and cost-conscious accommodations in an amply proportioned building erected in 1922. Only half of its rooms have been renovated, so your opinion of this hotel may depend on your room assignment. Naturally, the renovated ones go first. Rooms are neat and functionally furnished. Each unit has a well-kept bathroom with a tub/shower combination. Ask for one on the fifth floor if you'd like a good view of the sound. If you need to make a phone call, you can do so at the reception desk. The hotel lies behind a red-brick facade along a street running parallel to the port near the bus and train station and the departure point for the ferryboat to Sweden.

Bramstræde 1, DK-3000 Helsingør. © **49-21-09-02.** Fax 49-21-09-54. www.hotelskandia.dk. 44 units, 9 with bathroom. 650DKK ($111/£59) double without bathroom; 750DKK ($128/£68) double with bathroom; 925DKK ($157/£83) 3-bed family rooms with shower. DC, MC, V. **Amenities:** Lounge; nonsmoking rooms. *In room:* TV, no phone.

WHERE TO DINE

Typical Danish hot meals, such as *hakkebof* (hamburger steak), *frikadeller* (Danish rissoles or meatballs), rib roast with red cabbage, cooked or fried flounder or herring, and *æggekage* (egg cake) with bacon, are served in the local restaurants. In Helsingør you'll also find many fast-food places, and you won't want to miss the celebrated ice-cream wafers.

Ophelia Restaurant DANISH/FRENCH Naturally, in the town of Hamlet, some enterprising owner had to come up with a touristy name to lure visitors. Don't be put out by this conceit. Ophelia is one of the most appealing restaurants in town, its cooks using market-fresh ingredients. In the elegantly rustic dining room, photos of *Hamlet* productions from around the world line the brick walls. Specialties of the house include "Hamlet veal steak" and calorie-rich desserts. Lunches cost half as much as dinner. Although not overly imaginative, the cookery is very competent, with dish after tasteful dish emerging from the kitchen.

In the Hotel Hamlet, Bramstræde 5. 🕿 **49-21-05-91**. Reservations recommended. Main courses 90DKK–190DKK ($15–$32/£8.10–£17). AE, DC, MC, V. Daily noon–9:30pm. Bus: 801 or 802.

San Remo DANISH   A down-to-earth self-service establishment that nevertheless sports crystal chandeliers, the San Remo offers 35 different meals, including *frikadeller* and potatoes. The fare is robust, filling, and cheap—nothing more. The cafeteria is set in a traffic-free shopping mall half a block from the harbor, in a Dutch-inspired building dating from 1904.

Stengade 53 (at Bjergegade). 🕿 **49-21-00-55**. Main courses 32DKK–95DKK ($5.45–$16/£2.90–£8.55). MC, V. June–July daily 9am–9pm; Aug–May daily 11am–6pm. Bus: 801 or 802.

A DINING COMPLEX

Kærgaarden is the setting for a trio of international restaurants in what was Helsingør's Customs House back in 1770. This complex enjoys the dining monopoly in Helsingør and is frequented by passengers going to and from Sweden. Kærgaarden offers **Gringo's Cantina** (🕿 **49-26-14-47**), a Mexican restaurant where main courses cost 98DKK to 159DKK ($17–$27/£8.80–£14), with a fixed-price menu going for 149DKK to 346DKK ($25–$59/£13–£31). There is also the very competent **Bamboo** (🕿 **49-21-22-82**), a Chinese restaurant offering main courses for 100DKK to 150DKK ($17–$26/£9–£14). Both are open daily from noon to 10pm. All accept American Express, Diners Club, MasterCard, and Visa.

HELSINGØR AFTER DARK

The major center of nightlife is the previously recommended **Hotel Marienlyst,** which has a casino usually filled with Swedes. Charging an admission of 50DKK ($8.50/£4.50), it is open daily from 7pm to 4am. Games of chance include blackjack, roulette, Seven-card stud poker, and 60 slot machines. Bring a photo ID, and know that the minimum age is 18. A casino package, costing 2,690DKK ($457/£242), includes a welcoming drink, a four-course dinner in the Seaside restaurant, admission to the casino, and cash chips at a value of 100DKK ($17/£9).

4 Hornbæk

50km (31 miles) N of Copenhagen; 12km (7½ miles) west of Helsingør

New Englanders may sing of Cape Cod, but when the summer winds blow, islanders like to head for Hornbæk for "sea, suds, and sex," as one habitué told us. A 500-year-old fishing hamlet turned modern holiday resort, Hornbæk is one of the best places for a vacation on the north coast of Zealand—sometimes called the Kattegat coast. Coastal woodlands, heath, and sand dunes make for a uniquely Danish holiday.

Hornbæk has the best beach along the north coast, a wide expanse of soft white sands that runs the full length of the resort, set against a backdrop of beach grass and sand dunes. *Rosa rugosa,* a wild pink rose that flourishes in this salty air, blooms here all summer. The beach is pristine and is beautifully maintained; all the kiosks and facilities lie inland from the dunes.

The light found in Hornbæk attracted and continues to attract artists to this fishing hamlet. In 1870, the town was discovered by such artists as Kristian Zartmann, P. S. Krøyer, Viggo Johansen, and Carl Locher—all names you've never heard of unless you were born in Denmark. Krøyer often depicted the work of fishermen at sea and down the shore. Locher was so fascinated with his marine subjects that he lived at

Hornbæk from 1881 to 1889; his home still stands at Østre Stejlebakke but is not open to the public.

ESSENTIALS

GETTING THERE **By Train** From Helsingør (see above), which has frequent connections to Copenhagen, trains arrive about twice an hour during the day, pulling into the station at Hornbæk (trip time: 22 min.).

By Bus Bus no. 340 journeys here about once an hour, taking 30 minutes.

By Car Drive northeast along the coastal road (Rte. 237) from Helsingør, following the signs to Hornbæk and/or Gilleleje.

VISITOR INFORMATION Providing information for the area, **Hornbæk Turist-bureau,** Vester Stejlebakke 2A (© **49-70-47-47;** www.hornbaek.dk), is found inside the local library. Hours are Monday 10am to 7pm, Tuesday to Friday 10am to 5pm, Saturday 10am to 2pm.

FUN ON THE BEACH & ELSEWHERE

Hornbæk Beach is the big attraction, and swimming conditions are good. The dunes protect the beach from heavy winds. Danes, often from Copenhagen, flock here in summer, but there's always space for sunbathing. The beach offers views over the sea toward Kullen, the rocky promontory jutting out from the Swedish coast.

The municipality cleans the beach daily, and for several years it has been voted one of the cleanest beaches in Scandinavia. A host of activities are available, including water biking or even nude romping. Windsurfing can be arranged at **Surfudlejning** (© **49-70-33-75**), at Drejervej 19. Kiosks sell food and drinks; there are toilets, and, for persons with disabilities, boardwalks that are wheelchair-friendly lead to the sea.

The **Havnen** or **Hornbæk Harbor** is a modern, well-equipped harbor with mooring for 200 boats. It lies next to "shanty town," a collection of huts where fishermen check their tackle or hang flatfish out to dry. Facilities with showers are beside the harbor master's office. Charters for fishing trips can be arranged here, and the harbor here is the starting point of an annual Zealand regatta in June.

If you've arrived by train from Helsingør, the harbor is only a 5-minute walk from the depot. Head down Havnevej. After crossing the dunes, you're on the beach, and we hope the day is a sunny one.

At the harbor, you'll see a monument honoring the poet Holger Drachmann, who died here in 1908.

If you'd like to walk through the village, you'll come upon some old fishermen's cottages still standing, and a church from the 17th century with many votive ships hanging

---

Tips **Insider's Tip**

After you've explored the town of Hornbæk and hit the beach, consider taking a trail through a vast tract of public forest, **Hornbæk Plantage** , 3km (1¾ miles) east of the center of Hornbæk. The tourist office will give you a free map outlining the best hiking trails. You'll come across Scotch broom, wild roses, and hundreds of pine trees as you follow one of the trails along the coast. We recommend the coastal trail because of its more dramatic scenery, although some of the hiking routes cut inland.

from the ceiling. Votive ships are scaled-down replicas that have been blessed by a priest or minister and are designed to honor the sacrifices of men who labor at sea. The church was built in 1737 to take the place of two buildings that were blown down in fierce winds. A bit inland, many Danes have erected summer villas. City officials have planted tree plantations to give shelter from the frequent gales.

SHOPPING

The best outlet for handicrafts is found at **Sylvest Stentøj,** Klosterrisvej 2, Havreholm (© **49-70-11-20**), which specializes in beautiful handcrafted stoneware.

WHERE TO STAY

Ewaldsgaardeny *Value*   Small-scale and deliberately rustic, this hotel prides itself on its role as a simple boardinghouse with few if any of the extras of a full-fledged hotel. It was originally built in 1814 as a post office, with enough stables to house the horses needed for keeping mail deliveries timely. You'll be thrown into a closer series of contacts with the other guests here than in a more anonymous setting, thanks to the small dimensions and rather cramped rooms. Each of these is outfitted with a combination of wallpaper and painted surfaces, sometimes in bright colors, and contains many of the trappings of a thoughtfully decorated private home. Overall, thanks to genuine cheerfulness and thoughtful management, you can have a happy and successful overnight stay here.

Johs. Ewaldswej 5, DK-3100 Hornbæk. ©/fax **49-70-00-82.** 12 units, none with bathroom. 715DKK–750DKK ($122–$128/£64–£68) double. Rates include breakfast. V. *In room:* No phone.

Havreholm Slot *Finds*   The most elaborate and best-accessorized hotel in Hornbæk—and our personal favorite—occupies what was originally built in the 1870s as the private home of a lumber baron and paper manufacturer, Valdemar Culmsee. Designed with a mock-fortified tower and vaguely ecclesiastical Victorian-style ornaments, it sits 4km (2½ miles) south of Hornbæk, within a large expanse of privately owned field and forest. Overnight accommodations are in a series of independent bungalows set on the hillsides sloping down to a widening of the river on which the property sits. Each is cozy and attractively decorated in a way befitting an upscale private home, and all units have well-kept bathrooms with shower units.

Klosterrisvej 4, Havreholm DK-3100 Hornbæk. © **49-75-86-00.** Fax 49-75-80-23. www.havreholm.dk. 30 units. 1,850DKK ($315/£167) double; 2,350DKK ($400/£212) suite. AE, DC, MC, V. Take bus from central Hornbæk marked HAVREHOLM. **Amenities:** Restaurant; bar; 2 pools (1 indoor heated); 9-hole golf course; squash course; fitness room; Jacuzzi; sauna; laundry service; dry cleaning; nonsmoking rooms; rooms for those w/limited mobility; solarium. *In room:* TV, dataport, minibar, hair dryer, safe.

WHERE TO DINE

Havreholm Slot *Finds* FRENCH/INTERNATIONAL   Food-savvy yacht owners and their cronies head for the most appealing restaurant in the region, lying in the previously recommended Havreholm Slot hotel, in a grand 19th-century dining room whose original accessories remain for the most part intact. Part of its allure for art historians and Danish nationalists derives from the wall murals commissioned in 1872 by the owner of the house and painted by Danish artist Joakim Skovgaard. The result was an interpretation of the Creation and the Garden of Eden in 12 panels. In addition to the mural-decked dining room, there are three other dining areas, each with a fireplace. A well-trained chef produces the best food in town, with menu items that change with the seasons. The finest examples include a salad of fresh mussels, fresh salmon served with a vegetable terrine, breast of chicken delectably cooked with mushrooms and red-wine sauce, and an especially fine choice, roasted oxtail in red-wine sauce.

Klosterrisvej 4, Havreholm. (℃) **49-75-86-00**. Reservations recommended. Main courses 110DKK–135DKK ($19–$23/ £9.90–£12); fixed-price menu 405DKK ($69/£36). AE, DC, MC, V. Daily noon–2pm and 6–9pm.

Hornbæk Bodega DANISH/INTERNATIONAL   Set near the water, in a century-old building in the center of town, this deservedly popular place resembles an English pub more closely than anything else in Hornbæk. Surrounded by forest green walls, you'll be seated on the black leather upholstery of what used to serve as seats for an old-fashioned English train. No one will mind if you drop in for a drink. But if you're hungry, menu items include lots of American-derived items such as well-stuffed club sandwiches and juicy burgers, and such Danish standards as *frikadeller,* fish filets with shrimp and asparagus, liver pâté with bacon and mushrooms, and fried plaice. Fried plaice is to the Dane what Dover sole is to the English.

A.R. Friisvej 10. (℃) **49-20-00-12**. Main courses 65DKK–129DKK ($11–$22/£5.85–£12). DC, MC, V. June–Aug Sun–Thurs 11am–midnight, Fri–Sat 11am–4am; Sept–May Mon–Fri 5–11pm, Sat–Sun 5pm–2am.

Søstrene Olsen ⭐ DANISH/CONTINENTAL   Imagination is not this restaurant's strong point, but if you want time-tested dishes, prepared to lip-smacking delight, this is the place to dine. Set near the sea, close to the center of town, the building that houses this restaurant was originally constructed in the 1880s as the summer home of a wealthy woman who spent most of her winters in Copenhagen. Today, it's a winner, partly because of the flavorful cuisine that emerges on steaming platters from the hardworking kitchen staff. The well-chosen menu is changed every 2 weeks and is seasonally adjusted. We like the gratin of lobster with an herby green sauce so much it's hard to sample any other dish. But Danish friends recommend the filets of monkfish served with fresh shrimp and "liquefied" spinach, or the mussels marinara, a heaping bowl seasoned just right. Danes delight in the fried eel with mashed potatoes like grandma made, but you may happily settle instead for the tender filet of Danish beef with a savory tomato cream sauce.

Øresundsvej 10. (℃) **49-70-05-50**. Reservations recommended. Main courses 220DKK–260DKK ($37–$44/£20–£23); fixed-price dinner 438DKK ($74/£39). AE, DC, MC, V. Daily noon–4pm and 5:30–9pm. Closed Dec–Mar.

HORNBÆK AFTER DARK

Two of the busiest and most oft-mentioned watering holes in Hornbæk are particularly active during the summer months. Our preferred choice, and the more historic of the two, is **Hornbæk Bodega,** A.R. Friisvej 10 (℃ **49-70-28-88**), a previously recommended restaurant (see above). Set within what was originally conceived as the town's movie theater, it attracts socializing young Danes like a magnet every evening as the dinner service begins to wind down. Come here for a drink of beer or schnapps, or for some dance music if your visit happens to fall on a Friday or Saturday night (10pm to around 5am year-round). When there is dance music, a cover charge of 50DKK ($8.50/£4.50) pays for the first drink. The Bodega's most visible competitor is **Café Paradiso,** Havnevej 3 (℃ **49-70-04-25**). This is a lively and hell-raising English-inspired pub that offers live music every Friday and Saturday night 9pm to 5am, with no cover.

5 Gilleleje   ◆

59km (37 miles) N of Copenhagen; 30km (19 miles) NW of Helsingør

The great philosopher Søren Kierkegaard used Gilleleje as an escape from his world—and so can you. In World War II, it became the port for yet another escape, as Danish Jews fled here from the Nazis. The daring local fishermen in their colorful wooden-hulled fishing boats—sometimes under heavy gunfire—transported the refugees into neutral Sweden.

The northernmost town in Zealand, Gilleleje offers Blue Flag beaches (meaning their waters are not polluted), the leafy glades of the nearby Gribskov forest in the south, and a typical Danish landscape with straw-roofed houses and a large fishing harbor. In all, there are 14km (8⅔ miles) of coastline with plenty of sandy beaches for water lovers of all ages.

Gilleleje Harbor is the center of local life. As soon as dawn breaks, fishing boats of all sizes make their way into North Zealand's largest industrial port, and they can be seen unloading their catch. Look for the fish auction hall to see the night's catch being sold in a unique language understood only by the initiated. There are many smokehouses along the harbor used for smoking the fish.

Later you can go for a walk in the town itself, with its many small and large shops. On Thursdays and Saturdays you can experience a Zealand *mylder* (market), when the town square becomes a marketplace with stalls and booths vying to take your kroner. Horse-drawn carriage rides and street music provide an added bonus.

ESSENTIALS

GETTING THERE   By Train   During the day, two trains an hour arrive from Hillerød (trip time: 30 min.), and there is also frequent service from Helsingør (40 min.).

By Bus   Buses link all the towns of North Zealand. For example, bus no. 340 links Gilleleje with Hornbæk (20 min.), and with Helsingør (50 min.). Bus no. 363 links Gilleleje with Tisvildeleje, but the awkward route takes about an hour. The bus and train depot in Gilleleje adjoin each other. It's only a 5-minute walk from the bus and train stations down to the harbor.

By Car   Follow Route 237 west from Helsingør (see earlier in this chapter).

VISITOR INFORMATION   The **Gilleleje Turistbureau** is at Gilleleje Hovedgade 6F (© **48-30-01-74;** www.gilleleje-turistbureau.dk). June to August, it's open Monday to Saturday 10am to 6pm; September to May, it's open Monday to Friday 10am to 4pm and Saturday 10am to noon.

EXPLORING THE AREA

When you tire of the beaches, take a stroll through the old town, with its narrow streets and well-preserved old houses, no two alike. In the center of town stands the Sladrebænken, or "gossip bench," where you can rest and spread some rumors.

From the harbor you can take the signposted Gilbjergstien path, offering panoramic views over the sea. This will take you to the **Søren Kierkegaard Stone,** a monument to Denmark's most renowned philosopher. As long ago as 1835, he was one of the first visitors to appreciate the beauty and tranquillity of this place. If you want to get existential while standing here, you can repeat his words: "I often stood here and reflected over my past life. The force of the sea and the struggle of the elements made me realize how unimportant I was."

But most summer visitors come here for the beaches. Gilleleje has an unbroken coastline on either side, stretching from Gilbjerg to Kullen, running from Kattegat in the north to Øresund in the southeast. The city has lifeguards posted in several places along the coast. Many of the bathing beaches have modern toilets, little kiosks, and, often, good restaurants. Several beaches also have ramps leading down to the water for the benefit of wheelchair users.

Within a green space adjacent to the sea, an area that forms part of the landscaping around the recommended Gilleleje Museum and the town's public library, stands a bronze statue called *Teka Bashofar Gadol,* a Hebrew phrase meaning "Let the mighty *shofar* proclaim." The statue was donated by a wealthy Israeli patron of the arts, Yul Ofer, and was unveiled in the spring of 1997 to commemorate the flight of Danish Jews from the Nazis in 1943. Gilleleje was the point of departure for some 2,000 Jews who fled to Sweden from the town and other places along the North Coast. Risking their own lives, people in the town and country harbored Jews until they could secure passage on a ship to Sweden.

From a 19th-century fishermen's house to artifacts of the Middle Ages, curators have thrown relics of their past into a somewhat disorganized cultural stew at the **Gilleleje Museum,** Vesterbrogade 56 (© 48-30-16-31). The museum traces the development of the area from the early Middle Ages, although some exhibits go back before recorded history. Panoramas present both shorebirds and migratory birds. The museum, along with Gilleleje's library, is housed in the **Pyramiden,** the Pyramid cultural center where traditional and modern buildings have been integrated into a harmonious whole. There is a fascinating exhibit related to the rescue of the Danish Jews in 1943. The museum is open year-round, Tuesday to Sunday, 1 to 4pm. Admission costs 25DKK ($4.25/£2.25) for adults; children ages 18 and under are free.

Less than a kilometer (about ½ mile) east of town stands the world's first coal-fired lighthouse, **Nakkehoved Østre Fyr,** Fyrvej 20 (© 48-30-16-31). Dating from 1772, it has been restored and turned into a nautical museum. You can drive there—its location 2.5km (1½ miles) east of town is marked from the town center (follow the signs marked NAKKEHOVED ØSTRE FYR). But the more invigorating method of reaching the lighthouse involves walking along a coastal footpath beginning in Gilleleje at Hovedgade on the east side of the fishing museum. It's open only June to September, Wednesday to Monday 1 to 4pm, charging an admission of 10DKK ($1.70/90p) for adults; children ages 11 and under are free.

Fiskerhuset (Old Fisherman's House) and **Skibshallen** (Ship Hall) are at Hovedgade 49 (© 48-30-16-31). "We've always looked to the sea," a local fisherman told us. "It's sustained our lives. Sometimes it took the lives of our brave men, but, even so, the sea and the food it gave us has always made it our faithful friend, although it gets turbulent at times." This is a restored fisherman's dwelling from the 1820s. The Hall presents the history of fishermen in the area from the Middle Ages to the present day, using the fishing hamlets between Hundested and Helsingør as the points of departure. The museum—on the main street—uses a variety of panoramic scenes, models of the boats, and exhibits on trades associated with fishing, to reveal how the industry has dominated local life. The hours and prices are the same as those previously mentioned for the lighthouse.

At Dronningmølle, the **Rudolph Tegnersmuseum** *€,* Museumsvej 19, in Villingerød (© 49-71-91-77; bus: 340), is set 7km (4⅓ miles) southwest of Gilleleje. You can reach it by driving southwest along the coastal route (no. 237) and then following the signs pointing south to the museum from Dronningmølle. Surrounded by heather-covered hills that might remind you of Scotland (although this region of Zealand is often referred to as "Russia"), this museum is devoted to the artist Rudolph Tegner (1873–1950). "So why should I come here to see the works of what's-his-name?" you might ask. Tegner is worth discovering, as his art is provocative with disturbing elements. "He makes you think," the curator told us. "Isn't that reason enough to come here?" At the end of your visit, you'll have to answer the big question for yourself: Was Tegner, born in 1873, the great artist he considered himself to be, an art megalomaniac, a crazy genius, or the world's worst sculptor? Fourteen of his bronzes are displayed in an adjacent sculpture park, 17,000 hectares (42,000 acres) of protected countryside. The museum houses Tegner's collection of 250 sculptures in plaster, clay, bronze, and marble, some of monumental proportions. Selected pieces of furniture from the artist's home and a sarcophagus containing his body make the museum a monument to this individual and controversial avant-garde artist. It's open April 15 to May, Tuesday to Sunday noon to 5pm; June to August, Tuesday to Sunday 9:30am to 5pm; September to the third Sunday in October, Tuesday to Sunday noon to 5pm. It's closed the rest of the year. Admission costs 40DKK ($6.80/£3.60) for adults and is free for children under age 12.

OUTDOOR ACTIVITIES

An array of possibilities in North Zealand await you, none finer than the **Gilleleje Golf Klub** ✪✪, Ferlevej 52 (② **49-71-80-56**), one of Denmark's best golf courses, with 18 holes situated in gently undulating terrain. The course is of very high quality and often used for both national and international tournaments. A bar, restaurant, and golf shop are on-site. Greens fees are 350DKK ($60/£32) from Monday to Friday, rising to 450DKK ($77/£41) on weekends.

Gilleleje Tennis Klub, Øster Allé (② **48-30-22-29**), is a few minutes' walk from the beach. This tennis complex has eight hard courts, plus bathing and club facilities. The cost is 80DKK ($14/£7.20) per hour weekdays, and 110DKK ($19/£9.90) per hour on Saturday and Sunday.

Many other sporting possibilities are available—the tourist office (see "Visitor Information," above) has full details. The use of jet skis is prohibited, but the coast of Rågeleje is ideal for windsurfing. The beaches of Gilleleje and Dronningmølle also attract windsurfers, although you must exercise caution to avoid swimmers. If you'd like to go horseback riding across heath and sand dunes, contact the **Enggården Ridecenter,** Hellebjergvej 27, Dronningmølle (② **49-70-46-60**).

SHOPPING

There are more shops in Gilleleje, per capita, than virtually any other small town in Zealand. At least part of that is attributable to the discretionary income of many of the well-heeled vacationers who flock here, or perhaps it's the tradition of buying and selling antiques that has been a part of the civic consciousness here since the 1960s. In any event, a walk up and down the length of the **Vesterbrogade** will reveal lots of small boutiques whose collective inventories might enrich the aesthetics of your home or office.

J.S. Antiques, Ferlevej 55–57, Ferle (② **49-71-79-79**), is one of the biggest and most visible antiques stores in town. Another store that has garnered a devoted clientele from all around the world because of its knowledge of antique Danish porcelain, especially Royal Copenhagen, is **Antik Ulla,** Vesterbrogade 46 (② **48-30-07-58**).

Know before you begin your barnstorming of Gilleleje's antiques stores that opening hours are relaxed to the point of being almost chaotic. In *most* cases, shops open daily except Monday and Tuesday, roughly 11am to 4 or 5pm, depending on business and the mood of the shopkeeper. Most, however, maintain extensions of the phone numbers listed that ring in their homes, so a call in advance will sometimes do the trick in getting a shop to open.

WHERE TO STAY

Hotel Strand   If you were a bathing beauty who arrived in your bulky swimming costume for a dip in 1896, you wouldn't recognize this long-established hotel today. It's kept abreast of the times, but in doing so has lost a lot of its original architectural adornment. Nonetheless, if you're not a romantic, you'll find a well-managed hotel with functionally furnished, yet comfortable, rooms. Most of the fairly spacious bedrooms contain private bathrooms with showers; only a handful of occupants have to use the corridor bathrooms. Bookings are heavy in summer so reserve well in advance. The Strand is aptly named, as it lies only a 2-minute walk from the sands and the old fishing harbor.

Vesterbrogade 4D, DK-3250 Gilleleje. © 48-30-05-12. Fax 48-30-18-59. 25 units, 22 with bathroom. 990DKK ($168/£89) double with bathroom; 820DKK ($139/£74) double without bathroom; 1,100DKK ($187/£99) suite. Rates include breakfast. AE, DC, MC, V. **Amenities:** Breakfast room; bar; lounge; laundry service; dry cleaning; nonsmoking rooms. *In room:* TV, hair dryer.

WHERE TO DINE

Brasseriet *❀* DANISH   The setting is evocative: a yellow-brick building moving into its second century. Once it was a general store serving the fishing industry at the harbor. Today its hardworking staff attracts an array of visitors who come for the good-tasting food but like to avoid more formal dining choices. As so many Danish restaurants "go French," the owners here claim there's nothing wrong with serving their own version of regional food. Therefore, you get such classics as plaice sautéed in butter and served with new potatoes, chopped parsley, and browned butter. This is perhaps the most frequently served fish dish in the country. For something more exotic, order the steaming mussels flavored with saffron and fresh herbs. Each night a seafood kebab offers the market-fresh catch of the day studded with shrimp and scallops. The meat eater can take delight in the beautifully marbled and tender rib-eye steak. If you'd like to dine light at lunch, you can order *smørrebrød* along with freshly made salads.

Nordre Havnevej 3. © 48-30-21-30. Reservations recommended. Lunch *smørrebrød* 48DKK–98DKK ($8.15–$17/£4.30–£8.80); main courses 158DKK–240DKK ($27–$41/£14–£22); fixed-price menus 248DKK–288DKK ($42–$49/£22–£26). AE, DC, MC, V. Daily noon–4pm and 6–9:30pm.

Fyrkroen *❀* DANISH   When the lights go on in the harbor and the cool (often chilly) breezes blow in from Sweden, there is no more romantic place to be than sitting at a table at this first-class restaurant. You not only get panoramic views of the sea but can enjoy the restaurant's historic charm. Back in 1772 the setting was a lighthouse. A low-slung, white-painted stone building was erected adjacent to the lighthouse for the restaurant itself. If the weather is right, try for a table on the alfresco terrace or else retreat indoors to enjoy the nautical decor of ships and the sailors who manned them.

Using market-fresh ingredients, the chef gives each dish a personal stamp. The kitchen still prepares homemade soups every day, none better than the shrimp. You might also start with some delectable smoked salmon or a freshly made salad with crisp lettuce. The steaks are tender to the fork and the palate, but most diners opt instead for such freshly caught fish as halibut, salmon, and perch, which, more or less, can be cooked to your specifications.

Fyrvejen 29. © **48-30-02-25.** Reservations recommended, especially when weather is clear. Main courses 128DKK–178DKK ($22–$30/£12–£16). DC, MC, V. May–Oct daily noon–9pm; Nov–Dec and Mar–Apr Thurs–Sun noon–9pm. Closed Jan–Feb. From Gilleleje, drive 4km (2½ miles) west, following signs to Hornbæk.

6 Tisvildeleje

59km (37 miles) NW of Copenhagen; 25km (16 miles) W of Helsingør; 18km (11 miles) NW of Hillerød; 71km (44 miles) N of Roskilde

If heather-covered hills, gloriously wide sandy beaches backed by low dunes, and a forest of dramatic wind-tormented trees is your idea of a good time, make it to the seaside village of Tisvildeleje. We find it the most idyllic along the coast, the perfect place for a writer to complete that novel (more likely a screenplay these days). Tisvildeleje—the largest settlement in the region known as Tisvilde—opens onto the broadest stretch of white sandy beaches in Zealand, although the waters, even in July, will be too cold for you if you're accustomed to Florida-like temperatures. The best beach is less than 1.5km (1 mile) west of the center of the resort. It has a changing room and toilets and also a spacious parking lot.

People also come here for walks through **Tisvilde Hegn,** a windswept forest of heather-covered hills and trees twisted by the cold Nordic winds.

ESSENTIALS
GETTING THERE   By Train   From Hillerød trains run to Tisvildeleje once an hour during the day (trip time: 30 min.).

VISITOR INFORMATION   Tisvilde Turistinformation, Banevej 8 (© **48-70-74-51**), is open Monday to Saturday 9am to 4:30pm and Sunday 10am to 3pm, but only from June to August.

GETTING AROUND   Bike rentals are available at **Servicehjørnet,** Hovedgade 54 (© **48-70-80-13**). You can rent one for 80DKK ($14/£7.20) per day.

EXPLORING THE AREA
To the west of the center, running alongside Tisvilde Hegn, one of Denmark's largest forests, is a 1.2km (¾-mile) stretch of white sandy beaches lapped by clean salty waters and fringed by dunes and woodland. The surroundings here are exceptionally clean and unspoiled. Volunteers work to see that this whole area of coastline is the most thoroughly inspected and litter-free in Denmark. A blue flag flies over the beach, meaning that the waters are not polluted.

In town you can visit **Tibirke Kirke,** Tibirke Kirkevej (© **48-70-77-85**), which is open Monday to Saturday 8am to 4pm, with Sunday devoted to a church service. Admission is free. This church was probably built around 1120 on a pagan site. In the latter part of the 14th century, it was enlarged and the nave provided with arches. At that time, the small Roman windows were replaced with larger Gothic ones. In the middle of the 15th century a larger choir also replaced the original one. The tower was built during the first half of the 16th century, but has been reconstructed many times since. During a period of terrible sand drifts, the church was laid waste. But it was eventually restored, and in 1740 a baroque altarpiece was added, with a picture by J. F. Krügell depicting the Last Supper.

At the foot of the church is a spring that may have been the place where pilgrims came in olden days.

Tisvilde Hegn is enchanting and usually windblown. The forest is crossed with many trails, our favorite being a dirt path south to Troldeskoven, a distance of about 2.5km (1.5 miles). Nordic winds have turned the trees into "sculptures" of rather haunting shapes—one is called "Witch Wood." The tourist office (see "Visitor Information," above) will provide trail maps.

SHOPPING

Every Saturday between June and September, 10am to 2pm, a large, lively flea market, **Tisvilde Loppemarked** (Tisvilde Flea Market), is held at Birkepladsen, in front of Tisvildeleje's railway station. This is the time locals empty their attics, divesting themselves of things they might have inherited or acquired and don't really want. There's also a collection of crafts and, in some cases, used clothing.

WHERE TO STAY

Kildegaard *(Finds)* It's down-home and friendly, a most comfortable place to stay at a reasonable price. This is an engaging and likable small hotel whose owners, the Tetzschner family, work hard to create an intimate, cozy environment for guests who tend to return year after year. The centerpiece of the complex is a century-old farmhouse whose space is supplemented with outbuildings. Guests spend their days swimming at the nearby beach, playing volleyball or sleeping in hammocks strung across the garden, and enjoying a menagerie of family pets. Rooms are unpretentious and summery, and each is outfitted with a mishmash of simple contemporary furniture. Dinner platters are served only to residents who request them in advance. The establishment is located in the heart of town, a short walk from the tourist information office.

Hovedgaden 52, DK-3220 Tisvildeleje. © 48-70-71-53. 27 units, none with bathroom. 685DKK ($116/£62) double. Rates include breakfast. No credit cards. **Amenities:** Dining room; lounge. *In room:* No phone.

Tisvildeleje Strand Hotel If your needs are a little grander than Kildegaard can provide, then check into what locals call "the Strand." This is one of the few structures in Tisvildeleje that preceded the building boom of the 1920s, when wealthy Copenhagen families bought up much of the seafront and constructed summerhouses. Conceived in 1897 as a grocery store and livery stable, it has been rebuilt and expanded many times until it reached its present form: four interconnected buildings encircling a verdant courtyard and a massive chestnut tree. Don't expect a lot of amenities to amuse and entertain you, as the focus is on beach life (the sea is only 90m/295 ft. away) and walks in the nearby forest. Rooms are functionally comfortable, summery, and unpretentious, and eight have neatly kept bathrooms with shower units. The in-house restaurant is good and international in its tastes (see "Where to Dine," below).

Hovedgaden 75, DK-3220 Tisvildeleje. © 48-70-71-19. Fax 48-70-71-77. 29 units, 8 with bathroom. 695DKK ($118/£63) double without bathroom; 795DKK–1,095DKK ($135–$186/£72–£99) double with bathroom. Rates include breakfast. MC, V. **Amenities:** Restaurant; bar; lounge. *In room:* No phone.

WHERE TO DINE

Bio-Bistro *(Value)* DANISH/INTERNATIONAL "We will feed you well, and at a good price, but we don't expect you to call the gourmet magazines if you eat with us." That was a waiter's candid appraisal of this well-respected dinner-only bistro next to a movie theater. It offers food that is praised by the owners of various B&Bs in town without restaurants of their own. In a setting that's vaguely reminiscent of the kind of brasserie you might expect in Paris or Lyons, you can order good-tasting lunches (sandwiches, burgers, croque-monsieur), but only during the peak of midsummer. Like many regional restaurants, the bistro serves mainly French and Danish dishes—and does so rather well, in our view. The chicken with wine sauce is always a dependable choice, but we find the salmon with a mousseline sauce even more alluring. The tender, well-cooked steaks served here are a good advertisement for Danish beef.

Hovegården 38. ℭ **48-70-41-91**. Main courses 100DKK–235DKK ($17–$40/£9–£21). MC, V. June–Aug daily 6–10pm; Sept–May Fri–Sat 6–10pm.

Tisvildeleje Strand Hotel ℱ INTERNATIONAL   This is the most formal choice in town, and the cuisine has imagination and a discreetly exotic touch. Set in a big-windowed area of the previously recommended hotel, this brasserie-like eatery is the most cosmopolitan and internationally conscious restaurant in town. About the only thing that's Danish here is the clientele; menu options include selections from Thailand, the Philippines, Australia, and France, and all of the well-crafted dishes use very fresh ingredients. Expect an array of stir-fried fish and vegetable dishes, lemon grass soup and both green and red curry dishes from Thailand, satay skewers of beef and chicken served with peanut sauce, and, whenever the chef feels particularly French, an old-fashioned coq au vin or pepper steak.

Hovegården 75. ℭ **48-70-71-19**. Reservations recommended. Main courses 75DKK–175DKK ($13–$30/£6.75–£16); 2-course fixed-price menu 185DKK ($31/£17); 3-course fixed-price menu 220DKK ($37/£20). AE, MC, V. July to late Aug daily 11:30am–10pm. Closed Sept–June.

7 Roskilde ℱℱ

32km (20 miles) W of Copenhagen

If you have only 1 day for North Zealand, we'd skip the highly touted and touristy "Hamlet's Castle" and make the trek to Roskilde instead. It's that special.

Next to Copenhagen, this is Zealand's second-largest town, with one of its longest histories, dating back to 998. It's true that much of this thriving town is devoted to industry, but there are many remnants of its illustrious past as a royal residence in the 10th century and the spiritual capital not only of Denmark but of Northern Europe in the 12th century. The Vikings used Roskilde Fjord to sail in from the open sea after their conquests.

Royal tombs, Viking boats, and one of northern Europe's biggest open-air rock festivals keep the visitors coming.

Roskilde, once a great ecclesiastical seat, was Denmark's leading city until the mid–15th century. Today the twin spires of **Roskilde Cathedral** stand out from the Danish landscape like elegantly tapered beacons. These towers are the first landmark you see when approaching the city that celebrated its 1,000th anniversary in 1998.

Roskilde may be centuries past its peak, but it is no sleepy museum town. It's filled with a dynamic student community, boutique-filled walking streets, several landmarks and major sights, and a population of more than 52,000 people who call themselves *Roskildenser.*

Toward the end of the first millennium (A.D.), the Vikings settled the area, drawn, no doubt, by its sinuous coastline, where they could launch their ships. In 1957 divers in the Roskilde Fjord came upon shards of wood and reported their findings. Their discovery turned out to be bigger than anyone imagined. Here, sunken and mud-pre-served, were five Viking ships that presumably had been put there to block the passage of enemy ships.

Archaeologists began the painstaking job of building a water-tight dam and draining that section of the fjord, while keeping the chunks of splinters of wood wet enough so as not to cause them to disintegrate. Splinter by splinter they began the reconstruction and reassembly of the boats—a process that continues today. You can see their efforts on display at the **Viking Ship Museum** (see below), a modern museum that contains the five ancient ships.

Between A.D. 990 and A.D. 1000, Roskilde's prominence grew, becoming the home of the royal residence. By the 11th century, a Catholic church and a Bishop's Seat resided at Roskilde, which was to remain Denmark's capital until the Reformation in 1536.

At that time all the parish churches were abolished and the Catholic hierarchy disappeared. The government and the monarchy moved to Copenhagen. Nonetheless, at its peak, Roskilde's importance was expressed in its architecture. By 1150, it was surrounded by an embankment and a moat, inside of which stood 12 churches and a cathedral. In 1170, Bishop Absalon built a new church on the site where Harald Bluetooth had erected his church 2 centuries before. Though it took 300 years to construct, and was subsequently burned, destroyed, ravaged, and rebuilt, Absalon's cathedral laid the foundation for the existing Roskilde Cathedral or Domkirche, which today is a UNESCO World Heritage Site.

ESSENTIALS

GETTING THERE   By Train   Trains leave three times an hour from Copenhagen's Central Railroad Station on the 35-minute trip to Roskilde.

By Bus   Buses depart from Roskilde several times daily from Copenhagen's Central Railroad Station.

By Car   Take the E-21 express highway west from Copenhagen.

VISITOR INFORMATION   The **Roskilde-Egnens Turistbureau,** Gullandsstræde 15 (© **46-31-65-65**), provides pamphlets about the town and the surrounding area. The office is open August 23 to March 31 Monday to Thursday 9am to 5pm, Friday 9am to 4pm, and Saturday 10am to 1pm; April 1 to June 27 Monday to Friday 9am to 5pm and Saturday 10am to 1pm; June 28 to August 22 Monday to Friday 9am to 6pm and Saturday 10am to 2pm. While at the tourist office inquire about a Roskilde card, which costs 185DKK ($31/£17) adults, 95DKK ($16/£8.55) children 10 to 15, and free for children under 10. The card admits you to the 10 attractions in the area and is valid for 7 days from the date of issue. Without the card, it would cost 439DKK ($75/£40) to visit these same attractions.

SPECIAL EVENTS   The **Roskilde Festival** ★★ (© **46-36-66-13;** www.roskilde-festival.dk) is one of Northern Europe's best outdoor concerts. We first discovered it when we journeyed here to see David Bowie. It is held June 29 to July 2 on a large grassy field, attracting fans of rock and techno music. To get information on the festival—dates and performances—call the above number or contact the Roskilde-Egnens Turistbureau (see above).

SEEING THE SIGHTS

Roskilde Domkirke ★★★   There's no church in Copenhagen, or anywhere else in Denmark for that matter, to rival this towering edifice. This cathedral made Roskilde

Roskilde

the spiritual capital of Denmark and northern Europe. Today it rises out of a modest townscape like a mirage—a cathedral several times too big for the town surrounding it. Construction started in 1170 when Absalon was bishop of Roskilde. Work continued into the 13th century, and the building's original Romanesque features gave way to an early Gothic facade. The twin towers weren't built until the 14th century.

Today the cathedral's beauty goes beyond a single architectural style, providing almost a crash course in Danish architecture. Although damaged by a fire in 1968, the cathedral has been restored, including its magnificent altarpiece.

The Domkirke is the final abode of 38 Danish monarchs whose tombs are here, ranging from the modest to the eccentric. Not surprisingly, Christian IV, the builder king who was instrumental in the construction of nearly all of Copenhagen's famous towers and castles, is interred in a grandiose chapel here with a massive sculpture of

Czarina's Remains Returned to Russia

A historical footnote occurred in Denmark at the Roskilde Cathedral in 2006. In a bizarre episode, the remains of Czarina Maria Feodorovna, the mother of Russia's last emperor, made her final journey from Roskilde to St. Petersburg. Her saga began at birth in 1847 when she was born Princess Dagmar, the daughter of Denmark's King Christian IX and Queen Louise. She was later to marry Alexander and convert to the Russian Orthodox faith. She had six children, one of whom was Nicholas II, who became czar in 1894 and was executed a year after the Bolshevik Revolution. Fleeing from the Imperial capital, Maria Feodorovna made it to the Crimean Peninsula, where a British navy ship took her to London. She continued to Copenhagen, where she lived until her death in 1928. Buried at Roskilde, she rested along with other Danish royalty. In September of 2006 she was transferred to St. Petersburg, where she was reburied with relatives in the Peter and Paul Cathedral. Until the day she died, she refused to believe that her husband and children had been executed in 1918, 16 months after Czar Nicholas had abdicated the throne. "She is reunited with her beloved family once again," said Dimitry Romanoc, an 80-year-old retired bank clerk and a distant relative.

himself in combat, a bronze likeness by the Danish sculptor Bertel Thorvaldsen. In humble contrast is a newer addition, from 1972, of the simple brick chapel of King Frederik IX, which stands outside the church. This chapel is octagonal in shape and decorated with hand-painted tiles designed by the architects Johannes and Inger Exner and Vilhelm Wohlert. Other notable tombs include the white marble sarcophagus of Queen Margrethe I.

In King Christian I's Chapel, which dates from the 15th century, there is a column marked with the heights of several kings. The tallest monarch was Christian I, at 2.1m (6 ft. 9 in.). This, no doubt, was an exaggeration, as his skeleton measures only 1.9m (6 ft. 2 in.). A large, bright cupola graces the late-18th- and early-19th-century chapel of King Frederik V. Note also the Gothic choir stalls, each richly and intricately carved with details from both the Old and New Testaments.

The gilded winged altar in the choir was made in Antwerp in the 1500s and was originally intended for Frederiksborg Castle. Pictures on the wings of the altar depict scenes from the life of Jesus, ranging from the Nativity to the Crucifixion. Following the fire, the renowned artist Anna Thommesen created a new altar cloth.

For us, the most charming aspect of the cathedral is its early-16th-century clock poised on the interior south wall above the entrance. A tiny St. George on horseback marks the hour by charging a dragon. The beast howls, echoing through the cavernous church, causing Peter Doever, "the Deafener," to sound the hour. A terrified Kirsten Kiemer, "the Chimer," shakes in fright but pulls herself together to strike the quarters.

Insider's tip: Free concerts on the cathedral's pipe organ, which dates from the 1500s, are often presented at 8pm on Thursdays in summer. They are featured less frequently throughout the rest of the year. Check with the tourist office.

Domkirkestræde 10. ℂ 46-35-16-24. www.roskildedomkirke.dk. Admission 25DKK ($4.25/£2.25) adults, 15DKK ($2.55/£1.35) children 10–15, free for children under 10. Apr–Sept Mon–Fri 9am–4:45pm, Sat 9am–noon, Sun 12:30–4:45pm; Oct–Mar Tues–Sat 10am–3:45pm, Sun 12:30–3:45pm. Bus: 602, 603, or 604.

Vikingeskibshallen (Viking Ship Museum) ★★

If the cathedral weren't reason enough to visit Roskilde, the Viking ships displayed here certainly are. These types of ships sailed to England, to Hamburg on the German coast, and—dare we speculate?—even to the east coast of North America. Displayed here are five vessels found in Roskilde Fjord and painstakingly pieced together from countless fragments of wreckage. It's presumed that the craft were deliberately sunk about 20km (12 miles) north of Roskilde at the narrowest section of the fjord to protect the settlement from a sea attack. The discovery was relatively unpublicized until 1957, when the Danish National Museum carried out a series of underwater excavations.

A merchant cargo ship used by the Vikings, a small ferry or fishing boat, and a Danish Viking warship similar to the ones portrayed in the Bayeux Tapestry are also displayed, and a longship—a Viking man-of-war that terrorized European coasts—was also discovered. Copies of Viking jewelry may be purchased in the museum gift shop, and there's also a cafeteria.

To understand the attraction better, you can see a short film, *The Ships of the Vikings,* about the excavation and preservation of the ships and the building and navigation of *Roar Ege,* a Viking ship replica.

In 1997 the Viking Ship Museum opened a museum harbor for its collection of Nordic vessels, including *Roar Ege,* plus another Viking ship replica, *Helge Ask.* The museum's restored sloop, *Ruth,* is also moored here. And workshops where you can try your hand at old maritime crafts, such as rope- and sail-making, woodworking, and other activities, are located opposite the Boat Yard.

Vindebader 12. ℂ 46-30-02-00. www.vikingeskibsmuseet.dk. Admission May–Sept 80DKK ($14/£7.20) adults, 200DKK ($34/£18) family ticket; Oct–Apr 50DKK ($8.50/£5.40) adults, 130DKK ($22/£12) family ticket; free for children under 17. Daily 10am–5pm. Bus: 216 or 607.

Roskilde Museum

We didn't give this place any stars, and no one will beat you if you skip it, but we always find something intriguing here. Take the strange-looking pictures that satirist Gustav Wied took of his family, for example, or what passed for children's toys in the Middle Ages. Located 90m (295 ft.) from the Town Square, this museum, in a former merchant's house, features exhibits of the celebrated Hedebo embroidery, and regional costumes. Displays also include an *aurochs* (an ancient European ox) skeleton, a unique Viking tomb, and a large number of medieval finds from the town. The museum also has a grocer's courtyard, with the shop in operation.

Skt. Ols Gade 15–18. ℂ 46-31-65-00. www.roskildemuseum.dk. Admission 30DKK ($5.10/£2.70) adults, free for children under 12. Daily 11am–4pm. Closed Dec 24–25 and Dec 31–Jan 1. Bus: 601, 602, 603, or 605.

Museet for Samtidskunst (Museum of Contemporary Art)

This is the artistic center of Roskilde. Invariably, there's always a presentation of interest to "culture vultures." In a beautiful palace from the 18th century, this museum of modern art has frequently changing exhibitions, together with performances, films, and dance and classical-music concerts. It also houses a screening room presenting programs with Danish and foreign artists. "The Palace Collections" are also housed here, displaying objets d'art and paintings that rich Roskilde merchants and their families collected in the 18th and 19th centuries. Such local fat cats as the Brunns and the Borchs amassed an astonishing array of art and antiques on display today.

Stændertorvet 3D. ℂ **46-31-65-70**. www.mfsk.dk. Admission 30DKK ($5.10/£2.70) adults, 15DKK ($2.55/£1.35) seniors, free for children under 10. Tues–Fri 11am–5pm; Sat–Sun noon–4pm. Bus: 601, 602, 603, or 605.

MORE ATTRACTIONS

The **St. Jørgensbjerg quarter** was originally a small fishing village, and a number of old, half-timbered houses, some with thatched roofs, remain. These houses cluster around **Skt. Jørgensbjerg Kirke,** Kirkegade, which stands on the top of a hill with a panoramic view of Roskilde Fjord. This is one of the oldest and best-preserved stone buildings in Denmark. The nave and choir of the church date from the beginning of the 12th century, but the walled-up north door is even older, possibly dating from 1040. Slender billets, found only in wooden churches, are in the corners of the church and in the center of the nave. A model of a *kogge,* a medieval merchant vessel, has been engraved in a wall. The church is open only June 22 to August 31, Monday to Friday 10am to noon. To get here from Roskilde, take bus no. 607 toward Boserup.

The same bus will deliver you to **Skt. Ibs Kirke** ("The Church of St. James"), Skt. Ibs Vej (ℂ **46-35-29-66**), also in the north of Roskilde. Although no longer in use as a church, this ruin dates from around 1100. Abolished as a church in 1808, it was later a field hospital and a merchant's warehouse. Regrettably, the merchant destroyed the tower, the chancel, the porch, and the church vaults of this medieval relic, though he spared the nave. It is open for visits only April 4 to October 17, from sunup to sundown.

NEARBY ATTRACTIONS

Ledreborg Park Og Slot ✦   One of the last remaining aristocratic families of Denmark, the Holstein-Ledreborgs, still live in this castle and are willing to share their treasures with you in fair weather. A baroque manor house and French/English-style park 7km (4⅓ miles) southwest of Roskilde and 43km (27 miles) west of Copenhagen, Ledreborg is one of the best-preserved monuments in Denmark. Built by Johan Ludwig Holstein, a minister to Christian IV, the Holstein-Ledreborg family has owned this 33-room house with a landscaped garden and 88-hectare (217-acre) park for eight generations. Between 1741 and 1757 it was turned from a farmhouse into a baroque manor. Inside are a collection of 17th- and 18th-century antiques and a gallery of Danish paintings. It's approached by a 6km (3¾-mile) alley of lime trees, some 2 centuries old. Near the manor is a grave dating from the late Stone Age, approximately 3000 B.C.

Allé 2, Lejre. ℂ **46-48-00-38**. Admission 75DKK ($13/£6.75) adults, 45DKK ($7.65/£4.05) children 3–14. Mid-June to Aug daily 11am–5pm; May to mid-June and Sept Sun 11am–5pm. Closed Oct–Apr. From Copenhagen's Central Railroad Station, take the direct train to Lejre, which leaves hourly and takes 35 min.; from Lejre station, take the 3-min. bus 233 to the castle and park. From Roskilde, there are frequent buses to Lejre, followed by the short bus ride to the castle and park. Combined ticket for Ledreborg Park Og Slot and Lejre Research Center (see below) 130DKK ($22/£12) adults, 70DKK ($12/£6.30) children.

Lejre Research Center ✦ *Kids*   Imagine being able to wander back into a village reconstructed from the Iron Age. Not only that, but getting to see workers, wearing the costumes of the era, going about their daily chores. You're even invited to take part in these activities. Such a thing is possible if you head here and have some 2 hours to spare. Eight kilometers (5 miles) west of Roskilde, this archaeological research center, Lejre Research Center, is the site of a reconstructed Iron Age community on 10 hectares (25 acres) of woodland. The main feature is clay-walled and thatch houses built with tools just as they were some 2,000 years ago. Staffers re-create the physical working conditions as they thatch Iron Age huts, work fields with *ards* (oxen-pulled plows), weave, and make pottery by an open fire. They also sail in dugout canoes, grind corn with a stone, and bake in direct fire. Visitors can take part in these activities. Jutland black pottery is produced here, and handicrafts and books are for sale at the gift shop. There are tables where you can enjoy a picnic lunch.

Slagealléen 2, Lejre. © **46-48-08-78**. www.lejre-center.dk. Admission 95DKK ($16/£8.55) adults, 55DKK ($9.35/£4.95) children 3–14. Tues–Fri 10am–4pm; Sat–Sun 11am–5pm. Closed mid-Sept to Apr. Take the train from Copenhagen to Lejre, then bus 233 to the center. From Roskilde, there are frequent buses to Lejre; then take bus 233.

A BOAT TOUR OF THE ROSKILDE FJORD

Roskilde Fjord 𝕲𝕲 is one of the longest and largest in Denmark. A sail will take you along the same watery road that Viking ships used to traverse. The shores of this narrow fjord are peppered with tranquil landscapes set against a backdrop of rolling hills. Forests, windswept reeds, low-lying meadows filled with Danish cows, and little villages along the way greet you as you sail along.

You'll get a leisurely waterside view of the southern parts of Roskilde Fjord by participating in one of the frequent warm-weather tours offered aboard the *Sagafjord,* a steamer from the 1950s whose profile evokes a paddle-wheel steamer on the Mississippi. You can opt for either a lunch or a dinner cruise (2–2½ hr., and 3½ hr., respectively), or a shorter mid-afternoon cruise (90 min.), depending on your schedule. Regardless of what you select, you'll pay a base rate of 89DKK ($15/£8), after which your (optional) food costs are extra. Platters of food aboard the lunch cruise cost 85DKK to 245DKK ($14–$42/£7.65–£22) each. Evening fixed-price 3-course menus cost 310DKK to 405DKK ($53–$69/£28–£36) each. Tours are conducted only April to October. They operate daily in June, July, August, and September, and, depending on the schedule, 3 to 5 days a week in April, May, and October. Cruises depart from a prominently signposted (SAGAFJORD TOURS) pier in Roskilde Harbor. For schedules, information, and reservations, contact **Rederiet Sagafjord,** St. Valbyvej 154 (© **46-75-64-60**).

SHOPPING

The best streets for shopping are the pedestrian thoroughfares **Algade** and **Skomagergade.** Of these, we find that Skomagergade has the best shops. From the 12th century, its name, which literally means "shoemaker street," was where the cobblers of Roskilde plied their trade in the Middle Ages.

At either end of the street, a **triskelion** within a circle has been placed in the pavement. The symbol is three curved lines radiating from the center. It comes from the coins struck in Roskilde from 1018 to 1047. Today this silver coin has been re-created by one of the goldsmiths of Roskilde and is sold as a piece of jewelry at the tourist office (see "Visitor Information," above).

The best time for shoppers to be in Roskilde is for the **market days** every Wednesday and Saturday morning (go after 8am). Fresh fruit and vegetables of the season are sold from stalls on Stændertorvet, the main square by the cathedral, along with many stalls hawking fresh fish and Danish cheese. You can purchase the makings of a picnic, along with beautiful pieces of jewelry, and even mugs and pottery. Vendors also peddle a number of well-made children's clothes.

Roskilde also abounds in specialty shops, notably **Bydr. Lützhøfts,** Købmandsgård, Ringstedgade 6–8 (© **46-35-00-61**), a cozy old grocer's shop selling herring and other delicacies across the counter. The interior of the shop looks as it did during the 1920s, and goods for sale are typical of that era. The building at Ringstedgade 8 is a butcher's shop, **Slagterbutikken O. Lunds,** selling goods made according to recipes from about 1920. You can also explore the merchant's yard with 18th- and 19th-century buildings. Sometimes exhibitions are staged here—for example, depictions of merchants and trade in Roskilde over the past 1,000 years. This shop is open Monday to Friday 11am to 5pm and Saturday 10am to 2pm. Even if you don't purchase anything, this is one of the town's tourist attractions.

The town also has very excellent buys in handicrafts. Head first for **Glasgallerjet**★, Skt. Ibs Vej 12 (© **46-35-65-36**), a former gasworks near the harbor that now houses the open workshop of a glass blower. Here, the glass blower, who displays marvelous skill, shapes the most beautiful glasses, dishes, vases, and other items. Spectators are able to watch the transformation of a lump of melted glass into a beautiful Danish handicraft on sale at the gallery.

An unusual selection of crafts is found at **Jeppe,** Skomagergade 33 (© **46-36-94-35**), which is run collectively by 20 craftspeople from Roskilde and its environs. They make and sell their own crafts. These are definitely nonfactory goods, and exhibitions are always changing.

SWIMMING

You can swim both in- and outdoors in the Roskilde area, although outdoors might be a bit cool if you're not a Dane. There are several small bathing beaches along Roskilde Fjord, notably **Vigen Strandpark,** directly north of the town. Here you'll find a sandy beach with a jetty, set against the backdrop of green salt meadows. The blue flag flying at this beach means the waters are not polluted.

If you'd like to swim indoors, head for the **Roskilde Badet,** Bymarken 37 (© **46-31-63-63;** bus: 601 toward Vindinge from the center). Admission is 25DKK ($4.25/£2.25) adults, 13DKK ($2.20/£1.20) children 5 to 15, free for children under 5. Hours are Monday and Wednesday 1 to 6pm, Tuesday and Thursday 1 to 8:30pm, Friday 1 to 6:30pm, Saturday 7am to 4pm, and Sunday 8am to 1:30pm. Closed July 1 to 25.

WHERE TO STAY

Hotel Prindsen ★   Although surpassed by the Scandic (see below), the Prindsen has been an enduring favorite for 100 years. We still stay here on occasion and find that it has kept up with the times, even though its foundations date from 1695. Today it offers medium-size, smartly furnished rooms with bathrooms containing tub/shower combinations. Though a bit small, all in all the rooms are cozy nests. We prefer the five rooms on the top floor that have a view of the fjord. All the guest rooms in the newer wing are decorated in a Nordic style with wooden floors. Those in the older section are furnished in a more classic style. Take your choice, as rooms in both sections are equally comfortable. Our favorite pocket of posh here is the extremely spacious and elegant Hans Christian Andersen suite.

Algade 13, DK-4000, Roskilde. © 46-30-91-00. Fax 46-30-91-50. www.hotelprindsen.dk. 77 units. 1,325DKK–1,525DKK ($225–$259/£119–£137) double; from 2,150DKK ($366/£194) suite. Rates include breakfast. AE, DC, MC, V. Bus: 602 or 603. **Amenities:** Restaurant; bar; sauna; 24-hr. room service; laundry service; dry cleaning; nonsmoking rooms. *In room:* TV, dataport, minibar, hair dryer, trouser press.

Scandic Hotel Roskilde ★   If you don't mind being housed outside the historic core, this chain-run hotel from 1989 is the best in town if you like modern decor and good facilities. If you're seeking a more romantic atmosphere, head for Svogerslev Kro (see below). Rooms are average size, typically furnished, and very comfortable, with medium-size bathrooms containing shower units. The hotel also has a good restaurant serving Danish and international dishes, plus a bar. It's on the ring road less than a kilometer (about ½ mile) south of the green belt, Roskilde Ring, on the southern outskirts of the city.

Søndre Ringvej 33, DK-4000 Roskilde. ☎ **46-32-46-32**. Fax 46-32-02-32. www.scandic-hotels.com. 98 units. 726DKK–1,510DKK ($123–$257/£65–£136) double; 1,090DKK–2,190DKK ($185–$372/£98–£197) suite. Rates include breakfast. AE, DC, MC, V. Free parking. **Amenities:** Restaurant; bar; fitness center; sauna; children's playroom; babysitting; laundry service; dry cleaning; nonsmoking rooms; rooms for those w/limited mobility; solarium. *In room:* TV, minibar, hair dryer, trouser press, iron/ironing board.

Svogerslev Kro ☆ *Finds* If you've seen those touristy pictures of a thatched-roof Danish inn, with timeworn and exposed wooden beams, and want to stay in such a place yourself, head here as we so often do. We like to wander around the little village of Svogerslev at night, far removed from the bustle of Copenhagen. Since 1727 this old-time inn has been welcoming visitors who make the 4km (2½-mile) journey west of Roskilde's center. Rooms are medium size (some are a bit small), decorated in modern Danish styling, and well maintained. Many open onto the inn's garden and come equipped with tub/shower combinations. The well-respected kitchen serves open-faced sandwiches at lunch and an array of international dishes at night, including regional specialties, with main courses 98DKK to 210DKK ($17–$36/£8.80–£19). If you're adventurous, request the fried eel; if not, you might happily settle for the breast of guinea fowl with fresh herbs and a red-pepper cream sauce. The chef's stew is made with bacon, onions, and mushrooms, in a paprika sauce. You can always count on baked salmon and some good steak dishes. After a good night's rest under the eaves, you'll be fortified to continue with us on our journey through Denmark.

Hovedgaden 45, Svogerslev, DK-4000 Roskilde. ☎ **46-38-30-05**. Fax 46-38-30-14. www.svogerslevkro.dk. 18 units. 875DKK ($149/£79) double. Rates include breakfast. AE, DC, MC, V. Bus: 602 with hourly connections to the town center. **Amenities:** Restaurant; bar; laundry service; dry cleaning. *In room:* TV, dataport, hair dryer.

NEARBY ACCOMMODATIONS

Gershøj Kro ☆ *Finds* A visit here is like wandering back in time to experience Denmark as it used to be. The only problem with this atmospheric hotel is that it's open to individual travelers only 3 months a year, farming out its simple and old-fashioned rooms to members of corporate conventions the rest of the time. If you're lucky enough to arrive during midsummer, you'll be welcomed at an inn (dating from 1830) that's only a few paces from the docks of the fishing hamlet of Gershøj. Expect old-fashioned charm and a restaurant that's known for the variety of ways in which it prepares a time-tested local favorite, eels hauled in from the harbor. June to August, the restaurant is open daily for lunch and dinner.

Havnevej 14, Gershøj, DK-4050 Skibby. ☎/fax **47-52-80-41**. www.gershoejkro.dk. 11 units, none with bathroom. 400DKK–725DKK ($68–$123/£36–£65) double. Rates include breakfast. MC, V. Free parking. Closed Sept–May. From Roskilde, drive 14km (8⅔ miles) NW, following the signs to Frederikssund. **Amenities:** Restaurant; bar. *In room:* No phone.

Osted Kro & Hotel Frankly, we prefer Gershøj or Svogerslev Kro (see above), but you might not always get into those establishments. View Osted Kro as a lovely consolation prize. There has been a hotel on this site since 1521, functioning as a refreshment stopover for travelers migrating between Roskilde and Ringsted. The roadside inn you'll see today is much newer than that, with a rebuilt original core and a modern annex (constructed in 1985) that holds the establishment's 16 deliberately old-fashioned rooms. All units have well-maintained bathrooms with tub/shower combinations. Don't expect too many distractions here; other than a restaurant and bar, there isn't a lot to do. Nonetheless, meals are savory and prepared according to old-time Danish recipes.

Hovedvejen 151B, Osted, DK-4000 Roskilde. © 46-49-70-41. www.ostedkro.dk. Fax 46-49-70-46. 16 units. 825DKK ($140/£74) double. Rates include breakfast. AE, DC, MC, V. From Roskilde, drive 12km (7½ miles) south along Rte. 151, following the signs to Ringsted. **Amenities:** Restaurant; lounge. *In room:* TV.

Skuldelev Kro   A final choice for aficionados of old Danish inns is this solid and reliable choice. In all the years we've been publicizing it, we've yet to get a complaint about it. It is set behind a pale yellow facade in the hamlet of Skuldelev, less than 1.5km (1 mile) from the sea. This Danish inn was built in 1778 and was reconfigured and upgraded from a virtual ruin in the early 1990s. Since its reopening, several branches of Denmark's governmental bureaucracy have designated it as the site for some of their conferences. When one of these isn't going on, you can rent any of the simple but comfortable rooms, with well-kept bathrooms with tub/shower combinations.

Østergade 2A, Skuldelev, DK-4050 Skibby. © 47-52-03-08. Fax 47-52-08-93. www.hotel-skuldelevkro.dk. 31 units. 750DKK ($128/£68) double. Rate includes breakfast. MC, V. From Roskilde, take Rte. 53 north for 26km (16 miles), following the signposts to Skibby. **Amenities:** Restaurant; bar; outdoor pool; sauna; nonsmoking rooms. *In room:* TV, hair dryer.

WHERE TO DINE

La Brasserie ⚘ STEAK/DANISH/INTERNATIONAL   We've always found this first-rate restaurant, in the previously recommended Prindsen, to be one of the best places in town for dining. The food is well-prepared with market-fresh ingredients. The staff is perhaps the friendliest and most helpful in town, and the decor is in a stylish bistro style, like something in modern Paris. Everything is prepared from scratch, and handpicked Danish raw materials are used whenever possible. The chefs even get their butter from a special dairy; their herring is cured for 8 months in Iceland, and their virgin olive oil comes from a small privately owned farm near Madrid.

It's simple and standard but ever so good, as evidenced by the grilled entrecôte with baked herb butter, baked potato, and grilled tomatoes. For a hefty, succulent meal, opt for the sirloin steak cut from Angus beef. Tiger prawns are a delightful concoction served with a raw tomato salsa with lime and cilantro flavorings. Chicken breast with homemade pesto is another reliable dish, as is a lamb kebab marinated in garlic and rosemary. In fair weather, you can dine outside.

Algade 13. © 46-30-91-00. Reservations recommended. Main courses 138KK–248DKK ($23–$42/£12–£22). AE, DC, MC, V. Daily noon–10pm.

Raadhuskælderen ⚘ DANISH   Savvy foodies will often direct you to one of the oldest restaurants in Roskilde, a dining room at the street level of a building erected in 1430 across the street from the town's cathedral. Although it's tempting to remain within the vaulted interior, there's also an outdoor terrace that is pleasant during midsummer, especially because of its view of the cathedral. Menu items are carefully prepared using very fresh ingredients. Some of the chef's best dishes include salmon steak with tartar sauce and grilled and marinated filet of young chicken with sautéed vegetables and a cream sauce flavored with ginger and citrus. Rack of lamb is delectably roasted and served with a sauce made from fresh summer berries.

Stændertorvet, Fondens Bro 1. ℂ **46-36-01-00.** www.raadhusk.dk. Reservations recommended. Main courses 148DKK–218DKK ($25–$37/£13–£20); lunch main courses 128DKK–168DKK ($22–$29/£12–£15). DC, MC, V. Mon–Sat 11am–11pm.

Restaurant Toppen DANISH   We knew a travel writer who once wrote a book about where to dine with a view. We like views too, but we like the food to be good as well. Both the view and the good food are possible at Toppen. At the top of a 1961 water tower, 84m (276 ft.) above sea level, Restaurant Toppen offers a panoramic view of the whole town, the surrounding country, and Roskilde Fjord—all from the dining room. Begin with a shrimp cocktail served with dill and lemon. Main dishes include sirloin of pork a la Toppen with mushrooms and a béarnaise sauce. For dessert, try the chef's nut cake with fruit sauce and sour cream. The cookery has much improved, and there is a finesse and consistency that wasn't here before. The restaurant is less than 1.5km (1 mile) east of the town center between Vindingevej and Københavnsvej. The water tower doesn't revolve electronically, but some clients, in the words of the management, "get the feeling that it's turning if they drink enough." There's a free elevator to the top.

Bymarken 37. ℂ **46-36-04-12.** Reservations recommended. Main courses 69DKK–125DKK ($12–$21/£6.20–£11). DC, MC, V. Mon–Fri 3:30–10pm; Sat–Sun noon–10pm. Bus: 601.

A NEARBY PLACE TO DINE
Langtved Færgekro ★ (Finds DANISH   Frankly, with its romantic setting, this inn could probably get away with serving hot dogs. Fortunately for us, it offers so much more. This isolated Danish inn, a short walk from the hamlet of Munkholm Bro, 5km (3 miles) southwest of the town of Kirke Såby, was inaugurated 250 years ago when a need arose to feed passengers on a nearby ferryboat route. Clients who appreciate a walk in the surrounding forest or along the nearby shoreline before or after enjoying a meal in this historic dining room favor this black-and-white half-timbered restaurant. The seasonal menu items have received several awards for their flavors. The best examples include crepes stuffed with baby shrimp, feta cheese, and herbs; marinated salmon with homemade bread; tender steak with fried onions; and either freshly caught halibut or plaice with hollandaise sauce.

Munkholmvej 138. ℂ **46-40-50-53.** Reservations recommended. Main courses 138DKK–240DKK ($23–$41/£12–£22). No credit cards. Fri–Sun noon–8pm. 5km (3 miles) SW of Kirke Såby; from Roskilde, drive 26km (16 miles) NW, following the signs to Holbæk and then to Munkholm Bro.

ROSKILDE AFTER DARK
One of the most consistently fun and popular nightlife venues in Roskilde is the **Gimle Musikcafe,** Ringstedgade 30 (ℂ **46-35-12-13**), where the trappings and ambience of a battered English pub combine with recorded—and in rare instances live—music. A 5-minute walk west from the center of town, it serves simple lunches and dinners, endless steins of Danish and international beer, and a dose of good cheer that's often welcomed by the many regulars—often young—who define this place as their "local."

7

South Zealand & Møn

North Zealand and South Zealand are a study in contrasts. The great drama and all the three-star man-made attractions, such as "Hamlet's Castle" or the cathedral at Roskilde, lie in the north, and naturally that's where hordes of visitors go. We don't dispute this obvious choice. If you have only 2 or even 3 days for Zealand, the north is a more rewarding target.

But if you have at least 2 days extra to spare, you can take in all the highlights of South Zealand as travel times are short between sightseeing targets. Zealand may be the largest of all Danish islands, but it is only about the size of the state of Delaware. Even if you have only a day for South Zealand, you can visit it using Copenhagen as your base. If that's the case, we recommend that you confine your trip to the ancient "witch-burning," medieval city of Køge and the offshore island of Møn, both of which can be seen in just 1 day.

Sjælland Syd (its Danish name) is today called a "land of mist and moods," with its prehistoric monuments and ancient towns. Its "cities" are really overgrown towns, and it is blanketed with rolling farmlands, blighted in places by necessary industry. It is also filled with white sandy beaches opening onto rather cold waters.

The land is also filled with medieval churches (we've selected the best of them)

and a 1,000-year-old ring fortress at Trelleborg (p. 214). There are often festivals of fine food and music throughout the summer, and there are seemingly endless sailing clubs, which give the ports a real maritime atmosphere, filled with the heady scents of seaweed and tar.

Before Copenhagen or Roskilde emerged, South Zealand loomed large in history as the seat of the Valdemar dynasty of Danish kings. It was also a power player in the Middle Ages and Denmark's ecclesiastical center. In the 1600s, some of the most epic battles between Sweden and Denmark took place here, especially in the seas off Køge. One of Denmark's greatest moments of shame came in 1658 when King Gustav of Sweden marched across the fields of South Zealand heading for Copenhagen. Once here, he forced a treaty that nearly cost Denmark its sovereignty.

Motorists from Køge in the east heading to Korsør in the west (perhaps to cross the bridge over the Great Belt into Funen) would be wise to steer clear of the dull E20 motorway and follow the scenic and greener Route 150, which will take you through South Zealand's best villages and farmlands.

For Zealand rail or bus information, you can call ✆ 70-13-14-15.

1 Køge (★)

40km (25 miles) S of Copenhagen; 24km (15 miles) SE of Roskilde

The best-preserved medieval town on the island of Zealand lives in infamy as the town that "barbecued" old ladies suspected of witchcraft. "You had your Salem, Massachusetts, and we Danes, regrettably, had our Køge," a Danish historian once told us. The witch burning took place during the 17th century at the Torvet, the market square.

In about 3 hours, you can explore this old port city on Køge Bay, lying on the east coast of South Zealand. The city was granted a charter by King Erik VI in 1288, but its fame is of another day. The area grew up and prospered because of its natural harbor, becoming a bustling hub of seafaring trade with Germany and a thriving fishing center, exporting its fresh catches to feed the hungry masses of Copenhagen.

Every Danish schoolboy (or -girl) knows the story of the Battle of Køge Bay, fought here in 1677, one of the major conflicts in the eternal wars with Sweden. The Danish admiral Niels Juel defeated the attacking Swedish navy, thwarting their attempt to conquer Denmark. This made him a national hero, like Admiral Nelson to the British.

Køge, a bustling city of 40,000 with a modern commercial harbor, is visited mainly because it has preserved the narrow, historic streets of its inner core. A fire in 1633 leveled many of the buildings, but others were spared to greet visitors today—and still others were restored to their original appearance.

ESSENTIALS

GETTING THERE   By Train   Take the S-tog extension from Copenhagen, with service every 20 minutes throughout the day (trip time: 35 min.). You can also reach Køge by train from Roskilde (25 min.), and there are also rail links with Næstved (35 min.).

By Bus   Bus no. 21 departs for Køge frequently from Copenhagen's Central Railroad Station.

By Car   From Copenhagen, head south along the express highway E47/E55. Motorists from Roskilde can take Route 6, connecting with Route 151 south into the heart of Køge. Parking is available at Torvet (but only for an hour at a time); you'll find less restrictive parking at Havnen, north of the yacht harbor.

VISITOR INFORMATION   Guided tours of Køge are arranged through the **Tourist Office,** Vestergade 1 (© **56-67-60-01;** www.koegeturist.dk), open year-round Monday to Friday 9am to 5pm; June to August Saturday hours are 9am to 2pm; off season, Saturday hours are 10am to 1pm.

GETTING AROUND   By Bicycle   While at the tourist bureau you can ask for a free brochure published by the Dansk Cyklist Forbund (Danish Cyclists' Union). It's in English and outlines five biking tours of the nearby area, ranging from a 40km (25-mile) tour that features Vallø Slot (see "Easy Excursions from Køge," later in this chapter), to a 6km (3¾-mile) route that visits the grave of Danish philosopher Nikolai Frederik Grundtvig.

For bike rentals in Køge, contact **HH-Cykler,** Nørre Blvd. 59 (© **56-65-06-10**), costing 65DKK ($11/£5.85) per day, plus a deposit of 400DKK ($68/£36).

EXPLORING THE TOWN

Many Copenhageners, especially those with a boat or yacht, flock to **Køge Bay** (★★★) in the summer the way New Yorkers go to the Hamptons. We find the town very sleepy in winter, but in summer it bursts into bloom and its population swells. The bay is one vast pleasure-boat harbor set against a backdrop of beaches that we find bone-chilling even in July.

The harbor is only a short walk from the medieval center, and it has the same appeal for the people of Køge as Nyhavn does for Copenhageners. We enjoy the atmosphere here and like watching the action in the busy harbor, which is filled with Baltic freighters, fishing boats, and pleasure craft of all types. If you walk to the North Pier, you'll find a number of eating places and cafes in old-fashioned houses, where you can relax over a meal or order a cold Danish beer.

Opening onto the bay is a monument commemorating the battle in Køge Bay. You'll see it standing some 9m (30 ft.) high near the harbor. This granite obelisk bears the names of maritime heroes Niels Juel and Ivar Huitfeldt. Huitfeldt commanded the *Danebrog,* which burst into flames when bombarded by Swedish forces in 1710.

Before taking a look at the bay, wander the medieval streets of Køge's **Gamle Stan** ✸✸✸, or Old Town. You'll pass fish markets selling freshly caught flatfish, herring, and eel. Stroll through the town parks and surrounding woodland and peek into the courtyards of the old buildings left from the Middle Ages. In summer, live street entertainment will amuse you (giving a few kroner to the young musicians is always appreciated, of course).

The best street for wandering is **Kirkestræde,** lined with graceful old houses. A small building on the street, no. 20, is reputed to be the oldest half-timbered house in Denmark, dating back to 1527. A couple of porch stones from the Middle Ages, said to be the only pair in Denmark in their original position, are in front of a house at Smedegarden 13, near an ancient tree.

Of the town's churches, **Sankt Nicolai Church,** Kirkestræde 29 (✆ **56-65-13-59**), 2 blocks north of Torvet, is a Gothic structure dating from 1450 named after St. Nicholas, patron saint of mariners. History records that King Christian IV watched the Battle of Køge, in which Niels Juel sank many Swedish vessels, from the church tower. The church has a number of art treasures, including an altarpiece by Lorents Jørgensen and 100 tombs of Køge merchants. Note the carved angels on the pews—they are without noses, thanks to drunken Swedish troops who in the 1600s came this way, cutting off the noses with their swords. What sorry fun that must have been for them. Look for a little brick projection at the east end of the church tower. Called *Lygten,* it was for centuries a place where a burning lantern was hung to guide sailors safely back into the harbor. From mid-June to late August, hours are Monday to Friday 10am to 4pm, Sunday noon to 4pm; off season, Monday to Friday 10am to noon. Admission is 5DKK (85¢/45p).

On the north side of the Torvet (market square) is the **Køge Rådhus** ✸✸, believed to be the oldest town hall in Denmark still in use. The building in the rear was erected very early in the 17th century to serve as accommodations for King Christian IV on his trips between the royal palaces in Copenhagen and Nykøbing F (the "F" refers to the island of Falster). You can wander into the courtyard at the town hall to see a modern sculpture created by Jens Flemming Sørensen.

A path for walkers and cyclists leads along the Køge River with access from the center in several places. Go here to enjoy some peace and quiet—and take along a picnic lunch if the weather's fair. There are several delis in town where you can pick up some open-faced sandwiches and drinks to take along. At a park, **Lovparken,** only a 5-minute walk from the Torvet, a wooden bridge takes you across the river, where you have a panoramic view of the riverside and its gardens.

The coastline near Køge offers several fine spots for bathing. Directly north of Køge you'll come upon a land of dunes and lyme grass, with a sandy beach on **Ølsemagle Revle.** Near the city center, **Køge Sydstrand,** or south beach, offers camping sites, and a bit farther south, the beach at **Strøby Ladeplads** is ideal for windsurfers.

Among specific attractions, consider a visit to the following:

Køge Museum ✦ As provincial museums go, this is the best in South Zealand, and it can be visited in less than an hour, an especially amusing thing to do on one of the many rainy afternoons in Køge. The museum lies in an old merchant's home from 1610; it is surrounded by a beautiful garden near the town square and is devoted to the cultural history of South Zealand. It consists of six well-furnished rooms and a kitchen with implements used between 1640 and 1899. Displays of costumes, textiles, carriages, farm equipment, crafts from artisan's guilds, and other historical artifacts of the area are featured. Curiously, there's a windowpane where H. C. Andersen scratched the words OH, GOD, OH, GOD IN KØGE. The museum also displays many mementos and personal items belonging to this spinner of fairy tales. The museum also has a desk once owned by Nikolai Frederik Grundtvig, the Danish philosopher and theologian who used to live on the outskirts of Køge. Also on display are hundreds of silver coins, forming a treasure-trove that may have been hidden for safekeeping during the wars with Sweden in the 1600s. There's also a collection of 322 coins from all over Scandinavia and Europe—the oldest coin is a Palatinate taler from 1548. Your museum ticket, incidentally, is valid—if you use it on the same day—for admission to Vallø Slot, a charming castle that's recommended separately at the end of this section, under "Easy Excursions from Køge."

Nørregade 4. ℂ 56-63-42-42. Admission 30DKK ($5.10/£2.70) adults, free for children under 16. June–Aug daily 11am–5pm; Sept–May Tues–Sun 1–5pm.

Kunstmuseet Køge Skitsesambling ⭐ *(Finds*   Changing exhibitions and a rather large permanent collection of sketches, sculpture, and contemporary Scandinavian art draw visitors to this art museum devoted mainly to sketches. Its most viewed work is a series of studies that sculptor Edvard Eriksen did for *The Little Mermaid* statue in Copenhagen that's always being decapitated by someone. But there's so much more— some 7,500 models and studies of both paintings and sculptures, the latter conceived mainly for public parks in the country. In English the museum's name translates as "art and sketch collection." What makes this museum unique is that it traces the artist's creative process from conception to execution, from the advent of the idea to the unfolding of the "vision." Original drawings, clay models, and even mock-ups of a particular work are included so that the public can see how a piece of art looks while it's still in the conceptual stage. This approach is particularly fascinating for us to see when a piece of art undergoes a tremendous conceptual change along the way.

Nørregade 29. ℂ 56-67-60-20. Admission 30DKK ($5.10/£2.70) adults, 15DKK ($2.55/£1.35) children 5–15, free for children under 5. Thurs–Tues 10am–5pm; Wed 10am–8pm.

SHOPPING

We try to time visits to Køge on market days, which take place on Wednesday and Saturday (it's best to go in the morning) at the main market square, **Torvet** ⭐⭐, the best-preserved market square from the Middle Ages in Denmark. The town is crowded with people from the countryside, many of whom have products to sell, including fruits, vegetables, Danish cheese, and smoked fish, as well as handicrafts and even secondhand goods. If you have a choice of days, we have found that the Saturday market is livelier. You can wander from stall to stall as street musicians—most often jazz artists—entertain you from courtyards nearby.

The best and largest selection of Danish gifts is found at **Jørgen Müller,** Torvet 3–5 (ℂ 56-65-25-80), on the market square. Here you can pick up Georg Jensen silver, exquisite Royal Copenhagen porcelain, Holmegaard glass—you name it. The best selection for women's fashion is **Rokkjoer,** Torvet 2 (ℂ 56-65-02-58), which has an impressive array of continental coats, blouses, and dresses—many in what they call "oversize."

For South Zealand antiques, the best outlet is **Antik Bahuset,** Brogade 16E (© 56-66-17-19), selling old furnishings, pewter, brass, and a lot of pre-1900 items. It's open only Saturday 10am to 1pm unless you call for an appointment. Another good antiques store is **Tamalat Antik,** Brogade 22 (© 56-65-63-10), with a wide selection of furniture, and good buys in paintings, jewelry, glass, and porcelain. Finally, **Krybben,** Torvet 19 (© 56-63-02-01), offers a wide selection of clothing, crafts, shoes, and antiques—an odd mixture, but intriguing nonetheless. A special feature of Krybben is an upstairs gallery exhibiting the works of a talented local painter, Anne Kureer.

For the novelty alone, you might want to visit **Købmandshandel,** Vestergade 6 (© 56-66-30-67), a grocer's shop of yesterday. Two hundred different sorts of tea, spices from around the world, and everything from olive oils to licorice root to rock candy are on sale—you'll even find syrups, fruity jams, and handmade candles in rainbow colors.

Køge used to be known for its goldsmiths. Thriving since 1979, **Guldsmedien Ejvind Sørensen,** Nørregade 31 (© 56-66-19-91), is in a charming old building dating from 1612. A selection of gold and silver jewelry is sold here.

For the very best of Scandinavian, especially Danish, design, not only furnishings but also home accessories, head for **Hjelm's Bolighus,** Nørregade 32 (© 56-65-06-30), the leading design outlet in Køge for more than 4 decades.

WHERE TO STAY

Because of the demand from business travelers, some of these hotels charge higher rates in winter, granting discounts for tourists in summer.

Best Western Hotel Niels Juel ⭐ The town's best address since 1989 opens onto the harborfront, and is the place where we always lay our heads in modern comfort. To name the hotel after the town's 17th-century naval hero seemed a natural idea. Both the midsize bedrooms and the public lounges are designed with Feng Shui—the famous Chinese interior art—in mind. Each of the rooms is well maintained and comfortably furnished, with tiled bathrooms with tub/shower combos. On-site are a cozy bar and a first-class restaurant, **Quintus,** offering Danish and French food, including fresh salmon, oysters, and mussels, which we find the most tantalizing items on the menu. On the ground floor hotel guests are often invited for wine tastings from a well-stocked cellar, and there is also a library where guests relax while reading periodicals. The hotel is a safe, reliable, and substantial choice, and the staff is particularly helpful, including when they arranged for us to play on a golf course less than a kilometer (about ½ mile) from the hotel.

Toldbodvej 20, DK-4600 Køge. © **800/528-1234** in the U.S., or 56-63-18-00. Fax 56-63-04-92. www.hotelniels juel.dk. 50 units. Sept–June Sun–Thurs 1,225DKK ($208/£110) double, Fri–Sat 875DKK ($149/£79) double; July–Aug 875DKK ($149/£79) double. Rates include breakfast. AE, DC, MC, V. **Amenities:** Restaurant; bar; sauna; laundry service; dry cleaning; nonsmoking rooms; rooms for those w/limited mobility; solarium; wine cellar. *In room:* TV, dataport, minibar, hair dryer.

Centralhotellet Køge *Value* It calls itself a hotel, but it's really a glorified B&B hiding behind a pale blue facade in the heart of town, only a few feet from the tarmac of the street. There's the feeling of a cozy but restored 19th-century house here. Even though it's less well equipped than any other hotel in town, it's reasonably comfortable and most affordable—in fact, the best deal we find in town. The bedrooms are small and rather basic—and you can forget electronic extras such as TVs—but it's a good choice if you want only a bed for the night. Most of the bedrooms come with a tiny bathroom with shower; otherwise, you can use the facilities in the corridor.

Vestergade 3, DK-4600 Køge. ⓒ 56-65-06-96. Fax 56-66-02-07. 12 units, 3 with bathroom. 570DKK ($97/£51) double without bathroom; 670DKK ($114/£59) double with bathroom. Rates include breakfast. MC, V. **Amenities:** Breakfast room; bar; lounge. In room: No phone.

Hotel Hvide Hus   Washington isn't the only place with a White House. The White House (its English name) in Køge lies less than a kilometer (about ½ mile) east of the center, and is a good choice for motorists. Built in 1963 at the height of the Cold War, it reflects the dull architecture of that era, rising two floors in white brick with an angular, glass-and-chrome style. Its most winning features are the panoramic views from its windows of the Bay of Køge and a beach which lies about 180m (600 ft.) away. The midsize bedrooms are brightly decorated and furnished in Danish modern style, with well-kept tiled bathrooms with tub/shower combos.

Strandvejen 111, DK-4600 Køge. ⓒ **800/528-1234** in the U.S., or 56-65-36-90. Fax 56-66-33-14. www.hotelhvide hus.dk. 126 units. 1,075DKK–1,325DKK ($183–$225/£97–£119) double; 2,500DKK ($425/£225) suite. Rates include buffet breakfast. AE, DC, MC, V. **Amenities:** Restaurant; bar; sauna; room service (6am–9:30pm); laundry service; dry cleaning; nonsmoking rooms; rooms for those w/limited mobility. In room: TV, dataport, minibar, hair dryer.

Vallø Slotskro ⭐ *Finds*   This is one of the more enchanting little B&Bs on the southeast coast of Zealand, and it's surrounded by some of the most evocative landscapes on the island at a point 8km (5 miles) south of Køge near Vallø Slot (p. 206), a Renaissance castle from the 16th century. That's not all. The building was ordered built by a king, Christian VII in 1781, for overflow guests he didn't want running underfoot at his own castle abode. The years have brought changes architecturally— not all successful—and what awaits you today is a well-run guesthouse where each of the small-to-midsize bedrooms is decorated and furnished individually, all comfortably appointed. Only seven come with private bathrooms, each with a tub/shower combo, the occupants of the other rooms sharing the adequate corridor facilities. The best rooms here—and these are assigned first—are those with more space and such extras as minibars, Jacuzzis, and four-poster antique beds.

Slotsgade 1, DK-4600 Køge. ⓒ 56-26-70-20. Fax 56-26-70-71. www.valloeslotskro.dk. 13 units, 7 with bathroom. 770DKK ($131/£69) double without bathroom; 945DKK ($161/£85) double with bathroom. Rates include breakfast. AE, DC, MC, V. Free parking. **Amenities:** Restaurant; bar. In room: TV, minibar.

WHERE TO DINE

Horizonten Café & Restaurant ⭐⭐ DANISH/FRENCH   On a summer day when the sun's shining, we always request a table on the terrace overlooking the harbor that has played such a major role in Denmark's naval history. This is Køge's premier dining room; the chef and his kitchen brigade are devoted to the memorable dishes they turn out. They are especially skilled with Danish seafood, and whenever possible they use fresh Danish ingredients, although they freely "plagiarize" recipes from the continent, mostly from France. We have found that their fixed-price menu is the best offered by any major restaurant in South Zealand. Most clients wisely request that their fish be grilled, and it's done almost to perfection here and to your specifications. "Americans generally like their fish too dry," the chef told us. "Danes prefer it more juicy." After we devoured the halibut meunière and all the goodies served—yummy desserts, freshly made crisp salads, and vegetables cooked "to the point," never mushy—the summer day was ours.

Havnen 29A. ℂ 56-63-86-28. Reservations required. Main courses 175DKK–235DKK ($30–$40/£16–£21); fixed-price menus 425DKK ($72/£38). AE, DC, MC, V. Tues–Sun 6pm–midnight.

Restaurant Arken DANISH/FRENCH   The chefs here may not be quite as dazzling as those manning the stoves at Horizonten, but they will also feed you well. They, too, have a terrace overlooking the smaller of Køge's two harbors. This 1979 big-windowed restaurant is called "the Ark," because its architecture is like a large wooden boat that would have made Noah green with jealousy. The interior is flooded with sunlight and decorated with varnished wood that evokes the paneling you might find aboard a yacht. Our British dining companion, living an expat life in Køge, told us he comes here once a week for a "hearty tuck-in," appreciating the fact that they often serve English-style roast beef with horseradish sauce. During warm weather, we've often seen visitors from Germany devouring the fried eel with stewed potatoes. The cooks aren't interested in showstopping dishes but prefer to stick to old Danish favorites such as *frikadeller* (meatballs), fresh grilled salmon in a butter sauce, and sautéed beefsteak with mashed potatoes and golden fried onions.

Køge Lystbådehavn 21. ℂ 56-66-05-05. Reservations recommended. Main courses 135DKK–250DKK ($23–$43/£12–£23); fixed-price menu 192DKK ($33/£17). DC, MC, V. Daily 11:30am–10pm.

Skipperkroen ✦ DANISH/INTERNATIONAL   Sailors, yachties, and summer campers flock here for platters of hearty, good-tasting food within a restored 1600s building set across the road from Køge's harbor. Summer laughter and noise resound through the restaurant, where diners enjoy beer, wine, and Danish food. The drinking and dining overflow onto an outdoor garden with tables in summer, but for most of the year clients dine inside in one of two areas. The cooks are loyal to Danish products whenever they are available, both freshly caught fish and vegetables from the countryside. Plaice regularly appears on the menu, and, when the chefs get fancy, they dress it up with fresh shrimp and asparagus, even chunks of lobster meat. The cooks elevate the Danish staple of *biksemad* (beef hash with potatoes and onions, traditionally made with whatever happened to be lurking in a family's larder) to a high art form. Here, a platter of *biksemad,* with the promise of as many refills as you want, makes this one of the best dining deals in town.

Havnen 25. ℂ 56-65-02-64. Main courses 155DKK–185DKK ($26–$31/£14–£17). AE, DC, MC, V. Daily 10am–11pm.

KØGE AFTER DARK

Begin your nightly pub-crawl, as the locals do, at **Toldboden,** Havnen 27 (ℂ 56-65-50-75), built between 1833 and 1847. Carlsberg is served on draft, and you can also order Guinness, downing your suds in a summer courtyard. Live music is presented every Friday evening and on Saturday afternoons, but mostly it's a place to gather and meet the locals.

Our favorite spot to meet friends for a friendly chat at night is **La Fontaine,** Torvet 28 (ℂ 56-65-51-00), which somehow always manages to have the coldest beer in town. It's right on the market square by the old fountain and stays open Sunday to Thursday 10am to midnight, and Friday and Saturday 10am to 2am—late hours for sleepy Køge.

For young people, the hottest place to be at night is the **Ritz Rock Café,** Torvet 22 (ℂ 56-65-33-77), which is Køge's version of the fabled Hard Rock cafes. People come here for the dance music and to eat and drink, partaking of the American and Tex-Mex cuisine. On a busy night, it holds up to 1,000 patrons. On the ground floor you'll find the most impressive sound and light equipment, whereas the second floor is smaller and more formal, attracting a more mature clientele.

One of the most charming places for a quiet drink at night is **Hugos Vinkælder, Brogade 19** (© **56-65-58-50**), which opens its courtyard in fair weather. This cozy little wine bar retreat is found in the cellar of an antique building dating from 1392. Filled with atmosphere, it always has a well-chosen selection of wine, which it will sell by the half bottle if desired. Open Monday to Thursday 10am to 11pm, Friday and Saturday 10am to 1am.

Ask at the tourist office what's on the bill at **Køge Bugt Kulturhus,** Portalen 1 (© **43-97-83-00**); the Køge Bay Cultural Center is the venue for a wide range of concerts and theatrical performances. An exhibit of Danish and international art is displayed in its exhibition hall. Tickets for all types of cultural events are sold at the tourist office. Of course, you might want to skip the theatrical performances if you don't speak Danish, but concerts and other entertainment might interest English speakers.

EASY EXCURSIONS FROM KØGE
VALLØ & ITS CASTLE ⊛

This hamlet of mustard-yellow houses and cobblestone streets from the Middle Ages gets our vote as the most charming in South Zealand, lying only 7km (4⅓ miles) south of Køge. Off the beaten path, it's visited by those wanting to wander through the gardens of the red-brick **Vallø Slot,** dating from 1586 but rebuilt after a fire in 1893. Originally the palace housed "spinsters of noble birth," but today it is used for housing pensioners. You can't go inside but you can wander through the well-landscaped gardens with their little lakes, moats, rare trees, and rose and dahlia flower beds. The castle is surrounded by 2,800 hectares (6,920 acres) of woods and ponds and also enveloped by 1,300 hectares (3,210 acres) of cultivated fields that flow gradually to the coast. Charging no admission, the gardens are open April to October 10am to dusk.

On the grounds at the stables, **Hestestalden** (© **56-26-74-62**), there's an exhibition on the history of the castle from the days when it was the property of Queen Sophie Magdalene in 1737. It's open May to August 11am to 4pm. Admission is 30DKK ($5.10/£2.70) adults and free for children. The ticket, incidentally, is valid for a visit to the Køge Museum as well—but only if you use it on the same day.

GETTING THERE **By Train** Vallø station is two stops from Køge.

By Car Head south on Route 209, turning right onto Billesborgvej and left onto Valløvej.

By Bicycle Bicycling is the ideal way to reach Valløvej, as there's a cycle route signposted from Køge.

THE CHALK CLIFFS OF STEVNS KLINT ⊛

If you, like us, sometimes prefer to wander off the beaten track, we suggest an afternoon exploring **Stevns Peninsula** lying only 24km (15 miles) south of Køge, near Rødvig. The attraction here is the chalk cliffs of **Stevns Klint** (admittedly, they don't compare to the White Cliffs of Dover).

This chalk escarpment extends along the coastline, opening onto a panoramic vista of the sea, and it's one of our favorite places to wander and explore during an afternoon in southeast Zealand. The most stunning white chalk crag rises 43m (141 ft.) in the vicinity of Højerup. In the hamlet of Store Heddinge, you'll come across a little

Fun Fact **Zealand's Link to the Continent**

On June 14, 1998, one of the world's largest bridge links opened on the west coast of Zealand near the town of Korsør. Queen Margrethe II was here to cut the ribbon shortly before driving across the 18km-long (11-mile) **Great Belt Bridge.** After 10 years of construction, Zealand is linked to the mainland of Europe via Funen, which already has a bridge link to Jutland on the mainland. From Jutland, you can drive south into Germany.

The bridge has cut traveling time across the Belt by more than 1 hour compared to the ferries, which ceased operations with the opening of the bridge. At a speed of 105kmph (65 mph), crossing the Great Belt into Funen now takes only 10 minutes. By contrast, crossing by ferry took 1 hour, not including the waiting time at the port and embarkation and disembarkation from the ferries. For crossing the bridge, a one-way fare for a private car costs 200DKK ($34/£18). About 23,000 cars now cross the bridge each day.

The rail link across the Great Belt was opened in 1997, and since then Danish State Railways has seen a 60% rise in passenger volume on trains across the Great Belt.

Besides joining east and west Denmark, the bridge link across the Great Belt represented the first stage of an improved infrastructure between Scandinavia and the rest of Europe. The **Øresund Fixed Link** between Denmark and Sweden opened in 2000, establishing even more vital links between Copenhagen and Malmö, southern Sweden's largest city. With three million people living within a 50km (31-mile) radius of the link, the region has the largest population concentration in Scandinavia.

For more information about the bridge, call ℭ **33-93-52-00.**

church, **Højerup Kirke,** built here in 1357. Legend claims this church was erected by fishermen in gratitude for having been rescued at sea. There's another legend about this church as well. The sea continues to erode the chalk cliffs, and locals claim that each New Year's Eve the church moves a fraction inland to keep from falling into the sea. In 1928 it didn't move far enough and the choir collapsed, but the church has since been reinforced and made relatively safe. Hours are daily 10am to 5pm, but only May to September.

For more information about the area, consult the **Turistbureau** in Stevns at Havnevej 21 (ℭ **56-50-64-64**).

GETTING THERE   By Train and Bicycle   To get to Stevns Klint from Køge, take the train to Rødvig, where you'll rent a bicycle from the tourist office. From here, it's only about 5km (3 miles), heading east, following the signs to Højerup, to the cliffs. This is an easy bike ride and offers the best way to experience the bracing sea air and wind-swept panoramas.

By Car   From Køge to Stevns Klint, take Highway 261 to the village of Store Heddinge, then detour to the cliffs, following the signs to Højerup.

2 Ringsted

69km (43 miles) SW of Copenhagen; 24km (15 miles) W of Køge; 16km (10 miles) E of Søro; 28km (17 miles) N of Næstved

"Our glory was of another day," the curator of a local museum told us. "But life must go on." He was referring to both the days of those "raping, pillaging Vikings" who made Ringsted a major settlement and also an era during the Middle Ages when Ringsted was a powerful ecclesiastical center. "In those days, Ringsted for Denmark was just as powerful as the Vatican is today in Rome," wrote a long-ago (nameless) historian.

A sleepy provincial town today, this modern center of 30,000 people makes an ideal base for touring South Zealand, offering excellent rail and road conditions. Route 14 from Næstved (see below) to Roskilde intersects the east–west highway (E20) from Køge to Korsør, where you can take the bridge over the Great Belt into Funen.

As late as the 4th century, Ringsted was the site of "the thing," or *Landsting,* as the regional governing body was called, where justice was dispensed. In Torvet, the market square, you can still see a trio of three stones, the *Tingstener,* or "thing stones," recalling the days when Ringsted was a center of power in Denmark. Also on the square is a 1930s statue of Valdemar I sculpted by Johannes Bjerg.

In times gone by, Ringsted was where Valdemar kings and many of their successors were laid to rest, in Skt. Bendts Kirke (St. Benedict's Church), dating from the 12th century.

After a long period of slumber following the loss of its royal patronage, Ringsted revived again in the 19th century with the coming of the railway.

You could base in Ringsted for 2 nights if you want to use it as a center for exploring **Næstved** and **Slagelse** (see below), two neighboring towns within easy reach, both of which are of historic interest.

ESSENTIALS
GETTING THERE   By Train   Trains run frequently from Roskilde (trip time: 18 min.). Dozens of daily trains from Copenhagen pass through to Roskilde (see chapter 6, "North Zealand"). There are also rail connections from Næstved (20 min.). The center of Ringsted can be reached in a 10-minute walk north from the train depot.

By Car   Ringsted lies on Route 150 just off the E20 motorway coming in from Copenhagen in the east or Funen in the west. From Roskilde, follow Route 14 to Ringsted.

VISITOR INFORMATION   The **Ringsted Turistbureau,** Sankt Bendtsgade 6 (© **57-62-66-00**), stands opposite Skt. Bendts Kirke. May to August, its hours are Monday to Friday 10am to 5pm and Saturday 10am to 2pm. Off-season hours are Monday to Friday 10am to 5pm, and Saturday 10am to 1pm. The tourist office will advise you of the best cycling routes in the Ringsted area.

EXPLORING THE TOWN
Skt. Bendts Kirke ⊛⊛   The Domkirke at Roskilde (see chapter 6) is the major ecclesiastical site of Zealand, but this church has been the site of royal burials for 150 years. It was constructed by King Valdemar I (1157–82) on the site of a previous abbey. His original intent was that the church serve as a burial site for his father, Duke Knud Lavard, who was slain by Magnus the Strong, son of King Niets (1104–34). The beloved Knud Lavard was entombed here, beginning a tradition of using the church

as a burial site for the Valdemar dynasty. In 1169 Knud Lavard was canonized by the pope. The tradition of burying kings and queens of Denmark here continued until 1341. Valdemar I's larger motive in building the church was to use it to bring together the influences of the Catholic hierarchy and the Valdemar dynasty.

In the early 20th century, ill-advised restorers altered the style of the original church, but much remains from the Middle Ages, even the 11th-century travertine blocks from the older abbey church built on this site.

In 1885, King Frederik VII ordered that the royal tombs be unsealed. In a church chapel you can see the treasures found in these tombs, including a lead tablet from the tomb of Valdemar the Great, plus silks from the grave of Valdemar the Victorious. The tombs themselves—marked by a series of flat stones—were buried beneath the nave on the aisle floor. Such notables as Valdemar III and his queen, Eleonora; the twice-married Valdemar II with his queens, Dagmar and Benegærd; Knud VI; Valdemar I and his queen, Sofia; and the already-mentioned Duke Knud Lavard are all entombed here. Many long-forgotten royals suffered the indignity of having their tombs removed to make way for later royal personages. Chief among these was the beloved Queen Dagmar, born a princess in Bohemia and still revered in Danish folk ballads. Much loved by the people of Denmark, she died prematurely in 1212. When her grave was removed to make way for the tomb of Erik VI (Menved) and his Queen Ingeborg, a gold cross with detailed enamel work was found. The **Dagmar Cross** is believed to date from around 1000. Today it is displayed in the National Museum in Copenhagen, but local jewelry shops sell replicas of this pendant. Today, brides marrying in Skt. Bendts often wear replicas of the Dagmar Cross.

In the choir and on the cross vaulting, you can see some notable chalk paintings. Some of Zealand's best church frescoes are in the nave, especially a series depicting events in the life of King Erik IV. He was called "King Ploughpenny," because of a tax he imposed on ploughs throughout his kingdom. These frescoes were painted at the beginning of the 14th century in a failed attempt to have the king canonized (the pope declined). One fresco shows Queen Agnes, wife of Erik IV, seated on a throne; another immediately to her left depicts the murder of Erik IV, his attackers stabbing him with a spear. In another fresco the king's corpse is being rescued at sea by fishermen.

Other notable features in the church include pews from 1591 with dragon motifs. The richly adorned altarpiece is from 1699, and the even older pulpit dates from 1609. The **baptismal font** ✦ is the oldest relic of all, believed to date from some time in the 1100s.

Sankt Bendtsgade. ℂ **57-61-40-19**. Free admission. May to mid-Sept daily 10am–noon and 1–5pm; mid-Sept to Apr daily 1–3pm.

Ringsted Museum   This is another one of Denmark's provincial museums and is of such minor interest it could easily be skipped. Instead of the museum, we gravitate to the restored 1814 Dutch windmill next door, which is still in working order, grinding organic flour sold at a kiosk on-site. You can also stop for a coffee at the cafe before ducking inside the museum of local culture and history, presenting artifacts to illustrate the life of the locals long since departed. We learned more about the history of local farming than we wanted to know.

Køgevej 41. ℂ **57-61-69-00**. Admission 25DKK ($4.25/£2.25). Tues–Sun 11am–4pm. Closed Jan.

Eventyrlandet Fantasy World *(Kids)*   The fairy tales of Hans Christian Andersen still live on here, and many families from Copenhagen drive down for the day to relive

their childhoods and introduce their kids to a world of fantasy. Within a large, echoing room, you'll walk along simulations of paths through a magic forest. In the forest's clearings, mechanical dolls, each about 5m (16 ft.) high, simulate characters from the stories of Andersen as they dance, pirouette, and interact in their stiff but charming way. The assumption is that onlookers will have memorized the tales behind each tableau, but if you've forgotten one of them, virtually any Dane in the crowd will be able to recap it for you. There are also tableaux depicting folkloric dances in Mexico and China, plus hunting scenes in Greenland. There are also an outdoor playground, a cafe, and a gift shop.

Eventyrvej 13. ℭ **57-61-19-30**. Admission 75DKK ($13/£6.75) adults, 50DKK ($8.50/£4.50) children 2–11, 25DKK ($4.25/£2.25) kids under 2. Feb 7–15 daily 10am–4pm; May 28–Aug 28 daily 10am–5pm; Oct 2–Dec 30 daily 10am–5pm. Closed at other times. Bus: 14 or 401 from Ringsted. 1.5km (1 mile) northwest of Ringsted.

SHOPPING

Ringsted has a number of specialty shops. A covered shopping center, **Ringsted Centret,** Nørregade 15 (ℭ **57-67-38-05**), stands right in the middle of town, enabling you to shop and browse without having to worry about the weather. This is where you'll find the widest array of Danish products in various stores. The best place to go for copies of the Dagmar Cross (see Skt. Bendts Kirke, above) is **Klints Guld & Sølv,** Torvet 2 (ℭ **57-61-01-83**). The cross comes in gold, silver, and gold with enamel. In 1683 the cross—believed to date from 1000—was discovered when Queen Dagmar's tomb site was moved. Today nearly all brides married in Ringsted wear a reproduction of this cross, which makes an intriguing piece of jewelry even if you aren't a bride.

WHERE TO STAY

Scandic Hotel Ringsted *Kids*   Short on character, but big on comfort, this four-story red-brick hotel, lying a 5-minute walk south of the town center, opened in 1986, and no challenger has risen since to unseat it as the king hostelry of town. Despite the fact that it's newer and a lot less historic than the also-recommended **Sørup Herregård** (see below), we prefer it for its location near the town center and because the staff is a lot better organized. Its public areas host many of the region's conventions and business meetings, which is hardly a recommendation for the average visitor—in fact, we don't like to stay here at those busy times. The midsize bedrooms are streamlined in a Danish modern sort of way, with writing tables, functional furniture, and tile bathrooms with shower units. There's a respectable, rather standard restaurant onsite, which serves Danish dishes for lunch and dinner. This is one of the best hotels for families in the area, and kids are given a "surprise" when checking in and later can enjoy organized activities planned just for them.

Nørretorv 57, DK-4100 Ringsted. ℭ **57-61-93-00**. Fax 57-67-02-07. www.scandic-hotels.com. 75 units. 1,235DKK ($210/£111) double. Rates include breakfast. AE, DC, MC, V. **Amenities:** Restaurant; bar; fitness center; sauna; children's playroom; laundry service; dry cleaning; nonsmoking rooms; solarium. *In room:* TV, Wi-Fi, minibar, coffeemaker (in some), hair dryer, trouser press (in some).

Sørup Herregård *Finds*   If you're a motorist, and you like your hotels with a lot more character and atmosphere than Scandic (see above), drive 6km (3¾ miles) east of town to a restored old manor house surrounded by 385 hectares (951 acres) of rolling fields and forests. Of course, the red-brick manor didn't have 102 units, as does today's hotel, but modern wings were added in the 1980s with lots of glass allowing light to stream into the interior during those rare sunny days. The midsize-to-spacious bedrooms are conservatively but comfortably decorated in Danish modern, with small but well-appointed bathrooms with shower units. Public rooms evoke an upscale private home of the lord of the manor.

Sørupvej, DK-4100 Ringsted. (C) **800/528-1234** in the U.S., or 57-64-30-02. Fax 57-64-31-73. www.sorup.dk. 102 units. June to mid-Aug 590DKK ($100/£53) double; mid-Aug to May,198DKK ($204/£108) double; 2,050DKK ($349/ £185) year-round suite. Rates include breakfast. AE, DC, MC, V. **Amenities:** Restaurant; bar; indoor heated pool; tennis court; sauna; 24-hr. room service; laundry service; dry cleaning; nonsmoking rooms; rooms for those w/limited mobility; solarium. *In room:* TV, dataport, Wi-Fi, minibar, hair dryer.

WHERE TO DINE

Italy & Italy ⭐ ITALIAN   Thanks to good, market-fresh food and an emphasis on the olive oil–based cuisine of Italy, this is the most consistently popular restaurant in Ringsted, and well deserving of its celebrity. It sits very close to Ringsted's most famous church, in a dining room that's flooded with sunlight from big windows and lined with paintings that commemorate the architectural grandeur of Italy. Menu items cover all aspects of a well-orchestrated Italian meal, and include marinated seafood and vegetarian antipasti, and such succulent pastas as lasagna and fettuccine with Bolognese sauce. Two specialties that we've noted that the cooks do very well are medallions of veal Skt. Elisabeth, flamed in cognac, and a strong, powerful-tasting but nonetheless appealing plate of tender veal with a Gorgonzola sauce.

Torvet 1C. (C) **57-61-53-53.** Reservations recommended. Main courses 129DKK–189DKK ($22–$32/£12–£17); fixed-price menu 239DKK ($41/£22). AE, MC, V. Mon–Sat noon–9pm; Sun 5–9pm.

Rådhus Kro DANISH   The cooks at this restaurant don't set out to win awards, their main intent being to give you a satisfying meal made with fresh ingredients— everything offered at an affordable price. The inn is set across the street from the Rådhus (City Hall), but isn't really the *kro* (inn) of the Rådhus, as its name suggests. Erected in the mid-1980s, it occupies a modern-looking building short on style and character. Diners include many of the town's locals who have one or two meals here a week, especially members of the business and government communities.

There is a certain attention to detail and a proud professionalism, but what you get are such familiar dishes as filet of pork with white sauce and those boiled potatoes Danes are so fond of, or else a "competent" veal steak in a mushroom sauce. Norwegian haddock occasionally appears on the menu, and it's jazzed up with a red-wine sauce.

Skt. Bendtsgade 8. (C) **57-61-68-97.** Reservations recommended. Main courses 115DKK–195DKK ($20–$33/£10– £18). AE, DC, MC, V. Daily 11am–8:45pm.

RINGSTED AFTER DARK

You'll find pubs in virtually every neighborhood. Our favorite is the **Kong Valdemar Pub,** Nørregade 5 ((C) **57-61-81-32**), an antique-looking watering hole that has welcomed generations of drinkers to its paneled interior. Established in 1999, **Crazy Daisy,** Skt. Hansgade 31 ((C) **57-61-25-47**), is a two-floor drink and dance emporium that contains an active bar area, sometimes with live music, on its street level, and a busy dance club upstairs. Every night owl in town between the ages of 20 and 40 is likely to show up here to enjoy relaxed conversation and hot music. It's open only Friday to Sunday, 11pm to around 5am, charging a cover of 50DKK ($8.50/£4.50) per person.

3 Slagelse

99km (62 miles) SW of Copenhagen; 37km (23 miles) SE of Kalundborg; 19km (12 miles) NE of Korsør, 32km (20 miles) W of Ringsted

In the Middle Ages, this was a major trading center, with trade routes to Næstved in the south, Copenhagen in the east, and Kalundborg in the north. In the 11th century the town had its own mint, and its municipal charters were granted in 1288. Slagelse lies in the heart of Viking country and is the best center for visiting the nearby fortress at Trelleborg (see below).

Today the town of some 36,000 people is prospering, thanks largely to a lively economy. The area around here might be called Hans Christian Andersen Country, like Odense in Funen: The writer attended the local grammar school for several years but found the town a "nuisance." The school was founded after the Reformation and remained important until it closed in 1852.

After its heyday in the Middle Ages, Slagelse declined considerably, the victim of various wars and some raging fires that burned its major buildings. But with the coming of the rail lines, the economy recovered. Canning factories, distilleries, and breweries beefed up its economy.

Today it's a major city of West Zealand, a route along the important traffic artery, the E20, linking Copenhagen with the bridge across the Great Belt into Funen and the continent. Though often bypassed by rushed motorists, Slagelse has a number of treasures for those interested in the Viking period.

ESSENTIALS

GETTING THERE   By Train   Slagelse lies on the main east–west rail line between Copenhagen and the neighboring island of Funen (its subsequent link to the continent), and trains run here frequently (trip time: 1 hr.). There are also easy connections from Roskilde (35 min.) and from Korsør, near the bridge over the Great Belt (12 min.).

VISITOR INFORMATION   A 10-minute walk south of the train depot, the **Slagelse Turistbureau,** Løvegade 7 (© **58-52-22-06;** www.vikingelandet.dk), provides information about its own attractions and Trelleborg (see below) to the west. It's also helpful in hooking you up with any activities you may want to pursue and in providing directions for hiking and walking. Hours are Monday to Friday 10am to 5pm and Saturday 10am to 3pm, mid-June to August. Off season, it's open Monday to Friday 10am to 5pm and Saturday 10am to 1pm. The tourist office can arrange rooms in private homes with prices beginning at around 150DKK ($26/£14) per person for a B&B, plus a 40DKK ($6.80/£3.60) booking charge. You can rent bikes here or at **HJ Cykler,** Løvegade 46 (© **58-52-28-57**).

EXPLORING THE TOWN

If you follow the street, **Fisketorv,** it will lead to **Gammel Torv,** which, for many decades, was the thriving main square of town and a meeting place of locals. It's said that Queen Margrethe I crowned her 6-year-old son, Oluf, on this spot.

Slagelse possesses two historic churches and a minor museum, but, frankly, most sightseers use the town merely as a base for exploring the Viking reconstruction at **Trelleborg** (see below). If you're covering both Slagelse and Næstved in 1 day, you might skip the attractions in the center of Slagelse if you're pressed for time.

Skt. Mikkels Kirke (St. Michael's Church) dominates the town center. On the tallest hill in Slagelse, construction on this medieval church began in 1333, the architects preferring the Gothic style, using red brick made locally, in the construction. It was once the most important place for worship in town, but by the 1870s the townspeople seemed to have deserted it. Over the decades it had fallen into serious despair before a group of loyal church members raised the money for its restoration. If it was ever filled with art, it isn't anymore but it does have a historic memorial, honoring the brave members of the Danish Resistance movement in World War II. A noted Danish sculptor, Gunnar Slot, designed this memorial in 1959, and next to it is the church's other most noteworthy sculpture. Simply entitled *Woman* (and so it is), it is the work of Keld Moseholm Jørgensen.

Rosengade 4. ✆ **58-52-05-11**. Free admission. Daily 8:30am–5pm.

Skt. Peders Kirke If you like your churches dripping with more antiquity than Skt. Mikkels, then check out St. Peter's Church. Originally built in the Romanesque style around 1150, it was later—and regrettably—given a Gothic overlay. The vestry and porch came later, around 1500, and the present tower is from 1664, when it was reconstructed after the original collapsed. Of chief interest is a series of graves from the Middle Ages, which can be seen in a section that was once used for armament storage. The "big name" tomb here is that of St. Anders, who died in 1206, the first in a long line of vicars and one of the town's founding fathers. His tomb is in the northern tier of the church.

Bredegade 7A. ✆ **58-52-08-81**. Free admission. Daily 9am–5pm.

Slagelse Museum The town museum is relatively dull, not unusual for the provincial market towns of Denmark. Lying south of Nytorv, the main commercial square of town, this 1984 museum brings together exhibits devoted to both arts and crafts, as well as industry. Everybody gets in on the act here—the grocer, the carpenter, the joiner, the blacksmith, and even the barber. It's sort of a mishmash of everything valuable the town owned, including an exquisitely set dining table from the 19th century.

Bredegade 11. ✆ **58-52-83-27**. Admission 25DKK ($4.25/£2.25) adults, 5DKK (85¢/45p) children 15 and under. June 15–Aug daily noon–4pm; Sept–June 14 Sat–Sun noon–4pm.

SHOPPING

Slagelse is home of the **Vestsjællands Center,** Jernbanegade 10 (✆ **58-50-63-90**), a shopping mall with about 40 stores strong on Danish design and clothing, among other utilitarian shops.

If you're in the market for gold and silver jewelry, as well as the elegant products of Georg Jensen and Royal Copenhagen, the best outlet is **Guildsmed Carl Jensens,** Rosengade 17 (✆ **58-52-02-97**). But don't expect any discounts, as we found the prices charged here about the same as those of Copenhagen.

Finally, **Bahne** (✆ **58-52-00-75**) is located in the shopping complex in the heart of Slagelse, housing the largest collection of applied art in town, along with a wide range of pieces from Holmegaard glassworks and the Royal Danish Porcelain Factory. Again, prices are similar to what you'd pay in Copenhagen.

WHERE TO STAY

Hotel Frederik den II   In spite of its regal name, this sprawling, red-brick motel-style establishment is far better than the Bates Motel, but really no more than a refueling stop. Motorists stop here for the night, as the hotel lies a 10-minute drive south of the center at the junction of Route 22 and the E20 highway leading to Korsør and the neighboring island of Funen. Rooms are relatively small, but comfortably furnished in a standardized Danish modern way with tiny tiled bathrooms with shower stalls. The accommodations on the ground floor open onto private patios, and those upstairs open onto their own balconies. The on-site restaurant and bar is nothing special but will feed you well with Danish regional dishes.

Idagårdsvej 3, DK-4200 Slagelse. © **800/528-1234** in the U.S., or 58-53-03-22. Fax 58-53-46-22. www.frederik2.dk. 72 units. Mon–Fri 1,200DKK ($204/£108) double; Sat–Sun 945DKK ($161/£85) double; 1,700DKK ($289/£153) suite for 2. AE, DC, MC, V. **Amenities:** Restaurant; bar; sauna; laundry service; dry cleaning; nonsmoking rooms; rooms for those w/limited mobility. *In room:* TV, dataport (in some), hair dryer.

WHERE TO DINE

Pulcinilla ITALIAN   We won't pretend that this will be the finest Italian meal you've ever been served, but the food is well prepared with fresh ingredients, and it's good as a change of pace if you've tired of too much Danish fare. This likable dinner-only trattoria stands in the heart of Slagelse, with a white-walled interior whose roster of Italian art includes a blown-up version of the *Mona Lisa*. Menu items are flavorful and fun, and include a number of pizzas and pastas such as lasagna and fettuccine Bolognese, freshly made soups and crisp salads, with such standard main courses as veal parmigiana and entrecôte with pepper sauce.

Rosengade 7C. © **58-53-08-07.** Reservations recommended. Main courses 139DKK–179DKK ($24–$30/£13–£16). DC, MC, V. Daily 5–11pm.

SLAGELSE AFTER DARK

The municipality of Slagelse has converted an old power station into a splendid concert center. **Slagelse Musikhus,** Træskogården, Sdr. Stationsvej 1–3 (© **58-50-10-70**), is the venue for frequent musical events and also for changing art exhibitions. The old turbine hall can seat more than 400 patrons, and a cafe on-site serves refreshments. Ask at the tourist bureau (see "Visitor Information," above) whether any events are being staged at the time of your visit.

SIDE TRIPS: MEDIEVAL RUINS & VIKING RECONSTRUCTION

Slagelse makes a good base for exploring one of Scandinavia's major Viking reconstructions, Trelleborg, as well as a center for exploring Antvorskov, the ruins of a former royal palace and monastery. While still based at Slagelse, you can view both of these attractions in 1 busy day.

TRELLEBORG ✦✦

Although it's merely a mock representation, you can experience Viking life as lived 1,000 years ago at **Trelleborg Allé** (© **58-54-95-06**), the reconstructed fortress of **Trelleborg.** Trelleborg is the best preserved of the quartet of Viking ring fortresses in Denmark. Expect an agenda-loaded schedule once you arrive: You can feel replicas of Viking tools, see household items used by Mrs. Viking, view the inevitable weapons of the day, soak up the atmosphere in a re-created Viking house, and, best of all, enjoy the beautiful Danish countryside surrounding Trelleborg. You can also take part in various events staged throughout the summer, including longbow archery, Viking cooking, sailing, martial arts, games, a Viking pageant, and a Viking market.

A reconstructed Viking house at the entrance was built in the Viking stave style, with rough oak timbers rising above mud floors. Warriors and their families used the earthen benches inside for both sitting and sleeping. The central hearth, as in this house, usually had an opening in the roof for venting smoke. This house and other reconstructions were based on finds excavated from an actual settlement on this site, dating from 1000 to 1050.

The ring fortress consisted of a circular rampart with wooden stakes inserted in the earth, and it could be entered through four different gates. From these entrances four lanes led to the heart of the fortress. This divided the ring into four quadrants, with about 16 houses laid out in each quadrant. A moat protected the eastern side of the fortress, whereas two small rivers and a marshland secured the other three sides.

The Trelleborg Museum contains a shop selling reproduction Viking jewelry, books on the era, a film room, Viking exhibitions, ship models, ancient artifacts, and a cafe. The 20-minute video shown here will help you understand Trelleborg better before you actually explore it.

It is open Saturday to Thursday 10am to 5pm, and you can allow at least an hour for a visit, perhaps more if you find the site intriguing. Admission is 50DKK ($8.50/£4.50) adults, 35DKK ($5.95/£3.15) children 10 to 15, free for children under 10, a family ticket costing 130DKK ($22/£12).

GETTING THERE   By Car   Trelleborg is 6km (3¾ miles) west of Slagelse. Follow Strandvejen until its end at the village of Hejininge, where you'll see signs for Trelleborg, which is less than a kilometer (about ½ mile) away.

By Bus   You can take bus no. 312 from Slagelse right to the gate. There are several buses daily.

By Bicycle   You can cycle your way to Trelleborg on a rented bike from Slagelse. The tourist office will give you a brochure outlining points of interest along the cycle trail.

ANTVORSKOV

Today only the ruins of this former monastery and royal palace can be viewed, but much of Danish history happened on this spot, 2km (1¼ miles) south of the center of Slagelse near the road to Næstved. In 1164 King Valdemar I founded a monastery here, dedicated to the Order of St. John of Jerusalem. In time it became the major seat of the Order of St. John throughout the Nordic countries.

The monastery's chief legend centers on Hans Tausen (1494–1561), who preached a sermon in Antvorskov that paved the way for the Reformation in Denmark. This renegade monk, who trained at Antvorskov, then one of the richest monasteries in the country, became a disciple of Martin Luther, whom he had heard preach in Wittenberg. Tausen became so inflamed at the abuses of the Catholic church that he delivered a fiery speech upon his return to Antvorskov.

When the Reformation did come, the king confiscated Antvorskov, and it eventually was turned into a hunting manor. In time it fell into disrepair, its buildings sold or carted off. When it was deemed unsafe, the monastery church was torn down. The E20 motorway from Copenhagen buried about half of the former grounds of the monastery, but you can still see some of the brick foundations.

Don't expect a formalized museum if you opt to visit this site, as it's little more than a ruin, with no guardian, no fence or barricades, no telephone contact point, no formal hours, and no admission fee.

GETTING THERE **By Bicycle** To reach the site from Slagelse, follow Slotsalleén from the heart of town, turning right when you reach the end of this road, and then follow the signposts into Antvorskov.

BIRKEGÅRDENS HAVER ⍟

This is a large, privately owned park set in one of the most beautiful parts of Southwest Zealand, 23km (14 miles) north of Slagelse. The grounds contain a stunning **Japanese garden** ⍟ designed by the Danish landscape architect H. C. Skovgård, and also a young oak forest with a woodland lake. There are plenty of benches throughout the park, and packed lunches may be eaten in the courtyard garden. Here you can also see cows being milked, horses grazing, and goats, rabbits, and calves that come right up to you. There are also a playground for children, a cafe offering refreshments, and a kiosk selling ceramics, porcelain, and jewelry. Birkegårdens Haver lies at Tågerupvej 4 at Tågerup, near Kongsted (© **58-26-00-42**). It's open from April 10 to September 12 daily 9am to 6pm (July and August to 9pm). Admission is 70DKK ($12/£6.30) for adults, 20DKK ($3.40/£1.80) for children 10 to 15, free for children under 10.

GETTING THERE **By Car** To reach the gardens from Slagelse, drive north for 27km (17 miles) from the town center, following the signs that point to Kalundborg.

4 Næstved

80km (50 miles) SW of Copenhagen; 25km (16 miles) S of Ringsted; 35km (22 miles) SE of Slagelse

As your car roars on through rolling farmland and undiscovered villages, you come to the largest town in South Zealand, at the mouth of the Suså River, which made it a major Hanseatic port back in medieval times. The Danes themselves come here to enjoy the series of lakes and woodland that lie to the west and south of the town. Some visitors also like to go boating on the **Karrebæk Fjord,** forming a waterway linking Næstved with the scenic Karrebæksminde Bay.

Although there is industry here that sprouted up when the railway line came through in the 19th century, there is much of historic charm as well. The average foreign visitor can spend 2 to 3 hours exploring the historic core, with its Gothic churches, before setting out to take in the treasures of the environs.

Næstved sprouted up around a Benedictine monastery, whose buildings today house Herlufen, Denmark's most famous boarding school, similar in prestige to Eton in Britain. Today it's a garrison town and home to the **Gardehussar Regiment** or Hussars of the Household Calvary. The best time to catch these guards is on Wednesday morning when they ride through the center of town amid much fanfare.

Today much of the outlying area of the town is industrial, devoted to such businesses as timber, paper, engineering, and even ceramics. But in the immediate surroundings, beyond the fringe of town, lie a number of charming places to visit, ranging from manors to mansions, and from abbeys to beautiful parks (see "Easy Excursions," below).

ESSENTIALS

GETTING THERE **By Train** Næstved lies on two major train routes, one going via Ringsted (trip time: 20 min.), the other going via Køge (38 min.). Of course, Køge (see section 1) and Ringsted (see section 2) enjoy frequent rail connections from Copenhagen.

By Car   From Copenhagen, head south along E55 (also known as E47), cutting west along Route 54 into Næstved.

VISITOR INFORMATION   South of Axeltorv, **Næstved Turistbureau,** Havnen 1 (© **55-72-11-22**), is open January to June 14 and September to December, Monday to Friday 9am to 4pm, Saturday 9am to noon; June 15 to 30 and August, it's open Monday to Friday 9am to 5pm, Saturday 9am to 2pm; July it's open Monday to Friday 9am to 6pm, Saturday 9am to 2pm.

GETTING AROUND   By Bicycle   Bicycling is especially popular in Næstved, thanks to a relatively flat landscape and the fact that everyone in town seems to view it as a part of everyday life. You can pick up a bike from **Brotorvets Bicycles,** Brotorvet 3 (© **55-77-24-80**), costing 50DKK ($8.50/£4.50) a day, plus a 100DKK ($17/£9) deposit.

EXPLORING THE TOWN

Our favorite pastime here is a canoe ride on the River Suså, with its calm waters, running through the west side of Næstved. It doesn't have rapids and its current is negligible, so maneuvering by canoe is fairly easy. On summer weekends, the river is crowded with others who like to go canoeing too. Boats can be rented at **Suså Kanoudlejning,** Næsbyholm Allé 6, near Glumsø (© **57-64-61-44**), costing 100DKK ($17/£9) per hour or 370DKK ($63/£33) per day. The outlet for rentals lies at Slusehuset, at the southern end of Rådmanshavn.

As you stroll through the town, you'll come upon antique buildings, the most notable of which is **Apostelhuset,** a half-timbered house on Riddergade (just south of Skt. Mortens Kirke) that dates from the Middle Ages. "Apostle House" has carved figures of the apostles on the beams of its 16th-century facade; each carries an object that symbolizes his martyrdom. These are some of the oldest, and certainly the best-preserved, timber-frame carvings in the country. Nearby you'll see **Løveapoteket,** an old pharmacy in a restored half-timbered structure from 1853. The building is in the Dutch Renaissance style, and medicinal herbs and spices are still grown in a garden out back.

The central square of town is **Axeltorv,** and all of the major sights of town are within a short walk of this historic area. These include the following:

Skt. Peder Kirke   Dating from the early 1200s, St. Peter's Church is the largest Gothic church in Denmark, lying just to the south of Axeltorv. When it was restored in the 1880s, wall paintings from 1375 were uncovered in the choir area, one depicting Valdemar IV and his consort, Hedwig, kneeling at a penitent's stool. A Latin inscription reads, "In 1375, the day before the feast of St. Crispin, King Valdemar died—do not forget that!" You can also see a choir screen by Abel Schrøder the Elder (ca. 1600), plus an impressive crucifix by an unknown artisan dating from the 1200s and a pulpit dated 1671.

Skt. Peders Kirkeplads. © **55-72-31-90.** Free admission. May–Sept Tues–Fri 10am–noon and 2–4pm; Oct–Apr Tues–Fri 10am–noon.

Skt. Mortens Kirke   With a facade of red brick similar to that of St. Peter's, this church is of minor interest but worth 20 minutes or so of your time. It's found halfway between the rail terminal and that landmark square Axeltorv. Inside, the artistic highlight is a towering altar that was carved in 1667 by Abel Schrøder the Younger. The pulpit of the church is even older, dating from sometime in the early 1600s, and the work of the artist's father, Abel Schrøder the Elder.

Kattibjerg 2. ℂ 55-73-57-39. Free admission. July–Aug Mon–Fri 2–5pm; Sept–June Tues–Fri 9–11am.

Næstved Museum   Just when you thought you couldn't face another Danish provincial museum, along comes this one, which is better than most. Allow about an hour to visit its location north of Axeltorv, where it is divided into two sections. The best exhibits are in the town's oldest building, formerly the 14th-century **Helligånd-shuset** or "House of the Holy Ghost," which used to be the town hospital. Its collection is known for its medieval woodcarvings, although some contemporary works are also featured, and other artifacts illustrate the agricultural history of the region and the tools the peasants used. The second section, **Boderne,** at Skt. Peders Kirkeplads, displays local silver and crafts, including Holmegaard glass made locally. The buildings housing this section of the museum are period pieces, made of medieval brick with arched windows imbedded in mortar. Called *Stenboderne,* these 15th-century "stone booths" are the only remaining medieval terrace houses in Denmark. Craftspeople used to occupy them before they were turned into a museum.

Ringstedgade 4. ℂ 55-77-08-11. Admission 20DKK ($3.40/£1.80); free for children 17 and under. Tues–Sun 10am–4pm.

SHOPPING

There's plenty of shopping in Næstved itself, with no fewer than three major shopping centers. Every day in summer the streets in the heart of town echo with the sounds of a jazz band, and there's a market at **Axeltorv** Wednesday and Saturday mornings. All the shopping malls in Næstved stage free exhibitions and shows.

The best mall is the **Næstved Stor-Center,** Holsted Allée (ℂ **55-77-15-00;** bus: 2), the major shopping center for all of South Zealand, attracting shoppers from Møn, Falster, and various hamlets for many kilometers around. Located less than a kilometer (about ½ mile) north of the center, it's dominated by the giant Bilka supermarket (it's so large that they refer to it as a "hypermarket"). The mall's more than 50 specialist shops sell handicrafts, glass, jewelry, clothing, gifts, and dozens of other items.

WHERE TO STAY

Hotel Kirstine 🄰 *Finds*   The second-most-appealing hotel in Næstved originated in 1745, when a local alderman created it as a venue for town meetings in a carpenter-derived design that's part neo-Classical, part country baroque. Throughout most of the 1800s, it functioned as the home of the town's mayors, until around 1909, when it was transformed into a hotel that strictly prohibited any kind of alcohol on its premises, a policy long since abandoned. Today, the site is a half-timbered and romantic-looking monument to the elegant country life, thanks to a meticulous allegiance in all the public areas to a kind of well-scrubbed, prosperous-looking integrity that many visitors associate with rural Denmark. The midsize bedrooms are conservatively furnished and decorated, each with a private tiled bathroom with shower. There's glamour in some of the richly accessorized public areas, but only comfort in the bedrooms.

Købmagergade 20, DK-470 Næstved. ℂ 55-77-47-00. Fax 55-72-11-53. www.hotelkirstine.dk. 31 units. 895DKK ($152/£81) double; 1,200DKK ($204/£108) suite. Rates include buffet breakfast. AE, MC, V. **Amenities:** Restaurant; bar; laundry service; dry cleaning. *In room:* TV, dataport, minibar, hair dryer, safe.

Hotel Vinhuset ☆☆ *Finds*   The most distinctive and best hotel in the region was built in 1768 atop vaulted cellars that monks used to store wine as long ago as the 1400s. And although the site has always had a tradition of housing overnight guests and the worldly goods of an order of monks, it entered the world of modern tourism in earnest sometime after World War II, when it was transformed into a first-class hotel across the square from Sankt Peders Kirke. Inside, Persian carpets, antique furniture, and a romantic atmosphere add to the allure. The midsize-to-spacious rooms are comfortable, high ceilinged, and outfitted with a combination of modern furniture—especially good beds—and reproductions of antiques, each with neatly kept bathrooms with tub/shower combos. Even if you're not a guest, consider dining at this old hostelry (see below).

Skt. Peders Kirkeplads 4, DK-4700 Næstved. ☎ **55-72-08-07**. Fax 55-72-03-35. www.hotelvinhuset.dk. 57 units. 945DKK–1,445DKK ($161–$246/£85–£130) double. Rates include breakfast. AE, DC, MC, V. **Amenities:** Restaurant; bar; room service (7am–10pm); babysitting; laundry service; dry cleaning; nonsmoking rooms. *In room:* TV, hair dryer.

Mogenstrup Kro   If you can skip the fancy frills, this is an old Danish *kro* that has been putting up wayfarers for more than 2 centuries. It never pretends to be more than it is, and has a steady stream of customers, often weekenders escaping the congestion of Copenhagen. Its bedrooms, medium in size, are comfortably and tastefully furnished, though hardly memorable, and each unit comes with a tub/shower combo in each of the private bathrooms. Good Danish country cooking in its restaurant also attracts a local trade.

Præstø Landevej 25, DK-4700 Næstved. ☎ **55-76-11-30**. Fax 55-76-11-29. www.firsthotels.com. 99 units. 960DKK–1,350DKK ($163–$230/£86–£122) double. Rates includes breakfast. AE, DC, MC, V. **Amenities:** Restaurant; bar; sauna; room service (7am–9pm); laundry service; dry cleaning; nonsmoking rooms; rooms for those w/limited mobility. *In room:* TV, dataport, minibar (in some), hair dryer.

WHERE TO DINE

Restaurant Bytinget ☆ DANISH/FRENCH   In the previously recommended Hotel Vinhuset, the town's best restaurant lies within an 18th-century setting that originally was a warehouse for wine. Both the roast Danish lamb and the duckling are superb here, as the chefs are known for selecting the finest ingredients at the market that day. They can get fancy with their sauces but also turn out down-home fare such as *frikadeller,* browned steak with onions, and filet of plaice in a parsley butter sauce. Desserts are made fresh daily and are scrumptious.

In the Hotel Vinhuset, Skt. Peders Kirkeplads 4. ☎ **55-72-08-07**. Main courses 108DKK–198DKK ($18–$34/£9.75–£18). AE, DC, MC, V. Mon–Sat noon–3pm and 7–9:30pm.

NÆSTVED AFTER DARK

Each of the hotels recommended above maintains a bar, but in addition to those, you'll find easy access to at least three pubs, any of which might act as a backdrop for some drinks, dialogue, and people-watching. The watering holes follow an unpredictable, frequently changing schedule that incorporates an hour or two of live music, usually on Friday and/or Saturday nights beginning around 9pm. Everything in town, however, is very spontaneous, so be alert to whatever musical venue your hotel staff says is happening during the time of your arrival. A worthwhile bet for nautical atmosphere and camaraderie is **Rådhus Kroenm,** Skomagerrækken 8 (☎ **55-72-01-56**), rivaled only by **Underhuset Bar,** Axeltorv 9 (☎ **55-72-79-19**). Equally appealing is another pub, **Step Inn,** Ramsherred 14 (☎ **55-77-01-08**).

EASY EXCURSIONS

Herlufsholm is known to educators throughout Europe as the site of a famous prep school, less than a kilometer (about ½ mile) northwest of the center of Næstved. It was founded at the dawn of the 13th century as a Benedictine monastery known as Skovkloster. The monastery, abandoned at the time of the Reformation, was transformed into the **Herlufsholm Academy,** Herlufsholm Allée (© **55-75-35-01;** bus: 6A). To reach it from Næstved, follow the Slagelsevej from the town center. You can wander around the grounds, assuming you don't interrupt the flow of the academics, but if your time is limited, the crown jewel of the academy grounds is the monastery church, **Stiftskirke Herlufsholm.** Constructed in the late Middle Ages, it is one of the oldest brick churches in Denmark. It's noteworthy for its tombs, especially those of Admiral Herluf Trolle, who left an endowment to the monastery, and his wife, Birgitte Goye. The ivory Gothic crucifix inside dates from around 1230; the baroque pulpit was the creation of Ejler Abelsen in 1620. The church, which has an unusually wide nave, can be visited daily—except during religious services—during daylight hours. Admission is free.

One of the many stately homes surrounding Næstved is **Gavnø Slot & Park** (★, Gavnørej (© **55-70-02-00;** bus: 1A). Located 4km (2½ miles) south of town, it lies on a peninsula, on the opposite bank of the Karrebækfjord. The old rococo castle is surrounded by a delightful botanical garden and is also the site of **Butterfly World,** where exotic tropical butterflies are allowed to fly free. A former nunnery, Gavnø reverted to private ownership in 1584. When Otto Thott (1703–85) took over the property, he had it converted into the rococo-style mansion you see today. Thott also accumulated one of the largest picture collections and private libraries (about 140,000 volumes) in Denmark. The premises also contain a valuable altar and pulpit carved by Abel Schrøder the Elder. Although part of the interior remains a private residence, some sections of the castle can be visited. The best time to visit is when the tulips bloom in spring, these flowers later giving way to ornamental shrubs and roses. A ticket that combines admission to the castle, the castle gardens with its butterfly collection, and a nearby church (Gavnø Kirke) that has been associated with the castle for many generations costs 65DKK ($11/£5.85) adults, 30DKK ($5.10/£2.70) for children under 12. All three places are open only May to August, daily 10am to 4pm.

The manor house that we'd like to own is **Gisselfeld Slot** (★, Gisselfeldvej 3, Haslev (© **56-32-60-32**), a beautiful, step-gabled, brick Renaissance home dating from 1557. If you visit, you'll be wandering in the footsteps of Hans Christian Andersen, who found inspiration here for his fairy tale *The Ugly Duckling.* Although it has been much altered and changed over the centuries, it forms an impressive sight today, set in a well-laid-out park that evokes the countryside of England, with a fountain, a small lake, a grotto, and even a waterfall. You will have to be content to view the house from the outside, but you can wander through one of Denmark's finest private gardens, with some 400 different species of trees and bushes, including a rose island and a bamboo grove. The gardens are at their best in the late spring. The gardens can be visited daily 10am to 5pm (mid-June to mid-Aug to 6pm). It costs 25DKK ($4.25/£2.25) for adults, free for children under 12. The only time the interior can be visited is during July, when guided tours can be arranged, on a rotating and oft-changing schedule that must be reconfirmed prior to your arrival.

The little town of Vordingborg, 27km (17 miles) south of Næstved, was a power-house back in the Middle Ages, and the place where Denmark's first constitution was written. "It's our Philadelphia," the tourist manager told us.

Most visitors arrive to see the fabled "Goose Tower," once part of the sprawling royal cas-tle and fortress that stood here during the Middle Ages. The 14th-century **Gåsetårnet** ★★, Slotsruinen 1 (© **55-37-25-54**), is the best-preserved medieval tower in Scandinavia, the only structure remaining intact from the Valdemar era. The tower gets its name from 1368, when the king, Valdemar IV, ordered that a golden goose be placed on top of the tower to show his disdain for a declaration of war against Denmark by the Hanseatic League of Germany. He was hoping to suggest that the threats coming from the Hanseatic League were no more ominous to him than a flock of cackling geese. The pointed copper roof of the 37m (121-ft.) tower is still crowned by a golden goose, and the tower, of course, remains the town's landmark and source of historic pride. From the top of the tower a panoramic view of the countryside unfolds. In its heyday, the fortress had seven more towers, but they were demolished over the centuries. In recent years excavations have uncovered the ruins of the castle. Queen Margrethe visited in 1997 to view the excavation of a Viking quay. Visiting hours are June to August daily 10am to 5pm; off season, Tuesday to Sunday 10am to 4pm.

VORDINGBORG AFTER DARK

A good place to begin your evening is **Amigo Bar,** Algade 35 (© **55-37-60-65**), right in the center of town. It seems to attract the most simpatico crowd. The best alehouse is nearby: **Slots Kroen,** Algade 119 (© **55-37-02-61**). A lot of the locals will also direct you to **Willy Nilly,** Algade 1 (© **55-34-20-40**), a friendly English pub that seems to have the coldest beer in town, attracting a 20-to-40 age group. It's also the site of **Prinsen Diskotek,** Algade 1 (© **55-34-20-40**), which opens at 10 or 11pm, often staying open until 3 or 4am. It rarely charges a cover.

5 Møn

128km (80 miles) S of Copenhagen

In world War II almost every music hall in England had singers promising that blue-birds would return to the White Cliffs of Dover when the world was free. On the island of Møn, which also has spectacular white cliffs, it was the peregrine falcon that returned after a mysterious disappearance that lasted for the remaining 25 years of the 20th century. Off the coast of Southeast Zealand in a "corner" of Denmark, the island of Møn lures visitors with its white chalky cliffs, the 120m (394-ft.) **Møns Klint** that stretches for some 6km (3¾ miles), rising dramatically from the Baltic Sea. Møns Klint was formed by the Baltic, and made up of ice-transported chalk masses and glacial deposits formed from calcareous ooze 75 million years ago. The ooze enclosed shells of marine animals that are now fossils. The glacial deposit originated partly as boul-der clay deposited by inland ice and partly as bedded clay and sand containing mus-sels. The boulders on the beach long ago dropped from the cliff and have been rounded by wave erosion.

Although Møn's white chalk cliffs are its main appeal, once you get here you'll find an island of rustic charm and grace well worth exploring. Fewer than 12,000 people live here, and the residents of Møn zealously guard their natural environment where the beauty of their landscapes remains largely unspoiled. Sheltered by dunes, the white sandy beaches are a summer attraction, so it's not just the wild cliffs that draw visitors

---

(Finds) **Pottery Sales**

As you drive about Møn, note the many signs advertising *keramik*. On this slow-paced island, people everywhere seem to have taken up ceramics and pottery and are only too willing to sell their products to you. This interest in ceramics originated because of the rich clay deposits found here.

---

here. The island also boasts beautiful forests with a wide variety of wildlife and a trio of churches with the best frescoes in the country (more about that later), plus a lively market town in Stege.

Møn is also known for the prehistoric remains that are scattered about the island. For detailed information, the tourist office (see "Visitor Information," below) publishes a booklet called *Prehistoric Monuments of Møn*. Several Neolithic chambered tombs known as "giants' graves" were discovered. As the legend goes, the western part of the island was ruled by a "jolly green giant" called the Green Huntsman, and the eastern part of the island was the domain of another giant, Upsal.

Møn lies at the eastern edge of the Størstrommen, a channel dividing the island of Zealand and the island of Falster.

ESSENTIALS

GETTING THERE   By Car   Cross over from the island of Zealand on the Dronning Alexandrines Bridge, then proceed through the old country town of Stege.

VISITOR INFORMATION   The local tourist office, **Møns Turistbureau,** Storegade (© **55-86-04-00**), is open Monday to Friday 10am to 5pm and Saturday 9am to noon.

GETTING AROUND   Because bus service on the island is meager, you'll need a car or bike to explore.

By Bicycle   Many Danes prefer to explore Møn by bike. The best trail to follow is the signposted bike route going from the capital, Stege, to Møns Klint. Ask at the tourist office for a pamphlet outlining the best cycling tours of the island, which take in all of Møn's principal attractions. In Stege, bikes can be rented at **Dækaingen Cykler,** Storegade 91 (© **55-81-42-49**). Rates average 50DKK ($8.50/£4.50) a day.

STEGE ⊛: THE ISLAND'S CAPITAL

Time seems to have forgotten this sleepy little capital, and that is part of its charm. To the surprise of first-time visitors, Stege has preserved its moat and ramparts from the Middle Ages, whereas other Danish towns have torn them down. One of its original trio of town gates, **Mølleporten,** is still here to greet guests as in olden days. Mølleporten, which once allowed (or prohibited) entry to the town, stands on Storegade. Meaning "mill gate" in English, the gate bears a resemblance to the Stege church tower, and is made of red brick and lined with horizontal strips of white chalk from (where else?) Møns Klint.

After crossing the bridge from "mainland" Zealand on Route 59, take an immediate left and follow the road to the ancient market town of Stege, which is the ideal gateway to the island and the source of the best information about Møn (see "Visitor Information," above).

Møn

EXPLORING THE TOWN

Known for its primitive frescoes, **Stege Kirke** ⚸, Kirkepladsen (✆ **55-81-40-65**), is one of the largest churches in the country, with a massive tower striped in brick and chalk. Its oldest section, built in the Romanesque style, dates from the early 1200s and was constructed by the ruler of the island, Jakob Sunesen, who was a member of the powerful Hvide family. In the latter 1400s the church was expanded to its present size.

The principal nave is flanked by two smaller naves on each side and is filled with pointed arched windows and high vaulted ceilings. Rich frescoes by the Master of Elmelunde are found in the choir and main nave. Long covered with whitewash, they were discovered and restored in 1892. Many are quite whimsical in nature; and in the post-Reformation era, Lutheran ministers found the frescoes too evocative of Catholic themes, and ordered that they be whitewashed. Although this sounds bad, it was the whitewashing that actually preserved the frescoes so that they can still be enjoyed today. They were restored under the supervision of Denmark's national museum. Charging no admission, the church is open April to September Tuesday to Sunday 9am to 5pm; October to March Tuesday to Sunday 9am to 1pm.

Next to the old Mølleporten, or town gate, stands **Empiregården,** Storegade 75 (✆ **55-81-40-67**), housing the rather elegant **Møn Museum,** a repository of local cultural history. The collection is rich in artifacts from the Middle Ages, including coins and old pottery, but it also goes back to the Stone Age, displaying items like ancient fossilized sea urchins. The museum also exhibits Møn house interiors from the 1800s. It's open Tuesday to Sunday 10am to 4pm, charging 30DKK ($5.10/£2.70), free for children under 11.

SHOPPING

The island is known for its ceramics and pottery, whose production keeps dozens of artisans working long hours. Two of the best places to see, and buy, some of the goods produced here include a warehouse-size emporium 4km (2½ miles) east of Stege on the road leading to Møns Klint. **Ympelese,** Klintevej 110 (© **55-81-30-05**), stocks some of the most appealing handmade candles in Zealand, as well as a variety of ceramic pots, plates, and vessels. There's even men's, women's, and children's clothing for sale, some of it fabricated by local seamstresses, and some of it designed to protect its wearer from the midwinter gales that sweep in from the Baltic and North Seas.

WHERE TO STAY & DINE

Hotel Ellens Cabaret   This oddly named hotel is the site of a weekend cabaret that is pure country, certainly not of the "come to the cabaret" sophistication that would attract a Danish Liza Minnelli. One local told us that the humor is strictly for the islanders and even Copenhageners wouldn't understand it. But if you can get past this beer-and-booze attraction, you'll find a three-story motel-style building, standing at the edge of town near the sea. Bedrooms are fairly streamlined and small to midsize, the most desirable with large windows opening onto balconies. All the tiny but tiled bathrooms come with tub/shower combos and are well maintained. The bar with its large-screen TV attracts a lot of sports fans and traveling salespeople, and is said to be a good pickup spot for women.

Langelinie 48, DK-4780 Stege. © 55-81-54-54. Fax 55-81-58-90. 27 units. 770DKK ($131/£69) double. Rates include breakfast. MC, V. **Amenities:** Bar; nightclub; lounge; laundry service; dry cleaning. *In room:* No phone.

Præstekilde Kro & Hotel ☆☆   This is the most opulent and glamorous hotel on Møns—partly because of its upscale comforts and partly because of its association with the island's nearby golf course, opening onto a view of the Bay of Stege. Built in the early 1970s in a rambling compound of big-windowed, low-slung buildings, it lies 5km (3 miles) east of Stege, about 2.5km (1½ miles) from the nearest beach, Strand Wengensgaardsvej. Many, but by no means all, of the clients spend their day on the golf links; others decompress from urban life in Copenhagen, walking through nearby fields and forests or relaxing beside the seacoast. Bedrooms are not as plush as we would prefer, considering the public lounges, but, though small, they are tastefully and comfortably furnished, each with bathrooms that are well kept and come with tub/shower combos.

The on-site restaurant risks being fully booked throughout the fleeting months of a Danish summer, but is a lot more accessible throughout the rest of the year. Within a color scheme of yellow and white, with big-windowed views over the surrounding scenery of this isolated spot, it offers conservative Danish cuisine in the form of fresh fish and such specialties as meatballs and hash. It's one of the very few fully functioning restaurants that remains open throughout the year in this remote part of Denmark. A daily fixed-priced three-course lunch is 258DKK ($44/£23), with dinner main courses costing 158DKK to 210DKK ($27–$36/£14–£19). Service is daily 12:30 to 4pm and 6 to 9pm.

Klintevej 116, DK-4780 Stege. (✆ **55-86-87-88**. Fax 55-81-36-34. www.praestekilde.dk. 46 units. 925DKK–1,025DKK ($157–$174/£83–£92) double; 1,125DKK–1,225DKK ($191–$208/£101–£110) junior suite. Rates include breakfast. AE, DC, MC, V. **Amenities:** Restaurant; bar; indoor heated pool; sauna; 24-hr. room service; laundry service; dry cleaning; nonsmoking rooms; solarium. *In room:* TV, minibar, hair dryer.

STEGE AFTER DARK

Persons under age 25 on the island are quick to point out that there are no full-time dance clubs on Møn, unless a local church or civic group opts to hold a youth-group gathering in a communal basement somewhere. In lieu of that, the most convivial gathering place is the bar at the previously recommended **Præstekilde Kro & Hotel,** Klintevej (✆ **55-86-87-88**). Here you'll find an inkling of big-city style a la Copenhagen, but not so much that you won't realize that you're far from urban life. Still, the drinks taste good, and you're likely to meet a handful of other urbanites to swap stories with.

ULVSHALE 🎖🎖 & NYORD

After leaving Stege, you can follow a minor little road directly north 6km (3¾ miles) with signposts that will lead you to Ulvshale, or "Wolf's Trail" in English, a peninsula jutting west toward Zealand. It's one of the most beautiful spots on Møn, now preserved as a nature reserve, with gnarled old trees and rare birds such as snipe, razorbills, water rails, and others, which prefer to live on the mud flats. Ulvshale boasts one of the best beaches on the island and it also is home to one of the few virgin forests left in the country. The chilly beach is Ulvshale Strand, and the main road, Ulvshalevej, runs right along it. The forest is crisscrossed with a network of hiking routes.

Once at Ulvshale you'll see a bridge connecting Møn with the little offshore island of **Nyord.** You can walk across the bridge to get to this tiny speck of an island, which means "New Word" in English. It's been set aside as a sanctuary for rare birds, including rough-legged buzzards, snow buntings, hen harriers, and others. The birds are seen mainly in the east marshes. On the north side of the road, about a kilometer (⅗ mile) after crossing the bridge, you'll come to a tower that is the best vantage point for watching the birds, and the bridge itself is also a good bird-watching site.

The little village on the island is called **Nyord,** too, and it's a time capsule from the 1800s, with old thatched houses. Other than a tiny yacht harbor and a little church from 1846, there aren't a lot of attractions, but it's such an idyllic place it's worth the effort to get here.

After a look at the birds, head back in the direction of Stege, but when you see a turnoff to Keldby, follow the signs into this hamlet, 5km (3 miles) east of Stege.

KELDBY

This agrarian community is mainly visited by those who want a look at **Keldby Kirke** 🎖, Præstegårdstræde 1, Keldby (✆ **55-81-33-05**). Built of brick between 1200 and 1250, this is one of the island's special churches, celebrated for its frescoes that span 200 years, the oldest dating from 1275, with both Old and New Testament scenes included. No church in Denmark quite equals Keldby in medieval frescoes—note especially the dramatic representation of Cain and Abel and the horror show depicting Doomsday. Shepherds pictured with their flocks create a more bucolic scene. In addition to the frescoes, the church also contains a number of other treasures, notably a carved pulpit dated 1586, and, in the vaulting, paintings by the Master of Elmelunde, including a tender depiction of Joseph preparing gruel for his newly born infant son. A tombstone at the north side of the church dates from the mid–14th century. Admission is free, and the church can be visited April to September daily from 7am to 4:45pm, off season daily 8am to 3:45pm.

If you have time after viewing the church, visit the manor **Hans Hansens Gård,** Skullebjergvej 15 (© **55-81-40-67**), which lies about 1.5km (about a mile) south of Keldby Church. (Follow the signs to Keldbylille to reach it.) Dating from 1800, this is a thatch-covered building whose wings enclose an inner courtyard. Originally conceived as a farmhouse, it's the home of Møns Museumsgården, a monument that depicts what family life was like for homesteaders during the 1800s. The farm was kept in the same family for generations. When its last owner, a bachelor, Hans Hansens (for whom the property is named), died, he willed it to the people of Møns, who converted it into a museum. Furniture and utensils used by the Hansens family are on display. Open April to September, Tuesday to Sunday 10am to 4pm, charging 30DKK ($5.10/£2.70) for admission.

The highway (Rte. 287) continues directly east to Elmelunde.

ELMELUNDE

This tiny rural hamlet, roughly equivalent to Keldby in size and layout, is 7km (4⅓ miles) east of Stege and is the site of the island's second-most-visited church, **Elmelunde Kirke** ⍟, Klintevej, Elmelunde (© **55-81-33-05**). Dating from around 1080, it's one of the oldest stone churches in Denmark. During the Romanesque era, the nave was expanded. In the early 1300s, the distinctive tower was added, transforming it into a prominent landmark for sailors coming in from the turbulent sea. The interior of the church is known for its frescoes painted by the Master of Elmelunde. Here this rather mysterious artist left some of his masterpieces, including *Last Judgment, St. Peter with the Key to Heaven, Christ in Majesty, St. Paul with a Sword,* and his charming *Entry into Jerusalem,* along with the more sobering *Flagellation of Christ.*

He also painted lighter subjects, including autumn harvest and some plowing-the-fields scenes. Other frescoes depict Adam and Eve being thrown out of the Garden of Eden. The feudal lord Corfitz Ulfeldt and his consort, Queen Leonora Christina, donated the altar and pulpit. The intricately carved and painted altar dates from 1646; the pulpit was created about 3 years later. The carved pulpit is supported entirely on a figure of St. Peter. In 1460 the three-pointed vaults (seen over the altar) were added, and the Master of Elmelunde painted them as well. Admission free, the church is open daily 8am to 4pm.

WHERE TO STAY

Hotel Elmehøj   This place, one of the most stately looking guesthouses in Møn, has a real down-home feel, lying 4km (2½ miles) inland between Stege and Møns Klint, adjacent to the stop for buses that interconnect the two. The hotel actually started life in 1928 as a retirement home but was later successfully converted into a hotel. In 1991, it was acquired by Brit Olifent, a woman born and reared on Møn, who runs it today with her husband, Jonathan, who was born in Perth, Australia. Rooms are simple and very well maintained, with few frills and a sense of regimented orderliness. There's little to do on the property, other than taking promenades in the well-tended garden, exploring the nearby beach and forest, and visiting the 12th-century interior of the Elmelunde church, a short walk away. A communal TV room and a public kitchen that some guests use to prepare light lunches and snacks are on the premises.

Kirkebakken 39, Elmelunde, DK-4780 Stege, Møn. © **55-81-35-35.** Fax 55-81-32-67. www.elmehoj.dk. 23 units, none with bathroom. 470DKK ($80/£42) double. Rate includes breakfast. MC, V. Closed Jan. **Amenities:** Breakfast room; lounge; laundry service; dry cleaning. *In room:* No phone.

WHERE TO DINE

Kaj Kok ⓕ *Finds* DANISH   Good country cooking consistently lures us to this big-windowed restaurant from the 1970s, lying a kilometer (⅔ mile) from the hamlet of Elmelunde. Many locals praise it for its well-prepared versions of time-honored Danish specialties, and we agree with their enthusiasm. You'll recognize it by its red facade and a large garden in which tame goats munch on vegetables. The interior's modernity is disguised by a roster of old-fashioned decorative accessories. Launch yourself with the likes of a well-flavored garlic-laced crab bisque or else the smoked salmon. You won't shed tears of joy but might still delight in the filet of halibut in a white wine and parsley sauce or a particularly flavorful version of pepper steak, with just the right "bite." Lighter appetites appreciate the *smørrebrød* (open-faced sandwich), which usually sell for 30DKK ($5.10/£2.70), except for a deluxe version, with lobster, that costs 61DKK ($10/£5.50).

Klintevej 151, Elmelunde. ⓒ **55-81-35-85.** Reservations recommended. Main courses 92DKK–161DKK ($16–$27/ £8.30–£14). No credit cards. Daily noon–9pm. Closed Oct–Apr Mon–Wed.

LISELUND

After a meal at Kaj Kok, head east along Route 287 through the hamlet of Borre, where you'll pass a brick church built in the early 1200s. Continue through the village but turn left at the signpost to Sømarke. The next road to the right leads to Sømarkedyssen. At this point you'll come upon a round dolmen crowned by a huge capstone over an open chamber. From here there's a panoramic view over the entire island. After a look at the dolmen, continue on the same road, going left up a very narrow lane. At the peak, turn right along the road for about 90m (300 ft.), which will lead to the entrance of Liselund.

This thatched palatial summer home from 1795 is surrounded by lovely park grounds with artificial lakes and canals in the northeastern part of the island. H. C. Andersen wrote *The Tinder Box* while staying at the Swiss Cottage here. The park is called a "folly" of the 18th century, when it was constructed by Bosc de la Calmette, a royal chamberlain who was inspired by Marie Antoinette's Hamlet at Versailles. You can buy refreshments at a small chalet filled with antlers and antiques. The admission-free park is open daily until sunset year-round.

Other structures in the park were destroyed by a rockfall in 1905, but guided tours of the **Gamle Slot** (Old Castle) are available. Call ⓒ **55-81-21-78** for more details. Inside you'll find an architectural mélange of styles, with tiny canopied beds, a *trompe l'oeil* painting, and a Monkey Room painted with a jungle scene. Visits are possible Tuesday to Friday and Sunday, at 10:30am, 11am, 1:30pm, and 2 pm. Admission is 20DKK ($3.40/£1.80) adults, 10DKK ($1.70/90p) for children 10 to 15, free for children under 10.

WHERE TO STAY & DINE

Liselund Ny Slot   Don't let the *slot* (castle) reference in the name of this place mislead you—Buckingham Palace it isn't. Set amid the trees and rolling hills of a national park, this manor house was built in 1887 as an annex to a much older castle. Since the transformation of the original castle into a museum, most of the region's overnight guests seek accommodations in the yellow-colored stucco walls and soaring tower of the Ny Slot (New Castle). Rooms are simple but bright, outfitted with minimalist furniture and neatly kept bathrooms with shower units, offering views over fields, forests, a pond with swans, and the sea. Many of the public areas have high, frescoed ceilings that evoke a sense of the place's original grandeur.

You don't have to stay at the hotel to eat lunch in the establishment's basement-level cafe (served noon–6pm), or for dinner in the more formal dining room (6:30–8pm). Menu items include standard preparations of Danish lamb in rosemary sauce, Baltic or North Sea fish, and steaks. There's also an occasional Chinese or Asian dish to break the monotony. The restaurant is open daily in summer, with an occasional (unscheduled) closing 1 or 2 days a week in winter.

Langebjergvej 6, DK-4791 Borre. © 55-81-20-81. Fax 55-81-21-91. 15 units. 1,250DKK ($213/£113) double. Rate includes breakfast. MC, V. **Amenities:** Dining room; cafe; lounge. *In room:* No phone.

MØNS KLINT ★★

After a visit or even an overnight stay at Ny Slot, drive back to Route 287 and follow the road east to the highlight of the tour, **Møns Klint.** These impressive white chalk cliffs (see section 5, "Møn") stretch for several kilometers, with a sheer drop of 120m (394 ft.) at their highest point. Formed by glacial deposits combined with the action of a turbulent sea, they are one of the most dramatic natural sights in Denmark. Møns Klint was pocked throughout with nearly 100 Neolithic burial mounds. Paths lead through woodland to the towering edge of the cliffs, where one of the most panoramic views ★★★ in all of Denmark awaits you. For decades photographers have delighted in capturing the image of these brilliantly white cliffs against the azure blue of the sea. When the sun is out, the scene is especially breathtaking.

Footpaths are cut into the cliffs, and visitors are fond of hiking these towering trails. It takes about an hour's walk to appreciate the magnificence of the site. There's a wide expanse of beech trees along the top of the cliffs, providing shelter for rare plants, including 20 species of orchids hidden in the undergrowth. For the best view, follow the signs to the peak called Sommerspiret and hope that the sky is clear at the time of your visit. Fossils of marine animals—some long extinct—have also been discovered on the beach below these cliffs. Two steep flights of steps lead from both Storeklint and Jydeleje down to the sea, but be prepared for an exhausting climb back to the top. Once you're at the bottom, you can join Danish families who hunt for blanched fossils on the beach, usually sea urchins. Captains at sea use the cliffs as a navigational point since they stand out from Zealand's relatively flat topography.

The most dramatic hike, of course, is along the towering cliffs. But if time remains, you can also hike through **Klinteskoven** (Klinte Forest), a woodland area that grows right up to the edge of the cliffs. Horse trails and a network of paths have been cut through this forest. Trails start from the edge of the cliffs, and the best track to follow is about a kilometer (⅔ mile) west of Storeklint, which will take you to Timmesø Bjerg. Here you'll see the ruins of a castle built around 1100. If you visit, facilities for tourists are found at Storeklint, including a cafeteria and a parking lot, along with some routine souvenir kiosks.

At **Rent-A-Horse,** Langebjergvej 1 (© **55-81-25-25**), an outfitter near a local youth hostel at Møns Klint, you can book 2-hour guided horseback tours of Møns Klint or the bay at its base, the Klinteskoven. Equestrian treks are priced at 300DKK ($51/£27) per person per 1½ hours (including a guide).

KLINTHOLM HAVN

Returning to the parking lot at Møns Klint, you can continue south along a minor little road to the hamlet of Sandvej. Once here, turn right at the T-junction in the direction of Mandemarke. Before reaching this village, take a left turn down a lane marked KLINTHOLM HAVN. This will take you to an old village on the coast with a bustling fishing harbor and a modern marina. The seaside village, a bit of a holiday center, opens onto Hjelm Bay. It's best to visit here on a sunny day, as Klintholm Havn is mainly known for its beach.

Many wealthy Germans use the marina here to station their yachts. One harbor is filled with fishing boats, the other with these yachts, and the beach runs in both directions from these two harbors. We prefer the beach extending to the east, since it's well maintained and set against a backdrop of low-lying dunes; the sands aren't pure white, however, but more of an oyster gray. But if you want to venture into these usually cold waters, the safest swimming is on the beach extending to the west of the harbors. At the marina are public toilets and showers.

WHERE TO DINE

Chances are you'll be in the area for lunch. There are a few slightly formal places to eat, but our suggestion for a meal is to walk east along the coastal road from the fishing harbor until you come to a little outlet called **Klintholm Røgeri.** Here you can purchase fried or smoked fish and wash it down with a cold Carlsberg. This is an ideal place to enjoy a picnic, and there are picnic tables on-site.

SIGHTS IN WEST MØN

After a visit to Møns Klint, you'll have to take the same route back into Stege. But there are other attractions in Møn if time remains. From Stege, head south along Route 287 to **Grønjægers Høj,** an impressive long barrow surrounded by a stone circle, 6km (3¾ miles) south of Stege near the hamlet of Æbelnæs. Called "The Hill of the Green Huntsman," it's a Stone Age "passage grave." Nearly 150 large stones surround the megalithic tomb with three chambers, one of the largest such gravesites in all of Scandinavia.

The third church of Møn to have been decorated by the Master of Elmelunde lies in the area. To reach it, continue on Route 287 to Damsholte, then go left on a minor road following the sign to **Fanefjord Kirke** ⚜, Fanefjordkirkevej, Fanefjord (© 55-81-70-05). The frescoes in the chancel date from the mid–14th century, but the rest are by the master himself. The cycle of paintings was called *Biblia Pauperum,* or "Bible of the poor," since many of the peasants who formed the congregation did not read. Most of the themes were taken from the Old and New Testaments, and others are loosely based on Christian legends.

Depicted are the *Adoration of the Magi,* the *Baptism of Jesus,* the *Birth of Jesus,* and the *Annunciation,* among other subjects. *The Slaughter of the Innocents* is particularly moving. The most fun and amusing fresco is *St. George and the Dragon.* In the choir arch are some frescoes from the High Gothic period, around the mid–14th century, depicting St. Martin and St. Christopher, among other subjects, with St. Christopher seen carrying Christ across a fjord. The imagination that went into these frescoes shows amazing creativity and massive talent, and the refinement of color is also a remarkable achievement. They are well worth the detour here to reach them. The church itself overlooks Fanefjord and was constructed in the mid–13th century in the Gothic style. It's open Monday to Saturday 7am to 4pm, charging no admission.

After viewing the church, head 8km (5 miles) north in the direction of Tostenæs, where you'll see a sign to **Kong Asgers Høj,** a large passage grave, with a passageway leading to a vast burial chamber. The site lies in a farmer's field on Kong Asgers Vej. The burial chamber is 10m (33 ft.) long and some 2m (6½ ft.) wide. Duck as you go in or you'll crown yourself.

One final attraction remains for Møn, and it's actually an island unto itself. The island of **Bogø** at the southwestern edge of Møn is reached by continuing along Route 287. A causeway leads to what is called "The Island of Mills." Once many mills peppered the little island, but now there's only one remaining, **Bogø Molle,** which was constructed in 1852 and looks like a windmill from Holland.

Other than its bucolic charm, there isn't a lot to see and do on Bogø, but it has some of the most unspoiled scenery around and makes for a satisfying drive.

In the little hamlet you can pass by a medieval village church with some late-15th-century murals, but you will have seen better and more intriguing churches if you've already toured Møn. It isn't necessary to return to Møn to get back to Zealand. You can drive straight through Bogø until you come to the Farø bridges, which will connect you with Copenhagen in the north or to Falster in the south.

As you approach the ramp to the bridges, you'll see the **Farobroen Welcome Center,** with a cafeteria, money-exchange office, and toilets, and at the tourist kiosk here you can pick up brochures about Denmark if you wish to continue your journey into other parts of the country.

8

Bornholm

Bornholm is for connoisseurs and an acquired taste. We had discovered all of Denmark before getting around to Bornholm, writing it off as a Baltic island where Danish families who can't afford a Mediterranean holiday go to romp on the sandy beaches in summer. But after coming to know Bornholm in greater depth, we eventually succumbed to its peculiar charm.

The most hurried visitor to Denmark will still pass it by, and it's damn hard to get an accommodation in July and August unless you make reservations well in advance. Most of the holiday flats want a full week's booking, and very few foreign visitors, except perhaps Germans, have so much time to devote to Bornholm.

We like to skip the overcrowded summers altogether and visit in either the late spring or early fall, when Bornholm appears at its most dramatic seasonal change. Of course, that means you'll have to forego beach life, but the waters, even in July or August, are just too cold for us. Perhaps we grew spoiled after living for so many years in the Florida Keys.

Surrounded by the Baltic Sea, astride the important shipping lanes that connect St. Petersburg with Copenhagen and the Atlantic, Bornholm sits only 37km (23 miles) off the coast of Sweden, but about 153km (95 miles) east of Copenhagen and the rest of Denmark. Prized as a strategic Baltic military and trading outpost since the early Middle Ages, and sadly the site of many bloody territorial disputes among the Danes, Germans, and

Swedes, it's home to 45,000 year-round residents. An additional 450,000 visitors arrive during the balmy months of summer. Besides tourism, which is growing rapidly, the economy relies on trade, fishing, herring processing, agriculture, and the manufacture of ceramics. Thanks to the island's deep veins of clay, ceramics has been a major industry since the 1700s.

Covering a terrain of granite and sandstone is a thin but rich layer of topsoil; the island's rock-studded surface is made up of forests and moors. The unusual topography and surprisingly temperate autumn climate—a function of the waters of the Baltic—promotes the verdant growth of plants: figs, mulberries, and enough lavish conifers to create the third-largest forest in Denmark (right in the center of the island). This forest, Almindingen, has the only rocking stone which still rocks. Rocking stones are giant erratic boulders weighing up to 40 tons that were brought to Bornholm by the advancing glaciers during the last Ice Age. In addition, one of Denmark's largest waterfalls, Døndalen, lies in the north of Bornholm in a rift valley and is best viewed from spring to fall.

The island covers 945 sq. km (365 sq. miles), and most of the inhabitants live along 140km (87 miles) of coastline. Not only do the flora and fauna differ in many respects from the rest of Denmark, but its geology is unique as well. The island is divided into two geologic zones: 1,500-million-year-old bedrock to the north and a 550-million-year-old layer of sandstone

---

Tips Hassle on Bornholm

Don't expect to enjoy a holiday on Bornholm without some inconvenience: Boats from Copenhagen take either 5½ or 7 hours each way. And if you plan to visit in midsummer, firm reservations are essential because of the large numbers of Danes who come for the sandy beaches and the Baltic sunshine.

---

to the south. The best beaches of Bornholm lie in the southwestern section of the island, between the towns of Balka and the main beach town of Dueodde.

Bornholmers traditionally have been fishermen and farmers. Today their villages are still idyllic, evocative of the old way of life in their well-kept homesteads, as are fishing hamlets with their characteristic smokehouse chimneys, often used for smoking herring.

The island is still sparsely populated. Grand Canary, a Spanish island off the coast of Africa, for example, is the same size as Bornholm, but while that resort hosts some two million residents in high season, the greatest number of people ever seen on Bornholm at one time is 100,000.

Because of its location at the crossroads of warring nations, Bornholm has had a turbulent history, even as recently as 1945. Strongholds and fortified churches protected local inhabitants when the island was a virtual plaything in the power struggle between royal and religious forces. It was plundered by pirate fleets, noblemen, and the Hanseatic towns of Pomerania. It didn't experience peace until after it revolted against Swedish conquerors at the end of Denmark's war with Sweden in 1658. A group of liberators shot the island's Swedish Lord, and the Bornholmers handed their land over to the king of Denmark.

On a more modern and rather fanatical note, the liberation of Bornholm—unlike the rest of Denmark—was slow to come in 1945. Even when the Nazis had surrendered, the local German commandant on Bornholm refused to give up the island to the Allies. In response, the Soviets rained bombs down on Rønne and Nexø (the two main towns) and then invaded the island and occupied it for several months before returning it to the crown of Denmark. During the long Cold War, the Danes indulged in a little payback time with the Russians. Bornholm became one of NATO's key surveillance bases, spying on what Ronald Reagan called "The Evil Empire."

The island's cuisine is obviously influenced by the surrounding sea. Baltic herring, cod, and salmon are the traditional dishes. One of the most popular local dishes is called Sun over Gudhjem, a specialty of smoked herring topped with a raw egg yolk in an onion ring. It's served with coarse salt and chives, or, most often, radishes. In autumn, the small Bornholm herring are caught and used for a variety of spiced and pickled herring dishes. Another local dish is salt-fried herring served on dark rye bread with beetroot and hot mustard. When it comes to food, those Bornholmers are a hearty bunch.

ESSENTIALS
GETTING THERE

By Ferry   The most popular means of reaching the island from Copenhagen is the 7-hour ferryboat ride. Maintained by the **Bornholmstraffiken** (*©* **56-95-18-66**), these ferries depart year-round from the pier at Kvæsthusbroen once per evening at

11:30pm, with scheduled arrival the following morning at 6:30am. Late-June to mid-August there's an additional departure at 8:30am every day except Wednesday. Passage costs 33DKK ($5.60/£3) per person each way, plus an optional supplement of 221DKK ($38/£20) to rent a private cabin. These ferries are most often used to transport a car from Copenhagen, which costs 174DKK ($30/£16) each way.

Bornholm Ferries, Havnen, at Rønne (© **56-95-18-66**), operates 2½-hour ferries from Ystad on the southern coast of Sweden, with up to four departures daily. These ferries have tax-free shops onboard. A car with a maximum of five passengers costs 164DKK ($28/£15) each way. You can also travel from Sassnitz-Mukran (Rügen) in north Germany for a 3½-hour crossing to Bornholm, arriving at Rønne. Tax-free shopping is also found onboard during this crossing. From Germany, one-way passage for a car with a maximum of five passengers is 1,275DKK ($217/£115). Each of these ferries has a restaurant or bistro featuring a buffet with Danish and Bornholm specialties.

By Plane   **Cimber Air** (© **70-10-12-18**) has about nine flights a day from Copenhagen to Bornholm's airport, 5.5km (3½ miles) south of Rønne. Depending on restrictions, round-trip fares range from 567DKK to 1,680DKK ($96–$286/£51–£151).

VISITOR INFORMATION

The tourist office, **The Bornholm Welcome Center,** Kystvej 3, Rønne (© **56-95-95-00**), is open June to August daily 10am to 5:30pm; April, May, September, and October Monday to Friday 9am to 4pm, Saturday 10am to 1pm; November to March Monday to Friday 9am to 4pm.

GETTING AROUND

By Car   The best place on the island for car rentals is **Europcar,** Nodre Kystvej 1 in Rønne (© **877/940-6900** in the U.S., or 84-33-11-33). Its least expensive rentals begin at 2,750DKK ($468/£248) per week, including unlimited mileage and insurance coverage, as well as the government tax. In addition, **Avis** is located at Snellemark 19, in Rønne (© **800/230-4898** in the U.S., or 56-95-22-08).

By Bicycle   During sunny weather, biking around the island is almost as popular as driving. If you want to do as the Danes do, rent a bike; the prices are pretty much the same throughout the island—about 60DKK ($10/£5.40) a day. A suggested bike-rental company in Rønne is **Bornholms Cykleudleijning,** Nordre Kystvej 5 (© **56-95-13-59**). Open daily 8am to 4pm and 8:30 to 9pm.

EXPLORING THE ISLAND

Even if you have a car available, you might want to take a bike tour (see "Seeing the Sights," below). Ask at any tourist office for a map of the island's more than 190km (120 miles) of bicycle trails and divide this tour into several days, hitting the highlights mentioned below at your own pace.

The tour begins at Rønne, but you could join in at almost any point; basically, the route goes counterclockwise around the island's periphery. Be aware that Bornholm's highways do not have route numbers; even though some maps show the main east–west artery as Route 38, local residents call it "the road to Nexø."

1 Rønne

Your arrival point is Rønne, the capital of the island, but not the most compelling reason to visit Bornholm. There are far more rewarding targets away from the main town, which lies on the western coast facing the island of Zealand and is the site of the major harbor and airport.

But, once here, you'll find Rønne has a certain charm as you walk its historic Gamle Stan (Old Town), with its cobblestoned streets flanked by cross-timbered houses, many of them brightly painted in such "sunshine colors" as yellow and orange.

The best streets for seeing Bornholm as it used to be are **Laksegade** and **Storegade,** plus the triangular sector lying between **Store Torv** and **Lille Torv.** You'll find even more charm in many of the island's smaller towns or hamlets.

Because of Soviet aerial attacks in 1945, most of Rønne was left in shambles, so what you see today is essentially a modern town with a population of some 15,000. The parents of today's inhabitants rebuilt Rønne wisely in the postwar years, opting for an old-fashioned architectural look, which makes most of the houses look older than they actually are.

If you arrive by ferry, you'll notice **St. Nicolai Church,** dedicated to the patron saint of seafarers, on Harbor Hill, towering over the small South Boat Harbor just below. It wasn't until the 18th century that locals moved ahead with plans for a large trading harbor here. Even today the harbor is still expanding to service ferries and the many cruise ships that call at Rønne in increasing numbers.

Should you experience that rare hot day in Denmark, you'll find that vast stretches of sand lie both south and north of Rønne. These beaches are popular with Danish families, many from Copenhagen, in summer.

SEEING THE SIGHTS

If you have a car or are a great biker, you can also view some attractions in the environs. **Borgårdsten** lies 9km (5⅗ miles) north of Rønne along the road to the hamlet of Hasle. This is the most significant runic stone on the island. First found in 1868, it dates from the beginning of the 12th century. Some long-ago Viking inscribed "Svenger had this stone placed here for his father Toste and for his brother Alvlak and for his mother and sisters." Apparently, women weren't considered important enough to list their names.

If you visit Borgårdsten, you can continue for 2.5km (1½ miles) up the coast to the little port of **Hasle,** with its stone church from the 1300s and a half-timbered tower. Inside the church is an intricately carved and painted altar, the work of an unknown Lübeck artist, dating from the mid–15th century. In July a "herring festival" is celebrated here.

If you'd like to check out a west-coast Bornholm beach, you'll find the best one south of Hasle. It's quite sandy and set against a backdrop of pine trees.

While at Hasle you can see five smokehouses in a row, lying on the coastline. One of the smokehouses (which can be visited free) is preserved as it was originally built in 1897, the **Silderøgerierne I Hasle,** Sdr. Bæk 16–20 (© **56-96-44-11**). In one of the other smokehouses, you can watch herring and other kinds of fish being smoked the traditional way, in open chimneys. Afterward you can purchase smoked fish, pick up a beer, and find a nearby spot for an idyllic and quintessential Bornholm experience.

The major and more clearly defined attractions of Bornholm include the following:

Bornholm

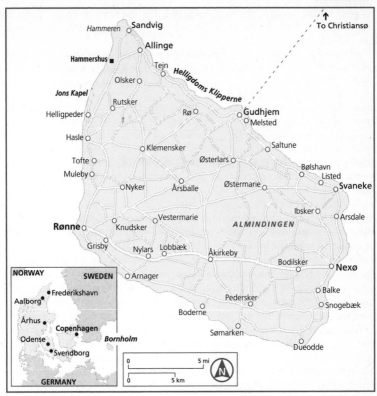

Ericksson's Gård (Farm) ⭐ *Finds* This is the most enchanting private home we've found on Bornholm, and the public can visit it and wander through its beautiful garden. Set on the outskirts of Rønne, just a short walk from the town center, this is the island's best-preserved example of an old-fashioned farm—the kind that once flourished on Bornholm. Originally constructed in 1806, it's a half-timbered, tile-covered building filled with antique furniture and oil paintings, many of them by the well-known Danish artist Kristian Zahrtmann. Some of the objects inside the house commemorate the marriage of a descendant of the farm's original owners—the Ericksson family. An Ericksson daughter married the Danish poet Holger Drachmann (1846–1908), whose works are studied by virtually every schoolchild in Denmark. Finally you can explore the remarkable **garden** ⭐⭐⭐, which horticulturists admire for its 160 species of nonhybrid roses and flowers. It's best seen in July.

Laksegade 7. *©* **56-95-87-35.** Admission 35DKK ($5.95/£3.15) adults, 10DKK ($1.70/90p) children 10–15, free for children under 10. July to mid-Aug daily 10am–5pm; mid-Aug to mid-Oct Mon–Sat 10am–5pm. Closed mid-Oct to June.

Forsvarsmuseet Today this museum attracts World War II buffs like us. But originally the citadel was built in 1650 for defensive purposes in the southern part of town. With its massive round tower, this old castle is like an armed fortress, with all its guns, blades, weapons, war maps, and models of fortification. There are even military uniforms of the men who fought each other, plus a rare collection of antique armaments.

By far the most intriguing exhibitions depict the Nazi occupation of the island from 1940 to 1945, followed by the aerial bombardment of Rønne and Nexø by the Soviet air force. The Soviets occupied the island when the Nazis either were killed or fled for their lives. Although the Soviets left in the spring of 1946, it was done with reluctance. Stalin felt that Bornholm would have made a great center for spying on the west.

Kastellet Galløkken. ℂ **56-95-65-83.** Admission 30DKK ($5.10/£2.70) adults, 10DKK ($1.70/90p) children 6–12, free for children under 6. June–Oct Tues–Sun 11am–5pm.

Hjorth's Fabrik (Bornholm Ceramic Museum) ☾

Bornholm has long been famed for its beautiful ceramics, and this "working ceramics museum" showcases the craft better than any other place on the island. The unusual geology of Bornholm includes deep veins of clay that potters have appreciated for many generations. Since the 1700s hundreds of island residents have produced large numbers of unusual pots, plates, and cups—many of which we find are whimsical and highly idiosyncratic reminders of another way of life. In 1858 a small-scale factory, Hjorth's Ceramics, was established to make pottery from the island's rich deposits of clay, surviving until 1993. In 1995 this museum was established in the company's original factory, a solid building dating back to 1860. Inside, you'll find an intriguing hybrid between an art gallery and an industrial museum. You'll see the island's best examples of the dark-brown, yellow, and gray pottery that was produced in abundance beginning in the 1700s; samples of the dishes and bowls made by the Hjorth company over the years; and some of the work of Bornholm's modern-day potters. Throughout the year several ceramic artists maintain studios inside, casting, spinning, or glazing pots in full view of visitors. Just follow the path of clay. Women descendants of the fourth generation of the Hjorth family run the museum. The museum shop sells modern-day replicas of Hjorth ceramics, and many exhibits trace the production process from start to finish. We once purchased a cherished "heirloom" set of old-fashioned pharmacy jars here.

Krystalgade 5. ℂ **56-95-01-60.** Admission mid-Apr to mid-Oct 35DKK ($5.95/£3.15) adults, 10DKK ($1.70/90p) children under 18; mid-Oct to mid-Apr 10DKK ($1.70/90p) adults, free for children. May–Oct Mon–Fri 10am–5pm, Sat 10am–2pm; Nov–Apr Mon–Fri 10am–5pm, Sat 10am–1pm.

Bornholms Museum ☾

To open this museum, islanders raided their attics for any curiosities that might be of interest to the general public, and they came up with a number of objects to intrigue, ranging from antique toys of the 19th century to gold objects discovered while farmers were plowing their fields. Even Roman coins are on display. The nautical exhibits are decked out like a ship's interior. Installed in what used to be the major hospital on the island, the museum traces the history of Bornholm's unique position in the Baltic through displays on archaeology, folkloric costumes, ethnology, and seafaring and agrarian traditions. Several rooms are outfitted with 19th-century antique furniture, island-made silverware, and accessories. Of special interest is the collection of Bornholm-made clocks, copied from a shipment of English clocks that was salvaged from a Dutch shipwreck in the late 1700s. Since Bornholm is known for its ceramics and glassware, it is entirely predictable that there are nearly 5,000 pieces of glassware and handcrafted ceramics.

Skt. Mortensgade 29. ℂ **56-95-07-35.** www.bornholmsmuseum.dk. Admission 40DKK ($6.80/£3.60); free for kids 12 and under. Mid-May to mid-Oct Mon–Sat 10am–5pm; mid-Oct to mid-May Mon–Sat 1–4pm.

SHOPPING

Despite its isolation in the middle of the Baltic, Bornholm offers many opportunities for acquiring some serious merchandise. Most of the island's shops line the streets funneling into the Lille Torv and the Store Torv. Part of the fun for us involves wandering aimlessly from shop to shop, but if you want specific addresses and ideas, consider any of the following.

Want to offer some flowers to the object of your most recent affections? Head for **Lilliendal Plantecenter,** Sagavej 1 (© **56-95-47-24**). Some of the most unusual and eccentric kitchen- and housewares in Bornholm are available at **Inspiration,** Lille Torv 1 (© **56-95-01-11**). Expect Danish functionalism combined with wrought iron, glass, ceramics, textiles, and wood; much of it is made within Scandinavia.

If you're looking for a garment of any degree of formality for the child or kids you left behind, the best clothing store on the island is **Kids' Shop,** Skt. Mortensgade 4 (© **56-91-00-17**). Is your camera running out of film? Film supply or development is available at **Ilsted Bech,** Snellmark 25 (© **56-95-00-23**).

A major outlet for some of the art glass produced in abundance on Bornholm is **Pernille Bülow Glas,** Lille Torv (© **56-95-43-05**).

The island is known for its unique Bornholmer grandfather clocks. The tradition began in 1744 when a Dutch ship was stranded on the way from Helsingør in Denmark to Tallinn in Estonia. In its hold were five clocks and a cask with weights for them. Dexterous young men made models of the clocks and, in so doing, founded a Bornholm clockmaking tradition, a craft that virtually disappeared at the end of World War II. The craft has now been revived, and the island's largest clockmaker workshop is located in Rønne. **Nye Bornholmerure** 😊😊, Torneværksvej 26 (© **56-95-31-08**), sells the finest handmade grandfather clocks in Denmark, although they can be very expensive depending on the model. These clocks sound the hour with music—everything from Mozart to Andrew Lloyd Weber.

Many Swedes come over to Bornholm just to shop for the island's famous ceramics. **Michael Andersen** 😊😊, Lille Torv 7 (© **56-95-00-01**), still preserves the old ceramics-making traditions but manufactures many modern products as well.

The island's best goldsmith—and he's a stunning talent—is Jørn-Ole Thomsen, who works at **Guldhuset** 😊😊😊, Bornholmercentret (© **56-95-02-70**), on Store Torv. Thomsen makes fine jewelry not only for the local shop but also for Georg Jensen, the world-famous silver and goldsmith company.

WHERE TO STAY

The island is essentially a fair-weather destination, and most hotels are likely to be closed in winter except for a few die-hards.

Hotel Griffen 😊 *Kids*   "You like to bike, of course," the manager said to us as we checked in. "You're in luck. The bike trail around the island begins right in front of your hotel. Of course, we can help you rent a bike. We'll even pack a picnic basket for you." This kind of assistance makes us vote the staff here as the most helpful on the island. This hotel is the largest on Bornholm, and may fall a few notches below the Radisson Hotel Fredensborg (see below), but it's one of the most inviting.

Even though it was constructed in the dull architectural era of the '70s, its buildings have a certain style, designed to evoke 18th-century hip-roofed manor houses. Two of the four buildings contain the bedrooms, which are separated from the dining, drinking, and convention facilities in the other structures.

Lying in the heart of Rønne, a 5-minute walk to the beach and the town center, the hotel is also close to a busy summer marina. We especially like the way the architects added plenty of windows so guests can take in views of the Baltic in many directions. Some rooms have floor-to-ceiling windows and glass doors.

The small-to-midsize bedrooms are furnished in a modern but minimalist style, each comfortable and tasteful and each with well-appointed private tiled bathrooms with tub/shower combos. We are especially fond of their "Sunset Menu," served every evening between 5 and 9pm, and based on the "freshest and best" found at the market that day, most often seafood from Baltic waters.

Ndr. Kystvej 34, DK-3700 Rønne. (C) **56-95-51-11.** Fax 56-95-52-97. www.hotelgriffen.dk. 140 units. 1,125DKK ($191/£101) double; 1,715DKK ($292/£154) suite. AE, DC, MC, V. **Amenities:** Restaurant; bar; indoor heated pool; kids' pool; use of tennis courts at Radisson; sauna; room service (7am–9pm). *In room:* TV, hair dryer.

Hotel Ryttergården ⭐ *Kids*   This is one of the best hotels—it's more of a holiday resort, really—on Bornholm, lying 2km (1¼ miles) south of Rønne. It is the most scenically located hotel in the area, enjoying its closeness to a sandy beach, a golf course, and woodland offering dozens of walks and hikes along the coast. Built in stages between 1986 and 1998, the compound of angular, big-windowed modern structures evokes a boxy, modern airport terminal with an ample use of glass.

The interior warms considerably, and you have a choice of standard doubles or else one-level holiday apartments, often booked by six persons, which makes them ideal for families. The midsize-to-spacious units have sleek modern styling, with comfortable and tasteful Danish furnishings in blond wood, with sliding glass doors opening onto balconies fronting the sea, and each comes with a small but well-kept bathroom with tub/shower combo. Guests enjoy drinks in an international bar with a starlit ceiling, later patronizing the 150-seat restaurant serving first-rate Danish and international cuisine with a focus on fresh seafood.

Strandvejen 79, DK-3700 Rønne. (C) **56-95-19-13.** Fax 56-95-19-22. www.hotel-ryttergaarden.dk. 103 units, 28 apts with kitchenette. 795DKK–995DKK ($135–$169/£72–£90) double; rates include breakfast. Apts for up to 6 occupants 2,895DKK–5,595DKK ($492–$951/£261–£504) per week, without breakfast, plus an obligatory one-time fee of 325DKK ($55/£29) for cleaning, plus 201DKK–320DKK ($34–$54/£18–£29) per apt per week for electricity. AE, DC, MC, V. Closed Oct–Apr. Bus from Rønne: 23 or 24. **Amenities:** 2 restaurants; bar; indoor heated pool; tennis court; fitness center; sauna; laundry service; dry cleaning; nonsmoking rooms; rooms for those w/limited mobility; solarium. *In room:* A/C, TV, minibar, hair dryer, trouser press.

Radisson Hotel Fredensborg ⭐⭐ *Kids*   There are hotels on Bornholm with more atmosphere and charm, but this chain hotel is clearly the market leader for international luxury. Of course, luxury is a relative term. What passes for luxe living on Bornholm wouldn't make the grade in Copenhagen. One of the few hotels on the island to remain open all year, Fredensborg lies in a wooded, tranquil location adjacent to a beach and less than a kilometer (½ mile) south of Rønne harbor. Its Danish modern style from the 1960s wouldn't win architectural awards, but its midsize-to-spacious bedrooms are the island's best appointed, each comfortable and tasteful with a private balcony or terrace overlooking the Baltic. Bathrooms are small but with sleek tiles, modern plumbing, and a tub/shower combo. The suites are really apartments with full kitchens, most often rented to families with small children. Some of the best food in Rønne is served at the well-respected **De 5 Stâuerna** restaurant here, specializing in Danish/French cuisine (see below). Guests are allowed to use the pool at the previously recommended Griffen.

Strandvejen 116, DK-3700 Rønne. © **800/333-3333** in the U.S., or 56-95-44-44. Fax 56-95-03-14. www.bornholm hotels.dk. 72 units. 1,195DKK–1,395DKK ($203–$237/£108–£126) double; 1,495DKK–1,795DKK ($254–$305/£135–£162) suite. Rates include buffet breakfast. AE, DC, MC, V. **Amenities:** Restaurant; bar; tennis court; sauna; room service (7am–10pm); babysitting; laundry service; dry cleaning; nonsmoking rooms. *In room:* TV, dataport, minibar, hair dryer.

Sverres Small Hotel *(Value* "Small Hotel" is an apt description for this ocher-colored antique building, which had its origins as a coaching inn, putting up wayfarers since 1850. It's tried to keep up with the times with some modern improvements. It lies in the center of Rønne only 200m (656 ft.) from the yacht-clogged harbor. The place is well maintained and an unpretentious choice if you don't mind the 1km (⅔-mile) trek to the best nearby beach. In keeping with the hotel's name, the bedrooms are small, but comfortably and tastefully furnished, coming with tiled bathrooms with shower units. Breakfast is the only meal served, although the neighborhood around the hotel offers a few dining choices.

Snellmark 2, DK-3700 Rønne. © **56-95-03-03.** Fax 56-95-03-92. www.sverres-hotel.dk. 22 units, 12 with bathroom. 460DKK ($78/£41) double without bathroom; 550DKK–630DKK ($94–$107/£50–£57) double with bathroom. MC, V. Rates include breakfast. **Amenities:** Breakfast room; lounge; room service (7am–10pm). *In room:* TV, no phone.

WHERE TO DINE

De 5 Stâuerna *★★* DANISH/FRENCH/INTERNATIONAL   When we told our Bornholm dining companion we were giving this restaurant two Frommer stars, he protested, "Give it three—be more generous!" But we're stubbornly sticking by our original position. It is, however, the best and the most upscale restaurant on the island, with a clientele that tends to select it for celebratory meals and family gatherings. Its name translates as "the five rooms," each of which is outfitted in a rustic country-Danish style. There's always a platter of the proposed fish of the day, which is usually fried in butter and served with new potatoes—a style that Bornholmers have witnessed since their childhood. Other more elaborate options include Hereford beefsteak prepared *cordon bleu* style, with salted cured ham and Emmenthaler cheese; tournedos of beef flambéed in Calvados and served with apples and onions; an exotic sautéed filet of ostrich with Mexican pimentos and peppers; marinated and minced beefsteak with chiles; and a dish that we personally prefer more than almost anything else on the menu: Bornholm lamb served with a sauce concocted from rosemary, olive oil, and tarragon.

In the Radisson Hotel Fredensborg, Strandvejen 116. © **56-95-44-44.** Reservations recommended. Main courses 75DKK–210DKK ($13–$36/£6.75–£19); fixed-price menu degustation 265DKK ($45/£24). AE, DC, MC, V. Daily 11:30am–9:30pm.

Rådhuskroen *★ (Finds* DANISH   This is the most visible and, in its own way, most charming restaurant in Rønne, although it doesn't use the pricey ingredients or employ the expensive chefs hired by the previously recommended De 5 Stâuerna. It's situated in the darkened and intimately illuminated cellar of the Town Hall, a 140-year-old building with a long history of feeding island residents—and feeding them well—in a cozy setting protected from blustering midwinter winds. Wall sconces cast romantic shadows over a collection of antique furniture and accessories, as a well-trained staff serves fresh and well-prepared dishes such as filet of salmon in a "summer sauce" of fresh tomatoes, chives, and herbs, and two different sizes of tender and well-prepared beefsteak ("Mr. Beef" and "Mrs. Beef").

Nørregade 2. © **56-95-00-69.** Reservations recommended on weekends. Main courses 100DKK–171DKK ($17–$29/£9–£15). AE, DC, MC, V. Mon–Sat noon–3pm and 5–9pm.

RØNNE AFTER DARK

Its role as Bornholm's largest settlement forces Rønne into the sometimes unwanted role as nightlife capital of the island. But don't expect too much glitter, as things on Bornholm tend to stay quiet.

For high-energy members of the under-30 generation, the most visible and popular dance club on the island is **Red Barone,** Skt. Mortensgade 48, in Rønne (© **56-95-06-88**). Victim to oft-changing ownership within the past decade, it offers high-volume mania that's associated with nightlife in bigger cities. The venue is a dark-painted, much-used environment with prominent bars, battered sofas and chairs, and a dance floor lit by colored lights that just might tempt you to get up and dance. A 40DKK ($6.80/£3.60) cover charge is imposed on Friday and Saturday; other times, entrance is free. If you're less interested in hanging out with the young crowd, consider a pint of Guinness at **O'Malley's Irish Pub,** Store Torvegade, in Rønne (© **56-95-00-16**), where clients older than 30 appreciate the Celtic conviviality and the recorded music.

Calm, cool, and mellow, **Dr. Jazz** ⚛, Snelle Mark 26 (© **56-95-50-26**), is Bornholm's leading emporium of jazz, which is produced by local combos as well as groups imported from other parts of Europe. Expect a crowd of drinkers and smokers over 25, and a spontaneity that can be rather charming. It's open daily 11pm to 5am. There's usually no cover charge.

FROM RØNNE TO NEXØ

From Rønne, drive east along the island's modern highway, A38, following the signs toward Nexø. Stop in **Nylars** (about 5km/3 miles from Rønne), a town that's known as the site of the best-preserved of Bornholm's four round churches. The **Nylarskirke** (© **56-97-20-13**), built around 1250 and rising prominently from the center of a community with no more than about 50 buildings, contains frescoes that depict the Creation and the expulsion of Adam and Eve from the Garden of Eden. The cylindrical nave has three floors, the uppermost of which was a watchman's tower in the Middle Ages. You can also view two fragments of a runic stone. From Rønne, you can take bus no. 6 if you don't have a car; the bike path from Rønne to Åkirkeby also passes by the church. Admission is free May to October 20, Monday to Friday 9am to 5pm.

Continue driving another 5km (3 miles) east until you reach **Åkirkeby,** the only inland settlement of any size. Its economy based on farming, the hamlet is small-scale and sleepy, and is Bornholm's oldest settlement (its town charter dates from 1346). The little town was important in medieval times when islanders had to move inland to avoid attacks from enemies at sea. Bornholm's regional council met here until 1776, and Åkirkeby was also the ecclesiastical center of Bornholm.

It's also home to the island's oldest and largest church, **Åkirke,** Torvet (© **56-97-41-03**), originally built around 1250. This church isn't as eccentric as some of the others. It's a sandstone-fronted monument built with defense in mind, as you'll note from the small windows. Inside, a Romanesque baptismal font is incised with runic inscriptions believed to be carved by the master craftsman Sigraf on the island of Gotland. Other runic inscriptions appear on the cloverleaf-shaped arches. The church is open daily 10am to 4pm, charging 6DKK ($1/55p) for visitors.

Åkirkeby is a good point to cut inland if you wish to see some of Bornholm's woodlands, among the densest in Denmark, with forests filled with oak, hemlock, fir, spruce, and beech trees. The tourist office in Rønne (see "Visitor Information," earlier in this chapter) will give you a map outlining the best of the trails that cut through Bornholm's largest forest, **Almindingen,** in the center of the island. It can be reached by following a signposted road north from Åkirkeby. The forest is also the location of the island's highest point, **Rytterknægten,** a 160m (525-ft.) hill with a lookout tower, Konge-mindet, with a staircase you can climb for a panoramic view of the dense woodlands.

You can also pick up information at a minor, rarely used tourist office that's much less visible than the island's main office in Rønne. It's the **Sydbornholms Turistbu-reau,** Torvet 2 (© 56-97-45-20), at Åkirkeby. Mid-May to mid-September, it's open Monday through Friday 9am to 6pm and Saturday 8am to 1pm. The rest of the year, hours are Monday to Friday 10am to 6:30pm, closed Saturday and Sunday.

A minor museum for devoted automobile fans is the **Bornholms Automobilmu-seum,** Grammegardsvej 1 (© 56-97-45-95), displaying vintage cars and motorcycles, plus some farm equipment and tractors that highlight the 20th century's advances in agrarian science. Antique cars and tractors derive from such manufacturers as Dela-haye, Opel, Ford, Adler, Singer, Jaguar, and Fiat. It's open May to October, Monday to Saturday 10am to 5pm. The rest of the year it's closed, and admission costs 30DKK ($5.10/£2.70) per person.

From Åkirkeby, cut southeast for 4.5km (2¾ miles), following the signs to **Peder-sker,** a hamlet with only three shops (which close down during the cold-weather months). Six kilometers (3¾ miles) later you'll reach **Dueodde,** the name of both a raffish beachfront community and the entire region around the southernmost tip of the island. The village of Dueodde marks the southern edge of a stretch of coastline that is the finest beach on the island. The oceanfront bounty—and the best beaches on the island—stretch northward and eastward to the town of **Balka,** 5km (3 miles) beyond, encompassing stretches of white sand whose grains are so fine that they were used for generations to fill hourglasses. The towns themselves are little more than backdrops for seasonal kiosks and a scattering of holiday homes for mainland Danes and Swedes. Most of the landscape is a virtual wilderness of pine and spruce trees, salt-tolerant shrubs, and sand dunes, some of which rise more than 12m (40 ft.) above the nearby sea.

The focal point of this southeastern coastline is the **Dueodde Fyr** (Dueodde Light-house), the tallest lighthouse on the island, built in 1962 to warn ships away from the extreme southern tip of the island. Weather permitting, you can climb to its top dur-ing daylight hours May to October for a fee of 5DKK (85¢/45p), which you pay directly to the lighthouse keeper. For information, call the tourist office in Dueodde © **56-49-70-79.**

From Dueodde, continue along the coast in a northeasterly direction, passing through the unpretentious fishing hamlets of **Snogebæk** and **Balka.** Immediately north of Balka the road will deliver you north to Nexø, the second major town of the island after Rønne, opening onto the eastern coast facing Sweden.

2 Nexø ⟨★

Nexø, 48km (30 miles) northeast of Rønne, has a year-round population of 3,900, which makes it the largest fishing port on the island. As is the case with Rønne, we like to wander around only for 2 hours or so before pressing on to the countryside. It's not an unattractive town because after Soviet bombings in 1945, its demolished build-ings were reconstructed more or less in the style of the 17th and 18th centuries. The

11th-hour World War II bombings of the town's once-fabled 900 antique buildings is the stuff of local legend—just ask any old-timer.

In May 1945, Nexø was heavily bombed by the Russians during 2 days of horror; this happened several days after the rest of Denmark had been liberated from the Nazis. Nexø was a final holdout of Nazi soldiers in the closing days of the war. Ironically, Bornholm was the last area of Denmark to get rid of its Russian "liberators," who didn't completely evacuate the island until 1946.

Before exploring the area, you can pick up good information at the **Nexø-Dueodde Turistbureau,** Sdr. Hammer 2A (© **56-49-70-79**). May to August, it's open Monday to Friday 10am to 5pm and Saturday 9am to 2pm. The rest of the year, it's open Monday to Friday 10am to 5pm and closed Saturday and Sunday.

One of the town's more eccentric and idiosyncratic monuments is the **Nexø Museum,** Havnen (© **56-49-25-56**), open only May to October, daily 10am to 4pm. For an entrance fee of 35DKK ($5.95/£3.15), you'll see displays of fishing-related equipment that has sustained the local economy, and memorabilia of the Danish author Martin Andersen (1869–1954)—better known as Martin Andersen Nexø, a pen name he adopted in honor of his native village. His novel *Pelle the Conqueror,* set in Bornholm and later made into an Oscar-winning film, revealed how Danish landowners in the early 20th century exploited Swedish newcomers to the island. Admittedly, this is hardly a subject that will interest most people, and you may want to pass it by in favor of outdoor fun, which is what Bornholm is all about.

WHERE TO STAY

In this southeastern corridor of Bornholm you aren't limited just to Nexø. In summer you can also stay at the seaside hamlets of **Dueodde** or **Snogebæk,** immediately south of Nexø. These are more scenic places to stay, and they also open onto the island's best beaches. Dueodde is Bornholm's number one beach area, and the entire stretch of coast is filled with rolling dunes and endless strips of white sand. Snogebæk is a little seaside settlement with holiday homes, but there's no village attached to Dueodde. For the most part, residents who live in Dueodde or Snogebæk use Nexø for their services and supplies. All these destinations are essentially summer ones, and most of the places to stay close for the winter.

AT NEXØ

Hotel Balka Strand   This is the only hotel along Bornholm's beach-fringed eastern coast that remains open year-round, so it stays busy even in midwinter, usually with conferences. Originally built in the 1970s and doubled in size in 1992, the hotel on its exterior could easily fit into any number of towns in America's heartland. There's nothing particularly Bornholmian about it; rather it's imbued with a more international aura. The government gives it four stars, based more on comfort and facilities than any particular winning atmosphere. Nonetheless, the hotel staff is helpful and personal in their welcome, and the building is laid out in a one-story format about 150m (490 ft.) from one of the island's best bathing beaches adjoining a protected nature preserve ideal for walks or hikes. The neatly kept midsize bedrooms, with a bathroom with tub/shower combo, are comfortably and tastefully furnished in Danish modern (if you travel in Denmark, you invariably get Danish modern in the bedrooms). A standard but good cuisine is served in a big-windowed dining room, where most Danish-style dinners conclude with live music, dancing, or some form of entertainment.

Boulevarden 9, DK-3730 Nexø. ℂ **56-49-49-49.** Fax 56-49-49-48. 95 units, half with kitchenettes. 975DKK–1,095DKK ($166–$186/£88–£99) double without kitchenette; 1,050DKK–1,315DKK ($179–$224/£95–£118) double with kitchenette. Rates include breakfast and dinner. MC, V. From Nexø, drive 2.5km (1½ miles) south along the coastal road, following the signs to Balka and Dueodde. **Amenities:** Restaurant; bar; outdoor heated pool; tennis court; sauna; 24-hr. room service; laundry service; dry cleaning; nonsmoking rooms; rooms for those w/limited mobility. *In room:* TV, dataport, hair dryer.

Strandhotel Balka Søbad *(Kids)*   This hotel is designed for those seeking summer fun at one of Bornholm's prettiest sandy beaches, the waters of which lie no more than 90m (295 ft.) from the hotel's door. A compound of five white-painted buildings were modern in 1972 and 1976 when they were first constructed and aren't as fresh as they were, but the hotel's maintenance is still good. The clientele consists mostly of families with children, many of which can be seen renting a bike to go on self-generated tours of the island. The midsize-to-spacious bedrooms were renovated between 2004 and 2006, and most are furnished in plain but comfortable Danish modern with a balcony or private terrace in most cases. Each comes with a small but tiled private bathroom with tub/shower combo. For the higher price you often get a second bedroom, ideal for the family trade.

Vestre Strandvej 25, DK-3730 Nexø. ℂ **56-49-22-25.** Fax 56-49-22-33. www.hotel-balkasoebad.dk. 106 units. 895DKK–1,641DKK ($152–$279/£81–£148) double. Rates include breakfast. MC, V. Closed Nov–Apr. From Nexø, drive 3km (1¾ miles) south, following the signs to Snogebæk. **Amenities:** Restaurant; bar; outdoor heated pool; tennis court; sauna; laundry service; dry cleaning. *In room:* TV, kitchenette (in some).

AT SNOGEBÆK

Snogebæk Hotelpension *(Value)*   This little boardinghouse began life as a rustic farmhouse at the turn of the 20th century, but in an expansion in the 1980s it turned itself successfully into a small hotel with motel-style wings that extend into a garden. Set about a kilometer (⅔ mile) west of the center of Snogebæk, we find it a refreshing place to stay. It lies inland about a kilometer (⅔ mile) from the nearest good beach, and it is near many good walking and hiking trails. The farmhouse's old, beamed interior was converted into a restaurant and social center for guests. The rooms are comfortable enough though hardly plush—in fact, about as basic as we'd want to recommend with small shower-only bathroom units. The rooms would be more claustrophobic if they didn't open onto well-maintained greenery that surrounds the hotel. The on-site restaurant serves Danish fare, with a lot of fish based on the catch of the day. Surprisingly such a simple place has one of the best hotel pools sheltered under an enclosed greenhouse-style canopy.

Ellegade 9, DK-3730 Snogebæk. ℂ **56-48-80-80.** Fax 56-48-81-31. www.zzz-zzz.dk. 25 units. 580DKK–1,160DKK ($99–$197/£52–£104) double. Rates include breakfast. MC, V. Closed Oct–Apr. **Amenities:** Restaurant; bar; indoor heated pool. *In room:* TV.

AT DUEODDE

Dueodde Badehotel *(★) (Kids)*   This hotel is very much a family affair, which could be a turnoff for romantic duos seeking a more secluded Bornholm hideaway. Well-designed and tasteful, this two-story motel-like structure was built in 1978 and remains the most southerly hotel in Bornholm, set in a private pine-wood forest. It's surrounded by scrub-covered sand dunes and is a short walk from the beach, one of the finest in Europe and riddled with sand dunes and a wide stretch of fine, white sand. If only the water were warmer, it would be perfect. When the weather is bad, guests have access to a public indoor swimming pool just 400m (1,312 ft.) from the hotel. Each accommodation is laid out something like an efficiently designed suite aboard a cruise ship, with compact dimensions, a color scheme of blue and white, modern furniture, and, in every case, a separate seating area and a balcony or terrace. Each has a neatly kept bathroom equipped with a shower unit. Families often book the apartments, which come in various sizes, although all of them have an up-to-date kitchen. There's a comfortable restaurant that charges 100DKK to 200DKK ($17–$34/£9–£18) for well-prepared Danish meals and is open to the general public.

Poulsker, DK-3730 Nexø. ℂ **56-48-86-49**. Fax 56-48-89-59. www.dueodde-badehotel.dk. 48 apts with kitchenette. 850DKK–1,170DKK ($145–$199/£77–£105) double. AE, DC, MC, V. Closed Nov–Apr. From Nexø, drive 9km (5⅓ miles) south along the coastal road, following the signs for Dueodde. **Amenities:** Restaurant; bar; cafe; tennis court; sauna; kids' playground; coin-operated laundry; nonsmoking rooms; rooms for those w/limited mobility. *In room:* TV, safe.

Hotel Bornholm *Kids*   This hotel is one of the most idyllic for families who don't require a lot of luxury. The beach here is good for kids because the waters are usually calm and shallow for some 100m (328 ft.) out. Built between 1972 and 1982 in a dull architectural style, the hotel evokes a roadside motel in the States. Its saving grace is a verdant garden, and each unit opens directly on this greenery replete with roses, flowering shrubs, and small patches of lawn, giving the impression of camping out in a natural setting.

The rooms, ranging from midsize to spacious, are durable, efficient, and practical—designed for hard use by occupants who spend most of their holiday on the beach. Each unit comes with a small but well-kept bathroom with a tub/shower combo. Families and even "friendly friends" (those who don't mind living as a family unit) have a choice of 44 apartments or 7 cottages, and, naturally, we go for those cottages, which offer more privacy and living space.

Pilegårdsvej 1, Dueodde, DK-3730 Nexø. ℂ **56-48-83-83**. Fax 56-48-85-37. 44 apts, 7 cottages. 1,095DKK–1,195DKK ($186–$203/£99–£108) double; 2,975DKK–5,975DKK ($506–$1,016/£268–£538) cottage for 4 people. Rates include breakfast; half-board 175DKK ($30/£16) extra per person per day. MC, V. Closed Oct–Apr. From Nexø, drive 5.5km (3½ miles) south along the coastal road, following the signs for Dueodde. **Amenities:** Breakfast room; bar; 2 heated pools (1 indoor); tennis court; exercise room; sauna; coin-operated laundry. *In room:* TV, safe.

WHERE TO DINE
AT NEXØ
Hotel Balka Strand DANISH   The cuisine, although not richly varied, is always reliable, especially in its selection of fish and seafood from the Baltic. We've found the portions quite large, filling, and most satisfying, and you can often dance at least part of the night away to live music. Although residents of the (previously recommended) hotel occupy much of its dining room, this restaurant opens its doors to nonresidents who phone ahead for reservations. Within an airy, sparsely decorated dining room, you can enjoy such traditional menu items as marinated or fried herring, various kinds of omelets, soups such as a creamy borscht, a standard fried steak with onions, and, best of all, a roster of fresh fish that includes our favorite—halibut with herbed wine sauce. Dessert might be a slice of chocolate layer cake, or perhaps a flan inspired by the chef's vacation visit to Spain.

Boulevarden 9. ℂ **56-49-49-49**. Reservations required for nonhotel guests. Main courses 100DKK–150DKK ($17–$26/£9–£14). AE, DC, MC, V. Daily noon–3pm and 6:30–9:30pm.

Tre Søstre *Kids* DANISH/SEAFOOD   Outside Rønne, there is no restaurant on the island that serves finer food than "The Three Sisters," standing right at the bustling little harbor of Nexø. The large dining room was created from a former storage warehouse, and it's named for the model of an old Danish ship on display. The decor honors artists of Bornholm, and even the ceramic plates and candlesticks are locally made by craftspeople on the island working through long dark winters. Island artist Kirsten Clemann, quite well known locally, created the ceramic fish suspended from the ceiling.

The rustic, somewhat nautical decor sets the stage for the tasty seafood you are likely to be served here. We take delight in the fresh turbot, which is roasted to perfection and served with "fruits of the sea"—in this case shellfish. The grilled salmon is equally delectable and served with a homemade hollandaise (this chef knows how to make hollandaise!). Nothing is finer, however, than the sautéed scampi splashed with cognac and flavored with curry powder and fresh garlic. The meat eater can always order a standard grilled sirloin of beef with mushroom sauce.

Havnen 5. ℰ 56-49-33-93. Reservations recommended. Main courses 100DKK–200DKK ($17–$34/£9–£18). AE, DC, MC, V. Daily 11:30am–10pm.

AT SNOGEBÆK

Den Lille Havfrue *(Value* DANISH   The cookery here is always reliably good tasting, and never makes any pretense of being anything more than it is. In other words, the cooks have no "shame" in serving plain old codfish with boiled potatoes and onions. "Most Danes grew up on that dish," one of the cooks told us. "Why not serve it?" Housed in a cozy, modern building erected in the 1980s, this is one of the least-pretentious but solidly good restaurants on the island. Local artist Kirsten Kleman accents its woodsy setting with dozens of pottery pieces. The hardworking staff will suggest any of various fish and meat dishes, including salmon with lobster sauce (a perennial favorite), beefsteak and calf liver, and broiled plaice with lemon and parsley-butter sauce. The menu includes an ample selection of homemade soups, fresh salads, and desserts based on recipes that some cook's grandmother must have taught him.

Hovedgaden 5, Snogebæk. ℰ 56-48-80-55. Reservations recommended. Main courses 100DKK–170DKK ($17–$29/£9–£15). AE, DC, MC, V. Daily 11:30am–10pm. Closed Oct–Apr.

3 Svaneke ⟨★⟩

After Nexø, the topography of the island gradually changes from tawny sandstone to a more heavily forested area with thin topsoil, deep veins of clay, and outcroppings of gray granite. From Nexø drive 5.5km (3½ miles) north along the coastal road, following the signs to Svaneke, Denmark's easternmost settlement, with fewer than 1,200 year-round residents, lying 20km (12 miles) east of Rønne.

An idyllic retreat from the urban life of Copenhagen, this is the one settlement where we'd like to anchor if we lived on Bornholm. Many writers, sculptors, and painters have acquired homes in Svaneke, a former fishing village and the most photogenic town on Bornholm. In 1975 it won the European Gold Medal for town preservation. Its most famous citizen was J. N. Madvig, Denmark's influential philologist, who was born here in 1804.

The little town bears some resemblance to certain eastern regions of the Baltic with which it has traded, and it still has many 17th- and 18th-century cottages along cobblestone streets leading to the harbor, where fishing boats bob idyllically at anchor. Sights are few here and easily covered on foot. It's the appealing town itself, filled with red-tile buildings, that's the attraction. The town's main square is the **Torv.** Directly south of here is **Svaneke Kirke,** which has a runic stone dating from the mid–14th century. The church itself was largely reconstructed in the 1800s and is only of minor interest.

In and around the area are a number of windmills, including an old post mill on the north side of town. At a point 3km (1¾ miles) south of Svaneke, in the hamlet of **Årsdale,** there is an old working windmill where corn is still ground and sold to locals.

For information about the area, contact **Svaneke Turistbureau,** Storegade 24 (© **56-49-70-79**), open Monday to Friday 12:30 to 4:30pm.

SHOPPING

Bornholm's east coast, particularly around Svaneke, contains the highest percentage of artists, many of whom display their creations within such art galleries as **Gallerie Hvide Hus** *(Finds*, Rand Kløvej 15, Saltuna (© **56-47-03-33**). Set midway between Svaneke and Gudhjem, it specializes in crafts, ceramics, and paintings, usually by Danish or Swedish artists, many of whom reside on the island. On the antiques front, **Svaneke Antikvitetshandel,** Kirkebakken 4 (© **56-49-60-91**), is one of the most appealing stores on Bornholm, with an inventory of nautical memorabilia, plus some of the curios and furnishings that long-ago merchant ships hauled here from all parts of the world.

WHERE TO STAY

Hotel Østersøen *(Finds* This is one of the oldest hotels on the island, having opened in 1873 when a former merchant's house was rebuilt as a hotel. In 1990 major construction took place again when the compound was converted to holiday apartments, each furnished with an individual character and containing a separate entrance opening onto a beautiful courtyard garden. Families settle in for a week, using the place as a base for exploring Bornholm. Rich with many of the architectural quirks of its original construction 400 years ago as a farmstead, this complex of apartments with kitchenettes is more charming and more authentically old-fashioned than its nearby competitors. It sprawls along a goodly portion of Svaneke's harbor, wrapping itself around three sides of an open-air courtyard. Apartments contain an appealing blend of old-fashioned buttresses, modern kitchenettes, and summery, airy furnishings. All units contain well-kept shower-only bathrooms. Overall, the venue is comfortable, cozy, and attractively positioned.

Havnebryggen 5, DK-3740 Svaneke. © **56-49-60-20.** Fax 56-49-72-79. www.ostersoen.dk. 22 apts. 2,495DKK–4,995DKK ($424–$849/£225–£450) double per week; 2,895DKK–5,995DKK ($492–$1,019/£261–£540) quad per week. Obligatory end-of-rental cleaning fee of 400DKK ($68/£36) for 2 persons, 450DKK ($77/£41) for 4. AE, DC, MC, V. **Amenities:** Lounge; outdoor heated pool; laundry service; dry cleaning. *In room:* TV, kitchenette.

Pension Solgården The only problem with this solidly built, family-style guesthouse is that it's open only 3 months a year, during the peak of midsummer. It was originally conceived in the 1930s as the quintessential red-brick schoolhouse, with a panoramic position adjacent to the sea, 3km (1¾ miles) south of Svaneke, beside the road leading south to Nexø. The small but cozy rooms are outfitted with the kind of furnishings you might see in a college dormitory of long ago. This place is one of the bargains of the area, especially if you're willing to forego a private bathroom and settle for the quite adequate hallway facilities. There's a dining room serving good, wholesome Danish meals, but it's open only to residents of the hotel. Outside you'll find lawns strewn with tables for sea gazing and sun worshipping.

Skolebakken 5, DK-3740 Svaneke. © **56-49-64-37.** Fax 56-49-65-37. www.pension-solgaarden.dk. 18 units, 9 with bathroom. 550DKK ($94/£50) double without bathroom; 650DKK ($111/£59) double with bathroom. Rates include breakfast. No credit cards. Closed Sept–May. **Amenities:** Dining room; lounge. *In room:* No phone.

Siemsens Gaard ⭐   This is a hotel with a history, its origins going back to the great day of the sailing ships in the Baltic beginning around 1650 when it opened as a merchant's store, supplying sailors. It's named for Johan P. Siemsens, who in 1827 married the widow of a rich merchant. As an inn, it dates from 1687, welcoming a visit by the Danish king, Christian V, and naval hero Admiral Niels Juel. In the 1930s it was rebuilt as a hotel. In the early 1990s, however, lightning struck one of the two buildings, burning it to the ground, and necessitating a rebuilding of about half of the hotel rooms. Today, you'll face a hotel with old and new rooms; both types are cozy and rustically appealing as weather-tight getaways. All units have well-maintained bathrooms with shower units. Its location a few steps from the Svaneke harbor adds a lot of charm to this property, as does the publike cocktail lounge and restaurant (see "Where to Dine," below).

Havnebryggen 9, DK-3740 Svaneke. © **56-49-61-49.** Fax 56-49-61-03. www.siemsens.dk. 50 units. 890DKK–1,190DKK ($151–$202/£80–£107) double. Rates include breakfast. AE, DC, MC, V. **Amenities:** Restaurant; bar; sauna; room service (7:30am–9:30pm); coin-operated laundry; all nonsmoking rooms. *In room:* TV, hair dryer, trouser press, iron, safe.

WHERE TO DINE

Siemsens Gaard ⭐ *Value* DANISH   Set directly on the Svaneke harbor, the building that contains this restaurant is one of the oldest in town. Half-timbered, and with a pale yellow facade, it serves the best food in the area. The artfully rustic dining rooms have thick walls and harbor views that evoke early-20th-century Denmark. If you're not sure what to order at lunch, consider a medley of *smørrebrød* (open-faced sandwiches) that some culinary experts think are almost too attractive to eat. An average lunch might consist of two or three of these. More substantial fare might include a selection of herring arranged onto a platter, steaming bowls of cream-of-shellfish soup, smoked and marinated salmon with crème fraîche, voluptuous grilled monkfish or haddock with herbs and red-wine sauce, and a dessert specialty of crepes with almond cream and fresh berries.

Havnebryggen 9. © **56-49-61-49.** Reservations recommended. Lunch main courses 100DKK–125DKK ($17–$21/£9–£11); dinner main courses 160DKK–215DKK ($27–$37/£14–£19); lunch *smørrebrød* 50DKK ($8.50/£4.50). AE, DC, MC, V. Daily 7am–10:30pm.

FROM SVANEKE TO GUDHJEM

From Svaneke, you can leave the Baltic coastline and head inland through the northern outskirts of the third-largest forest in Denmark, **Almindingen.** (The western part of this forest is best explored by heading north from Åkirkeby; see "From Rønne to Nexø," earlier in this chapter.) Dotted with creeks and ponds, and covered mostly with hardy conifers, it's known for the profusion of its wildflowers—especially lily of the valley—and well-designated hiking trails. Head first for **Østerlars,** home to the largest of the island's distinctive round churches, the **Østerlarskirke,** at Gudhjemsveg 28 (© **56-49-82-64;** bus: 9 from Gudhjem). It's open early April to mid-October, Monday to Saturday 9am to 5pm, charging 10DKK ($1.70/90p) adults; children 15 and under enter free. The Vikings originally built it around 1150, using rocks, boulders, and stone slabs. The church was dedicated to St. Laurence and later enlarged with chunky-looking buttresses; it was intended to serve in part as a fortress against raids by Baltic pirates. Inside are several wall paintings that date from around 1350, depicting scenes from the life of Jesus.

After exploring the area and dipping south along forest roads, you can follow the signposts to **Østerlars,** southwest of Gudhjem, or else drive back along the coast to Svaneke and take the coastal road northwest into Gudhjem.

4 Gudhjem ⟨★⟩

If you're in this little town on a summer's day, you'll know why it's called "God's Home." Tiny cross-timbered houses in bright colors flank the cobblestone streets. The fig and mulberry trees, plus the steep slopes, give it a vaguely Mediterranean feeling. Boats clog the harbor, and for lunch you go for the alder-smoked golden herring from one of the local smokehouses—and the day is yours.

From Østerlars, drive 3km (1¾ miles) north, following the signs to Gudhjem, a steeply inclined town that traded with the Hanseatic League during the Middle Ages. Most of its population died as a result of plagues in 1653 and 1654, but Danish guerrilla fighters and sympathizers, following territorial wars with Sweden, repopulated the town some years later.

Before setting out to explore the area, you might want to call first at the **Gudhjem Turistbureau,** Åbogade 9 (© **56-48-52-10**), a block inland from the harbor. It's open only in summertime, May to September. May to mid-June, and mid-August to September, hours are Monday to Saturday 1 to 4pm. During the peak of midsummer, from mid-June to mid-August, hours are Friday to Wednesday 10am to 4pm.

SEEING THE SIGHTS

Especially charming are Gudhjem's 18th-century half-timbered houses and the 19th-century smokehouses, known for their distinctive techniques of preserving herring with alder-wood smoke. Its harbor, blasted out of the rocky shoreline in the 1850s, is the focal point for the town's 1,200 permanent residents.

Gudhjem Museum   Frankly, we find the temporary art exhibits and the outdoor sculptures more intriguing than the permanent collection of locomotives and other rail-related memorabilia housed here in an old station that existed from the early 20th century until 1952. Its exhibits depict the now-defunct rail line that once crisscrossed the island. But if you're a railroad buff, you'll really get off on this museum's nostalgic "remembrance of things past," to borrow from Marcel Proust.

Stationsvej 1. © **56-48-54-62**. Admission 25DKK ($4.25/£2.25) adults, 10DKK ($1.70/90p) children 10–15, free for children under 10. Mid-May to mid-Sept Mon–Sat 10am–5pm, Sun 2–5pm. Closed mid-Sept to mid-May.

Landsbrugs Museum (Bornholm Agricultural Museum)   This is a timbered, thatched-roof farmhouse that originally was built in 1796, and it's been preserved much as it was back then. The farmhouse and its surrounding garden is a journey back in time. You can go inside the brightly colored interior of the house, which has been preserved with artifacts that were used by its occupants in the 1800s. Outside it's like Ma and Pa Kettle on the farm, the barnyard complete with pigs, goats, cows, and chickens. On-site is a little shop selling woolen sweaters and wooden spoons, as well as some of the tastiest jars of homemade mustard we've found in Denmark.

Melstedvej 25. © **56-48-55-98**. Admission 30DKK ($5.10/£2.70) adults, 10DKK ($1.70/90p) children 10–15, free for children under 10. Mid-May to mid-Oct Tues–Sun 10am–5pm. Closed mid-Oct to mid-May. 1km/⅔ mile south of Gudhjem.

SHOPPING

For some of the best glass objects in the area, head for **Gallerie Baltic See Glass** (*R*, Melstedvej 47 (*C* **56-48-56-41**), lying 3km (1¾ miles) south of Gudhjem along the coastal road. Although much of this glass has a practical value, some works are so stunningly beautiful that they should be treated like objects of art. One of the best art galleries in the area is **Gallerie Kaffslottet,** Duebakken 2 (*C* **56-48-56-18**), which displays the finest works from local artists, some of whom are expats from Copenhagen who have escaped from the urban jungle.

WHERE TO STAY

Casa Blanca   Efficient, well run, and carefully scrutinized throughout its summer-only rental season by its welcoming owners, Elly and Preben Mortensen, this is a three-story, red-roofed, motel-style structure in the center of Gudhjem. The white rooms are somewhat cramped and outfitted with simple yet comfortable furniture that, in some instances, is covered with leather upholstery. Glass doors in every room open onto private balconies or terraces, and all units have well-maintained shower-only bathrooms. The hotel restaurant, the Flagermusen (see "Where to Dine," below), functions as a social center for residents.

Kirchevej 10, DK-3760 Gudhjem. *C* 56-48-50-20. Fax 56-48-15-58. Casablanca@adr.dk. 33 units. 700DKK–760DKK ($119–$129/£63–£68) double. Rates include breakfast; supplement for half-board 100DKK ($17/£9) per person. AE, DC, MC, V. Closed Oct–Apr. **Amenities:** Restaurant; bar; outdoor heated pool. In room: TV, no phone.

Gudhjem Hotel & Feriepark   To stay in this holiday apartment complex you have to agree to a booking of 3 or 4 days, which is enough time to explore Bornholm in depth. The location is south of Gudhjem, about midway between that town and its satellite hamlet of Melsted; the hotel is a 5-minute walk from either center. Most guests can be found during the day enjoying the wide, sandy expanse of beach lying a few steps from the hotel, or else taking in the view from the summer terrace. The complex consists of tastefully designed, masonry-sided cottages, each with a sky-lit terra-cotta roof and a cement-paved patio extending the living area out onto the carefully clipped lawns. The living isn't fancy—strictly utilitarian though comfortable. Apartments come with two bedrooms, each equipped with two single beds, plus a living room with a sofa converting at night into a bed for a cozy twosome. The bathrooms are small but well kept with a shower unit, not a tub. There are small markets nearby where you can purchase food to cook in your fully equipped kitchen. If you want more style and glamour, book into the Jantzens (see below).

Jernkåsvej 1, DK-3760 Gudhjem. *C* 56-48-54-44. Fax 56-48-54-55. www.hotelgudhjem.dk. 102 apts. 490DKK–1,020DKK ($83–$173/£44–£92) double. Supplemental charges include 175DKK ($30/£16) for electricity, a nominal fee for the rental of linens and towels, and a one-time cleaning charge of 325DKK ($55/£29). Discounts available for stays of more than 3 days. MC, V. Closed Nov–Apr. **Amenities:** Lounge; outdoor heated pool; 2 tennis courts; sauna; coin-operated laundry. In room: TV, kitchen.

Jantzens Hotel *RR* (*Value*   This is where we like to hang our hat, and it's one of the best deals on the island—not only affordable but filled with an old-fashioned charm and many grace notes including an idyllic terrace and rose garden in the rear, which fronts a trio of small cottages with private terraces. Opened in 1872, the buttercup-yellow structure with wrought-iron balconies opens onto the Baltic Sea. The owners have recaptured the ambience of the early 1900s, with hardwood floors and rattan furnishings. Bathrooms were added as an afterthought and are a bit cramped, but adequate for your needs. All the bedrooms come with a small refrigerator. You don't have to journey outside at night but can dine at the on-site Andi's Kokken, serving a Danish and French menu. What do we like most about the cook here? As we were hiking one summer day, we came across him picking fresh berries in a nearby meadow, so we knew in advance what dessert to order that night.

Brøddeg 33, DK-3760 Gudhjem. ⓒ 56-48-50-17. 16 units. 875DKK–1,050DKK ($149–$179/£79–£95) double. Rates include breakfast. MC, V. Closed Nov–Apr. **Amenities:** Restaurant. *In room:* TV (in some).

Melsted Badehotel   This is a classic Bornholm beach hotel that satisfies the needs of all but the most demanding clients. Originally built in 1942, during the darkest days of World War II, in a boxy format with white-painted bricks and soft blue trim, this is the most prominent and visible building in the seaside hamlet of Melsted, a kilometer (⅗ mile) south of Gudhjem. Part of its allure derives from its location just 12m (39 ft.) from the edge of the sea—occupants of its well-maintained and cozy rooms can hear the sounds of the surf throughout the night. Most of the rather small rooms have private terraces or balconies; all units contain well-kept bathrooms with shower units. If you'd like more space and grander comfort, opt for one of the apartments in a half-timbered house next to the hotel. These apartments are attractively and comfortably furnished and one of the best deals on the island, the largest unit sleeping four adults and two to three kids. There's a coffee shop/bistro that serves simple lunches every day when the hotel is open, but never dinner. Much of this establishment's conviviality is exhibited on the wooden terrace that extends out over the sands, where outdoor tables, sun parasols, and chairs provide a space for sunbathing, people-watching, and dining on meals from the hotel's bistro.

Melstedvej 27, DK-3760 Gudhjem. ⓒ 56-48-51-00. Fax 56-48-55-84. www.melsted-badehotel.dk. 21 units. 930DKK–1,330DKK ($158–$226/£84–£120) double; 1,550DKK ($264/£140) apt. Rates include breakfast. DC, MC, V. Closed Nov–Apr. Bus: 7. **Amenities:** Restaurant; cafe; lounge; all nonsmoking rooms. *In room:* TV.

WHERE TO DINE

Bokulhus ⊛ DANISH   For the best food locally, head to this converted 1932 private home, lying only a 5-minute walk from the harbor. Its name derives from the Bokul, which in Gudhjem refers to the highest elevation in town—an undulating, gentle knoll. It was built in 1932 as a private home. Menu items are authentically Danish and, in many cases, designed so that a platter of food is all most warm-weather diners really want. The best example is a *Dansk-platte,* which is loaded with herring, salmon, an assortment of cheeses, chickpeas, and hand-peeled shrimp. Other well-prepared choices include beef tournedos with baked sweet peppers, yellowfin tuna with saffron sauce, and veal cutlets with potatoes and a shallot and parsley sauce. There's nothing imaginative about this fare but it's good tasting, wholesome, and market fresh.

Bokulvej 4. ⓒ 56-48-52-97. Reservations recommended. *Smørrebrød* platters 75DKK ($13/£6.75); main courses 170DKK ($29/£15). AE, DC, MC, V. Wed–Mon 11:30am–10pm. Closed mid-Oct to mid-Apr.

Restaurant Flagermusen *Value* DANISH   Locals flock to this wood-paneled restaurant in a hotel we previously recommended, knowing they can get solid, reliable, time-tested Danish cooking, prepared without frills to spoil the natural flavor. It's a sort of brasserie with a Danish accent, offering personalized service that is polite, but a bit slow when the house is full. We wisely turned down the mushroom soup as an appetizer, going for a delectable cream of clam instead. We also had a side order of smoked salmon, which always tastes better than what you find in the grocery store. Many savvy diners like the pan-fried herring, although those with more moderate palates opt for the filet of plaice with a butter-and-parsley sauce. From Norway comes a marvelous haddock which the chefs grilled just right and served with a Béarnaise sauce.

In the Casa Blanca, Kirchevej 10. (© **56-48-50-20.** Main courses 100DKK–160DKK ($17–$27/£9–£14); fixed-price menu 80DKK ($14/£7.20). AE, DC, MC, V. May–Sept daily 11:30am–9pm. Closed Oct–Apr.

GUDHJEM AFTER DARK

Consider a drink at the **Café Klint,** Egn Mikkelsensvej (© **56-48-56-26**), where a cozy ambience that might remind you of a Danish version of an English pub welcomes you with pints of ale in an old-fashioned setting. And for something a bit more electronic, with more emphasis on rock-'n'-roll music, have a drink or two at the **Café Gustav,** St. Torv 8 (© **56-91-00-47**), where at least one or two of the many artists living on the island's east coast are likely to congregate.

FROM GUDHJEM TO ALLINGE

For our next journey, head west along the coastal road. Between Gudhjem and Allinge, a distance of 14km (8⅔ miles), you'll enjoy dramatic vistas over granite cliffs and sometimes savage seascapes. The entire coastline here is known as **Helligdoms Klipperne** (Cliffs of Sanctuary), for the survivors of the many ships that floundered along this granite coastline over the centuries.

Midway along the route, the **Bornholms Kunstmuseet** (Art Museum of Bornholm), Helligdommen (© **56-48-43-86**), which opened in 1993, contains the largest collection of works by Bornholm artists, including Olaf Rude and Oluf Høst. It's open June to August, daily 10am to 5pm; April, May, September, and October, Tuesday to Sunday 10am to 5pm; November to March, Tuesday and Thursday 1 to 5pm, Sunday 10am to 5pm. Admission is 50DKK ($8.50/£4.50) adults, free for children ages 15 and under. From the rocky bluff where the museum sits, you can see the isolated and rocky island of **Christiansø** (see below), about 11km (6¾ miles) offshore, the wind-tossed home to about 120 year-round residents, most of whom make their living from the sea.

5 Christiansø ⭐

This is where TomKat should have gone for their honeymoon. Even Brooke Shields, trying to present her wedding gift of a blender, wouldn't have found them here in this remote outpost of 100 islanders, much less the paparazzi.

The island is only 500m (1,640 ft.) long and can be explored in about an hour. Should there be too much "excitement" on Christiansø, you can walk over a footbridge to the smaller island of **Frederiksø,** which is so tranquil it seems asleep. Christiansø and Frederiksø are the only inhabited islands in the Ertholmene archipelago, the others being set aside as bird sanctuaries.

Both Christiansø and Frederiksø are spring breeding grounds for eider ducks. Not only are cars forbidden on the island, but so are cats and dogs, each viewed as a predator to the rich bird life here, which includes puffins.

This remote place used to be a vital link in Denmark's defense when Christian V established a naval fortress here in the wake of a Swedish invasion in 1658. By the 1850s, when Sweden was no longer viewed as an enemy, the naval forces withdrew and the island went into a long decline, which continues to this day. The naval cottages housing the sailors were taken over by fishermen who still eke out a living here. A few artists, seeking a retreat from the world, have also established little studios here.

Other than the island's beauty, the only major—and clearly visible—sight is the **Store Tårn** (Great Tower) on Christiansø. Constructed in 1684, it measures 25m (82 ft.) in diameter and has a century-old **lighthouse** that offers the most panoramic view of the island. If you pay 4DKK (70¢/35p) you can scale the stairs to the top—that is, if anybody is around to let you in—things are very laid back here. An even grander thrill is a walk along the once-fortified stone walls with their cannon-studded batteries.

Lille Tårn (Little Tower) lies on Frederiksø and dates from 1685. It's been turned into a small museum of local artifacts that holds almost no interest at all—some old cannons, fishing equipment, iron works, and fishing gear. We suggest you skip it.

Ferryboats depart from the "mainland" of Bornholm one to seven times a day, depending on the season. For ferry schedules from Allinge and Gudhjem, call ℂ **56-48-51-76**; from Svaneke, ℂ **56-49-64-32**. Round-trip transit of 60 to 90 minutes costs 160DKK ($27/£14).

If you become enchanted with Christiansø and want to move in, at least for the night, there is the following charming accommodation.

WHERE TO STAY & DINE
Christiansø Gæstgiveriet ⚡ *(Finds* Of all the places we recommend in this guide, this is the ultimate retreat for the escapist. There is no better place for an off-the-record weekend. Once the home of a naval commander, the 18th-century, solidly built house is the only place to stay on the island. The small bedrooms are decorated in a style that evokes a private home as it might have looked in 1910. Bedrooms are comfortably furnished, but you must share the corridor bathrooms with the other guests—no great hardship. Residents and day-trippers meet in the nautically decorated bar on-site, and there is also a good restaurant serving typically Danish meals, most often seafood. Even if you aren't staying here, you might visit for lunch—platters cost from 50DKK to 60DKK ($8.50–$10/£4.50–£5.40). At dinner the fare is more elaborate, with main courses going from 89DKK to 160DKK ($15–$27/£8–£14). The only entertainment you'll find here is what you'll create for yourself, talking with fellow guests, or exploring the local bird and wildlife habitats. Don't even consider, especially during July and August, heading out here from Bornholm without an advance reservation, as it's very popular in midsummer.

DK-3740 Christiansø. ℂ **56-46-20-15.** Fax 56-46-20-86. 6 units. 800DKK ($136/£72) double. Rates include breakfast. AE, DC, MC, V. Closed mid-Dec to mid-Feb. **Amenities:** Restaurant; bar; coin-operated laundry; all nonsmoking rooms. *In room:* No phone.

6 Allinge & Sandvig

Continue driving northwest until you reach the twin communities of **Allinge** and **Sandvig.** Allinge, whose architecture is noticeably older than that of Sandvig, contains 200- and 300-year-old half-timbered houses built for the purveyors of the long-ago herring trade, and antique smokehouses for preserving herring for later consumption or for export abroad.

The newer town of Sandvig, a short drive to the northwest, flourished around 1900 when many ferryboats arrived from Sweden. Sandvig became a stylish beach resort, accommodating guests at the Strandhotellet.

The forest that surrounds these twin communities is known as the **Trolleskoe** (Forest of Trolls), home to wart-covered and phenomenally ugly magical creatures that delight in brewing trouble, mischief, and the endless fog that sweeps over this end of the island.

From Allinge, detour inland (southward) for about 4km (2½ miles) to reach **Olsker,** site of the **Olskirke** (Round Church of Ols), Lindesgordsvej (☎ **56-48-05-29**). Built in the 1100s with a conical roof and thick walls, it's the smallest of the island's round churches. It was painstakingly restored in the early 1950s. Dedicated to Skt. Olav (Olav the Holy, king of Norway, who died in 1031), it looks something like a fortress, an image that the original architects wanted very much to convey. June to September, and October 17 to 18, it's open Monday to Saturday 2 to 5pm; April and May, and October 1 to 16, it's open Monday to Friday 10am to 1pm. It's closed the rest of the year. Entrance costs 7DKK ($1.20/65p).

Now retrace your route back to Allinge and head northward toward Sandvig, a distance of less than a kilometer (about ½ mile). You'll soon see **Madsebakke,** a well-signposted open-air site containing the largest collection of Bronze Age rock carvings in Denmark. Don't expect a building, any type of enclosed area, or even a curator. Simply follow the signs posted beside the main highway. The carvings include 11 depictions of high-prowed sailing ships of unknown origin, and were made in a smooth, glacier-scoured piece of bedrock close to the side of the road.

From here, proceed just less than a kilometer (about ½ mile) to the island's northernmost tip, **Hammeren,** for views that—depending on the weather—could extend all the way to Sweden. Here you'll see the island's oldest lighthouse, **Hammerfyr,** built in 1871.

WHERE TO STAY IN SANDVIG

Strandhotellet *(ℛℛ (Finds* There is a romantic nostalgia about this place. In 1896 it was built as stables but a decade later was converted to the largest and most stylish hotel in Bornholm. Those days are gone forever. Today the venerable old hotel is a remote outpost and a reminder of days gone by when Sandvig was a viable port and commercial center before losing out to Rønne. A worthy detour for diners who drive from other parts of the island, the hotel offers three floors of spartan accommodations with lots of exposed birch wood and (in most cases) sea views. Each unit has a well-maintained bathroom with a tub/shower combo.

Strandpromenaden 7, DK-3770 Sandvig. ☎ **56-48-03-14.** Fax 56-48-02-09. 49 units. 650DKK–950DKK ($111–$162/£59–£86) double; 900DKK–1,400DKK ($153–$238/£81–£126) suite. AE, DC, MC, V. **Amenities:** Restaurant; bar; sauna. *In room:* TV.

WHERE TO DINE IN SANDVIG

Strandhotellet Restaurant DANISH/SEAFOOD "There's nothing wrong with having an extra *akvavit* or two," a diner visiting from Copenhagen told us at table. "There's not much to do here at night except eat. At least the food is delicious." That about sums it up.

Today's hotel dining room, attracting both residents and visitors to the island, grew out of a 1930s dance hall and supper club that once flourished here. The chefs have to import a lot of their produce but use whatever is fresh at the local markets. The smoked filet of wild salmon with a savory tomato tapenade got us off to a fine start, and was followed by a platter of various fish, the actual dish varying depending on the catch of the day. The meat devotee will also find a few good choices, such as beef medallions with a ragout of fresh vegetables.

Strandpromenaden 7, Sandvig. ℂ **56-48-03-14.** Lunch main courses 59DKK–69DKK ($10–$12/£5.30–£6.20); dinner main courses 93DKK–130DKK ($16–$22/£8.40–£12). AE, DC, MC, V. Daily noon–10pm.

FROM ALLINGE & SANDVIG BACK TO RØNNE

For our final adventure, turn south, following the signs pointing to Rønne. After less than a kilometer (½ mile) you'll see the rocky crags of a semiruined fortress that Bornholmers believe is the most historically significant building on the island—the **Hammershus Fortress** ℱ, begun in 1255 by the archbishop of Lund (Sweden). He planned this massive fortress to reinforce his control of the island. Since then, however, the island has passed from Swedish to German to Danish hands several times; it was a strategic powerhouse controlling what was then a vitally important sea lane. The decisive moment came in 1658, when the Danish national hero Jens Kofoed murdered the Swedish governor and sailed to Denmark to present the castle (and the rest of the island) to the Danish king.

Regrettably, the fortress's dilapidated condition was caused by later architects, who used it as a rock quarry to supply the stone used to construct some of the buildings and streets (including Hovedvagten) of Rønne, as well as several of the structures on Christiansø, the tiny island 11km (6¾ miles) northeast of Bornholm. The systematic destruction of the fortress ended in 1822, when it was "redefined" as a Danish national treasure. Much of the work that restored the fortress to the eerily jagged condition you'll see today was completed in 1967. Hammershus escaped the fate of the second-most-powerful fortress on the island, Lilleborg. Set deep in Bornholm's forests, Lilleborg was gradually stripped of its stones for other buildings after its medieval defenses became obsolete.

Some 4km (2½ miles) south of Hammershus—still on the coastal road heading back to Rønne—is a geological oddity called **Jons Kapel** (Jon's Chapel); it can be seen by anyone who'd like to take a short hike (less than 1km/½ mile) from the highway. Basically it's a rocky bluff with a panoramic view over the island's western coast, where, according to ancient legend, an agile but reclusive hermit, Brother Jon, preached to the seagulls and crashing surf below. For those who would like to enjoy a panoramic view, signs point the way from the highway.

From here, continue driving southward another 13km (8 miles) to Rønne, passing through the hamlet of **Hasle** en route. And so ends our discovery of the island. If you followed us all the way, you've seen the best of Bornholm.

9

Funen

After Copenhagen and after a visit to "Hamlet's Castle" in North Zealand, nearly all foreign visitors head for **Odense,** the capital of the island of Funen (*Fyn* in Danish), lying to the west of Zealand. And rightly so. Hans Christian Andersen was born in Odense, and houses and memorabilia associated with him are the big attractions.

But there is so much more here, including the most fantastic island in Scandinavia, little old "time-warp" Ærø of the southern coast. Hop gardens, Viking runic stones, orchards of fruit trees, busy harbors, market towns, swan ponds, thatch-roof houses, once-fortified castles, and stately manor homes invite exploration by car.

Funen has some 1,125km (700 miles) of coastline, with wide sandy beaches in some parts, and woods and grass that grow all the way to the water's edge in others. Steep cliffs provide sweeping views of the Baltic or the Kattegat.

Although ferryboats have plied the waters between the islands and peninsulas of Denmark since ancient times, recent decades have seen the development of a network of bridges. In 1934 the first plans were developed for a bridge over the span of water known as the **Storebælt** (Great Belt), the 19km (12-mile) silt-bottomed channel that separates Zealand (and Copenhagen) from Funen and the rest of continental Europe. After many delays caused by war, technical difficulties, and lack of funding, and after the submission of 144 designs by engineers from around the world, construction began in 1988 on an intricately calibrated network of bridges and tunnels.

On June 14, 1998, her majesty, Queen Margrethe II, cut the ribbon shortly before driving across the Great Belt Bridge. The project incorporated both railway and road traffic divided between a long underwater tunnel and both low and high bridges. (The rail link has operated since 1997.) Only some aspects of the Chunnel between England and France are on par with the staggering scale of this project.

Visitors can view exhibitions about the bridge at the **Great Belt Exhibition Center** (🕿 **58-35-01-00**), located at the entrance to the bridge and hard to miss. It's open July to August, Wednesday to Monday 11am to 4pm, and the admission is free.

1 Nyborg: Gateway to Funen

130km (81 miles) W of Copenhagen; 34km (21 miles) E of Odense

One of the oldest towns in Denmark, founded 7 centuries ago, Nyborg lies at the western terminus of the Storebælt bridge and is the easternmost town on the island of Funen. Local residents thought the opening of the bridge would boost tourism, but that has happened only marginally. Most motorists, especially foreigners, rush through town en route to Odense to pay their respects to the memory of Hans Christian Andersen.

Tips Around the Island by Rail & Bus

Funen has a good system of buses and trains that fan out from the central depot in Odense in all directions. Although public transport obviously takes longer than driving a car, it's possible to see the highlights of Funen without your own vehicle. It's also possible to base yourself in Odense, and visit the island's intriguing towns such as Svendborg as day trips. See the individual town listings for more details. For rail information or schedules throughout Funen, call ℂ 70-13-14-15, and for bus routes on the island, call the tourist office (ℂ 65-31-02-80).

That's a shame, really, because Nyborg is deserving of at least 2 hours of your time, which will allow you to visit its old **Torvet** (the market square in the center), the ruins of a medieval castle, and some cross-timbered old houses. Like so many other cities or towns of Denmark, Nyborg was more strategic in the Middle Ages than it is today.

Its location in the middle of the trade route between Zealand in the east and Jutland in the west helped boost its importance. In medieval times, about 1200 to 1413, Nyborg was the capital of Denmark. Medieval buildings and well-preserved ramparts are testaments to that era. Nyborg's town square, the Torvet, was created in 1540, when a block of houses was demolished to make room for the royal tournaments of Christian III.

In summer, Denmark's oldest open-air theater, **Nyborg Voldspil,** is the setting for musicals or operettas under the leafy beeches on the old castle ramparts. Throughout the summer, classical music concerts (featuring international soloists) are performed in the castle's Great Hall. Inquire at the tourist office (see "Essentials," below) for further details.

Dating from the mid-1600s, the "Tattoo" is an ancient military ceremony with musical accompaniment. This old custom has been revived to honor the corps who played an important role in the Schleswig wars in 1848 and again in 1864. In tribute to the old corps, the present-day Tattoo participants wear a green uniform with its characteristic cap, or *chakot.* The corps marches through the center of town at 9pm each year on June 30, thereafter every Tuesday in July and August.

ESSENTIALS
GETTING THERE   By Train or Bus   You can reach Nyborg by train or bus (via ferry). Trains leave Copenhagen every hour, and there's frequent bus service from Copenhagen as well. From Odense, east-bound trains arrive 2 times an hour.

VISITOR INFORMATION   The **Nyborg Turistbureau,** Torvet 9 (ℂ **65-31-02-80;** www.nyborgturist.dk), is open June 15 to August, Monday to Friday 9am to 5pm and Saturday 9:30am to 2pm; September to June 14, Monday to Friday 9am to 4pm and Saturday 9:30am to 12pm.

GETTING AROUND   Bus nos. 1, 3, and 4 serve all in-town destinations listed below.

SEEING THE SIGHTS
Mads Lerches Gård (Mads Lerches House) ⊕   Of all the places in Funen, this 1601 house, the former home of Mads Lerche, the town mayor, provides the best insight into what life was like in the 17th century—that is, if you had some money in

the bank. The house, painted a reddish pink, is filled with exhibitions on local history, but far more intriguing than that are the antique-filled period chambers spread over 30 rooms on two floors. There's even a small brewery on-site, which every home in the 1600s should have had but didn't.

Slotsgade 11. © 65-31-02-07. www.museer-nyborg.dk. Admission 30DKK ($5.10/£2.70) adults, 15DKK ($2.55/£1.35) children 6–14, free for children under 6. Apr–May and Sept–Oct 21 Tues–Sun 10am–3pm; June and Aug Tues–Sun 10am–4pm; July Tues–Sun 10am–5pm. Closed Oct 22–Mar. Bus: 1, 3, or 4.

Nyborg Slot (Nyborg Castle) ⚔

This hardly compares to Windsor Castle in England but to the Danes it's just as important; yet it comes as a disappointment that there's so little left to evoke all the momentous historical events that occurred here in the Middle Ages. Dating from 1170, this is one of the oldest of Denmark's royal castles. Originally it was built to defend the country from the Wends of North Germany. King Erik Glipping signed Denmark's first constitution in this moated castle in 1282, and Nyborg became the seat of the Danish Parliament, the Danehof, until 1413, when Copenhagen took over.

In a regrettable decision, much of the Slot was demolished in 1722 to provide building materials for Odense Castle. Nonetheless, part of the original ramparts remain. From these bastions, Danes rained down hot tar on their invaders. If you walk these ramparts today, you'll have a **panoramic** view of Nyborg and the sea. The terrace in front is still lined with bronze guns facing the town center. The town gate, **Landporten** , can still be seen just north of the castle.

Most intriguing is the still-remaining **Danehof** , the hall where Parliament met. The walls are painted with geometric murals, and there is an extensive collection of armaments such as guns and swords, suits of armor (rather impressive), and old royal paintings (not too impressive). Other rooms open to view include the King's Room, the Knights' Hall, and even the apartment once occupied by the royal kids, heirs apparent to the throne.

Slotspladen. © **65-31-02-07**. www.museer-nyborg.dk. Admission 30DKK ($5.10/£2.70) adults, 15DKK ($2.55/£1.35) children 10–15, free for children under 10. Apr–May and Sept–Oct 21Tues–Sun 10am–3pm; June and Aug Tues–Sun 10am–4pm; July Tues–Sun 10am–5pm. Closed Oct 22–Mar. Bus: 1, 2, or 3.

Vor Frue Kirke   The Church of Our Lady, as it's called in English, is still a place of worship even though it dates from the Middle Ages. Unfortunately, restorers and decorators descended on the church in 1870 and completely changed it, so we're not able to see the purity of its original simple architectural details. Even so, it's still a worthy place to wander about for 30 to 45 minutes. We found that the greatest treasure here is a **baroque pulpit** in stunning detail, the work of Odense-born Anders Mortensen in 1653. He depicted some of the epic moments in the Bible, including the Baptism of Christ, the Birth of John the Baptist, the Transfiguration, and both the resurrection and the Ascension, the subject of countless medieval paintings.

The Gothic spire of the church is a landmark for miles around, and the interior is split into a trio of aisles and endowed with woodcarvings, carved old epitaphs, candelabra, and model ships. The elegant wrought-iron gate you see was forged in 1649 by Casper Fincke, the court-appointed craftsman to King Christina IV. The most evocative aspect of the church, which we discovered while strolling about Nyborg one night, is that at 9:45pm the Watchman's Bell from 1523 is still rung, a tradition that dates back for centuries. Lying at the end of Kongegade in the town center, Vor Frue Kirke can be entered through its south door. Nearby at Adelgade and Korsbrodregade stands a large stone-built house, **Korsbrodregården,** dating from 1396. This was the Chapter House of the Order of St. John, its vaulted cellar converted today into a gift shop.

Adelgade. © **65-31-16-08**. Free admission. Daily 9am–6pm.

SHOPPING

The open workshop of the town's most talented potter and ceramicist can be visited at **Ida Rostgård,** Holken Havn 1 (© **65-30-23-02**).

WHERE TO STAY

Hotel Hesselet   Such an elegant hotel of a high international standard comes as a surprise in this sleepy, provincial town. One of the most stylish hotels in Funen, outclassing most of those in Odense itself, is idyllically set among beech trees, opening onto a view of the Great Belt with its Storebælt suspension bridge. Opt for a room with a view of this sea spectacle, or else you'll be assigned an accommodation opening onto a forest.

Inside, the hotel creates a glamorous aura in its public lounges with its use of Asian artifacts and plush Oriental carpets, its large fireplace, its sunken living rooms, and a cozy library lined with leather-bound volumes. Bedrooms are sumptuously furnished and spacious, each with tasteful appointments and the best bathrooms of any hotel along the east coast of Funen, coming with granite floors, double wash basins, bathtubs, and separate shower cabins, plus plenty of toiletries.

Even if you're not a guest, consider a meal here preceded by an aperitif on the patio or by the open fireplace in cold weather. A first-rate chef, Tina Møhring Madsen composes her dishes incorporating fresh seasonal produce.

Christianslundsvej 119, DK-5800 Nyborg. ⓒ **65-31-30-29.** Fax 65-31-29-58. www.hesselet.dk. 47 units. Mon–Thurs 1,580DKK–1,780DKK ($269–$303/£142–£160) double; Fri–Sun 1,280DKK–1,680DKK ($218–$286/£115–£151) double; 2,400DKK–2,800DKK ($408–$476/£216–£252) suite. Rates include breakfast. AE, DC, MC, V. Free parking. **Amenities:** Restaurant; bar; indoor heated pool; 2 tennis courts; sauna; room service (7am–10pm); babysitting; laundry service; dry cleaning; nonsmoking rooms; rooms for those w/limited mobility; solarium. *In room:* TV, dataport, minibar, hair dryer, safe.

Hotel Nyborg Strand 🏆 (Kids)   The only thing that turns us off about this hotel, managed by Best Western, is its tendency to book noisy conference groups. That's the bad news. The good news is that it's a most recommendable choice in summer when there are no conventions. For years, it was the flag bearer in Nyborg, since 1899 in fact, until that "upstart," the Hesselet (see above) came along to absorb all the glory. The location near a forest-blanketed beach lies less than a kilometer (about ½ mile) from the train station. At the water's edge, the hotel, like its rival, opens onto a fine view of the bay and the Great Belt Bridge.

They cost more; but the junior suites in the hotel tower not only command the most panoramic views through their round windows but also have private balconies, and one comes with a private sauna. The midsize-to-spacious standard rooms also have great views and are tastefully and comfortably furnished. Each comes with a bathroom with a tub/shower combo, and an extra bed can be added if requested by a family. Head chef Erik Møllerand commands a brigade of highly skilled cooks, offering a choice of two restaurants, the accurately named **Panorama** with a formal French/Danish cuisine, and the more informal and family-friendly **Bistro,** specializing in grills. It also has the largest and best salad buffet in town. All menus are adjusted to take advantage of the best produce of any season.

Østersvej 2, DK-5800 Nyborg. ⓒ **800/528-1234** in the U.S., or 65-31-31-31. Fax 65-31-37-01. www.nyborgstrand.dk. 300 units. Mon–Thurs 1,055DKK–1,420DKK ($179–$241/£95–£128) double; Fri–Sun 695DKK–995DKK ($118–$169/£63–£90) double; 1,970DKK–2,280DKK ($335–$388/£177–£205) junior suite. Rates include breakfast. AE, DC, MC, V. Closed Dec 16–Jan 3. **Amenities:** 2 restaurants; bar; indoor heated pool; fitness center; sauna; room service; babysitting; laundry service; dry cleaning; nonsmoking rooms; rooms for those w/limited mobility. *In room:* TV, dataport (in some), hair dryer.

WHERE TO DINE

Central Cafeen 🏆 DANISH/FRENCH   When we first discovered this restaurant many years ago, we were put off by its name of "Central Café." Only after dining here did we discover that this is one of the finest restaurants along the east coast of Funen, set directly across the street from City Hall in a house from 1787 that has contained some kind of restaurant since 1854. With a sense of local history and a deep-seated pride, it offers four separate, cozy dining rooms, each outfitted with sepia-toned photographs of four generations of Danish monarchs, plus a quirky collection of ladies' hats tucked museum-style in glass cases.

The composition of the fixed-price menus changes every month to take advantage of seasonal produce. First-rate ingredients are used, often fresh shrimp and lobster. Begin perhaps with a bowl of the creamy lobster bisque, going on to the fried plaice with a lobster-and-shrimp sauce. Roasted salmon appears with fresh spinach, and meat eaters gravitate to the fried pork cutlets in a parsley sauce. The sumptuous desserts are made daily, and there is an impressive but pricey wine list to back up the cuisine.

Nørregade 6. ✆ 65-31-01083. Reservations recommended. Main courses 128DKK–198DKK ($22–$34/£12–£18). Fixed-price menu 208DKK ($35/£19); 3-course menu 238DKK ($40/£21). AE, DC, MC, V. Mon–Sat 11am–9:30pm. Bus: 1, 3, or 4.

Restaurant Østervemb ✪ DANISH/FRENCH   The down-home Danish cooking here is as heartwarming as that provided by a nourishing Danish aunt, although the chefs get a bit fancy at times and "Frenchify" some of their more elegant offerings. In the east of Nyborg, Østervemb has been feeding locals since 1924, and feeding them well, to judge by some of the waistlines we noted on diners. The market-fresh fish is one of the culinary attractions here, as we realized when we dived into a platter piled high with three different preparations of herring. The main courses are carefully wrought and the ingredients "married well," as evoked by the breast of Danish hen served with fresh spinach and mushrooms. The curried chicken salad was given extra flavor by crispy bacon bits, and a grilled beef tenderloin, tender and moist, came with a tarragon-flavored glaze and a "side" of a fricassee of oyster mushrooms. As elsewhere in Denmark, desserts are predictably good.

Mellemgade. ✆ 65-30-10-70. Reservations recommended. Lunch platters 190DKK ($32/£17); dinner main courses 187DKK–235DKK ($32–$40/£17–£21); fixed-price 2-course menu 280DKK ($48/£25), 3-course 328DKK ($56/£30). DC, MC, V. Tues–Sat noon–2:30pm and 5:30–10:30pm.

NYBORG AFTER DARK

The town's most consistently popular bar and pub is **Café Anthon,** Mellemgade 25 (✆ **65-31-16-64**), where sports enthusiasts, students, and anyone who happens to want to be convivial gather in a publike ambience that's cozy and warm. For the release of spontaneous energy on a dance floor, head for **Crazy Daisy,** Strandvejen 10 (✆ **63-31-08-28**), open Friday and Saturday from 11pm to dawn.

2 Odense: Birthplace of Hans Christian Andersen ✪✪

96km (60 miles) W of Copenhagen; 34km (21 miles) W of Nyborg; 43km (27 miles) NW of Svendborg

Many people make their living off Hans Christian Andersen and all the visitors his memory brings to Odense. But the town never seemed to appreciate the boy until the world discovered his writing. In some respects, he was treated like Salzburg treated Mozart. Actually, the storyteller had a very unhappy childhood in Odense and left as soon as he was old enough to make his way to Copenhagen.

His cobbler father was always out of money, and had been forced to marry Hans's ill-tempered, peasant mother when she was 7 months pregnant. The Andersen grandmother was insane and, as noted by Andersen himself, was a pathological liar. No wonder the boy wanted to get out of Odense.

But those unpleasant memories are long gone today, and Odense is proud of its world-famous son, hawking souvenirs of him and dusting off the writer's memorabilia to each new generation. This ancient town, the third largest in Denmark, has changed greatly since Andersen walked its streets. But its historic core still evokes the fairy-tale town that Andersen knew so well.

In the heart of Funen and home to more than 185,000 inhabitants, Odense is one of the oldest cities in the country, with a history stretching back some 1,000 years. The

Odense

ATTRACTIONS ●

Brandts Klædefabrik **17**
Bymuyseet Møntegården **7**
Carl Nielsen Museet **5**
Danmarks Jernbanemuseum **3**
Den Fynske Landsby **26**
Fyns Kunstmuseum **14**
H.C. Andersen's Barndomshjem **23**
H.C. Andersens Hus **11**
Skt. Knuds Domkirke **22**
Superbowl **15**

ACCOMMODATIONS ■

Best Western Hotel Knudsens Gaard **25**
City Hotel Odense **6**
Clarion Hotel Plaza **1**
Comfort Windsor Hotel **13**

First Hotel Grand **19**
Hotel Ansgar **2**
Hotel Domir / Hotel Ydes **18**
Næsbylund Kro **4**
Radisson SAS H.C. Andersen Hotel **8**
Scandic Hotel Odense **24**

DINING ◆

Den Gamle Kro **20**
Den Grimme Æling **10**
La Brasserie **16**
Målet **17**
Marie Louise **21**
Restaurant Klitgaard **12**
Sortebro Kro **27**
Under Lindetræt **9**

city's name stems from two words—*Odins Vi* (Odin's shrine), suggesting that the god Odin must have been worshipped here in pre-Christian times. Long before Odense became a pilgrimage center for fans of Andersen, it was an ecclesiastical center and site of religious pilgrimage in the Middle Ages.

Odense today is not just a fairy-tale town, but an industrial might in Denmark, its harbor linked by a canal to the Odense Fjord and thus the Great Belt. It's a center of electro-technical, textile, steel, iron, and timber production.

In summer Odense takes on a festive air, with lots of outdoor activities, including all types of music, drama, and street theater taking place on its squares and in its piazzas. Cafes and pubs are lively day and night.

ESSENTIALS

GETTING THERE   By Train or Bus   You can easily reach Odense by train or bus from Copenhagen, as about 12 trains or buses a day leave Copenhagen's Central Railroad Station for Odense (trip time: 3 hr.).

By Car   From Nyborg, head west on E20 to Allerup and then follow Route 9 north to Odense.

VISITOR INFORMATION   Odense Tourist Bureau is at Rådhuset, Vestergade 2A (© **66-12-75-20;** www.visitodense.com). It's open mid-June to August, Monday to Friday 9am to 6pm, Saturday and Sunday 10am to 3pm; September to mid-June, Monday to Friday 9:30am to 4:30pm and Saturday 10am to 1pm.

Besides helping you arrange excursions, the tourist bureau sells the **Odense Adventure Pass,** giving you access to 16 of the city's museums, the Odense Zoo, six indoor swimming pools, and unlimited free travel on the city buses and DSB trains within the municipality. It also entitles you to discounts on river cruises and admission to the summer-only presentation of the city's Hans Christian Andersen plays (see "Seeing the Sights," below). Passes are valid for 1 or 2 days. A 1-day pass is 125DKK ($21/£11) for adults, 65DKK ($11/£5.85) for children under 14; 2-day passes cost 160DKK ($27/£14) and 85DKK ($14/£7.65).

GETTING AROUND   By Bus   Bus no. 2 serves all in-town destinations listed below.

SEEING THE SIGHTS

The Odense Tourist Bureau offers a 2-hour **walking tour** conducted in July and August, every Tuesday, Wednesday, and Thursday at 11am, from a meeting place behind its office. Covering the town's major sites, it costs 50DKK ($8.50/£4.50) adults and 25DKK ($4.25/£2.25) children 10 to 15; free for children under 10. Reservations are recommended.

Also at the tourist office, you can get information about the **Hans Christian Andersen plays,** which are presented every year mid-July to mid-August. The plays are given on an outdoor stage in the Funen Village, where members of the audience sit on blankets on the grass (if it's dry) or stand (if it's raining or if the ground is wet). Even if you don't understand Danish, there's lots of entertainment value in the visuals. Plays begin every day at 4pm, last around 90 minutes, cost 70DKK ($12/£6.30) adults and 45DKK ($7.65/£4.05) children 10 to 15, and are usually mobbed with H. C. Andersen fans.

Less than a kilometer (½ mile) west of the city center is **Superbowl,** Grøneløkkenvej (© **70-11-11-55;** bus: 91 or 92), a complex of amusements and diversions that are entirely devoted to popular American culture. It incorporates facilities for indoor go-cart racing, an indoor version of American-style miniature golf, several bowling alleys, and a small-scale collection of rides and games inspired by the theme parks of Florida. Each individual attraction within the park maintains its own hours and entrance policies, but the best way to appreciate this site's activities is to head here any-time daily between 10am and 6pm, when for an all-inclusive fee of 80DKK ($14/£7.20), you'll have unlimited access to all of them.

Brandts Klædefabrik (Brandt's Textile Mill) ⚔   An antique textile factory has been successfully converted into an artifact- and art-filled compound with four muse-ums spread across its precincts. You can spend 3 or more hours here and only scratch the surface of its exhibits. At the very least you should ascend to the roof terrace for a panoramic view of Odense. The **Danish Museum of Printing** and the **Danish Press Museum** (© **66-12-10-20**) show the development of the printing press in the coun-try for at least 3 centuries. The museum also houses papermaking, bookbinding, and lithography workshops. Also on-site is the **Kunsthallen Brandts** (© **66-13-78-97**), the art gallery filling four spacious rooms that once housed weaving machines. The exhibitions vary here depending on the season. Some of these have been of world-class interest, with stunning displays of paintings and sculpture, even avant-garde Danish design. Of special interest is a library of art films open to the viewing public. The **Museum of Photographic Art** (© **66-13-78-97**), the only one of its kind in the country, offers not only a permanent collection but at least 10 special exhibits a year. Exhibits go all the way back to August 19, 1839, the official "birthday" of photogra-phy in Denmark. Christian Tuxen Falbe, a former marine officer, was the first Dane to make daguerreotypes in Paris, sending them back to his patron in Copenhagen, Prince Christian Frederik (later King Christian VIII). Finally, **The Time Collection** (© **65-91-19-42;** www.tidenssamling.dk) allows you to travel through time by follow-ing its exhibitions of housing interiors and changing fashions. The exhibits focus on six interior designs, typical living rooms from the beginning of the 20th century until the '70s. You're allowed to actually enter the room and sit on the furniture. You can even play the old gramophones. Nostalgic fashion shows are presented on certain occasions.

Brandts Passage 37–43. © **66-13-78-97.** www.brandts.dk. Combined ticket 50DKK ($8.50/£4.50); 25DKK–30DKK ($4.25–$5.10/£2.25–£2.70) for each attraction. July–Aug daily 10am–5pm; Sept–June Tues–Sun 10am–5pm.

Bymuseet Møntegården (Odense City Museum) ⚔   Not the typical dull city museum with dusty artifacts, of which we've seen too many, this museum traces Odense's history back to the Viking era and has a number of half-timbered houses from the 1500s and 1600s you can actually walk through. In a snug little alleyway off the main courtyard stands a row of workmen's cottages from the same period. The museum is particularly rich in artifacts from the Middle Ages, and there are interiors from the 17th and 18th cen-turies, as well as exhibits that go right up to the 1950s. In the Nyborgladen—the open storehouse of the museum—there are thousands of items exemplifying everyday life from the Middle Ages to the present day. These artifacts cover a vast range, with exhibits from the Middle Ages, including church carvings, rare archaeological digs unearthed on Funen, and rooms filled with period furnishings, mostly from the 19th century, and even church carvings. The exceptional **coin collection** ⚔ spans the mil-lennium, showcasing such rare numismatic items as coins minted during the Danish rule over Estonia.

Overgade 48–50. © **65-51-46-01.** Free admission. Tues–Sun 10am–6pm.

Carl Nielsen Museet   Judge Carl Nielsen by his great music, not his purple prose, as evoked by such rhapsodic lines about the Funen landscape as "Even trees dream and talk in their sleep with a Funen lilt." At the Odense Concert Hall, you can learn about the life and music of Denmark's greatest composer, Carl August Nielsen (1865–1931), the second-most-famous son to come out of Odense.

This towering musician developed a unique polytonal and contrapuntal musical form, his operas including *Saul and David* in 1903 and *Maskerade* in 1906. He also composed symphonies, concertos, and choral and chamber music. Nielsen single-handedly "woke up" Danish music after its sleepy decline of decades. In the museum you can listen to some of his greatest works, even a polka he penned as a child before joining the Odense Military Band as a trumpet player at the tender age of 14.

A biographical slideshow brings to life once again this cultural icon, whose six symphonies and several operas, as well as his hymns and popular songs (many of which are patriotic) are still played around the world today.

Nielsen married a famous sculptor of her day. She changed her name to Anne Marie Carl-Nielsen, strangely keeping her husband's first name in her full name. Although hardly as well known as her husband, she created works still on view in Denmark, including her equestrian statue of Christian IX that stands outside the Royal Stables in Copenhagen.

Although "Anne and Carl," as they were known to their intimates, remained married until he died, they had long periods of marital strife, including a lengthy separation and mutual accusations of infidelity.

Claus Bergsgade 11. ℭ **65-51-46-01**. www.odmus.dk. Admission 25DKK ($4.25/£2.25) adults; free for children 16 and under. Tues and Fri 4–8pm; Sun noon–4pm.

Danmarks Jernbanemuseum (Railway Museum) ℛ (Kids   This is one of the best transportation museums in Scandinavia, appropriately located adjacent to the Odense train station. It's a very active museum and not some dull depot of long-abandoned locomotives, although there are those here too, the best of which is a **royal carriage** ℛ that once carried his majesty King Christian IX.

From the first train in Denmark, dating from 1847, until more modern times, the history of locomotives and carriages is on display, even a "B-Machine," a moving vehicle from 1869. A replica of a 19th-century train depot is on view along with two dozen engines and various saloon cars. Model ferries, buses, model railway tracks, and even Wagons-Lits restaurant cars and ferries are on view. The entire family can go on the minitrains and take a simulated ride in a large diesel locomotive.

Dannebrogsgade 24. ℭ **66-13-66-30**. www.jernbanemuseum.dk. Admission 48DKK ($8.15/£4.30) adults, 20DKK ($3.40/£1.80) children 10–15, free for children under 10. Daily 10am–4pm.

Den Fynske Landsby (Funen Village) ℛℛ (Kids   If Hans Christian Andersen himself were to come back to life and land in this village, he'd feel that the world had never changed. This is the Danish version of Scotland's mystical "Brigadoon," where some 30 buildings, dating from the 17th to the 19th century, keep alive the village milieu of yesterday, with half-timbered houses, flower gardens, a communal pond, and a grazing cow (or goat) that characterized village life of long ago.

In a scenic setting in the Hunderup Woods, these old buildings include a tollhouse, weaver's shop, windmill, farming homestead, vicarage, village school, brickworks, and the inevitable jail. Each was reassembled on this site and authentically furnished. You can visit workshops to see craftspeople, including a basket maker, a spoon cutter, a weaver, and the village blacksmith.

As an added treat, plays and folk dances are staged at a Greek-style theater. The best way to get here is to ignore the bus suggestion below and take a boat from Munke Mose in Odense down the river to Erik Boghs Sti. After you disembark, it's a 15-minute scenic walk to the museum. A one-way fare is 40DKK ($6.80/£3.60) for adults or 30DKK ($5.10/£2.70) for children 10 to 15, free for children under 10.

Sejerskovvej 20. © **65-51-46-01**. Admission 55DKK ($9.35/£4.95) adults, 15DKK ($2.55/£1.35) children 10–15, free for children under 10. Mid-June to mid-Aug daily 9:30am–7pm; Apr to mid-June and mid-Aug to mid-Oct Tues–Sun 10am–5pm; mid-Oct to Mar Sun 11am–3pm. Bus: 21 or 22 from Flakhaven.

Fyns Kunstmuseum (Funen Art Museum) ✦

The founding fathers of one of the oldest, largest, and best art museums outside of Copenhagen wanted it to be a miniature version of the Statens Museum for Kunst in the Danish capital. Opening the Odense museum in the early 1880s, they long ago succeeded in their ambition. Their once-stated goal of "a little bit of everything" is clearly on display today, with a collection dating from 1750 to the present, going from the classics to abstract modern. The permanent exhibitions are beefed up with special shows presented several times a year, some of them world-class in interest, depth, and perspective (often devoted to themes featuring one artist or a collective group such as the French Impressionists). There are some fine sculptures but it is Danish painting that is clearly the star attraction here. Predictably the largest array of paintings is devoted to the artists of Funen, particularly Peter Hansen and Johannes Larsen. Our favorite painting here is the evocative, powerful *Udslidt*, meaning "worn out," the work of the enormously talented H. A. Brendekilde.

Jernbanegade 13. © **65-51-46-01**. www.museum.odense.dk. Admission 30DKK ($5.10/£2.70) adults, 15DKK ($2.55/£1.35) children 10–15, free for children under 10. Tues–Sun 10am–4pm.

H. C. Andersens Barndomshjem (H. C. Andersen's Childhood Home) (Kids)

Visit Andersen's humble childhood abode, where the fairy-tale writer lived from 1807 to 1819. From what is known of Andersen's childhood, his mother was a drunken, superstitious washerwoman, and Andersen was a gawky boy, lumbering and graceless, the victim of his fellow urchins' cruel jabs. However, all is serene at the cottage today; in fact, the little house with its tiny rooms has a certain unpretentious charm, and the "garden still blooms," as in *The Snow Queen*. The museum is only mildly diverting, worth no more than 15 or 20 minutes of your time.

Munkemøllestræde 3. © **65-51-46-01**. www.odmus.dk. Admission 25DKK ($4.25/£2.25) adults, free for children under 17. June–Aug daily 10am–4pm; Sept–May daily 11am–3pm.

H. C. Andersens Hus (H. C. Andersens Museum) ✦✦ (Kids)

Though not the rival of the Shakespeare properties in Stratford-upon-Avon, the object of most Funen pilgrimages is to the house of the greater spinner of fairy tales himself, Hans Christian Andersen. When it opened in 1908, it became one of the first museums in the world focusing on the life and work of a single author. In various memorabilia, such as hundreds of documents, manuscripts, and reprints of his books in 100 languages (including Zulu), you learn of the writer's life from his birth as the son of a poor cobbler in Odense, to his hard times in Copenhagen, until his eventual debut upon the world stage.

We even learn about some aspects of his love life, as when he fell for Jenny Lind, "the Swedish Nightingale," who did not return his affection. Letters to such fellow famous writers as Charles Dickens are also on exhibit. The storyteller lives again as you get to see some of his "props," such as his famous walking stick, Fred Astaire–like top hat, and battered portmanteau.

On one visit we encountered an Arab journalist who claimed "Andersen stole his fairy tales from *The Arabian Nights*." That provocative statement simply isn't true. It'd be better to say that he was "influenced" by the Arabian classic.

Bangs Boder 29. ✆ 65-51-46-01. Admission 55DKK ($9.35/£4.95) adults, free for children under 17. June 16–Aug daily 9am–7pm; Sept–June 15 Tues–Sun 10am–4pm.

Skt. Knuds Domkirke ⚔ Dating from the 13th century, this is the only purely Gothic cathedral in Denmark. It was named after King Knud (Canute), who reigned from 1080 to 1086. Of a certain ghoulish interest in the crypt is the skeleton of Knud II, who was slain in 1086 by farmers angered at the taxes he'd imposed on them. Amazingly, he was canonized 15 years later when the furor had died down. The crypt lay buried for centuries until it was rediscovered and opened in the 1870s, at which time tombstones of several royal personages were discovered. The *kirke*'s chief treasure— indeed the finest piece of art on Funen—is the intricate wooden **altar** ⚔⚔⚔ in gold leaf, carved by Claus Berg, the German sculptor, in 1526. The 5m (16-ft.) triptych is practically luminous—no doubt because of its whitewashed walls—and it contains some 300 intricately carved figures, the central panel of which depicts the Crucifixion. All this work was done at the bequest of Queen Christina. Other notable treasures include some wrought-iron pieces by Caspar Fincke, who was the official craftsman to King Christian IV.

Klosterbakken 2. ✆ 66-12-03-92. www.odense-domkirke.dk. Free admission. Apr–Oct Mon–Sat 10am–5pm, Sun and holidays noon–2pm; Nov–Mar Mon–Sat 10am–4pm.

NEARBY ATTRACTIONS

Carl Nielsens Barndomshjem (Carl Nielsen's Childhood Home)   Thirteen kilometers (8 miles) from Odense, the childhood house of the famous composer is now a museum and archive of his life. Nielsen lived here until his confirmation in 1879. He was born as one of a dozen children to a poor peasant family, his father a house painter and amateur musician. For more about Nielsen's early days, you can read a delightful memoir called *My Childhood on Funen*. Two studies have been made into commemorative rooms, where the collections illustrate the composer's life.

Odensevej 2A, near Lyndelse. ✆ 65-51-46-01. Admission 25DKK ($4.25/£2.25) adults, free for children 17 and under. Tues–Sun 11am–3pm. Closed Oct–Apr. Bus: 960 or 962.

Egeskov Castle ⚔⚔⚔   This moated Renaissance island castle is the best preserved of its type in Europe. Plan to spend at least a morning or an afternoon viewing the castle and its historical gardens. Constructed in 1554, it is still privately owned and still inhabited by the descendants of Henrik Bille, who purchased the castle in 1784. The location of Denmark's most splendid fortified manor is outside of the town of Kværndrup, lying 29km (18 miles) south of Odense.

The castle was built on oak pillars in the middle of a small lake, for which thousands of oak trees in the neighboring forests were cut down.

The most dramatic story in the castle's history is about an unfortunate maiden, Rigborg, who was seduced by a young nobleman and bore him a child out of wedlock. Banished to the castle, she was imprisoned by her father in a tower from 1599 to 1604.

Because of private living quarters, only some of the castle is open to view, including the restored **Great Hall** ⚔⚔, which is now a venue for chamber music concerts on 10 summer Sundays beginning in late June and starting at 5pm. The inhabitants of this castle were great hunters, and you can visit a hunting room with some of their most prized trophies, including elephant tusks and the heads of tigers. You can also view precious antiques and classical paintings.

For us the spectacular **gardens** 𝒜𝒜𝒜 in the 12-hectare (30-acre) park are even more beautiful than the interior. Laid out in the 1730s, the gardens are among the most dramatic in Denmark. The **Fuchsia Garden** 𝒜𝒜𝒜 contains the largest collection of fuchsias in Europe, about 75 different species. The English Garden with its tree-studded green lawns sweeps down to the streams and the castle lake. In summer the rose beds are a delight to behold, the prize flower being the pink "Egeskov Rose." At a kiosk onsite you can purchase rose jelly. There is also a maze made of cut beech hedges several centuries old, and it's the world's largest maze.

Also on the grounds is a museum of antique cars, old airplanes, and even horse-drawn carriages.

Egeskovgade 18, Kværndrup. 𝒞 62-27-10-16. www.egeskov.dk. Admission including castle, park, and maze 150DKK ($26/£14) adults, 77DKK ($13/£6.95) children 4–12; park, maze, and museum 77DKK ($13/£6.95) adults, 52DKK ($8.85/£4.70) children 4–12. Free for children under 4. July park daily 10am–8pm, castle daily 10am–7pm; June and Aug park daily 10am–6pm, castle daily 10am–5pm; May and Sept park and castle daily 10am–5pm. Closed Oct–Apr. Train: From Odense or Svendborg every hour. Bus: 920 from Nyborg.

Frydenlund *Kids*   Sometimes when we've had enough of H. C. Andersen and his fairy tales, we like to secure the makings of a picnic lunch and escape to this bird sanctuary and park 20km (12 miles) southwest of Odense near the village of Tommerup. Some 200 different species of pheasants, ducks, geese, storks, ostriches, parrots, owls, and other birds from all parts of the world live here. There are more than 120 aviaries and some 20 parkland areas in an old farm setting, with many flowers, bushes, and trees. You can enjoy coffee and homemade pastries in the cafe on-site.

Skovvej 50, Naarup, near Tommerup. 𝒞 64-76-13-22. Admission 60DKK ($10/£5.40) adults, 30DKK ($5.10/£2.70) children 10–15, free for children under 10. Daily 10am–6pm.

Ladbyskibet   Admittedly, the ruins of a 10th-century Viking ship, discovered in 1935, don't equal those vessels discovered in the Oslofjord and displayed on Oslo's Bygdøy peninsula. But if you're not going on to Oslo, this is your best shot at seeing what one of those ships that terrified the coastal settlers of Britain looked like. "The Vikings are coming!" was a scream heard throughout the land.

This is one of the few Viking ships discovered to date in Denmark. Archaeologists are puzzled as to why more Viking ships haven't been unearthed in Denmark because they were used as coffins for burying chieftains. In this one, the corpse of the pagan chieftain buried was never found, just the bones of nearly a dozen horses and dogs. Other utensils, believed to be of use in Valhalla, were also interred with the corpse. Remains of the ship are displayed in a burial mound along with replicas from the excavation (the originals are in the National Museum of Copenhagen).

Vikingevej 123, Ladby. 𝒞 65-32-16-67. www.kert-mus.dk. Admission 40DKK ($6.80/£3.60) adults, free for children under 15. May 15–Sept 14 daily 10am–5pm; Mar–May 14 and Sept 15–Oct daily 10am–4pm; Nov–Feb Wed–Sun 11am–3pm. Bus: 482 from Kerteminde. 19km (12 miles) northeast of Odense.

SHOPPING
Inspiration Zinch 𝒜, Vestergade 82–84 (𝒞 **66-12-96-93**), offers the widest selection of Danish design and handicrafts on the island of Funen. All the big names are here, everything from Royal Copenhagen to Georg Jensen, but you will also come across

younger and more modern designers, with whose names you might be unfamiliar. In the heart of the old town, opposite Hans Christian Andersen's house, you'll find a display of Danish crafts and Christmas decorations in a typical atmosphere of Old Funen at **Klods Hans,** Hans Jensens Stæde 34 (© **66-11-09-40**). Another outlet is **Smykker,** 3 Klaregade (© **66-12-06-96**), which offers museum copies of Bronze Age, Iron Age, and Viking jewelry—all made in gold, sterling silver, and bronze in the outlet's own workshop. **College Art,** Grandts Passage 38 (© **66-11-35-45**), has assembled a unique collection of posters, lithographs, silk-screens, original art, and cards. The best gallery for contemporary art is **Galleri Torso,** Hasselvej 25 (© **66-13-44-66**). Finally, if none of the above shops has what you want, head for **Rosengårdcentret** at Munkerisvej and Ørbækvej. It's Denmark's biggest shopping center, with nearly 110 stores all under one roof.

WHERE TO STAY

Some hotels in Odense charge higher rates in winter because of the demand from business travelers at that time.

EXPENSIVE

Clarion Hotel Plaza (★★★   This is Odense's classiest address with far more personality, atmosphere, and glamour than its closest rival, the also-recommended Radisson SAS (see below). One of Funen's most alluring hostelries, the Plaza lies less than .5km (¼ mile) outside of the town center, yet only a 5-minute walk from the train station. A stately place to stay, it fronts the city's finest and leafiest park, Kongens Have.

After checking in and inspecting the formal lounges, an old-fashioned early-20th-century elevator takes you to the midsize-to-spacious bedrooms, many of which evoke life in an English country home, opening onto scenic views. The rooms are handsomely decorated, often with antique reproductions, and they escape the curse of too much Danish modern, each coming with a tiled bathroom with tub/shower combos. The hotel's terrace overlooks the park and a garden. A first-class cuisine of both Danish and international specialties is served in the Plaza's formal restaurant, known for its attentive service and impressive wine list.

Østre Stationsvej 24, DK-5000 Odense. © 877/424-6423 in the U.S., or 66-11-77-45. Fax 66-14-41-45. www.hotel-plaza.dk. 68 units. July–Aug 925DKK ($157/£83) double, 1,840DKK ($313/£166) suite; Sept–June 1,350DKK ($230/£122) double, 1,845DKK ($314/£166) suite. Rates include breakfast. AE, DC, MC, V. Free parking. Bus: 31, 33, 35, or 36. **Amenities:** Restaurant; bar; 24-hr. room service; laundry service; dry cleaning; nonsmoking rooms. *In room:* TV, dataport, minibar, hair dryer, safe.

Radisson SAS H.C. Andersen Hotel (★★   It may lack the nostalgic charm of the Plaza, but commercial travelers find this first-class hotel more convenient with a livelier roster of facilities, including a casino. In summer, fans of Andersen from abroad fill its 1960s Nordic-style bedrooms near a former Hans Christian Andersen residence in the heart of the city. This red-brick hotel, one of the finest on the island of Funen, welcomes you into a plant-filled lobby and a glass-roofed reception area, where you encounter the most efficient staff in Odense.

The tasteful, conservatively decorated, and comfortably appointed bedrooms come in a variety of sizes—some large, others, especially the singles, a bit cramped—with the most tranquil rooms opening onto the interior. Each of the bathrooms, though small, is well equipped with thoughtful extras such as makeup mirrors along with tub/shower combos.

Overlooking the market square, the hotel's formal restaurant is known for catering to special requests, such as vegetarian or other diets. It serves a refined international and Danish cuisine and does so exceedingly well, using market-fresh ingredients.

Claus Bergs Gade 7, DK-5000 Odense. © 800/333-3333 in the U.S., or 66-14-78-00. Fax 66-14-78-90. www.radisson sas.com. 145 units. 850DKK–1,665DKK ($145–$283/£77–£150) double. Rates include breakfast. AE, DC, MC, V. Bus: 4 or 5. **Amenities:** Restaurant; bar; fitness center; sauna; room service (7am–10pm); laundry service; dry cleaning; nonsmoking rooms; rooms for those w/limited mobility; casino; solarium. *In room:* TV, dataport, Wi-Fi, minibar, hair dryer, safe.

Scandic Hotel Odense ✔ *Kids*   This chain-run hotel is sort of a glorified roadside motel, dating from 1986, when it was built 5km (3 miles) southwest of the city center in an industrial neighborhood that's convenient to the E20 express highway. Motorists, especially families, are attracted to it because of its comfortable midsize bedrooms, many of which sleep up to two adults and two children. The rooms are in a three-story, low-slung building, with contemporary Danish modern decor, plus a good-size bathroom with shower unit. You don't have to go back into town for dinner, as the hotel operates a good restaurant on-site serving both Danish and international dishes. There is a big playroom with a large selection of books and toys.

Hvidkærvej 25, DK-5250 Odense SV. © 66-17-66-66. Fax 66-17-25-53. www.scandic-hotels.com. 100 units. 1,325DKK–1,525DKK ($225–$259/£119–£137) double; 2,150DKK ($366/£194) suite. Rates include breakfast. AE, DC, MC, V. Bus: 835 or 840. **Amenities:** Restaurant; bar; fitness center; sauna; children's playroom; room service (7am–10pm); babysitting; laundry service; dry cleaning; nonsmoking rooms; rooms for those w/limited mobility; solarium. *In room:* TV, dataport, Wi-Fi, minibar, hair dryer, trouser press.

MODERATE

Best Western Hotel Knudsens Gaard   This is a serviceable chain-operated hotel—and not a lot more—and still imbued with a slight aura of 1955 when it first opened less than a kilometer (½ mile) south of the town center. Once it was a half-timbered old Danish farmhouse, but those days are long gone. Today it attracts many families in town to check out the H. C. Andersen sights. Even so, it is not especially geared to families. The previously recommended Scandic (see above) caters better to kids. Nevertheless, the compact bedrooms are comfortably furnished, each containing a neatly kept bathroom with tub/shower combo. The on-site restaurant serves a standard and affordable cuisine.

Hunderupgade 2, DK-5230 Odense. © 800/528-1234 in the U.S., or 63-11-43-11. Fax 63-11-43-01. www.bestwestern.com. 72 units. 1,095DKK–1,695DKK ($186–$288/£99–£153) double. Rates include breakfast. AE, DC, MC, V. **Amenities:** Restaurant; bar; room service (7am–10pm); laundry service; dry cleaning; nonsmoking rooms; rooms for those w/limited mobility. *In room:* TV, dataport, Wi-Fi, minibar, hair dryer.

City Hotel Odense   This hotel is down the pecking order from those previously recommended, but you forget all that as you sit out on summer furniture enjoying one of the best panoramic views of the city. Built in 1988, the hotel offers standard comforts and an affordable price without generating any raves. Lying only 2 blocks from the train station, this hotel often caters to conventions. Its midsize bedrooms are comfortably but rather blandly furnished in an uninspired style, each with a neatly kept, small bathroom with shower. There is a certain coziness here even in winter when you can sit in the lounge enjoying a cup of coffee in front of an open fire. Other than breakfast, no meals are offered, although a 300-year-old Danish inn, Den Gamle Kro, run by the same owner, serves flavorful meals a 5-minute walk away.

Hans Mules Gade 5, DK-5000 Odense. © 66-12-12-58. Fax 66-12-93-64. www.city-hotel-odense.dk. 43 units. Mon–Fri 905DKK ($154/£81) double; Sat–Sun 805DKK ($137/£72) double. From 1,095DKK ($186/£99) apt. Rates include breakfast. AE, DC, MC, V. Bus: 41 or 42. Free parking. **Amenities:** Breakfast room; bar; game room; laundry service; dry cleaning; nonsmoking rooms. *In room:* TV, dataport, Wi-Fi, hair dryer.

First Hotel Grand *(Value)*

In those halcyon Belle Epoque days of 1897, this grand hotel opened near the rail depot to greet arriving passengers from Copenhagen. At that time it was the grandest hotel in town, losing that position in 1915 to the Clarion Hotel Plaza (see above), which is still the market leader today. But the Grand holds its own and is our second choice for Odense, rising four floors in a brick-built structure shaped like a triangle and studded with old-fashioned dormers. The ground-floor reception will provide you with an ornately shaped brass key for your bedroom door. Bedrooms, in the 19th-century tradition, are large, and each is comfortably furnished, with an adjoining good-size bathroom with tiles and a tub/shower combination. On-site are a relatively good restaurant serving Danish regional food and a cozy bar that makes an ideal place for a rendezvous.

Jernbanegade 18, DK-5000 Odense. © **66-11-71-71.** Fax 66-14-11-71. www.firsthotels.com. 147 units. 798DKK–1,598DKK ($136–$272/£72–£144) double; 1,688DKK–2,503DKK ($287–$426/£152–£225) suite. Rates include breakfast. AE, DC, MC, V. Parking 50DKK ($8.50/£4.50). **Amenities:** Restaurant; bar; sauna; room service (7am–10pm); laundry service; nonsmoking rooms. *In room:* TV, dataport (in some), minibar, hair dryer.

Hotel Ansgar *(Kids)*

In 1902, when this hotel opened a 5-minute walk from the train depot, it attracted clean-living, nondrinking Christian clients. But those religious associations are long gone, and even some hard-drinking Danes check in here today. The original founders would shout hell and damnation, because there's even a bar on-site. Behind a brick-and-stone facade, the hotel has been considerably renovated, with the installation of modern furniture and double-glaze windows to cut down on the traffic noise. As befits the style of the hotel's era, the rooms range from small to spacious, each comfortably furnished with Italian pieces, and each with adequate and well-kept bathrooms with tub/shower combos. The staff does much in summer to attract the family trade, even giving kids a coupon for free ice cream. A wide range of dishes from both the Danish and international kitchens is served, and one of the best food values in town is the restaurant's two-course fixed-price dinner at 150DKK ($26/£14).

Østre Stationsvej 32, DK-5000 Odense. © **66-11-96-93.** Fax 66-11-96-75. www.hotel-ansgar.dk. 64 units. June–Aug 750DKK ($128/£68) double; Sept–May 1,050DKK ($179/£85) double. Rates include breakfast. Extra bed 150DKK ($26/£14). AE, DC, MC, V. Free parking. Bus: 31, 33, 35, or 36. **Amenities:** Restaurant; bar; kids playroom; laundry service; dry cleaning; nonsmoking rooms. *In room:* TV, dataport, Wi-Fi, minibar, hair dryer.

INEXPENSIVE

Comfort Windsor Hotel

Even though its prices have risen in recent years, this is still viewed as an affordable choice, since most of its bedrooms are at the lower end of the price scale. Since 1898, this cozy, well-furnished, red-brick hotel building has come as a welcome relief to travelers who arrive at the rail station. The Windsor, in spite of its royal name, was never regal in any sense, but is a decent, well-run, and inviting hotel. Comfortably furnished and tasteful, it offers high-ceilinged bedrooms that are well maintained and tasteful, although small for our tastes, as are its equally small shower-only bathrooms. Furnishings are in sleek, not very exciting, Danish modern, with double-glazing on the windows to cut down on the street noise. The food is plain Danish, but prepared with fresh ingredients, a two-course dinner costing 155DKK ($26/£14) and attracting many locals to its dining room, which is open only Monday to Thursday from 6 to 9:30pm.

Vindegade 45, DK-5000 Odense. ✆ **66-12-06-52.** Fax 66-91-00-23. www.choicehotels.dk. 62 units. 795DKK–1,145DKK ($135–$195/£72–£103) double. Rates include breakfast. AE, DC, MC, V. **Amenities:** Restaurant; bar; laundry service; dry cleaning; nonsmoking rooms. *In room:* TV, dataport, minibar.

Hotel Domir/Hotel Ydes *(Value)*

When antiquities dealer Eigil Johns opened what is now the Domir, he romantically called it "The Gaslight," evocative of the street lighting of the time. A few years later, the Ydes was opened nearby. Today, these are still among the finest affordable lodgings in Odense and are under the same ownership. If there is no room at one, chances are you'll be housed in another. Each hotel has comfortable but small rooms, with the Ydes (28 rooms) focusing a bit more on old-fashioned decor, and the Domir (35 rooms) going for brighter colors and a more indulgent approach to pop culture. Every room has a well-kept bathroom with a shower unit. You'll have a greater sense of camaraderie at the Domir, where a live receptionist will check you in; at the Ydes, a TV monitor will beam you the instructions from the manager (who works in the Domir).

Hans Tausensgade 11 and 19, DK-5000 Odense. ✆ **66-12-14-27.** Fax 66-12-17-82. www.domir.dk; www.ydes.dk. 63 units. Domir 595DKK ($101/£54) double; Ydes 550DKK ($94/£50) double. Rates include breakfast. AE, DC, MC, V. **Amenities:** Breakfast room; bar. *In room:* TV, dataport, trouser press.

Næsbylund Kro

For greater tranquillity, many motorists like to stay out of town. If so, our choice for such lodgings is this *kro* (inn) lying 4km (2½ miles) north of Odense. The Danish word *kro* often suggests an antique inn, but in this case the compound is modern, dating from 1983. It's basically a roadside motel, with midsize bedrooms, many with balconies, and each furnished in a conservatively modern style, although the look is somewhat impersonal. Each accommodation comes with a neatly kept shower-only bathroom. For an overnight stopover, it's just fine, but there are far more attractive places to go for the rest of your stay in Funen. In a separate building, the Carolinenkilde restaurant serves dinner nightly 5 to 9:30pm, with a fixed-price menu going for 165DKK ($28/£15).

Bogensevej 105–117, DK-5270 Odense. ✆ **66-18-00-39.** Fax 66-18-29-29. 53 units. 775DKK ($132/£70) double. Rates include breakfast. AE, DC, MC, V. Bus: 91 or 92. **Amenities:** Restaurant; lounge; indoor pool. *In room:* TV, dataport.

WHERE TO DINE
EXPENSIVE

Den Gamle Kro ⋆ DANISH/FRENCH   For all we know, Hans Christian Andersen used to drop into this place—after all, it's been serving food and drink to the locals since 1683, and at one time or another nearly every resident of Odense has eaten or drunk here. Set a 5-minute walk from the center, it is unusual architecturally in that it was constructed within the courtyard of several antique buildings, but has been modernized with its timeworn stone capped by a sliding glass roof.

A cellar-level bar is lined with antique masonry and the street-level restaurant rests under centuries-old beams. The food has remained consistently good over the years, and we've often dropped in for lunch for some of the best *smørrebrød* (open-faced sandwich) selections in town, especially when shrimp and dill is stacked on top of a freshly baked bread.

If you return for dinner, you'll find some of the best fixed-price meals in town. There's nothing you're served here that you haven't tasted before, including beef tenderloin flavored with herbs or herb-sprinkled trout sautéed in butter, but the ingredients are market fresh and skillfully prepared by the kitchen staff, who also serve yummy, freshly made desserts.

Overgade 23. ℭ **66-12-14-33.** Reservations recommended. Main courses 179DKK–278DKK ($30–$47/£16–£25); fixed-price meals 298DKK–358DKK ($51–$61/£27–£32). AE, DC, MC, V. Mon–Sat 11am–10:30pm; Sun 11am–9:30pm. Bus: 2.

Le Brasserie ℛ FRENCH/ASIAN   For years this restaurant was fondly known as LPC, or "La Petite Cuisine," and it's still here, only with a name change. It offers the same bistro fare that you might find in a provincial town somewhere in the heart of France. Set on a narrow, partially covered passageway in the heart of town, it features contemporary-looking decor and a soothing color scheme. The only change is that some of the dishes are inspired by an Asian fusion cuisine such as the marinated duck breast, which is delectable. The basically French menu is composed only after the shopping at the market is completed so that everything will be fresh. We can't predict what you will be served, but expect such delights as marinated wild Scottish salmon with pickled watercress and a mild mustard sauce with passion fruit oil. Thinly sliced scallops are "escorted" with foie gras, wild watercress, and slices of pickled pumpkin. For a main course, the chef proposes a delicious duet of Danish veal and French duck aromatically served with anise-poached fennel, or else the crisp fried filet of redfish with roasted artichoke hearts.

Brandts Passage 13. ℭ **66-14-11-00.** Reservations recommended. Main courses 169DKK–250DKK ($29–$43/£15–£23); 4-course fixed-price menu 305DKK ($52/£27). DC, MC, V. Mon–Sat 5:30–10pm. Bus: 2.

Marie Louise ℛℛℛ FRENCH/INTERNATIONAL   You'd have to return to Copenhagen to order French food as fine as that served here in an antique house sheltering one of the smallest and most exclusive—also the best—restaurants in Odense.

Its dining room is a white-walled re-creation of an old-fashioned country tavern, although closer inspection reveals a decidedly upscale slant to the furnishings, accessories, silver, and crystal. A polished staff serves well-planned dishes based mainly on French recipes, with more and more international recipes appearing on recent menus.

The chef prepares dishes with a certain precision and sensitivity, as evoked by such delectable specialties as a salmon-and-dill mousse with shrimp sauce. Most savvy diners order the fresh fish dishes of the day, perhaps turbot in Riesling or a champagne sauce. The chef gets an extra point for that divine lobster he served us in Danish country butter. An array of enticing desserts is laid out like works of art for your selection.

Lottrups Gård, Vestergade 70–72. ℭ **66-17-92-95.** Reservations recommended. Main courses 318DKK–387DKK ($54–$66/£29–£35); fixed-price menu 345DKK–565DKK ($59–$96/£31–£51). V. Mon–Sat noon–midnight. Closed July. Bus: 2.

Restaurant Klitgaard ℛℛℛ *(Finds)* CONTINENTAL/DANISH   Although Marie Louise is still number one in Odense, this 1998 restaurant is the most innovative in town, serving a cuisine that is cutting edge—and not traditional like the time-honored favorite. The setting is woodsy and appealing in monochromatic tones of brown and beige, with room for only 30 guests at a time. The feeling you might get, except for its view over the other buildings of Odense's historic core, is that of a Tuscan farmhouse. Jacob Klitgaard, born about 30km (19 miles) from the town of Svendborg, is the chef and very hip namesake of this place, personally selecting impeccably fresh ingredients, many of them produced or cultivated in and around Odense. Menu items make ample use of both foie gras and shellfish. Ingredients such as herbs come from the restaurant's own kitchen garden, and produce is sourced from local growers, breeders, and local game hunters. Inspired by the bounty of Funen, you are likely to be served roast trout with a rosemary-scented olive oil or else a saltwater catfish with a ragout of basil-flavored minestrone. The chef also keeps his customers happy with such marvelous dishes as braised pheasant with wild mushrooms in a beer sauce or else fricassee of guinea fowl with savory herb sauce.

Gravene 4. ℂ **66-13-14-55.** Reservations recommended. Fixed-price menus 395DKK–595DKK ($67–$101/£36–£54). DC, MC, V. Tues–Sat 6–9pm (last order). Closed July. Bus: 2.

Under Lindetræet ✦ DANISH/INTERNATIONAL   In summer make your way past the artists who invariably sit out sketching the home of Hans Christian Andersen to this inn from 1704 located across the street from the storyteller's museum. Since the 1960s it's been a landmark and local favorite. Since everyone visits *The Ugly Duckling's* home, it's the most popular restaurant in town. That could mean it is no more than a tourist trap. It isn't—rather, it's one of the finest restaurants in town with a menu based on fresh, first-class ingredients. Skillfully prepared dishes include tender Danish lamb, filet of plaice with butter sauce, escallop of veal in sherry sauce, fried herring with new potatoes, and an upscale version of *skipperlabskovs,* the famed sailors' hash. The atmosphere is Old World, and in summer, meals and light refreshments are served outside under linden trees.

Ramsherred 2. ℂ **66-12-92-86.** Reservations required. Main courses 225DKK–495DKK ($38–$84/£20–£45); fixed-price menus 395DKK–595DKK ($67–$101/£36–£54). AE, DC, MC, V. Mon–Fri 11am–11pm; Sat–Sun 6–11pm. Closed July 4–24. Bus: 2.

MODERATE

Sortebro Kro *Value* DANISH/FRENCH   Even though it serves good food, this is a very touristy inn because it lies just outside the entrance to Funen Village (p. 264). The open-air culture museum is about 2.5km (1½ miles) south of the center. Sortebro was a coaching inn from 1807, but later in its life was moved to this location. The interior is an attraction in its own right: long refectory tables, sagging ceilings with overhead beams, three-legged chairs, florid handmade chests, and crockery cupboards. Expect a vast array of meat, poultry, and seafood dishes, plus a groaning table filled with freshly made desserts. The chef, John Kofod Pedersen, creates classic, time-tested dishes based on the freshest and finest produce from the Funen countryside.

Sejerskovvej 20. ℂ **66-13-28-26.** Reservations required. Main courses 265DKK–385DKK ($45–$65/£24–£35). AE, DC, MC, V. Mon–Sat noon–10pm; Sun noon–5pm. Closed Dec 23–26. Bus: 21 or 22 from Flakhaven.

INEXPENSIVE

Den Gremme Æling ✦ *Kids* DANISH   Part of its charm derives from its name (which translates as "The Ugly Duckling"), and its location is very close to the former home of Hans Christian Andersen. It's set on a cobblestone street in Odense's historic core, in an ocher-colored building from around 1850 that emulates an old-fashioned Danish *kro.* Attracting a large family trade, it specializes in well-stocked buffets manned by uniformed staff members who will cook your steak, fish, omelet, or whatever into virtually any Danish-inspired configuration you want. There are no *smørrebrød,* but because the buffet contains a roster of sliced cheeses, breads, meats, and condiments, you can always make your own. The staff speaks excellent English, and if buffet dining appeals to you, you might have a wonderful time here, as we always do.

Hans Jensens Stræde 1. ℂ **65-91-70-30.** Sun–Thurs buffet 112DKK ($19/£10), Fri–Sat 125DKK ($21/£11). MC, V. Daily noon–2:30pm and 5:30–10:30pm.

Målet DANISH   This is the leading sports pub in town and also a restaurant serving an acceptable (predictably not gourmet) cuisine. Don't expect the high-tech, big-screen bombast of sports bars you might visit in the U.S. Instead, you'll see a cramped bar for around 15 drinkers in one corner, two small-screen TVs projecting sports events from around the world, and years of collected memorabilia pertaining to soccer. No one will mind if you simply drink your way through the evening with the locals. But if you want a meal, try the house specialty, a large portion of pork schnitzel, priced at 89DKK ($15/£8), served with potatoes, and prepared in any of 10 different ways. Otherwise, you can order fish or beefsteak, and even an occasional vegetarian dish, but the schnitzels are simply the most appealing dish in the house. *Målet,* incidentally, translates as "soccer goal post," and management has erected one as an admittedly ugly decorative centerpiece in a prominent position against one wall.

Jernbanegade 17. (℃ 66-17-82-41. Reservations recommended. Main courses 55DKK–135DKK ($9.35–$23/£4.95–£12). No credit cards. Tues–Sat 11am–11pm.

ODENSE AFTER DARK

There are lots of cultural events in Odense, foremost among which are performances by the **Odense Symphony Orchestra.** Throughout much of the year, concerts are presented in the **Carl Nielsen Hall,** Claus Bergs Gade 9 (℃ **66-12-00-57** for ticket information). Tickets cost 60DKK to 160DKK ($10–$27/£5.40–£14), depending on the event. During the warm-weather months, the orchestra's role is less formal. In August, for example, the group is more likely to play outdoors at the marketplace in front of the vegetable stands. Because of their location, these performances have been referred to as "the Vegetable Concerts." On Saturdays at 11am in August the orchestra presents free live music at Skovsoen park.

The **casino** at the Radisson SAS H.C. Anderson Hotel, Claus Berg Gade 7 (℃ **66-14-78-00;** www.casinoodense.dk), is one of only six casinos in the entire country. Dress is casual, and it is open daily from 7pm to 4am, charging a cover of 60DKK ($10/£5.40). A driver's license or passport is required to enter.

Odense offers several places for dancing. By far the most popular and entertaining is **Congress Disco,** Asylgade 9 (℃ **66-11-63-02**), which opens at 11pm only on Friday and Saturday and offers a sometimes crowded dance floor in its cellar; upstairs, very high ceilings help reduce the noise a bit. Only a bit less visible is **Boogies,** Nørregade 21–23 (℃ **66-14-00-39**), which attracts the most mixed crowd in town, including some of Odense's gay and lesbian population, who blend in with an otherwise straight clientele. Other than hanging out at Boogies (see above), gay people either drive to Copenhagen for evening events, or stay alert to the special activities sponsored by **Lambda** (℃ **66-17-76-92**), which offers a Friday and/or Saturday (depending on the schedule) dance club in the cellar of Vindegade 100.

At Odense's railway station, **Frank A.'s Café,** Jernbanegade 4 (℃ **66-12-27-57**), operates as a cafe throughout the day, and as such, draws a respectable crowd of drinkers and diners who appreciate the tasty Danish platters, which cost from 69DKK to 198DKK ($12–$34/£6.20–£18). But the real heart and soul of the place doesn't become visible until after 10pm, when all pretenses of culinary skill are abandoned, and the cafe becomes one of the loudest, wildest, and most raucous nightlife venues in town. Then, live music—Brazilian, Latin, or simple rock 'n roll—transforms the room into everybody's favorite rendezvous. Come here to be convivial, amid a setting that's loaded with kitschy bric-a-brac and dozens of single or wannabe-single local residents.

Food service is daily 10am to 10pm; nightlife action runs 10pm to at least 3am, and sometimes later.

3 Svendborg ★

43km (27 miles) S of Odense; 146km (91 miles) W of Copenhagen, 25km (16 miles) E of Faaborg

Svendborg, with 42,000 residents, is the second-biggest town in Funen and a major commercial and touristic hub for South Funen, but it has none of all that fairy-tale overlay that Odense hypes. It's a sailors' town—beloved of Danish yachties—and has had a long history as a maritime center. Until 1915, it was the home port for a big fleet of sailing ships because of its position on the beautiful Svendborg Sound, which provides convenient access to Baltic ports.

Although shipbuilding is a ghost of itself, there are still a couple of shipyards left that construct wooden-hulled ships and are around to repair visiting yachts plying the waters off the coast of South Funen.

Frankly, we'd spend only a night here as the islands of Ærø and Tåsinge (see later in this chapter) are more alluring. But if you give Svendborg a day, you'll find much to do.

You'll see yachts, ketches, and kayaks in the harbor. The town still retains some of its medieval heritage, but much of it has been torn down in the name of progress and industry.

Today Svendborg is a lively modern town, with museums, constantly changing art exhibitions, and sports. It has swimming pools, beaches, and a yachting school. Its best beach, **Christiansminde,** is one of several in Funen flying the blue flag that indicates nonpolluted waters.

Svendborg is also a market town, and on Sunday morning, you visit the cobblestone central plaza where flowers and fish are sold. Wander through the many winding streets where brick and half-timbered buildings still stand. On **Ragergade** you'll see the old homes of early seafarers. **Møllergade,** a pedestrian street, is one of the oldest streets in town, with about 100 different shops.

Literary buffs know that the German writer Bertolt Brecht lived at Skovsbo Strand west of Svendborg from 1933 to 1939, but he left at the outbreak of World War II. During this period he wrote *Mother Courage and Her Children,* which is still performed all over the world.

ESSENTIALS

GETTING THERE   By Train   You can take a train from Copenhagen to Odense, where you can get a connecting train to Svendborg, with frequent service throughout the day.

By Car   From our last stopover in Odense, head south on Route 9, following the signs into Svendborg.

VISITOR INFORMATION   Contact the **Svendborg Tourist Office,** Centrumpladsen (© **62-21-09-80;** www.visitsydfyn.dk), open June 20 to August 21, Monday to Friday 9:30am to 6pm and Saturday 9:30am to 3pm; January 2 to June 19 and August 22 to December 22, Monday to Friday 9:30am to 5pm, and Saturday 9:30am to 12:30pm; closed December 23 to January 1.

GETTING AROUND   By Bus   Bus no. 200 serves all in-town destinations listed below, except for Vester Skerninge Kro, for which you need a car.

By Bike   Bike rentals for hotel guests, at 60DKK ($10/£5.40) per day, can be obtained at the Hotel Svendborg, Centrumpladsen 1 (𝄞 **62-21-17-00;** bus: 200 or 204). Biking routes and maps are available at the tourist office.

SEEING THE SIGHTS

Anne Hvides Gård   This cross-timbered house looks a little tipsy, like it's had too much to drink, lying as it does in the center of the Torvet, the old market square. Actually it's the oldest secular house in Svendborg, dating from 1558 and operated today as a branch of the County Museum. This is another one of those "let's raid the attic to see what we can find" type of museums. Its most dramatic features are the re-creations of interiors from the 18th and 19th centuries, and there are plenty of silver objects, glassware, copper and brass utensils, and the inevitable faience. Temporary cultural exhibitions are also presented here.

Fruestræde 3. 𝄞 62-21-34-57. www.svendborgmuseum.dk. Admission 25DKK ($4.25/£2.25) adults, 15DKK ($2.55/£1.35) seniors, free for children 14 and under when accompanied by an adult. Apr–Sept Tues–Sun 10am–5pm; off season by arrangement with the main office.

Skt. Jørgens Kirke   Only the Church of Skt. Nicolai (see below) exceeds the beauty of St. George's church, whose origins go back to the 12th century when it was originally a chapel for lepers who were forced to live outside the town in an attempt to control spread of the disease. The church itself was named for that fearless knight St. George, patron of lepers. The core of the church is a Gothic longhouse with a three-sided chancel from the late 13th century. During restoration of the church in 1961, an archaeological dig of the floor disclosed traces of a wooden building believed to be a predecessor of the present house of worship.

Strandvej 97. 𝄞 62-21-14-73. Free admission. Mon–Fri 8am–4pm.

Skt. Nicolai Kirke   Svendborg's oldest church is situated among a cluster of antique houses off Kyseborgstræde, in the vicinity of Gerrits Plads just south of the market square. Built of bricks before 1200 in the Romanesque style and last restored in 1892, its red-brick walls and white vaulting complement the fine altarpiece by Joachim Skovgaard in 1894. The magnificent **stained-glass windows** (𝄐 were designed by Kræsten Iversen during Denmark's darkest days in recent history, the Nazi occupation that lasted from 1940 to 1945. Nearby you can admire a statue by Kai Nielsen (1820–1924), a native son who went on to greater glory and became a famous sculptor.

Skt. Nicolajgade 2B. 𝄞 62-21-28-54. Free admission. May–Aug daily 10am–3pm; Sept–Apr daily 10am–noon.

Naturama   Formed from a zoological collection started in 1935, Naturama was greatly expanded, changing its name from the zoo to a new moniker based on "nature" and "drama." In both skeletons and mounted animals, the exhibition raids the land, sea, and air, including the great whales of the North Atlantic—in fact, Naturama is Denmark's largest display of not only whales but other sea mammals. The center also displays the largest forest mammals in Scandinavia, including everything from bears to bison. Advanced lighting techniques, sound, and even films supplement the exhibitions. On top of the building you'll be introduced to 500 woodland birds, everything from eagles to owls, from Woody Woodpecker to the most beautiful of songbirds.

Dronningemæn 30. 𝄞 62-21-06-50. www.naturama.dk. Admission 90DKK ($15£8.10) adults, 70DKK ($12/£6.30) seniors, free for children under 18. Mid-June to mid-Aug daily 10am–5pm; mid-Aug to mid-June Tues–Sun 10am–5pm. Bus: 205, 206, or 208.

Svendborg

Legend:
- Church
- Ferry Lines
- Information *(i)*
- Parking **P**
- Post Office ⊠
- Railway —

DRONNINGEMAEN

VIEBÆLTET

HAVNEGADE

NORDRE HAVNE VEJ

Centrum-pladsen *(i)*

Torvet

Rådhus

Train Station

Svendborg Hospital

SWEDEN
- Frederikshavn
- Aalborg
- Århus
- Odense
- Copenhagen
- Svendborg

GERMANY

ATTRACTIONS ●
Anne Hvides Gård **6**
Naturama **2**
Skt. Jørgens Kirke **12**
Skt. Nicolai Kirke **11**
Viebæltegård **3**
Vor Frue Kirke **5**

ACCOMMODATIONS ■
Hotel Christiansminde **8**
Hotel Garni **7**
Hotel Svendborg **4**
Majorgården **1**
Missionshotellet Stella Maris **13**

DINING ◆
Restaurant Marco Polo **10**
Svendborgsund **9**

277

Viebæltegård   Time for a confession. We view this museum as being of such minor interest that we rarely give it more than 30 or 40 minutes. If the day is sunny, we prefer to come here to enjoy a picnic lunch in the museum garden. The headquarters for the county museum is housed in a former poorhouse/workhouse from 1872, the only one of its kind still existing in Denmark. The complex of "social welfare" buildings has been converted into museums of history, displaying artifacts from ancient times to the Middle Ages, including finds from fields around Svendborg and South Funen in general. More intriguing is to visit the crafts workshops on-site, watching goldsmiths, potters, and printers at work, and there's also an on-site museum shop that has some wonderful crafts for sale.

Grubbemøllevej 13 (near Dronningemæn). ☎ 62-21-02-61. www.svendborgmuseum.dk. Admission 40DKK ($6.80/£3.60) adults, free for children under 18 when accompanied by an adult. Open year-round Tues–Sun 10am–4pm.

Vor Frue Kirke   On the hill where the old Castle Swineburg stood, this Romanesque-Gothic church, dating from 1253, has a carillon of 27 bells, which ring four times a day. From the tourist office at Torvet, walk up the steps leading to the rise on which the church stands, overlooking the Old Town and the harbor, for a grand view. The church has a late-16th-century pulpit and altar, but nothing else to hold your attention for very long.

Frue Kirkestræde 4. ☎ 62-21-01-35. Free admission. Daily 8am–4pm.

SHOPPING

The widest selection of Danish design, from household utensils to prestigious china from Royal Copenhagen, and even silver from Georg Jensen, is found at **Inspiration Zinck,** in the Svendborg Bycenter, Tinghusgade (☎ 62-22-35-93). The best source of glass is **Glasblæseriet,** Brogade 37 (☎ 62-22-83-73), where glass can be blown to your own design specifications. Of course, regular glass products, created by others, are also for sale.

WHERE TO STAY

Hotel Christiansminde   According to photographs we saw, the history of this hotel dates from 1830, although in its present reincarnation the building was constructed in the 1970s, lying 3km (1¾ miles) east of Svendborg's center on a grassy knoll close to the sea. Many visitors come here for a summer holiday beside the beach; others arrive as part of corporate conventions whose sponsors rent virtually every room for inspiration-building discussions over long weekends. Midsize rooms have balconies or private terraces, neatly kept bathrooms with shower units, and functional, unpretentious, yet comfortable furniture. Some contain small kitchens, although there's no additional cost for such added luxuries. There are a restaurant and a series of convention rooms with up-to-date electronic and broadcast facilities. Walks into Svendborg are made easier thanks to a network of hiking trails, most of which avoid active roadways. Other than that, there aren't a lot of sport facilities and diversions at this property—only easy access to the great Danish outdoors and the nearby sea.

Christiansmindevej 16, DK-5700 Svendborg. ☎ 62-21-90-00. Fax 62-21-60-82. www.christiansminde.dk. 98 units. 945DKK–1,095DKK ($161–$186/£85–£99) double. Rates include breakfast. AE, DC, MC, V. Closed Jan–Mar. Bus: 201 from Svendborg. **Amenities:** Restaurant; lounge; indoor heated pool; laundry service; dry cleaning; solarium. *In room:* TV, dataport.

Hotel Garni   If you're not supposed to judge a book by its cover, perhaps you'll extend the same courtesy to this hotel, one of the most affordable in town, long attracting the frugal traveler to its location opposite both the rail and bus stations. Behind a plain facade, it is a bastion of comfort and convenience, its front rooms opening onto the harbor. The small-to-midsize bedrooms are more inviting than stylish, and though the furnishings are in plain Nordic design they are nonetheless suitable for an overnight stay, each room coming with a small bathroom equipped with shower. Only breakfast is served, but it's a generous one, and there are many taverns and restaurants nearby for lunch or dinner.

Toldbodvej 5, DK-5700 Svendborg. ⓒ/fax **63-20-30-51.** www.hotel-garni.dk. 18 units. 685DKK ($116/£62) double. Rates include breakfast. MC, V. Bus: 200, 208, or 980. **Amenities:** Breakfast room; lounge. *In room:* TV, hair dryer.

Hotel Svendborg ⋆
Built in the 1950s, not a great decade for architecture, this hotel nonetheless is stylish inside and offers the best accommodations in Svendborg, the rooms spread across four floors above the commercial core of town. It's never been our favorite, as we prefer more evocative or romantic addresses, but during the two nights we spent here we were exceedingly comfortable and found the English staff helpful and informative about the area. The bedrooms range from small to spacious, and each is furnished in a tasteful Scandinavian modern design with excellent bathrooms with tub/shower combos. The eight apartments, each with kitchen, can be rented to one to four guests. On-site is the first-class restaurant Krinsten, serving menus based on the seasons.

Centrumpladsen 1, DK-5700 Svendborg. ⓒ **62-21-17-00.** Fax 62-21-90-12. www.hotel-svendborg.dk. 133 units (8 apts). 995DKK–1,245DKK ($169–$212/£90–£112) double; 1,750DKK–2,300DKK ($298–$391/£158–£207) suite; 1,450DKK ($247/£131) apt for 2; 1,750DKK ($298/£158) apt for 4. Rates include breakfast. AE, DC, MC, V. Free parking. Bus: 200 or 204. **Amenities:** Restaurant; bar; room service (7am–10pm); laundry service; dry cleaning; nonsmoking rooms; rooms for those w/limited mobility. *In room:* TV, dataport, Wi-Fi, minibar, hair dryer, safe.

Majorgården ⋆ *Finds*
It had to happen. We just had to find a cozy nest on Funen that we liked above all others—and this is it. On the coast road, 11km (7 miles) from Svendborg and 30km (19 miles) from Nyborg, such illustrious Danes as tenor Lauritz Melchior have cherished this 1761 white-brick inn. Outside, a bower of roses grows against the walls, low white tables on the lawn are great for sipping coffee, and a little pond at the rear is filled with ducks. An old horse stable has been turned into a congenial bar. The rooms sit above the restaurant under the roofline. If you're just driving by, stop in for a "plate of the inn"—two kinds of herring, plaice, meatballs, meat sausages, liver paste, and cheese. A large selection of fish and meat dishes is also available. Fixed-price menus cost 100DKK to 145DKK ($17–$25/£9–£13) and meals are served every day noon to 9:30pm.

Landevejen 155, DK-5883 Oure. ⓒ **62-28-18-19.** Fax 62-28-18-13. 4 units, none with bathroom. 450DKK ($77/£41) double. Rates include breakfast. MC, V. Bus: 910 from Svendborg and Nyborg. **Amenities:** Restaurant; bar; lounge. *In room:* No phone.

Missionshotellet Stella Maris ⋆ *Value*
A Danish countess with a staff of 18 servants once occupied this 1904 estate, naming it Stella Maris, meaning "Star of the Sea," because of its location southwest of the city in a lovely old-fashioned seaside villa. In time it became part of a Christian hotel chain—it used to maintain a smoke- and alcohol-free atmosphere, and was a place where "preaching the word of God (was) the most important thing."

This old-fashioned world of charm and nostalgia is today one of the undiscovered allures of Svendborg, with its English-style drawing room (with piano), overstuffed chairs, and antiques. Surrounded by well-landscaped gardens, it offers midsize-to-spacious bedrooms, each with an individual color scheme, or else rose wallpaper and white-lace curtains. The rooms in front opening onto Svendborg Sound are the more expensive options, and you can follow a private path leading directly to the water.

Kogtvedvænget 3, DK-5700 Svendborg. © **62-21-38-91.** Fax 62-22-41-74. www.stellamaris.dk. 26 units, 19 with bathroom. 680DKK ($116/£68) double without bathroom; 750DKK–900DKK ($128–$153/£68–£81) double with bathroom. Rates include breakfast. DC, MC, V. Bus: 202. From Svendborg head west along Kogtvedvej. **Amenities:** Breakfast room. *In room:* No phone.

WHERE TO DINE

Restaurant Marco Polo 🛪 ITALIAN   Housed in a former ironmonger's smithy, this appealing and congenial restaurant serves the best food in town. It just happens to be Italian, not Danish. Chef and owner Mr. Nikolaj is the host with the most, attracting foodies to his dining room at the edge of Svendborg's harbor. Perhaps the steady stream of locals want to remember some sunny holiday in Italy by dining here. To get you going, the chef might tempt with his ravioli and a freshly made pesto and tomato sauce. A well-crafted mating of products comes together in the golden brown roasted chicken with a Gorgonzola sauce. Our favorite of his pastas is a delectable fettuccine with strips of salmon, and we are forever tempted by the grilled lamb entrecôte when it comes in a whisky sauce.

Kullinggade 1B. © **62-22-92-11.** Reservations recommended. Main courses 99DKK–159DKK ($17–$27/£8.90–£14). MC, V. Mon–Sat 5–10pm.

Svendborgsund DANISH/FRENCH   Many Danes, often sailors and visiting yachties, come here just to drink in the separate bar area, but the food in the restaurant is good and wholesome, the cooks following recipes familiar to their grandmothers'. In summer, the terrace is a magnet, and you can sit out taking in a picture-postcard view of all the ferryboats, trawlers, and pleasure yachts in the harbor. The waterfront restaurant is the oldest in town, built of white-painted stone in the 1830s and lying about a 5-minute walk south of the center of town. The food is for the meat-potatoes-and-onion crowd—in fact, that is the most popular dish to order here. It's called *biksemad* in Danish. The chef specializes in fresh fish, and does so exceedingly well, but he also provides a few dishes for the carnivore, notably some tasty pork chops or tender Danish lamb.

Havnepladsen 5A. © **62-21-07-19.** Reservations recommended. Main courses 100DKK–188DKK ($17–$32/£9–£17); lunch *smørrebrød* 60DKK–100DKK ($10–$17/£5.40–£9). MC, V. Daily 11am–10pm.

Vester Skerninge Kro 🛪 *Finds* DANISH   Frankly, for a special dinner in an old-fashioned setting, we prefer to leave Svendborg altogether and drive to the hamlet of Vester Skerninge, 11km (6¾ miles) west of Svendborg along Route 44. This is our favorite inn in the southeastern corner of Funen, and it's been dispensing food and drink to wayfarers since 1772. Behind a half-timbered facade, you dine in cozy, traditional surroundings, enjoying the type of Danish food served here for decades. An energetic kitchen staff never seem to lose their cool regardless of how many orders are being called out to them. Those orders are often for halibut from Greenland (a Danish colony). It's made into a rather zesty dish by being served with a caper sauce. Parsley sauce is used to enliven other dishes such as freshly caught plaice, which is pan-fried or else roasted filet of pork. A trusty tenderloin of steak with fresh vegetables always appears on the menu, as does a satisfying baked veal in a fresh mushroom sauce.

Kravej 9, Vester Skerninge. © **62-24-10-04.** Main courses 89DKK–195DKK ($15–$33/£8–£18). AE, MC, V. Wed–Sun noon–3pm and 6–9pm.

SVENDBORG AFTER DARK

The most popular dance club in town, with the most appealing clients, is **Crazy Daisy,** Frederiksgade 6 (℃ **62-21-67-60**). Outfitted with bright lights and loud music deriving from Los Angeles, New York, and London, it spreads its clients—mostly people ages 20 to 35—over two floors that have easy access to three separate bars. Upstairs is disco music from the 1980s; downstairs, the dance music is newer, more cutting edge, and more experimental. It's open only on Wednesdays, Fridays, and Saturdays 10pm till dawn. Cover is 50DKK ($8.50/£4.50). Attracting a diverse age group, the town's best pub, **Børsen,** Gerritsgata 31 (℃ **62-22-41-41**), is also the largest. The tavern itself dates from 1620. We like its old-style atmosphere, but as the night ages, the patrons grow younger and rowdier. And during the warm-weather months, the outdoor decks of the ship **Orangi,** Jessens Mole (℃ **62-22-82-92**), is a late-night venue for drinks and live jazz, but only May to September, daily from 9pm to around 1am.

NEARBY ATTRACTIONS

ON THURØ ✿

Too often overlooked by the hurried visitor, this horseshoe-shaped island is one of the most beautiful off the coast of Funen. Its gardens and fruity orchards have earned for it the justified title of the "Garden of Denmark." In one scenic hour, you can explore about all there is to see here. The island used to belong to the manor house, Bjornemose; but the Thurineans wanted liberty, so they joined together to buy back Thurø in 1810, an event commemorated by a stone proclaiming freedom from manorial domination.

It's the island itself that's the attraction, because of its scenic beauty. However, if you want a specific target to visit, make it the little **Thurø Kirke** (℃ **62-20-50-92**), open daily 7:30am to 4pm, charging no admission. The best beaches can be found at Smørmosen, Thurø Rev, and Grasten. When you take the causeway over from Funen, you'll be entering another world.

ON TÅSINGE ✿✿

Ærø (see section 5, later in this chapter) is the major tourist attraction of Funen, outside Odense, but the lesser known island of Tåsinge is for lovers, the most romantic hideaway in all of Denmark. Although sleepy, it is still the largest island in the South Funen archipelago, and it's been connected to Funen by the Svendborg Sound Bridge since 1966. The location is only 3km (1¾ miles) south of Svendborg via the bridge, but a distance of 43km (27 miles) south of Odense.

Route 90, which is the main road, crisscrosses the island, but we'll let you in on a secret. When you see a signpost marked TÅSINGE, take it to the northeastern sector of the island. Once here, you'll find the "skipper town" of **Troense** ✿✿, one of the best-preserved and most idyllic villages in all of Denmark. Many half-timbered houses in gay colors still stand on **Badstuen** and **Grønnegade** ✿, the latter declared by many makers of landscape calendars "the prettiest street in Denmark." While exploring Troense, you can also dart in for a quick look at the town's maritime museum, **Sofartssamlingerne I Troense** (p. 282). You can also visit **Valdemars Slot** nearby (see below).

The island was the setting for a famous tragic love story depicted in the 1967 film *Elvira Madigan.* After checking out of a hotel in Svendborg, Danish artist Elvira Madigan and her lover, Sixten Sparre, a Swedish lieutenant, crossed by ferry to Tåsinge, where together they committed suicide. The Romeo and Juliet of Denmark were

buried in the Landet Kirkegård, Elvira Madigansvej, at Landet, in the middle of
Tåsinge, where many brides, even today, throw their wedding bouquets on their graves.
The 100th anniversary of the death of these two lovers was widely observed in 1989
throughout Scandinavia; many ballads were written to commemorate the date.

The island is best explored by car—follow Route 9 and drive over the causeway—
or you could take local bus no. 980. You can also take the vintage steamer MS *Helge*
(℘ 62-21-09-80 for information), which departs several times daily from the harbor
at Svendborg. The steamer operates from May 7 to September 5. A one-way ticket
costs 35DKK ($5.95/£3.15); a round-trip, 70DKK ($12/£6.30). Tickets are sold
onboard or at the Svendborg Tourist Office (see earlier in this section).

Seeing the Sights

Bregninge Kirkebakke (Bregninge Church Tower)
Lying on Route 9, the
small village of Bregninge doesn't have the charm of Troense, but it's a rewarding target for those who want to stop over here and climb its church tower for one of the
greatest **panoramic views** ⊛⊛⊛ in all of Denmark, a clear sweep (that is, on a fair
day) of Funen and its southern archipelago. To the south are the Bregninge Hills,
whose wooded slopes are popular for outings. Originally Romanesque, the church has
a porch that dates from the 16th century, and its north wing was built in the 18th century. Inside you'll see a Romanesque granite font, a head of Christ on the north wall
dating from about 1250, and a 1621 pulpit with rich ornamentation. In the porch is
a tombstone with arcade decoration, the image of a vicar, and runic letters. Except for
that view from the tower, it's not much of an attraction, but you may want to give it
20 minutes or so. After seeing the church, you can also visit Tåsinge Skipperhjem og
Folkemindesamling (see below).

Kirkebakken 1, Bregninge. Admission to tower 7DKK ($1.20/65p) adults, 3DKK (50¢/25p) children 10–15, free for chil-
dren under 10; free admission to church. Tower daily 6am–10pm. Church Apr–Sept Mon–Sat 8am–6pm, Sun
8am–noon; Oct–Mar Mon–Sat 8am–4pm, Sun 8am–noon. Bus: 980 from Svendborg.

Sofartssamlingerne I Troense (Maritime Museum of Troense)
Funen sailors
once traversed the trade routes from Scandinavia to China and East India. Along the
way, they picked up rare curiosities of all shapes and sizes (some of which are too erotic
to put on display), and many of those long-ago artifacts, often from the early 19th
century, have been put on display here. It's a flotsam-and-jetsam type of ships-in-a-
bottle museum that has such mismatched exhibits as Sunderland china, rope-work art,
and Staffordshire figures, along with model ships and figureheads. Surely you'll find
something to amuse you here, as we always do. This museum, a branch of the County
Museum, is housed in a 1790s school, with a rooftop belfry.

Strandgade 1, Troense. ℘ 62-22-52-32. Admission 25DKK ($4.25/£2.25) adults, free for children 15 and under. May
to Oct daily 10am–5pm. Cross the causeway to Tåsinge, turn left and then left again, heading down Bregingevej
toward the water; turn right at Troensevej and follow the signs to the old port of Troense and to the village school
(now the museum) on Strandgade.

Tåsinge Skipperhjem og Folkemindesamling (Tåsinge Museum)
The young
Romeos and Juliets of Denmark today go to this 1826 former school building to bathe
in the aura of memorabilia linked to the tragic love affair of Lt. Sixten Sparre and the
artist Elvira Madigan depicted in film and literature. How romantic can you get? "The
death of these tragic lovers in 1889, who chose suicide to separation, is a story that
will live forever in Denmark," the curator assured us. In addition to memorabilia of

these lovers, you can see another one of those flotsam-and-jetsam type exhibits that Danes like to collect before opening museums. The inevitable ship models or ships in a bottle are here, along with ancient coins and other not-very-intriguing artifacts from the attics of Tåsinge. In another building you can see what a typical sea captain's house looked like some 100 years ago.

Kirkebakken 1, Bregninge. ℂ 62-22-71-44. www.taasinge-museum.dk. Admission 40DKK ($6.80/£3.60) adults, 5DKK (85¢/45p) children. June–Aug daily 10am–5pm. Bus: 980 from Svendborg. From Valdemars Slot (see below), turn right by 2 thatched cottages and left again at the next junction; follow the signs to Bregninge.

Valdemars Slot (Valdemar's Palace) *Kids* Although not quite as stellar an attraction as Egeskov (p. 266), this palace is our second favorite on Funen, and it looms large in history, having been given to naval hero Niels Juel for his third victory over the Swedes in 1678. The castle itself was built between 1639 and 1644 by Christian IV for his son, Valdemar, in a romantic style, and is still occupied today by a charming, handsome couple, Caroline and Rory Fleming, who welcome guests (some groups) to stay overnight.

You can eat here after enjoying one of four museums, including a big-game trophy room, a toy museum, and a yachting museum. Children take special delight in the toy museum, whose collection covers the past 125 years. Along with several thousand toys, there are books, comics, and other delights for kids, such as model cars. By far the most intriguing are the room interiors themselves, filled with artifacts and antiques. Guests today treat the property better than the Swedish soldiers who once occupied it, sending the copper roof back home to Sweden to make bullets and stabling their horses in the church.

Valdemars Slotskirke (Valdemar's Castle Church), in the south wing, cleaned up by Admiral Juel, was consecrated in 1687, and has been used for worship ever since. Two stories high, it's overarched by three star vaults and illuminated by Gothic windows.

Slotsalléen 100, Troense. ℂ 62-22-50-04. www.valdemarsslot.dk. Admission 90DKK ($15/£8.10) adults, 45DKK ($7.65/£4.05) children 4–12, free for children under 4. Apr–June and Aug daily 10am–5pm; July daily 10am–6pm; Sept Tues–Sun 10am–5pm; Oct 1–19 Sat–Sun 10am–5pm. Take the MS *Helge* from Svendborg Harbor. By car, from Troense, follow Slotsalléen to the castle.

WHERE TO DINE

Restaurant Slotskælderen DANISH/FRENCH In a wing of the main attraction of Tåsinge, Valdemars Slot, you can dine like royalty or else more democratically at a bistro. Inside the thick stone walls of one of the region's most foreboding castles, this restaurant is divided into an unpretentious Danish bistro and an upscale French restaurant. The bistro serves such down-home dishes as schnitzels, *lobscouse* (hash), and roulades of beef with Danish beer and *akvavit*. The views over the tidal flats and sea are better from the restaurant, but most visitors prefer the informality and lower prices of the bistro. For more elegant dining, with formal place settings, you can enjoy haute cuisine like that served in the best of Paris's luxe restaurants, feasting on venison in the autumn, a delicate foie gras, a velvety lobster bisque, and only the choicest cuts of tender beef.

In Valdemars Slot, Slotsalléen 100, Troense. ℂ 62-22-59-00. Restaurant main courses 68DKK–398DKK ($12–$68/£6.10–£36); bistro main courses 158DKK–210DKK ($27–$36/£14–£19). MC, V. June to mid-Sept daily 11:30am–5pm; Apr–May and mid-Sept to mid-Dec Tues–Sat 11am–9pm. Closed mid-Dec to Mar.

4 Faaborg ⟨⋆⟩

25km (16 miles) W of Svendborg; 179km (111 miles) W of Copenhagen; 37km (23 miles) S of Odense

Far removed from the commerce and industry of Svendborg, Faaborg is more a sleepy dream of long ago. It's a "Gone with the Wind" situation, as its heyday was in the 1600s when it was a thriving harbor town containing one of the country's biggest commercial fleets.

Today you can wander those same streets where wealthy merchants and ship-builders lived. The best collection of these crisscrossed, half-timbered houses in pastel colors is along **Adelgade, Tarngade,** and **Holkegade.** For some reason, many home-owners like to plant hollyhock around their doorways.

Funen has more attractive villages, but Faaborg is its most beautiful small town, lying on the sunny south coast and a magnet for Danish and German sunbathers in summer.

In the Middle Ages Faaborg was a fortified town, with a castle and defensive walls, which were torn down, although you can still see some of the fortifications in the western gate on Vestergade. The West Gate, dating from the 1400s, lies 500m (1,640 ft.) north of Torvet.

Gamle Stan (Old Town) is centered around the Torvet (market square), where you can enjoy a coffee in a cafe while taking in Funen's most controversial sculpture, the bronze fountain, *Ymerbrønd,* by Kai Nielsen. For more information about the original, refer to the Faaborg Museum, below.

ESSENTIALS

GETTING THERE   By Bus   From Odense, bus nos. 960, 961, or 962 run hourly from sunrise to about 11pm (trip time: 1¼ hr.). Bus no. 930 from Svendborg also arrives frequently throughout the day (40 min.). The bus station lies on Banegård-spladsen, site of the old rail train depot at the southern rim of town. *Note:* There is no longer **train service** to Faaborg.

By Car   From Svendborg, head west on Route 44; from Odense, go south on Route 43.

VISITOR INFORMATION   The **Faaborg and District Tourist Association,** Banegårdspladsen 2A (© **62-61-07-07;** www.faaborg.dk), is open May to mid-September Monday to Saturday 9am to 5pm, Sunday 10am to 3pm.

GETTING AROUND   You can cover the sites below **on foot** from the Faaborg bus station with the exception of Korinth Kro, which can be reached by **bus** no. 930.

SEEING THE SIGHTS

Den Gamle Gaard (The Old Merchant's House)   Hans Christian Andersen came this way, falling in love with Riborg Voigt, the daughter of a rich merchant. The relationship was brief, but he maintained a longing and infatuation for her that lasted most of his life. In one room of this museum are personal mementos of his stay here, even a lock of his hair.

There's much more here than that, however, including 22 rooms that are decorated mostly with antiques from the 19th century, along with displays related to life even as far back as the 1700s. The house itself dates from 1725 and was established as a museum back in 1932, complete with glassware, china, and faience, much of it left over from the days when Faaborg was an important trading and shipping center.

In the town center near the marketplace and harbor, the museum also displays some beautiful textiles and embroidery, but these are of such minor interest they rarely hold one's attention. There is one ghoulish-looking exhibit of a hearse carriage that carried the dead for burial back in the 1800s.

Holkegade 1. ⓒ **63-61-20-00**. www.fkm.nu. Admission 30DKK ($5.10/£2.70) adults, free for children under 14. May 15–Sept 15 daily 10:30am–4:30pm; Sept 16–Oct 31 Sat–Sun 11am–3pm. Closed Nov 1–May 14.

Faaborg Museum ⓐ   This collection of the works of Funen artists, known for depicting the "dusky light of the overcast Danish sky," was founded in 1910 by a wealthy art patron with what to us at least is the most amusing nickname in Denmark—"Mads Tomato." Actually, he was named Mads Rasmussen. All the major Funenite artists are represented here with their best works, including painters Jens Birkholm, Karl Schou, Harald Giersing, Anna Syberg, Alhed Larsen, and Christine Swane. But the real showstopper of the group is the sculptor Kai Nielsen (1882–1924), whose bronze fountain *Ymerbrønd* ⓐ★★ is found here. We know of no other piece of sculpture in Denmark that is as controversial as this one, and it caused a rage among local citizens when first shown. The sculptor depicts a naked giant suckling at the udder of a bony cow which licks a baby. Denounced as obscene by some critics, Ymer Wall (its English name) was praised by others for its originality. A copy stands on the Torvet, the main market square of town. The museum is installed in an impressive neoclassical building with a rotunda, which was once a former winery.

Grønnegade 75. ⓒ **62-61-06-45**. www.faaborgmuseum.dk. Admission 40DKK ($6.80/£3.60) adults, free for children under 18. Apr–Oct daily 10am–4pm; Nov–Mar Tues–Sun 11am–3pm.

Klokketårnet   In the center of town near the marketplace stands Faaborg's major landmark, an old belfry which is all that remains from the Church of St. Nicolai, the town's first church, which was built in the 16th century but demolished by 1600 because of structural flaws. For reasons known only to themselves, the town fathers did not rebuild the church but kept the belfry, whose carillon bells play hymns four times a day. Visitors are allowed to climb the tower in summer for a view of the town.

Tarnstræde. ⓒ **63-61-20-00**. Admission 10DKK ($1.70/90p) adults, free for children 15 and under. Mon–Fri 11am–4pm; Sat 10am–1pm. Closed mid-Sept to mid-June.

WHERE TO STAY

Faaborg Fjord ⓐ   This is a modern year-round resort that is one of the largest and best in the area, opening onto one of Funen's most famous fjords at a location in its own parklike setting at the eastern edge of Faaborg. Because of its size, it has more facilities than most in the area, including an indoor heated pool and fitness center. The bedrooms are midsize to spacious, each with comfortable furniture in Danish modern along with a bathroom with a tub/shower combo or else just a shower. Opening onto a panoramic view of the water, the first-class restaurant hires chefs skilled in a French-inspired Danish cuisine, and they purchase locally caught fish and produce at the market and seasonally adjust their menus.

Svendborgvej 175, DK-5600 Faaborg. ⓒ **62-61-10-10**. Fax 63-60-61-60. www.hotelfaaborgfjord.dk. 126 units. 820DKK–1,125DKK ($139–$191/£74–£101) double. Rates include breakfast. AE, DC, MC, V. **Amenities:** Restaurant; bar; indoor heated pool; fitness center; sauna; laundry service; dry cleaning; nonsmoking rooms; rooms for those w/limited mobility. *In room:* TV.

Falsled Kro ⓐ★★   The epitome of a Danish roadside inn, this former 15th-century smuggler's inn has been converted into a premier Relais & Châteaux property, the finest hotel in Funen. When Hans Christian Andersen passed through here, he wrote, "it was glorious out in the country." And so it is today. In fact, much of the landscape around here is as the 19th-century Funen artists depicted it. Perhaps our most delightful memory of a stay here is when the owner allows mushroom gatherers with their baskets to come onto the property and pick wild mushrooms, including cèpes, horn of plenty, chanterelles—some with an apricot aroma—and field mushrooms tasting of aniseed. The most delectable of all, morels, are available as early as the month of April.

The *kro* offers tradition and quality in its colony of beautifully furnished thatched buildings clustered around a cobblestone courtyard with a fountain. The spacious rooms are often furnished with antiques, and some of the units are in converted outbuildings, others in cottages across the road. Regardless of your room assignment, expect the comfort to be equal. The inn is filled with grace notes such as stone fireplaces, and, as a piece of enchantment, a lovely garden leads to the water and the yacht harbor. The *kro* is not only the finest address on the island, better than anything in Odense, but also offers the island's premier restaurant (see below).

Assensvej 513, Falsled, DK-5642 Millinge. © **62-68-11-11.** Fax 62-68-11-62. www.falsledkro.dk. 20 units. 1,350DKK–2,450DKK ($230–$417/£122–£221) double; 2,675DKK–2,900DKK ($455–$493/£241–£261) suite. AE, DC, MC, V. Bus: 930. **Amenities:** Restaurant; bar; 24-hr. room service; babysitting; laundry service; dry cleaning. *In room:* TV, dataport (in suites), minibar, hair dryer.

Hotel Mosegaard *Finds*

Here is a rare chance to live on a genuine Funen farm in a compound built around a quadrangle and converted into a modern hotel with an inviting atmosphere and complete comfort. The hotel lies in a tranquil, isolated spot in a setting of field and woodland opening onto the sea at a point 5km (3 miles) east of Faaborg. Most of the clients are the Danes themselves, some of whom book in here with their families for a week or more.

The small-to-midsize bedrooms are well maintained, tastefully and comfortably furnished—all rather snug and cozy—and each equipped with a little shower-only bathroom. The most desirable accommodations open onto a sea view and contain private balconies. The cuisine is Danish regional fare, with such familiar dishes as roast veal with boiled potatoes or breaded plaice meunière with fresh lime. Fixed-price meals in the hotel's informal, family-style dining room go for 205DKK ($35/£18) for two courses or 235DKK ($40/£21) for three courses.

Nabgyden 31, DK-5600 Faaborg. © **62-61-56-91.** Fax 62-61-56-96. www.hotelmosegaard.dk. 22 units, 15 with bathroom. 525DKK ($89/£47) double without bathroom; 680DKK–995DKK ($116–$169/£61–£89) double with bathroom. Rates include breakfast. AE, DC, MC, V. **Amenities:** Restaurant; breakfast room; lounge. *In room:* TV, hair dryer (in some).

Hvedholm Slot

Would you like to stay in a romantic castle mentioned in the writings of Hans Christian Andersen? The choice is yours. One of the region's most evocative castles enjoys a recorded history going back to 1231, and a sweeping view over the fjord and the Faaborg harbor. The grand and ornate brick-and-sandstone facade you'll see today was rebuilt during the late 19th century, when it gained the soaring tower and elaborate gables and ornamentation that make it so charming. When its owners ran out of money after World War I, the contents were sold at auction by the Danish government, and the site functioned as a mental hospital beginning in 1928. In 1996, it was bought by a team of bold and imaginative entrepreneurs, Gorm Lokdam and Ann Vibeke, who added it to their already-functioning chain of three other stately hotels in Denmark. Today, you'll find a tasteful medley of conservative reproductions vaguely inspired by the stately homes of England. Bedrooms are spacious and comfortably and tastefully furnished, containing well-kept bathrooms with tub/shower combos.

Breakfast and dinner are the only scheduled meals, although someone on the staff might prepare you a platter of food around noontime if you ask. Dinner is daily 6 to 10pm, and priced as part of sumptuous table d'hôte meals at 325DKK ($55/£29), plus drinks. Nonguests who phone in advance are welcome. There's a great deal of charm about this place, and a vivid history, despite a certain spartan look.

Hvedholm Slot 1, DK-5600 Faaborg. © 63-60-10-20. Fax 63-60-10-29. www.royalclassic.dk. 42 units. 1,000DKK–1,300DKK ($170–$221/£90–£117) double. Rates include breakfast. AE, DC, MC, V. 7km (4½ miles) west of Faaborg; follow Rte. 8 and signs for Bøjden. Bus: 920 from Faaborg center stops .5km (⅓ mile) from hotel. **Amenities:** Restaurant; room service (7am–10pm); laundry service; dry cleaning; rooms for those w/limited mobility. *In room:* TV, dataport (in some), hair dryer, minibar.

Korinth Kro (*Value* This is one of the oldest inns in Funen, dating back to 1801 when it first opened its doors as a *kro*. Before that, this 1758 building had been a school teaching weaving to local farm girls. Today it still exudes an old-fashioned aura although it's been brought up-to-date with modern amenities. Bedrooms are midsize to spacious, each with comfortable, tasteful furnishings; most of them come with a small private bathroom with shower. Occupants of the bathless rooms share adequate corridor facilities. The good country cooking attracts both locals and nonresidents to a location 8km (5 miles) northeast of Faaborg along Route 8.

Reventlowsvej 10, DK-5600 Faaborg. © 62-65-10-23. www.korinth-kro.dk. 26 units, 17 with bathroom. 525DKK ($89/£47) double without bathroom; 695DKK ($118/£63) double with bathroom; 795DKK ($135/£72) suite. Rates include breakfast. DC, MC, V. Bus: 930. **Amenities:** Restaurant; bar. *In room:* TV.

Steensgaard Herregårdspension (*Finds* It doesn't pretend to have the glamour of Falsled Kro or Hvedholm Slot, but Steensgaard is the best place in Funen that is evocative of a bygone manorial life. This brick-and-timber house is set in an area of scenic beauty with a private lake and nearly 10 hectares (25 acres) of lovely parkland with old trees and a game reserve, lying at the foot of the so-called "Funen Alps." About 6.5km (4 miles) northwest of Faaborg, the oldest section dates from 1310, possibly earlier. The midsize-to-spacious rooms are comfortably and tastefully furnished, often with antiques, and all units contain well-kept bathrooms with tub/shower combos. Even if you're just passing through for the day, consider a stopover here for either lunch or dinner, as you get atmosphere and good food at an affordable price. Dinner is served nightly 6:30 to 9:30pm. If you aren't a guest you should reserve a table. You can also visit for lunch daily 12:30 to 2pm. Some of the best dishes include champagne soup, roe deer with juniper berries, or salmon *en papillote* with local herbs. Fresh from the sea, Danish lobster or baby shrimp are also featured.

Steensgaard, DK-5642 Millinge. © 62-61-94-90. Fax 63-61-68-61. www.herregaardspension.dk. 20 units. 1,145DKK–1,695DKK ($195–$288/£103–£153) double. Rates include breakfast. AE, DC, MC, V. Bus: 920 or 930. **Amenities:** Restaurant; bar; tennis court; 24-hr. room service; laundry service; dry cleaning; nonsmoking rooms. *In room:* Dataport, minibar, hair dryer.

WHERE TO DINE

Falsled Kro (★★★ DANISH/FRENCH Not only is this previously recommended inn the finest on the island of Funen, but it is one of the premier choices for cuisine outside Copenhagen. Moneyed, cosmopolitan Danes, along with savvy foodies from abroad, book in here for a gourmet weekend. The chefs know how to work wonders with fresh ingredients, and they grow many of their own vegetables, and secure the best game from hunters in the autumn. As a sign of their extreme dedication to cuisine, the owners also breed quail locally, cooking the birds to perfection in a port-wine sauce.

The chefs even bake their own delectable breads and rich, yummy cakes, and back up all their food with the most impressive—but also pricey—wine *carte* on the island.

Some of the restaurant's most noted dishes are among the simplest, as evoked by a succulent salmon smoked on the premises in one of the outbuildings. Flavor and harmony combine in the fish-and-shellfish soup with sorrel, and the spicy lobster "Tiger Lee" borrows "the best secrets" from Asian cuisine. Also deserving of your attention is a warm salad of smoked haddock with roast eggplant. The chef's seafood platter is a gift to put before Neptune, and French duck liver with wild rice and the saddle of rabbit are hard to resist.

Assensvej 513, Falsled, Millinge. ☏ **62-68-11-11**. Reservations required. Main courses 280DKK–395DKK ($48–$67/ £25–£36); 3-course fixed-price menu 565DKK–730DKK ($96–$124/£51–£66); 6-course fixed-price menu 895DKK ($152/£81). AE, DC, MC, V. Mon noon–2:30pm; Tues–Sun 6:30–9pm. Closed Mon Oct–Mar.

Restaurant Klinten 🎯 DANISH   Come here as we do for dining with a view, either on the terrace or through big windows opening onto a panoramic view of a verdant offshore island. The forest setting for this restaurant is near the sea, about half a kilometer (1/3 mile) east of the center of Faaborg. Fortunately, the cooks here don't depend just on that view, but imbue dishes with a lot of flavor and show respect for fresh ingredients. On the terrace is a barbecue grill with a bar of freshly made salads, and, on occasion, the cooks stage an all-you-can-eat barbecue for 160DKK ($27/£14).

In a relaxed and friendly setting, you can try the fresh salmon in puff pastry with spinach and lobster as a divine appetizer. You can later, as a main course, sample such well-loved dishes as spicy steak in a tomato sauce, served with a medley of fresh vegetables, or else fresh salmon cutlet in a well-made white-wine sauce. Desserts are country fresh and rich in calories, but a delight to the palate.

Klintallée 1. ☏ **62-61-32-00**. Reservations recommended. Main courses 120DKK–195DKK ($20–$33/£11–£18); fixed-price lunch 150DKK ($26/£14); fixed-price dinner 198DKK ($34/£18). DC, MC, V. Daily 9am–10pm. Bar open until 11pm.

Tre Kroner DANISH   This is the oldest pub and restaurant in Faaborg, with a pedigree going back to 1821, when it was established as an inn, and a stone-sided architectural layout that dates back to sometime in the 1600s. The venerable, informal, and somewhat cramped setting is the first to be cited by townsfolk as a cozy site for drinks. Meals focus on traditional Danish recipes, and include a lunchtime roster of *smørrebrød,* platters of herring, homemade soups, and freshly tossed salads. All this is predictable fare, which some Danes never tire of day after day. Dinners are more elaborate, but the cooks still stick to time-tested recipes, including some longtime favorites such as grilled steaks, calf liver with onions, and roasted pork with braised red cabbage. Occasionally they get fancy and pour a brandy sauce over the chicken breasts and fresh mushrooms.

Strandgade 1. ☏ **62-61-01-50**. Reservations recommended. Lunch main courses 50DKK–100DKK ($8.50–$17/ £4.50–£9); dinner main courses 90DKK–115DKK ($15–$20/£8.10–£10). MC, V. Daily 11am–3pm and 6–10pm. Bar daily 10am–11pm or midnight, depending on business.

FAABORG AFTER DARK

Our leading choice for a drink in comfy and historic surroundings is the previously recommended restaurant **Tre Kroner.** Even during peak dinner hours, someone is likely to be here just for drinks, and after the rush of the evening meal service ends (around 9:15pm), the entire place is reinvented as a hard-drinking pub until closing at around midnight.

A viable competitor for the after-dark favors of Faaborgians is **The Train,** Banegård-spladsen 21 (no phone), occupying a former movie theater. Its pub section opens daily at noon and continues until at least midnight. Live music is heard on Fridays and Saturdays 9pm till closing. A weekend nightclub transforms the place into a rock-'n'-roll emporium every Friday and Saturday 10pm to around 6am, and admission to the club ranges from 30DKK to 60DKK ($5.10–$10/£2.70–£5.40).

5 Ærø ★★★

29km (18 miles) across the water S of Svendborg; 176km (109 miles) W of Copenhagen; 74km (46 miles) S of Odense

If this small Danish island, off the southern coast of Funen, didn't exist, Hans Christian Andersen would have invented it. It's that special. Its capital of Ærøskøbing is a Lilliputian souvenir of the past. Walt Disney must have gone through this town with a paintbrush and a bucket of rainbow colors.

Many of Denmark's offshore islands are dull and flat with red-brick market towns best passed through hurriedly. But Ærø is a place at which you'll want to linger, wandering its sleepy one-lane roads, walking the cobblestone streets of its hamlets—or merely spending a day at the beach. The best sands are along the northern and eastern coastlines. Take your pick. Chances are, even in July, you'll end up with a strip of sand all to yourself.

The place is small so it's easy to get around—30km (19 miles) long and 8km (5 miles) at its widest point. The number of windswept "souls" is also small, no more than 7,000 hearty islanders, with less than a thousand centered in the capital of Ærøskøbing itself.

There are only three towns that could even be called that. If time is fleeting, explore only **Ærøskøbing,** the best preserved town of 18th-century Denmark. The largest town is the ancient seaport of **Marstal,** where mariners once set out to conquer the Seven Seas. Its maritime glory a distant memory today, it has a bustling marina and a shipyard that still makes some wooden vessels as in Viking days. Yachties sail into **Søby,** the third town with a still-active shipyard and a sizable fishing fleet. Everyone's lifeblood here seems drawn from the sea.

Small fishing harbors, wheat fields swept by the winds, storybook hamlets of half-timbered houses, a dilapidated church or two from the Middle Ages, beer gardens filled with raucous laughter during the too-short weeks of summer, old windmills, and yacht-filled marinas make Ærø the kind of island you search for—but rarely find—in all of Scandinavia. Sure, Ærø is all clichéd charm, but a cliché wouldn't be that unless it existed once in time. A local resident put it this way: "We didn't change after our seagoing heyday in the 17th century. We were too poor to modernize. When we finally started earning money centuries later, we were a valuable antique, and we learned there was money to be made from visitors who wanted to see Denmark the way it used to be."

ESSENTIALS

GETTING THERE   By Ferry   The only way to reach Ærø is by ferry; car ferries depart Svendborg six times daily; trip time: 1 hour). For a schedule, contact the tourist office or the ferry office at the harbor in Svendborg. Bookings are made through **Det Æroske Færgegraf-Ikselskab** in Ærøskøbing (© **62-52-40-00**).

GETTING AROUND   By Bus   It's best to take a car on the ferry since there's limited bus service on Ærø (© **62-53-10-10** in Ærøskøbing for bus information). Bus no. 990 runs every hour on the hour in the afternoon between Ærøskøbing, Marstal, and Søby, but there's only limited morning service. Tourist offices (see below) provide bus schedules, which change seasonally. Tickets are 62DKK ($10/£5.60) for the day and can be bought on the bus.

If you'd like to take a bus tour of the island, call **Jesper "Bus" Jensen** (© **62-58-13-13**). His bus holds 12 to 14 passengers, costing 50DKK ($8.50/£4.50) per person.

EXPLORING THE ISLAND

Most visitors go to Ærøskøbing, or perhaps Marstal, then return to the pleasures of south Funen. But if you like to cycle or have rented a car in Funen, you can explore the southern tier of the island, going from Marstal, the port in the east, all the way to Søby at the northern and far western tip of Ærø. There are several attractions along the way, although you can just enjoy the landscape for its own idyllic beauty.

Take the coastal road going west from Marstal (signposted VEJSNÆS). From here continue west, following the signs to Store Rise, where you can stop and visit **Rise Kirke,** originally a Romanesque church dating from the latter part of the 12th century. Later, vaults were added and the church was enlarged twice, the last time in 1697. The altarpiece inside dates from 1300 and depicts the suffering and resurrection of Christ. Its carved work is from the town of Schleswig, now in northwestern Germany. The tower is similar to that of the church at Bregninge. It was originally roofed in oak tiles but these were replaced in 1957. In the churchyard wall facing the vicarage garden an old porch known as "the Monks Door" (ca. 1450) can be seen.

In a field in the rear of the church you can view **Tingstedet,** a 54m (177-ft.) Neolithic passage grave believed to be at least 5,000 years old. Archaeologists have claimed that the cuplike markings in the biggest stone (close to the church) indicate the site may have been used by a "fertility cult." A footpath leading from the church to the Neolithic site only a short walk away is clearly marked.

If you'd like to break up the driving tour, you can drive less than a kilometer (½ mile) south of the village to **Risemark Strand,** one of the island's few sandy beaches. Many of the other beaches on Ærø consist of shingles.

CYCLING AROUND THE ISLAND

Ærø is one of the best islands in Denmark for cycling because of its low-lying terrain and scenic paths. Local tourist offices provide maps outlining routes for 15DKK ($2.55/£1.35), and you can use these maps for bike rides but also for walks. Numbers 90, 91, and 92 mark cycle trails around the coast. Bike rentals cost 45DKK ($7.65/£4.05) a day, and rentals in Ærøskøbing are available at the **Ærøskøbing Vandrerhjem,** Smedevejen 15 (© **62-52-10-44**); at Marstal at **Nørremark Cykelforretning,** Møllevejen 77 (© **62-53-14-77**); and at **Søby Cykelforretning,** Langebro 4A (© **62-58-18-42**).

The road continues west to Tranderup, where you can visit **Tranderup Kirke,** a Romanesque building with Gothic vaulting. Inside, the large carved figure depicting Mary and the infant Jesus dates from around the 14th century and is one of the oldest ecclesiastical pieces on the island. The triptych is from around 1510, and the large mural over the chancel arch reveals the date of its execution in 1518. Originally, the spires of Tranderup resembled those of Bregninge (see below). But they were rebuilt in a neoclassical style in 1832; the largest bell was cast in 1566 and is still in use.

After a visit follow the signs west to the village of **Vodrup,** which originally was founded in the 13th century and is mentioned for the first time in 1537 as "Wuderup." The village disappeared in the 17th century when the land became part of Vodrup Estate. When the estate was dissolved, the village came back.

The cliffs at Vodrup, **Vodrup Klint** 🏖🏖, have an unusual geology: Large blocks of land have slipped down and resemble huge steps. The soil lies on top of a layer of gray clay, which can be seen at the base of the cliffs by the beach. The layer of clay is full of snail and cockleshells, left here by the sea. Water seeping down through the earth is stopped by the clay. When the clay absorbs enough water, it becomes so "movable" that it acts as a sliding plane for the layers above. The last great landslide here occurred in 1834.

Vodrup Klint is one of the most southerly points in Denmark, attracting creatures such as lizards and many species of plants that thrive here—the carline thistle grows on these cliffs, blooming from July to September. An unusual characteristic of the cliffs is a proliferation of springs, where water bubbles out by the foot of the slopes. When the cattle need water, farmers need only push a pipe into the cliff face and let the water collect in a pool.

Fyn County has bought the cliffs, roughly 35 hectares (86 acres), and set them aside for the use of the public, which has access to the area. Animals are allowed to graze the fields in the summer months, and you can walk on all areas of the land. Cycle trail 91 runs right past Vodrup Klint, so it's often a stopover for bikers.

The route continues west to Bregninge and **Bregninge Kirke,** a 13th-century building with grandiose vaults that were added during the late 15th century. Its impressive spire shows the influence of east Schleswig (Germany) building traditions, and is roofed with oak tiles. The murals inside date from around 1510—one, for example, depicts the Passion of Christ, another the life of John the Baptist. The magnificent **triptych** 🏖 dates from shortly before the Reformation, and was made by the German sculptor Claus Berg. The crucifix in the nave is from the latter Middle Ages, and the 1612 pulpit was executed in the Renaissance style.

After your visit along the southern part of Ærø, you can continue northwest into Søby.

ÆRØSKØBING 🏖🏖🏖

The neat little village of **Ærøskøbing** is a 13th-century market town, which came to be known as a skippers' town in the 17th century, with its small gingerbread houses, intricately carved wooden doors, and cast-iron lamps. Few Scandinavian towns have retained their heritage as well as Ærøskøbing. In the heyday of the windjammer, nearly 100 commercial sailing ships made Ærøskøbing their home port.

Lying in the middle of the island, the town looks as if it were laid out by Walt Disney—in fact, it's often known as "the fairy-tale town" because it looks more like a movie set than a real town. Filled with cobblestone streets, hollyhocks, and beautifully painted doors and windows, the town invites wandering and exploring at random.

During the summer its shops, cafes, and restaurants are bustling with life. At the old market square you can still see the pumps that supplied the town with its water until 1952; they are still in working order. The marina and nearby beach are ideal spots for enjoying outdoor activities. At the end of a busy day, we suggest you stroll over to the **Vesterstrand,** where the sunset (in our view) is the most romantic and evocative in all of Denmark.

The town of Ærøskøbing was founded in the 12th century, and it was granted town privileges in 1522 on orders of King Christian II. As visitors wander through the town, many wonder why the houses are still original and weren't torn down to make way for modern structures. The main reasons were the hard times and poverty that prevented many citizens from tearing down their old structures and rebuilding. However, when prosperity did come, the locals realized their old buildings were a treasure, so instead of tearing them down they restored them—and they're waiting for you to see them today. Preservation societies are particularly strong on the island.

ESSENTIALS

VISITOR INFORMATION   The **Ærøskøbing Turistbureau,** Vestergade 1 (© 62-52-13-00), is open June 15 to August, Monday to Friday 10am to 3:30pm, Saturday 10am to 3pm; September to June 14, Monday to Friday 10am to 3pm, Saturday 10am to 1pm.

SEEING THE SIGHTS

Ærøskøbing Kirke, Søndergade 43 (© 62-52-11-72), was built between 1756 and 1758 to replace a rather dilapidated church from the Middle Ages. In the present reconstructed church, the 13th-century font and the pulpit stem from the original structure, and were donated by Duke Philip of Lyksborg in 1634, the year he bought Gråsten County on the island of Ærø. The year before, he had inherited the market town of Ærøskøbing and an estate in Vodrup. The altarpiece is a copy of Eckersberg's picture hanging in Vor Frue Kirke in Svendborg. The colors selected for the interior of the church, along with the floral motifs, were the creation of Elinar V. Jensen in connection with an extensive restoration project carried out in 1950. The church can be visited every day 8am to 5pm; admission is free.

Flaskeskibssamlingen, Smedegade 22 (© 62-52-29-51), is a nautical museum dedicated to the seafaring life documented by Peter Jacobsen's ships in bottles, which represent his life's work. Upon his death in 1960 at the age of 84, this former cook, nicknamed "Bottle Peter," had crafted more than 1,600 bottled ships and some 150 model sailing vessels built to scale, earning him the reputation in Ærøskøbing of "the ancient mariner." The museum also has Ærø clocks, furniture, china, and carved works by sculptor H. C. Petersen. Admission is 25DKK ($4.25/£2.25) adults, 10DKK ($1.70/90p) children 3 to 15, free for children under 3; open daily 10am to 5pm.

Ærø Museum, Brogade 35 (© 62-52-29-50), is the best local museum, found at the corner of Nørregade and Brogade. In the old days it was inhabited by the bailiff, but today you'll find a rich exhibit of the island's past. The collection includes antiques and paintings from the mid-1800s. It's open Monday to Friday March 19 to October 22, 10am to 4pm; off-season hours are Monday to Friday 10am to 1pm. Admission is 20DKK ($3.40/£1.80).

Of minor interest, **Hammerichs Hus,** Gyden 22 (© 62-52-29-50), at the corner of Brogade and Gyden, is the home of sculptor Genner Hammerich and now a museum with a collection of his art and tiles. The half-timbered house also has period furnishings, antiques, and china, all gathered by the artist in Funen and Jutland. In one of the rooms you'll find a pair of porcelain dogs, which were brought home from

England by sailors. Prostitutes placed these dogs on their windowsills; if the dogs faced each other, callers were welcome. Since prostitutes were not allowed to charge for their favors, they sold the dogs to their customers instead. It's said that the North Sea is paved with porcelain dogs that the sailors did not dare bring home. It's open June to August, daily noon to 4pm; admission is 25DKK ($4.25/£2.25).

SHOPPING
Shopping options in Ærøskøbing blossom like flowers in summer, but are greatly reduced after the crush of seasonal tourists retreats. Two particularly worthwhile options that remain open most of the year include **Ærøskøbing Antiks,** Vestergade 60 (© 62-52-10-32), which sells a remarkable collection of antiques, many of them nautical in their inspiration, and some of them imported from faraway St. Petersburg, Estonia, or northeastern Germany during Ærø's maritime heyday. Gift items, souvenirs of Ærø, newspapers, and books in Danish, German, and English are available from **Creutz Boghanel,** Vestergade 47 (© 62-52-10-22). And in addition to those year-round staples, some of the best shopping is available simply by wandering among the seasonal kiosks and boutiques that line either side of the Søndergade and the Vestergade, the town's main shopping emporiums.

WHERE TO STAY
Hotel Ærøhus *Cozy* intimacy and nostalgia are combined at this classic Danish inn, with many traditional features from its past, such as copper kettles hanging from the ceiling and warm lamps glowing, but it has modern amenities as well. We like to hang out here on a summer evening at the barbecue grill that keeps glowing long after everyone has been fed. An old-fashioned lounge, a typical Danish courtyard, and a luxuriant garden are part of the allures of this place.

The midsize-to-spacious bedrooms are traditionally furnished in a vaguely French boudoir style for the most part; most of them come with private bathrooms with shower, although some units lack facilities and guests share the adequate corridor bathrooms. The good island cooking, based on fresh produce, is a reason to stay here, and tables are placed on the terrace in summer. Offering live music on most summer weekends, the inn lies a 3-minute walk from the harbor.

Vestergade 38, DK-5970 Ærøskøbing. © 62-52-10-03. Fax 62-52-21-23. www.aeroehus.dk. 30 units, 18 with bathroom. 700DKK ($119/£63) double without bathroom; 1,190DKK ($202/£107) double with bathroom. Rates include breakfast. MC, V. Free parking. **Amenities:** Restaurant; bar. *In room:* TV, dataport, hair dryer, safe.

Pension Vestergade 44 *Value* One of the most historically appealing buildings of Ærøskøbing is in the center of the village, 180m (591 ft.) from the ferryboat piers, within an antique (ca. 1784) half-timbered structure that the Danish historical authority considers almost sacrosanct. This allegiance to maintaining the building in its pristine original condition has restricted its owner, English-born Susanna Greve, from adding private bathrooms to its venerable interior. But because of its history and atmosphere, the guests don't seem to mind. This enormous apricot-colored building was built by a local sea captain for his two daughters, and it's divided into two almost exactly equal halves. Only half of the house is occupied by this B&B. (The other half is the home of a local doctor, and is not open for view.) Within Susanna's half, you'll find scads of Danish and English antiques, substantial and bracing breakfasts, midday coffee that's served every day, and a distinctive (and rather philosophical) sense of humor. Local fire codes demand an absolute no-smoking policy on the building's upper floors. As for plumbing issues, know in advance that the inn maintains five bathrooms, each opening onto corridors and public areas, for six accommodations, more than most other B&Bs in Denmark, so most visitors find the bathroom situation acceptable. Susanna knows the ins and outs of virtually every tourist facility in town, and is generous about transmitting information about local restaurants and bike-rental facilities to her guests. There's a communal TV in one of the public areas.

Vestergade 44. DK-5970, Ærøskøbing. © 62-52-22-98. www.pension-vestergade44.dk. 6 rooms, none with private bathroom. 680DKK–780DKK ($116–$133/£61–£70) double. No credit cards. *In room:* Dataport, no phone.

WHERE TO DINE

Ærøskøbing Røgeri *Value* SMOKED FISH   The setting is anything but glamorous, and your meal will be served on paper plates with plastic knives and forks. And if you're looking for wine to accompany your meal, forget it, as the beverage of choice is beer. Nevertheless, this is one of the most popular places in town, a culinary landmark that patrons describe with nostalgia and affection. Set beside the harbor in a raffish-looking house built in the old Ærø style, it serves only fresh fish that has been smoked (usually that morning) in electric and wood-fired ovens on the premises. You specify what kind of fish you want (salmon, herring, filet or whole mackerel, trout, or shrimp) and which of a half-dozen seasonings you want (dill, parsley, pepper, paprika, garlic, or "Provençal"), then you carry your plate to outdoor seating overlooking the harbor, or haul it back to wherever you're staying. The most expensive thing on the menu is a slab of fresh-smoked salmon accompanied by bread, butter, and a portion of potato salad; the least expensive is a make-it-yourself *smørrebrød* that includes a smoked herring, a slice of rough-textured bread, and Danish butter.

Havnen 15. © 62-52-40-07. Platters 19DKK–26DKK ($3.25–$4.40/£1.70–£2.35). No credit cards. May–Aug daily 10am–6pm (until 8pm mid-June to mid-Aug). Closed Sept–Apr.

Restaurant Mumm *&* AMERICAN/INTERNATIONAL   In a simple house whose foundation dates from 1780, this restaurant enjoys a reputation for well-prepared dishes that sometimes carry a North American (or at least an international) flavor. Inside, you'll find a pair of dining rooms; the less formal one offers a view into a very busy kitchen. There's also a terrace set up in the garden in back, where parasols and candles usually adorn the outdoor tables. The restaurant offers an unusual combination of American- and Danish-style dishes (a former owner was a chef at a Florida resort). There's a copious salad buffet, well-flavored steaks, and an abundance of seafood (most of which comes from local waters), including filet of plaice, grilled salmon with hollandaise sauce, sole in parsley-butter sauce, and various preparations of shrimp and snails.

Søndergade 12. © 62-52-12-12. Main courses 120DKK–188DKK ($20–$32/£11–£17). AE, DC, MC, V. June–Aug daily 11:30am–2:30pm and 6–9:30pm; May and Sept Tues–Sun 11:30am–2:30pm and 6–9:30pm. Closed Oct–Apr.

ÆRØSKØBING AFTER DARK

In summertime, you'll find sidewalk cafes and bars that come and go with the seasons (and which sometimes don't return the following year) along either side of the Vestergade and the Søndergade. One of the most reliable and enduring of these seasonal joints is the **Café Andelen,** Søndergade 28A (© 62-52-17-11), which presents live jazz that begins around 9pm most nights June to August. Two year-round pubs that are favored by local residents and fishermen are **Aarebo Pub,** Vestergade 4 (© 62-52-28-50), which offers some kind of live music every Friday and Saturday throughout the year, and its nearby competitor, **Landborgården Pub,** Vestergade 54 (© **62-52-10-41**), which is a site just for drinking and socializing for all ages.

MARSTAL ⊛

Marstal is the second city—really, an overgrown town of 2,500 people—standing at the eastern end of the island. Its marina is busy in summer with yachts, and there's even a shipyard, but its glory days are long gone. Back in the 1800s as many as 300 merchant ships called Marstal their home port.

The harbor is protected by a granite jetty, forming one of Denmark's largest yacht basins. It's idyllic for all with nautical interests, but if you have time for only one town on Ærø, make it Ærøskøbing (see above). Otherwise, wander the streets of Marstal for an hour or two, the names of which still evoke the town's seafaring past—**Skonnertvej, Barkvej,** and **Galeasevej** (Schooner, Bark, and Ketch roads).

SEEING THE SIGHTS

In summer, consider an offbeat side trip to **Birkholm Island,** which is ideal for exploring, relaxing, and swimming. Twice a day a mail boat takes a limited number of passengers on this 45-minute trip from Marstal. Except for service and utility vehicles, there are no cars allowed on the island. For information and reservations, call **Birkholm Færgen** at © **62-54-17-77.** The price of round-trip passage from Marstal to Birkholm Island is 130DKK ($22/£12) per person.

Maren Minors Minde   This is the once-prosperous, once-private home of a successful sea captain, Rasmus Minor, whose other bequests to Ærø included an orphanage and a retirement home. In the 1950s his widow, Maren Minor, willed the house and its collection of nautical artifacts to the municipality as a museum. It's not much of a sight, but in its own way is some kind of immortality for the captain. If he hadn't given his home, his name would certainly be forgotten today. Give it 20 minutes or so. Although Minor always declared his love for his native Ærø, he eventually left the island and sailed for a new life in the United States.

Teglgade 9. © 62-53-23-31. Admission 40DKK ($6.80/£3.60) adults, 10DKK ($1.70/90p) children 5–15, free for children under 5. Daily 10am–3pm. Closed Sept–May.

Marstal Kirke   Built in 1738, the church was enlarged twice—once in 1772 by adding an extension and later in 1920 with a tower to commemorate the reunification of southern Jutland with Denmark. Seven votive ships inside indicate the growth of shipping in the town from the 18th to the 20th century, and Marstal's close links to the sea. The font dates from the Middle Ages, and the blue color of the benches symbolizes the sea and eternity, whereas the red colors of the altar and pulpit evoke the blood shed by Christ. Red is also the color of love. Carl Rasmussen, a maritime artist who usually specialized in the motifs of Greenland, painted the 1881 altarpiece, depicting Christ stilling a storm. In the old churchyard are memorials and tombstones honoring the sailors of Marstal who died at sea during two world wars.

Kirkestrade 14. © 62-53-10-80. Free admission. Daily 9am–5pm.

Marstal Søfartsmuseum ⊛   This museum is an evocative reminder of Marstal's heyday as a center of shipping. It's larger than you expect, spread across a trio of old buildings with three dozen different showrooms illustrating a maritime past. It has Funen's best collection of ship models, more than 200 in all, plus 100 "bottle ships," even full-size boats and a lot of flotsam-and-jetsam junk Danish sailors of yore picked up in foreign ports, often while cavorting with prostitutes. At least the museum reveals what some of these sailors thought were objects valuable enough to bring home with them.

We are drawn to the works of an island-born artist, Carl Rasmussen, who sailed to Greenland and was captivated by its landscapes and its turbulent sea. He painted a large collection of works, some of which are on view today. Of course, some of the rooms are more worthwhile than others, especially when you get to see the 19th-century parlors of skippers of yore. There are many antiques and a lot of nautical memorabilia to check out. Some of these types of museums are boring, but this one has much to intrigue you, including an on-site shop selling unusual gifts and souvenirs.

Prinsensgade 1. ℂ **62-53-23-31**. www.marmus.dk. Admission 40DKK ($6.80/£3.60) adults, 10DKK ($1.70/90p) children under 18. Oct–Apr Tues–Fri 10am–4pm, Sat 11am–3pm; May and Sept daily 10am–4pm; June and Aug daily 9am–5pm; July daily 9am–8pm.

SHOPPING

Marstal's most densely packed shopping streets are the **Kirkestræde** (which is transformed into a pedestrians-only walkway July–Aug) and **Kongensgade.** Many of the boutiques and kiosks that flourish there during midsummer disappear altogether the rest of the year, so the best way to appreciate the shopping scene involves spontaneously dropping in and out of boutiques as they catch your fancy. The best, and most enduring, venue for souvenirs from Ærø and the rest of Denmark is **Emerto,** Kirkestræde 10 (ℂ **62-53-13-91**). Its owner, Bille Knusen, accumulates porcelain, crystal, woodcarvings, nautical memorabilia, and pots and pans into an all-inclusive emporium. Nearby is **Fruhøst,** Kongensgade 22 (ℂ **62-53-24-09**), a store specializing in odd bits of handmade paraphernalia that for the most part are made on Ærø. Owner Elizabeth Jørgensen sells weavings, homemade wine, homemade chocolates, candles, and bric-a-brac.

WHERE TO STAY

Hotel Ærø Strand ✦   Surrounded by sea grass and sweeping vistas of the water, this first-class hotel is the largest and most up-to-date on the island, even though it opened back in 1989. It is a 5-minute walk from the center and less than half a kilometer (¼ mile) from the beach. The hotel is about the only place on Ærø that could be called a holiday resort, offering midsize-to-spacious bedrooms, each decorated in Danish modern set against pastel-colored walls, and each containing a sleek tiled bathroom with tub/shower combo. The suites are twice the size of the regular rooms and worth the extra money if you can afford it. The restaurant is right by the harbor, and during the day fishermen can be seen bringing in the catch. In winter you can retreat to one of the cozy nooks inside, or else dine in summer close to the giant heart-shaped swimming pool.

Egehovedvej 4, DK-5960 Marstal. ℂ **62-53-33-20**. Fax 62-53-31-50. www.hotel-aeroestrand.dk. 100 units. 925DKK ($157/£83) double; 1,295DKK ($220/£117) suite. Rates include breakfast. DC, MC, V. Free parking. Closed Dec 20–Jan 2. Bus: 990 to Marstal. **Amenities:** Restaurant; bar; indoor heated pool; tennis court; Jacuzzi; sauna; solarium; dance club. *In room:* TV.

Hotel Marstal   This is a classic Danish waterfront inn, drawing more locals and visitors to its drinking and dining facilities than it does to the rather Spartan bedrooms upstairs. The location is in the town center, and the look is a bit nautical, with a ship's wheel on the wall along with old-fashioned wood-beamed ceilings and subdued lighting.

You may want to dine here even if you're not an overnight guest (see below). The small-to-midsize bedrooms are well maintained and functionally furnished in Danish modern, two with windows that open onto a view of the sea—naturally, these are the most frequently requested. Bathrooms are a bit small but tidily kept and equipped with tub/shower combos; otherwise, you can use one of the corridor bathrooms.

Droningstræde 1A, DK-5960 Marstal. © **62-53-13-52**. www.hotelmarstal.dk. 18 units, 12 with bathroom. 575DKK–850DKK ($98–$145/£52–£77) double. Rates include breakfast. MC, V. **Amenities:** Restaurant; bar. *In room:* TV, no phone.

WHERE TO DINE
Den Gamle Vingård ⊛ DANISH   On the Torvet (main square) of Marstal, this restaurant is set in a relatively new building, despite the fact that its name means "the old vineyard." It is, nonetheless, one of the best restaurants in Marstal, with engravings and oil paintings of antique ships and lots of woodsy-looking memorabilia of old Ærø. Your meal might consist of something as simple as pasta or pizza, or more substantial fare, which includes tender steaks, veal, chicken, fried filet of pork, or any of a half-dozen kinds of fresh fish. Each is prepared with the sauce suited to its individual flavors: Salmon, for example, is grilled and accompanied by an herb-and-butter sauce; herring is best either marinated, or fried and served with a lime-vinegar sauce. Plaice, depending on the mood of the chef, might be stuffed with shrimp and asparagus.

Skolegade 15. © **62-53-13-25**. Reservations recommended. Pizzas and pastas 50DKK–68DKK ($8.50–$12/£4.50–£6.10); main courses 64DKK–142DKK ($11–$24/£5.75–£13). No credit cards. May and Sept daily 5–10pm; June–Aug daily noon–10pm. Closed Oct–Apr.

Hotel Marstal Restaurant ⊛ STEAKS/SEAFOOD   The other leading restaurant in town is this dark-toned replica of an English pub, where lots of varnished paneling, flickering candles, and nautical accessories contribute to a general coziness at all times of the year. There's lots of beer on tap, as well as a menu that focuses on grilled steaks, some of them with pepper sauce; veal *cordon bleu;* and fresh seafood that might have arrived that morning from local fishermen. Especially flavorful are any of the beef dishes, or the grilled salmon steak with potatoes, asparagus, and either a lemon-butter or hollandaise sauce.

Dronningestræde 1A. © **62-53-13-52**. www.hotelmarstal.dk. Reservations recommended. Main courses 104DKK–178DKK ($18–$30/£9.35–£16); fixed-price menus 110DKK–175DKK ($19–$30/£9.90–£16). AE, DC, MC, V. Daily noon–2pm and 4–9pm.

MARSTAL AFTER DARK
Our favorite pub in Marstal is **Toldbohus,** Prinsensgade 7 (© **62-53-15-41**), which opens every day at 8am and which transforms itself from a cafe into a bar and pub as the day progresses. People of all ages converge here in a convivial atmosphere.

10

South Jutland

This is a tough call for us to make, but if you have time to visit only one part of the peninsula of Jutland, we'd opt for the south as opposed to central and northern Jutland. Each has its peculiar charm, but South Jutland can be a joyful celebration in summer, with its old seafaring towns, miles of sandy beaches, North Sea islands, and Jutland's oldest and most beautiful town, Ribe.

South Jutland (*Syd Jylland* in Danish) is the part of Denmark that's on Continental Europe, with Germany its immediate neighbor to the south. As the southernmost part of the Jutland peninsula, it is dotted with heather-covered moors, fjords, farmlands, lakes, and sand dunes. It's 400km (250 miles) from the northern tip of Jutland to the German frontier, and the North Sea washes up on kilometers of sandy beaches, making this a favorite holiday place.

The meadows of Jutland are filled with rich bird life and winding rivers, and nature walks are possible in almost all directions. Gabled houses in the marshlands of South Jutland add to the peninsula's charm. The two most popular vacation islands are **Rømø** and **Fanø,** off of the southwestern coast. Here many traditional homes of fishermen and sea captains have been preserved. Of all the towns of South Jutland, none has more particular appeal and charm for the visitor than **Ribe,** fabled for its storks' nests.

You can do as the Danes do and cycle through the countryside of South Jutland, which is crisscrossed by a fine network of bicycle paths. Stop in at one of the tourist offices and pick up a detailed map of the region, which often outlines the best bike paths.

A dike evocative of the Netherlands stretches along the coast of southwest Jutland, built to protect the land here from the tempestuous North Sea. Nature lovers flock here to enjoy walks along the Wadden Sea, and at low tide they can even explore the seabed itself. You can also bicycle along the dike, but the westerly winds make this a difficult run.

Some of the finest beaches in northern Europe are found in South Jutland, especially on the island of Rømø. When the winds blow, these long beaches are ideal for kite flying. In the little villages and towns, the past meets the present as you walk along narrow, cobbled streets, admiring the half-timbered houses that look as if they've emerged from a Hans Christian Andersen fairy tale. To experience an authentically Danish meal, order the traditional lunch of pickled herring, rye bread, and schnapps.

There are many museums of local history, showing you how life was lived long before you arrived. Many include workshops where artisans still practice the old crafts—for example, the lacemaking that made Tønder famous in the 18th century.

Mainly, South Jutland is a place to go to recharge your batteries.

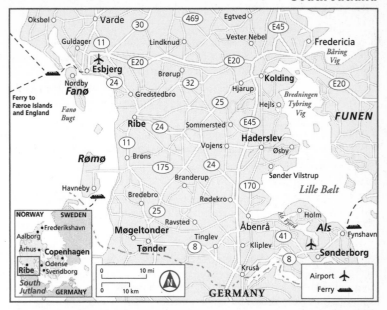

1 Kolding

208km (129 miles) SW of Copenhagen; 71km (44 miles) NW of Odense; 82km (51 miles) N of the German border; 70km (43 miles) SW of Århus

Our South Jutland adventure begins in the gateway city of Kolding, nestled on the scenic **Kolding Fjord.** The sixth-largest city in Denmark can become an overnight stopover or else the object of a short visit of 2 to 3 hours depending on your schedule.

There are more young designers running around the streets of Kolding than even in Copenhagen itself, as it is home base for the **Danish School of Art & Design,** attracting students from throughout Scandinavia who dream of becoming the Arne Jacobsen of tomorrow. The center is comparable to the Parsons School of Design in New York. Many devotees of art and design visit Kolding just to see the **Trapholt Museum for Moderne Kunst** (p. 300), devoted to 20th-century and modern art.

Kolding is hardly one of the "must-see" sites for Jutland, but tourism is on the rise, mainly because of its hilltop castle, that modern art museum, and its historic Gamle Stan (Old Town) in the center. If you'll ignore the industrial suburbs, the cobblestoned streets and gaily painted half-timbered houses make a visit worthwhile. The center is surrounded by thriving industries such as iron, engineering, and textiles.

Dating from 1321, Kolding was a battleground in the Middle Ages, which led to the erection of Koldinghus Slot (castle) in 1248. The town stood as disputed territory of Schleswig-Holstein, which is now part of Germany. Prussian troops wanted to make it part of the German empire but by 1864 at the signing of the Treaty of Vienna it was returned to Danish hands, except for its Nazi occupation from 1940 to 1945.

ESSENTIALS

GETTING THERE   By Train   Trains run frequently between Kolding and Padborg on the northern German border (trip time: 70 min.). Frequent trains also arrive from Frederikshavn in the north of Jutland (4 hr.). Trains also cut across Jutland, reaching Esbjerg in the west in just under an hour.

By Car   After taking the bridge from Funen in the east, follow Route 161 into Kolding. If you're already in West Jutland, perhaps in Esbjerg, you can cut across Jutland along motorway E20 until you reach Kolding as you near the east coast.

VISITOR INFORMATION   Kolding Tourist Information, Akseltorv 8 (© **76-33-21-00;** www.visitkolding.dk), is open Monday through Friday 9:30am to 5:30pm and Saturday 9:30am to 2pm.

SEEING THE SIGHTS

Kolding Fjord ⋇ attracts anglers, swimmers, and boaters, and **Kolding Marina** is one of the largest in Denmark. The fjord is also lined with beaches with plenty of recreational areas.

The town's two main attractions include the following:

Koldinghus Slot ⋇⋇   This castle from the Middle Ages is the most happening spot in town. We'd visit it for no other reason than to see the **panoramic view** ⋇⋇ of the fjord and the town from its observation deck. But there is so much more here, even cultural events such as classical music concerts presented every Thursday evening (inquire at the tourist office for details). These take place in the Great Hall.

The last royal castle built in Jutland, the domain of King Erik Glipping, the castle became a royal residence, although its original purpose was as a defense against the Duchy of Schleswig to the south. Christian IV spent much of his boyhood here, adding a landmark tower in 1600. Fire and bombardment has destroyed the castle over the years, but it always bounced back, its oldest sections dating from around the mid-1400s. In 1808, Denmark was allied with France under Napoleon Bonaparte. Napoleon commanded Spanish troops because his brother occupied the Spanish throne, and at the time Spanish soldiers were billeted in Koldinghus Slot. The Spanish soldiers, not used to Danish winters, built a roaring fire that not only kept them warm, but set the castle on fire.

Until 1890 the castle was left in ruins. A north wing was restored to house a museum. Reconstruction continued slowly over much of the 20th century, with the Christian IV tower restored by 1935. The exterior has a baroque facade evocative of the 18th century. Today the castle shelters a **Historical and Cultural Museum,** with exhibitions tracing the town's history. The castle is rich in Romanesque and Gothic sculptures, plus such handcrafted articles as silver, stoneware, and porcelain. A special exhibit documents the wars against Prussia from 1848 to 1850 and in 1864.

Rådhustrasse. © **76-33-81-00.** www.koldinghus.dk. Admission 60DKK ($10/£5.40) adults, 30DKK ($5.10/£2.70) students, free for children 12 and under.

Trapholt Museum for Moderne Kunst (Museum of Modern Art) ⋇⋇⋇   This is one of Denmark's greatest museums outside of Copenhagen. After viewing too many badly lit and dusty country museums throughout Denmark, it's refreshing to visit this sprawling complex that's been incorporated into its landscape opening onto scenic views over Kolding Fjord. Housing one of the country's most sophisticated collections of visual arts, sculpture, furniture design, applied art, and design produced after 1900, the museum is a stunner with state-of-the-art lighting and floor-to-ceiling windows. The **ceramic art collection** 🎯🎯 is one of the finest in the country, the works often called "studio pieces." All the pioneers in Danish ceramic art are represented here, including Jais Nielsen and Gutte Eriksen.

Begun in 1988, the **furniture collection** 🎯 charts Danish design from the 1900s to the present day, with a broad selection from the kingpin of them all, Arne Jacobsen. The museum also stages special exhibits where the best in new Danish furniture design is on parade. A full array of Danish painters can be viewed, from the CoBrA movement to abstract artists of today. The works of one of our favorite Skagen artists, Ann Ancher, are particularly impressive. Pieces of sculpture by leading Danish artists are viewed in the museum garden. Near the main entrance is the Museum Shop, where many items on sale have been produced exclusively for Trapholt by leading Danish designers.

Overlooking the fjord, a cafe with a summer terrace features a selection of hot main dishes, salads, and homemade cakes.

Æblehaven 23. ℂ 76-30-05-30. www.trapholt.dk. Admission 60DKK ($10/£5.40); free for children 15 and under. Daily 10am–5pm. Closed Dec 21, 24, and 25.

Geografsisk Have og Rosehave (Geographical Garden) 🎯 (Finds An idyllic spot, but most often overlooked by visitors, is this "Garden of Eden" on the southern border of the town, housing some 2,000 species of trees and shrubs from all over the globe, including North and South America, and what used to be Burma. It's the perfect place for a picnic lunch either on the grounds or at one of the on-site garden pavilions. This vast nursery, the creation of green thumb Axel Olsen, also is home to the largest **bamboo grove** 🎯🎯 in Northern Europe.

Chr. d. 4 Vej. ℂ 75-50-38-80. Admission 35DKK ($5.95/£3.15) adults, 15DKK ($2.55/£1.35) children 10–16; free for children 9 and under.

SHOPPING

A network of pedestrian streets flanked with shops lies in the town center. On Tuesday and Friday 7am to 1pm there's an open-air market at Akseltorv where traders sell flowers, fruit, vegetables, cheese, fish, and much more.

One of the largest shopping malls in Denmark, **Kolding Storcenter,** Skovvangen 42 (ℂ 75-50-96-06), lies 4km (2½ miles) north of Kolding's center (follow the signs to Vejle from the town center). Home to some 60 shops, it attracts an astonishing 80,000 visitors a week. In a style that evokes a megamall in California, it's especially crowded whenever it's raining, when hundreds of local residents come here just to hang out.

Another intriguing shopping possibility is the **Kolding Antiques & Stall Market** held at Haderslevvej and Sdr. Ringvej on Saturday and Sunday 10am to 5pm.

The best art galleries in town are **Galleri Elise Toft,** Låsbygade 58 (ℂ 20-96-54-14), and **Galleri Pagter,** Adelgade 3 (ℂ 75-54-09-30).

WHERE TO STAY

Comwell Kolding 🎯 (Finds This hotel is not exactly a spa, but it's the best in the area for R&R as well as the active life. Opening onto a small lake northwest of the town center, it does have a small spa as well as a pool. The staff will hook you up to play at two nearby 18-hole golf courses or else will rent you a bike for trailblazing through the beautiful forest, Marielundskoven.

The hotel is a showcase for Danish modern design, with exposed and varnished pine-wood trim with touches of brass, big windows opening onto views, and cozy public areas, including a wood-burning fireplace in one lounge. The bedrooms are tastefully and comfortably furnished, also in a contemporary Danish design, and they are decorated in bright, cheerful colors and well maintained, each with a small bathroom with a tub/shower combo. First-class international and Danish cuisine are served in the on-site restaurant, **Repos,** and you can also enjoy lighter fare and drink in the bar with an unusual name: Jes or No.

Skovbrynet 1, DK-6000 Kolding. ✆ 76-34-11-00. Fax 76-34-12-00. www.comwell.com. 180 units. 1,465DKK ($249/£132) double. Rates include breakfast. AE, DC, MC, V. Bus: 1, 5, or 6. **Amenities:** Restaurant; bar; indoor heated pool; exercise room; spa; sauna; room service (7am–10pm); laundry service; dry cleaning; nonsmoking rooms; solarium. *In room:* TV, dataport, minibar, hair dryer.

Hotel Byparken *Kids* The owners of this hotel built it in 1972 as a motel right next to the city park, Legeparken, which offers many free activities for children of all ages, such as rides, video games, and biking. It's a good base for touring South Jutland as it lies just 3km (1¾ miles) from the express highway. Outside it's not distinguished architecturally, although the owners have done much in recent years to make the interior more relaxing and cozy in the public rooms. Each of the midsize bedrooms is furnished in standard Danish modern with comfortable, tasteful furnishings, plus a small bathroom with shower units. The best deal here is one of the renovated junior suites with more living space and a more upmarket decor. The staff can make arrangements for you to use the spa and Slotssøbadet (which includes a water slide and pools) lying just a few minutes' walk from the hotel.

Byparken, DK-6000 Kolding. ✆ 75-53-21-22. Fax 75-50-40-64. www.hotelbyparken.dk. 76 units. 945DKK ($161/£85) double; 1,395DKK ($237/£126) junior suite. Rates include breakfast. AE, DC, MC, V. **Amenities:** Restaurant; bar; fitness center; sauna; room service (7am–10pm); laundry service; dry cleaning; nonsmoking rooms; rooms for those w/limited mobility. *In room:* TV, dataport, safe.

Kolding Byferie *Kids* Although right in the heart of Kolding's Gamle Stan (Old Town), this is a series of modern cement-and-glass buildings erected in 1994 and shaped into different architectural forms, including squares, rectangles, octagons, circles, and stars—we kid you not. Many of the "flats" open onto a scenic view of Lake Slotssøen and the castle, Koldinghus. The apartments, each tastefully and comfortably furnished, come in various sizes, housing from two to eight visitors, which makes them ideal for families traveling together. Children will not only find a playground on-site, but will enjoy the location near the watersports center and baths at Slotssøbadet. The staff is one of the most helpful in the area, and will give touring guidance, or even rent you a bike for the day. A 3-night booking is preferred, which means you can use the hotel as a base for day tours of South Jutland, visiting some of the towns we'll discuss later.

Kedelsmedgangen 2, DK-6000 Kolding. ✆ 75-54-18-00. Fax 75-54-18-02. www.kolding-byferie.dk. 85 units. 750DKK–850DKK ($128–$145/£68–£77) double. AE, DC, MC, V. **Amenities:** Restaurant; indoor heated pool; bike rentals; playground; nonsmoking rooms. *In room:* TV, full kitchen, safe.

Koldingfjord Hotel *** You're close to town but can still feel you're in the country if you check into this vast compound at the edge of the fjord and surrounded by beautiful beech forests. Formerly a Radisson SAS hotel, this is the most appealing hotel in the region, lying on the opposite bank of Kolding Fjord, a 5km (3-mile) drive from the center. The ostentatious and somewhat grandiose complex began life in 1911 as a neo-Classical palace erected on 20 hectares (49 acres) of forested land. After a stint as a hospital and later a school, the site was transformed into a first-class hotel in 1988. Each of the midsize-to-spacious bedrooms is individually designed in a combination of classic decor and modern Danish design. Rooms open onto views, of either the forest or the fjord, and are spread across the main building and three of the original outbuildings, each offering "separate but equal" facilities. Also on the premises are a brand-new, very large convention center and a recommended restaurant (see "Where to Dine," below).

Fjordvej 154, Strandhuse, DK-6000 Kolding. (C) **75-51-00-00.** Fax 75-51-00-51. www.koldingfjord.dk. 134 units. 950DKK–1,485DKK ($162–$252/£86–£134) double. AE, DC, MC, V. From Kolding, follow the signs to the E45; before you reach it, detour northward along the Lushojalle and drive 3km (1¾ miles). **Amenities:** Restaurant; bar; indoor heated pool; tennis court; sauna; room service (10am–10pm); laundry service; dry cleaning; nonsmoking rooms; rooms for those w/limited mobility; solarium. *In room:* TV, Wi-Fi, minibar, hair dryer, trouser press.

Saxildhus Hotel ★★ Although the competition is keen today, since 1915 this architecturally graceful hotel was the traditional choice, lying right at the train station. With its dormer-studded rooftop, valuable antiques, and painted beams, it's been our preferred stopover for years. We applaud the postmillennium renovations that have returned some of the bedrooms to those glory days before World War II. Not all the bedrooms are the same—some have nostalgic decor with antique mahogany four-poster beds and others are furnished in Danish modern. As befits a hotel of its day, bedrooms come in various sizes, but each is equipped with a good-size private bathroom with tub/shower combo. Even if you're not a guest, consider stopping off at the hotel restaurant, as it features superb Danish regional specialties, most of which come from the sea.

Banegårdsplatz, DK-6000 Kolding. (C) **75-52-12-00.** Fax 75-53-53-10. www.saxildhus.dk. 87 units. 935DKK–1,195DKK ($159–$203/£84–£108) double; 1,295DKK ($220/£117) suite. Rates include buffet breakfast. AE, DC, MC, V. **Amenities:** 2 restaurants; bar; 24-hr. room service; laundry service; dry cleaning; nonsmoking rooms. *In room:* TV, Wi-Fi, minibar.

WHERE TO DINE

Hotel Koldingfjord ★ DANISH/CONTINENTAL The menu is adjusted seasonally because the cooks like freshness, such as lobster with asparagus, which the chef called his "*terroir* specialty." If a dish from the sea could be labeled "earthy," we'd give the honor to the gratin of fresh tuna with a ragout of fish roe. The chef also makes the most of local produce in such dishes as a warm salmon pudding with fresh spinach or a crabmeat bouillon with fresh tomatoes. The filet of monkfish—a delectable offering—comes with either a citrus sauce or else *beurre blanc*. The dessert specialty consists of a medley of summer berries with freshly made vanilla cream.

Fjordvej 154, Strandhuse. (C) **75-51-00-00.** Reservations recommended. Main courses 85DKK–260DKK ($14–$44/£7.65–£23). AE, DC, MC, V. Daily noon–2pm and 6–10:30pm. From Kolding, follow the signs to the E45; before you reach it, detour northward along the Lushojalle and drive 3km (1¾ miles).

Repos DANISH/FRENCH The only drawback to this well-orchestrated restaurant is its lack of a view over the nearby lake. Other than that, the place is cozy, inviting, and appealing, thanks to well-prepared food. The copious lunchtime buffet (the best in town) includes an all-Danish medley of hot and cold dishes that feature *frikadeller* (meatballs), many different preparations of herring, freshly made salads, casseroles, an impressive collection of fresh-baked breads, and an artful medley of Danish and European cheeses. Our favorite dish here is North Sea turbot with white asparagus stalks, baby cabbage, and a reduction of fresh tomatoes. You might also find other delectable dishes offered, especially a ragout of anglerfish with scallops and fresh vegetables. A classic Dover sole meunière is on the menu, as is a tender, flavorful tournedos of beef "perfumed" with onions and confit of sweet red peppers.

In the Hotel Comwell, Skovbrynet 1. (📞 76-34-11-00. Reservations recommended. Lunch 170DKK ($29/£15); dinner main courses 184DKK–220DKK ($31–$37/£17–£20); fixed-price dinners 298DKK–468DKK ($51–$80/£27–£42). AE, DC, MC, V. Mon–Sat noon–2pm and 6–10pm. Bus: 1, 5, or 6.

KOLDING AFTER DARK

Three sites compete with one another for the title of most popular nightlife option in Kolding. They include the **English Pub,** A. L. Passagen (📞 **75-50-80-44**), open Monday to Friday 2pm to 2am, Saturday 2pm to 4am, and Sunday 2 to 8pm, serving hundreds of pints of English and Danish beer every night until closing. Equally popular, but with shorter hours, is the **Crazy Daisy,** Jernbanegade 13 (📞 **75-54-16-88**), a pub and nightclub that's open for drinking every night 9pm to midnight, and which becomes a dance club every Tuesday, Friday, and Saturday night 9pm to around 4am. A fashionable venue that combines hi-tech decor with food service and occasional bouts of live jazz is the **Blue Café,** Lilletorv (📞 **75-50-65-12**). Light platters of passable food are served daily 10am to around 9:30pm; cappuccino, wine, beer, and schnapps are available every day till at least midnight, and sometimes later, depending on the size of the crowd.

AN EASY EXCURSION FROM KOLDING

Directly to the south of Kolding, a distance of 9km (5⅔ miles)—follow the signs pointing to Christiansfeldt—is one of the most powerful but understated monuments of Denmark, **Skamlingsbanken.** A rolling hill that rises to a height of 113m (370 ft.), it commemorates the survival of the Danish language and the Danish nation against German incursions throughout the centuries. Its location marks the frontier between Denmark and North Schleswig, a hotly contested territory that was bounced around between Germany and Denmark repeatedly throughout modern times. In 1920, as part of the settlement at the end of World War I, the Danish-German border was moved 82km (51 miles) to the south, where it has remained ever since. Today, few Danes can articulate the reason for the emotion associated with this site. (In the words of one tourist official, "Today, we're all part of the European Community, and we really don't like to talk about that.") For reasons of tact, since the 1960s, the site has been downplayed within the Danish national psyche. Beginning in 1998, it has been the site of a concert presented the first Sunday in August, for which the Royal Danish Opera travels down from Copenhagen to present operatic works by archetypal German and Danish composers Richard Wagner and Karl Nielsen. The event is free, with further details available at the tourist office in Kolding (see earlier in this section).

2 Haderslev ⊛

248km (154 miles) SW of Copenhagen; 31km (19 miles) S of Kolding; 51km (32 miles) E of Ribe

This is not an imperative stopover on one's itinerary for South Jutland, but if you have 2 hours or so, it's a rewarding visit. If it's a choice between Kolding or Haderslev, make it Kolding. Some visitors see Kolding in the morning, reserving Haderslev for an afternoon checkout.

At the head of the **Haderslev Fjord,** this appealing town of 32,000 inhabitants is known for having one of the oldest and best-preserved historic cores in Denmark. In

1995 it was awarded the Europa Nostra Prize for its old, beautifully restored buildings, which center around Torvet, the historic market square in the center. In spite of some minor attractions, there's nothing better here than walking through its narrow cobblestone streets with buildings dating back all the way to 1570. In 1971 the people of Haderslev launched this massive preservation effort to save their Gamle Stan (Old Town), and they succeeded beautifully.

Although built on the banks of a fjord, Haderslev actually lies 15km (9⅓ miles) inland. It has always depended on trade for its livelihood, and by 1292 it already had a city charter. Christian I came here in 1448, signing a charter that allowed him to become king of Denmark. Another Christian (this time King Christian IV) came here in 1597 to celebrate his wedding to Anne-Catherine of Brandenburg. From 1864 to as late as 1920 Haderslev was part of the duchy of Schleswig-Holstein and controlled by Prussia (and later Germany). When the Duchy of Schleswig was divided in 1920, Haderslev became part of Denmark, and remains so to this day.

ESSENTIALS

GETTING THERE   By Train   The nearest train depot is at the town of Vojens. It is possible to arrive by train at Vojens, then take a 30-minute bus ride over to Haderslev.

By Bus   Bus no. 34 runs hourly between Kolding and Haderslev (trip time: 45 min.).

By Car   From Kolding, head south on Route 170 or go east from Ribe along Routes 24 and 47.

VISITOR INFORMATION   The **Haderslev Turistbureau,** Honnørkajen (© 74-52-55-50; www.haderslev-turist.dk), is open January 2 to March, Monday to Friday 9:30am to 4:30pm; April to mid-June and September to December 22, Monday to Friday 9:30am to 4:30pm, Saturday 9:30am to 12:30pm; mid-June to August, Monday to Friday 9:30am to 6pm and Saturday 9:30am to 2pm.

EXPLORING THE AREA

Haderslev is situated in a **subglacial stream trench** ℛ that is 24km (15 miles) long and stretches from the Little Belt to the neighboring town of Vojens. A beautiful landscape has been created by nature. In 1994, Denmark's second-largest nature reserve opened south of Haderslev Dam, stocked with fallow deer. Near the reserve, the large marsh area of Hindemade was flooded, and today the whole area has a rich bird and animal life. Hindemade has been designated a bird sanctuary by the European Union, and you can walk about in the area along the Tunneldal paths, which run through most of the subglacial trench between Haderslev and Vojens.

Back in the center of Haderslev, you can wander through the town's historic core, an area so well preserved it was voted "European Town of the Year" in 1984. The old town grew up around its Domkirke (see below), which stands on high ground.

Ehlers-samlingen (Ehlers Collections) ℛ   The Ehlers family set out to collect pottery from the Middle Ages to the present and ended up with one of the biggest collections in Europe. All of this vast array can be seen in this historic timber-framed building from 1577, which has preserved many of its original decorative wall panels. You can also see many antique domestic utensils and some 16th-century wall paintings. Slotsgade 20. © **74-53-08-58.** Admission 30DKK ($5.10/£2.70); free for children 15 and under. Tues–Fri 10am–5pm, Sat–Sun 1–5pm. Closed Mon in winter.

Haderslev Domkirke 🏛🏛   The origins of this red-brick cathedral go back to the 13th century; but over the years it's been torn down, rebuilt, destroyed, rebuilt, and so on, so what you see today is a mishmash of styles. The transept and nave are the most ancient parts of the cathedral, dating from the mid–13th century. Many additions, however, were made over the years, including the bronze font from the late 1400s and a baroque pulpit added in 1636. A restored Sieseby organ has a beautifully clear sound, and is played regularly. At the altar you'll see a Romanesque crucifix, probably from the beginning of the 14th century, and statues of Mary and John along with alabaster figures of the Apostles. The church played an important part in the Reformation, becoming the first Lutheran church in the country. A disastrous fire swept over the Domkirke in 1627, destroying much of the building, but a restoration was completed by 1650. When Haderslev reunited with Denmark in 1920, a new diocese was established, making the Domkirke a true cathedral. In August concerts are given on the previously mentioned organ at 8pm on Tuesday and at 4:30pm Friday. These days might vary, depending on the availability of performers, so a call in advance to the tourist office might clear up any confusion. The Friday concert is usually free, while admission to the Tuesday concert is 80DKK ($14/£7.20).

Torvet. ✆ **74-52-36-33**. Free admission. May–Sept Mon–Sat 10am–5pm, Sun 11:30am–5pm; off-season daily 10am–3pm.

Haderslev Museum   This two-part museum is only of passing interest and need occupy less than an hour of your time. Lying a kilometer (⅔ mile) northwest of the market square, Torvet, it contains one of South Jutland's most extensive collections of archaeological artifacts, most of which were dug up from nearby bogs. The best part are the reconstructed street scenes of the 19th century and the entire re-created and antique-filled rooms. Adjacent to the museum is a small open-air museum with an old farmstead, several period structures, and even a windmill.

Dalgade 7. ✆ **74-52-75-66**. Admission 25DKK ($4.25/£2.25); free for children 16 and under. June–Aug Tues–Sun 10am–4pm; off-season Tues–Sun 1–4pm.

SHOPPING

Two of the most appealing shops in Haderslev include **Stentebjerg**, Storegade 8 (✆ **74-52-02-09**), which specializes in pottery from the region and from throughout Denmark. For more options on how to make your home or apartment look a little more Danish, head for **Stolen**, Møllepladsen 2 (✆ **20-16-02-16**).

WHERE TO STAY

Hotel Harmonien 🏛🏛   Established in 1793, this is one of the oldest and most historic hotels of South Jutland, receiving its share of royal visitors over the years, ranging from King Christian VII in the 1800s to today's Queen Margrethe II. Much of the historic atmosphere has been maintained, although the hotel has been completely modernized over the years. The staff is one of the most hospitable we've encountered in Jutland, advising about the touring in the area and attending to your personal needs. Even so, much of the allure of this place still derives from its cozy restaurant (see "Where to Dine," below). The midsize-to-spacious bedrooms are attractively and tastefully decorated with a combination of Danish modern and antiques, each unit coming with a well-kept bathroom with shower unit. There is no array of spas or gyms here, but plenty of charm and lots of comfort—and that's why we love it so.

Gåskærgade 19, DK-6100 Haderslev. © **74-52-37-20.** Fax 74-52-44-51. www.harmonien.dk. 33 units. 795DKK–1,200DKK ($135–$204/£72–£108) double. Rate includes breakfast. AE, DC, MC, V. **Amenities:** Restaurant; bar; room service (7am–10pm); laundry service; dry cleaning; nonsmoking rooms. *In room:* TV, dataport (in some), hair dryer.

Hotel Norden 🐾🐾 Harmonien may have the history, but Norden offers the most facilities in the area and is also the best and most scenically positioned, placed directly by the sea on a beautiful lake with a view to the cathedral. To make the place more charming and personal, the owners of the hotel have placed original oil paintings and sculptures by the internationally known Robert Jacobsen throughout. As a curiosity, Jacobsen coated with pure gold the motorcycle from the world champion Ole Olsen, which can be seen in the reception. The midsize-to-spacious bedrooms are done in a stylish Danish modern, with the best units, called VIP rooms, costing more, but, worth it if you want the ultimate in local comfort.

Storegade 55, DK-6100 Haderslev. © **74-52-40-30.** Fax 74-52-40-25. www.hotel-norden.dk. 68 units. 1,145DKK–1,445DKK ($195–$246/£103–£130) double year-round. Rates include breakfast. AE, DC, MC, V. **Amenities:** Restaurant; bar; indoor heated pool; exercise room; sauna; room service (7am–10pm); laundry service; dry cleaning; nonsmoking rooms; 1 room for those w/limited mobility; solarium. *In room:* TV, dataport, minibar, hair dryer.

WHERE TO DINE

Restaurant Harmonien 🐾 DANISH/INTERNATIONAL   There isn't culinary greatness here, but you get the sense that the kitchen staff really cares about the meals it serves guests. The 19th-century setting in the town center is both charming and historic, and the dining room is frequented by royalty. This is the coziest place in the area for a fine Danish meal without too much emphasis on big-city glamour. The long and narrow dining room has only 10 tables and an oversized fireplace that's ablaze in the evening. The kitchen staff prepares dishes that are well crafted and expertly seasoned, including venison with red-wine sauce or a tournedos of beef with several kinds of peppercorns. The repertoire is familiar—no inventiveness or experimentation here—but the "classics" are done with great competence, including Dover sole meunière or roasted breast of duck with a piquant sauce.

In the Hotel Harmonien, Gåskærgade 19. © **74-52-37-20.** Reservations recommended. Main courses 80DKK–250DKK ($14–$43/£7.20–£23). Daily 11:30am–10pm. AE, DC, MC, V. Closed Dec 20–Jan 4.

Restaurant Svanen 🐾 DANISH/FRENCH   This hotel restaurant is in a neck-and-neck race for culinary supremacy with the previously recommended Harmonien. Unlike the antique dining room of the Harmonien, the Norden offers a modern, airy, high-ceilinged, and spacious setting, which is decorated with art. The food is flawlessly prepared and beautifully presented by a helpful staff, which is both unobtrusive and prompt. Some of the most successful dishes emerging from the kitchen include North Sea turbot roasted with lemon juice and wine and served with white asparagus and braised cabbage. We also recommend that you try the Danish veal cutlet with ham, shallots, parsley, and a morel sauce, or the delectable noisettes of lamb sautéed in virgin olive oil and served with a Dijon mustard sauce and Swiss-style *spätzle* (egg noodles).

Storegade 55. © **74-52-40-30.** Reservations recommended. Main courses 76DKK–218DKK ($13–$37/£6.85–£20). AE, DC, MC, V. Daily 6–10pm.

HADERSLEV AFTER DARK

Most of the after-dark activities in town take place at one of only two hangouts. One of them, **Buch's Vinstue,** Nørregade 9 (© **74-53-09-53**), is an old-fashioned Danish beer and wine house that gets very crowded with friends and acquaintances from throughout the district. They select it as a rendezvous point for ongoing discussions about politics, art, business, or just casual conversation. It opens daily at 2pm, closing at 1am. A competitor that's a bit more modern in its approach to entertainment is **Huset,** Nørregade 10 (© **74-53-43-73**). Opening around 6pm, it functions as a well-used bar most nights, except on Thursdays and Fridays, when live music is presented beginning around 10pm; it closes at 2am. There's never any cover charge, and the under-40 residents of Haderslev tend to flock to the changing musical fare at this local landmark.

3 Tønder ⟨★⟩

277km (172 miles) SW of Copenhagen; 77km (48 miles) S of Esbjerg; 85km (53 miles) SW of Kolding, 195km (121 miles) SW of Århus

Tønder, on the banks of the River Vidå, is called the capital of the marshland, the oldest town in Denmark holding official town rights, with a municipal charter granted in 1243. In medieval times, it was an important port and a place of disembarkation for horses and cattle. Its surrounding marshland, even Tønder itself, was often flooded by the North Sea. By the middle of the 15th century, townspeople started to erect dikes. But the end result was that Tønder lost its position as a port. The sea eventually receded, leaving Tønder landlocked.

In the 17th century, the townsfolk turned to lacemaking, and eventually 12,000 lacemakers were employed in and around the town. The many rich lace dealers built the beautiful patrician houses adorning the streets today.

From 1864 Tønder and the region of North Schleswig were part of Germany. But a plebiscite in 1920 led to the reunion of North Slesvig with Denmark. Even so, Tønder is still influenced by German traditions, as it is only 4km (2½ miles) north of the German frontier. The town still has a German school, kindergarten, and library, and a German vicar is attached to Tønder Christ Church.

ESSENTIALS

GETTING THERE   By Train   The train depot lies on the west side of Tønder, less than a kilometer (½ mile) from Torvet (the market square) and reached by going along Vestergade. Monday to Friday, trains arrive every hour during the day from Ribe (trip time: 50 min.) and Esbjerg (trip time: 1½ hr.). There's less frequent service on Saturday and Sunday.

By Car   From Kolding (see earlier in the chapter), take Route 25 southwest to the junction with Route 11, which will carry you for the final lap to the turnoff for Tønder, reached along Route 419 heading west.

VISITOR INFORMATION   The **Tønder Turistbureau,** Torvet 1 (© **74-72-12-20;** www.visittonder.dk), is open June 15 to August Monday to Friday 9am to 5pm and Saturday 9am to noon. Otherwise, hours are Monday to Friday 9am to 4pm and Saturday 9am to noon.

GETTING AROUND   By Bicycle   Tønder Campingplads, Holmevej 2A (© **74-72-18-49**), rents bikes and, mid-May to mid-August, water bikes from 60DKK ($10/£5.40) a day. Bicycling maps are available at the tourist office.

SPECIAL EVENTS   Beginning rather modestly in 1975, the **Tønder Festivalen,** Vestergade 80 (© **74-72-46-10**), held every year August 25 to 29, has turned into an international musical event. The Tønder Festival, covering a wide range of music styles, presents musicians from all over the world playing blues, bluegrass, Cajun, zydeco, jazz, gospel, and traditional Irish, Scottish, English, and American folk music. Names as well as unknowns play their instruments in the streets, squares, pubs, and on seven official stages. More than 25,000 visitors flock to Tønder annually for this event. Tickets cost 110DKK to 220DKK ($19–$37/£9.90–£20).

SEEING THE SIGHTS

To see the antique homes built by the lacemakers during the heyday of Tønder's prosperity, wander up and down the main street, which changes its name several times: **Østergade** becomes **Storegade,** and finally **Vestergade.** Most of these stately mansions, which are characterized by richly carved portals, were built in the 17th and 18th centuries. The actual lacemakers lived on the smaller side streets, Uldgade and Spikergade, and their houses were more modest, but still worthy to explore. Most of these houses on the latter two streets were built in the 1600s with bay windows. Actually, in our view, **Uldgade** ✪ is the most colorful street in Tønder. A narrow cobblestone lane, it is in many ways the street in Tønder most evocative of old Denmark.

All that remains of the ancient **Tønder Castle,** victim of border wars with the Germans, is this gatehouse housing the local history of the area, including its lacemaking heyday, with lacy baptismal gowns and fragile doilies of another era. The collection of tiles is exceptional, as they were hand-painted in the Netherlands and brought back home by sailors from the 1600s and 1700s, when they were used as ballast. Once they were in Tønder, locals used them to decorate their homes. Other artifacts and exhibits include regional costumes and even elegant table silver owned by prosperous merchants in the area. The wooden figure with cane, *Kagmand,* once stood at the Torvet, the marketplace. At one time any citizen who had committed a crime was tied to this figure and publicly whipped—real S&M stuff.

In the same building as the Tønder Museum is the **Sønderjyllands Kunstmuseum,** which holds a fine collection of Danish surrealistic art and a collection of contemporary works. Besides the permanent exhibitions, changing art shows are staged here as well.

Follow a glass corridor to the old water tower, which has been converted into a museum:

Museumstårnet & H. J. Wegner udstilling (Tower Museum and H.J. Wegner Exhibit) In 1995, the town's old water tower was converted into an exhibition center for the works of the celebrated furniture designer, native son H. J. Wegner, whose designs during the 1950s and 1960s were precursors of the style that became known as Danish modern. His best-known design is called—rather simply—"The Chair." If you're of a certain generation, you may have seen this chair during the famous Nixon/Kennedy debates. Both presidential aspirants sat in Wegner's chair, a debate that some historians claim cost Nixon, with his five o'clock shadow, the election. The top floor of the tower offers panoramic views over the surrounding marshlands.

Kongevej 55. ℂ 74-72-89-89. Admission 40DKK ($6.80/£3.60); free for children 12 and under. May–Oct daily 10am–5pm; off-season Tues–Sun 1–5pm.

Kristkirken (Christ's Church) ✪ Religious lace merchants and cattle barons in the surrounding area were devout followers of this church and used part of their personal treasures to richly decorate the interior, which is one of the finest in Denmark in terms of furnishings and art from the Renaissance and baroque eras. The present church dates from the end of the 16th century, although the 50m (164-ft.) tower is actually from the earlier Skt. Nicolai Kirke that stood on this spot before it became too small. Inside the church are a mid-14th-century font, a pulpit from 1586, and a series of memorial tablets, some dating from the 1400s.

Kirkepladsen. (✆ 74-72-20-80. Free admission. Mon–Sat 10am–5pm.

Dröhse's Hus (Dröhse's House)   In this little museum—strictly for aficionados in our opinion—Tønder pays homage to its lacemaking past. Other exhibits focus on artifacts of the area, including antique furniture and glass. The museum is only of passing interest, and you may not want to give it more than 20 minutes unless you plan to take up lacemaking.

Storgade 14. (✆ 74-72-49-90. Admission 20DKK ($3.40/£1.80); free for children 15 and under. Apr–Dec Mon–Fri 10am–5pm, Sat 10am–1pm.

SHOPPING

According to long tradition, the shopkeepers of Tønder—dressed in old-fashioned costumes—arrange a pedestrian-zone market in the center of town July 17 and 18. On Saturday, the final market day, there are live music and drinks in the main square, Torvet. Another shopping adventure occurs on August 1 when there's a feast in the pedestrian zone. Shops remain open until 10pm, offering amusements to visitors, with plenty of food and drink, climaxed by a concert in the main square.

On Tuesday and Friday local vendors sell fish, fruit, cheese, and fresh vegetables in the main square. We always like to gather the makings for a picnic here, to be enjoyed later in the marshland surrounding Tønder.

For such a small town, Tønder has a large number of specialty shops. Many Germans drive across the border to shop here. Various gifts and souvenirs can be purchased at **Andersen & Nissen**, Storgade 26 (✆ 74-72-13-42).

Back in 1671, **Det Gamle Apotek** (The Old Pharmacy), Østerg 1 (✆ 74-72-51-11), opened as a pharmacy. But today it's been converted into one of the best Danish handicrafts shops in the area, although the landmark antique structure was left as it used to be, just restored. Even the medicine jars and pharmaceutical equipment are intact, except instead of headache remedies and cures for the gout, you get Danish glassware, handmade ceramics, and various other quality crafts. **Din Grønne Skobutik,** Østergade 3 (✆ 74-72-48-93), features one of the best collections of women's shoes in town, everything from high heels to the kinds of boots a woman might want for treks through the marshes and forests of Denmark.

Gaveboden, Østergade 10–12 (✆ 74-72-58-29), sells sweaters—the kind of garments that ward off the fog and damp of a Danish winter yet still manage to make a wearer look appealing. Specialties of the store include alpaca, Angora, and woolen tops with unusual patterns, including plaids. There's even a scattering of garments by Finnish designer Marimekko.

WHERE TO STAY

Bowler Inn *Kids*   If you're a bowler, this is your number one place to stay in all of Denmark. Adjoining the hotel is a series of 10 state-of-the-art bowling alleys, even two other lanes set aside for young children, as they are equipped with "ball walls" to prevent the ball from going off the lane. Rental of a bowling alley for up to six players costs 100DKK to 145DKK ($17–$25/£9–£13), depending on the time of day. Even if you're not a bowler, consider staying here as the midsize bedrooms are tastefully furnished in Danish modern, each with a private bathroom with shower unit. Just north of the city center, the Bowler Inn also contains an English-inspired pub attracting bowlers (but of course) and a good family-style restaurant serving mostly Danish regional specialties.

Ribe Landevej 56, DK-6270 Tønder. © 74-72-00-11. Fax 74-72-65-11. www.hotelbowlerinn.dk. 10 units. 795DKK ($135/£72) double. Rate includes breakfast. AE, DC, MC, V. **Amenities:** Restaurant; bar. *In room:* TV, dataport (in some), minibar.

Hostrups Hotel ✿   On the banks of the Vidæn River, this classically designed hotel dates from 1904, when it was erected on the southern tier of town. Today it projects an aura of calm, manicured charm, alluring to those who seek a bastion of tranquillity in the "capital of the marshlands." As befits a hotel of its era, bedrooms come in widely different sizes, shapes, and decor, but all of them are comfortable, tastefully furnished, and equipped with well-maintained bathrooms with tub/shower combos. We've found the staff most helpful in guiding you for outings and excursions. An informal on-site restaurant and bar specializes in good-tasting Danish specialties with a scattering of continental dishes.

Søndergade 30, DK-6270 Tønder. © 74-72-21-29. Fax 74-72-07-26. www.hostrupshotel.dk. 18 units. 725DKK ($123/£65) double. Rates include breakfast. AE, DC, MC, V. **Amenities:** Restaurant; bar. *In room:* TV, hair dryer.

Hotel Tønderhus ✿✿   This is Danish country living at its best, even superior to the also highly recommended Hostrups. A government-rated, four-star hotel, it is a family-run operation that we've always found most welcoming and inviting. The hotel was built in 1943, which is unusual in itself in that this was the time of the Nazi occupation—not a good time to be opening hotels in Denmark. In 1986 the owners extended the hotel with 21 rooms, and again in 1993 they added a dozen more units. In 2004 the hotel was so successful that they added another two dozen rooms. We still prefer the older and more spacious rooms in the main house, enjoying the bathrooms with the large tubs. However, the modern rooms are comfortable and tasteful as well, many with balconies. Tradition or Danish modern—the choice is yours.

A basement-level party room with a glass ceiling was originally a cistern. A glass-sided cafe serves tasty snacks and coffee, and the cozy restaurant is so good that we're recommending it separately even if you aren't staying here.

Jomfrustien 1, DK-6270 Tønder. © 74-72-22-22. Fax 74-72-05-92. www.hoteltoenderhus.dk. 65 units. 950DKK–1,050DKK ($162–$179/£86–£95) double. AE, DC, MC, V. **Amenities:** Restaurant; lounge; room service; laundry service; dry cleaning. *In room:* TV, Wi-Fi, minibar, hair dryer, trouser press.

WHERE TO DINE
Hotel Tønderhus ✿ DANISH   This is a model of successful innkeeping, not only the previously recommended hotel, but the restaurant, which uses the finest ingredients handled with a razor-sharp technique by the kitchen chefs. In an artfully old-fashioned setting, accessorized with rustic farm implements, you can order copious portions of such tried-and-true Danish specialties as cold potato soup with bacon and chives, fried fish cakes, a platter of assorted marinades of tangy herring, tender brisket of beef with horseradish, and a savory afterthought that might include fried Camembert with black currant jam. Between the lunch and dinner hour, the place remains open for coffee, tea, drinks, and a selection of such cold platters as marinated herring with various types of Danish cheeses.

Jomfrustien 1. © 74-72-22-22. Main courses 175DKK–235DKK ($30–$40/£16–£21); fixed-price menus 250DKK–300DKK ($43–$51/£23–£27). AE, DC, MC, V. Daily noon–2pm and 6–9:30pm.

Torvets Restaurant *(Finds* DANISH   The stately main floor of this former 1930s bank is divided into a formal, antiques-laden restaurant and a less elegant bistro where food is cheaper and culinary pretensions are a lot lower. In the bistro, you can order platters of *smørrebrød* (open-faced sandwich), pastas, pizzas, and cold assortments of Danish cheese, herring, and fresh vegetables. In the restaurant, expect more elaborate concoctions that change with the season. As our dining companion told us, "I grew up on mother's fried plaice with hollandaise sauce and boiled potatoes, and I'm still ordering it today. Why not?" Why not indeed. If you want something more exciting, try the grilled trout with roasted fresh tomatoes, Danish shrimp, asparagus recently picked from the fields, and button mushrooms. The chef "stuffs" a steak with roast onions, bacon, and mushrooms—and it's quite a savory concoction. The staff also serves a roasted salmon "spiced up" for more flavor.

Storegade 1. *©* **74-72-43-73.** Reservations recommended in restaurant only. Restaurant main courses 89DKK–218DKK ($15–$37/£8–£20); bistro platters 45DKK–69DKK ($7.65–$12/£4.05–£6.20). AE, DC, MC, V. Daily noon–11pm.

TØNDER AFTER DARK

There isn't much activity here at night. Your best bet is **Hagge's Musik Pub,** Vestergade 80 (*©* **74-72-44-49**), which lies opposite the post office. You can order pub grub and both Irish and Danish beer on draft here. Although it's not a nightly event, it's a frequent venue for live music, including blues, jazz, and Danish or Scottish folk. Open Tuesday to Thursday 4 to 11pm; Friday 3 to 11pm; Saturday noon to 11pm.

A VISIT TO OLD-WORLD MØGELTØNDER

Even if you have to skip Tønder itself, head for the little village of **Møgeltønder** *ℛℛ,* only 4km (2½ miles) west of Tønder via Route 419. Bus no. 66 from Tønder runs here about every hour during the day (trip time: 10 min.).

Once at Møgeltønder, you'll find a charming old-world village, which filmmakers have called "a fairy-tale setting." Its long and narrow street, **Slotsgade** *ℛℛ,* is lined with low gabled houses, some with thatched roofs and most dating from the 1700s. The street is also planted with a double row of lime trees, making it even more colorful and photogenic.

At the end of the street stands a small castle, **Schackenborg Slot,** which can be viewed only from the outside, as it's owned by the Queen of Denmark and currently functions as the principal residence of her younger son, Prince Joachim. After his marriage to Hong Kong–born Alexandra, in 1995, the couple lived here until their divorce in 2004. Today, Prince Joachim wanders the lonely castle alone, although many attractive young women write him daily, volunteering to become his "new princess." The king presented Field Marshall Hans Schack with the castle in 1661, in the wake of his victory over the Swedes during the battle of Nyborg. Although security is tight and you can't visit the interior of the castle, you can tour the moat-enclosed grounds that begin on the opposite side of the street. June, July, and August, two 30-minute tours are conducted daily at 2pm and 2:30pm. The price is 25DKK ($4.25/£2.25) for adults, 20DKK ($3.40/£1.80) for children 5 to 15, for the carefully supervised trek. The rest of the year, visits to the gardens are not possible.

At the other end of the Slotsgade stands the 12th-century **Møgeltønder Kirke,** Slotsgade (*©* **74-73-89-40**), which contains frescoes—the oldest from 1275—under the chancel's arch. In the chancel itself are some mid-16th-century frescoes. The altarpiece is probably early 16th century, and you can also see such treasures as a Romanesque font, a late-17th-century baroque pulpit, and a church organ made in Hamburg in 1679. The admission-free church is open daily from 8am to 4pm, closing at 3pm October to March.

WHERE TO STAY

Schackenborg Slotskro 🔆🔆🔆 *Finds*   After checking in here, you can always tell the folks back home that you were the guests of the Danish royal family. This venerable, thick-walled 17th-century structure is set on the historic, picture-perfect main street of the hamlet Møgeltønder. Owned but not operated by the queen's son, Prince Joachim, the Royal-licensed coaching inn takes great pains to project an aura of aristocratic well-being and glamour, despite occasional streamlined, modern touches in an otherwise old-world setting. Princess Alexandra, now divorced from the prince, personally decorated each of the bedrooms. Each room is named after one of the palaces or fortresses of Denmark and contains a condensed history of its namesake. Both the furnishings and the bathrooms with tub/shower combos are tidily kept. Expect a relatively luxurious Danish manor house at its most intimate. Even if you opt not to spend the night, consider a meal in the formal **dining room,** which, frankly, is a lot more appealing than the hotel (see "Where to Dine," below).

Slotsgaden 42, Møgeltønder, DK-6270 Tønder. ℂ **74-73-83-83.** Fax 74-73-83-11. www.slotskro.com. 25 units. 1,190DKK–1,400DKK ($202–$238/£107–£126) double. Rates include buffet breakfast. AE, DC, MC, V. **Amenities:** Restaurant; bar; car rental; room service (7am–10pm); laundry service; dry cleaning; nonsmoking rooms. *In room:* TV, hair dryer, safe.

WHERE TO DINE

Schackenborg Slotskro 🔆🔆🔆 DANISH/INTERNATIONAL   The most stylish and prestigious restaurant in South Jutland lies on the street level of the inn owned by Prince Joachim. In an ocher-colored dining room that reeks of 18th-century elegance, you'll be seated at formally accessorized tables. The restaurant is famous for a distinctive specialty—salmon soufflé encased in a fish mousse. Yours will come with a number indicating where it falls on the historical tally (at this writing, the restaurant had served more than 72,000). Another specialty that we like equally is quail in Madeira sauce, along with various versions of market-fresh seafood and fish. The chefs cook with a flawless technique, using local ingredients and seasonal produce. For us, dining here is about not just the cuisine, but the "regal experience." Expect a leisurely, rather elegant reflection of the image that's preferred by Denmark's royal family, and a bit of social posturing on the part of the other guests.

Slotsgaden 42, Møgeltønder. ℂ **74-73-83-83.** Reservations recommended. Main courses 200DKK–300DKK ($34–$51/£18–£27); fixed-price menus 400DKK–600DKK ($68–$102/£36–£54). AE, DC, MC, V. Daily noon–2pm and 6–8:30pm. Closed Dec 1–28.

A TRIP TO LØGUM KLOSTER & MEMORIES OF A MONASTERY

In sad decline today, our final excursion is through a marshy plain to an abbey that knew its greatest days in the Middle Ages. Journey to the hamlet of Løgum, 18km (11 miles) north of Tønder. (From Tønder, follow the road signs to Ribe, then to Kolding and, a bit later, to Løgum Kloster.) **Løgum Kloster (Løgum Abbey),** Klostervej (ℂ **74-74-41-65**), once competed with Tønder as a lacemaking center. Built in what was then an uninhabited area, the abbey—today an ecclesiastical administrative center—was founded in 1173. Once impressive in size, the abbey today has been reduced to its east wing, with the sacristy, library, chapter house, and church remaining. Constructed from red brick, the abbey church grew and changed over a period of years from 1230 to 1330. It was built when Europe was changing from the Romanesque to the Gothic style, so the abbey reflects both periods of architecture. In the nave are traces of frescoes, and other treasures include a winged altar and elegantly carved choir stalls from the early 16th century, and a reliquary with wings and a Gothic triumphal cross (ca. 1300). Opposite the main building stands a 24m (79-ft.) tower with a carillon named in honor of King Frederik IX. It strikes a concert every Wednesday at 8pm (only June–Aug).

Between May and October, the admission-free abbey church can be visited Monday to Saturday 10am to 6:30pm; Sunday noon to 5pm. The rest of the year it's open Monday to Saturday from 10am to 4pm and Sunday noon to 4pm.

4 Rømø ⋆

288km (179 miles) SW of Copenhagen; 15km (9⅓ miles) W of Skærbæk; 5km (3 miles) N of Sylt

We've never recovered from our first visit here when we saw three Anita Ekberg–style blondes chasing a Danish man into the sand dunes. Germans, some sans clothing, flock to this North Frisian island for nude sunbathing like that practiced on their own island of Sylt to the immediate south.

In summer, it's a wild romp, straight, gay, or whatever, but it settles down for a long winter nap when the cold winds blow in from North Sea. Rømø is the largest Danish island in the North Sea, which borders its western shore. The east coast faces the Danish mainland and is bounded by tidal shallows, and the northwest corner of the island is a restricted military zone. In all, Rømø is 9km (5⅗ miles) long and 6.5km (4 miles) wide.

Wild and almost constantly windswept, Rømø is separated from Germany by the Lister Dyb (Lister Deep) body of water. Midway between Ribe and Tønder, Rømø is connected to the mainland by a 10km (6¼-mile) causeway that passes over a panoramic marshland filled with wading seabirds and grazing sheep in summer. Exposed to the North Sea, the western edge of the island is the site of the best sandy beaches and is a magnet for windsurfers. The most popular beach area is at Lakolk on the central western coastal strip. Here the beach is under a kilometer (½ mile) wide. The main hamlets are on the eastern coast along a 6km (3¾-mile) stretch from the causeway south to the little port of Havneby.

ESSENTIALS

GETTING THERE   By Train   Skærbæk is linked by rail to the towns of Tønder, Ribe, and Esbjerg.

By Bus   You can take a bus south from Ribe to Skærbæk and then bus no. 29 across the tidal flats to Rømø.

By Car   Take the 10km (6¼-mile) stone causeway from mainland Jutland, a half-hour's drive on Route 175 from either Tønder or Ribe (there are no tolls en route).

⎛*Moments*   **Wildlife on Rømø**

Many visitors come to Rømø to seek out its plentiful bird life on the west coast, which is also home to some 1,500 seals. You can see them sunbathing during the day.

By Ferry If you'd like to continue your trip to Sylt from Rømø, a car ferry departs six times daily from the Danish fishing village of Havneby to the far northern German town of List (trip time: 1 hr.). For schedules and more information, call **Rømø/Sylt Linie** (© **74-75-53-03**). The price for a car (up to five passengers) is 290DKK to 323DKK ($49–$55/£26–£29), depending on the size of the car.

VISITOR INFORMATION **Rømø Turistbureau,** Havnebyvej 30 (© **74-75-51-30;** www.romo.dk), is open June to August daily 9am to 6pm. It's closed every Sunday off season November to April.

GETTING AROUND **By Bicycle** The best way to get around Rømø is by bike. Rentals, costing from 45DKK ($7.65/£4.05) a day, are available at **Garni,** Nørre Frankel at Havneby (© **74-75-54-80**).

SEEING THE SIGHTS

The island of Rømø has one of the widest **beaches** in Denmark flying the blue flag (indicating nonpolluted waters). The nude beach, frequented by Germans, is at Sønderstrand on the southwestern tip of the island. Windsurfing is popular here, mainly on the west coast, the best area being at the southern side of Lakolf. *Note:* Windsurfers must bring their own equipment to Rømø, as there is no outlet locally to rent equipment.

Other than the beaches and windsurfing, the most popular outdoor pursuit is horseback riding, available at **Rømø Ranch,** Lakolk Strand (© **74-75-54-11**), a stable right on Lakolk Beach. It offers rides to experienced as well as novice riders, and most jaunts take place right on the beach, for 59DKK to 95DKK ($10–$16/£5.30–£8.55) per hour.

At the rear of the tourist office (see "Visitor Information," above) you'll find the **Naturcentret Tønnisgård,** Havnebyvej 30 (© **74-75-52-57**), in an old thatched farmhouse from the island of Rømø. It contains modest displays of the island flora and fauna, and there is also a cafeteria serving drinks and Danish pastries. Tønnisgård is open Monday to Friday 10am to 4pm except November to January. Admission is 15DKK ($2.55/£1.35) adults and 5DKK (85¢/45p) children 14 and under. The center also conducts 90-minute nature tours of the local wetlands June to September. Four or five of these depart every day during that period, depending on demand, for 45DKK ($7.65/£4.05) adults, 20DKK ($3.40/£1.80) children 13 and under. Phone ahead for schedules and departure times.

Other attractions include **Kommandørgården** (The National Museum's Commander House), Guvrevej 60, in the hamlet of Toftum (© **74-75-52-76**). The house dates from 1748 and is evocative of the great prosperity enjoyed by ship commanders in the sailing heyday of Rømø in the 18th century. The house is fully restored, including its panels, ceilings, and doors. The walls are covered with Dutch tiles and the furnishings are lavish. About 50 sailors from Rømø served simultaneously as captains on Dutch and German ships that sailed on whaling expeditions to Greenland. May to September the house is open Tuesday to Sunday 10am to 5pm. In October it's open Tuesday to Sunday 10am to 3pm and closed off season. Admission costs 15DKK ($2.55/£1.35) adults, 10DKK ($1.70/90p) seniors and students, free for children 15 and under.

In the village of **Jurve,** there is a fence of whale jawbone made in 1772, which has been preserved and is now under the protection of the National Museum in Copenhagen. As no wood or stone was available on the island at the time, the locals made use of this unusual building material, a remnant of the whaling ships' catches in Greenland.

Rømø Kirke at Kirkeby also merits a visit. The church was originally built in the late Gothic style, but was greatly extended in the 17th and 18th centuries. It is consecrated to St. Clemens, the patron saint of seafarers, and contains a number of ship models, as well as three large chandeliers, all donated by sailors. Admission is free, and it is open year-round Tuesday to Friday 8am to 4pm.

SHOPPING

At the center of the island in Kongsmark, Rømø's major gallery is known by its English name **Art House,** Gamle Skolevej, 8A (© **74-75-61-36**). Here you can experience and purchase Danish and European handicraft products. April to October, a new exhibition of glass and pottery by leading Danish and international artisans is presented every month. If weather allows, you can enjoy freshly brewed coffee and other refreshments in a beautiful garden surrounding the Art House. The only way to stop in is by appointment.

WHERE TO STAY

Danland RIM & Feriecenter   If you want to spend a few days devoted to a beach holiday on Rømø, this is the best choice without breaking the bank. Germans fleeing here from the North Sea's highest-priced island of Sylt claim that the tariffs charged here were prevalent in Germany 20 years ago. This is the largest and most visible hotel on Rømø, with a northern European clientele (Danish, Dutch, and German) that tends to stay for several days or more. The setting is a compound of gabled brown-brick houses, each of which contains between two and four well-equipped apartments. Inside, you'll find angular modern furnishings, lots of exposed wood, neatly kept bathrooms with shower units, and an overall unfrilly, anonymous setting. Don't expect verdant gardens or forests, as the venue is based on the fragile ecology of tenacious sea grasses that grow under streaming sunlight and almost constant ocean winds. There's easy access to the largest beach in northern Europe, a windswept stretch of sand almost 3km (1¾ miles) wide by 7km (4⅓ miles) long. Unlike many other apartment-style beachfront hotels in Denmark, this one remains open year-round.

Vestergade 159, DK-6792 Rømø. ℂ 74-75-57-75. Fax 74-75-57-36. www.feriecenter-rim.dk. 207 units, each with kitchenette. 718DKK–1,190DKK ($122–$202/£65–£107) apt for 1–4 occupants; 813DKK–1,327DKK ($138–$226/£73–£119) apt for 1–6 occupants. AE, DC, MC, V. **Amenities:** Restaurant; bar; 4 pools (2 heated indoor); fitness center; sauna; laundry service; dry cleaning; nonsmoking rooms; solarium. *In room:* TV.

Kommandørgården ⊀ *Kids*   Far superior to Feriecenter, this is the island's best holiday resort, offering you a choice of living styles—hotel rooms, a fully equipped apartment, or an Abe Lincoln log cabin. The hotel rooms are rather standard—nothing special here, but the apartments are generous in size, with beds for two to four guests, including bunk beds for families traveling with kids. Added features include a private terrace or balcony with garden furniture and a large shared barbecue by the pool. Log cabins house two adults and two children, with a terrace filled with garden furniture and a barbecue, each coming with a kitchenette. In some cases, a bathroom is shared by other guests at the campsite. Other better-equipped cabins contain their own bathroom. Of all the hotels of Rømø, this one offers the most activities, including beach sailing, trips by horse carriage, and rides on Icelandic horses. A special feature is a small Tepidarium, which is said to "rid your body of toxins." On-site dining is possible, though many families prefer to cook their own meals in their apartment rentals.

Havnebyvej 201, Mølby DK-6792. ℂ **74-75-51-22.** Fax 74-75-59-22. www.kommandoergaarden.dk. 56 units. 715DDKK–916DKK ($122–$156/£64–£82) double; 715DKK–1,020DKK ($122–$173/£64–£92) apt; log cabins 506DKK–1,020DKK ($86–$173/£46–£92). MC, V. Free parking. **Amenities:** Restaurant; bar; cafe; 2 pools (indoor and outdoor); 2 playgrounds; 2 volleyball courts; laundry service; nonsmoking rooms; rooms for those w/limited mobility. *In room:* TV, Wi-Fi, kitchenette (in apts and cabins), beverage maker, hair dryer.

WHERE TO DINE

Otto & Ani's Fisk SEAFOOD   You'll find this place either authentic and appealingly raffish, or hopelessly informal, depending on your temperament. Expect a self-service format in a brown-brick building that's among the least stately looking in Rømø. English-speaking proprietor Susan Jensen will help you select from a Danish-language menu that lists various platters of fish, most of which compose a filling meal in their own right. Some taste treats include everything from a fresh filet of cod served sandwich-style, with fresh home-baked bread, butter, and a handful of freshly peeled shrimp, to a dinner-sized filet of sole with baked potato, mixed salad, and—again—a handful of shrimp. Beer or wine might accompany your meal, which you'll consume either at picnic tables set up outside or in a severe all-white room. Despite its shortcomings, the place has thrived for more than a dozen years because of its low prices and fresh fish.

Havnepladsen, Havneby. ℂ **74-75-53-06.** Main courses 55DKK–135DKK ($9.35–$23/£4.95–£12). No credit cards. Apr–Oct daily 11am–9pm.

RØMØ AFTER DARK

There are very few options for nightlife on this island that is notoriously sleepy, even by the Danish island standards. Our best suggestion is to have a drink and do some dancing at **Make Up Diskotek,** Lakolk Butikstorv (© **74-75-59-23**), open summer only Thursday to Saturday 10pm to 4am and Sunday to Wednesday 10:30pm to 2am. Cover is 60DKK ($10/£5.40).

5 Ribe ★★

150km (93 miles) SW of Århus; 298km (185 miles) W of Copenhagen; 47km (29 miles) N of Tønder

This is one of Denmark's oldest towns, and if you have to miss all the other cities of Jutland, spend a night here where local residents ponder the question, "Will the storks return on April 1?" Every year some storks—now an endangered species—fly to Ribe to build their huge nests on top of the red-roofed, medieval, half-timbered, and crooked houses of Ribe which flank the narrow cobblestone lanes.

One of New York's most legendary citizens, Jacob A. Riis, was born in Ribe. When "the town's prettiest girl" broke his heart, he headed for New York in 1870. Once there, he was shocked by the city's inhumane slums, which he wrote about in his first book in 1890, *How the Other Half Lives.* A friend of Theodore Roosevelt, Riis was offered the job of mayor of the city but turned it down to pursue his efforts to get a million people off the streets and into decent housing. For such work, he became known as "the most beneficial citizen of New York." In time, he returned to Ribe, where "the prettiest girl" said yes this time. His former residence lies at the corner of Skolegade and Grydergade, a plaque marking his former abode.

As a former port, Ribe was an important trading center during the Viking era (around A.D. 900) and became an Episcopal see in 948, when one of the first Christian churches in Denmark was established here. It was also the royal residence of the ruling Valdemars around 1200.

In medieval days, sea trade routes to England, Germany, Friesland, the Mediterranean, and other ports linked Ribe, but then its waters receded. Today it's surrounded by marshes, much like a landlocked Moby Dick. On a charming note, the town watchman still makes his rounds—armed with his lantern and trusty staff—since the ancient custom was revived in 1936.

ESSENTIALS

GETTING THERE   By Train   There's hourly train service from Copenhagen (via Bramming). The schedule is available at the tourist office.

By Car   From Kolding (see earlier in this chapter), head west across Jutland on the E20 motorway, but cut southwest when you reach Route 32, which will carry you into Ribe.

VISITOR INFORMATION   The **Ribe Turistbureau,** Torvet 3 (© **75-42-15-00;** www.ribetourist.dk), is open June 15 to August, Monday to Saturday 9:30am to 5:30pm, and Sunday 10am to 2pm; April to June 14 and September to October, Monday to Friday 9am to 5pm and Saturday 10am to 1pm; and November to March, Monday to Friday 9:30am to 4:30pm and Saturday 10am to 1pm.

GETTING AROUND   By Bicycle   If you'd like to bike your way around the area, you can rent bikes for 60DKK ($10/£5.40) at **Ribe Vandrerhjem** (Youth Hostel), Skt. Pedersgade 16 (© **75-42-06-20**).

ATTRACTIONS ●
Det Gamle Rådhus
  (Town Hall Museum) **7**
Ribe Domkirke (Cathedral) **4**
Ribe Kunstmuseet **11**
Ribe Legetøjsmuseum
  (Toy Museum) **8**
Ribe Vikingcenter **12**
Ribe Vikinger
  (Museum of the Viking Age
  and the Middle Ages in Ribe) **14**
Skt. Catharine Kirke **9**

ACCOMMODATIONS ■
Den Gamle Arrest **5**
Hotel Dagmar **3**
Hotel Fru Mathies **10**

DINING ◆
Restaurant Backhaus **2**
Restaurant Dagmar **3**
Restaurant Kammerslusen **13**
Restaurant Sælhunden **1**
Weis' Stue **6**

SEEING THE SIGHTS

Gamle Stan ✸✸✸   The historic core of Ribe is the gem of all Old Towns on the peninsula of Jutland. Beginning at the **Torvet** ✸✸✸ or old market square, you can fan out in all directions, covering most of the major streets or lanes of interest within 2 hours, maybe more if you have the time. The well-preserved Ribe of the Middle Ages surrounds the cathedral, the Ribe Domkirke (see below).

Instead of wandering at random, you can visit the tourist office, which sells a copy of a guided walking tour of Ribe for 5DKK (85¢/45p). Our favorite hotel (Dagmar) and our favorite Ribe restaurant (Weis Stue) open onto the main square.

From Torvet many streets radiate out—take **Skolegade,** for example, opening onto the west side of the Domkirke. Riis spent his final decade on the street at **Hans Tausen's House,** which dates from the early 17th century. A plaque marks the spot. At the corner of Sønderportsgade and Stenbrogade stands **Det Gamle Rådhus** (see below), the oldest existing town hall in Denmark.

A memorial tablet at the corner of Sønderportsgade and Bispegade marks the spot where on November 9, 1641, Maren Spliid was burned at the stake, the last victim of Denmark's witch hunts, evocative of those of Salem, Massachusetts.

To the east of Torvet lies **Skt. Catharine Kirke** (p. 321), the only remaining church built before the Reformation.

Arm yourself with a tourist-office map and discover other streets that evoke the Middle Ages, of which **Fiskergade** is one of the most evocative, with its offshoot alleys that lead to the riverfront. Talk about narrow alleys.

Det Gamle Rådhus (Town Hall Museum)   Perhaps the most exciting thing to look at in Denmark's oldest existing town hall are storks building a nest on top. You'll be lucky if you chance upon this. Originally built in 1496, the Town Hall Museum today houses some rather unimpressive artifacts and archives from Ribe's illustrious past. These include a gruesome 16th-century executioner's axe, ceremonial swords, the town's money chest, antique tradesmen's signs, and a depiction of the "iron hand," still a symbol of police authority.

Von Støckends Plads. ℂ 79-89-89-55. Admission 15DKK ($2.55/£1.35) adults, 5DKK (85¢/45p) children 7–14, free for children under 7. June–Aug daily 1–3pm; May and Sept Mon–Fri 1–3pm. Closed Oct–Apr.

Ribe Domkirke 𝄞𝄞   Denmark's earliest wooden church, built around A.D. 860, once stood on this spot. In 1150 it was rebuilt in the Romanesque style, opening onto the main square of town, but over the years has been remodeled and altered considerably. The **south portal** 𝄞 remains a rare example of Danish Romanesque sculpture, and is known for its carved tympanum depicting the *Descent of Christ from the Cross.* Most of the *kirke* was built of a soft porous rock (tufa) found near the German city of Cologne and shipped north along the Rhine River. Before the Dom was completed, 100 years would go by. Several Gothic features such as arches were later added, but the overall look is still a Rhineland Romanesque. The wide nave is flanked by aisles on both sides, and the church is surmounted by a dome. The interior holds treasures from many eras, including mosaics, stained glass, and frescoes in the eastern apse by the artist Carl-Henning Pedersen, who created them in the 1980s. Older treasures include an organ designed by Jens Olufsen in the 1600s plus an elaborate altar from 1597 by the renowned sculptor Kens Jens Asmussen.

The Devil, or so it is said, used to enter the Domkirke through the **"Cat's Head Door"** 𝄞𝄞, once the principal entryway into the church. The location is found at the south portal of the transept. The triangular pediment depicts Valdemar II and his queen, Dagmar, positioned at the feet of Mary and her infant son. Talk about tradition: Daily at noon and 3pm the cathedral bell still tolls in mourning of Dagmar's death during childbirth.

For the most **panoramic view** 𝄞𝄞 of Ribe and the surrounding marshes, climb the 248 steps to the cathedral tower left over from 1333. A watchman once stood here on the lookout for floods, which frequently inundated Ribe.

Torvet (town center) off Sønderportsgade. ℂ 75-42-06-19. www.ribe-domkirke.dk. Admission 12DKK ($2.05/£1.10) adults, 5DKK (85¢/45p) children 3–14. June–Aug daily 10am–5:30pm; May and Sept daily 10am–5pm; Oct–Apr Mon–Sat 11am–3pm, Sun 1–3pm.

Ribe Kunstmuseet (Ribe Art Museum)   Of minor interest, this museum with its more than 600 paintings and sculpture is dedicated to art from various epochs in Danish history, from around 1750 to 1940, which marked the beginning of the Nazi occupation. There are masterpieces from artists from all the major eras in Danish painting—the Golden Age, the Realistic Period, the Skagen and Funen artists, Modernism, and the period "between the wars." The Golden Age is best evoked by P. C. Skovgaard's *Møns Cliff* (1852), the Skagen painters by Michael Archer's *baptism of the Painter's Daughter* (1888). The museum is housed in a stately villa in a garden on the

Ribe River, the former residence of a factory owner built from 1860 to 1864 based on drawings made by the royal surveyor L. A. Winstrup.

Skt. Nicolai Gade 10. © **75-42-03-62**. Admission 40DKK ($6.80/£3.60) adults, free for children under 16. July–Aug daily 11am–5pm; Sept–Dec and Feb 12–June Tues–Sun 11am–4pm. Closed Jan–Feb 11.

Ribe Legetøjsmuseum (Toy Museum) 🐾 *Kids*
The only problem with taking your children to this museum is in convincing them that none of the several thousands of toys made from 1850 to 1980 is for sale. Spread across two floors—there are more than 500 dolls alone—the collection ranges from toy cars to the first horseless carriages to today's model cars. There are also wooden toys, old games, robots, antique teddy bears, and much more.

Von Støckens Plads 2. © **75-41-14-40**. Admission 35DKK ($5.95/£3.15) adults, 15DKK ($2.55/£1.35) children 3–12, free for children under 3; family ticket 100DKK ($17/£9). Jan–Mar and Nov–Dec Mon–Sat 1–4pm; Apr–May and Sept–Oct daily 1–5pm; June–Aug daily 10am–noon and 1–5pm.

Ribe VikingeCenter 🐾
You don't see too many Vikings running around Ribe anymore except at this center, 2km (1¾ miles) south of the center. Just follow your nose: The smell of baking bread will lure you here. The bread is baked over open fires by women dressed in early medieval costumes. Such crafts as pottery making and leather work are demonstrated, but it's the falconry demonstrations that lure the visitors. The aim of the center is to reenact Ribe's Viking age, and locals do so by reconstructing buildings, costumes, utensils, tools, and equipment—even the food. Horses, cows, sheep, hens, and geese run about as in olden days. The centerpiece of the re-created town is a "great house" revealing an early Danish manor reserved for the town's most powerful baron. Other buildings from around 1050 can also be entered.

Lustrupvej 4. © **75-41-16-11**. ribevc.dynamicweb.dk. Admission 70DKK ($12/£6.30) adults, 35DKK ($5.95/£3.15) children 3–14, free for children under 3. May–June and Sept Mon–Fri 10am–3:30pm; July–Aug daily 11am–5pm. Guided tours in English are offered May–June and Sept daily at 10:10am; July–Aug daily at 11:10am. Tours cost 200DKK ($34/£18) for 30 min. or 375DKK ($64/£34) for 1 hr.

Ribe Vikinger (Museum of the Viking Age and the Middle Ages in Ribe)
This museum showcases Ribe in both its Viking era and its medieval epoch. Beginning in the year 700 when a marketplace was established on the banks of the Ribe River, thousands of archaeological finds have been dug up to reveal how the Vikings lived and traded with Europe to the south. Pottery, even skeletons, are exhibited from the Middle Ages when Ribe was one of Denmark's major commercial towns. Justice was harsh in those times, as you can see from the re-created Debtors' Prison, with its spiked maces, thumbscrews, and executioner's swords. Most bizarre of all is a multimedia room, Wodan's Eye, where you can explore the Viking age via computer, lights, and sound. A Viking marketplace from around 800 is re-created, as well as a church from around 1500.

Odins Plads. © **76-88-11-22**. www.ribesvikinger.dk. Admission 60DKK ($10/£5.40) adults, free for children 15 and under; family ticket 130DKK ($22/£12). Apr–June and Sept–Oct daily 10am–4pm; July–Aug Thurs–Tues 10am–6pm, Wed 10am–9pm; Nov–Mar Tues–Sun 10am–4pm.

Skt. Catharine Kirke 🐾
The Spanish Black Friars (Dominicans) came to Ribe in 1228 and began constructing a church and chapter house (the east wing of a monastery). Parts of the original edifice can still be seen, especially the southern wall. The present church, near Dagmarsgade, with nave and aisles, dates from 1400 to 1450, the tower from 1617. Only the monks' stalls and the Romanesque font remain

from the Middle Ages, with the delicately carved pulpit dating from 1591, the ornate altarpiece from 1650. The brothers were kicked out in 1536 at the time of the Reformation, and in time the complex became both an asylum for the mentally ill and, later, a wartime field hospital. You can walk through the cloisters and see ship models and religious paintings hanging in the southern aisle. Tombstones of Ribe citizens from the Reformation and later can be seen along the outer walls of the church.

Skt. Catharine's Plads. (✆ 75-42-05-34. Free admission to church; cloisters 5DKK (85¢/45p) adults, 1DKK (17¢/9p) children under 14. May–Sept daily 10am–noon and 2–5pm; Oct–Apr daily 10am–noon and 2–4pm. Closed during church services.

OUTDOOR ACTIVITIES

You can evoke yesteryear by riding a horse-drawn carriage through the cobblestone streets of Ribe. In summer, you can hire a carriage in Torvet, the central market square. The cost is 60DKK ($10/£5.40) per person for a ride of about 15 minutes, with carriages holding up to five passengers each. For more information, call ✆ **75-42-19-94.**

Anglers and fishermen head for **Storkesøen,** an interconnected trio of artificial lakes that are kept well-stocked with fish, especially trout. Known for their appeal to escapists and for their verdant beauty, they lie less than 1.5km (¾ mile) south of Ribe. A permit allowing 4 consecutive hours of fishing costs 100DKK ($17/£9); 6 hours costs 140DKK ($24/£13); 9 hours go for 225DKK ($38/£20); and a permit good for 24 hours of fishing is priced at 420DKK ($71/£38). For more information, contact Storkesøen, Haulundvej 164 (✆ **75-41-04-11**).

Horseback riding in the area can be arranged through **Gelsådalens Ridelejr,** Ribelandevej 17 at Gram (✆ **74-82-21-22**), costing 100DKK ($17/£9) per hour.

SHOPPING

Ribe has some of the best shopping in Jutland. The best selection of antiques is at **Antik Gaarden,** Overdammen 5 (✆ **75-44-19-47**). The best clothing store is **Mr. Lundgaard,** Saltgade 3 (✆ **75-42-42-40**), which has the town's largest selection, everything from high-quality clothes to Marlboro classics, catering to both women and men. A wide range of footwear for adults and children is available at **Sara Sko,** Skoringen Ribe, Tømmergangen 3 (✆ **75-42-11-24**). At **Ribe's Broderi & Garn,** Dagmarsgade 4 (✆ **75-42-16-75**), you'll find the finest selection of needlework—some of the pieces are exquisite—and woolen items. **Bentzons Boghandel,** Mellemdammen 16 (✆ **75-43-57-51**), is the best bookstore, with many English-language titles. **Alisson-Dansk Naturkosmetik,** Nederdammen 32 (✆ **75-41-09-01**), is an intriguing store with a varied selection of products from a well-known Danish company, Alisson of Denmark, which makes skin-care and cosmetic products.

If your tastes run to handicrafts, gifts, and souvenirs, you'll find that Ribe is loaded with boutiques. The most amusing outlet is **Ryk Ind,** Sønderportsgade 7 (✆ **75-42-29-69**), which is stuffed with gifts—everything from classic model cars to china dolls. A large assortment of artwork, porcelain, glass, paper collages, and mobiles, plus other decorative items for the home, is sold at **Overdammens Idebutik,** Overdammen 5 (✆ **75-42-14-14**). For generations, Ribe citizens have patronized **Børge Bottelet Guldsmedie,** Mellemdammen 14 (✆ **75-42-02-26**), for exquisite jewelry.

WHERE TO STAY

Weis Stue and Restaurant Backhaus (see "Where to Dine," below) also rent rooms. Parking at the following hotels is available on the street.

Den Gamle Arrest ★★ *Finds*   Among hotels, this is the most amazing job of recycling on the peninsula of Jutland. The town jail from 1546 to 1989 has been turned into a hotel of charm albeit with some cramped "jail cells." Right on the main square of town, it was constructed from the same russet-colored bricks as the town's more prestigious addresses. On the top floor the rooms are . . . well, "cozy," with sloping attic walls. There are also various prison cells on the second floor, but how did a bridal suite with a four-poster manage to appear on the ground floor? The prison garden courtyard has been transformed into a sensuous garden with fragrant roses, trickling fountains, and stone sculptures. The brick walls bear the prisoners' inscriptions, including their names, addresses, the date and year, even the length of their sentences, and, of course, their longing for wine, women, and song.

Torvet 11, DK-6760 Ribe. © **75-42-37-00.** Fax 75-42-37-22. www.dengamlearrest.dk. 12 units, 2 with bathroom. 565DKK–765DKK ($96–$130/£51–£69) double without bathroom; 855DKK–965DKK ($145–$164/£77–£87) double with bathroom. Rates include breakfast. No credit cards. **Amenities:** Restaurant; bar. *In room:* TV (in some), no phone.

Hotel Dagmar ★★★   The most famous hotel in Denmark outside Copenhagen is also the oldest in the country, dating from 1581. Converted from a private home in 1850, it's also the most glamorous hotel in South Jutland, taking its name from the medieval Danish queen. The bedrooms have been carefully restored, respecting the hotel's age while adding modern conveniences. Most of the units, as befits a building of this vintage, have low ceilings, sloping floors, and windows with deep sills. Textiles are in autumnal colors, and the walls are decorated with original paintings. Each bedroom is also individually decorated and comes in various shapes and sizes. Some of the rooms are equipped with slower-only bathrooms, others with complete old-fashioned bathtubs with sitz baths, and some of the accommodations even have phones in the bathrooms. Dagmar also offers the best food in Ribe; see "Where to Dine," below.

Torvet 1, DK-6760 Ribe. © **75-42-00-33.** Fax 75-42-36-52. www.hoteldagmar.dk. 50 units. 1,125DKK–1,525DKK ($191–$259/£101–£137) double. Rates include breakfast. AE, DC, MC, V. **Amenities:** 3 restaurants; bar; room service (7am–10pm); laundry service; dry cleaning; nonsmoking rooms. *In room:* TV, minibar, hair dryer, safe.

Hotel Fru Mathies *Value*   For those who like to travel the B&B route, this is one of the best choices in town—and extremely affordable. Set behind a bright yellow stucco facade, a very short walk from the city's pedestrian zone, this hotel was named after its present guardian and supervisor, *Fru* Inga Mathies. There's a shared TV/living room on the premises, and the small bedrooms are simple but cozy affairs, each with a bathroom equipped with a tub/shower combo and a modest number of old-fashioned accessories. Breakfast is the only meal served, and it's generous and satisfying, fit for-tification for a morning wandering the streets of Ribe.

Saltgade 15, DK-67660 Ribe. © **75-42-34-20.** 6 units, 4 with bathroom. 590DKK ($100/£53) double without bathroom; 640DKK ($109/£58) double with bathroom. Rates include breakfast. AE, DC, MC, V. **Amenities:** Breakfast room; bar; lounge. *In room:* TV, minibar, no phone.

WHERE TO DINE

Restaurant Backhaus DANISH   This place has served as a restaurant or an inn for as long as anyone in Ribe can remember. Today, steaming platters of all-Danish food arrive in generous portions at reasonable prices. Menu specialties include a Danish platter containing artfully arranged presentations of herring, cheeses, and vegetables that taste wonderful with the establishment's earthy, rough-textured bread. Tomato soup with sour cream comes with a surprising but refreshing dab of horseradish. The chef tells us that the most frequently ordered dish is tender pork schnitzels with boiled potatoes and braised red cabbage, a favorite of German visitors. However, we found that the sautéed strips of beef tenderloin with fried onions hit the spot better on one cold, windy, rainy day. Dessert might be a hazelnut pie with vanilla ice cream.

On the premises are seven simple rooms, stripped-down but comfortable hideaways that are well maintained. With breakfast included, doubles cost 500DKK ($85/£45). With the exception of about a week every year at Christmas, the hotel is open year-round.

Grydergade 12. ⓒ 75-42-11-01. Reservations recommended. Main courses 100DKK–170DKK ($17–$29/£9–£15). MC, V. Daily 11am–9:30pm. Closed 1 week around Christmas.

Restaurant Dagmar ⓡⓡ DANISH/INTERNATIONAL Honoring a beloved medieval queen, this restaurant opposite the cathedral is a major stopover for those making the gastronomic tour of Denmark. Its four dining rooms are a 19th-century dream of ornate furnishings and objets d'art, a tribute to the heyday of the Belle Epoque. In such fancy surroundings, they could get away with ordinary food, but the chefs showcase a varied cuisine that is refreshingly authentic in that it's based on the best of market-fresh ingredients in any season. Care, craftsmanship, and a concern for your palate go into every dish served by the best staff in town.

We opt for one of the two fresh North Sea fish dishes of the day as they are just caught and prepared with flavor without spoiling their natural taste. The scallops are topped with a sweet-potato crisp, and in autumn we go for the sautéed stuffed quail with mushrooms accompanied by beurre blanc sauce. We feel the chefs shine brighter with their regional cuisine, but they also borrow freely from international larders, serving a tender veal tenderloin with one of the tastiest shallow mousses we've ever sampled— plus a delectable port-wine sauce as well. Talk about gilding the lily.

In the Hotel Dagmar. ⓒ 75-42-00-33. Reservations required. Main courses 165DKK–265DKK ($28–$45/£15–£24); fixed-price lunch 200DKK ($34/£18). AE, DC, MC, V. Daily noon–10pm.

Restaurant Kammerslusen ⓡ *Finds* DANISH Quite by accident we discovered this place while driving through the marshlands, and we've been a loyal customer ever since. This restaurant lies between the seacoast and the canal that connects Ribe to the sea; to reach it, drive 15km (9⅓ miles) east of Ribe, across flat and sandy terrain, until you reach this red-brick, old-fashioned-looking hideaway. There's no public transport to this hotel. The cooking is always reliable and tasty, and it's easy to understand why this place has blossomed into a local favorite. Menu items derive from long-standing regional traditions, and include fried filets of eel with white sauce and new potatoes, poached red salmon with au gratin potatoes, and a popular house specialty of grilled steak with barbecue sauce and fried onions. There's nothing too fancy here, nothing you've not had before, but we like the congenial premises, the old-fashioned flavors, and the sense of a nostalgic charm that hangs over the place.

Bjerrumvej 30. ⓒ 75-42-07-96. Fax 75-42-29-32. Reservations recommended. Main courses 125DKK–250DKK ($21–$43/£11–£23); fixed-price menu 210DKK ($36/£19). DC, MC, V. Daily 11am–9pm.

Restaurant Sælhunden ⓡ DANISH/INTERNATIONAL One of the most evocative and cheerful restaurants in Ribe occupies a venerable but cozy brick building whose history goes back to 1634. Set beside the river that flows through Ribe, within full view of the craft that kept its commerce alive during its mercantile heyday, it has flourished as a restaurant since 1969. Today, you're likely to find an engaging staff hailing from every corner of Europe, and an old-fashioned format whose size is doubled during mild weather thanks to an outdoor terrace. The cuisine is based on fresh ingredients and, for the most part, sticks to tried-and-true favorites so beloved by the Danish palate, including smoked salmon or platters of ping-pong-size meatballs. The dish that most locals seem to order is the fried filets of plaice with boiled potatoes, a dish that—no doubt—their mamas made for them. Other items include at least three kinds of steaks that feature T-bone, French-style entrecôte, and something known as "English steak." A local delicacy is smoked and fried dab, a flat fish not unlike flounder that flourishes in the local estuaries. No one will mind if you come here just for a beer or a simple snack. In summertime, it's one of the closest approximations in town to the kind of beer garden you might expect to find in Hamburg.

Skibbroen 13. ⓒ 75-42-09-46. Reservations recommended. Main courses 136DKK–210DKK ($23–$36/£12–£19). MC, V. Daily 11am–10pm. Beer served till 11pm.

Weis Stue ⓐ DANISH   For old-fashioned dining in a mellow atmosphere of long ago, there is no better place in Ribe than this small, charming, brick-and-timber inn sitting on the market square near the cathedral and the Hotel Dagmar which owns it. Originally built in the 1500s, the half-timbered inn you see today dates mainly from 1704. The food here is plentiful and well prepared, based on the best from field, air, and stream.

When in Denmark, we always do as our fellow Danish diners do and launch a repast with marinated herring with raw onions and the always-divine little shrimp they serve with mayonnaise. For something more substantial, we join our fellow guests in feasting on smoked Greenland halibut with scrambled eggs, a local favorite, as is the liver paste with mushrooms. For more standard dishes, you can order a very good filet of beef flavored with onions. We ended our meal, as did our dining companions, with a selection of Danish cheese and almost found ourselves agreeing with our hosts—"It's the best in the world."

The inn also has four upstairs guest rooms that are cozy but don't have private bathrooms. A double costs 645DKK ($110/£58), including breakfast.

Torvet 2. ⓒ 75-42-07-00. Reservations recommended. Main courses 140DKK–195DKK ($24–$33/£13–£18); 2-course fixed-price menu 158DKK ($27/£14). AE, DC, MC, V. Daily 11am–10pm.

RIBE AFTER DARK

The Hotel Dagmar, on the market square, is the most happening place in Ribe. If it's winter, visit their cellar-level restaurant, **Vægterkælderen** (ⓒ 75-42-14-00), the place to enjoy a good meal in informal and traditional surroundings, or else to savor a glass of frothy, newly drawn ale in the company of locals. The kitchen serves homemade pickled herring, fresh fish dishes, and juicy steaks, but many locals just come in for a drink. In the summer months you might want to sit outside in the Dagmar's courtyard, enjoying the **Pavillionen** (ⓒ 75-42-00-33). Hot drinks are served on cooler days, but if it's hot you can order draft beer or lemonade. Light summer meals, including fresh fish, are served. You can listen to the bells in the cathedral tower, admire the storks in their nests, and, if you're still around at 10 o'clock at night, see the night watchman as he prepares for his rounds.

The market square is also the home of the **Stenbohus Pub & Bar,** entered at Stenbogade 1 (ⓒ 75-42-01-22), where live music can be heard at least once a week—folk, rock, soul, or blues. Otherwise, it's one of the most congenial taverns in town to meet locals over a glass of beer with a good head on it. Vægterkælderen (see above) is a classier joint for a drink; this one is more informal, attracting a more youthful crowd.

A SIDE TRIP TO MANDØ 🔊

The island of Mandø, 10km (6¼ miles) off the coast of Jutland southwest of Ribe, is one of the most tranquil island hideaways in Denmark. Surrounded by the Wadden Sea, it has remained almost untouched by tourism, partly because of the awkwardness involved in getting here. Other than privately owned watercraft, the only way to reach the island is via a bumpy stone-and-gravel drive (the Låningsvejen) that's completely submerged during high tide, usually twice a day.

Under normal conditions, and whenever seas aren't particularly rough, access is possible some 15 to 18 hours during every 24-hour period in summertime. The island itself is a low-lying marshland that's protected from erosion by a man-made dike that surrounds it. Massive sandbanks and dunes that are infertile, uninhabited, and completely surrounded by water during high tides, and that change their size and locations after storms, also protect the island.

To reach Mandø from Ribe, drive 10km (6¼ miles) southwest of town to the coastal hamlet of Vester Vedsted, which marks the beginning of the Låningsvejen. The distance from Vester Vedsted to Mandø is 11km (6¾ miles), of which 5.5km (3½ miles) are submerged by the high tides of the Wadden Sea. If you respect the clearly posted safety notices and the schedule of tides, a conventional car can make the trip out to Mandø without incident. You can also get there as a passenger in the **Mandø Bussen (Mandø Bus)**, a heavy-duty tractor-bus that's equipped with large-tread tires. It departs from the parking lot just to the west of Vester Vedsted at least twice a day May to September, charging 50DKK ($8.50/£4.50) per passenger. Except under optimum circumstances, it doesn't run at all from October to April. For information about departure times, call either the tourist office in Ribe (p. 318) or the Mandø Bussen at ✆ 75-44-51-07.

The first recorded mention of Mandø appeared in 1231, when it was claimed in its entirety by the Danish monarch. In 1741, the inhabitants purchased the island from the king at auction. Then, and throughout the rest of the 18th and 19th centuries, the island's men were involved with shipping while the women took care of the farms. In 1890, the island's population was 262; today, the island has a year-round population of only 70.

A few meters from where the bus stops in Mandø village stands **Mandøhuset** (✆ 75-42-60-52), an old skipper's home, now a lackluster museum of local artifacts. Entrance is 10DKK ($1.70/90p) adults and 5DKK (85¢/45p) children, and visits are possible Monday to Friday 10am to 4pm.

To the south stands **Mandø Kirke** (✆ 75-44-51-80), dating from 1639. The entrance costs 30DKK ($5.10/£2.70), but you have to call ahead to have the church opened. An old mill, built in 1860, can be seen in the northern part of the village.

"Birders" flock here to see thousands of breeding pairs, including eider ducks, sandpipers, and oystercatchers.

The tidal flats on the island are neither land nor sea. One moment they are dry, but for 6 hours a day they are covered by vast quantities of water. These flats are spawning grounds for several species of edible fish, including plaice and cod. It is estimated that every year 10 to 12 million birds fly over these tidal flats. These flats are Denmark's largest nature reserve. For those who like bird-watching, the spring and autumn migration periods are the best times to visit.

If you look anywhere to the southwest of Mandø, you'll get a view of what's sometimes referred to as Denmark's largest desert, an uninhabited expanse of sand dunes surrounded like an island by tidal flats that are submerged during high tides and storms. With borders and *prieler* (channels) whose positions are constantly changing because of storm and wave actions, the dunes and sand deposits are known as **Koresand.** Although a visit in winter is not advisable, during calm seas in summer, the site attracts ecologists and bird-watchers as part of twice-per-week half-day tours that are arranged by the same entrepreneurs who manage the above-mentioned **Mandø Bussen** (*©* **75-44-51-07** for reservations and departure times).

Tours depart from and return to Mandø in open trailers drawn by tractors that resemble the Mandø Bussen. En route, you'll pass some of the largest seal colonies in the Baltic. (These are most active during Aug.) You'll also be able to see the island of Rømø to the south and the island of Fanø to the northwest. There's usually a chance to search for amber on the beaches of Koresand, depending on the waves and the weather. The whole experience covers about 25km (16 miles) and takes about 2 hours, and the cost of the excursion is 70DKK ($12/£6.30) adults and 50DKK ($8.50/£4.50) children under 12.

6 Fanø ★★

47km (29 miles) NW of Ribe; 282km (175 miles) W of Copenhagen

Off the coast of South Jutland, Fanø, at least in our view, is the most beautiful of all North Sea islands—and we've sailed to all of them. It is the one place in Denmark which we most prefer for some R&R. Perhaps you will join us in the fun, which is what Fanø is all about. Go here to enjoy the outdoors and nature, ducking into the man-made attractions only if it's a rainy day.

Consisting of a landmass of some 54 sq. km (21 sq. miles), with a population of 3,500, it is known for its white sandy beaches, which have made it a popular holiday resort in summer. Set against a backdrop of heath-covered dunes, the best beaches are in the northwest, mostly in and around the hamlets of Rindby Strand and Fanø Bad.

Nordby, where the ferry arrives, is a logical starting point for exploring the island of Fanø. Here you'll find heather-covered moors, windswept sand dunes, fir trees, wild deer, and bird sanctuaries. From Ribe, Fanø makes for a great day's excursion (or longer if there's time).

Sønderho, on the southern tip, and only 14km (8⅔ miles) from Nordby, with its memorial to sailors drowned at sea, is our favorite spot—somewhat desolate, but that's its charm.

It was a Dutchman who launched Denmark's first bathing resort at Nordby in 1851. It consisted of a raft on which some bathing huts had been set up. The bathers entered the huts, undressed, put on different clothes, pulled down an awning to the water's surface, and bathed under the awning. How modest of them.

Until 1741 Fanø belonged to the king, who, when he ran short of money, sold the island at auction. The islanders themselves purchased it, and the king then granted permission for residents to build ships, which led to its prosperity. From 1741 to 1900, some 1,000 sailing vessels were constructed here, with the islanders often manning them as well. Inhabitants built many beautiful houses on Fanø with monies earned, and some of these thatched Fanø homes stand today to greet visitors. There are some charmers in the northern settlement of Nordby, but more gems in the south at Sønderho.

Although Nordby and Sønderho are the principal settlements, beach lovers head for the seaside resort of **Fanø Bad,** which is also a popular camping area. From Fanø Bad the beach stretches almost 4km (2½ miles) to the north. Bathing here is absolutely safe as a sandy bottom slopes gently into the North Sea, and there are no ocean holes and no dangerous currents.

Fanø adheres to old island traditions almost more than any other island in Denmark, with the exception of Ærø. As late as the 1960s some of the elderly women on Fanø still wore the "Fanø costume," the traditional dress, although today you'll see it only at special events and festivals. This dress originally consisted of five skirts, but today's costumes are likely to have only three. When the skirt was to be pleated, it was wet, laced up, and sent to the baker, who steamed it in a warm oven.

ESSENTIALS

GETTING THERE   By Car and Ferry   From Ribe, head north on Route 11 to Route 24. Follow Route 24 northwest to the city of Esbjerg, where you can board a ferry operated by **Scandlines** (© 70-10-17-44; www.scandlines.dk for information and schedules). May to October, ferries depart Esbjerg every 20 minutes during the day (trip time: 12 min.). In winter, service is curtailed, with departures during the day every 45 minutes. A round-trip ticket costs 30DKK ($5.10/£2.70) adults or 15DKK ($2.55/£1.35) children 5 to 15, and one average-size car, along with five passengers, is carried for 340DKK ($58/£31) round-trip.

VISITOR INFORMATION   The **Fanø Turistbureau,** Færgevej 1, Nordby (© 75-16-26-00), is open Monday to Friday 9am to 4pm, Saturday 9am to 1pm, and Sunday 11am to 1pm, except from June 6 to August 23, when hours are Monday to Friday 9am to 6pm, Saturday 9am to 7pm, and Sunday 9am to 5pm.

GETTING AROUND   By Bus   Local buses meet passengers at the ferry dock, crisscrossing the island about every 40 minutes, with vastly curtailed service in winter. The bus will take you to the communities of Nordby in the north and Sønderho in the south, with stops at Rindby Strand and Fanø Bad. For information, call **Fanø Rutebiler** at Sønderho (© 75-16-40-10), or pick up a bus timetable at the tourist office.

By Bicycle   Many visitors like to explore Fanø by bike, and rentals cost from 60DKK ($10/£5.40) per day, at **Unika Cykler,** Mellemgaden 12 (© 75-16-24-60).

SPECIAL EVENTS   A summer highlight on Fanø is **Fannikerdagene,** the second weekend in July, which offers traditional dancing, costumes, and events connected with the days when sailing ships played a major part in community life. If you miss the festival, try to be on Fanø the third Sunday in July for **Sønderho Day.** The high point of the festival day is a wedding procession that passes through the town to the square by the old mill. Traditional costumes and bridal dances are some of the attractions.

SEEING THE SIGHTS

Most explorations of the island begin where the ferry docks at the settlement of Nordby. While here, and before setting out to explore the rest of Fanø, you can stop in at the **Fanø Skibsfarts-og Dragtsamling** (Fanø Shipping & Costume Collection), Hovedgaden 28 (© 75-16-22-72). The museum traces the maritime heyday of the island in the 19th century, its boom period, when Fanø had the largest fleet outside of Copenhagen. Exhibits reveal that husbands often left their families for years at a time for a life at sea. The maritime collection incorporates many ship models, details of Fanø's fleet, and displays depicting a sailor's life aboard ship and in port. The costume collection shows both the working dress of the island women and those special costumes they wore for festivals. May to September, the museum is open daily 11am to 4pm. Off season, it's open Monday to Saturday 11am to 1pm. Admission is 15DKK ($2.55/£1.35) adults and 5DKK (85¢/45p) children under age 12.

Housed in a 300-year-old building, the **Fanø Museum,** Skolevej 2 (no phone), houses a comprehensive collection of period furniture, utensils, tools, and other island artifacts. There's also an exotic collection of mementos sailors have gathered on their voyages. The museum is open in June, Monday to Saturday 10am to 1pm, and July and August, Monday to Friday 11am to 4pm and Saturday 10am to 1pm. In September it's open Monday to Friday 10am to 1pm. Admission is 15DKK ($2.55/£1.35) adults, 5DKK (85¢/45p) children under age 12.

Near the most southerly tip of the island, in the settlement of Sønderho, you can visit the island's most beautiful building, **Sønderho Kirke,** Strandvejen (© 75-16-40-32), open daily during daylight hours, with free admission. The church has a strong maritime influence—in fact, it displays 14 votive ships, more than any other church in Denmark. The baroque altarpiece dates from 1717, the pulpit from 1661, and the organ loft with a painting from 1782. This is an assembly-hall church, seating some 800 members of a congregation.

While at Sønderho you can also visit **Fanø Kunstmuseum** (Fanø Art Museum) Norland 5 (© 75-16-40-44), which in 1992 opened in Kromanns Hus, a former store and factory. The old shop dating from 1868 has been restored and now serves as the entrance to the museum. Fanø attracted a number of artists who moved here, and this museum showcases their most outstanding paintings, the collection based on pictures first assembled by Ruth Heinemann, who founded an art association on Fanø. The museum shows art inspired by the Frisian coast, past and present, with both permanent and temporary exhibitions. April 3 to October, it is open Tuesday to Sunday 2 to 5pm, charging 25DKK ($4.25/£2.25) or 15DKK ($2.55/£1.35) children under age 12.

Less than half a kilometer (¼ mile) north of Sønderho, on the road to Nordby, stands the **Sønderho Mølle,** Vester Land 44 (© 75-16-44-29), a restored windmill. Once islanders were obliged to use the crown's mill at Ribe, but in 1701 they received permission to construct one here. Several mills have stood on this site since then, and one burned down in 1894 but was replaced by another the following year, which was in use until 1923. A preservation-minded group purchased the mill in 1928 and restored it. It's open to the public June 26 to August 29 and during October, daily 3 to 5pm; and from August 30 to September 30, Wednesday, Saturday, and Sunday 3 to 5pm. Admission is 15DKK ($2.55/£1.35) or 5DKK (85¢/45p) for children 11 and under.

Hannes Hus, Østerland 7 (© 75-16-44-29), is one of the most typical of old Fanø structures, and it's in Sønderho, which contains Denmark's highest proportion of protected buildings. Hannes Hus faithfully maintains the atmosphere of a 17th-century captain's home. Hanne, a captain's widow, and her daughter, Karen, lived here until 1965, when it was acquired by the Village Trust. Inside are original furnishings, a stove, pictures, a sheep stable, and souvenirs from the captain's travels. Here's your chance to see what a Fanø sailor's private home looked like. It's open July and August, daily 3 to 5pm, and September, Saturday and Sunday 3 to 5pm. Admission is 15DKK ($2.55/£1.35) adults, 5DKK (85¢/45p) children under age 12.

SHOPPING

For an antiques store, combined with a flea market, head for **Vestergårdens Antik,** Vestervejen 47 (© 75-16-68-00), also at Nordby. For the best collection of the tiles for which the island is known, shop at **Den lille butik,** Landevejen 3 (© **75-16-43-58**), at Sønderho. You'll also find an array of exquisite silk items, many of them hand-made, at **Jane Heinemann,** Landevejen 15 (© **75-16-42-90**), also at Sønderho. The best art gallery is at Sønderho: **Galleri Anne,** Østerland 15 (© **75-16-43-05**), is open in July and August, Monday to Friday noon to 3pm. Island artists are showcased here.

WHERE TO STAY

Fanø Krogaard (see "Where to Dine," below) also has some of the best rooms to rent on the island.

Hotel Fanø Badeland *(Kids)*   This hotel takes no chances with the quite likely possibility that fog or rain might ruin the swimming. Although it sits on Fanø's western edge, close to one of the best beaches on the island, it has the added benefit of a glass-enclosed complex of indoor pools creating an impressive array of year-round swimming options. Located 3km (1¾ miles) south of the hamlet of Nordby, it was built amid windswept scrubland. The midsize rooms are urban-looking, minimalist, and angular, with well-kept shower-only bathrooms and small kitchenettes nestled into the corners of the living rooms. Each has either one or two bedrooms outfitted with simple, durable furniture and no-nonsense accessories. The atmosphere is rather impersonal, not snug and cozy, but it's perfectly suited for families who want to spend most of their time outdoors, enjoying comfortable living and plenty of facilities when they nestle in for the night. You'll pay an additional 65DKK ($11/£5.85) per person for a package containing sheets and towels, unless you opt to bring your own.

Strandvejen 52–56, DK-6720 Fanø. © **75-16-60-00.** Fax 75-16-60-11. www.fanoebadeland.dk. 126 units, each with kitchenette. 820DKK–945DKK ($139–$161/£74–£85) 1-bedroom unit for up to 4 occupants; 925DKK–1,225DKK ($157–$208/£83–£110) 2-bedroom unit for up to 6 occupants. Discounts offered for stays of 5 nights or more. MC, V. Bus: 631. **Amenities:** Restaurant; bar; swimming complex; tennis court; fitness center; sauna; room service (8am–10pm); laundry service; dry cleaning. *In room:* TV.

Sønderho Kro *(★★★)*   This is an unbeatable choice. Dating from 1722, it is one of Denmark's oldest inns—not only that, but one of its most charming and atmospheric. A Relais & Châteaux property, the thatch-roof inn in the heart of the village of Sønderho is the best we've ever encountered in South Jutland. There's also a beautiful garden where guests drink and dine on a summer night in the shade of towering trees.

Niels and Birgit Steen Sørensen are the "hosts with the mostest" on Fanø, pampering guests and feeding and housing them in elegant style. The building is under the protection of the National Museum, which closely supervised its expansion in 1977. Each of the bedrooms comes in a different shape and size, and each is individually decorated in a tasteful way, complete with a modern private bathroom with tub/shower combo. The windows open onto views over a nearby dike, the marshlands, and the North Sea. Lace curtains, lovely tapestries, and four-poster beds add to the old-fashioned allure.

Guests meet in the first-floor lounge, opening onto views of tidal flats. The *kro* (inn) lies 13km (8 miles) south of the Nordby ferry dock, where a bus carries nonmotorists the final distance into Sønderho.

Kropladsen 11, Sønderho, DK-6720 Fanø. © **75-16-40-09.** Fax 75-16-43-85. www.sonderhokro.dk. 13 units. 1,030DKK–1,410DKK ($175–$240/£93–£127) double. Rates include full breakfast. AE, DC, MC, V. Free parking. **Amenities:** Restaurant; lounge; room service (7am–10pm); laundry service; dry cleaning. *In room:* TV, hair dryer.

WHERE TO DINE

Café Nanas Stue ⭐ *Finds* DANISH

If it's a summer night and you're on Fanø, head to this 1855 half-timbered farmhouse for a rollicking good time. It's likely that a group of local musicians will be playing typical island music using such instruments as the harmonica and the bagpipe. You get not only entertainment, but a display of tiles as well: The cafe is also the site of the **Fanø Tile Museum,** and its walls and hand-made wood cupboards are filled with Dutch blue-and-white tiles brought by Fanø sailors from the 1600s to the 1800s. Each tile depicts a representational scene, often taken from the Bible.

Wooden tables fill up with both islanders and visitors who come here to enjoy a typical Fanø kitchen that offers regional specialties. At lunch you can partake of those Danish open-faced sandwiches—count on three making a really satisfying meal. At night you can enjoy more elaborate fare such as a tender and perfectly cooked pepper steak topped with a cognac sauce. Other tasty dishes include shrimp and salmon with asparagus or else a "Paris steak" with such accompaniments as horseradish and capers. Most habitués finish off their repast by asking the bartender to make his specialty, which is a powerful *akvavit* ("water of life") flavored with coffee beans, vanilla, and orange zest.

Sønderland 1. ☎ 75-16-40-25. Reservations recommended. Main courses 95DKK–148DKK ($16–$25/£8.55–£13). MC, V. July–Sept Tues–Sat 11am–midnight, Sun 11am–5pm; off season Fri–Sun 5pm–midnight.

Fanø Krogaard ⭐ DANISH

Set within 90m (295 ft.) of the point where ferry-boats arrive from the Danish "mainland," this is one of the most historic inns on the island. Originally built of russet-colored bricks in 1624, with a rich patina that has accumulated thanks to many generations of diners and drinkers, it offers three cramped but cozy dining rooms that specialize exclusively in Danish food. The market-fresh cuisine is satisfyingly good, reasonably priced, well prepared, and nutritious, served by an extremely efficient and congenial waitstaff. You'll find the usual array of herring, fried beef with onions, and roasted chicken you'd expect in such a conservative setting. But you'll also find a house specialty of roasted rack of veal with a cream sauce, fresh green beans, two kinds of potatoes, and a garnish that's a hollowed-out apple filled with red currant jelly. Desserts are sumptuous, and the wine *carte* is well chosen but pricey. The old *kro* also rents 17 units, each attractively furnished with comfortable pieces and each with a well-kept bathroom with a tub/shower combo. With breakfast and dinner included, double rooms range from 595DKK to 735 DKK ($101–$125/£53–£66) per person; suites from 695DKK to 835DKK ($118–$142/£63–£76) per person.

Langelinie 11, Nordby. ☎ 75-16-20-52. Reservations recommended. Main courses 150DKK–200DKK ($26–$34/£13.50–£18). AE, DC, MC, V. May–Sept Sun–Thurs noon–midnight, Fri–Sat noon–1am; Oct–Apr Mon–Thurs 3–11pm, Fri 3pm–midnight, Sat noon–midnight, Sun noon–11pm.

Kromann's Fisherestaurant DANISH/GERMAN

Far from the fancy *kros* of Fanø, this is a local hangout where the cookery is solid, filling, reliable, and afford-able—nothing more, nothing less. But isn't that enough? In the heart of the village, near its famous church, this restaurant occupies a red-brick building originally constructed as a private house during the early years of World War I. Menu items include a wide roster of meats and fish, especially plaice and salmon, which the chef prepares in any of at least three different ways. There are also shrimp, crayfish, and fried eel served in the traditional way—with potatoes and parsley. Obviously there's nothing served that taxes the imagination of the chef, but the food is fresh and well flavored.

Kropladsen, Sønderho. © **75-16-44-45.** Reservations recommended. Main courses 110DKK–170DKK ($19–$29/ £9.90–£15). No credit cards. Easter–Oct daily 11am–midnight. Closed Nov–Easter.

Sønderho Kro 🐸🐸🐸 INTERNATIONAL   Over the years we have found no finer cuisine in South Jutland than that served here. It's as bracing and fresh as the North Sea breezes that blow this way. A Relais & Châteaux property, this is the most prestigious and elegant restaurant on the island. The setting is adjacent to the harbor within what was established as an inn in 1722; it has gained steadily in influence and glamour ever since. Your meal is likely to include some form of smoked fish, prepared in-house with smoke from juniper wood, in a custom-built oven whose construction was inspired by designs perfected by the Inuit of Greenland.

Only the best local produce is used by the hotel chefs, who make their own jams and preserves. You can purchase some of the hotel's products to take home—like strawberry jam with almonds and French black-currant liqueur. All of their dishes are superb, especially some of the best beef sausage you are likely to taste—it's also smoked with juniper wood. A juniper schnapps sausage and a superb smoked leg of lamb are also likely to be offered. These meats are without artificial coloring and have a low-fat content. Move on to an array of perfectly prepared dishes, a splendid gourmet feast that comes as a surprise in a country inn. Save room also for one of the harmoniously composed desserts. The international wine list is no less delightful than the friendly, efficient service.

Kropladsen 11, Sønderho. © **75-16-40-09.** Reservations necessary. Main courses 235DKK–255DKK ($40–$43/ £21–£23); fixed-price menus 298DKK–378DKK ($51–$64/£27–£34). AE, DC, MC, V. Apr–Sept daily noon–2:30pm and 6–9pm; Oct–Mar Thurs–Tues noon–2:30pm and 6–9pm.

FANØ AFTER DARK

Your best bet is any event sponsored by the **Fanø Jazzklub,** Bavnebjergtoft 7 (© **75-16-28-52**), at Fanø. The club has various events in summer, and the tourist office keeps a schedule. Tickets cost 80DKK ($14/£7.20) and can be purchased at the door.

Don't expect glitter or glamour on Fanø, as virtually everyone who lives here seems to believe in honest industry and an early-to-bed kind of entertainment agenda. For an after-dark diversion in Nørdby, head for the previously recommended **Fanø Krogaard,** Langelinie 11 (© **75-16-20-52**), which has a cozy bar and a cold-weather fireplace to keep you warm when the North Sea winds blow in. In Sønderho, a fun bar is **Nanas Stue** (© **75-16-40-25**), which is lively and comfy with live music and good food.

11

Central Jutland

The central part of Jutland cuts across a broad swath of the country, extending from the gateway city of Fredericia in the south to Viborg and Limfjord (a large inland fjord) in the north. The east side of Central Jutland is more populous than the west, which is a wide plain of windswept moors bordered by a rugged coastline of beach flats and sand dunes.

Small farms and rich fertile land characterize the rolling hills of the central belt's eastern shores. But since the 19th century, much of the land in the west has also been reclaimed; great parts of it have been transformed into pastureland and fields against the competition of North Sea winds.

Central Jutland contains some of the most sparsely populated regions of Denmark, although it has cities too—notably Århus (the largest city in the region), as well as Silkeborg, Randers, and others.

It is also one of the most hospitable regions of Denmark. Locals are proud of a landscape that ranges from wide expanses of heath to lovely fields of heather to charming towns. Central Jutland also has some of the best beaches in Denmark, with vast stretches of white sand. Art museums, galleries, concerts, and beautiful old churches add to the allure.

The best towns in east Central Jutland are Jelling, Vejle, and Århus. If you'd like to base your travels in the Lake District, favorite spots include Ebeltoft, Silkeborg, and Ry. In the interior, Randers makes the best stopover, and if you want a base on the central west coast, make it Ringkøbing.

Jelling is one of the most historic spots in Denmark, and **Legoland** is Jutland's most visited attraction. The liveliest and most diverse cultural scene is found in Århus, Denmark's second-largest city with some quarter of a million residents.

For rail and bus information to any town, call ✆ **70-13-14-15.**

1 Vejle ⟨★

199km (124 miles) W of Copenhagen; 72km (45 miles) SW of Århus; 30km (19 miles) N of Kolding; 25km (16 miles) NW of Fredericia; 27km (17 miles) E of Billund

Admittedly, there are more enticing destinations in Central Jutland than the ancient old city of Vejle. But there is a certain charm here which you'll soon discover if you stop over for 2 or 3 hours.

The setting of the city is spectacular, set against a backdrop of tree-clad hills facing the Kattegat, that body of water that separates the island of Funen from mainland Jutland. Lying near the top of the blue waters of the Vejle Fjord, the thriving town invites hikes into its tall wooded slopes, fertile dales, and deep gorges. This area of Central Jutland has long been known for its scenic beauty and hilly countryside, and Vejle is smack in the middle of it.

One evocative moment we experienced in Vejle was the chiming of an old Dominican monastery clock. The clock still chimes even though its monastery is gone with the wind, having given way in the 1800s to the construction of the town's imposing City Hall.

Lying in a sheltered hollow, the city has a thriving economy based on exports of sausage, textiles, and chewing gum, among other products, as well as an ever-increasing tourist industry. Highway 3 goes through the town, and the railway also brings passengers and goods here.

Vejle is close to the coast of East Jutland, and lies north of Kolding and northwest of Fredericia. The entire Vejle region stretches from the Vejle Fjord through Grejsdalen to Jelling, going through the river valley of Vejle Adal to Egtved.

The town was granted its charter in 1327. But wars with Prussia hurt its economy, and Vejle suffered great hardship in the 1600s due to the Black Plague and economic deprivation brought on by wars. In the 1820s the construction of a new harbor brought it increased prosperity. By that time, the making of *akvavit* (schnapps) played an important role in its economy. In the wars of the 19th century with Schleswig-Holstein in the south, Vejle was occupied several times by German troops, and until 1956, it was a garrison town.

ESSENTIALS

GETTING THERE   By Train   Trains arrive frequently throughout the day from Copenhagen, as Vejle is on the main Jutland line. The town also has good rail links to the other major towns in Jutland—it's only 45 minutes by rail to Århus or 35 minutes to Kolding.

By Car   If you've used Fredericia as your gateway to Central Jutland, follow Route 28 northwest into Vejle.

VISITOR INFORMATION   The **Vejle-Egnens Turistbureau,** Banegårdspladsen 6 (© 75-82-19-55; www.visitvejle.dk), is open June to August, Monday to Friday 9:30am to 5:30pm, Saturday 9:30am to 1:30pm; off season, Monday to Thursday 10am to 5pm, Friday 10am to 4:30pm, Saturday 10am to noon.

SEEING THE SIGHTS

Charming small squares, old houses, courtyards, and pedestrian streets provide the town center with a distinctive atmosphere. Even from the center of town, there are views of the blue waters of Vejle Fjord and its forest-clad hills.

The chief attraction is **Sankt Nicolai Kirke** ✸, Kirketorvet (© 75-82-41-39; www.aabenraasogn.dk), a 10-minute walk from the tourist office. The Gothic church is one of the town's oldest buildings, its north wall dating back to the mid–13th century. The church contains one of Denmark's finest bog findings, an **Iron Age woman** ✸✸ from 450 B.C., discovered in the Haraldskaier bog in 1835. She can be seen through a glass-topped case. Many guidebooks report that this is the preserved body of the Viking queen Gunhilde. However, recent scientific studies have shown that the corpse is much older, dating from the early Iron Age. The skulls of 23 beheaded robbers caught in the Nørreskoven woods some 3 centuries ago have been gruesomely bricked into the outer north wall of the church. Special features of the church include a classical reredos (the screen behind the altar), the work of sculptor Jens Hiernoe in 1791, plus a 16th-century Renaissance pulpit and a processional crucifix. Admission free, it's open Monday to Friday 9am to 5pm, Saturday and Sunday 9am to noon.

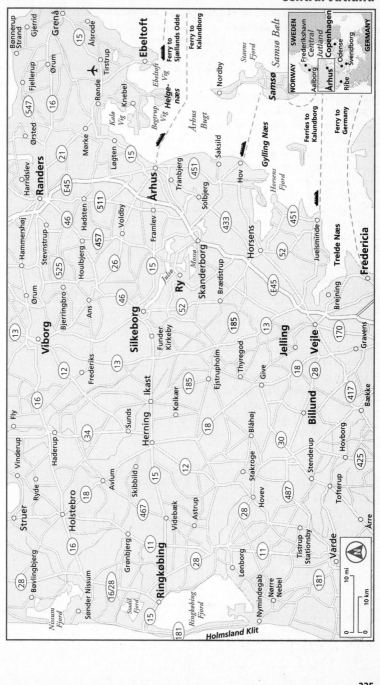

Vejle Kunstmuseum ✸, Flegborg 16 (℃ **75-72-31-99;** www.vejlekunstmuseum.dk), comes as a surprise for such a provincial town. Many large Danish towns have provincial art museums, but it's rare to find works by such famous Old Masters. Of course, Danish art from the beginning of the 20th century to the millennium is the one primarily showcased. The museum's prize is a remarkable **self-portrait of Rembrandt** ✸✸ dating from 1563. Founded back in 1899, the museum houses some 12,000 prints and drawings, including foreign prints from 1450 to 1800. The treasure-trove here is 2,000 prints and drawings, forming the **Eckardts Sambling Collection** ✸✸, donated at the turn of the 20th century, providing the reason for the museum to come into existence. The collection comprises Old Master prints by Albrecht Dürer, among others, and there are some 50 prints from Rembrandt alone. Just to see this collection is reason enough to visit the museum in the first place. Landscape painting is a strong feature here, including some rare art from the Danish-affiliated and faraway Faroe Islands. Charging no admission, the museum is open Tuesday to Friday 10am to 3pm.

A far less intriguing museum, **Vejle Museum,** Flegborg 18 (℃ **75-72-31-99;** www. vejlekunstmuseum.dk), adjacent to the art museum, could be skipped if time is running short. It also was founded in 1899, offering an exhibit called "Man and Nature— Archaeology in the Vejle Area." Exhibits trace the history of Vejle over the past 8 centuries, including life in the Middle Ages, Vejle as a 17th-century theater of war, and, finally, Vejle's rise as an industrial town. We were not overly enchanted, but you might find it of passing interest. Admission free, the museum is open Tuesday to Sunday 10am to 4pm.

For your farewell to Vejle, you can take a moving stairway in town up to the "mountain" known as **Munkebjerg,** to the southeast of Vejle. At an elevation of 90m (300 ft.), you'll enjoy a panoramic view of Vejle and the fjord. The yew—that most Scandinavian of trees—and other rare trees and plants can be seen here.

If you have a car, arm yourself with a good map (available at the tourist office) and explore **Grejsdalen,** 7km (4⅓ miles) from Vejle. This valley is one of Denmark's most beautiful areas, with densely wooded hillsides and many lookout points. The preserved part of the valley is also the home of a richly varied bird life. Near Grejs itself are some limestone deposits resembling cliff caverns.

SHOPPING

The main pedestrian zone in the heart of town features more than 220 specialty shops, restaurants, and department stores, so there's a wealth of shopping opportunities here, more so than nearly any other place in Jutland.

The best and most innovative ceramics are sold at **Ulla Møller,** Havnegade 21 (℃ **75-83-71-21**). For a gift shop featuring local crafts, head to **Allehånde,** Søndergade 14 (℃ **75-83-83-66**).

WHERE TO STAY

Best Western Torvehallerne ✸   Its construction in 1993 was viewed as a vital part of the success of the Torvehallerne—Vejle's largest conglomeration of cultural, dining, drinking, and nightlife facilities. Consequently, in any season or weather you'll be able to migrate from your room at this three-story hotel through the big-windowed, greenhouse-inspired spaces of the market hall for diversions of the kind you might expect in a mall in California. Rooms are well maintained and comfortable, and contain angular, modern furnishings that are both comfortable and tasteful, along with small private bathrooms with neatly tiled shower units. In spite of its charms, we still gravitate to the Munkebjerg.

In the Torvehallerne, Kirketorvet 12, DK-7100 Vejle. ℂ **800/528-1234** in the U.S., or 79-42-79-10. Fax 79-42-79-01. www.torvehallerne.dk. 43 units. 1,195DKK ($203/£108) double. Rate includes breakfast. AE, MC, V. **Amenities:** 2 restaurants; bar; 24-hr. room service; laundry service; dry cleaning; nonsmoking rooms; rooms for those w/limited mobility. *In room:* TV, dataport, minibar, hair dryer.

Munkebjerg Hotel 🏨🏨 This is the most stylish and prestigious hotel in the region, with the most panoramic setting, and a professional and sensitive staff that's capable of dealing with delicate temperaments. South of the center, it sits in isolated but contemporary grandeur on a panoramic hilltop within the Munkebjerg Forest. Originally built in 1967, and renovated and enlarged many times since, it's the preferred stopover for clients as diverse as Little Richard and Chuck Berry, as well as the prime minister of Denmark. Expect dramatic, impeccably maintained public areas in a big-windowed and angular modern style, and very comfortable, soothing accommodations that range from midsize to spacious. Rooms are flooded with sunlight thanks to sliding glass windows, and offer private balconies overlooking the forest. The furniture is soft and comfortable, with deep cushions, and each midsize bathroom has a tub and shower. From the three large suites with Jacuzzi and a separate living room, there is a panoramic view of the fjord.

Munkebjergvej 125, DK-7100 Vejle. ℂ **76-42-85-00.** Fax 75-72-08-86. www.munkebjerg.dk. 158 units. 1,485DKK–1,885DKK ($252–$320/£134–£170) double; 2,985DKK–3,685DKK ($507–$626/£269–£332) suite. Rates include buffet breakfast. AE, DC, MC, V. From Vejle's center, drive 7km (4⅓ miles) south, following the signs to Vejle Sid. **Amenities:** 3 restaurants; 2 bars; indoor heated pool; gym; sauna; room service (7am–10pm); babysitting; laundry service; dry cleaning; nonsmoking rooms; casino. *In room:* TV, dataport, minibar, hair dryer.

Quality Hotel Australia 🏨🏨🏨 This is one of the most modern and state-of-the-art hotels in Central Jutland, and is even better than the superb Munkebjerg. It rises 11 stories and is in a central location in the heart of town. Originally built in 1958, and radically upgraded in 1996, the hotel has a name that derives from its creator's fascination with Australia, thanks to the many trips he took there. As such, the hotel has (unofficially) spurred a flood of Danish visitors to Australia. Inside, you'll find all the amenities that several corporations would need to host simultaneous conventions. Public areas are spacious and modern. The public lounges are also spacious and decorated in Danish modern, as are the midsize-to-large bedrooms, which are well maintained and both comfortably and tastefully furnished, with small bathrooms coated with tiles and equipped with showers. Because of its first-class restaurant on-site, many visitors eat in at night.

Dæmningen 6, DK-7100 Vejle. ℂ **76-40-60-00.** Fax 76-40-60-01. www.choicehotels.dk/hotels/dk014. 102 units. 1,175DKK–1,275DKK ($200–$217/£106–£115) double; extra bed 200DKK ($34/£18). Rates include breakfast. AE, DC, MC, V. **Amenities:** Restaurant; bar; exercise room; sauna; room service (7am–10pm); babysitting; laundry service; dry cleaning; nonsmoking rooms; 1 room for those w/limited mobility. *In room:* TV, dataport, Wi-Fi, minibar, hair dryer, trouser press, iron.

WHERE TO DINE

Treetops Restaurant 🏨🏨 DANISH/INTERNATIONAL This restaurant in the previously recommended Munkebjerg Hotel is celebrated throughout the region for its contemporary glamour and its devotion to fine cuisine. A meal is always prefaced with a guided tour of the establishment's wine cellar, where a glass of something tasty is part of the experience. After that, a table is prepared within a high-ceilinged room that's spanned with artfully arranged tree limbs that provide a cozy, forest-like tone.

Menu items change frequently, but count on the ingredients being first-rate and market fresh. Finely balanced sauces are one of the culinary highlights here. Our appetizer contained two of our favorite foods—smoked salmon and foie gras. For a hearty regional dish guaranteed to put hair on your chest, try the breast of goose with pork jaw. More tempting to most diners are a succulent version of filet of lamb roasted with garlic and served with a lemongrass sauce or tournedos of veal with ratatouille and a flavoring of balsamic vinegar. The pastry chef always manages to delight with such concoctions as white chocolate mousse with mango and pistachio.

In the Munkebjerg Hotel, Munkebjergvej 125. (℃) 76-42-85-00. Reservations required. 4-course fixed-price menu 555DKK ($94/£50); 8-course fixed-price menu 750DKK ($128/£68). AE, DC, MC, V. Daily 6:30–9:30pm. From Vejle's center, drive 7km (4⅓ miles) south, following the signs to Vejle Sid and the Munkebjerg Hotel.

VEJLE AFTER DARK

At the **Casino Munkebjerg Vejle,** Munkebjergvej 125 (℃ **76-43-50-00**), you can play roulette, blackjack, the slot machines, and—if you're willing to learn—"Viking poker." A photo ID is required to gain entrance and there is an admission fee of 50DKK ($8.50/£4.50). The major cultural venue for the city is the **Musik Theatret Vejle,** Vedelsgade 25–31 (℃ **79-43-20-20**), the setting for operas, musicals, shows, and theater. You can check with the tourist office (see "Visitor Information," above) to see if any events at the time of your visit appeal to you.

Also consider a visit to the complex **Torvehallerne,** Kirketorvet 10–16 (℃ **79-42-79-00**). A large, spacious palm garden, Væksthuset, forms the center of a complex that includes restaurants, a hotel, a cafe, a stage, and a pub. There is always something going on here—jazz, dancing under the palm trees, concerts, or theatrical performances. We can't predict what will be going on at the time of your visit, but it's always a lively place to drop in on at night.

Vejle is also a town rich in pub life, our favorite being **Seven Oaks,** an old English-style pub at Dæmningen 42G (℃ **75-72-07-77**). Another good choice is the dance club **Crazy Daisy,** Nørregade 65–67 (℃ **75-83-23-03**).

2 Jelling ⟨⋆

11km (6¾ miles) NW of Vejle; 144km (89 miles) W of Copenhagen

It seems almost impossible to wander this sleepy little village today and realize that it was the site of riotous pagan festivals and celebrations. At the peak of the Viking era, a thousand years ago, Jelling was the Danish Royal Seat, the birthplace of the Danish monarchy. Although the site of Gorm the Old's castle has never been discovered, he was the first in a millennium-long string of Danish kings that continues today in an unbroken line to Queen Margrethe herself.

Gorm the Old and his son, the amusingly named "Harald Bluetooth," left behind two large burial mounds and two runic stones from their reigns. In 1994 these Viking monuments were declared a World Heritage Site. Bluetooth is a towering figure in Danish history, having driven the Swedes from his lands and having begun the conversion of his people from pagan rituals to Christianity. See the box "Discovering a Viking Past" (below) for more details.

Most visitors come for the meager glimpse into the secrets of the Viking era, but some remain to wander around the village of Jelling itself, which enjoys idyllic surroundings set against a backdrop of forests and lakes.

Discovering a Viking Past

In the center of town, **Jelling Kirke** ⛪ (📞 **75-87-16-28**) was erected at the beginning of the 12th century, and is one of the oldest churches in Denmark. The church is visited mainly because of its two well-preserved runic stones, which sit outside the door. You should look inside the church as well to see its restored 12th-century frescoes. Admission is free, and the church is open Monday to Friday 10am to 5pm, and Saturday 10am to 2pm. It's closed for visits on Sunday because of Mass. You can attend Mass then, but casual sightseeing in the church is discouraged when it's being used as a place of worship.

Both **Gorm the Old** (883–940) and his son, **Harald Bluetooth** (935–85), lived in Jelling, and they left behind two large burial mounds and two runic stones—one small, one large. The small stone bears the inscription "King Gorm made these sepulchral monuments to Thyra, his wife, the grace of Denmark." The large stone is inscribed "King Harald had these sepulchral monuments made to Gorm, his father, and Thyra, his mother, the Harald who conquered all Denmark and Norway and made the Danes Christians."

The latter part of the inscription has often been called Denmark's baptismal certificate, though this is something of an exaggeration. But King Harald and his people were undoubtedly converted to Christianity, even if it was a century before the country as a whole can be said to have become Christian.

The north's oldest depiction of Christ is seen over this part of Harald's runic lettering. The Christlike figure appears with his arms spread out but without a cross. This may have been because the artist at the time wanted to depict Christ as a victorious Viking king—hence no cross. The significance of the other depiction on the stone isn't known. It shows a snake locked in deadly combat with a mythical animal. The stones, decorated in the typical Viking style, with interlacing leaf and creeper-work, were originally painted in bright colors.

Excavations of the two barrows began in 1820, when the north barrow was dug up. It revealed a burial chamber but no human remains, only a few objects and fragments, including a silver goblet, later dubbed the Jelling goblet. It's thought that grave robbers may have plundered the site over the years. In 1861 King Frederik VII, who had a keen interest in archaeology, excavated the south barrow, but it didn't even have a burial chamber. It is now believed that both Gorm and Thyra had been buried in the north mound and that the empty south barrow was merely a memorial mound.

In modern times, the area beneath the church was excavated, and archaeologists discovered the remains of three wooden churches. The oldest was King Harald's and was even bigger than the present Jelling Kirke, earning the nickname "the Cathedral of the Viking Age."

The discovery of a burial chamber beneath the choral arch revealed human bones, but they were in complete disorder, indicating that they had been moved. The skeletal remains are believed to be those of Gorm, which were probably moved over from the north mound when Harald became Christian. It has never been determined where Queen Thyra was reburied.

ESSENTIALS

GETTING THERE **By Train and Bus** Jelling is a 20-minute train ride from Vejle on the run to Struer and Herning. Trains depart about once an hour Monday to Friday, less frequently on weekends. Connections are possible by bus no. 211 from Vejle's bus station.

By Car From Vejle, take Route A18 north. If you're using Fredericia as your gateway to Central Jutland, go to Vejle first, then continue into Jelling.

VISITOR INFORMATION **Jelling Turistbureau,** Gormsgade 23 (© **75-87-13-01;** www.visitvejle.com), is open daily June to August, 10am to 5pm. At other times of the year, contact the tourist office at Vejle (see "Visitor Information," above).

WHERE TO STAY

Jelling Kro 🌟 *Value* The most evocative and appealing hotel in town occupies the dignified yellow-fronted premises of what has functioned since 1780 as a *kro* (old-fashioned inn). Capped with a terra-cotta roof and positioned in the center of town, across from the country's most famous burial site, the hotel offers a well-recommended restaurant (see "Where to Dine," below). Each of the comfortable, well-maintained rooms is slightly different from its neighbor, and all have a shared bathroom. If you opt to stay in this hotel, know in advance that you'll share it with good company. In 1842, just before an overnight visit from the Danish king, it was reclassified as one of only about 30 hotels in Denmark suitable then and thereafter for overnight visits from a Danish monarch.

Gormsgade 16, DK-7300 Jelling. © **75-87-10-06.** Fax 75-87-10-08. www.jellingkro.dk. 6 units, all without bathroom. 495DKK ($84/£45) double. Rates include breakfast. AE, MC, V. Bus: 214. **Amenities:** Restaurant. *In room:* TV, no phone.

WHERE TO DINE

Jelling Kro 🌟 *Value* DANISH Good, wholesome cookery greets visitors in Jelling to pay homage to a Viking past. The most appealing restaurant in Jelling is in the previously recommended hotel. The dining room is much more modern than the historic setting would imply. Menu items usually stress fish that's parceled out into several kinds of platters, served either as a starter or in a more elaborate form as a main course configured into a "symphony of fish." Although the composition of each platter changes according to availability, you can almost always expect an emphasis on marinated salmon and fresh shrimp. Other excellent dishes include cream of leek soup with bacon, tournedos of beef garnished with mushroom stew and potato dish of the day, or breast of chicken with white-wine sauce.

Gormsgade 16. © **75-87-10-06.** Reservations recommended. Main courses 140DKK–195DKK ($24–$33/£13–£18); fixed-price menus 220DKK–250DKK ($37–$43/£20–£23). AE, MC, V. June–Aug daily 5–9pm; Sept–May Wed–Sun 5–9pm.

3 Billund 🌟 & Legoland 🌟🌟

228km (142 miles) W of Copenhagen; 59km (37 miles) NE of Esbjerg; 27km (17 miles) W of Vejle

The "Disneyland of Denmark," Legoland, an amusement park less than a kilometer (about ½ mile) north of the small Central Jutland town of Billund, is the second-most-visited tourist attraction in the country, after Tivoli in Copenhagen. Since it opened in 1968, some 28 million visitors from around the world have arrived. It can be a lot of fun if you're traveling as a family. Adults exploring Denmark without children in tow might want to seek other diversions (unless, of course, they are hard-core Lego aficionados).

ESSENTIALS

GETTING THERE **By Plane** Planes fly into **Billund Airport,** just across the road from Legoland—a 5-minute walk from the arrival lounge to the park. **SAS** (© **800/ 221-2350** in North America, or 32-32-22-33 in Billund; www.scandinavian.net) has frequent daily flights from Copenhagen (26 flights a week from Copenhagen). **Sterling Airlines** (© **70-10-84-84;** www.sterling.dk) has direct flights from London and Stockholm, to Billund.

By Bus There is no train service. Rail passengers get off at Vejle (see earlier), then take a bus marked LEGOLAND for the final lap of the journey. In summer, more buses run from Vejle, and there is also bus service from Esbjerg (© **75-16-26-00**).

By Car After crossing the bridge linking Funen and Jutland, continue northwest toward Vejle on the E20, linking up with Route 18, which connects with Route 28 going west into Billund.

LEGOLAND ⓖ

Legoland theme park (www.legoland.dk) is constructed from—what else?—plastic Lego blocks, and boasts 50 "fun activities." The greatest attraction is Castleland, which opened in 1997. Home to the King's Castle, a faux-medieval fairy-tale castle, it offers an action-adventure ride on one of two 212-seat "dragons" that fly around this re-created world. On the upper floor is the Knight's Barbecue, a restaurant decorated with suits of armor and shields.

Miniland is the second major attraction, with miniature models of famous buildings and monuments from around the world. The entire medieval town of Ribe is re-created, for example, as is Amalienborg Castle in Copenhagen. Other thematic attractions in the park include Legoredo Town, a re-creation of a western town with an Indian camp and a sheriff's office, plus Pirateland, where you can take a boat trip through caves. There's even a Lego Safari, where children steer small zebra-striped jeeps on a ride through a faux savanna. There are dozens of amusement rides, mostly for children, including merry-go-rounds and Ferris wheels. All the rides, including the miniature train and boat trips, are included in one admission price.

Hours are subject to change based on seasonal and weather conditions. Always call for the latest information before heading here. In general, the park is open Monday to Friday in April, May, September, and October from 10am to 8pm. In June and the last days of August, it is usually open daily 10am to 8pm. At the time of peak visitation, July to late August, hours are daily 10am to 9pm. Admission is 225DKK ($38/£20) for those 13 and over, or 195DKK ($33/£18) for ages 3 to 12; free for children 2 and under. For more information, call © **75-33-13-33.**

WHERE TO STAY

Hotel Legoland ⓖ *Kids* As the manager boasted to us, "The family that goes to Legoland together stays together." This is the only hotel associated with Jutland's most famous theme park, and as such, it does a thriving summer business renting overnight accommodations to families with children. In fact, we find it the most kid-friendly hotel in Denmark. During the winter, the clientele shifts to more of a business-oriented crowd that checks in as part of an ongoing schedule of corporate conventions.

It was originally built in 1968, and it's predictably permeated with a Legoland theme. There are lots of Disney-style Legoland sculptures in the lobby, and a chipper and perky multilingual staff that's often preoccupied with the care, feeding, and amusement of children. Like everything else in Legoland, a bit of this goes a long way, especially if you happen to be traveling without children. Rooms have less of an emphasis on the Legoland theme than you'll find in the public areas. Suites are larger, and contain minibars. Each accommodation comes with a private bathroom—some with tub and shower, others with just shower. In 2000, the hotel opened up an additional wing with 22 "Kids' House Rooms," ideal for families. Some of the rooms, suitable for boys, are called "Knights' Rooms," whereas those for little girls are known as "Princess Rooms." Both of these types of rooms feature a mock wooden castle door in the middle of a wall that converts to a bunk bed. Every accommodation includes a dragon made of 8395 Lego bricks.

Aastvej 10, DK-7190 Billund. (�C) **75-33-12-44.** Fax 75-35-31-79. www.hotellegoland.dk. 176 units. 1,845DKK ($314/£166) double; 3,345DKK ($569/£302) junior suite. AE, DC, MC, V. Free shuttle bus to the hotel from the airport at Billund. **Amenities:** Restaurant; bar; gym; 24-hr. room service; laundry service; dry cleaning; nonsmoking rooms. *In room:* TV, dataport, Wi-Fi, minibar (in suites), hair dryer, trouser press, iron.

WHERE TO DINE

Le Petit 𝓻𝓻 DANISH/INTERNATIONAL   By creating this *luxe* restaurant in 1998, the owners more or less admitted that you can carry the kiddie theme too far. So instead of another pirate's restaurant or one with a Viking dragon decor, they went upmarket and created a first-rate international restaurant. Le Petit especially appeals to the corporate convention crowd, whose clients dominate when the kiddies go back to school. Consequently, you might be relieved to discover a mostly adult crowd in this attractively formal venue within the resort's only hotel. The decor is urbane and postmodern, and cuisine draws its inspiration from big-city venues. Don't expect a wide variety of menu items, as there might be only three or four starters, main courses, and desserts. Examples include roe of salmon garnished with red onions and sour cream, *Bündnerfleisch* (air-dried beef) with Parma ham served with exotic lettuces and marinated artichokes, a savory ragout of halibut and shellfish in a saffron sauce with wild rice, tuna steak with fresh spinach in a pasta basket on a bed of tomato sauce, and a succulent version of tenderloin of lamb with *Rösti* potatoes with rosemary-flavored gravy and glazed onions. One particularly delicious dessert is a chocolate basket filled with berries of the season and served with a Grand Marnier–flavored parfait. A drink within the Concorde Bar is a welcome preface to a meal here.

In the Hotel Legoland, Aastvej 10. (℃) **75-33-12-44.** Reservations recommended. Lunch 60DKK–145DKK ($10–$25/£5.40–£13); main courses 165DKK–200DKK ($28–$34/£15–£18). AE, DC, MC, V. Daily noon–2pm and 6–10pm.

4 Ringkøbing 𝓻

320km (199 miles) W of Copenhagen; 9km (5⅔ miles) E of the North Sea; 85km (53 miles) W of Silkeborg; 100km (62 miles) W of Århus

Århus and Silkeborg (see later in this chapter) justifiably attract more visitors, but count yourself lucky if you can spare a day for one of Denmark's most attractive towns left over from the Middle Ages.

We used to exclude Ringkøbing from our Danish itinerary until a broken vehicle forced us to overnight here one rain-lashed night. In the morning the sun broke through, and we set out to discover the charms, both obvious and hidden, of Ringkøbing, and have been including it on our stopovers ever since. The physical setting alone is dramatic, lying to the east of the gigantic **Ringkøbing Fjord,** which is separated by a narrow strip of land, Holmsland, from the turbulent North Sea to the west.

This old market town, lying on the north side of the lagoon-like Ringkøbing Fjord, is the seat—albeit tiny, with only 9,000 inhabitants—of the regional government. Its oldest known municipal charter dates from 1443, but the earliest archaeological finds establish its origins some time around the mid–13th century. At that time there was no outlet from the western end of Liim Fjord to the North Sea, so Ringkøbing Fjord was the only natural harbor in the area. It became one of the most important harbor cities on the west coast of Denmark with trading links extending to Norway, Germany, and Holland.

In time, though, especially during the 17th century, the approach at Nymindegab began to fill with sand and move south. With the opening of the West Jutland trunk line in 1875, shipping for Ringkøbing stopped almost immediately, leaving the town to reinvent itself. It wasn't until a lock at Hvide Sande was constructed in 1931 that Ringkøbing was once again assured of a passage to the North Sea. However, its role as a port for ships was never to return to its former glory. It did, however, become the first small town in Denmark to provide free universal education.

That falloff in commerce is what has kept Ringkøbing looking as old-fashioned and splendid as it does today. The townspeople also have a lively, cooperative spirit. For example, they have a beachcombing event to clean the town's 11km (6¾ miles) of coastline to ensure that the blue flags (symbol of unpolluted waters) fly over their beaches in summer.

ESSENTIALS

GETTING THERE   By Train   Ringkøbing lies on the main rail lines between Esbjerg (trip time: 1¼ hr.) and Struer (1 hr.).

By Car   From Silkeborg (see later in this chapter), continue west along Route 15 into Ringkøbing.

VISITOR INFORMATION   Ringkøbing Turistbureau, Torvet (© **70-22-70-01;** www.ringkobingfjord.dk), is open mid-June to August, Monday to Friday 9am to 5pm, Saturday 10am to 2pm; September to mid-June, it's open Monday to Friday 9:30am to 5pm and Saturday 10am to 1pm.

GETTING AROUND   By Bicycle   The surrounding scenic flatlands are ideal for cyclists. Bikes can be rented at **Børgensen Cykler,** Nørredige 10 (© **97-32-36-01**) for 50DKK to 60DKK ($8.50–$10/£4.50–£5.40) per day.

SEEING THE SIGHTS

Ringkøbing's townscape takes its characteristic look from houses mostly built from 1700 to 1800. The dominant building style—dark red houses with white cornices and semihipped rooftops—developed in the late 18th century. Ringkøbing's leading citizens were its merchants, whose large houses lined the narrow streets, particularly **Algade** and **Østergade.** Some have remained in a well-preserved condition, especially the addresses of Nørregade 2 and Algade 4–6. Much effort still goes into preserving Ringkøbing's mellow old-town atmosphere, and a walk through the town's narrow cobblestone streets brings its own reward.

If you're standing at the Torvet (marketplace) seeking a way to the harbor, the obvious choice is **Vester Strandgade** ★. This is an old street whose earliest homes date from the early 1800s. The street was always known for its merchants, including a plumber, butcher, baker, grocer, and shoemaker, as well as a bike shop and an inn. We always like to smell fresh bread from the local bakery and to stop for a delicious Danish pastry at a coffee shop, chatting with the locals.

For us, no visit is complete without time spent wandering **Ringkøbing Harbor** ✦, dating from 1904 when it was a bustling fishing port until the town lost out to Hvide Sande to the south. Today, it's much sleepier and filled with yachts, smaller pleasure craft, and fjord fishing boats. You can see fishermen from Ringkøbing Fjord pulling in here with their catch of the day, earmarked for private homes or restaurants. We like to attend the daily auction at 9:30am in a red-painted wooden structure at the harbor's edge. Here salmon, trout, flounder, perch, eel, and sea trout are hawked to the highest bidder and might be resting on your plate if you stick around Ringkøbing for dinner.

At the edge of the town center, **Alkjær Lukke** is a lovely park, idyllic for a picnic lunch. Ducks quacking in the pond tell you they want to be fed. In the airy beech woods the forest floor is covered with wood anemones, buttercups, and lilies of the valley. It's a good place to stop and enjoy "the sound of silence."

The town's main attraction—other than the town itself—is **Ringkøbing Museum Østerport,** Herningvej 4 (© 97-32-16-15; www.ringkobing.dk). A few blocks east of the Torvet, this museum is a virtual attic of local history, including coins and ecclesiastical artifacts, ships' figureheads, and even pictures of stranded ships in the North Sea. Someone at the museum is likely to show you what a chastity belt from 1600 looked like. We find the most intriguing exhibits to be those devoted to Ludwig Mylius-Erichsen (1872–1907), who led an expedition to Greenland in 1906. Regrettably, he died on the return journey. July and August, the museum is open daily 11am to 5pm; September to June, Monday to Thursday 11am to 4pm, and Saturday and Sunday 1 to 4pm. It's closed Friday during off season. Admission costs 30DKK ($5.10/£2.70) adults, 10DKK ($1.70/90p) children 8 to 12, free for children 7 and under.

SHOPPING

Some of the town's most sophisticated ceramics are sold at **Keramikkens Hus,** Ndr. Ringvej 14 (© 97-32-05-88).

One of the most intriguing shopping prospects is not in Ringkøbing itself, but directly south of the town at the hamlet of Stauning. Follow the secondary road along the east side of Ringkøbing Fjord until you come to the village, where you'll see a sign indicating **Bousøgaard** ✦, Bousøvej 6, Stauning (© 97-36-91-72). This is an old thatched West Jutland farm with four wings. The attractive barn is an art gallery, the biggest in West Jutland, with oils, graphics, and sculptures by well-known Danish artists. There's also an on-site potter's workshop, where the old potter's craft is still practiced. Next to the workshop is a museum of Danish decorated pottery from the 1800s to about 1950. Hours are Monday to Saturday 11am to 5pm.

WHERE TO STAY

Hotel Fjordgården ✦ *Kids*　Head for the Hotel Ringkøbing for an older pedigree but check in here for greater comfort and superior facilities. The best hotel in Ringkøbing lies less than half a kilometer (about ¼ mile) north of the town center, on sandy flatlands 8km (5 miles) from the coast. Built in 1967 in a sprawling, generously proportioned format with between one and two stories, white walls, and a prominent brown roof, it has the most comfortable accommodations—and better dining—than any competitor. Rooms are good size with firm beds, small but spanking-clean bathrooms (with tub and shower), and big windows that grant views over the surrounding land and seascape. Many of the units are large enough to use as family rooms. The hotel boasts an indoor subtropical water land, with spa, sauna, children's pool, and water slide.

Vesterkær 28, DK-6950 Ringkøbing. © **800/528-1234** in the U.S., or 97-32-14-00. Fax 97-32-47-60. www.hotel fjordgaarden.dk. 98 units. 1,295DKK ($220/£117) double; 1,595DKK ($271/£144) suite. AE, DC, MC, V. **Amenities:** Restaurant; bar; indoor heated pool; gym; spa; sauna; room service (7am–10pm); laundry service; dry cleaning; nonsmoking rooms; solarium. *In room:* TV, Wi-Fi, minibar, coffeemaker, hair dryer.

Hotel Ringkøbing Set on a cobble-covered square in the heart of town, near a quartet of linden trees, this is the second-oldest hotel in Jutland, established in its present format in 1833. The hotel is cozy but somewhat kitschy. Rooms are banal, even a bit dowdy, thanks to overly frilly bedcovers and clumsy attempts at gussying up relatively plain spaces. Two are in a nearby annex, and all units contain a private bathroom with shower. On the premises are an English-style pub serving lots of suds and occasional live rock-'n'-roll sessions and a restaurant that looks like it hasn't been redecorated since the 1960s.

Torvet 18, DK-6950 Ringkøbing. © **97-32-00-11.** Fax 97-32-18-72. www.hotelringkobing.dk. 47 units. 845DKK– 995DKK ($144–$169/£76–£90) double; 1,195DKK ($203/£108) suite. Rates include breakfast. DC, MC, V. **Amenities:** 2 restaurants; bar; gym; laundry service; dry cleaning. *In room:* TV.

WHERE TO DINE

Restaurant Helten 𝒜 DANISH/INTERNATIONAL   This is the showplace dining room of the only government-rated four-star hotel in Ringkøbing, and as such, you receive more internationally conscious culinary finesse, and more diligent service, than elsewhere in town. Within a very modern dining room with a view of the dunes and the sea, you'll find a lunch venue centered around the most appealing buffet in town. Look for a savory collection of homemade soups, salads, open-faced sandwiches, Danish cheeses, smoked meats and fish, seasonal berries, and pastries. Dinners are more elaborate. We highly recommend, when it's available, a platter of smoked *helten* (a small, herring-shaped fish that's the restaurant's namesake). Found only in the nearby fjord, and traditionally served salted or smoked, it's prized as one of the unusual delicacies of Denmark. Among the menu items we've enjoyed here is fried North Sea plaice with brown butter, or else the fresh salmon cutlet with vegetables, pasta, and herb butter. Also delectable is the guinea fowl with mushroom fricassee.

In the Hotel Fjordgården, Vesterkær 28. © **97-32-14-00.** Reservations recommended. Dinner main courses 165DKK–215DKK ($28–$37/£15–£19); fixed-price dinner menus 250DKK–315DKK ($43–$54/£23–£28). AE, DC, MC, V. Mon–Fri 7am–10pm; Sat 7am–1:30pm; Sun 7am–9pm.

EXPLORING RINGKØBING FJORD 𝒜

Long straight sandy beaches, nature reserves, drifting North Sea sands, and heathercovered dunes create a dramatic West Jutland landscape on the narrow isthmus running south from Ringkøbing along Route 181. To reach the road that takes you along the western side of the fjord, head directly east of Ringkøbing along Route 15, turning south when you see the junction with Route 181, going to the small town of Hvide Sande.

HVIDE SANDE

Midway along the isthmus, Hvide Sande (whose name translates as "white sands") is a typical West Jutland fishing town, founded in 1931 when it grew up around the large lock and sluice between the North Sea and Ringkøbing Fjord. Today, with its splendid beach on the seaside, it's the fifth-largest fishing port in Denmark. A path follows along the windswept dunes between the sea and Ringkøbing Fjord, with panoramic views in all directions.

The most intriguing attraction here is the picturesque fishing harbor, the heartbeat of the town. Catches of fish are unloaded at the auction building here. The auction is held every Monday to Friday at 7am, and again at 10am if the catch is heavy. A small nod or a lifted eyebrow is caught immediately by the auctioneer, and the purchase is registered. When the fish is sold, the catch is taken by truck for processing at local plants or exported directly in large refrigerated vans.

While in the area, you can visit the **Vestkyst Akvariet** (also known as Fiskeriets Hus), Nørregade 2B (© **97-31-26-10;** www.wja.dk/vestkystakvariet/de), a museum devoted to anything and everything to do with fishing. The museum has a saltwater aquarium with fish from both the North Sea and Ringkøbing Fjord. It also includes tanks for large fish such as piked dogfish, rays, and big gadoids. April to October, the fish are fed every Tuesday and Friday at 3:30pm. Displays also include fishing tackle, and children can go on a voyage in the wheelhouse of a real cutter. While below deck, visitors experience the cramped conditions under which fishermen live at sea. April to October, it's open daily 10am to 6pm; November to March, daily 10am to 4pm. Admission is 50DKK ($8.50/ £4.50) adults, 25DKK ($4.25/£2.25) children under age 12.

At Hvide Sande you'll find information available at **Holmsland Klit Turistforening,** on the premises of the **Vestkyst Aquarium,** Nørregade 2B (© **97-31-18-66**). The office is open year-round, Monday to Friday from 9am to 4pm. From June to August, it's also open Saturday noon to 5pm and Sunday 11am to 4pm.

Where to Dine in Hvide Sande

Restaurant Slusen SEAFOOD/DANISH   In a building from the 1940s, directly astride the harbor, this is the most appealing restaurant in Hvide Sande, thanks to well-conceived cuisine and a helpful staff. Menu items include fried filets of plaice or turbot, different preparations of herring and salmon, a succulent seafood platter, and filets of catfish with mustard sauce. Lobster is available, kept fresh in an on-site aquarium. The dessert specialty is a Grand Marnier soufflé served on a purée of fresh peaches. The helpings are generous, the food flavorful, the fish fresh and well prepared, and the price right. Not only that, but the staff assured us readers will have "great fun" here. What more could you ask?

Bredgade 3. © **97-31-27-27.** Reservations recommended. Main courses 163DKK–260DKK ($28–$44/£15–£23); fixed-price menu 258DKK ($44/£23). AE, DC, MC, V. Daily 1–4pm and 5–10pm. Closed Oct–Mar Sun 5–10pm and Mon.

TIPPERNE NATURE RESERVE ✦

You can continue south to Nymindegab, the gateway to the isthmus, if you're coming from Esbjerg. In times gone by, Nymindegab was the home of a small fishing harbor. From here you can explore **Tipperne Nature Reserve.** A small road, signposted from Nymindegab, leads into this tiny peninsula jutting into Ringkøbing Fjord. The flats and water surrounding the peninsula are one of the best bird sanctuaries in West Jutland. The area's bird life is protected to establish undisturbed breeding. Today it is a favorite stopover for migratory birds. During both spring and autumn, thousands of ducks, geese, and waders stop here to rest. In July and August, when migration is at its peak, the sandpiper, curlew, snipe, and golden plover are some of the many species

Windsurfing on Ringkøbing Fjord

Ringkøbing Fjord is one of the most popular places for windsurfing in the north of Europe. The area has Denmark's excellent breezes, and the shallow fjord waters are ideal for beginners. When the wind blows from the west, it comes in directly from the North Sea. Having passed the dunes, it accelerates across the fjord, creating a strong and constant wind. A wind from the east brings heat and sun, which in turn ensures increasing winds in the afternoon, so that surfing is generally possible every day. The wind is strongest in March, April, September, and October.

The best conditions are found at Hvide Sande, the venue for international and national speed weeks. This is the largest center around the fjord, with Denmark's best shallow water area for speed and slalom surfing. The center has a well-stocked shop with a school providing windsurfing instruction, equipment for hire, and a cafeteria with wind gauge. You'll be kept up-to-date on weather forecasts. You can stop in at **Westwind Nord** (℡ **97-31-25-99**), where you can get an introductory 3-hour course for 410DKK ($70/£37). They also rent gear in summer months.

to be seen here. In the winter season, the swan, Denmark's national bird, is one of the species finding shelter at Tipperne. April to August, the bird reserve is open to visitors Sunday 5 to 10am only. September to March, the reserve can be visited every Sunday 10am to noon. You should continue by car until you reach a building marked TIPPERHUSET. You're not allowed to stop until you come to the parking lot, but once here you can climb a viewing tower to observe the birds. A 1.5km (1-mile) nature path departs from the bird tower, and all walking in the area is restricted to this one path to protect bird life.

5 Ry ⓧ

256km (159 miles) W of Copenhagen; 24km (15 miles) SE of Silkeborg; 35km (22 miles) SW of Århus

In the heart of Jutland, the little old town of Ry makes a less commercialized center than Silkeborg (see below) for visiting the mid-Jutland Lake District, one of the most beautiful areas of Denmark. Ry lies in a rural setting of extensive forests and rolling hills, valleys, gorges, and lakes, all linked by the Gudenå (also spelled Gudenåen), the longest river in Denmark. The region is filled with numerous sites of historical interest, including old churches, abbey ruins, villages with thatched roofs, and a number of small museums. Other than a walk through the town of Ry itself, there aren't many notable sights in the historic center. We use Ry as a base, branching out to see attractions in its environs.

ESSENTIALS

GETTING THERE   By Train   Ry lies on the main rail route linking Silkeborg (trip time: 20 min.) and Århus (trip time: 30 min.). There's also a bus from Århus, but it takes twice as long.

By Car   From Silkeborg (see below), take Route 15, heading east, and following the signs to Århus. Veer right (south) when you reach the town of Låsby, following the signs to Ry.

VISITOR INFORMATION   The **Ry Turistbureau,** Klostervej 3 (© **86-89-34-22;** www.visitry.dk), is open June 15 to August 31, Monday to Saturday 9am to 4:30pm. Off-season hours are Monday to Friday 9am to 4pm and Saturday 9am to noon.

GETTING AROUND   By Bicycle   For many Danes, the only way to see the lake district and its little hamlets is by bike. **Ry Cykel,** Skanderborgvej 19 (© **86-89-14-91**), will rent you a bike for the day for 75DKK ($13/£6.75).

By Canoe   Instead of a bike, you might prefer to explore the river and the beautiful lakes in the area by canoe. Brochures about canoeing are available from the Ry Turistbureau or from **Ry Kanofart,** Kyhnsvej 20 (© **86-89-11-67**), which will rent you a canoe for 300DKK ($51/£27) per day.

EXPLORING THE AREA

A 10-minute drive west of Ry via Route 445, **Himmelbjerget** ☆ (Sky Mountain) is the most visited spot in the Lake District. You can also get here by taking bus no. 104 from the train station at Ry. Himmelbjerget rises 147m (482 ft.) above sea level, the highest point in Denmark. In 1871, the Danish crown obtained the property and turned it over to the people of Denmark as a sightseeing attraction.

Himmelbjerget towers majestically over the surrounding countryside, not only when viewed from the lake, but from the many footpaths in the woods as well. Two modern tourist boats, the *Viking* and the *Turisten,* run summer cruises between Ry and Himmelbjerget. For information and schedules, call © 86-82-88-21 in Ry. The one-way cost is 45DKK ($7.65/£4.05) adults and 30DKK ($5.10/£2.70) children 3 to 12.

Himmelbjerget Tower, rising 25m (82 ft.), was designed by the architect L. P. Fenger and erected in commemoration of King Frederik VII, who, on June 5, 1849, gave the Danish people a new constitution. From the tower you'll have the most panoramic view of the area. It's open daily May and June, 10am to 5pm; July, 10am to 9pm; August to September 15, 10am to 6pm. From September 16 to October, it's open only on Saturday and Sunday from 10am to 5pm. Admission is 10DKK ($1.70/90p).

Even more than Ry, we are attracted to the hamlet of **Gamle Ry (Old Ry)** ☆, directly west of Ry along Route 461. This is called the "village of kings and springs." The name "Ry" comes from *rydning,* Danish for "clearing." In the Middle Ages this was a spiritual center of Denmark because of its "holy springs." The village gets its royal associations through Frederik II, who built a mansion here in 1582.

From the center you can follow a sign directing you to Skt. Sørens spring in Rye Sønderskov (Rye Southwood). This is a wonderful walk through a subglacial stream trench, called Jammerdalen, or "The Vale of Tears." The water of this spring, thought to have curative powers, attracted many pilgrims, launching Gamle Ry on its heyday of medieval glory. In gratitude, pilgrims contributed to the funding of a granite church on the nearby hill where the present Sct. Sørens Kirke is situated. After the Reformation, when the pilgrimages stopped, the church fell into disrepair. In 1912, a rich farmer had the old tower reconstructed. The original church was the scene of the election of Christian III as king of Denmark on July 4, 1534, leading to the collapse of the Catholic Church in Denmark.

From the church you go east past a mill to **Galgebakken** (The Gallows Hill), a protected nature reserve set in lovely heather-clad hills.

East of Gamle Ry, if you cross the Gudenå at Emborg Bridge, you will come to the ruins of the largest Cistercian abbey in Denmark, the **Øm Kloster** (monastery). In the 12th century, a group of Cistercian monks left the Vitskøl Kloster monastery in Himmerland and arrived at Øm, where they founded the Øm Kloster monastery in 1175. The Cistercians were skilled farmers and preferred sites in forests and remote areas, where their hard work turned barren land into exemplary farms. During the Reformation, the monastery ceased to exist and the lands were taken over by the king. The monastery itself was pulled down. However, excavations in modern times have revealed one of the best-preserved ground plans of a medieval monastery to date. There is a little museum here open April, May, September, and October, Tuesday to Sunday 10am to 4pm; June to August, Tuesday to Sunday 10am to 5pm. The cloister is always closed on Monday. Admission is 40DKK ($6.80/£3.60) adults, 15DKK ($2.55/£1.35) children 7 to 12, free for children 6 and under. This minor museum has a historical medical exhibition, an herb garden, and a collection of skeletons discovered in the area. The plants in the herb garden date back to the days when the monastery flourished here. We find it an evocative, nostalgic place worthy of your discovery. For information, call ℂ **86-89-81-94** or visit www.klostermuseet.dk.

You can take Route 461 south from Gamle Ry until you see the turnoff east to the hamlet of Emborg. This takes you to **Mossø,** the largest lake in Jutland. To the west of the lake are the Højlund Forest and the Sukkertoppen Hill, rising 108m (354 ft.).

The longest watercourse in Denmark, the **Gudenå,** also passes through Mossø en route from Tinnet Krat to Randers Fjord. Closer to the river are valley terraces created by water that melted after the Ice Age. The sandy surfaces are covered with heather and coniferous plants, but make for poor farmland.

Mossø is the habitat of many types of birds. The sanctuary at Emborg Odde is a breeding site for a colony of black-headed gulls, which are extremely aggressive, thus providing protection from predators. The black-necked grebe takes advantage of this and breeds among the gulls. In the late summer, grebes can be seen along the edges of the reed banks, feeding on small animals.

WHERE TO STAY

Gamle Rye Kro ⟨ℛ⟩ *(Finds)*   Our favorite nest and the most historic hotel in Ry lies in the satellite town of Gamle Ry. The place looks like a large white farmhouse, set 180m (590 ft.) north of the village church and the town market square. It has a history stretching back 400 years, to the time when pilgrims heading for the nearby (now ruined) monastery extolled the healing powers of local springs. Don't expect your accommodations—or even the public rooms—to drip with a sense of antique nostalgia, as much of the inn's historic charm was erased during its renovations in the early 1990s. Overall, however, there's a sense of hospitality from the youthful and entrepreneurial staff, and a restaurant with good regional Danish cooking (see "Where to Dine," below).

Ryesgade 8, DK-8680 Ry. ℂ **86-89-80-42.** Fax 86-89-85-46. www.krohotel.dk. 20 rooms. 735DKK ($125/£66) double. AE, DC, MC, V. From Ry, drive 5km (3 miles) southwest, following the signs to Gamle Ry. **Amenities:** Restaurant; indoor heated pool; fitness room; laundry service; dry cleaning; nonsmoking rooms; solarium. *In room:* TV, no phone (in some).

Hotel Himmelbjerget ⟨ℛ⟩ *(Kids)*   Set at a higher altitude than any other hotel in Denmark, this charming, rustic, old-fashioned venue has changed little, despite subtle modernizations, since it was built in 1922. It lies 7km (4⅓ miles) northwest of the center of Ry, on a rocky plateau of its own, within a 10-minute walk of the Himmelbjerget Tower. Rooms retain some of their old-time paneling and accessories, and in many cases have terraces or balconies overlooking the nearby tower or the fields, lakes, and forests. Each has a writing table and twin beds that can be separated or moved together. On the premises are a bar and an appealing restaurant that serves generous portions of conservative, time-tested Danish recipes (see "Where to Dine," below). On-site is a children's cafeteria with direct access to a playground. The hotel's name, incidentally, translates from the Danish as "Heaven Mountain." It's not quite that, but is a worthy contender nonetheless.

Ny Himmelbjergvej 20, DK-8680 Ry. ℂ 86-89-80-45. Fax 86-89-87-93. www.hotel-himmelbjerget.dk. 18 units, none with bathroom. 575DKK ($98/£52) double. Rates include breakfast. AE, DC, MC, V. Bus: 411. **Amenities:** Restaurant; cafeteria; bar; laundry service; dry cleaning; kids' playground.

Nørre Vissing Kro 🏰 Set 11km (6¾ miles) northwest of Ry, amid rolling farmlands dotted with stately trees, this century-old inn has received many awards for the excellence of its cuisine. (See "Where to Dine," below.) It also maintains artfully decorated and stylish rooms, each with a small tiled bathroom with shower. Each has a scattering of rustic antiques that were in most cases acquired within Jutland. There are few amenities per se, but the staff is very hip, and we find the owners charming.

Låsbyvej 122, Nørre Vissing, DK-8660 Skanderborg. ℂ 86-94-37-16. Fax 86-94-37-57. 16 units. 795DKK ($135/£72) double. Rates include breakfast. DC, MC, V. Drive north from Ry, following the signs from Låsby; at Låsby, turn southwest, following the signs to Nørre Vissing. **Amenities:** Restaurant; bar; room service (7am–10pm); nonsmoking rooms. *In room:* TV.

Ry Park Hotel Set in the center of Ry, this is one of the oldest *and* newest hotels in town. Originally built in 1888, it was radically reconfigured into a more streamlined and comfortable venue a century later. About 20 rooms are in a comfortable annex across the road. We find the accommodations in the annex more sterile and prefer to stay in the main building. Regardless of your room assignment, all units come with a small private bathroom with tub or shower. Regrettably for the casual visitor, the inn is frequently reserved for conventions. If one is not taking place, the more relaxed and less harassed staff can arrange many sports for you, including fishing, canoeing, kayaking, cycling, and yachting.

Kyhnsvej 2, DK-8680 Ry. ℂ 86-89-19-11. Fax 86-89-12-57. www.ryparkhotel.dk. 76 units. 850DKK–1,250DKK ($145–$213/£77–£113) double. Rates include breakfast. AE, DC, MC, V. **Amenities:** Restaurant; bar; indoor heated pool; sauna; room service (7am–10pm); laundry service; dry cleaning; nonsmoking rooms. *In room:* TV, hair dryer, iron, safe.

WHERE TO DINE

Gamle Rye Kro 🏰 *Finds* DANISH It's the always-reliable grandmotherly Danish cookery—and not the hotel rooms (see above)—that attracts a steady stream of visitors and locals to one of the oldest inns in the region. Although the place has been renovated and modernized a little too much for our tastes, the generous portions of food are still traditional. Menu items include all the Danish staples, such as *frikadeller* (meatballs), platters with several different preparations of herring, smoked salmon with chive-flavored cream sauce, roasted pork with red cabbage and onions, Dover sole meunière, and filet of plaice stuffed with asparagus and baby shrimp. Fried eel is even available on occasion.

Ryesgade 8. ℂ 86-89-80-42. Reservations recommended. Main courses 75DKK–260DKK ($13–$44/£6.75–£23). AE, DC, MC, V. Daily noon–10pm. From Ry drive 5km (3 miles) southwest, following the signs to Gamle Ry.

Nørre Vissing Kro FRENCH/ITALIAN/DANISH This is one of the most sophisticated and urbane restaurants in Jutland, with a string of awards for its culinary excellence and flair. Most of the dinner guests combine their meal with an overnight stay (see above). Luncheons, however, tend to include greater numbers of guests en route to somewhere else, and are lighter and less elaborate. The dining room is a spacious, all-blue affair dotted with country antiques and artfully chosen accessories. Menu items change with the seasons. A well-conceived meal, however, might include foie gras with cherry sauce served on a bed of sautéed summer cabbage, poached lobster with a spinach flan and orange sauce, a medley of French and Italian cheeses, and a layer cake stuffed with summer berries marinated in rum, served with strawberry sorbet. There is a robust quality to the cuisine, yet each dish is imbued with a subtle texture that only a master chef—one who knows how to turn simple, natural produce into a gastronomic experience of unmistakable quality—can achieve.

Låsbyvej 122, Nørre Vissing, Skanderborg. © 86-94-37-16. Reservations recommended. Main courses 85DKK–235DKK ($14–$40/£7.65–£21); fixed-price menus 335DKK–1,045DKK ($57–$178/£30–£94). AE, DC, MC, V. Daily noon–3pm and 6–9pm. Drive north from Ry, following the signs to Låsby; at Låsby, turn southwest, following the signs to Nørre Vissing.

Restaurant Himmelbjerget DANISH At a higher altitude than any other in Denmark, this is an appealingly old-fashioned restaurant where white napery, high ceilings, and old-world service are still offered. The recipes haven't changed in a century—and that's exactly what the locals depend upon when they book a table here. Menu items include most traditional Danish specialties, including marinated salmon with mustard and dill sauce and fresh-baked bread, filet of beef with onions and red-wine sauce, filet of veal with fresh vegetables and mushroom sauce, cold potato soup with bacon and chives, brisket of beef with horseradish sauce, or tenderloin of beef with fried onions. Any of these might be followed by selections from a carefully arranged platter of Danish cheeses.

Ny Himmelbjergvej 20. © 86-89-80-45. Reservations recommended. Main courses 145DKK–210DKK ($25–$36/£13–£19). AE, DC, MC, V. Daily 10am–10pm. Bus: 411 from Ry.

6 Silkeborg

43km (27 miles) W of Århus; 279km (173 miles) W of Copenhagen; 37km (23 miles) S of Viborg

If you go on a TV trivia quiz show and are asked the question, "How old is the oldest man in the world and where does he reside?" remember that the answer, hopefully for $100,000, is the "Tollund Man," who is in pretty good shape, having been born 2,400 years ago. He resides in Central Jutland in the little town of Silkeborg. To make his acquaintance, read on.

In the heart of the Danish lake district, this town of 35,000 opens onto the waters of Lake Longsø, where we like to go for a stroll at night to see the largest color fountain in Scandinavia. If you don't like the lake (highly unlikely), there is always the Gudenå River, the longest in Denmark. The Danes themselves come here to go canoeing, hiking through the surrounding hills, or boating on the lake. Silkeborg has some notable attractions, as we will soon see, but many locals prefer it for the joy of its setting "in the great outdoors," as a local proudly informed us.

In 1845, Michael Drewsen, whose statue is seen in the heart of town on the Torvet (main square), built a paper mill here on the east side of the river, and in time other industries sprouted up, leading to great prosperity for the town. Unlike some little towns of Denmark, with their narrow cobblestone streets, Silkeborg is spaciously laid out. A progressive town, it is scenic, historic, but also modern, with a vast shopping district of 200 specialty stores, the largest marketplace in Central Jutland, a multiplex cinema, dozens of restaurants, and a convention center.

ESSENTIALS

GETTING THERE   From Århus, follow Route 15 west to Silkeborg. If you aren't driving, there's frequent train service from Copenhagen via Fredericia.

VISITOR INFORMATION   The **Silkeborg Turistbureau** is at Godthåbsvej 4 (© 86-82-19-11; www.silkeborg.com). It's open June 15 to August, Monday to Friday 9am to 5pm, Saturday and Sunday 10am to 2pm; September, October, and April to June 14, Monday to Friday 9am to 4pm, Saturday 10am to 1pm; November to March, Monday to Friday 10am to 3pm. In December the office is also open Saturday 10am to 1pm.

GETTING AROUND   Numerous **bus routes** service the city; all local buses depart from the stop on Fredensgade. There's no number to call for information. Tickets cost 20DKK ($3.40/£1.80) per individual ride, or 23DKK ($3.90/£2.10) if you need a transfer.

SEEING THE SIGHTS

Although we can never resist the charms of the **Tollund Man** (see "Silkeborg Museum," below), the greatest adventure for us is to sail aboard the world's last coal-fired paddle steamer, the *Hjejlen* 𝕬𝕬𝕬, which has been sailing since 1861. It follows the route of the Gudenå River, going along a waterway of about 150km (100 miles) through Jutland's lake district. Himmelbjerget, or "Sky Mountain" (p. 348), is the major attraction along the route. Departures are daily from Silkeborg harbor at 10am and again at 2pm from mid-June to mid-August. With a round-trip costing 117DKK ($20/£11) for adults or half-price for children 3 to 12. For schedules and more information, call **Hjejlen Co., Ltd.**, Havnen (© 86-82-07-66).

AQUA Ferskvands Akvarium og Museum 𝕬 𝕂𝕚𝕕𝕤   North Europe's largest freshwater aquarium is called "the inside-out aquarium." Now just what does that mean? The circular building is placed in the waters of the lake, which makes it a reverse aquarium, with you inside of it. Through the large seascape windows, you can look into the lake and watch both fish and water plants. In a beautiful park at AQUA, you can observe bird life with plenty of beavers around to amuse you. We forego the ferocious pikes to find fun with the diving ducks.

The spookiest part is called "The Bog," a dark, mysterious place where the big carp dwell, as does the tench and the elusive eel. Rare European otters can be seen hunting live fish in "The Otter Lake." One section, "The Darkness of the Night," is devoted to nocturnal animals that come out in moonlight, especially the Danish owl. This section also boasts AQUA's largest indoor aquarium with its "dancing eels," along with zander, sturgeon, crayfish, and the freshwater turbot. Another section of the park is set aside for children where they can actually feel the big sturgeon, carp, flounder, or other fish. You can have lunch or picnic in the park or pay a visit to the AQUA Café.

Vejsøvej 55. © 89-21-21-89. www.ferskvandscentret.dk. Admission 85DKK ($14/£7.65) adults, 50DKK ($8.50/ £4.50) children 3–12. July and Aug daily 10am–6pm; off season Mon–Fri 10am–4pm, Sat–Sun 10am–5pm.

Silkeborg Kunstmuseum (Silkeborg Museum of Art) 𝕬𝕬   This is one of the great provincial art museums of Scandinavia. The moment you arrive you know you're in for something special when you are greeted by two large ceramic walls by Jean

Dubuffet and others. In one of the most beautiful areas of Silkeborg, in old parkland bordering the banks of the Gudenå River, Asger Jorn, a leading figure in 20th-century European art, donated his impressive collection of 5,000 paintings by 150 artists he collected up until his death in 1973. Many of the works were by his friends, artists he met in Paris "between the wars."

Jorn is famous today for having founded the fabled CoBrA group, based on the first letters of Copenhagen, Brussels, and Amsterdam where most of the artists originated. The Jorn collection includes impressive works by Le Corbusier, Léger, Max Ernst, Dubuffet, Miró, and Picasso.

Jorn himself was a virtual Renaissance man when it came to art, excelling in painting, sculpture, ceramics, tapestries, drawings, and graphics. His *Moon Dog* from 1953 is amusing, but he is at his most frightening in his masterpiece, *Stalingrad* 𝒦𝒦.

The museum is also richly imbued with an important collection of Danish art 𝒦 from the 20th century. Of the CoBrA group and their paintings, Jorn once said, "We are in violent reaction against the social disorder brought about by war. We also renounce all other artistic trends of our day." The privately owned gallery supplements its permanent collection with changing exhibitions of paintings and sculpture.

Gudenåvej 9. ⒸⒸ **86-82-53-88.** www.silkeborgkunstmuseum.dk. Admission 50DKK ($8.50/£4.50) adults, free for children under 18. Apr–Oct Tues–Sun 10am–5pm; Nov–Mar Tues–Fri noon–4pm, Sat–Sun 10am–5pm. Bus: 10.

Silkeborg Museum   One of the world's greatest human treasures from antiquity is the world-famous and much-photographed **Tollund Man** 𝒦𝒦𝒦. Discovered in a peat bog in 1950, he is the most perfectly preserved human being to have survived the ages. When he lived during the Iron Age (roughly 500 B.C. to A.D. 500), the great city of Athens was in decline, the second Punic War was being fought, the finishing touches were being put on the Great Wall of China, and Hannibal was trying to get those damn elephants to cross the Alps.

Just how well preserved is the Tollund Man? When his body was discovered, locals called the police, thinking it was a recent murder. You can even see the wrinkles in his forehead. He had good cause for wrinkles. His head capped by fur, the Tollund Man was strangled by a plaited leather string, probably as part of a ritual sacrifice for a successful peat harvest. He was also a vegetarian, as scientists have determined, his last meal consisting of flax and barley. An American woman student, standing next to us, was overheard saying: "My God, this guy is 2,400 years old and has fewer wrinkles than Mick Jagger."

Sleeping near the Tollund Man for centuries is the **Elling Woman** 𝒦𝒦, whose body was discovered in 1938 about 60m (200 feet) from where the Tollund Man was later discovered. Wrapped in a sheepskin cape, she had been hanged with a leather thong, the V-shaped furrow still to be seen around her neck today. Scientists estimate that she was about 25 years old when she died in 210 B.C., probably the result of another ritual sacrifice.

After seeing these rather gruesome sights, you can admire the setting of the museum in a manor house by the Gudenå River, directly east of the Torvet. The building itself dates back to 1767 and is the oldest structure in Silkeborg.

In addition to its gruesome corpses, the museum also displays exhibits devoted to regional history and local handicrafts, especially an antique glass collection, the renowned **Sorring ceramics** 𝒦. Interiors have been arranged to illustrate antiques from the mid–19th century.

The museum also has a special exhibition of a clog maker's workshop, a collection of stone implements, antique jewelry, and artifacts from the ruins of Silkeborg Castle. In the handicraft and Iron Age markets, artisans use ancient techniques to create iron, jewelry, and various crafts.

Hovedgaardsvej 7. (*C*) **86-82-14-99.** www.silkeborgmuseum.dk. Admission 45DKK ($7.65/£4.05); free for children 17 and under. May to mid-Oct daily 10am–5pm; mid-Oct to Apr Sat–Sun noon–4pm. Bus: 10.

NEARBY ATTRACTIONS

Jysk Automobilmuseum (Jutland Car Museum) *A*   Ever since a long-ago friend let us drive custom-made 1920s cars, originally created for silent-screen vamps around Hollywood, we've been addicted to vintage cars. Outside Silkeborg at the village of Gjern, our fantasies live again with a collection of 150 vintage vehicles made as far back as 1900 and as recently as 1950. Many rare European and American vehicles and motorcycles can be viewed, not only the Rolls Royce and Maserati, but the famous Renault Taxis de la Marne or a V12 Cadillac or the 1947 Crosley. A local mechanic, Aagi Louring, not only collected these vehicles but restored them to working order, opening the museum in 1967.

Skovvejen, Gjern. (*C*) **86-87-50-50.** www.jyskautomobilmuseum.dk. Admission 70DKK ($12/£6.30) adults, 30DKK ($5.10/£2.70) children 6–14; free for children under 6. May 16–Sept 15 daily 10am–5pm; Apr 1–May 15 and Sept 16–Oct 31 Sat–Sun and holidays 10am–5pm. Closed Nov 1–Mar. Bus: Take the bus marked RANDERS from Silkeborg. 15km (9½ miles) northeast of Silkeborg, it's accessible by following the road signs to the town of Hammel, then turning off when you see the signs for Gjern and the Jysk Automobilmuseum.

SHOPPING

The main market is held at **Torvet** (town square) on Saturday mornings, starting around 7am. It's always best to go before noon. A smaller market begins about the same time every Wednesday at **Nørretorv.** Among specialty stores, **Bon Sac,** Søndergade 2C ((*C*) **86-82-60-55**), has an intriguing collection of fashionable leather goods. **Inspiration,** Østergade 5 ((*C*) **86-82-50-11**), offers a large array of gift items for the home.

WHERE TO STAY

The Silkeborg Turistbureau (see above) can book you into nearby **private homes.**

MODERATE

Gl. Skovridergaard *A*   This historic and luxurious complex would be a complete delight if it weren't conference-crazed. Rooms during the peak of winter might not always be available if a convention is booked. But when midsummer arrives, and most Frommer's readers are in the Silkeborg area, a stay here can be one of the most rewarding in Central Jutland. The location itself is idyllic—close to the Gudenå River. All the accommodations contain private bathrooms, some with tub, others with shower. Set within a well-maintained park, the hotel originated in the 1700s, when the manager of the surrounding game reserve and forest built a well-appointed home for himself. In the mid-1980s, under the ownership of Silkeborg's largest bank (which books at least 30% of all convention space for its own managers and staff members), it was expanded into the convention center and hotel you'll see today.

Rooms are larger than you might expect, and filled with comfortable furnishings. Cafe tables are set up on the hotel's verdant lawns during mild weather, and the hotel's restaurant offers well-prepared, carefully choreographed meals. The restaurant merits special mention because of its ability to cater with aplomb to small or large groups.

Lunches are almost always configured as a buffet; dinners are sit-down, internationally inspired meals served by a staff at artfully decorated tables.

Marienlundsvej 36, DK-8600 Silkeborg. © 87-22-55-00. Fax 87-22-55-11. www.glskov.dk. 68 units. 1,245DKK ($212/£112) double; 1,540DKK ($262/£139) junior suite. Rates include buffet breakfast. AE, DC, MC, V. From Silkeborg, drive less than a kilometer (½ mile) south of town, following the signs to Horsens. **Amenities:** Restaurant; bar; sauna; room service (7am–10pm); babysitting; laundry service; dry cleaning; nonsmoking rooms. *In room:* TV, minibar (some units), coffeemaker, hair dryer, iron (in some).

Hotel Dania ☆

If you want modernity, plus facilities, check into the Radisson SAS (see below). But if you desire tradition, you could find no better choice than the town's oldest hotel, dating from 1848. Much improved over the years, it's been modernized without losing its charm. The bedrooms either overlook the lake or else the Torvet, the main square of town. Antiques fill the corridors and reception lounge, but the midsize-to-spacious guest rooms have been decorated in Danish modern, each unit containing a neatly kept bathroom with tub/shower combo. Outdoor dining on the square is popular in the summer, and the **Underhuset** restaurant serves typical Danish food along with Scandinavian and French dishes. The hotel's dining room is physically one of the longest restaurants in Denmark.

Torvet 5, DK-8600 Silkeborg. © 86-82-01-11. Fax 86-80-20-04. www.hoteldania.dk. 49 units. 1,069DKK–1,478DKK ($182–$251/£96–£133) double; 1,675DKK–2,405DKK ($285–$409/£151–£216) suite. Rates include breakfast. AE, DC, MC, V. Free parking. Bus: 3. **Amenities:** Restaurant; bar; room service (7am–10pm); babysitting; laundry service; dry cleaning; nonsmoking rooms. *In room:* TV, minibar, hair dryer, trouser press, safe.

Radisson SAS Hotel ☆☆☆

In hotels, this is the best case of recycling in all of Central Jutland. It was converted from a historic, 150-year-old paper factory into the most modern and up-to-date hotel in the area. The location is not quite as central as the Dania, but the Radisson rises right by the harbor, a short walk from attractions, shops, and restaurants. The chain hotel is also a favorite venue in Silkeborg for conferences, as the town's concert and theater facility, Jysk Musik & Teaterhus, lies nearby. The hotel offers the finest and most modern doubles and suites in Greater Silkeborg, successfully combining Danish modern with traditional styling, including state-of-the-art bathrooms with tub/shower combos. When it's snowing outside, the lobby bar with its fireplace is the best place to be in Silkeborg. During fair weather, the restaurant, with its spacious terrace offering panoramic views of the Remstrup River, is a favorite spot.

Papirfabrikken 12, DK-8600 Silkeborg. © 88-82-22-22. Fax 88-82-22-23. www.radissonsas.com. 86 units. 1,205DKK–1,345DKK ($205–$229/£108–£121) double; 1,945DKK–2,260DKK ($331–$384/£175–£203) suite. Rates include continental breakfast. AE, DC, MC, V. **Amenities:** Restaurant; bar; Jacuzzi (in suites); sauna; 24-hr. room service; laundry service; dry cleaning; nonsmoking rooms; rooms for those w/limited mobility. *In room:* A/C, TV, dataport, Wi-Fi, minibar, fridge, hair dryer, iron.

Scandic Hotel Silkeborg ☆ *Kids*

This chain-run hotel hardly has the glamour of the Radisson, but it is one of the better choices in the area for overnighting, especially for motorists, as it lies 2.5km (1½ miles) west of the town center in a residential neighborhood surrounded by fields and forests. The hotel has a certain charm and family appeal, with its playroom for kids and indoor heated pool. Bedrooms are small to midsize, each furnished in a chain format of Danish modern, with well-equipped tiled bathrooms with shower. In winter commercial travelers dominate the clientele, giving way by midsummer to vacationers from abroad. The hotel dining room, **Guldanden** (Golden Duck), is a glamorous spot serving Danish and international cuisine.

Udgårdsvej 2, DK-8600 Silkeborg. © 86-80-35-33. Fax 86-80-35-06. www.scandic-hotels.dk/silkeborg. 117 units. 880DKK–1,190DKK ($150–$202/£79–£107) double; 1,500DKK–1,700DKK ($255–$289/£135–£153) suite. AE, DC,

MC, V. Bus: 3 from rail station. **Amenities:** Restaurant; bar; indoor heated pool; gym; sauna; children's playroom; laundry service; dry cleaning; nonsmoking rooms; rooms for those w/limited mobility; solarium. *In room:* TV, Wi-Fi, minibar, coffeemaker (in some), trouser press, iron.

INEXPENSIVE

Kongensbro Kro 🌟🌟   Although a tavern stood on this site from 1663, it was little more than a ruin when members of the Andersen family bought and rebuilt it in 1949. The family's matriarch, Else, authored five Danish-language cookbooks during her active years here, and became something of a legend throughout Denmark. Today the charming and well-kept inn is directed by her son, Øle, and his hardworking staff. Accommodations are pleasant and cozy, and all contain private bathrooms with tub or shower.

Meals are served daily noon to 3pm and 6 to 9pm. A two-course fixed-price menu is available at lunch and dinner for 220DKK to 250DKK ($37–$43/£20–£23), although most serious gastronomes opt for a la carte meals. The inn lies between Ans and Århus, about a 10-minute drive north of Silkeborg.

Gamle Kongevej 70, DK-8643 Ans By. ✆ **86-87-01-77.** Fax 86-87-92-17. www.kongensbro-kro.dk. 15 units. 785DKK–985DKK ($133–$167/£71–£89) double. Rates include breakfast. AE, DC, MC, V. Closed Dec 23–24 and Dec 31–Jan 15. **Amenities:** Restaurant; room service (7am–10pm); laundry service; dry cleaning; nonsmoking room. *In room:* TV.

Svostrup Kro 🌟 *Finds*   The hotel advertises itself as "sweet as the good ole times"—and so it is. This is one of the least-modernized inns around Silkeborg, with more of its original architectural features than many of its competitors. On farmland between the Gudenå River and the Gjern hills, it was built in the 1600s as a bargeman's inn and designated by the Danish monarchy in 1834 as one of the inns suitable for a visit from the Danish king. Because of its authenticity and its hardworking, tactful staff, it's sought out by aficionados of old Danish inns, who appreciate its antique paneling and an interior that evokes the Denmark of long ago. Rooms contain appealing antique (or at least old) furnishings, with charmingly dowdy touches. The restaurant is open 7am to 11pm every day. Many of the food items include old-fashioned Danish cuisine such as herring platters with new potatoes, or fried steak with onions. Others are more modern, such as venison steak braised with red wine, and served with caramelized apples, nuts, celery, mushrooms, and a confit of baby onions.

Svostrupvej 58, Svostrup, DK-8600 Silkeborg. ✆ **86-87-70-04.** Fax 87-57-23-26. www.svostrup-kro.dk. 15 units. 895DKK ($152/£81) double; 1,095DKK ($186/£99) suite. Rates include breakfast. AE, DC, MC, V. Bus: 313 from Silkeborg. From Silkeborg, drive 10km (6¼ miles) north, following the signs to Randers and then the signs to Svostrup. *In room:* No phone.

WHERE TO DINE

Piaf 🌟 *Finds* MEDITERRANEAN   The most exotic and deliberately counterculture restaurant in town occupies a solid, 80-year-old brick building in the historic core. It was named after the uncanny resemblance of its owner, Anni Danielsen (who's known for her fondness for black dresses), to the late French chanteuse Edith Piaf. Artwork within the restaurant is offset with brick walls, potted plants, poster-image testimonials to the late Gallic sparrow, and deliberately mismatched tables, plates, ashtrays, and accessories. Lunch platters tend to be light, airy, and flavorful; dinners, more substantial with excellently chosen ingredients—always fresh—deftly handled by a skilled kitchen staff. Both are inspired by the tenets of Spanish, Greek, Provençal, and Italian cuisine. Look for heaping platters of paella, roasted lamb with rosemary, carpaccio, and sliced veal, with bowls of bouillabaisse. What's the only item you're likely not to find on the menu? Pork, since it reminds most of the clients of the cuisine served in

The Riverboat Jazz Festival

In late June of every year you'd think you were in pre-Katrina New Orleans. For 4 days, the sound of jazz music—Dixieland, swing, gospel, big band, street parades, and jam sessions fill the air. The festival takes place on the town squares, in the streets, and on the lakes, but most of all in four great tents erected for the occasion, two at the harbor, one on Bindslevs Plads, and another on Torvet (the main square). Concerts at these tents are always free. Jazz lovers from all over Europe flock here. For more information, contact the Turistbureau (see earlier in this chapter) or log onto **www.riverboat.dk**.

Denmark during their childhood, and which is consequently something avoided within this consciously exotic setting.

Nygade 31. *C* **86-81-12-55**. Reservations recommended. Fixed-price menus 240DKK–990DKK ($41–$168/£22–£89). DC, MC, V. Tues–Sat 6–10pm.

Spiesehuset Christian VIII 🏵🏵 DANISH/FRENCH   The best restaurant in Silkeborg, this establishment was founded in 1992 in what was originally a private house built in the late 1700s. It seats only 30 people in a dining room painted in what the owners describe as the color of heaven (cerulean blue), accented with modern paintings. "Give the chef a toque!" our dining companion urged, before we explained the Frommer's star system. "You'll shed tears of joy over the lobster ravioli." The dish didn't make us cry but we had praise for the chef. We also thought his carpaccio of marinated sole and salmon with a saffron sauce had a touch of brilliance, as did the filet of beef with truffle sauce. The multifariously flavored medallions of veal came stuffed with a purée of wild duck and herbs. Of course, you can go for the classics, none better than the tender rack of Danish lamb with garlic sauce.

Christian VIII Vej 54. *C* **86-82-25-62**. Reservations required. Main courses 170DKK–260DKK ($29–$44/£15–£26). AE, DC, MC, V. Mon–Sat 4–10pm.

SILKEBORG AFTER DARK

Available at any bar in town is *Neptun,* the local brew. According to a panel of expert tasters in Paris in 1986, it was then the world's best beer. Since that time, it's been challenged by other suds, but as any loyal native of Silkeborg will tell you, all other beers "taste like p . . ." We don't dare complete the word but it rhymes with *hiss.*

Rather historic is the **Underhuset Pub,** part of the dining and drinking facilities within the also-recommended Hotel Dania, Torvet 5 (*C* **86-82-01-11**), which is charmingly old-fashioned. The town's swankiest bar is in the previously recommended Radisson SAS (see above). It was designed by Botikken, a well-known retail design store, and is the trendiest place for a drink in town.

7 Århus 🏵🏵🏵

159km (99 miles) NE of Fanø; 175km (109 miles) W of Copenhagen; 43km (27 miles) E of Silkeborg

Some locals call it "the world's smallest city." Actually, it is the second-largest city in Denmark and the capital of Jutland. Because Copenhagen is so far to the east, Århus has also been called "the capital of the West." A large student population makes for a vast cultural life, which reaches its peak in late summer when visitors flock here for an arts festival.

There is much to see and do. More than any man-made attractions in Århus, we like its bustling life, which takes place in the best bars in Jutland and in its sidewalk cafes. There are sandy beaches nearby and a number of museums. Even more than the actual museums to explore, you can experience Århus life with a close encounter by walking its cobblestone streets and taking a picnic lunch to one of the city parks on a sunny day.

The city's economic growth today is based on communications, the food industry, electronics, textiles, iron and steel, and Danish design, as well as the harbor, which is now the second most important in Denmark, rivaled only by Copenhagen.

Originally Århus was a Viking settlement, founded as early as the 10th century; its original name, Aros, meaning estuary, comes from its position at the mouth of a river, Århus Å. The town experienced rapid growth and by 948 it had its own bishop. An Episcopal church was built here in 1060, and a cathedral was started at the dawn of the 13th century. This prosperity came to a temporary end in the late Middle Ages when the town was devastated by the bubonic plague. The Reformation of 1536 also slowed the growth of Århus. But the coming of the railway in the 19th century renewed prosperity, which continues to this day.

Try to plan at least a full day and night here—or two if you can spare the time.

ESSENTIALS

GETTING THERE   **By Plane**   **Århus Airport** is in Tirstrup, 43km (27 miles) northeast of the city. **SAS** (© **800/221-2350** in North America, or 70-10-20-00 in Århus; www.aar.dk) operates some 12 flights a day from Copenhagen, Monday to Friday, and about 6 on Saturday and Sunday. SAS also operates an afternoon flight most days between Århus and London. An airport bus runs between the train depot at Århus and the airport, meeting all major flights. The cost of a one-way ticket is 85DKK ($14/£7.65).

By Train   About five or six trains a day travel between Århus and Copenhagen (trip time: 4½ hr.). Some 20 trains a day connect Aalborg with Århus (1 hr., 40 min.). From Frederikshavn, the North Jutland port and ferry-arrival point from Norway, some 20 trains a day run to Århus (3 hr.).

By Bus   Two buses daily make the run to Århus from Copenhagen (4 hr.).

By Car   From the east, cross Funen on the E20 express highway, heading north at the junction with the E45. From the north German border, drive all the way along the E45. From Frederikshavn and Aalborg in the north, head south along the E45.

VISITOR INFORMATION   The tourist office, **Tourist Århus,** Banegårdspladsen 20 (© **87-31-50-10;** www.visitaarhus.com). Open June 26 to September 10 Monday to Friday 9:30am to 6pm, Saturday 9:30am to 5pm, and Sunday 9:30am to 1pm; September 11 to April 30 Monday to Friday 9am to 4pm, Saturday 10am to 1pm; May 1 to June 25 Monday to Friday 9:30am to 5pm and Saturday 10am to 1pm.

GETTING AROUND   A regular bus ticket, valid for one ride, can be purchased on the rear platform of all city buses for 17DKK ($2.90/£1.55). You can buy a **tourist ticket** for 50DKK ($8.50/£4.50) at the tourist office or at news kiosks throughout the city center. The 24-hour ticket covers an unlimited number of rides within the central city and includes a 2½-hour guided tour of Århus.

Århus

ATTRACTIONS ●
Århus Domkirke **9**
Århus Kunstmuseum **1**
Besættelsesmuseet **23**
Den Gamle By **6**
Marselisborg Slot **15**
Moesgård Museum **13**
Naturhistorisk Museum **2**
Rådhuset (Town Hall) **20**
Steno Museet **3**
Vikingemuseet **10**
Vor Frue Kirke **8**

ACCOMMODATIONS ■
Best Western Ritz Hotel **14**
Comfort Hotel Atlantic **23**
Hotel Guldsmeden **4**
Hotel La Tour **2**

Hotel Marselis **19**
Hotel Mercur **21**
Hotel Philip **12**
Hotel Royal **8**
Radisson SAS
  Scandinavia Hotel Århus **17**
Scandic Plaza **18**

DINING ◆
Gastronomica **15**
Hotel Philip Restaurant **12**
Ministeriet **7**
Prins Ferdinand **16**
Restaurant Margueritten **5**
Restaurant Skovmøllen **22**
Teater Bodega **11**

(*Value* **The Århus Pass**

The **Århus Pass** allows unlimited travel by public transportation and free admission to many museums and attractions. It also includes a 2½-hour guided tour. A 2-day pass costs 149DKK ($25/£13) for adults and 67DKK ($11/£6.05) for children 3–12; 1-week passes are 206DKK ($35/£19) and 91DKK ($15/£8.20) for children. The Århus Pass is sold at the tourist office, many hotels, camping grounds, and kiosks throughout the city.

SEEING THE SIGHTS

For the best introduction to Århus, head for the town hall's tourist office, where a 2½-hour **sightseeing tour** leaves daily at 10am June 24 to August 31, costing 80DKK ($14/£7.20) per person (free with the Århus Pass; see above).

In addition to the more major museums listed below, you can also visit two museums on the grounds of Århus University, Nordre Ringgade. They include **Steno Museet,** C. F. Møllers Allé (© **89-42-39-75;** www.stenomuseet.dk; bus: 2, 3, or 4), which displays exhibits documenting natural science and medicine. You'll see beautiful 19th-century astronomical telescopes, a 1920s surgical room, and some of the first computers made in Denmark in the 1950s. Posters, models, and do-it-yourself experiments, including tests of Galileo's demonstrations of gravity and of electromagnetism, are also on display. In addition, you can walk through an herbal garden with some 250 historical medicinal herbs. There is also a Planetarium, with daily shows Tuesday to Sunday at 11am, 1pm, and 2pm, or Saturday and Sunday at noon and 2pm. Hours for the museum are Tuesday to Sunday 10am to 4pm (until 7pm Oct to Mar), costing an admission of 45DKK ($7.65/£4.05), with children 17 and under admitted free.

Also at the university is a **Naturhistorisk Museum,** Block 210, Universitetsparken (© **86-12-97-77;** www.naturhistoriskmuseum.dk; bus: 2 or 3), filled with mounted animals from all over the world, some of which are displayed in engaging dioramas. The collection of Danish animals, especially birds, is unique within Denmark. Skeletons, minerals, and a display devoted to the evolution of life are some of the other exhibits. It's open daily 10am to 4pm (to 5pm July–Aug). It's closed on Mondays November to March. Admission is 40DKK ($6.80/£3.60) adults, and free for children 17 and under.

Århus Domkirke (Cathedral of St. Clemens) ✦ As European city cathedrals go, the Domkirke at Århus is low on the totem pole. When it was built in 1201 in the Romanesque style, it probably had greater style. But in the 1400s, after a fire, it was rebuilt in the Gothic style, with a soaring whitewashed nave that makes it the longest in Denmark, practically as deep as its spire is tall (96m/315 ft). Today's Gothic interior is relatively plain except for one of the few pre-Reformation survivors, a grand **tripartite altarpiece** ✦✦, by the noted Bernt Notke. The pipe organ is from the 1700s. Behind the altar is a painted glass window, the creation of Emmanuel Vigeland, brother of the more celebrated Gustav Vigeland of Norway. In shades of lavender and black, among other colors, chalk frescoes date from medieval times, depicting scenes from the Bible. Our favorite is a depiction of St. George slaying that dragon to save a princess in distress. Also depicted is the namesake of the church, St. Clement, who drowned with an anchor around his neck, making him the patron saint of sailors. The best for last: Climb the tower for a **panoramic view** 🟊🟊 over Århus and its surrounding area. (After the cathedral, we suggest a visit to the nearby medievalesque compound at Vestergade 3, with half-timbered buildings, rock garden, aviary, and antique interiors.)

Bispetorvet. 🕻 **86-20-54-00**. Free admission. May–Sept Mon–Sat 9:30am–4pm; Oct–Apr Mon–Sat 10am–3pm. Bus: 3, 11, 54, or 56.

Århus Kunstmuseum (Århus Museum of Art) 🟊

Crouching down and looking at you from 5m (16 ft.) above is Ron Mueck's controversial sculpture of a boy, called simply *Boy* 🟊🟊🟊, which is eerily lifelike. This avant-garde sculpture sets the tone for one of the best provincial art museums in all of Denmark. The collection is strong on Modernism from the turn of the 20th century to the 1960s.

The museum is also strong on paintings from the so-called Golden Age of art in Denmark in the 1800s. The Romantics, the Realists, the Impressionists—they are all here, along with contemporary works not only from Denmark but from such countries as the United States and Germany as well. The museum is spread over several floors, which are linked by a footbridge. On the top floor is a first-class restaurant and rooftop patio, from which panoramic views of Århus can be seen. Often a venue for temporary exhibitions, the museum owns about 10,000 pieces of art, the oldest of which date from 1770.

Aros Allé 2, Århus C. 🕻 **87-30-66-00**. www.aros.dk. Admission 60DKK ($10/£5.40) adults, free for children under 18. Tues–Sun 10am–5pm (Wed to 10pm). Bus: 2 or 3.

Besættelsesmuseet (Occupation Museum)

Dating from 1857 in what was the old town hall and police station, this building had a grim role to play in World War II. It was here that the Nazis interrogated prisoners and subjected them to torture in the cellars now housing this museum that illustrates the dramatic events of the German takeover of the city in 1940 until liberation in 1945. This was the Gestapo headquarters during the war. In the basement of the building, this Occupation Museum details a most troubled time, depicting Allied air raids on Århus, weapons, documents, World War II photo displays, guns, and even instruments of torture. The museum also describes sabotage carried out by the local resistance movement. One display documents Allied, Nazi, and Danish propaganda.

Mathilde Fibigers Have 2. 🕻 **86-18-42-77**. www.besaettelsesmuseet.dk. Admission 20DKK ($3.40/£1.80) adults, free for children under 12. June–Aug Tues, Thurs, and Sat–Sun 11am–4pm; off season Sat–Sun 11am–4pm. Bus: 3 or 7.

Den Gamle By (The Old Town) 🟊🟊🟊 *Kids*

Outside of Copenhagen, this is Denmark's only government-rated three-star museum, a journey back to yesterday as you wander through a Danish market town as it appeared in olden days. More than three million visitors descend on this museum where history comes alive. More than 75 historic buildings, many of them half-timbered, were uprooted from various locations throughout the country and placed down here to illustrate Danish life from the 16th to the 19th centuries in a re-created botanical garden. The open-air museum differs from similar attractions near Copenhagen and Odense in that this one focuses more on rural life. Visitors walk through the authentic-looking workshops of bookbinders, carpenters, hatters, and other craftspeople. There is also a pharmacy, a school, and an old-fashioned post office. A popular attraction is the Burgomaster's House, a wealthy merchant's antiques-stuffed, half-timbered home, built at the end of the 16th century. Be sure to see the textile collection and the Old Elsinore Theater, erected in the early

19th century. The museum also houses a collection of china, clocks, delftware, and silverware. Summer music programs are staged, and there are a restaurant, tea garden, bakery, and beer cellar. Many activities and programs are designed especially for kids.

Viborgvej 2. ✆ **86-12-31-88**. www.dengamleby.dk. Admission 80DKK ($14/£7.20) adults; free for children 16 and under. Sept–Oct and Apr–May daily 10am–5pm; June–Aug daily 9am–6pm; Nov–Dec and Feb–Mar daily 10am–4pm; Jan daily 11am–3pm. Bus: 3, 14, or 25.

Moesgård Museum ⋆ It's not quite the rival of the Tollund Man in Silkeborg (see earlier in this chapter), but this manor house museum shelters the 2,000-year-old **Grauballe Man** ⋆⋆⋆, whose well-preserved body was found in a bog. Apparently, the poor wretch had been sacrificed to some pagan gods. Discovered in 1952, Mr. Grauballe was so well preserved you can still see the wrinkles on his face. Centuries of "life" in the bog tanned his skin, making it very brown and leather-like. The museum lies in a 100-hectare (247-acre) forest about 8km (5 miles) south of Århus. It's really a Prehistoric Museum with exhibits on archaeology, featuring digs from the area, and ethnography.

If you take the Prehistoric Trail through the forest, you will come to reconstructed houses from the Viking area, even prehistoric houses and grave monuments. A still-active water mill stands on the grounds.

The Viking Market in July and the Willow Festival in August attracts visitors from all over Denmark (ask at the tourist office above for exact dates). As part of the landscape, a path leads to **Moesgård Strand,** the best sandy beach outside Århus.

Moesgård Manor, Moesgård Allé 20, Højbjerg. ✆ **89-42-11-00**. www.moesmus.dk. Admission 45DKK ($7.65/£4.05); free for children 17 and under. Apr–Sept daily 10am–5pm; Oct–Mar Tues–Sun 10am–4pm. Bus: 6 from railway station. Positioned 9km (5⅓ miles) south of Århus's center.

Rådhuset (Town Hall) Just before the outbreak of World War II, Arne Jacobsen, one of Denmark's greatest designers, drew up the plans for this Town Hall. Built between 1936 and 1941 to commemorate the 500th anniversary of the Århus charter, it's been the subject of controversy ever since. For us, it's too raw and functional to earn our press. The outer skeleton of the building evokes scaffolding that was abandoned, although the interior has light, open spaces and plenty of glass. It can be seen only on a guided tour. An elevator (and 346 steps) runs to the top of the 60m (197-ft.) tower, where a carillon occasionally rings. *Note:* The guided tour at 11am includes the tower. The elevator and stairs are open three times a day: 11am, noon, and 2pm.

Rådhuspladsen. ✆ **89-40-20-00**. Admission to tower 5DKK (85¢/45p); guided tour 10DKK ($1.70/90p). Tower 11am, noon, and 2pm; guided tour of hall and tower Mon–Fri 11am. Closed Sept–June 23. Bus: 3, 4, 5, or 14.

Vikingemuseet In the Viking era a rampart protected Århus, and in 1963 some archaeologists went digging to find whatever they could to learn of life in centuries past. The finds were impressive, including many artifacts, even a human skeleton. Remains of the town's Viking walls can still be seen. The most precious artifacts of the Viking era are displayed in the basement of Unibank, close to the cathedral. You'll find reconstructions of Viking houses—that is, a stave church and one of the small pit houses found during the excavation at the site. Objects illustrate how life went on in this bustling merchant city from its foundation in about A.D. 900 until around 1400.

Skt. Clemens Torv 6. ✆ **89-42-11-00**. www.vikingemuseet.dk. Free admission. Mon–Wed and Fri 10am–4pm; Thurs 10am–5:30pm. Bus: 3, 11, 54, or 56.

Von Frue Kirke   "The Church of Our Lady," lying to the northwest of Århus Domkirke, was built between the 13th and 15th centuries but was originally part of a Dominican priory. The original Århus Cathedral was erected on this site in 1060. Today's church, built of red brick, has a largely whitewashed interior. It's mainly a Gothic building with frescoes and a significant altarpiece from the workshop of Claus Berg, painted in 1520. The altarpiece depicts a scene from the Passion, in a stunningly expressive style that is often compared to the work of Pieter Bruegel the Elder. Restoration work was begun here in the 1950s, and the crypt of the original Romanesque church from 1060 was uncovered under the chancel. Its early date makes it the oldest vaulted building in all Scandinavia. This vaulted crypt is now virtually "a church within a church." In addition, a chapter house, which once was a hospital for the elderly in the Reformation era, has been dedicated as a church and incorporated into the general structure. So "Our Lady" is actually three churches in one. Wall paintings from the Middle Ages adorn the walls of the chapter house. Because of all these multiple layers beneath the surface, Von Frue Kirke is often likened to a Russian matryoshka doll.

Frue Kirkeplads. © 86-12-12-43. www.aarhusvorfrue.dk. Free admission. Sept–Apr Mon–Fri 10am–2pm, Sat 10am–noon; May–Aug Mon–Fri 10am–4pm, Sat 10am–noon. Bus: 7, 10, or 17.

NEARBY ATTRACTIONS

The summer residence of Denmark's royal family, **Marselisborg Slot** ✯, at Kongevejen 100, less than 2.5km (1½ miles) south of Århus's center (bus: 1, 18, or 19), is one of the most famous and symbolic buildings in Denmark. If you visit at noon on days Her Majesty and family are in residence, you can see the changing of the guard. It's announced on the local news and in the newspapers when Her Majesty is here. The royal family has used this white manor house since 1902.

It is not possible to visit the interior of the palace, but the castle grounds, even the Queen's rose garden, are open to the public admission-free 9am to 5pm when the castle is not occupied.

The setting is a large forest belt stretching for some 10km (6¼ miles) along the coast. The entire area is ideal for hikes, as nature trails have been cut through the forests. Bikers also like the terrain. Less than 1.5km (1 mile) from the royal palace on the main road south lies **Dyrehaven** (deer park), a protected forest area where you can see fallow deer, and even sika. The more elusive wild roe deer also live here, as well as wild boar, although you're unlikely to spot the latter. For more information visit www.kongehuset.dk.

THE MANOR HOUSES OF EAST JUTLAND

Clausholm   Seventeenth-century Clausholm is a splendid baroque palace, one of the earliest in Denmark. It was commissioned by Frederik IV's chancellor, whose adolescent daughter, Anna Sophie, eloped with the king. When Frederik died, his son by his first marriage banished the queen to Clausholm, where she lived with her court until her death in 1743.

The rooms are basically unaltered, but few of the original furnishings remain. The salons and ballroom feature elaborate stucco ceilings and decorated panels, and an excellent collection of Danish rococo and Empire furnishings has replaced the original pieces. The Queen's Chapel, where Anna Sophie and her court worshipped, is unchanged and contains the oldest organ in Denmark. In 1976 the Italian baroque gardens were reopened, complete with a symmetrically designed fountain system.

Clausholm is about 13km (8 miles) southeast of Randers and 31km (19 miles) north of Århus.

Voldum, Hadsten. © 86-49-16-55. www.clausholm.dk. Admission (including guided tour) 70DKK ($12/£6.30) adults, free for children under 14. Castle July only daily 11am–4pm; park May–Sept only daily 11am–4pm. Bus: 221 from Randers.

The Museums at Gammel Estrup ⍟   One of the most elegant Renaissance manors in Central Jutland lies 39km (24 miles) northeast of Århus. Today this compound of buildings is the site of the **Jutland Manor House Museum,** complete with a great Hall, a chapel, and richly decorated stucco ceilings; and the **Danish Agricultural Museum,** which celebrates the role of Danish farming over the past thousand years. The entire compound dates from the 14th century, but the structures you see were extensively rebuilt and remodeled in the early 1600s. Expect a glimpse into medieval fortifications, baronial furnishings, the changing nature of tools and machines used during Danish plantings and harvests, and an enormous sense of pride in Denmark and its traditions.

Jyllands Herregårdsmuseum, Randersvej 2, Auning. © 86-48-30-01. www.gl-estrup.dk. Admission 70DKK ($12/ £6.30) adults, free for children 17 and under. Agricultural Museum Jan–Mar and Nov–Dec Tues–Sun 10am–3pm; Apr–June and Sept–Oct daily 10am–5pm; July–Aug daily 10am–6pm. Manor House Museum Apr–June and Sept–Oct daily noon–4:30pm; July–Aug daily noon–4:30pm. Bus: 119. From Randers, take Rte. 16 east to Auning.

Rosenholm Slot (Rosenholm Castle) ⍟   One of Jutland's stateliest Renaissance manors was built in 1559 on a small island in the middle of a lake. Stone lions guard the bridge that leads to the castle where the Rosenkrantz family has lived for more than 4 centuries. The four-winged castle is encircled by 14 hectares (35 acres) of landscaped parkland. We find Rosenholm far more impressive than the queen's more modest digs at Marselisborg (see above). The Great Hall is graced with a portrait of King Frederik V, and most of the other salons and galleries are furnished and decorated in a Moorish-inspired Spanish style—or else with rococo adornments (a bit much at times). The Winter Room is walled with leather, and French and Flemish tapestries, some 3 centuries old, adorn the Tower Room and the Corner Room. The castle is 21km (13 miles) north of Århus and a kilometer (⅔ mile) north of the village of Hornslet.

Hornslet. © 86-99-40-10. www.rosenholmslot.dk. Admission 60DKK ($10/£5.40), free for children under 6. June 1–19 Sat–Sun 11am–4pm; June 20–Aug 31 daily 11am–4pm. Closed Sept–May. Bus: 119 or 121 from Århus.

SHOPPING

Århus is the biggest shopping venue in Jutland, with some 400 specialty stores, each of them tightly clustered within an area of about 1.3 sq. km (½ sq. mile). The centerpiece of this district is the Strøget, whose terminus is the Store Torv, dominated by the Århus Domkirke. You might try a large-scale department store first. One of the best is **Salling,** Søndergade 27 (© 86-12-18-00), with some 30 specialty boutiques, all under one roof. A wide range of articles for the whole family is sold here, including body-care items, clothing, gifts, toys, music, and sports equipment. **Magasin du Nord,** Immervad 2–8 (© 86-12-33-00), is the largest department store in Scandinavia, in business for more than 125 years. The staff will assist foreign visitors with tax-free purchases.

"The greatest silversmith the world has ever seen" is the praise often used to describe **Georg Jensen,** Søndergade 1 (© 86-12-01-00). A tradition since 1866, Georg Jensen is known for style and quality, producing unique silver and gold jewelry, elegant clocks and watches, and stainless steel cutlery, among other items. A leading goldsmith, **Hingelberg,** Store Torv 3 (© **86-13-13-00**), is the licensed Cartier outlet, and offers a wide selection of top-quality designer jewelry.

Galleri Bo Bendixen, Store Torv 14 (© **86-12-67-50**), offers the brilliantly colored designs of Bo Bendixen, the famous Danish graphic artist. The shop also sells a wide range of gifts and garments for children and adults. **Volden 4 Kunsthåndværk,** Volden 4 (© **86-13-21-76**), specializes in top-quality applied art, and glass made by some of the leading artisans of the country. Silver, copper, and brass ornaments are for sale, as are exclusive bronze candlesticks.

Bülow Duus Glassblowers, Studsgade 14 (© **86-12-72-86**), is a working glassblowing shop open to the public. At an attractive old house in the heart of the city, you can watch the fascinating work of glass blowing. Drinking glasses, candlesticks, bowls, and other items are for sale. For traditional Danish pottery, head for **Favlhuset,** Møllestien 53 (© **86-13-06-32**).

If you haven't found what you're looking for after all that, head for **Inspiration Buus,** Ryesgade 2 (© **86-12-67-00**), which sells top-quality gifts, kitchenware, tableware, and toiletry articles, much of it of Danish design.

WHERE TO STAY

Low-cost accommodations in this lively university city are limited. Those on a modest budget should check with the tourist office in the Rådhuset (© **87-31-50-10**) for bookings in **private homes.**

Depending on the day of the week or the time of the year you check in, rooms in many of the hotels labeled inexpensive aren't inexpensive at all, but more moderate in price.

EXPENSIVE

Hotel Marselis *⭐*   This is the most scenically located, isolated, and nature-conscious of the grand modern hotels of Århus, thanks to a long, narrow layout that rambles along a grass-covered bluff, a few steps from the sea, about 5km (3 miles) south of the city center. Built of earth-colored bricks in 1967, it plays up its views over the water and an interior decor that's the most nautical of all the hotels in the area. Rooms are smaller and less imaginatively decorated than those in, for example, the SAS Radisson, but overall, the setting is better with the windows opening on to views of the water. Each unit is equipped with a full bathroom with tub and shower. Corporate conventions sometimes come here, but less often than the hotel would really like.

The **Restaurant Marselis** and its bar, the **Café Nautilus,** provide food, piano music, drink, and a log-burning fireplace. A less formal dining and drinking venue, open only during mild weather, is the **Beach Café,** whose tables are arranged on a sunny terrace. This is one of the few modern hotels in Århus with its own swimming pool, an indoor affair with big windows overlooking the sea.

Strandvejen 25, DK-8000 Århus C. © **86-14-44-11.** Fax 86-11-70-46. www.marselis.dk. 101 units. 1,600DKK ($272/ £144) double; 1,950DKK ($332/£176) suite. Rates include buffet breakfast. AE, DC, MC, V. Bus: 6. **Amenities:** Restaurant; bar; indoor heated pool; gym; sauna; 24-hr. room service; laundry service; dry cleaning; solarium. *In room:* TV, dataport, minibar, hair dryer.

Hotel Philip *⭐⭐⭐ (Finds*   This hotel represents a dream come true for its famous owner. This discovery offers the finest accommodations in Århus and some of the best lodgings in Central Jutland, a 5-minute walk from the bus station. The hotel is owned by Marc Rieper, a former player on the Danish soccer team, who headed the ball at the crossbar—narrowly missing a goal—in the final moments against Brazil during the semifinals of the 1998 World Cup. Opening onto a canal, the building housing this boutique hotel has been vastly renovated, each accommodation turned into a luxury suite. The six regular suites have been lavishly decorated in a French and Italian style, and the two remaining suites on the top floor are even more luxuriously equipped in a romantic style. Jutlanders on their honeymoon often book this pair of suites. All the suites are spacious, containing Oriental carpets and works of art. Each bedroom has a king-size bed, and all the units come with a first-class bathroom with tub and shower. The service is the best in Århus—for example, you're greeted with fresh flowers. Even if not a guest, consider a meal at the Hotel Philip's on-site **restaurant.** See "Where to Dine," below.

Åboulevarden 28, DK-8000 Århus. ② **87-32-14-44.** Fax 86-12-69-55. www.hotelphilip.dk. 8 units. 1,495DKK ($254/£135) suite. Rates include breakfast. DC, MC, V. **Amenities:** Restaurant; cafe; bar; room service (7am–10pm); laundry service; dry cleaning; nonsmoking rooms. *In room:* TV, dataport, Wi-Fi, minibar, hair dryer, iron, safe.

Hotel Royal 𝕂𝕂𝕂   For the best in modern facilities, check into the Radisson SAS (see below). But for traditional extravagance and royal luxury, make this aptly named hotel your choice. This is the most glamorous accommodation in town, attracting such cultural greats of yesterday as Marian Anderson and Arthur Rubenstein or such current celebs as Madonna and Sting (but not in the same suite). The gilt date on its neo-baroque facade commemorates the hotel's establishment in 1838. There have been numerous additions and upgrades since. The Royal stands close to the city's symbol, its cathedral. A vintage elevator takes you to the guest rooms, many of them quite spacious. They're modernized, with good-size bathrooms containing tub/shower combos. Beds are refurbished and accommodations are fitted with high-quality furniture, carpeting, and fabrics. The ground floor houses the Royal Scandinavian Casino and night club, offering such games of chance as international roulette, blackjack, and seven-card stud poker.

Stove Torv 4, DK-8000 Århus. ② **86-12-00-11.** Fax 86-76-04-04. www.hotelroyal.dk. 102 units. 1,595DKK ($271/£144) double; 1,995DKK ($339/£180) suite. Rates include breakfast. AE, DC, MC, V. Parking 150DKK ($26/£14). Bus: 56 or 58. **Amenities:** Restaurant; bar; sauna; room service (7am–10pm); babysitting; laundry service; dry cleaning; nonsmoking rooms; casino. *In room:* TV, dataport, Wi-Fi, minibar, beverage maker, hair dryer.

Radisson SAS Scandinavia Hotel Århus 𝕂𝕂𝕂   This is one of the most modern and dynamic hotels in Denmark, and a city showplace that municipal authorities show off to visiting dignitaries. It was built in 1995 above the largest convention facilities in Jutland, and is the most popular convention hotel in the region. Of course, for that reason we like it less. However, should you arrive when a convention isn't taking place, the hotel can be a honey. Bedrooms occupy floors 4 to 11 of a glass-and-stone–sheathed tower that's visible throughout the city. Lower floors contain check-in, dining, drinking, and convention facilities. The standard bedrooms are outfitted in plush upholstery with bright colors. Each has a tasteful decor that's different from its immediate neighbor, incorporating Scandinavian, English, Japanese, or Chinese themes, and each has a well-kept bathroom with a tub/shower combo, and large-windowed views over the city. Costing more are the upgraded business-class rooms, with newspaper delivery, turndown service, and free entrance to the fitness suite.

Margrethepladsen 1, DK-8000 Århus C. ② **800/333-3333** in the U.S., or 86-12-86-65. Fax 86-12-86-75. www.aarhus kongrescenter.dk/hotellet. 234 units. 1,540DKK–1,685DKK ($262–$286/£139–£152) double; from 2,260DKK

($384/£203) suite. Rates include breakfast. AE, DC, MC, V. Bus: 1, 2, 6, or 16. **Amenities:** Restaurant; bar; fitness center; sauna; 24-hr. room service; massage; babysitting; laundry service; dry cleaning; nonsmoking rooms; rooms for those w/limited mobility. *In room:* TV, dataport, Wi-Fi, minibar, hair dryer, trouser press, safe.

Scandic Plaza ⊕ (Kids)   The massive bulk of this chain-run hotel rises imposingly in the heart of the city, and we think it's a most reliable and comfortable choice for overnighting, without reaching the pinnacle scaled by the Radisson SAS. Actually it opened in 1930 but has been vastly improved and enlarged since that time. The hotel never escapes the "chain format" of its bedroom decor, but the furnishings are first-class and the decoration is tasteful, with well-maintained private bathrooms that come with tub/shower combos. The on-site **Restaurant Brazil** comes as a surprise with its Latin cuisine. Before dinner, head for the cozy bar, where six exotic cocktails await your selection every evening along with the standard beer and liquors. This is one of the best hotels for families traveling with children, as it offers a playroom with all those games, toys, books, and crayons that kids demand. There's even a wooden train to amuse.

Banegårdspladsen 14, DK-8100 Århus C. ⓒ **87-32-01-00.** Fax 87-32-01-99. www.scandic-hotels.com/aarhus. 162 units. 1,025DKK–1,695DKK ($174–$288/£92–£153) double; from 1,865DKK ($317/£168) suite. Rates include breakfast. DC, MC, V. Bus: 3, 17, 56, or 58. **Amenities:** Restaurant; bar; fitness center; Jacuzzi; sauna; kids' playroom; room service (7:30am–10:30pm); laundry service; dry cleaning; nonsmoking rooms. *In room:* TV, dataport, Wi-Fi, minibar, hair dryer, iron, safe.

MODERATE

Best Western Ritz Hotel ⊕⊕ (Value)   Since 1932 when this hotel first opened its doors, it's been known for its fair-value rooms, its comfort, and its helpful staff. The good news is that it has been carefully restored and redecorated, with the original architecture still intact. Tradition is respected here. The location is convenient, opposite the central rail station and the airport bus terminal, close to entertainment, restaurants, and the best shopping. It is also near the major attractions of the city, including the Town Hall, which stands opposite the Ritz.

Don't be misled by the "Ritz" in its title. The Århus version is far less grand. The hotel takes its name from a large painting in its Art Deco restaurant that depicts the superswanky Ritz in Paris, where Princess Di spent her final hours. The hotel offers midsize-to-spacious bedrooms, which are rated "standard" and "standard plus." The main difference between the two is that the standard plus units are larger with bathtubs as well as a shower and a big comfortable queen-size bed (or twins), and some of these superior units also have a private balcony. The best of this lot that we inspected were also equipped with beautiful four-poster beds.

One real plus for the hotel is its on-site **restaurant** under the baton of master chef René Rohde Knudsen, who is known for his first-rate French/Danish cuisine. "Instead of serving just food, I prefer to take my diners on a gastronomic journey," he assures us. In the closets of the hotel, René discovered a treasure-trove of blue-fluted porcelain, which he has rescued along with old-fashioned silverware, jugs, candelabra, and centerpieces. The hotel also has the best wine cellar in town, with some 8,000 bottles spanning an impressive 150 years from old Madeiras to more recently arrived bottles of Beaujolais shipped up from France.

Banegårdspladsen 12, DK-8000 Århus. ⓒ **800/528-1234** in the U.S., or 86-13-44-44. Fax 86-13-45-87. www.hotel ritz.dk. 67 units. 1,350DKK ($230/£122) double. Rates include breakfast. AE, DISC, MC, V. Free parking. Bus: 3, 17, 56, or 58. **Amenities:** Restaurant; cafeteria; laundry service; dry cleaning; nonsmoking rooms. *In room:* TV, Wi-Fi, hair dryer.

Comfort Hotel Atlantic   This is a standard, durable choice for overnighting, though it lacks the style and glamour of some of our previous selections. Since its opening in 1964, it's provided good comfort and a fair price in one of the city's tallest buildings, rising 11 floors, with good views from the top-floor bedrooms, some of which open onto a balcony with a view of the water. Bedrooms range from small to midsize, but each is tastefully and agreeably furnished, with well-kept bathrooms with tub/shower combos. Breakfast is the only meal served, although there are many eateries nearby—the helpful staff will advise. They will also arrange for you to have access to a nearby health club and tennis courts.

Europlads 12–14, DK-8000 Århus. ✆ **86-13-11-11.** Fax 86-13-23-43. www.choicehotels.dk. 102 units. 1,295DKK ($220/£117) double; 1,595DKK ($271/£144) suite. Rates include breakfast. AE, DC, MC, V. Bus: 3. **Amenities:** Breakfast lounge; bar; laundry service; dry cleaning; nonsmoking rooms. *In room:* TV, dataport, minibar, hair dryer, safe.

INEXPENSIVE

Hotel Guldsmeden ★ *Value*   In its price range, this small, intimate hotel is our favorite hideaway in Århus. This affordable choice lies in a former town house from the 1800s that was completely renovated and turned into a cozy little place. We like to stop off here in the summer, when the garden is at its peak, and enjoy breakfast on the terrace outdoors. It's the best and healthiest breakfast in town—all organic, with fresh fruit, muesli, and the like. The bedrooms are small to midsize, and each is furnished tastefully, most often cheerfully, in soothing shades. Some of the rooms contain a small bathroom with shower; in units without bathrooms, corridor facilities suffice.

Guldsmedgade 40, DK-8000 Århus. ✆ **86-13-45-50.** Fax 86-13-76-76. www.hotelguldsmeden.dk. 27 units, 20 with bathroom. 845DKK ($144/£76) double without bathroom; 1,095DKK ($186/£99) double with bathroom; 1,495DKK ($254/£135) suite. Rates include buffet breakfast. AE, DC, MC, V. **Amenities:** Breakfast room; lounge. *In room:* TV, Wi-Fi.

Hotel La Tour *Kids*   If you're not too demanding, this is quite a good choice, especially for families on a holiday. Since its construction in 1956, and its rebuilding in 1986, this hotel has followed a conscious policy of downgrading (yes, downgrading) its accommodations and facilities from a once-lofty status to a middle-brow formula. The result is a hotel that's far from being the best in town—viewed, we imagine, as a great success by the management—that attracts hundreds of foreign visitors. The hotel, housed in an unimaginative two-story building, is 3.5km (2¼ miles) north of Århus center. It offers well-maintained, simple bedrooms with small bathrooms containing tub/shower combos. There is a patio-style restaurant serving competently prepared Danish and international food, as well as a bar, and a children's playroom (open May–Sept only).

Randersvej 139, DK-8200 Århus. ✆ **86-16-78-88.** Fax 86-16-79-95. www.latour.dk. 101 units. 825DKK ($140/£74) double; 1,045DKK ($178/£94) suite. Rates include breakfast. AE, DC, MC, V. Bus: 2, 3, or 11. **Amenities:** Restaurant; bar; room service (7am–10pm); laundry service; dry cleaning. *In room:* TV, minibar, hair dryer, safe.

Hotel Mercur   For motorists this is one of the most ultramodern hotels in town, 4km (2½ miles) south of the center and less than a kilometer (½ mile) from the park that surrounds Queen Margrethe's summer house (Marselisborg Slot). Overall, it's warmer and cozier than some of its most visible competitors. Rooms are masculine looking and conservatively contemporary with views that encompass panoramas over the town and the seacoast. Some have narrow, rarely used balconies, and each unit is equipped with a small bathroom with shower. There are a restaurant, the **Mercur,** and a bar on the premises, both of which are appealing and warmly decorated. There are also two bowling alleys in the hotel's cellar, and a larger bowling alley complex a few blocks away. A shopping mall, Viby Centret, with about 50 shops, is found on

Skanderborgvej, a short walk from the hotel. In spite of its name, this hotel is not associated with the French-based chain.

Viby Torv, DK-8260 Århus, Viby J. ⓒ 86-14-14-11. Fax 86-14-46-41. www.hotel-mercur.dk. 107 units. Mon–Thurs 700DKK–990DKK ($119–$168/£63–£89) double, 990DKK ($168/£89) suite; Fri–Sun 700DKK–790DKK ($119–$134/£63–£71) double, 790DKK ($134/£71) suite. Rates include buffet breakfast. AE, DC, MC, V. Bus: 5, 15, or 25. **Amenities:** Restaurant; bar; laundry service; dry cleaning; nonsmoking rooms. *In room:* TV, Wi-Fi.

WHERE TO DINE
EXPENSIVE
Hotel Philip Restaurant 🏵🏵🏵 DANISH/FRENCH   In the most exclusive hotel in Århus, a delightful restaurant is imbued with a romantic atmosphere and serves quality food prepared with the best and freshest of ingredients—an unbeatable combination. Tables are placed on beautiful hardwood floors, and elegantly set and lit by brass candleholders. The ceiling is adorned with a metal tapestry in the Art Nouveau style, and the walls are painted dark but brightened with summery yellow ornaments.

The front part of the restaurant, as can be viewed from the street, is decorated as an elegant cafe, with the luxurious dining found in the rear. Inventiveness goes hand in hand with solid technique. The kitchen also takes full advantage of the region's riches, with seafood predominating.

We like the way the chefs seasonally adjust the menu to take advantage of the best produce in any month—fresh asparagus in late spring, the finest of game dishes in the autumn, and always—but always—the freshest catch of the day. We can't recommend specific dishes because they are forever changing. But take that old standby cannelloni. As an example of the chef's technique, he stuffs it with Serrano ham, seafood, and Danish cheese—and that's not all. He serves it with truffles. Cannelloni will never taste the same again. Appetizers and desserts, as well as the meat and poultry dishes, have always tasted sublime to our palates.

Åboulevarden 28. ⓒ 87-32-14-44. Reservations required. Main courses 160DKK–200DKK ($27–$34/£14–£18). DC, MC, V. Mon–Sat noon–10:30pm.

Prins Ferdinand 🏵🏵🏵 DANISH/INTERNATIONAL   This is the only restaurant in town to give Philip a run for its kroner. Its name is actually a reference to the notoriously carousing Prince Frederik (1792–1863), who spent most of his nights in Århus gambling or pursuing wine and women. On the edge of Århus's historic center in a former tea salon, this is one of the city's finest restaurants. It was established in 1988 by different owners, but is run today by the hospitable Tonny Hansen and Martin Lemvig, who welcome the local business community and also the most discerning of visiting foodies into their lovely luxe restaurant. In two pink-toned dining rooms laden with flickering candles and flowers, you can order a platter of fresh smoked salmon served with tartare of salmon and pepper-cream sauce, turbot with Russian caviar and a drizzle of olive oil, sea devil with lobster prepared Thai-style with lemon grass, or boneless pigeon stuffed with fresh gooseliver served with a raspberry sauce. A dessert specialty is pears cooked with elderberries and served with vanilla ice cream, nougat, and almonds. The restaurant's array of dessert cheeses, the most unusual array in Jutland, includes artisan creations produced by small farmers.

Viborgvej 2. ⓒ 86-12-52-05. Reservations recommended. Lunch main courses 140DKK–175DKK ($24–$30/£13–£16); dinner main courses 160DKK–250DKK ($27–$43/£14–£23); fixed-price lunch menus 175DKK–235DKK ($30–$40/£16–£21); fixed-price dinner menus 395DKK–995DKK ($67–$169/£36–£90). AE, DC, MC, V. Tues–Sat noon–3pm and 6–9pm. Bus: 3.

MODERATE

Restaurant Margueritten DANISH/FRENCH/ITALIAN One of the town's better restaurants was carved out of what used to be stables for horses that pulled the carriages through Århus. It's a cozy place for lunch, and an ideal venue for a romantic dinner under old beamed ceilings. Old Danish furniture enhances the ambience, and in summer a beautiful little garden in the rear is open. This isn't grandmother-type cooking, as the fare is as modern as tomorrow, but it always uses the freshest regional produce. Chefs offer such dishes as guinea fowl with a stuffing of tiger shrimp; the distinctive flavor comes from the marinade of yogurt and tandoori spices. Some of the best dishes we found on the menu included filet of wild pork with a balsamic chocolate sauce (yes, you read that right), medallion of beef in a cognac sauce with mixed vegetables, and a tangy breast of duck with a raspberry sauce and fresh plums which have been marinated in port. The English-speaking waitstaff is polite and helpful.

Guldsmedgade 20. © **86-19-60-33**. Reservations required. 1-course fixed-price menu 159DKK ($27/£14); 2-course menu 179DKK ($30/£16); 3-course menu 209DKK ($36/£19). Mon–Sat 11:30am–11pm.

INEXPENSIVE

Gastronomica FRENCH/ITALIAN "The Ugly Duckling" (the former name of this restaurant) has blossomed into a swan. In its latest incarnation, this cost-conscious eatery, with one of the best fixed-price menus in town, has a continental flair, without charging the prices usually associated with Paris or Rome. Grilled salmon invariably appears on the menu as it does in most Danish restaurants, but other dishes are far more enticing to us, especially a veal scaloppini with a red-wine sauce. We'd also recommend their *pasta alla marinara* (seafood pasta), one of the best dishes we discovered on the menu. Save room for the desserts, especially if the cooks are inspired that night to make such delights as tiramisu, crème brûlée, or crepes with velvety ice cream.

Østergade 12. © **86-13-99-63**. Reservations recommended. Main courses 138DKK–192DKK ($23–$33/£12–£17); 2-course fixed-price menu 149DKK ($25/£13); 3-course menu 189DKK ($32/£17). MC, V. Mon–Thurs noon–9:30pm; Fri–Sat noon–10pm. Bus: 2, 6, or 17.

Ministeriet DANISH/MEDITERRANEAN The student from the University of Århus who first took us here was right on target: "You can eat well in Århus if you know the secret little places where students who don't have too much money go." This small and cozy inn with a courtyard is in the old Klostertorv across from Frue Kloster Abbey. You'll invariably stumble upon the charming old place if you're out sightseeing. It's a cafe-style place serving very good food, with lots of fish such as plaice, offered at reasonable prices. The chefs offer various menus depending on the season, using fresh Danish produce whenever available. There's a strong Mediterranean influence here.

Klostertorvet 5. © **86-17-11-88**. Reservations required. Main courses lunch 60DKK–140DKK ($10–$24/£5.40–£13); fixed-price dinner menus 150DKK–300DKK ($26–$51/£14–£27). AE, DC, MC, V. Mon–Sat 9:30am–1pm; Sun 10am–6pm. Bus: 1, 2, 6, or 9.

Restaurant Skovmøllen ★ *(finds* DANISH/INTERNATIONAL Since it was constructed of straw, wood, and stone more than 300 years ago, this building has functioned as a farmhouse, a gristmill, and a simple cafe. It's set beside the Giber River, 10km (6¼ miles) south of Århus, close to the Moesgård Museum. Beneath a beamed ceiling and frequent reminders of old-time Denmark, you can order typically Danish platters at lunchtime, and straightforward, not particularly esoteric dishes that are just a bit more cosmopolitan at night. Lunches might include meatballs, *smørrebrød* (open-faced sandwiches), herring platters, or roasted pork with onions and braised cabbage. Dinners are more elaborate, featuring shrimp cocktails, steak with french fries, stuffed filets of plaice with new potatoes, and salmon chops with garlic-flavored butter sauce. The place is always dependable, the cookery always reliable, but its main allure is that it's a charming, country-flavored getaway from the city center.

Skovmøllenvej 51. ⓒ 86-27-12-14. Reservations recommended. Main courses 48DKK–200DKK ($8.15–$34/ £4.30–£18); fixed-price menus 148DKK–298DKK ($25–$51/£13–£27). MC, V. June–Aug Tues–Sun noon–6pm; Sept–May Fri–Sun noon–5pm. From downtown Århus take bus no. 6.

Teater Bodega DANISH   Originally established at a different address in 1907, Teater Bodega in 1951 moved across the street from both the Århus Dramatic Theater and the Århus Cathedral. Here in its new setting it offers an amusing dining ambience for local actors and theatergoers, its walls covered with illustrations of theatrical costumes and other thespian memorabilia. The food is solid and flavorful in the Danish country style. Various kinds of Danish hash, including *biksemad,* are served along with regular or large portions of Danish roast beef. Although the beef dishes are good, a waiter assured us that most locals go for a platter of the freshly caught plaice or flounder. "Fish is the faithful friend to the Danish palate," he so accurately claimed.

Skolegade 7. ⓒ 86-12-19-17. Reservations recommended. Main courses 89DKK–198DKK ($15–$34/£8–£18); lunch *smørrebrød* 48DKK–89DKK ($8.15–$15/£4.30–£8); 3-course fixed-price lunch or dinner 258DKK ($44/£23). DC, MC, V. Mon–Sat 11am–11:30pm. Bus: 6.

ÅRHUS AFTER DARK

The city of Århus has the richest and most varied cultural life in Jutland. Its chief attraction, and a major venue for cultural events, is the Musikhuset Århus (see below). The Århus Symphony Orchestra and the Danish National Opera perform here frequently, among other attractions. For a look at what's happening here and in other venues, pick up a copy of the monthly booklet *What's On in Århus* at the tourist office (see "Visitor Information," earlier in this chapter).

CULTURAL ÅRHUS

You'll have to speak Danish to enjoy most productions at the **Århus Theater,** Bispetorv (ⓒ 89-33-23-00), which has five stages with a total of 1,200 seats. It was designed by Hack Kampmann and opened in 1900. Local actors and visiting stars entertain in a wide repertoire early September to mid-June.

Svalegangen, Rosenkrantzgade 21 (ⓒ 86-13-88-66), presents an up-to-date repertoire, the latest in Danish drama, music, cabaret, modern dance, and guest artists. The company stages about 40 productions annually. **Entré Scenen,** Grønnegade 93B (ⓒ 86-20-15-36), is an experimental feature of Århus's dramatic life. A varied range of performances, often by foreign artists, appeals to a wide spectrum of ages here. Guest opera and dance theater productions are also staged at **Gellerupscenen,** Gudrunsvej 78 (ⓒ 86-25-03-66).

Opened in 1982, **Musikhuset Århus,** Thomas Jensens Allé (ⓒ 89-40-90-00), is the home of the Århus Symphony Orchestra and the Danish National Opera. Tickets for most events range from 50DKK to 1,000DKK ($8.50–$170/£4.50–£90). Programs are presented on the great stage, the small stage, and the cabaret stage, as well as in the amphitheater and on the foyer stages, where free performances are presented year-round. The foyer, open daily 11am to 9pm, is the site of the box office, an information desk, a cafe/restaurant, and souvenir shops.

DANCE CLUBS

The most popular, charming, and fun dance club in town is **Train** ⚔, Toldbodgade 6 (© **26-12-58-00**), where a crowd that's under 35 or 40-ish dances on any of three floors of what used to be a warehouse down beside the waterfront. The top floors feature disco music from the '70s and '80s; the middle and lower levels are devoted to an English-style pub and louder, more jarring techno. The site is also a venue, at irregular intervals, for live concerts. There's sometimes, but not always, a cover charge that can range from 40DKK to 70DKK ($6.80–$12/£3.60–£6.30), depending on what's on that night.

BARHOPPING

Århus abounds in bars and taverns, most of which charge no cover unless there's live music on special nights. The oldest hostelry in town, **Thorups Kælder,** Store Torv 3 (© **86-12-04-14**), was founded by Cistercian monks in the 13th century. Here you can quench your thirst in historic surroundings. You'll find us at our favorite bar and cafe, **Café Under Masken,** Bispegade 3 (© **86-18-22-66**), next door to the Royal Hotel. This is the creation of a well-known local artist, Hans Krull, who designed the iron sculptures adorning the gateway to the hotel. If Salvador Dali were alive and could see the decor, he would call it surreal. Krull and some of his patrons apparently picked up the flotsam and jetsam of the world for decor. The only Aussie bar in Århus, **The Billabong Bar,** Skolegade 26 (© **86-13-27-15**), is a typical Outback-style bar, its raw edge adding to its charm. There's live music every weekend, and sports fans gather here to watch major events on TV, all the time sipping Australian beverages. **Gyngen,** Mejlgade 53 (© **86-19-22-55**), is the venue for rock, techno, and the like.

Bryggeriet Sct. Clemens ⚔, Kannikegade 10–12 (© **86-13-80-00**), is a combined brewery and public house which offers freshly tapped, frothy draft beer brewed in coppers in the cellar, matured, and served in glasses. The bartender's special is a 1-liter *kwak glas* (a round-bottomed glass held upright on a wooden stand). Regardless of which beer you select, this glass is designed for massive consumption. In addition to the pub, you can also order various Danish dishes here if you decide to stick around and dine.

Gays and lesbians gather to dance and enjoy the cafe at **Pan Club,** Jægergårdsgade 42 (© **86-13-43-80**). The cafe is open Friday and Saturday 10pm to 6am; the dance club is open Friday and Saturday 11pm to 5am. Cover is 50DKK ($8.50/£4.50) after midnight.

AN AMUSEMENT PARK

Tivoli-Friheden, Skobrynet (© **86-14-73-00;** www.friheden.dk; bus: 4), is a pale imitation of the Tivoli in Copenhagen; the scale is much smaller here, but there is some of the same sense of fantasy. Set in a forest about 3.5km (2¼ miles) south of Århus, it's bright and modern, appealing to families and couples from the city and the surrounding communities. Entertainment includes an open-air theater, art shows, concerts, clowns, rides, and a scattering of restaurants. The park is open only mid-April to mid-August. Although the park opens every day at noon, the rides and attractions don't open until 2pm. Everything closes down at 11pm. Admission is 60DKK ($10/£5.40) adults, 40DKK ($6.80/£3.60) children 4 to 11.

THE TOWN'S ONLY CASINO

Hotel Royal Casino, Stove Torv 4 (© **86-12-00-11**), is one of only four in Jutland and one of a handful in the entire country. Blackjack—also French roulette on weekends—plus other games of chance are offered daily 3pm to 4am. Admission is 50DKK ($8.50/£4.50). No jeans and no sports shoes are allowed; a jacket is preferred, although a tie isn't necessary.

8 Ebeltoft ★

96km (60 miles) E of Silkeborg; 53km (33 miles) NE of Århus; 335km (208 miles) W of Copenhagen

Wandering the cobblestone streets of Ebeltoft is like going back to a town 200 years ago. Why has so little changed in its historic core? That's because this town of half-timbered houses had a long slumber of about 2 centuries, when it economically stagnated. When it woke up in the 1960s, it found its old buildings and streets had become a tourist attraction. So instead of tearing down buildings, locals restored them with their increased prosperity.

Meaning "apple orchard" in Danish, Ebeltoft is the capital of the Mols hill country, an area of great scenic beauty in Central Jutland. Allow at least 3 hours to wander its streets—in some cases, hidden-away lanes—and to explore its old inns. Sometimes a ruddy-faced fisherman will consent to have his picture taken, assuring you that he is still following the same profession as his grandfather.

Ebeltoft's Viking-age wooden "dragon boats" have given way to expensive yachts in the harbor today. Life at Ebeltoft developed around this beautiful harbor and its scenic bay, Ebeltoft Vig.

In the Middle Ages, Ebeltoft was a thriving port, enjoying trade with Germany, Sweden, and, of course, Copenhagen. However, in 1659, after a dispute, the Swedish army invaded, sacking the port and setting fire to the merchant fleet. Ebeltoft never really recovered from this almost fatal blow until it became a tourist destination in the 1960s. Ironically, it was Swedish tourists who first discovered the antique charms of Ebeltoft, with its timber-framed buildings topped with red tile roofs.

ESSENTIALS

GETTING THERE   By Train and Bus   There's no direct train service to Ebeltoft. From Copenhagen, take the train (via Fredericia) to Århus; at Århus Central Station, board bus no. 123 for Ebeltoft.

By Car   From Silkeborg head east on Route 15 through Århus and continue around the coast, then follow Route 21 south to Ebeltoft.

VISITOR INFORMATION   Contact the **Ebeltoft Turistbureau,** Strandvejen 2 (© **86-34-14-00;** www.ebeltoftturist.dk), open June 15 to August Monday to Saturday 10am to 6pm and Sunday 11am to 4pm; and September to June 14 Monday to Friday 9am to 4pm and Saturday 10am to 1pm.

GETTING AROUND   By Bicycle   Bikes can be rented at **L&P Cykler,** Nørre Allé 5 (© **86-34-47-77**), open Monday to Friday 8am to 5:30pm, Saturday 8am to noon. Rental fees cost around 60DKK ($10/£5.40) per day.

SEEING THE SIGHTS

Det Gamle Rådhus (The Old Town Hall)   This is the smallest town hall in Denmark. It looks like something erected just for kindergarten children to play in—a

1789 building, blackened half-timbering, a red-brick with timbered facade, and a bell tower. Its museum houses an ethnographic collection from Thailand and artifacts from the town's history. It's in the town center north of Strandvejen.

Torvet. © **86-34-55-99.** Admission 25DKK ($4.25/£2.25); free for children under 18. Apr–Aug daily 10am–5pm; Sept–Oct Tues–Sun 11am–3pm; Nov–Mar Sat–Sun 11am–3pm.

Fregatten Jylland 🛈 Moored at the harbor, the *Jylland* is the oldest man-of-war in Denmark (1860) and the world's longest wooden ship at 71m (233 ft.). The vessel is an impressive monument to Ebeltoft's maritime heyday, and the restoration of the three-masted ship was financed by Mærsk McKinney Møller, a local shipping tycoon. Stand on the bridge and gun deck, imagining the harbor 2 centuries ago, and, down below, check out the captain's room and the galley with several miniature sea-battle scenarios on display.

Strandvejen 4. © **86-34-10-99.** www.fregatten-jylland.dk. Admission 80DKK ($14/£7.20) adults, 40DKK ($6.80/£3.60) children 4–12; free for children under 4. Jan 2–Mar 21 and Oct 25–Dec 30 daily 10am–4pm; Mar 22–June 13 and Aug 23–Oct 24 daily 10am–5pm; June 14–Aug 22 daily 10am–7pm.

Glasmuseet Ebeltoft (Ebeltoft Glass Museum) Unless you have a fascination with glass, you might want to pass by this attraction. At Ebeltoft harbor stands one of Denmark's most important glass museums, housed in a building that was once a customs and excise house. It displays both decorative and functional glass, ranging from the symbol-laden works of Swedish glass guru Bertil Vallien to the luminous gold pavilions of Japanese artist Kyohei Fujita. The artists exhibited decide which of their pieces they want to represent their work; this has resulted in a large permanent exhibition. May to September young glass students work with blowing irons and modern "syrupy" blobs of glass in the museum garden.

Strandvejen 8. © **86-34-17-99.** Fax 86-34-60-60. www.glasmuseet.dk. Admission 60DKK ($10/£5.40) adults, 10DKK ($1.70/90p) children 6–17; free for children under 6. Jan–June and Aug–Dec daily 10am–5pm; July daily 10am–7pm. Closed Dec 24–25, Dec 31, and Jan 1.

Vindmølleparken (Windmill Park) Don Quixote chased windmills across the plains of La Mancha, and you can follow in his tracks by heading to this offbeat attraction. Five kilometers (3 miles) south of Ebeltoft, adjacent to the ferryboat terminal, 16 windmills sit on a curved spit of land open to gusts of wind from the Baltic to generate electricity for some 600 families. To see it, drive south of town, following the signs toward the hamlet of Øer, or the signs pointing to the ferryboat to Zealand. If you phone in advance, in some rare instances a free, 30-minute guided tour during open hours can be arranged by the city council.

Færgehavnen. © **89-52-11-11.** Free admission. Mon–Fri 10am–4pm.

SHOPPING

Since the mid-1980s, Ebeltoft has become Denmark's "glass kingdom." There are no fewer than six local glassworks producing and selling blown-glass items. At several of the studios, it's possible to see the workshops where glass bowls, vases, wine glasses, and beautiful dishes are created in the glowing furnace. You can visit various workshops and purchase glass at such outlets as **Glasværkstedet,** Skindergade 5 (© **86-34-08-89**); **Glaspusteriet,** Kystvejen 169 (© **86-34-49-58**); and **Ebeltoft Glas,** Nedergade 19 (© **86-34-35-66**).

WHERE TO STAY

Hotel Ebeltoft Strand ⭐ *(Kids)*   This hotel is the best choice in the town center, although summer visitors will find the swanky Molskroen (see below) along the coast more inviting. Constructed in 1978, the comfortable, well-furnished guest rooms often have a private balcony or terrace, overlooking Ebeltoft Bay or the Mol hills. Each of the units, painted in pastel-like Nordic colors, comes with a well-kept bathroom with tub/shower combo. Family rooms can be composed by joining another room, with an extra bed for kids (providing they are under the age of 18) for 1,295DKK ($220/£117) for four guests. Kids have their own room but with a connecting door leading to where their parents sleep. In winter guests retreat to a cozy lounge with a fireplace, but in summer the terrace with a view of the water is preferred. The restaurant serves the best lunch buffet in town, and the chef relies on the fresh produce of the season to create an enticing menu. The location is a 5-minute drive from the ferry dock and a 15-minute jaunt from Tirstrup Airport.

Nordre Strandvej 3, DK-8400 Ebeltoft. ⓒ **86-34-33-00.** Fax 86-34-46-36. www.ebeltoftstrand.dk. 72 units. 1,195DKK ($203/£108) double. Rates include buffet breakfast. AE, DC, MC, V. Free parking. Bus: 123 from Århus. **Amenities:** Restaurant; bar; indoor heated pool; kids' playroom; 24-hr. room service; laundry service; dry cleaning; nonsmoking rooms; rooms for those w/limited mobility. *In room:* TV, dataport, minibar, hair dryer, safe.

Molskroen ⭐ *(Finds)*   Perched northwest of Ebeltoft on the coast, this half-timbered structure began life in 1923 as a private manor, but has been expanded and altered over the years. This hotel was vastly upgraded, and its prices have risen dramatically. Nevertheless, it's the best place to stay in the area. Many rooms have terraces overlooking Mols Hills, and a fine white sandy beach is only 100m (328 ft.) away. The *kro* is in the center of an area of summer houses mostly built in the 1920s and 1930s. The midsize guest rooms are now sleek, functional, and most comfortable, with freshly tiled bathrooms equipped with tub/shower combos. Ten of the bedrooms are found in the annex, a red-brick building with a tiled roof. Accommodations here are every bit as good in the main building. Nine of these annex accommodations are individually furnished junior suites set on two floors, with four beds in each room, making them suitable for families. Even if you're not a guest, consider a stopover at the on-site French restaurant, which offers the most imaginative cuisine in the area, the specialty being roast duck filled with dates, apricots, and figs in an Arabian style. Note the four original Warhol prints of famous queens, including Denmark's own Queen Margrethe. In winter, when the terrace closes down, you can sit and enjoy your brandy in front of a fireplace.

Hovegaden 16, Femmøller Strand, DK-8400 Ebeltoft. ⓒ **86-36-23-00.** Fax 86-36-23-00. www.molskroen.dk. 18 units. 1,380DKK–1,680DKK ($235–$286/£124–£151) double; 2,300DKK–3,500DKK ($391–$595/£207–£315) suite. Rates include breakfast. AE, DC, V. Free parking. Closed Dec 24–Jan 8. Bus: 123 from Århus. **Amenities:** Restaurant; bar; room service (7am–10pm); babysitting; laundry service; dry cleaning; rooms for those w/limited mobility. *In room:* TV, fax, dataport, minibar, hair dryer, safe.

WHERE TO DINE

Harriet ⭐ DANISH/FRENCH/ITALIAN   Our favorite restaurant in Ebeltoft, occupying a former general store built in 1775 in the heart of town, presents a sophisticated, carefully choreographed cuisine. Lunches include stable and relatively conservative platters, the most popular of which are salmon fish cakes with salad and fresh bread, or plates piled high with an assortment of various preparations of herring. Dinners are more elaborate, with menus that change frequently, according to the season, but which might include veal roasted with a ragout of locally picked forest mushrooms, veal cutlets in wine sauce, or filets of plaice with lemon-butter sauce. Any of these can be preceded with such exotica as Mediterranean-inspired carpaccio Piemontese with truffle oil, or hot pecorino cheese drizzled with hot maple syrup.

Adelgade 62. © **86-34-44-66**. Reservations recommended. Main courses 172DKK–210DKK ($29–$36/£15–£19); 2-course fixed-price menu 225DKK ($38/£20). AE, DC, MC, V. Daily 11:30am–10pm.

Restaurant "Mellem Jyder" ✦ DANISH The oldest and most historically evocative restaurant in Ebeltoft occupies a half-timbered building (ca. 1610), a few steps from the old Town Hall. Inside, you can order a roster of ultratraditional Danish dishes whose authenticity seems to go well with the antique setting. The chefs don't have any great surprises up their sleeves but turn out the tried-and-true, dishes such as filet of sole meunière or marinated salmon with dill sauce. They still make that old-fashioned sailors' favorite, Danish hash—*biksemal.* Desserts are nothing special. On afternoons, a beer garden in back—like you might expect in neighboring Germany—is popular during mild weather.

Juulsbakke 3. © **86-34-11-23**. Reservations recommended. Main courses 95DKK–170DKK ($16–$29/£8.55–£15); 3-course fixed-price menu 225DKK ($38/£20). MC, V. Daily noon–8pm.

EBELTOFT AFTER DARK

The best place to gather in the evening is **Den Skæve Bar,** Overgade 23 (© **86-34-37-97**), an English-style pub in a building dating from 1683. This is often the venue for live music, including folk, rock, blues, and jazz.

12

North Jutland

"**W**hy do we live here in such a rugged environment?" asked a painter in Skagen, who answered his own question: "The real Denmark is a winter day at the North Sea with the wind blowing back your hair and making your skin salty, a trip in the autumn forest to gather mushrooms, or a romantic stroll in the newly leafed beech forest."

The first visitors arrived in North Jutland some 4,000 years ago in a land created by the Ice Age some 10,000 years earlier. Many places in Vendsyssel (the name of the province) still bear traces from the Stone Age, the Iron Age, and certainly the Viking Age. You can see history at many ancient monuments and relics of antiquity on display in the area.

In 1859, Hans Christian Andersen said it best: "If you are a Painter then follow us here, here are Subjects for you to paint, here is Scenery for Writing." In the 19th century, the Skagen painters—the Danish equivalent of the French Impressionists—were attracted to North Jutland for its intense light, the region's natural surroundings, the sea, and the people. Many of

their paintings can be seen at the Skagens Museum. Some of their homes have been turned into museums.

After a long slumber, the towns of North Jutland are more alive than ever. Young people, who used to head for the bright lights of Copenhagen, often remain in the area of their birth, bringing new energy to its once-dull towns and hamlets.

Separated from the rest of Jutland (and also the mainland of Europe) by the Limfjord, North Jutland is a land unto itself. It's a landscape of North Sea beaches, coastal hamlets, fishing harbors, and wild heaths. It has only one large city, Aalborg, which lies at the narrow point of Limfjord, plus a number of midsize towns, notably Frederikshavn. Any of these would be a suitable base for exploration, but for scenic beauty we'd choose Skagen, at the northernmost boundary of Denmark, which has long attracted some of Denmark's leading artists and artisans.

Because of bridges linking Funen with Zealand and Jutland, you can drive to North Jutland from Copenhagen in 4½ hours.

1 Mariager ⍟

58km (36 miles) N of Århus; 341km (212 miles) NW of Copenhagen

There's a little nugget of a town that thrives in North Jutland that is most often overlooked by visitors on their trek to the more famous Aalborg. For a preview of Denmark of long ago, nothing evokes a time gone by in all of North Jutland more than the charming little town of Mariager overlooking the Mariager Fjord, an idyllic setting.

The locals certainly adore summer roses—planting them everywhere along their cobblestone streets and in front of their half-timbered, red-roofed antique structures. If your time is short and you want to see the most picturesque streets, stroll down

---

Tips **Getting to North Jutland**

For rail information to any town in North Jutland, call ℭ **70-13-14-15**; for bus schedules, ℭ **98-11-11-11**.

Kirkegade and **Postgården.** But the best collection of buildings with crisscross timbers envelops the **Torvet** ★★, the market square in the exact center of town. Some of our rival guidebooks (we won't name them) ignore Mariager completely—and that is a shame as it deserves at least a morning or an afternoon of your time.

Mariager was only a small fishing hamlet at the ferry crossing on the way between Randers and Aalborg before the foundation of Bridgettine Abbey in 1410. The abbey led to a flourishing trade and commerce in the area, and the town became a popular resort for the worshipping nobles. However, with the coming of the Reformation in 1536, the tide turned. When Mariager was granted its city charter in 1592, only 500 inhabitants remained. Many of the old buildings constructed in Mariager's heyday remain for us to appreciate today. Industrialization did not come until 1960, and by that time the town had become preservation-minded, as a walk through its cobbled streets will reveal.

ESSENTIALS

GETTING THERE   By Train and Bus   There are no direct trains to Mariager. Trains run from Aalborg to Hobro, east of Mariager, every 30 minutes, and from Århus to Hobro hourly. Take the bus from Hobro. Buses to Mariager run hourly from Hadsun, Hobro, or Randers. The ride on all three takes about a half-hour.

By Car   From Randers, take the E45 north, then head east at the junction of Route 555.

VISITOR INFORMATION   The **Mariager Tourist Association,** Torvet 1B (ℭ **98-54-13-77;** www.mariagerturist.dk), is open June 15 to August Monday to Friday 9am to 5pm, Saturday 9am to 2pm; off-season hours generally are Monday to Friday 9:30am to 4pm, Saturday 9am to noon. It is closed on Saturday from November to January.

SEEING THE SIGHTS

Mariager is connected to the Baltic via the **Mariager Fjord** ★★★, a deep but narrow saltwater inlet favored by sailors and yachties because of its smooth surface. You can sail aboard a small-scale cruise ship, the *Svanen,* as it circumnavigates the western recesses of the fjord. About four times a day, the ship touches down at such towns as Mariager, Hadsun, and Hobro, taking 2½ hours for a complete circuit that's priced at 100DKK ($17/£9) per person. You can get off at any of five villages en route, and wait for the next boat to pick you up two hours later and carry you on to the next town. There's a cafeteria onboard, and a sun deck where guests can improve their suntans during the short Nordic summer. Call ℭ **98-54-14-70** for more information.

Another ride you may not want to miss is aboard the smoke-belching **Mariager-Handest Veteranjernbane,** Ny Havnevej 3 (ℭ **98-54-18-64**), which takes riders on an hour-long joy ride from Mariager to the village of Handest. After a stopover of half an hour, the little steam train makes the return journey to Mariager. The summer-only

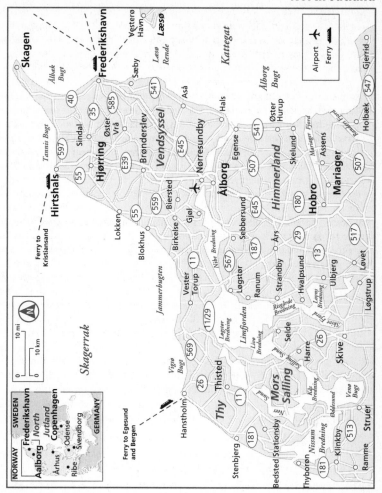

train departs daily at 11am, noon, 2pm, and 3pm, charging 100DKK ($17/£9) for a round-trip ticket. For more information visit **www.jernbaner.dk/mhvj.**

Although it's the old town itself that is the most alluring attraction, you may want to call on the abbey church, Mariager Kirke, Klostervej (© **98-54-15-95**), which was constructed in the 15th century as part of a nunnery. It was given to the town as its parish church following the Reformation. Although it has been largely reconstructed over the years, it's still a fine and lofty building with a magnificent carved altarpiece depicting the Last Supper and the Crucifixion, surrounded by 11 of the apostles. A memorial tablet to the last abbess can be seen in the south transept. Hours are Monday to Saturday 8am to 3:30pm; admission is free.

One of the most beautiful buildings in Mariager is an 18th-century merchant's house, now the **Mariager Museum,** Kirkegade 4B (© **98-54-12-87**). In the museum you can see an attractive collection of domestic utensils and tools. The museum also contains relics from the ancient history of both Mariager and the surrounding district. Of special interest is a minireconstruction of the abbey and its church, an exhibit established in 1981 in connection with the 500th anniversary of the church. Frankly, the antique building itself is more intriguing to us than the rather lackluster exhibits inside. If you're pressed for time, you can hop, skip, and jump by its doorstep, just enjoying its 1700s facade. It's open May 15 to September 15, daily 1 to 5pm. Admission is 15DKK ($2.55/£1.35) adults; free for children under 15.

Even if you like to take a shaker and sprinkle extra salt on your food before tasting it, a visit to a salt museum may not be your idea of a good time. It's not at all surprising to learn that when the **Danmarks Saltcenter** (Havnevej; © 98-54-18-16) opened in 1998 it became the only science center in Denmark devoted to salt. But the museum is far more of an adventure than you might think. Salt, formed some 250 million years ago, was once considered such an invaluable ingredient for food it was called "white gold." Of course, it's so commonly available today and in such wide use, that doctors and new cookbooks try to get us to cut down on its usage. Lying on the harbor at Mariager, close to the water, the museum traces the methods for extracting salt since the Middle Ages. You can explore in the tunnels of the salt mine and experience what it was like to work in a mountain salt mine a century ago. You can watch a foreman at the salt works boil the salts in a boiling hut as they did in the Middle Ages. That's not all. You can actually float in the **Dead Sea Pool**, the liquid of which is 30% salt. The curiosity of the museum is a collection of salt cellars that have been entered into the *Guinness Book of World Records*. The salt garden is planted with plants that obviously can tolerate salt, and this is the setting for the museum's Salt Café, where, naturally, dishes connected with salt are served. There are also many activities for children, including, among others, shallow pools in the outdoor water playground. Tickets are 80DKK ($14/£7.20) adults, 60DKK ($10/£5.40) children 3 to 11, and free for children 2 and under. Hours are June 19 to August 8 daily 10am to 6pm; January 3 to June 18 and August 9 to December 23 Monday to Friday 10am to 4pm, Saturday and Sunday 10am to 5pm. Closed December 24 to January 2.

WHERE TO STAY

If you can't find a hotel room, the **Mariager Tourist Association** (see above) will help book you into a private home or boardinghouse.

Hotel Postgården   There is just no contest about where to stay here. This old charmer—known for its warm hospitality, comfort, tradition, and elegance—is clearly the leader of a very limited pack. The most authentically historic hotel in Mariager has extended hospitality to travelers since it was established in 1710 in the heart of town, near the main square and Town Hall. It was restored in 1982 and has been upgraded many times since. The building's facade and public areas, especially its pub and restaurant, are the most popular places in town. About two-thirds of the rooms have been stripped of their historic charm and upgraded to a modern international style that nonetheless is still comfortable and cozy. If you insist on antique decor, request room no. 305 (one that the hotel usually assigns to anyone claiming to be a honeymooner); or, to a lesser extent, room nos. 201, 203, or 307. Some of the bedrooms contain tubs, but most of them offer showers. Even if you don't stay here, stop in for the best food and drink in town (see below).

Torvet 6A, DK-9550 Mariager. ✆ **98-54-10-12.** Fax 98-54-24-64. www.hotelpostgaardenmariager.dk. 14 units. 750DKK ($128/£68) double. Rates include breakfast. AE, DC, MC, V. **Amenities:** Restaurant; bar; sauna. *In room:* TV.

Motel Landgangen *Value* We've obviously made our preference known for the Postgården, but if for some reason that hotel is fully booked (a likely possibility in midsummer), this motel provides alternative accommodations—and good ones at that. Set beside the river, a 5-minute walk north of the abbey, this is not a dreary motel, even though its white exterior and simple architecture date from the late 1960s. Rooms are cozy and inviting, well kept and neat, including the bathrooms, which contain either shower or tub. The place is even better known for its restaurant, which features Danish specialties and comfy furniture with a view of the water. It's open in summer daily noon to 8pm, and off season Friday to Sunday noon to 8pm.

Oxendalen 1, DK-9550 Mariager. ✆ **98-54-11-22.** 6 units. 550DKK ($94/£50) double. Rates include breakfast. AE, DC, MC, V. **Amenities:** Restaurant; bar. *In room:* TV.

WHERE TO DINE

Restaurant Postgården DANISH/FRENCH Many diners appreciate this restaurant for its old-time decor and the sense of intimacy created by its small but bustling dining rooms. During mild weather, tables are set up outside. There's nothing particularly avant-garde about the food served here. Luncheon favorites include such tried-and-true favorites as *smørrebrød* (open-faced sandwiches) piled high with baby shrimp or Danish ham, and platters of herring or roasted pork with red cabbage and new potatoes. Dinners are more elaborate and might feature such good-tasting dishes as bacon-wrapped salmon with fettuccine in a saffron sauce or else lemon sole with crab in a lime-laced white-wine sauce with dill potatoes. A special treat is the marinated leg of duck with sautéed cabbage and mushrooms served in a sweet pepper sauce with a potato soufflé.

In the Hotel Postgården, Torvet 6A. ✆ **98-54-10-12.** Reservations recommended. Lunch main courses 82DKK–130DKK ($14–$22/£7.40–£12); dinner main courses 128DKK–195DKK ($22–$33/£12–£18); fixed-price menus 148DKK–298DKK ($25–$51/£13–£27). AE, DC, MC, V. Daily 11am–9pm.

MARIAGER AFTER DARK

The town's most consistently popular pub is in the **Hotel Postgården,** Torvet 6A (✆ **98-54-10-12**). Within a room sheathed with old-fashioned paneling, near a bar with antique-looking beer pulls, you'll find an animated crowd of office workers and the after-dinner set taking refuge from the confines of their homes, with lots of options for meeting and making new friends. Open daily 11am to 11pm, it serves platters of food, including herring, that taste good with the Carlsberg, and which cost 30DKK to 55DKK ($5.10–$9.35/£2.70–£4.95).

2 Aalborg ✭

132km (82 miles) NW of Ebeltoft, 383km (238 miles) W of Copenhagen

We won't pretend that Aalborg is our favorite city in Jutland—Århus is. But once in this city opening onto the Limfjord, we always manage to have a good time, and so will you if you avail yourself of all its attractions, especially some of those in the environs. We like to stand at Aalborg harbor, watching ships head out for sea, sailing to faraway Iceland and even the Faroe islands, and most definitely to Britain and Ireland.

The largest city in North Jutland, Aalborg is known worldwide for its *akvavit.* Although essentially a shipping town and commercial center, Aalborg makes a good base for sightseers, with its many hotels and attractions, more than 300 restaurants, and diverse nightlife.

History is a living reality in Aalborg. The city was founded 1,000 years ago when the Viking fleets assembled in these parts before setting off on their predatory expeditions. The city's historic atmosphere has been preserved in its old streets and alleys. Near the Church of Our Lady are many beautifully restored and reconstructed houses, some of which date from the 16th century.

Denmark's largest forest, **Rold,** where robber bandits once roamed, is just outside town. **Rebild National Park** is the site of the annual American Fourth of July celebration.

Not far from Aalborg, on the west coast of North Jutland, some of the finest beaches in northern Europe stretch from Slettestrand to Skagen. The resort towns of **Blokhus** and **Løkken** are especially popular with Danes, Germans, and Swedes.

ESSENTIALS

GETTING THERE   By Plane   You can fly from Copenhagen to Aalborg; the **airport** (© **98-17-11-44;** www.aal.dk) is 6.5km (4 miles) from the city center.

By Train   There is frequent train service from Copenhagen by way of Fredericia to Århus; there you can connect with a train to Aalborg, a 90-minute ride.

By Bus   Aalborg's bus station is the transportation center for North Jutland and is served from all directions. For all bus information in North Jutland, call **Nordjyllands Trafikselskab** (© **98-11-11-11**).

By Car   From Ebeltoft, follow Route 21 north until you reach the junction with Route 16. Drive west on Route 16 until you come to E45, which runs north to Aalborg.

VISITOR INFORMATION   The **Aalborg Tourist Bureau** is at Østerågade 8 (© **99-30-60-90;** www.visitaalborg.com). It's open June and August, Monday to Friday 9am to 5:30pm, Saturday 10am to 1pm; September to May, Monday to Friday 9am to 4:30pm, Saturday 10am to 1pm. In July it is open Monday to Friday 9am to 5:30pm, Saturday 10am to 4pm.

GETTING AROUND   For bus information, call © **98-11-11-11.** Most buses depart from Østerågade and Nytorv in the city center. A typical fare costs 16DKK ($2.70/£1.45), although you can buy a 24-hour tourist pass for 110DKK ($19/£9.90) to ride on all the city buses for a day. Information about bus routes is available from the *Aalborg Guide,* which is distributed free by the tourist office.

SPECIAL EVENTS   The **Aalborg Carnival** 𝕜𝕜, scheduled each year on May 25 and 26, is one of the major events of spring in Jutland. Streets are filled with festive figures in colorful costumes strutting in a parade. Up to 100,000 people participate in this annual event, marking the victory of spring over winter's darkness. The whole city seems to explode in joy. There's also the **Aalborg Jazz and Blues Festival** August 13 to 19. Jazz fills the whole city at dozens of clubs, although most activity centers on C. W. Obels Plads. Every year on the Fourth of July, Danes and Danish Americans meet to celebrate America's **Independence Day** in the lovely hills of Rebild.

SEEING THE SIGHTS

Aalborg Marinemuseum *Kids*   If you've ever fantasized about having a close encounter with the dinghy that Queen Margrethe sailed in while still a princess, here is your chance. Seriously, this museum is more enthralling than that, as it gives you a

Aalborg

Castle ♜
Church ♰
Information ⓘ

Limfjorden

Havnen

Aalborghus

Gammel Torv

SWEDEN

Aalborg ● ●Frederikshavn

Århus ●
● Copenhagen

Odense ●
● Svendborg

GERMANY

ATTRACTIONS ●
Aalborg Marinemuseum **1**
Aalborg Tårnet **21**
Aalborg Zoologiske Have **22**
Budolfi Domkirke **18**
Helligåndsklostret **16**
Jens Bangs Stenhus **10**
Nordjyllands Kunstmuseet **23**
Tivoliland **27**

ACCOMMODATIONS ■
First Slotshotel Aalborg **28**
Helnan Phønix Hotel **17**
Hotel Hvide Hus **14**
Hotel Scheelsminde **26**
Park Hotel **24**
Park Inn Chagall **15**
Prinsen Hotel **19**
Radisson SAS Limfjord
    Hotel **3**

DINING ◆
Duss Vinkælder **9**
Fyrtøjet **7**
Holles Vinstue **25**
Hos Boldt **2**
Il Mundo **11**
Kniv og Gaffel **8**
Layalina **4**
Mortens Kro **20**
Provence **5**
Restaurant Benzons **12**
Restaurant Kilden **13**
Ristorante Fellini **6**

hands-on experience with the interior of a submarine, *Springeren,* which is primed and ready for action. The 23m (75-ft.) sub was one of the last to be designed and built in Denmark. Also on-site is the torpedo boat *Søbjørnen,* the world's fastest such boat. You can see the inspection ship, *Ingolf,* that was on active duty in the bone-chilling waters around Greenland until 1990. Other exhibits depict life at sea, the port of Aalborg, and activities at the Aalborg shipyard. At the Café Ubåden (submarine), you can order food and drink. There's also a playground on-site.

Vester Fjordvej 81. ℂ **98-11-78-03.** www.aalborgmarinemuseum.dk. Admission 65DKK ($11/£5.85) adults, 30DKK ($5.10/£2.70) children 6–14, free for children under 6. May–Aug daily 10am–6pm; off season daily 10am–4pm. Bus: 12 or 13.

Aalborg Tårnet (Aalborg Tower)   Whenever we visit a city or town, and if there is a lookout point, we always head there first for a panoramic overview. In Aalborg, that perfect view (that is, if it's a clear day) is seen from this tower, rising 105m (344 ft.) into the air. Reached by stairs or elevator, its view takes in everything from the smokestacks to the beautiful Limfjord. Weather permitting, you can see the North Sea and even Rold Forest in the south. The tower itself is no beauty—rather ugly in fact—but it does have its rewards, including its location on a hill in back of the Nordjyllands Kunstmuseum and at the border of Mølleparken, the best woodland for walking or hiking in the area.

Søndre Skovvej, at Skovbakken. ℂ 98-77-05-11. www.aalborgtaarnet.com. Admission 25DKK ($4.25/£2.25) adults, 15DKK ($2.55/£1.35) children 3–14, free for children under 3. Apr–June daily 11am–5pm; July–Aug 8 daily 10am–7pm; Aug 9–Sept 26 and Oct 14–Oct 22 daily 11am–7pm. Closed Oct–Mar, except for 1 week in Oct. Bus: 11, 14, or 16.

Aalborg Zoologiske Have (Aalborg Zoo) 👍👍 *(Kids)*   We've seen bigger and better zoos in our lives, but this remains one of our favorites because of its success in the breeding of near-extinct animals such as the Siberian tiger. More than 1,300 animals are on parade here, including crocs, zebras, tigers, giraffes, polar bears, and orang-utans. Apes and beasts of prey are kept under minimal supervision. They live in such simulated conditions as an African savanna or a rainforest from South America. With the opening of a large playground, Oasen, for children, kids can romp around like the resident monkeys. Other adventures include a riverbank for crocs, a pampa for anteaters, or a forest full of bears.

Mølleparkvej 63. ℂ 96-31-29-29. www.aalborg-zoo.dk. Admission 95DKK ($16/£8.55) adults, 50DKK ($8.50/£4.50) children 3–11, free for children under 3. Jan–Feb and Nov–Dec daily 10am–2pm; Mar daily 10am–3pm; Apr and Sept–Oct daily 10am–4pm; May–Aug daily 9am–6pm. Last ticket is sold 1 hr. before closing. Bus: 11. 4km (2½ miles) south of Aalborg.

Budolfi Domkirke (Cathedral of St. Budolf)   Even if you don't visit this church, you'll be made aware of its presence. A carillon makes beautiful music daily every hour from 9am to 10pm, when it mercifully shuts down to allow the early-to-bed crowd to get some sleep. This elaborately decorated and whitewashed cathedral is dedicated to the patron saint of sailors. The baroque spire of the church is Aalborg's major land-mark. The church you see today is the result of 800 years of rebuilding and expansion. On the south wall is a fresco depicting St. Catherine of Alexandria and some grotesque little centaurs. Look for the altarpiece from 1689 and the pulpit from 1692—both carved by Lauritz Jensen. The marble font from 1727 was a gift to the church. Note too the gallery in the north aisle with its illustrations of the Ten Commandments. A similar gallery in the south aisle illustrates the suffering of Christ and also bears the names of a number of prominent Aalborg citizens from around the mid–17th century, which seems to be of no interest to anyone anymore. A series of cocks crow the hour from four matching clock faces on the church's tower.

Algade. ℂ 98-12-46-70. Free admission. Bus: 3, 5, 10, or 11. June–Aug Mon–Fri 9am–4pm, Sat 9am–2pm; Sept–May Mon–Fri 9am–3pm, Sat 9am–noon.

Helligåndsklostret (Monastery of the Holy Ghost)   Once when we were doing a magazine article on the Danish resistance movement during the Nazi occupation from 1940 to 1945, our trail led us to this site, often called the "Aalborg Kloster." Here we learned that it was the secret headquarters of the "Churchill Club," which was the first Resistance group established in Denmark to fight the Nazi menace. This vine-covered monastery is the oldest social-welfare institution in Denmark, as well as the oldest building in Aalborg. Built near the heart of town in 1431 and designed with step-shaped gables, it contains a well-preserved rectory, a series of vaulted storage cellars— some of which occasionally functioned as prisons—a whitewashed collection of cloisters, and a chapter house whose walls in some areas are decorated with 16th-century frescoes. The complex can be visited only as part of a guided tour.

C. W. Obels Plads. (*C* 99-30-60-90. Guided tour 40DKK ($6.80/£3.60) adults, 10DKK ($1.70/90p) children 3–12. Guided tour late June to mid-Aug Mon–Fri 1:30pm. Bus: 1.

Jens Bangs Stenhus (Jens Bang's Stone House) ☆ This is the finest example of Renaissance domestic architecture in the north of Europe. This glittering six-floor mansion, built in 1624, once belonged to a wealthy merchant, Jens Bang. Bang was gifted but also argumentative and obstinate. He deliberately made his house rich with ornamentation and ostentation as a challenge to the other good citizens of the town. It was rumored that he revenged himself on his many enemies by caricaturing them in the grotesque carvings on the facade of the house. In spite of his wealth, he was never made a member of the town council, and to this day his image is depicted on the south facade sticking his tongue out at the Town Hall. The historic wine cellar, Duus Vinkjælder, is the meeting place of the Guild of Christian IV. On the ground floor is an old apothecary shop. The mansion itself is still privately owned and is not open to the public.

Østerågade 9. www.kulturrejsen.dk/story.asp?id=517. Bus: 3, 5, 10, or 11.

Nordjyllands Kunstmuseet (Museum of Modern and Contemporary Art) ☆ *Kids* This building is a prime example of modern Scandinavian architecture. Built from 1968 to 1972, it was designed by Elissa and Alvar Aalto and Jean-Jacques Baruël as a showplace for 20th-century Danish and international art. The nucleus of the collection dates from 1850 but it's been added to over the years with many purchases and bequests. The Carlsberg Foundation, those beer barons, have donated some of the most notable works, including William Scharff's *Nocturne Series* and J. F. Willumsen's *War Invalids*. We find that the museum's most romantic picture is Harald Slott-Møller's *Spring* (1901). The greatest treasure-trove of art came from two dental technologists, Anna and Kresten Krestensen, who amassed a notable collection of Danish and international art from 1920 to 1950. In later years, as funds became available, the museum purchased works by great international artists including Fernand Léger, Max Ernst, and Wassily Kandinsky. Many events are staged for children, including picture hunts, family tours, and children's museum exhibits. On the ground floor is a good cafe overlooking the sculpture park. In 1994 artist Paul Gernes decorated the walls of the cafe, which serves a light lunch menu and open-faced sandwiches. Ask about musical concerts frequently staged here all year.

Kong Christians Allé 50. (*C* 98-13-80-88. www.nordjyllandskunstmuseum.dk. Admission 40DKK ($6.80/£3.60) adults, free for children. Free admission in Dec. Tues–Sun 10am–5pm (Feb–Apr and Sept–Nov Tues to 9pm).

NEARBY ATTRACTIONS

Less than 4km (2½ miles) north of Aalborg, you'll find some of the oldest grave sites in all of Scandinavia, not just of the Viking era but even Iron Age burial grounds. The Viking settlement of Nørresundby is the location of more than 700 cremation graves, and contains the charred remains of more than 150 Viking boats and ships that were ceremonially burned as part of the cremations. Set within a park, the excavations are open to the public year-round 24 hours a day. Most of the graves are marked with stones placed in the form of a triangle, an oval, or a ship. The deceased person was usually cre-mated. North of the burial ground lay the associated village, where the finds include the remains of houses, fences, wells, and fire pits. The area was subject to drifting sand. About A.D. 1000, the whole burial ground became covered with sand, which meant that the stone markings and even a newly plowed field were preserved until this day.

Further details about the excavations are on view in the **Lindholm Høje Museet,** Lindholmsvej 65 (© **96-31-04-10;** www.nordjyllandshistoriskemuseum.dk; bus: 2). The museum contains archaeological finds from the excavations and illustrates how the inhabitants of Lindholm Høje lived at home and traded abroad. It is open Easter to mid-October daily 10am to 5pm; mid-October to Easter Tuesday through Sunday 10am to 4pm. Admission costs 30DKK ($5.10/£2.70) adults, 15DKK ($2.55/£1.35) children 5 to 11, free for children 4 and under.

Voergård Slot 🟊🟊, Voergård 6, Dronninglund (© **98-86-71-08;** www.voergaard slot.dk), is enveloped by Denmark's widest moat, and is one of the best preserved Renaissance castles in the land. Its oldest section was constructed in 1481, its most "recent" in 1590. What makes this a special place is that it is furnished with an excep-tional **collection of European art and furniture** 🟊🟊🟊, including paintings by Goya, Rubens, El Greco, and Raphael. The antique treasures come from the eras of Napoleon, Louis XIV, and Louis XVI. A special section displays some of the **personal furniture** 🟊🟊 of Marie Antoinette. Two magnificent sideboards with gilted bronze plates and ornaments by Gouttiers were made by cabinetmaker Riesener for Louis XVI's court. Many of these rare treasures came from Count Ejnar Oberbech-Clausen, who took over Voergård in 1955 and filled it with art, antiquities, and furniture, mak-ing it one of the most spectacular private homes in Denmark.

Denmark's most famous ghost, Ingeborg Skeel, still resides at the castle, or so locals believe. As the owner of the castle, she is said to have drowned the architect, Philip Brandin, in the moat to prevent him from ever building a castle as splendid as Voergård ever again. Admission costs 65DKK ($11/£5.85) adults, 25DKK ($4.25/£2.25) chil-dren. Take the E45 from Aalborg, cutting east on Route 559 to Droningland, and then follow the signs to Voergård Slot. May 1 to June 13 and August 21 to October 17, it's open Saturday 2 to 5pm, Sunday 10am to 5pm; July 10 to 18, daily 10am to 5pm.

Americans who are in Jutland for the Fourth of July should make a beeline to the **Rebild National Park,** 29km (18 miles) south of Aalborg. On these heather dunes, Danes, Danish Americans, and Americans celebrate America's Independence Day. The program often features opera singers, folk dancers, choirs, and glee clubs, together with well-known speakers.

A 1-hour drive from Aalborg takes you to the resort town of **Blokhus** and the broad white beaches of the North Sea coast. Not far from here is a 50-hectare (124-acre) amusement park, **Fårup Sommerland & Waterpark** (© **98-88-16-00;** www.faarup sommerland.dk; bus: 200). Expect lots of noise, lots of families, and lots of emphasis on good, clean fun in a style that might remind you of a small-scale version of Dis-neyland. It's open mid-May to early September, daily 10am to 7pm. Admission: May 12 to June 23 145DKK ($25/£13), seniors over 65 85DKK ($14/£7.65); June 24 to early September 170DKK ($29/£15), seniors over 65 100DKK ($17/£9). Admission is reduced in late afternoon; see website for further details.

FOR FAMILY FUN

Tivoliland 🟊🟊, Karolinelundsvej (© **98-12-33-15;** www.tivoliland.dk), is an amuse-ment park for the entire family, with lots of snap and sparkle, although a pale imitation of the more famous one in Copenhagen. A tradition since 1946 in the center of Aalborg, it's one of the most attended attractions in the North Jutland. In addition to rides, there are beautiful gardens with thousands of flowers and fantastic fountains. You've seen it all before, but it's still an amusing and delightful way to spend an evening, as you can take everything from a flying carpet ride to a spin on Scandinavia's only boomerang roller coaster (which screws and loops both forward and backward). China Town is one of the most visited attractions, containing such features as the China dragon, the fun house, and a cycle fun rail. Other attractions include a Gravity Tower with a 55m (180-ft.) free-fall, and a Hall of Mirrors, a labyrinth showing you amazing dimensions of yourself. An open-air stage, restaurants, a pizzeria, dancing areas, and singalongs—it all makes for one big day. The attraction is open May to June daily noon to 9pm; July to September 6 daily 10am to 10pm. Admission is 50DKK ($8.50/£4.50) adults, 25DKK ($4.25/£2.25) children 3 to 13, free for children under 3. However, you'll pay separately for the various attractions, with tickets ranging from 15DKK to 45DKK ($2.55–$7.65/£1.35–£4.05). An unlimited ticket for all rides, good for 1 day only, costs 200DKK ($34/£18).

SHOPPING

This North Jutland city abounds in specialty stores. For the best collection of gold and silver jewelry, patronize **Aalborg Guld & Solvhus,** Gravensgade 8 (✆ 98-16-57-11). The most sophisticated handicrafts—many quite amusing—are sold at **Lange Handicrafts,** Hjelmerstald 15 (✆ 98-13-82-68). To watch a glass blower in action, and perhaps make some purchases, go to **Glaspusteriet,** Nørregade 6 (✆ 98-13-01-20).

The largest shopping center in North Jutland lies about 6.5km (4 miles) south of Aalborg's center. The **Aalborg Storcenter,** Hobrovej 452 (✆ 98-18-23-10; bus: 11, 14, or 16), contains at least 50 specialty shops and kiosks, as well as the all-inclusive **Bilka Department Store** (✆ 98-79-70-00).

Aalborg also has some other department stores that bring a vast array of Danish merchandise together under one roof, including **Salling,** Nytorv 8 (✆ 98-16-00-00; bus: 1, 11, or 14), with 30 specialty shops. It has the city's largest selection of fashion, plus lots of other good stuff, including books and toys. A major competitor is **Magasin,** Nytorv 24 (✆ 98-13-30-00; bus: 1, 11, or 14). **Gavlhuset,** Algade 9 (✆ 98-12-18-22; bus: 16 or 18), has a little bit of everything—Indian silver, "dancing beans," old Kilim carpets, masks from around the globe, knitted goods, "gods" in bronze, exotic spices, wooden toys in bright colors, and even African woodcarvings. To look at and perhaps purchase some of the city's best contemporary art, head for **Galerie Wolfsen,** Tiendeladen 6 (✆ 98-13-75-66).

WHERE TO STAY

The **Aalborg Tourist Bureau** (see earlier in this chapter) can book a room for you in a private Danish home—double or single, with access to a shower. Bed linens are included in the price, and all rooms are situated within the city limits and reached by bus. In July and August, the peak tourist months, Helnan Phønix slashes its rates and becomes a moderately priced choice, because it's primarily a business hotel, and for them, high tourist season is their low season. Although many rooms at the Limsford Hotel are labeled expensive, the hotel rents dozens of more affordable accommodations as well.

EXPENSIVE

First Slotshotel Aalborg ⚑   You can have a drink while taking in views of the beautiful Limfjord. Although down several notches from other recommended choices in this category, this is still a comfortable, tasteful, and well-designed hotel. Since its opening in 1986, it's been a preferred choice to stay for those seeking a central location near the harbor. Tired of their yachts, the boating crowd often stops over here for a real bath and a real meal. The location is also close to the major attractions of town. Bedrooms are larger than those of the average Danish hotel, and they have extrawide beds and plenty of space to store your possessions. The well-kept bathrooms are frequently renewed on an as-needed basis and come with a tiled shower unit. Some of the accommodations can easily be converted into family units.

Rendsburggade 5, DK-9100 Aalborg. ⓒ **98-10-14-00.** Fax 98-11-65-70. www.firsthotels.com. 154 units. 1,253DKK ($213/£113) double; 1,650DKK ($281/£149) suite. Rates include buffet breakfast. AE, DC, MC, V. Free parking. Bus: 1, 3, 5, or 7. **Amenities:** Breakfast lounge; bar; gym; sauna; breakfast-only room service; laundry service; dry cleaning; nonsmoking rooms; rooms for those w/limited mobility; solarium. *In room:* TV, dataport, Wi-Fi (in most), minibar.

Helnan Phønix Hotel ⚑⚑⚑   In the town's most sumptuous mansion, you'll find the oldest, largest, most historic, and most prestigious hotel in Aalborg, lying close to the bus station. It originated in 1783 on the main street of town as the private home of the Danish brigadier general assigned to protect Aalborg from assault by foreign powers. In 1853, it was converted into a hotel. Today, it appears deceptively small from Aalborg's main street, and very imposing if you see its modern wings from the back. Bedrooms are tastefully and elegantly appointed with dark wood furnishings. Some of the rooms have exposed ceiling beams, and all of them are equipped with neatly tiled bathrooms with tub and shower combos.

The hotel's restaurant, **Brigadieren,** serves a sophisticated Danish and international cuisine.

Vesterbro 77, DK-9000 Aalborg. ⓒ **98-12-00-11.** Fax 98-10-12-20. www.helnan.dk. 210 units. Summer 955DKK ($162/£86) double, 2,500DKK ($425/£225) suite; winter 1,180DKK ($201/£106) double, 2,500DKK ($425/£225) suite. AE, DC, MC, V. **Amenities:** Restaurant; bar; gym; Jacuzzi; sauna; room service (7am–10pm); massage; laundry service; dry cleaning; nonsmoking rooms; solarium. *In room:* TV, dataport, minibar, hair dryer, safe.

Hotel Hvide Hus ⚑   If you're willing to forego the antique charms of the Phønix, or prefer a more modern high-rise address, then the Hvide Hus is one of the most viable candidates for overnighting. The first-rate "White House Hotel" is in Kilde Park, about a 12-minute walk from the heart of Aalborg and close to the bus station. Many international businesspeople now stay here instead of at the traditional Phønix. In cooperation with well-known galleries, the hotel is decorated with works by some of Denmark's leading painters. The guest rooms are well furnished in fresh Scandinavian modern style; all have private balconies with a view of Aalborg. Each unit is also equipped with a well-maintained bathroom with a tub/shower combo. This hotel is a member of Best Western hotels. The restaurant **Kilden** and the bar **Pejsebar** are both on the 15th floor and offer city views.

Vesterbro 2, DK-9000 Aalborg. ⓒ **800/780-7234** in the U.S. and Canada, or 98-13-84-00. Fax 98-13-51-22. www. hotelhvidehus.dk. 198 units. Mon–Fri 1,325DKK–1,495DKK ($225–$254/£119–£135) double, 2,430DKK ($413/£219) suite; Sat–Sun 925DKK ($157/£83) double, 1,860DKK ($316/£167) suite. Rates include buffet breakfast. AE, DC, MC, V. Free parking. **Amenities:** Restaurant; bar; room service (7am–11pm); massage; babysitting; laundry service; dry cleaning; nonsmoking rooms. *In room:* TV, minibar, hair dryer, trouser press.

Radisson SAS Limfjord Hotel ⚑⚑   Check into the Phønix for traditional comfort and into the Radisson SAS for the modern comfort of its up-to-date facilities. This is the most avant-garde hotel in town—a five-story yellow-brick structure with huge expanses of glass in a streamlined Danish modern layout. In the center of town, a 3-minute walk east of the cathedral, the hotel opens onto the famous Limfjorden Canal. It's near Jomfru Anegade, a street packed with bars and restaurants. The public rooms are sparsely furnished with modern, streamlined furniture. Many of the midsize-to-spacious bedrooms overlook the harbor, and each is well maintained with tasteful, comfortable furnishings. All rooms have a tub/shower combo, and the suites are blessed with a Jacuzzi. The hotel offers some of the best drinking and dining facilities in town, and its casino is a lively hub of nighttime action.

Ved Stranden 14–16, DK-9000 Aalborg. © 800-333-3333 in the U.S., or 98-16-43-33. Fax 98-16-17-47. www.radisson sas.com. 188 units. 995DKK–1,615DKK ($169–$275/£90–£145) double; 2,215DKK ($377/£199) suite. Rates include breakfast. AE, DC, MC, V. Parking 75DKK ($13/£6.75). Bus: 1, 4, 40, or 46. **Amenities:** Restaurant; pizzeria; bar; fitness center; sauna; 24-hr. room service; laundry service; dry cleaning; nonsmoking rooms; rooms for those w/limited mobility; casino. *In room:* TV, dataport, Wi-Fi, minibar, hair dryer, trouser press.

MODERATE

Check into the Chagall on any Friday, Saturday, and Sunday night, and you'll find you're staying at an inexpensive hotel instead of a moderate one. Prinsen also rents a number of inexpensive rooms, although most of its accommodations are moderate. Likewise, the Park also rents a number of inexpensive rooms in addition to some pricey selections.

Hotel Scheelsminde ☆ *Finds* We'll let you in on a secret: For a stopover in Aalborg, we often like to drive out of town for 4km (2½ miles) south to an old but beautifully restored manor house from 1808. If you've been doing the whirlwind tour of Jutland, this is one of the best places we've found to wind down, enjoying total comfort, fresh air, and a market-fresh regional cuisine. A modern extension was built to accommodate tasteful, comfortably furnished, and completely up-to-date bedrooms, with the restaurant remaining inside the original manor. Each of the midsize bedrooms has a private bathroom—some with tub, others with shower. During the day you can go for walks through the hotel's large private grounds.

Scheelsmindevej 35, DK-9100 Aalborg. © 98-18-32-33. Fax 98-18-33-34. www.scheelsminde.dk. 96 units. 950DKK–1,850DKK ($162–$315/£86–£167) double. Rates include breakfast. AE, DC, MC, V. Bus: 5 or 8. **Amenities:** Restaurant; bar; indoor heated pool; gym; sauna; room service (6:30am–midnight); laundry service; dry cleaning; nonsmoking rooms; room for those w/limited mobility. *In room:* TV, dataport (in some), minibar, hair dryer.

Park Hotel ☆ This hotel has been putting up wayfarers who arrive at the rail terminus opposite the building since 1917. One of the oldest hotels in the city, the Park (not to be confused with Park Inn Chagall) became so popular that a modern block of tasteful, comfortable rooms was added when an extension was tacked on in 1990. Each unit comes with an immaculate private bathroom—some with showers, others with old-fashioned tubs. The original architectural details of the main building remain relatively intact in spite of modernization. Today the hotel enjoys a well-deserved reputation for its coziness and comfort, with personal service a hallmark. On-site is a first-class restaurant and bar, and in summer guests spill out onto chairs in front of the hotel.

J. F. Kennedys Plads 41, DK-9100 Aalborg. © 98-12-31-33. Fax 98-13-31-66. www.park-hotel-aalborg.dk. 81 units. 950DKK–1,060DKK ($162–$180/£86–£95) double; 1,160DKK–1,360DKK ($197–$231/£104–£122) suite. Rates include buffet breakfast. AE, DC, MC, V. **Amenities:** Restaurant; bar; room service (7am–10pm); laundry service; dry cleaning; nonsmoking rooms; rooms for those w/limited mobility. *In room:* TV, hair dryer.

Park Inn Chagall   Now part of the Park Inn chain, this hotel has been much improved since its takeover. Ever since the 1950s, it's been an affordable choice in pricey Aalborg. In honor of its namesake, most of the bedrooms have reproductions of Marc Chagall's paintings. As a grace note, the hotel offers an inner courtyard where you can sit out in summer, enjoying the far-too-few nights of warm weather. The mid-size bedrooms are designed in sophisticated Danish modern, with such features as individual climate control. All the units come with a well-kept, tiled bathroom with tub or shower. On-site is a cafe-style area in the lobby where breakfast is served.

Vesterbro 36–38, Postboks 1856, DK-9000 Aalborg. ⓒ 98-12-69-33. Fax 98-13-13-44. www.parkinn.dk. 89 units. 981DKK–1,290DKK ($167–$219/£88–£116) double; 1,385DKK ($235/£125) suite. Rates include breakfast. AE, DC, MC, V. **Amenities:** Breakfast lounge; fitness center; Jacuzzi; sauna; laundry service; dry cleaning; nonsmoking rooms; solarium. *In room:* TV, Wi-Fi (in some), minibar, coffeemaker, hair dryer.

Prinsen Hotel *Value*   Local residents often cite the Prinsen to us as "the place we store our relatives when we don't have room at home." They seem to know they'll get a square deal here. Opposite the railroad station, this 1906 landmark doesn't have the glamour of our previous choices, but it's still a good deal in our opinion. The small-to-midsize bedrooms, in spite of their age, are decorated in a light, modern Danish style, with comfortable, tasteful furnishings and well-kept private bathrooms with tub or shower. The hotel may be aging, but it's kept up-to-date with the times with frequent renovations and modernization. There is a family-style welcome here, and we like the touch of providing free coffee, tea, or hot chocolate (especially welcoming when you come in on one of the frequent snowy nights).

Prinsensgade 14–16, DK-9000 Aalborg. ⓒ 98-13-37-33. Fax 98-16-52-82. www.prinsen-hotel.dk. 40 units. 645DKK–995DKK ($110–$169/£58–£90) double. Rates include buffet breakfast. AE, DC, MC, V. Free parking. Closed Dec 23–Jan 1. Bus: 1, 3, or 5. **Amenities:** Breakfast lounge; bar; Jacuzzi; sauna; laundry service; dry cleaning; non-smoking rooms; solarium. *In room:* TV, dataport, Wi-Fi, hair dryer.

WHERE TO DINE

Jomfru Anegade is the most famous restaurant-filled street in Jutland. If you can't find good food here, you didn't try. It's got something for most palates and most pocketbooks.

EXPENSIVE

Hos Boldt *☞* DANISH/FRENCH   We once knew this place as a good tavern filled with suds-loving drinkers. The setting in a building from the 1800s was always antique, and the family owners have kept the rooms deliberately old-fashioned. In 1992 they decided to transform the place into an upmarket restaurant while keeping the quaint atmosphere of antique furniture and candles. One of our closest friends in Aalborg claimed that "this is my favorite, a pet spot I keep coming back to." His reason is obvious, as the food is consistently good. Menu items change with the season and the availability of ingredients. If featured, the lobster bisque seems the peak among all other appetizers. One intriguing main course is salmon presented with various preparations. The sea bass is cooked in a salt crust to preserve its aroma and its juices, and the tender rack of Danish lamb is made even more savory with the rosemary-laced wine sauce that comes with it. You just might smack your lips at the steamed freshly caught turbot with a julienne of leeks, or else the consommé of veal with herbs and quail eggs—a real gourmet dish.

Ved Stranden 7. ⓒ 98-16-17-77. Reservations recommended. Main courses 208DKK–228DKK ($35–$39/£19–£21); fixed-price menus 275DKK–400DKK ($47–$68/£25–£36). AE, DC, MC, V. Mon–Sat 5pm–midnight. Bus: 1, 4, 40, or 46.

Mortens Kro ★★★ *Finds* FRENCH/DANISH   This artful restaurant is the domain of Morten Nealsen, the most gifted chef in Aalborg. It is the best place to dine in the city, offering classic dining chairs and luxurious sofas. The chef wanted a "New York look but with Parisian ambience," the latter evoked by the champagne bar. The rustic brickwork and glass and steel form a backdrop for fine dining. DJs entertain during the weekends. This is really a top-rate restaurant with a lot of flair. The results are achieved with well-rehearsed rules of cooking technique, and the classic schooling of French cuisine has been beautifully blended with Danish flavors. Passionately fond of his trade, the chef is the supreme professional. To get you launched he takes great care with his appetizers, as evoked by such choices as a seafood plate with a sauté of mint- and lemon-flavored rice noodles. For a main course, the chef has several surprising delicacies up his sleeve. Try his filet of seawolf marinated with chili and lemon and served with a golden saffron risotto. The fresh lobster is divine—boiled to perfection and served with a lemon-flavored homemade mayonnaise that is so good we wanted to bottle it. Our favorite dessert is the passion fruit sorbet with pieces of rose hip served in a meringue "nest" with rose-hip syrup.

Mølleå 4–6, Mølleå Arkaden. ☎ **98-12-48-60**. Reservations recommended. Main courses 138DKK–228DKK ($23–$39/£12–£21); fixed-price menus 298DKK–648DKK ($51–$110/£27–£58). DC, MC, V. Mon–Sat 5:30–10pm. Bus: 3, 5, 10, or 11.

MODERATE

Il Mulino ITALIAN   Although under separate management, the best Italian restaurant in Aalborg occupies the street-level floor of the previously recommended Radisson SAS hotel. Come here for your Italian fix. We first discovered this place when it occupied a 1737 warehouse in another location. We were impressed then, and we're even more impressed with the restaurant after its move into sleeker, more sophisticated surroundings. The chefs moved their full-flavored dishes intact into the hotel space.

The pastas are homemade and rolled out fresh every day, and then the cooks do their magic, taking linguini, for example, and serving it with a savory seafood sauce. We usually find vegetarian lasagna a rather dull dish, but here it's spiced up. The main courses are seasoned with flair, the grilled veal cutlets, for example, drizzled with truffle oil and served with a zucchini-laced sauce. The grilled quail is especially appealing to us as it's seasoned with spices and served with a zesty tomato sauce laced with black olives.

Ved Stranden 14–16. ☎ **98-12-39-99**. Reservations recommended. Main courses 175DKK–195DKK ($30–$33/£16–£18); fixed-price menu 245DKK–389DKK ($42–$66/£22–£35). AE, DC, MC, V. Tues–Fri 11:30am–3:30pm and 5:30pm–midnight, Sat 5:30pm–midnight. Bus: 1.

Kniv og Gaffel FRENCH/DANISH   This is a romantic choice for dining, housed in the oldest preserved citizen's house, dating from 1552, in Aalborg. The street takes its name from Maren Turis, a woman who lived here in the 16th century and was accused of witchcraft, tried, but found not guilty. Those terrifying memories are long erased today—you'll experience only lots of atmosphere, and wonderful food served by candlelight. Its old oak tables fill up every night, and the wooden floors are buckled and slanted with age. The house specialty is thick steaks, the best in Aalborg, although you can order an array of other dishes as well, each prepared with first-rate ingredients plucked from the markets that very morning. On our most recent rounds, we enjoyed fresh Norwegian salmon baked with mushrooms and served with a béarnaise sauce. The chicken breast platter is delectably cooked here with homemade basil and tomato sauce and served with a garden salad and baked potato.

Maren Turis Gade 10. 𝘾 **98-16-69-72**. Reservations recommended. Main courses 42DKK–160DKK ($7.15–$27/ £3.80–£14). DC, MC, V. Mon–Sat noon–midnight. Bus: 1, 3, or 5.

Provence DANISH/FRENCH   This is Aalborg's foremost purveyor of Danish cuisine that's influenced in almost every case by the culinary traditions of France. Across from the Radisson SAS in the center of town, it offers a cozy, small-scale brown-and-white interior that's illuminated by a stained-glass skylight. The only complaint ever expressed is that its younger staff is not as well trained as those at some of its competitors. Even though the service isn't always faultless, the cuisine itself usually is, as the food is classical and always reliable. A wonderful menu begins with a tasting of the sea, with fresh Danish lobster appearing in a cocktail or in a velvety soup laced with cognac. The cuisine lately seems touched with a special grace, including a Dutch sole with a salmon soufflé and fresh spinach or a "fired" sea bass with a leek sauce. As on most elegant French menus, tournedos appear in their own juices or else layered with foie gras. We are not that enthralled with the dessert list, our dining companion complaining that the chocolate mousse brought back "memories of the nursery."

Ved Stranden 11. 𝘾 **98-13-51-33**. Reservations recommended. Main courses 119DKK–248DKK ($20–$42/£11– £22); fixed-price menus 110DKK–248DKK ($19–$42/£9.90–£22). AE, DC, MC, V. Sun–Thurs 5–10pm; Fri–Sat noon–10:30pm. Bus: 2, 12, or 13.

Restaurant Benzons 𝓡 DANISH/FRENCH   The inviting decor, summer terrace, attentive service, and finely honed cuisine make this pair of restaurants the very best on a street crammed with places to eat. The same kitchen prepares the tempting specialties served in the downstairs bistro and in the more formal upstairs restaurant. The menu, prices, and hours are the same in both. Appetizers include the best chunky lobster soup in the region, served with sour cream; sautéed Skagen shrimp; and delectable fish pâté. The main courses are prepared with equal flair, as you'll realize by savoring the roast breast of duck with Madeira sauce. The chefs also captivated our taste buds with the tender Dijon-style beef.

Jomfru Anegade 8. 𝘾 **98-16-34-44**. Reservations required. Main courses 59DKK–128DKK ($10–$22/£5.30–£12); fixed-price menus 119DKK–129DKK ($20–$22/£11–£12). AE, DC, MC, V. Daily 11:30am–11:30pm.

Restaurant Kilden 𝓡 DANISH/INTERNATIONAL   Set on the second-highest (15th) floor of the Hotel Hvide Hus, in the center of town near the bus station, this is a contemporary, stylish, and highly recommended restaurant that attracts crowds of office workers to its attractively priced luncheon buffet, and both local residents and hotel guests to its smoothly choreographed evening meals. Some of its allure derives from the views that sweep over the nearby municipal park (the Kilden Park, after which the restaurant is named) and the seacoast. Menu items are all elegant dishes, beautifully prepared by a skilled chef, using the freshest ingredients possible. Each year the chefs make their reputations anew with such classics as lobster soup or a tender, well-flavored pepper steak. The medallions of veal become a delicacy when "married" to a truffle sauce, and the roasted rack of lamb with garlic sauce almost bursts with flavor.

In the Hotel Hvide Hus, Vesterbro 2. 𝘾 **98-13-84-00**. Reservations recommended. Main courses 138DKK–168DKK ($23–$29/£12–£15); fixed-price menus 235DKK–355DKK ($40–$60/£21–£32). AE, DC, MC, V. Daily noon–10pm.

Ristorante Fellini SOUTHERN ITALIAN   Although not quite as superb as the previously recommended Il Mulino, this is another chance to break from too constant a diet of Danish food. As good as the local food is, change is always nice, or so we think as we head for this trattoria run by a hardworking staff in the center of Aalborg.

The staff comes from Campania, the region around Naples, so they are skilled in preparing succulent Mediterranean cuisine. Their display of fish and marinated vegetable antipasti is Aalborg's finest. No pasta tastes better to us than their spaghetti *con vongole* (with clams). Nightly you face a choice of fresh shellfish mingled with the catch of the day. Though the fish may come from the North or Baltic Seas, it's prepared with Italian verve, especially the risotto *alla pescator* (with both shellfish and fish) and the grilled shrimp resting on a bed of fresh radicchio. There's also a succulent version of lamb roasted with herbs and potatoes in a style perfected over the centuries by cooks in the highlands of Italy's south-central regions.

Vestergade 13. ✆ **98-11-34-55**. Main courses 139DKK–199DKK ($24–$34/£13–£18); 3-course fixed-price menu 279DKK ($47/£25). AE, DC, MC, V. Mon–Sat 11:30am–11pm; Sun 5–10pm. Bus: 1 or 2.

INEXPENSIVE

Duus Vinkjælder DANISH   The atmospheric setting alone would justify a visit here, but fortunately the snacks are also good and most affordable. This old-world 1624 cellar lies beneath one of the most famous private Renaissance mansions (Jens Bangs Stenhus), a 2-minute walk east of the cathedral. It features a selection of beer and wine (ever had Rainwater Madeira?), but it's a bit skimpy on the food. It's more of a snack restaurant and a wine bar than a full-fledged restaurant. However, you can order a plate of Danish *biksemad* (hash), a burger, or perhaps some pâté.

Østerågade 9. ✆ **98-12-50-56**. Snacks 30DKK–138DKK ($5.10–$23/£2.70–£13); wine by the glass 32DKK ($5.45/ £2.90). MC, V. Mon–Fri 11am–midnight; Sat 10am–2am.

Fyrtøjet DANISH/INTERNATIONAL   This cozy, small restaurant in the center of town never pretends to be more than what it is—an affordable food joint with competently prepared, filling dishes made with fresh ingredients. The cooks never scale any culinary heights, but we've always left here satisfied, especially after sampling the house specialty, an *almueplatte* (peasant's plate) with marinated herring, curry salad, two warm rissoles, cold potato salad flecked with fresh chives, and a deep-fried Camembert cheese with black currant jam. Sitting one night under a glass-covered courtyard, as the rains came down, our party sampled what was on each other's plates and dug into some tasty main courses that included a tender, cognac-flavored pepper steak, a savory roast breast of duck, and a freshly caught plaice stuffed with tiny Danish shrimp.

Jomfru Anegade 17. ✆ **98-13-73-77**. Reservations recommended. Main courses 100DKK–190DKK ($17–$32/£9– £17). AE, DC, MC, V. Daily 11:30am–10pm. Bus: 1, 3, 5, or 15.

Holles Vinstue DANISH   Much of the cookery here is designed to appeal to old Norsemen of the North Sea instead of foodies. We come here mainly to sample wine by the glass. In most Danish restaurants, the tax on a bottle of wine is so high that if you purchase one you'll be putting someone's kid through college. With an inviting atmosphere, welcoming a convivial crowd (often young), this combined wine bar/ restaurant combo serves the best *smørrebrød* in town until 3pm. We found that many dishes are designed to help you brace for the cold winds blowing in from the north— a platter-size Wiener schnitzel, for example, or else some "granny" stews and hashes. Lighter fare is available if you order one of the various omelets or else the filets based on the catch of the day. The location is one of the most convenient in town, lying just a 4-minute walk west of Nytorv.

Algade 57. ✆ **98-13-84-88**. Main courses 50DKK–90DKK ($8.50–$15/£4.50–£8.10); smørrebrød from 28DKK ($4.75/£2.50). Mon–Fri 11am–8pm; Sat 11am–4pm. Bus: 1, 3, or 5.

Layalina LEBANESE *Layalina* means "our pleasant nights" in Arabic. Its owners are Lebanese, and they have decorated the restaurant warmly with handmade Middle Eastern artifacts. Exotic dishes (at least by Danish standards) such as shish kebab and hummus are served in an atmosphere of genuine Middle Eastern hospitality. The house special is three brochettes with lamb, meatballs, and spicy sausage. Two other house specials include a vegetarian dish of hummus, eggplant, falafel, and sautéed cauliflower, or else chicken on a brochette flavored with a sauce with Asian spices. Although a true Lebanese might find fault with the cookery here, it comes as a wonderful change of pace for most of us after too many nights of unvarying Danish cuisine.

Ved Stranden 7–9. (© 98-11-60-56. Main courses 109DKK–179DKK ($19–$30/£9.80–£16); 2-course fixed-price menu 119DKK–139DKK ($20–$24/£11–£13); 3-course menu 129DKK–149DKK ($22–$25/£12–£13). MC, V. Mon–Thurs and Sun 5–10pm; Fri–Sat 5–11pm. Bus: 1, 4, 40, or 46.

AALBORG AFTER DARK

Hot summer days and long, mild evenings are ideal for open-air concerts of various kinds. Each year Aalborg hosts several major rock concerts in **Mølle Park,** with up to 16,000 attending. There are also rock concerts in **Skovdalen,** behind Nordjyllands Kunstmuseum, all through the summer. **Kilden Park** is also a setting for summer concerts. Information about these summer concerts becomes available at the tourist office (see "Visitor Information," earlier in this chapter) beginning in April.

The home of the Aalborg Symphony Orchestra is **Aalborg Kongres og Kultur Center,** Europa Plads 4 (© **99-35-55-55;** bus: 15), north of Kilden Park. Opera and ballet performances are also presented here. The tourist office keeps complete data on all cultural events staged here.

DANCE CLUBS

Young people gravitate to **Musik Keller,** in the basement of the previously recommended restaurant Provence, Ved Stranden 11 (© **98-13-51-33**). Neither the wildest nor the most conservative club in town, it's a bit staid by New York standards, although its DJ plays the most recent music arriving from London, Los Angeles, and elsewhere. There's never any live music, however. Admission is free, and the Keller is open Friday and Saturday 9:30pm to 6am.

Rendez-Vous, Jomfru Anegade 5 (© **98-16-88-80**), offers drinking facilities on its street level, and a dance floor upstairs, attracting university students and folks under 40. Or else head for **Cube,** Jomfru Anegade 10 (© **98-10-33-10**), a bar and dance club that's open every Friday and Saturday 11pm to 6am.

A CASINO

On the site of the Radisson SAS Limfjord Hotel, **Casino Aalborg,** Ved Stranden 14–16 (© **98-10-15-50**), offers such games of chance as American roulette, blackjack, stud poker, and the inevitable slot machines. It's open daily 7pm to 4am, charging 50DKK ($8.50/£4.50) for entrance. No one under age 18 is allowed.

3 Frederikshavn

64km (40 miles) NE of Aalborg; 381km (237 miles) NW of Copenhagen; 40km (25 miles) S of Skagen

Most visitors use Frederikshavn as a ferryboat terminus for trips to and from Norway. Playing host to some three million passengers annually, the port is the busiest international ferry terminal in all of Jutland. Unless you're passing to and from Norway, there are far more glamorous destinations in Jutland, which have already been documented.

Frederikshavn

ATTRACTIONS ●
Bangsbo Museum **13**
Cloostårnet **14**
Fiskerkylyngen **1**
Frederikshavn Kirke **4**
Krudttårnet **5**

ACCOMMODATIONS ■
Frederikshavn
  Sønabdshjem & Hotel **7**
Herman Bang Hotel **6**

Hotel Lisboa **12**
Hotel Mariehønon **2**
Hotel 1987 **10**
Park Hotel **3**
Radisson SAS Jutlandia Hotel **9**
Scandic Stena Hotel Frederikshavn **8**

DINING ◆
Gastronomen **3**
Restaurant Bacchus **11**
Restaurant Grå-Ander **9**

There is a good chance you'll be passing through this town—briefly, at least. Because it's such a vital link for so many passengers, we're including information about this port of some 26,000 people, the largest town in North Jutland north of Aalborg.

A relatively young town, it has a number of attractions but few historic sites. At first glance, however, you'll think the whole town is one vast supermarket, filled with Swedes or Norwegians on shopping expeditions. Danish food products are cheaper here than they are back in Sweden or Norway.

A strong maritime aura permeates the town, and there are seven municipal harbors alone where the ferries leave or arrive from Norway and Sweden. Just north of Frederikshavn lies the fishing hamlet of Standby, where most of the famous "Frederik-shavner plaice" are landed.

In the Middle Ages the fishing settlement here was called Fladstrand. During the Thirty Years' War the site became a defense entrenchment, and in time a powder tower surrounded by a wall was erected. But it wasn't until as late as 1818 that Fladstrand was granted its municipal charter and the new name of Frederikshavn. In addition to tourists, ferry passengers, and shoppers from other Scandinavian countries, Frederik-shavn also depends on fishing to spark its economy, and is the site of such industries as iron foundries, shipbuilding, and engineering.

ESSENTIALS

GETTING THERE **By Train** Trains leave from Aalborg hourly during the day.

By Bus Frequent buses run between Aalborg and Frederikshavn.

By Car Head north from Aalborg along the E45 to Frederikshavn.

By Ferry **Stena Line** (© **96-20-02-00**), one of Europe's largest and most reliable ferryboat operators, runs the two most popular routes in and out of town. Passengers to and from Norway have the option, with or without their cars, of a daily, 9-hour ferryboat transit between Frederikshavn and Oslo. Depending on the season, pedestrians pay between 175DKK and 300DKK ($30–$51/£16–£27) each; transport of a car with its driver costs from 380DKK to 1,140DKK ($65–$194/£34–£103), depending on the season and the size of the car. Be warned in advance that southbound boats originating in Oslo depart after dark, and consequently, all passengers are required to rent an overnight cabin for the 9-hour transit. Cabins, each suitable for two passengers, rent for between 380DKK and 1,560DKK ($65–$265/£34–£140) each. Stena also maintains five ferryboats a day between the Swedish port of Gothenburg and Frederikshavn. Transit time is between 2 and 3 hours, depending on the boat, all of which are capable of transporting cars. Pedestrians pay between 125DKK and 170DKK ($21–$29/£11–£15) each way. Transport of a car with its driver, depending on the speed of the boat and the season, costs between 650DKK and 980DKK ($111–$167/£59–£88). If you're traveling with a car during the midsummer crush between mid-June and August, advance reservations are advised. Stena also operates three catamaran crossings every day that are much faster than the ferries.

VISITOR INFORMATION The **Frederikshavn Turistbureau,** Skandiatorv 1 (© **98-42-32-66;** www.frederikshavn-tourist.dk), near the ferry dock, is open January 2 to June 23 and August 21 to December 30 Monday to Friday 9am to 4pm, Saturday 11am to 2pm; June 24 to August 20 Monday to Saturday 9am to 6pm, Sunday 9am to 2pm.

SEEING THE SIGHTS

Although most of Frederikshavn is modern, the oldest part of town, **Fiskerkylyngen,** lies to the north of the fishing harbor. Here you'll encounter a number of 17th-century houses, each well preserved. You can also see a former military fortification, **Norde Skanse** (North Entrenchment), which was constructed by the troops of Wallenstein during the Thirty Years' War.

Opposite the railway station rises Frederikshavn's most famous symbol, **Frederik-shavn Kirke,** Kirkepladsen (© **98-42-05-99;** www.frederikshavnkirke.dk). Most of this church dates from 1690, although it was significantly rebuilt in 1892. Inside you can see its major attraction, an altarpiece painted by Michael Ancher, the Skagen artist. The cemetery at the church contains graves of both Allied and German soldiers killed in World War II. Admission is free, and the church is open Tuesday to Saturday 9am to noon.

You can climb the whitewashed gun tower, **Krudttårnet,** at Havnepladsen (© **98-43-19-19**), a remnant of the famed citadel that stood here in the 1600s. The tower actually stood at another place in Frederikshavn, but when the shipyards had to be expanded it was moved here instead of being torn down. The former gunpowder magazine, built of stone in 1688, has been turned into a Museum of Military History, displaying weapons from the 17th to the 19th century. Admission is 15DKK ($2.55/£1.35), free for children 17 and under. Hours are June to mid-September Tuesday to Sunday 10am to 5pm.

Another tower worth a visit is **Cloostårnet** (© **98-48-60-69**), lying 4km (2½ miles) southwest of town at an altitude of 165m (541 ft.) above sea level. This observation tower rises 60m (197 ft.) above that, offering panoramic views over the sea and the countryside of Vendsyssel. An elevator will take you to the top, and in fair weather you can see most of the surrounding district. Admission is 15DKK ($2.55/£1.35) adults or 5DKK (85¢/45p) children. Hours are May to mid-June Wednesday to Monday 1 to 5pm, Saturday and Sunday 10am to 5pm; mid-June to mid-August daily 10am to 5pm; mid-August to August 31 Wednesday to Monday 1 to 5pm. Closed the rest of the year.

Bangsbro Museum 🅚 *Kids*   One of the premier open-air museums of Jutland, this place is in a wooded area beside the Deer Park, 3km (1¾ miles) south of the town center, and contains a cluster of 18th-century buildings near the remnants of a moated 14th-century manor house. Of special interest is an old barn built in 1580, one of the oldest in Denmark, which houses antique farm equipment and implements. The main house has such curiosities as a collection of handicrafts made from human hair, a display of relics from World War II, and a nautical section including ship models, figureheads, and other mementos. An early ship, *Ellingå,* similar to the vessels used by the Vikings, is in one of the buildings. It's the reconstructed remains of a Viking-style merchant ship excavated 5km (3 miles) north of Frederikshavn. Linked to the museum is the Bangsbo Botanical Gardens, with an herb garden and a deer park, plus a playground for the kids.

Dronning Margrethesvej 6. © **98-42-31-11.** www.bangsbo-museum.dk. Admission 45DKK ($7.65/£4.05) adults, free for children 17 and under. June–Oct daily 10:30am–5pm; Nov–May Tues–Sun 10:30am–5pm.

SHOPPING

Frederikshavn is an active shopping town, with boutiques and emporiums that line both sides of the **Gågade,** one of the longest all-pedestrian streets in Denmark.

One of the most intriguing shopping possibilities, **Dot Keramik** is at Skagensvej 270, Nielstrup, Standby (© **98-48-14-10**), 7km (4⅓ miles) north of Frederikshavn. Here you'll find a wide display of hand-thrown ceramics, plus an array of applied art, gift articles, and intriguing decorations. At **Birgitte Munch** ℱ, Daanmarksgade 42C (© **98-43-80-66**), you can see the town's most talented goldsmith producing jewelry according to the best traditions of workmanship. A wide range of high-quality, locally designed jewelry is on sale.

WHERE TO STAY

In case you miss the boat and need a room, the Frederikshavn Turistbureau (see above) will book you into a private home if you'd prefer that to a hotel.

EXPENSIVE

Radisson SAS Jutlandia Hotel ℱℱ   This is the largest and the best-rated hotel in town, and as such, it's the site where members of the Danish royal family have stayed during several of their visits. It's also the closest hotel to the dock where the ferryboats pull in. The lobby, a study in high-ceilinged, 1960s-style architecture, is one of the best examples of Scandinavian design of any hotel in town. Ranging from midsize to spacious, the bedrooms are the best furnished and most comfortable in town, beginning with the cheapest—the standard doubles—and ranging upward to deluxe suites. The decor is harmonious, with a perfect match in colors and natural materials. Bathrooms are first-rate with tub/shower combos. One exceptional accommodation is the Thai Suite, the largest in the building, outfitted in carved teak-wood furniture.

Postboks 89, Havnepladsen, DK-9900 Frederikshavn. © 800-333-3333 in U.S. or Canada, or 98-42-42-00. Fax 98-42-38-72. www.radissonsas.com. 95 units. 1,160DKK ($197/£104) double; 2,460DKK ($418/£221) suite. Rates include breakfast. AE, DC, MC, V. **Amenities:** Restaurant; bar; health club; sauna; room service (7am–1am); babysitting; laundry service; dry cleaning; nonsmoking rooms; rooms for those w/limited mobility. *In room:* TV, Wi-Fi, minibar, hair dryer.

Scandic Stena Hotel Frederikshavn ℱ *Kids*   Different from all other hotels in North Jutland, this longtime favorite has a special feature, Aqualand, where you can splash your way down water slides and enjoy foaming waterfalls, summery wavelets (even in the dead of winter), and even a "water flame." Talk about family fun, no wonder kids like it so. The hotel is made even more attractive to families with its playroom with the usual—balls, building bricks, crayons, a slide—but, get this, even a cinema for kids. In the center of town, near the pedestrian shopping area and not far from the harbor, this 1987 hotel, one of the largest hotels in Denmark outside of Copenhagen, is not as fancy or as highly rated as the Jutlandia. Rooms are well furnished and well maintained; and some can be converted into three- or four-bed accommodations, so the Stena has long been a favorite with families. All the bedrooms come with tiled private bathrooms with tub or shower. Good food is served in the hotel's premier dining room, **Det Gulge Pakhus,** or you can dine more informally in the **Brasserie Søhesten.**

Tordenskjoldsgade 14, DK-9900 Frederikshavn. © **98-43-32-33.** Fax 98-43-33-11. www.scandic-hotels.com. 215 units. 1,095DKK–1,895DKK ($186–$322/£99–£171) double; 1,495DKK–2,295DKK ($254–$390/£135–£207) suite. AE, DC, MC, V. **Amenities:** 2 restaurants; bar; nightclub; indoor heated pool; gym; sauna; children's playroom; 24-hr. room service; massage; laundry service; dry cleaning; nonsmoking rooms; rooms for those w/limited mobility. *In room:* A/C, TV, dataport, minibar (some units), hair dryer, trouser press, iron.

MODERATE

Frederikshavn Sømandshjem & Hotel *(Kids)* *(Value)* Everyone from families on vacation to sailors check into this hotel offering one of the best deals in town. In the center of town, near the shopping area and close to the harbor, this old-fashioned hotel was founded in 1880 as the Seamen's Mission. However, restored in 2003, it offers some of the best lodgings for your kroner in town. Many of its functionally furnished bedrooms can be converted into three- or four-bed rooms suitable for families, although this hotel is hardly the family favorite that the Scandic Stena (see above) is. The restaurant serves good Danish food of the meat-and-potatoes-with-gravy variety.

Tordenskjoldsgade 15B, DK-9900 Frederikshavn. © **98-42-09-77.** Fax 98-43-18-99. www.fshotel.dk. 47 units. 775DKK–950DKK ($132–$162/£70–£86). Rates include breakfast. AE, DC, MC, V. **Amenities:** Restaurant; laundry service; dry cleaning; nonsmoking rooms. *In room:* TV, hair dryer.

Hotel Lisboa Outfitted in a blue-and-white color scheme, and with polished stone floors of the type you might expect in a hotel in Portugal, this hotel was named in honor of a holiday that its founders had taken in Lisbon just before the hotel's construction in 1958. In 1978, it was enlarged with an annex. In many hotels, the annex contains less desirable rooms, but in the case of the Lisboa they are larger, more modernized, and better furnished. With good views of the sand dunes and the beach, it appeals to a nature-loving, escapist crowd year-round. Rooms are spartan and uncomplicated, with comfortable but strictly functional furniture. Each accommodation comes with a small bathroom with shower. Public areas and the restaurant are outfitted with the blue-and-white abstract paintings of Danish artist Peder Meinert.

Søndergade 248, DK-9900 Frederikshavn. © **98-42-21-33.** Fax 98-43-80-11. www.lisboa.dk. 32 units. 750DKK–850DKK ($128–$145/£68–£77) double. Rates include breakfast. MC, V. From Frederikshavn, take bus no. 1, 2, 3, or 4. **Amenities:** Restaurant; bar. *In room:* TV, hair dryer.

Hotel 1987 Check in here for the price—not for any great luxury or glamour. "Danish modern" is taken a bit to the extreme here—just how functional can furniture get? This hotel was configured from a 130-year-old marine warehouse in 1987— hence its name. Today, only the symmetrical yellow facade and massive interior beams and trusses remain from the original construction. Rooms are comfortable, cozy, and snug, each equipped with a small, shower-only bathroom. The staff is helpful, and although the hotel serves only breakfast, it's not far from the bars and restaurants of the rest of the town.

Damsgaards Plads 8E, DK-9900 Frederikshavn. © **98-43-19-87.** Fax 98-43-19-42. www.hotel1987.dk. 28 units. 600DKK–750DKK ($102–$128/£54–£68) double. Rates include breakfast. AE, DC, MC, V. **Amenities:** Breakfast room. *In room:* TV, minibar.

Park Hotel *(F)* An atmospheric choice with a certain charm, this hotel was built in 1880 in a combination Old French and Old English style. Many of the handsomely furnished midsize rooms have marble bathrooms. Only the suites have tubs in the bathrooms; the doubles contain only showers. The Park is known for its gourmet restaurant, **Gastronomen,** which serves an international cuisine (see "Where to Dine," below). The hotel doesn't just wait until dinner to feed you well; we found its breakfast buffet the most bountiful in town. In fair weather (not guaranteed in Denmark) breakfast—or even dinner on a warm summer night—can be served in a courtyard. On our last visit, we could imagine we were in the south of France.

Jernbanegade 7, DK-9900 Frederikshavn. ☎ **98-42-22-55**. Fax 96-20-17-98. www.parkhotelfrederikshavn.dk. 30 units, 20 with bathroom. 590DKK ($100/£53) double without bathroom; 990DKK ($168/£89) double with bathroom; 1,490DKK ($253/£134) suite. Rates include breakfast. AE, DC, MC, V. **Amenities:** Restaurant; bar; 24-hr. room service; laundry service; dry cleaning; nonsmoking rooms. *In room:* TV, minibar, hair dryer, iron, safe.

INEXPENSIVE

Herman Bang Hotel ⓡ ⓥalue   Over the years we've spent many a comfortable night here waiting for a ferryboat headed in the morning for Norway. As the Hoffmann Hotel, it was founded in 1882 and is today the oldest hotel in town. The hotel is now named for the well-known author Herman Bang, who used to be a frequent visitor back in the days when the hotel was a bohemian hangout, attracting writers and painters. Until 1999 the hotel was owned by the Stena shipping line.

Under new management, the hotel not only experienced a name change but a wholesale renovation, making it better than it ever was in its past. The midsize bedrooms are attractively furnished and maintained, each with a tiled bathroom with shower. As a grace note, the private bathrooms are candlelit and you can recline in luxurious comfort, using the aromatic oils and stimulating mineral salts. That's not all— the hotel has the best spa facilities in town, both indoor and outdoor. The spa is aptly named "Seventh Heaven." On-site is a good family-style restaurant that offers not only breakfast but lunch and dinner inspired by both American and Italian cuisine.

Tordenskjoldsgade 1, DK-9900 Frederikshavn. ☎ **98-42-21-66**. Fax 98-42-21-07. www.hermanbang.dk. 54 units, 39 with bathroom. 495DKK–695DKK ($84–$118/£45–£63) double without bathroom; 695DKK–895DKK ($118–$152/£63–£81) double with bathroom; 1,395DKK–1,795DKK ($237–$305/£126–£162) suite. Rates include breakfast. AE, DC, MC, V. **Amenities:** Restaurant; spa. *In room:* TV, hair dryer, iron.

Hotel Mariehønen   More people come here to dance at the bar, Sussi & Leo, to recorded music than they do to stay in the rooms. But if you've danced yourself out, you can sleep in comfort at an affordable price here. This hotel is among the most convenient in town, only 5 minutes from the ferry terminal and 3 minutes from the train depot. Most of its guests are passengers waiting overnight to catch ferries to Oslo or Gothenburg. A family-run hotel, Mariehønen offers rooms that are basic, functionally although comfortably furnished, and well maintained, some coming with a small bathroom with shower. There's no restaurant, but there are several places to eat nearby.

Scoolagade 2, DK-9900 Frederikshavn. ☎ **98-42-01-22**. Fax 98-43-40-99. www.hotelmariehoenen.dk. 32 units, 18 with bathroom. 390DKK–525DKK ($66–$89/£35–£47) double without bathroom; 490DKK–725DKK ($83–$123/£44–£65) double with bathroom. Rates include buffet breakfast. AE, DC, MC, V. **Amenities:** Restaurant; bar (w/dancing). *In room:* TV.

WHERE TO DINE

EXPENSIVE

Gastronomen ⓡⓡⓡ FRENCH   Long known for its cuisine, this gourmet restaurant has an engaging appeal and infectious charm. The food is several notches above that of a typical French bistro, relying on quality ingredients served in formal, traditional surroundings. The menu lists an exciting assemblage of food, often served in perfect combinations, such as the Norwegian lobster with asparagus, or the grilled filet of beef in a velvety smooth tarragon sauce. As a nouvelle dish, the grilled tenderloin of veal appears with chanterelles and a raspberry sauce. Old Danish tradition is followed with the fried plaice with white potatoes and parsley, but you can try more daring innovations as well, like the light and tasty watercress soup with champagne. Marinated salmon with freshly chopped herbs is always welcome, and the fish of the day is usually your safest bet. For your grand finale, opt for the walnut nougat cake with rhubarb purée or some other concoction of the day, or else settle for a dish of sorbet or perhaps a selection of cheese.

In the Park Hotel, Jernbanegade 7. ℂ 98-42-22-55. Reservations required. Main courses 158DKK–198DKK ($27–$34/£14–£18); 2-course fixed-price menu 258DKK ($44/£23); 3-course fixed-price menu 328DKK ($56/£30). AE, DC, MC, V. Mon–Sat 7am–10pm.

Restaurant Grå-Ander 🐦🐦 *Finds* FRENCH   Under the new policy of the "Gray Duck," only fixed-price menus are offered, and they're among the best and most finely honed in the area, rivaling but not topping the food at Gastronomen. This is one of the best-recommended dining rooms in Frederikshavn, with a reputation that the managers of the Hotel Jutlandia work hard to maintain. There's room inside for only 34 diners, who enjoy their meal in a dining room with windows overlooking the blue-gray expanse of the sea. Menu items are based on inspirations from France, and might include such starters as a seafood cocktail, a spinach crepe, or smoked duck breast. Two dishes to rave about include lemon sole in a ragout of mussels and curried cream, and quail with foie gras and a red-wine flambé. Dessert might be a raspberry Napoleon with a honey parfait and chocolate sauce. The staff are justifiably proud of their food and the service they provide, which are both excellent. There are many luxury ingredients on the menu but prices are not as daunting as you might fear.

In the Hotel Jutlandia, Havnepladsen. ℂ 98-42-42-00. Reservations recommended. Fixed-price 2-course menu 178DKK ($30/£16); 3-course menu 208DKK ($35/£19); 4-course menu 228DKK ($39/£21). AE, DC, MC, V. Mon–Sat 6–10pm.

INEXPENSIVE

Restaurant Bacchus MEXICAN/ITALIAN   View this more as a place for food on the run between ferryboat stopovers than as a venue for serious dining. Set near the harbor within a simple building dating from the 1850s, this is an unassuming, unpretentious bistro. Although there's a well-chosen wine list, it's a lot less comprehensive than you might assume from the restaurant's name. Within an old-fashioned dining room with only 40 seats, you can order such standard fare as pizza, succulent pastas, burritos, and a spicy chili con carne.

Lodsgade 8A. ℂ 98-43-29-00. Reservations recommended. Main courses 95DKK–160DKK ($16–$27/£8.55–£14); fixed-price dinner 75DKK–210DKK ($13–$36/£6.75–£19). AE, DC, MC, V. Mon–Sat 5–10pm.

FREDERIKSHAVN AFTER DARK

In Frederikshavn, nightlife simmers away in quiet, not particularly demonstrative ways, most visibly at the **John Bull Pub,** Havnepladsen (ℂ **98-42-42-00**), a clone of an English pub adjacent to the Jutlandia Hotel.

4 Skagen 🌟🌟

104km (65 miles) NE of Aalborg; 485km (301 miles) W of Copenhagen

Since the 19th century, Skagen—pronounced *skane*—has been the leading artists' colony of Denmark. As is inevitable in such cases, hordes of tourists followed in the footsteps of the artists to discover the northernmost tip of Jutland on its east coast. A sort of "bony finger" of land points into the North Sea at the second-biggest fishing port in Denmark.

"It was the light that first drew me here," said Phil Burton, an expat artist from Wales. "It's always mystical, even purple-peach at times, but always radiant. This special light can't be described—you must see it for yourself—but it imbues each of my paintings. It's inspired dozens of artists, even poets."

We find the combination today of Nordic sailors—Skagen has been a fishing port for centuries—and a colony of artists an intriguing mix. At least the two disparate elements make for lively conversation in the bars. The early artists were more isolated here, but the coming of the railway in 1890 opened up Skagen to the world with its link to the terminus of Frederikshavn.

By the end of July, the visitors are in retreat, and Skagen happily reverts to the locals again. We've spent hours here in both September and October wandering the heather-covered moors, the undulating stretches of dunes, and some of the best, but not the warmest, beaches in Europe. We particularly like to stand at the point where the North Sea meets the Baltic, the subject of countless landscape paintings. It's not unknown to have visitors applaud the spectacular sunsets here.

One of the founders of the Skagen School of Paintings, the poet and artist Holger Drachmann (1846–1908), once said, "Unlike so much of the rest of Europe, Skagen still retains its soul."

ESSENTIALS

GETTING THERE **By Car** Take the E45 northeast to Frederikshavn. From there, head north on Route 40 to Skagen.

By Train Several trains a day run from Copenhagen to Århus, where you connect with another train to Frederikshavn. From Frederikshavn there are 12 daily trains to Skagen.

VISITOR INFORMATION The **Skagen Turistbureau** is at Vestre Strandvej 10 (© **98-44-13-77;** www.skagen-tourist.dk). Open January 3 to March 31 and November 1 to December 23 Monday to Friday 10am to 4pm, Saturday 10am to 1pm; April, May, and August 29 to October 30 Monday to Friday 9am to 4pm, Saturday 10am to 2pm; June 1 to 26 and August 1 to 28 Monday to Saturday 9am to 5pm, Sunday 10am to 2pm; and June 27 to July 31 Monday to Saturday 9am to 6pm, Sunday 10am to 4pm.

SEEING THE SIGHTS

Since it opened in 1907, **Skagen Havn** (Skagen Harbor) ♠ has been one of the major attractions of the town. It's seen at its best when the boats come back to land their catches (times vary). For early risers, the fish auction at the crack of dawn is a popular attraction. Mid-May to mid-October, the oldest part of the harbor is a haven for the boating crowds centered around one of the marinas. Many yachting people in Jutland use Skagen as their favorite harbor haven.

Gammel Skagen (Old Town) ♠ lies 2.5km (1½ miles) from Skagen Havn. Signs point the way. Originally Gammel Skagen was the fishing hamlet—that is, until Skagen Havn opened in 1907. Today, Gammel Skagen is a little resort town with large beach hotels that are mainly timeshares.

An attraction worth exploring is **Rådjerg Mile,** a migrating dune moving at the rate of about 11m (36 ft.) annually. Located 16km (10 miles) south of town, it can be reached via Kandestederne. This dune was formed on the west coast in the 16th century during the great sand drift that characterized the landscape until the 20th century. The dune continues to move yearly, eastward toward the forest.

Den Tilsandede Kirke (Sand-Buried Church)   This church buried in sand dunes 1.5km (1 mile) south of town is an amusing curiosity. The only part that's visible is the upper two-thirds of the tower. When Hans Christian Andersen visited in 1859, he called the church "The Pompeii of Skagen." The only things hidden under the dunes are the remnants of a wall and the old floor and perhaps the baptismal font. By 1775, the church had fallen into disrepair and was used by fewer and fewer members. By 1795 it was closed down, and in 1810 it was partly demolished, the stones sold to people in the area as building materials for their private houses. Today red stakes in the ground indicate the placing and extent of the nave and vestry.

(ⓒ) **98-44-43-71.** Admission 10DKK ($1.70/90p) adults, 5DKK (85¢/45p) children 5–12. June–Aug daily 11am–5pm; Sept–May Sat–Sun 11am–5pm.

Drachmanns Hus   Built in 1828, the house was home to poet and artist Holger Drachmann until his death in 1908. Now a museum, it's filled with mementos of the artist. On his first visit to Skagen in 1872, he fell in love with the village and its surroundings—"Here there is sand, more sand, nothing but sand. And then, here there is the sky with large floating clouds, and finally the sea, Kattegut's shining surf on one side and the distant roar of the North Sea on the other." Following many illnesses and professional disappointments, Drachmann died and was buried in the sand dunes around Skagen.

Han Baghsvej 21. (ⓒ) **98-44-51-88.** Admission 25DKK ($4.25/£2.25) adults, free for children under 15. June 1–14 and Sept 16–Oct 16 Sat–Sun 11am–3pm; June 15–Aug 15 daily 10am–5pm; Aug 16–Sept 15 daily 11am–3pm. Closed Oct 17–May.

Michael og Anna Ancher Hus 𝄢   If you visit the Skagens Museum (see below), you will see work by talented artists Michael and Anna Ancher, who originally purchased this house back in 1884. After their daughter, Helga, died in the 1960s, it was converted into a museum of their work. It's preserved rather like it was in the lifetime of these artists. Michael painted the doors throughout the house, and some 240 paintings by all three family members adorn the walls. In the parlor the antique oil lamps and the lace curtains speak of a time long ago. Bathed in the fabled light of Skagen, Anna's studio still contains the easel she abandoned upon her death.

Markvej 2–4. (ⓒ) **98-44-30-09.** Admission 50DKK ($8.50/£4.50) adults, free for children 3–13. May–Sept daily 10am–5pm; Apr and Oct daily 11am–3pm; Feb–Mar and Nov Sat 11am–3pm. Closed Dec–Jan.

Skagen By- & Egnsmuseum (Skagen Open-Air Museum)   This museum, a 15-minute stroll from the train depot, is evocative of a time long gone. The lifesaving station here reminds us of how the seas sometimes violently clash in the depths of winter, as demonstrated by the dramatic photographs of ships and men in distress. In this open-air museum, the homes of both well-to-do fishermen and their poorer cousins were moved here to demonstrate how life was lived in Skagen from 1830 to 1880. A maritime museum is filled with nautical memorabilia, and an original Dutch windmill is all that's left of the many that used to dot the landscape.

P. K. Nielsensvej 8–10, Fortidsminderne. (ⓒ) **98-44-47-60.** www.skagen-bymus.dk. Admission 35DKK ($5.95/£3.15); free for children 17 and under. May–June and Aug–Sept Mon–Fri 10am–4pm, Sat–Sun 11am–4pm; July Mon–Fri 10am–5pm, Sat–Sun 11am–4pm; Mar–Apr and Oct Mon–Fri 10am–4pm; Nov–Feb Mon–Fri 11am–3pm.

Skagens Museum 😊😊😊 *(Finds)*   The glory days of the artists of the Skagen School of painting live again at this impressive museum. The apogee of their art was created from the beginning of the 1870s until the turn of the 20th century. The Skagen artists were inspired by naturalism and open-air painting, their favorite motif being the fishermen working on local beaches or else their quaint cottages. The artists came to celebrate the North Sea landscape, everything bathed in that special light that seems to exist in Skagen.

The major artists of this period included Michael Ancher (1849–1909) and his wife, Anna Ancher (1859–1935). You'll also see works by another of the school's leading paintings, P. S. Krøyer (1851–1909), plus many more—the entire collection consists of 1,800 paintings, sculptures, drawings, and graphic works. The museum opened its doors in 1928 but with only 325 works of art.

Brøndumsvej 4. (© **98-44-64-44**. www.skagensmuseum.dk. Admission 60DKK ($10/£5.40), free for children 17 and under. May–Sept daily 10am–5pm; Apr and Oct Tues–Sun 11am–4pm; Nov–Mar Wed–Fri 1–4pm, Sat 11am–4pm, Sun 11am–3pm.

Nordsømuseet 😊😊😊   The denizens of the deep who live in the North Sea come alive for you here in the town of Hirtshals. The main attraction of this two-story Oceanarium is the giant aquarium itself, containing some 4.5 million liters of seawater. Visitors can gaze upon an 8m-high (26-ft.) column of water or view the "ocean" through an aquarium window, the thickest in the world.

The large aquarium has been designed to house fish of the North Sea. Through the huge windows viewers can watch fascinating schools of herring, mackerel, gar, and horse mackerel, and see them react as predatory fish approach. Among other large creatures, several species of North Sea sharks can be viewed. Each day divers feed the shoal fish and the sharks and describe life in the aquarium to visitors.

The museum is devoted to modern Danish sea fishing, detailing man's exploitation of the North Sea—for better or worse. Displays of the daily lives of fishermen, equipment, and vessels are placed alongside exhibits depicting the resources of the North Sea. Seals are common along the coast of Denmark, but you seldom spot them. However, in the on-site seal pool, you can observe the animals at close range—above as well as underwater. Feeding times for the seals are daily at 11am and 3pm.

Willemoesvej, Hirtshals. (© **98-94-44-44**. www.nordsoemuseet.dk. Admission 110DKK ($19/£9.90) adults, 55DKK ($9.35/£4.95) children 3–11, free for children under 3. July–Aug daily 10am–6pm; Sept–June daily 10am–5pm. From Skagen take Rte. 40 south to the junction with Rte. 597 heading west into Hirtshals, a distance of 50km (31 miles).

SHOPPING

Since so many artists live in Skagen, many visitors purchase art here. The best gallery is **Galerie Skagen,** Trondsvej 16 (© **98-44-44-25**), which also has a tasteful collection of handicrafts. The most sophisticated collection of pottery is found at **Skagen Potteri,** Skt. Laurentivej 27 (© **98-44-69-29**). Stunningly designed modern jewelry is sold at **Smykkekunstner,** Sct. Laurentivej 48 (© **98-44-11-08**), in Gammel Skagen. Some of Jutland's finest glass pieces—often works of art—are on display and for sale at **Skagen Glasværksted,** Sct. Laurentivej 95 (© **98-44-60-50**).

WHERE TO STAY

Color Hotel Skagen 😊 *(Finds)*   This is more of a place to settle in for 2 or 3 days for a beach holiday, exploring the North Sea coast, than for an in-and-out overnight stopover. Southwest of Skagen, beside the only road leading into town from the rest of Jutland, this sprawling, one-story hotel lies 2km (1¼ miles) from the sea. Alone on sandy flatlands, it possesses an almost otherworldly sense of isolation. Unlike many of its competitors, which cater to families with children, this place appeals mostly to couples. Built in 1969, the hotel has a formal restaurant. The spacious, attractively furnished guest rooms contain hardwood floors, padded armchairs, and big windows. Each unit also contains neatly kept bathrooms with tub/shower combos. Of the accommodations, 45 are listed as apartments, which are rented only for 3 days at a time except during midsummer, when they are rented per week.

Gammel Landevej 39, DK-9990 Skagen. © 98-44-22-33. Fax 98-44-21-34. www.skagenhotel.dk. 153 units. 950DKK–1,395DKK ($162–$237/£86–£126) double; 1,695DKK–2,395DKK ($288–$407/£153–£216) suite; 6,500DKK–9,900DKK ($1,105–$1,683/£585–£891) apt per week. AE, DC, MC, V. From Skagen, drive 2km (1¼ miles) southwest along Rte. 40. **Amenities:** Restaurant; bar; outdoor heated pool; fitness center; sauna; 24-hr. room service; nonsmoking rooms; rooms for those w/limited mobility. *In room:* TV, dataport, hair dryer, safe.

Finns Hotel Pension   Originally built in 1909 in a style that the owner refers to as "a Norwegian wood house," this old-fashioned Danish homestead is designed like houses that Scandinavian immigrants made popular during the 19th century in American states such as Minnesota. In a residential neighborhood of Skagen, a 10- to 15-minute walk northeast of center and a 3-minute walk from the beach, it's furnished with old furniture and antiques. Many rooms have beamed ceilings and a charming but vaguely claustrophobic allure. Our only warning involves a rigidity on the part of the hardworking managers and staff, who establish very clear-cut rules for new arrivals; they aren't noted for their flexibility, and maintain an aggressive "take it or leave it" approach to their unique hotel. If you give advance notice, they'll prepare a three-course evening meal, which is served only to residents, for a price of 300DKK ($51/£27) per person. If you agree to this, on pain of severe reproach, don't be late for dinner. Children 14 and under are not accepted.

Østre Strandvej 63, DK-9990 Skagen. © 98-45-01-55. Fax 98-45-05-55. www.finnshotelpension.dk. 6 units, 3 with bathroom. 950DKK ($162/£86) double with bathroom; 675DKK–825DKK ($115–$140/£61–£74) double without bathroom. Rates include breakfast. MC, V. Closed Oct–Mar. **Amenities:** Dining room. *In room:* No phone.

Ruth's Hotel 🌟🌟🌟   This is a bastion of both comfort and gastronomy—its restaurant, in fact, is one of the greatest outside Copenhagen. Located in the sand dunes of Old Skagen, it stands by the beach just 4km (2½ miles) from the center of modern Skagen. It takes its name from its founders, Emma and Hans Christian Ruth. The bedrooms are superior to anything at Skagen, beautifully furnished and designed, exuding spaciousness and light. Each comes with a private tiled bathroom with a tub/shower combo, and some units even have a Jacuzzi. A private balcony or terrace opens onto a view of the sea.

The spa is one of the best in Jutland, complete with solarium, sauna, Turkish baths, therapy pool, and gym. The hotel restaurant, **Ruth's Gourmet,** is one of the top five in the country outside of Copenhagen, yet we hesitate to recommend it because it requires reservations a month in advance. If you're lucky enough to get a table, you'll be rewarded with Chef Michel Michaud's repertoire of sublime dishes, which embrace the best of fine French cuisine and tradition, with a carefully chosen wine carte. You stand a better chance of dining on the airy, sunlit terrace of the on-site Brasserie; the food here is watched over by Chef Michaud himself.

Hans Ruths Vej 1, Gammel Skagen, DK-9990 Skagen. © 98-44-11-24. Fax 98-45-08-75. www.ruths-hotel.dk. 26 units. 1,625DKK–1,975DKK ($276–$336/£146–£178) double; from 1,875DKK ($319/£169) suite. AE, DC, MC, V.

Amenities: Restaurant; brasserie; bar; heated indoor pool; gym; spa; limited room service; laundry service. *In room:* TV, Wi-Fi, hair dryer.

Strandhotellet/Strandhuset ⊀   This hotel at Gamle Skagen is for wild romantics who like the wind from the North Sea blowing through their hair. Built in 1912 as a holiday home, it lies only a stone's throw from the sea and incorporates the dunes and buildings of a historic farm into the main building. The compound also contains four other outbuildings, each with an individual atmosphere. The newest addition is Strandhuset, which was built in the 1990s with a prominent hip roof. The suites with kitchens within Strandhuset are evocative of a tasteful private summer home. The suites have tub/shower combos, the regular doubles coming with shower. Everything has a warm, cozy atmosphere, helped along by the original works of art on the walls, the wicker furnishings, and the painted wood furnishings. Breakfast is served within a semicircular greenhouse-style extension jutting out from one end of the house.

Jeckelsvej, Gammel Skagen, DK-9990 Skagen. ⓒ **98-44-34-99**. Fax 98-44-59-19. www.strandhotellet.glskagen.dk. 14 units, 6 suites with kitchenette. 1,000DKK–1,700DKK ($170–$289/£90–£153) double; 1,200DKK–1,950DKK ($204–$332/£108–£176) junior suite; 1,600DKK–2,850DKK ($272–$485/£144–£257) senior suite. AE, DC, MC, V. 4km (2½ miles) south of Skagen. **Amenities:** Restaurant (summer only); bar; room service (7am–10pm). *In room:* TV, Wi-Fi, hair dryer, iron.

WHERE TO DINE

Skagen Fiske Restaurant ⊀⊀ SEAFOOD   One of the best-known fish restaurants in Jutland occupies the red-sided, gable-roofed building that was erected directly beside the harbor in 1907. You'll enter a bar on the establishment's street level, where the floor is composed of the actual beachfront—nothing more than sand. Climb to the nautically decorated dining room one floor above street level for meals. Lunches usually include flavorful platters that might contain fish cakes, Norwegian lobster, peel-your-own-shrimp, three different preparations of herring, or grilled filets of sole with lemon sauce. Dinners are more elaborate, consisting of whatever fish has been hauled in that day by local fishermen, prepared any way you specify, with virtually any sauce that's reasonably available.

Fiskehuskai 13. ⓒ **98-44-35-44**. Reservations recommended. Lunch platters 58DKK–73DKK ($9.85–$12/£5.20–£6.60); dinner main courses 255DKK–288DKK ($43–$49/£23–£26); fixed-price menus 395DKK–495DKK ($67–$84/£36–£45). AE, DC, MC, V. Daily 6–10:30pm. Closed Jan–Feb.

Appendix:
Denmark in Depth

The Danes may live in a small country, but they usually extend an enthusiastic welcome to visitors. The British novelist Evelyn Waugh called the Danes "the most exhilarating people of Europe." Few Danes would dispute this—and neither would we.

Made up mostly of islands, Denmark is a heavily industrialized nation, known for its manufactured products as well as its arts and crafts. However, it also boasts a quarter of a million farmers.

1 Denmark Today

Denmark has been called a bridge because it links northern Europe with the Scandinavian Peninsula. In 2000 that became literally true, as the Øresund Bridge opened across the sound, connecting the island of Zealand, on which Copenhagen sits, with southern Sweden, at the city of Malmö, for the first time in history.

The smallest of the Scandinavian countries (about half the size of Maine), its total land mass equals about 41,400 sq. km (16,000 sq. miles), most of which is on the peninsula of Jutland, which borders Germany. The major islands are Zealand, Funen, and Bornholm. Denmark has adequate space for its population of

5.5 million people, but its population density is much greater than that of the other Scandinavian countries. About 1.4 million Danes live in the capital city, Copenhagen, on the island of Zealand.

About 98% of all native-born Danes belong to the Danish Lutheran Church, the state church, although church attendance is actually low. The second-largest group is Catholics (30,000), and there are about 6,500 Jews.

Only 4.5% of the population is made up of immigrants, including refugees identified as Palestinians, Somalis, Bangladeshis, Kurds, and Iraqis, among others. Some immigrants, such as the Vietnamese, seem to fit smoothly into Danish life. Among

---

Fun Fact **Did You Know?**

- Denmark is a nation of nearly 500 islands.
- The reigning queen, Margrethe II, designs postage stamps, as well as opera and ballet sets.
- Second only to the Bible, the writings of Hans Christian (H. C.) Andersen are the most widely translated literary works in the world.
- Some historians argue that the fairy-tale writer Andersen wasn't the son of a poor cobbler but the child of the 19th-century Danish king Christian VIII.
- Denmark has the highest proportion of female clerics per capita.
- The country has a celebration honoring America's Fourth of July.
- Chilly Denmark used to grow grapes for winemaking in the Middle Ages.
- Danes pay the highest taxes on earth.

some members of the Muslim and Arab communities, there have been cultural conflicts—as blaring world headlines about those Danish cartoons revealed.

Technically, Denmark is a parliamentary democracy and constitutional monarchy. Its territories include the Faroe Islands (an autonomous area under the Danish Crown) and Greenland (which was granted regional autonomy in 1985). The sovereign is Queen Margrethe II, who ascended the throne in 1972; her husband is a Frenchman, Prince Henrik. Margrethe is the first woman sovereign in Denmark in 6 centuries. Real power is vested in the unicameral parliament (the *Folketing*), which citizens over the age of 23 elect every 4 years. The royal family's primary function is ceremonial.

Although it has been a NATO member since 1949, Denmark does not permit nuclear weapons to be deployed on its soil. Denmark became the first NATO country to grant women the right to serve in frontline units. It's also an active member of the European Union (but not part of the Eurozone, having voted in Sept 2000 to retain the Danish kroner), and enjoys harmonious relations with its Scandinavian neighbors and other European countries.

Denmark boasts one of the world's highest standards of living plus a comprehensive social welfare system, which is funded through extremely high taxes. Danes enjoy 7½-hour workdays, cradle-to-grave security, state-funded hospitals and schools, and a month-long vacation every year. During their vacations, Danes tend to travel extensively. By and large the Danes are extremely well educated; they have pioneered the establishment of adult education centers (for those ages 18–35), a movement that has spread to other countries of Europe.

No country in the European Union has less poverty or a fairer distribution of wealth than Denmark. Both the poor and the rich get richer, and in most cases young people have little trouble finding employment.

Although a progressive, modern, and liberal state (it was one of the first countries to recognize same-sex marriages), Denmark has its share of problems. Drug use among young people is a growing concern, and the young are increasingly rejecting the institution of marriage, with common-law relationships becoming the norm. Also, the divorce rate is rising.

The "melancholy Dane" aspect of their character (if there is one) is reflected in a relatively high suicide rate. Otherwise, their general health is excellent—a Danish girl born today has a life expectancy of 78 years; a Danish boy, 72 years.

Culturally, Denmark is an avid producer and consumer of art and culture. Some 12,000 books a year are published in Denmark. There are 42 newspapers, and the theater and film industries are thriving in spite of cutbacks in government funding.

Denmark in the late '90s built bridges to the world. On June 14, 1998, Queen Margrethe II cut a ribbon before driving across the Great Belt Bridge, a span that links the island of Zealand (on which Copenhagen sits) with the island of Funen. Because Funen is linked by bridge to Jutland (part of mainland Europe), and with Malmö across the Øresund Sound, Copenhageners can now drive to Germany or Sweden without having to rely on ferries.

Impressions

If I were a dictator, I would not occupy Denmark for fear of being laughed to death.

—John Steinbeck

Composed of a flat and sandy peninsula and a cluster of islands, Denmark is tiny. But despite its small size, its strategic position at the mouth of the Baltic has made Denmark one of the most coveted terrains in the world. Consequently, Denmark's struggles to secure its sovereignty and independence from the larger, stronger military forces that surround it on every side have repeatedly shaped Danish history. And although modern Danes are somewhat embarrassed when confronted with their country's militaristic past, Denmark used to be known as a fiercely aggressive nation, jockeying for territory, prestige, and strategic advantage with other empire-building nations such as England, Austria, and the precursors of modern-day Germany.

PREHISTORIC DENMARK & THE ROMANS

The mystery that surrounds early Denmark stems from the fact that the Romans and their legions never managed to transform it into a colony. Consequently, while former Roman provinces like France and Germany were depicted by numerous historians, including Julius Caesar himself, little was ever recorded about ancient Denmark. There is evidence of early trade. Amber found only in the Baltic has been identified within Egyptian jewelry, and some historians cite Danish trade with the Eastern Mediterranean, in which the Danes exchanged fur and slaves for bronze utensils and gold jewelry.

Concentrations of bones from various grave sites, and stone implements that archaeologists estimate at 80,000 years old, have been unearthed in regions of Jutland, but despite those discoveries, Denmark has never produced the wealth of archaeological finds that are commonplace, say, in Greece, Italy, or Egypt. Part of the reason might stem from the great ice sheets that made much of Denmark uninhabitable for thousands of years.

Later, as the ice sheets receded northward, hunter-gatherers eked out a modest living. Their communal grave sites and the stone dolmens that mark their entrances show proficiency at erecting stone lintels and markers.

Ironically, the high acid and iron content within Denmark's peat bogs has had the macabre effect of preserving the bodies of at least 160 unfortunates, all of whom died violently, in some cases many thousands of years ago, and all of whom appear to have been unceremoniously dumped into bogs. Among the most famous of these is the well-preserved, 2,400-year-old body of the Tollund Man,

Dateline

- **810** The reign of the first recorded Danish king, Godfred, ends.
- **811** The southern boundary of the Danish kingdom is established at the banks of the Eider River, where it remains for almost a thousand years.
- **800–950** Vikings emerge to plunder the monasteries and settlements of England, France, and Russia.
- **940–985** Harald Bluetooth brings Christianity to Denmark.
- **1013–43** The crowns of Denmark and England are united.
- **1104** The foundation is laid for a Danish national church that is distinctly different from that within German lands to the south.
- **1397** The Union of Kalmar, under the leadership of Queen Margrethe, unites Denmark, Norway, and Sweden. Meanwhile, high percentages of Danes are allowed to work their own farmland, forming the basis of Denmark's eventual strength as an agrarian nation.
- **1471** Sweden abandons the union; Denmark and Norway remain united under Christian I (1426–81).

(continued)

who was probably strangled to death, and whose body was discovered in the 1950s in a Jutland peat bog. His body revealed some clues about what life was like in prehistoric Denmark: A wool cap covered his head, stubble on his chin and cheeks indicated that the fashion at the time involved shaving, and the remains in his stomach showed that his last meal consisted mostly of barley.

As for literary references, other than a few cryptic comments that appear within such early English sagas as *Beowulf*, and the cryptic descriptions by the medieval Scandinavian historian Saxo Grammaticus of a long line of (otherwise undocumented) early medieval Danish warlords, there isn't a lot of documentation about post-Roman Denmark. Historians conclude that Denmark was a land of frequent migrations, frequent annihilations of one tribal unit by another, and continual changeovers of the racial texture of the peninsula as one tribe of people was either annihilated or ousted by others.

VIKINGS TERRORIZE EUROPE

Denmark developed a reputation for violence as the Vikings ravaged regions of central and southern Europe.

So ironically, the country with one of the most peaceful reputations in Europe today was originally a hell-raising land that, along with such other Viking areas as Norway and Sweden, was associated with terror for the rest of Europe. Lustfully pagan and undeterred by the belief that Christian churches and monasteries were sanctified, they exacted rich plunder from whatever monastery or convent they happened to judge as weak enough to be attractive.

Their longboats were especially feared: Measuring about 18m (60 ft.) from the dragon-shaped prow to stern, longboats were powered by 30 oars and a sail. They were still light enough, however, that their crews could drag them across land, thereby "hopping" from rivers to lakes, across sandbars, and across isthmuses that would otherwise have been unnavigable. It's no small wonder that the Danes would eventually become proficient as both mariners and traders.

Through rape and intermarriage, the Vikings mingled bloodlines with future English, French, Germans, and Russians. Despite the mayhem they unleashed on conquered lands, Vikings brought with them regimented rituals; for example, unlike most European peoples at the time, they bathed every Sunday, regardless of temperature or weather.

The most distinct threat to Danish territoriality came from Charlemagne, whose Frankish empire covered what is today France and Germany. If Charlemagne

---

- **1530** Lutheran preachers bring the Reformation to Denmark.
- **1536** After a siege of Copenhagen, most of the lands and assets owned by the Catholic Church are seized by the Danish crown.
- **1577–1648** The long reign of Christian IV brings prosperity but ends in a losing war with Sweden.
- **1675–79** The Skane War is fought, and Denmark loses

large territories to Sweden, including the "château country" of southern Sweden.
- **1801–07** England, in a black chapter of its foreign policy, bombards Copenhagen and confiscates the ships of Denmark's navy as a means of ensuring that the Danes don't cooperate with Napoleon.
- **1813** The national treasury of Denmark, faced with punitive clauses in the treaty at

the end of the Napoleonic Wars, goes bankrupt.
- **1810–30** The golden age of Danish literature, as defined by the creation of works by Søren Kierkegaard and Hans Christian Andersen.
- **1849** Simultaneous with revolutions that break out across Europe, liberal reforms are activated in the form of a new Danish constitution.
- **1866** Denmark loses Schleswig-Holstein to Prussia.

hadn't focused most of his territorial ambitions on richer, more fertile lands in central Europe and Spain, it's likely that what's known today as Denmark would have become a vassal state of the Franks. As it was, the Franks only took a slight imperial interest in Jutland. Godfred, the first recorded Danish king, died in 810 after spending most of his reign battling the Franks.

Godfred's successor, Hemming, signed a treaty with the Franks marking the Eider River, an east–west stream that flanks southern Jutland, as the southern boundary of his sovereignty. That boundary functioned more or less as the Danish border until 1864.

Two famous kings emerged from Denmark during the 10th century, Gorm the Old (883–940) and his son, Harald Bluetooth (935–85). Their reigns resulted in the unification of Denmark with power centralized at Jelling in Jutland. Harald, through the hard work of a core of Christian missionaries trained in Frankish territories to the south (especially in Hamburg), also introduced Christianity, which eventually became the country's predominant religion. As part of his attempt to obliterate Denmark's pagan past, he transformed his father's tomb, which honored a roster of pagan gods and spirits, into a site of Christian worship.

Harald eventually extended Danish influence as far as neighboring Norway. The links he established between Denmark and Norway weren't severed, at least politically, until the 1800s. Harald's son, Sweyn I, succeeded in conquering England in 1013, more than 50 years before the Norman invasion in 1066. The Normans, ironically, were also of Danish origin, through invasions several centuries before.

Under Sweyn's son, Canute II (994–1035), England, Denmark, and part of Sweden came under the rule of one crown. After Canute's death, however, the Danish kingdom was reduced to only Denmark. Canute's nephew, Sweyn II, ruled the Danish kingdom, and upon his death his five sons governed Denmark successfully. In 1104, the foundation was laid for a Danish national church that was distinct from the ecclesiastical administration in Hamburg.

THE BALTIC: A DANISH "LAKE"

The few remaining links between Denmark and the Frankish Holy Roman Empire were severed under Archbishop Eskil (1100–82) and King Valdemar I (1131–82). During a celebration at Ringsted in 1190, the Danish church and state were united, partly because of the influence of Archbishop Absalon (1128–1201),

- **1890s** Many liberal reforms in education and health insurance act as precursors of the liberal social policies of Denmark in the 20th century.
- **1914** Denmark struggles to maintain neutrality in World War I.
- **1915** A new constitution gives Denmark universal suffrage.
- **1916** Denmark sells Virgin Islands to the U.S. for $25 million.

- **1926–40** Economic depression causes great suffering in Denmark.
- **1940–45** Denmark is invaded and occupied by Nazi Germany.
- **1949** Over some protests, Denmark joins NATO.
- **1953** A new constitution provides for a single-chamber parliament.
- **1972** Denmark joins the European Economic Community; Margrethe, daughter of

Frederik IX, becomes queen of Denmark.
- **1982** Poul Schluter becomes the first Conservative prime minister since 1894.
- **1989** Denmark leads the world in certain social policies: the first NATO country to allow women in front-line military units and the first country to recognize same-sex marriages.

(continued)

"Denmark"

It was during the early Middle Ages that the name "Denmark" was introduced to the consciousness of northern Europe. The name was inspired by the word for a primitive stone and earth barricade, known as the *Dannevirk* or *Danewerk,* which was erected in an ultimately futile attempt to shut out invaders from the south.

a soldier and statesman who is honored today as the patron saint of Copenhagen. Inspired by monarchical ideas, Absalon became a fierce and militaristic guardian of Danish independence. The hostilities became a religious confrontation, pitting the Christian Danes against the pagans to the south, as well as a territorial conflict. Absalon's most dramatic disfigurement of a pagan god occurred on the now-German island of Rügen around 1147, when he chopped *Svantevit,* the four-headed wooden figure, into little pieces and distributed them as firewood among his nominally Christian soldiers.

In 1169, Denmark began what would evolve into a long series of conquests that increased its sphere of influence within city-states along the Baltic, including the ports of Estonia (which was conquered by the Danes in 1219), Latvia, eastern Germany, Poland, Sweden, and Russia. Part of Denmark's military and mercantile success derived from the general weakness of the German states to the south; part of

it was because of a population explosion within Denmark, which increased the pressure for colonization.

Valdemar II (1170–1241) strengthened Denmark's control over the Baltic and came close to transforming it into a Danish lake. Grateful for their help, he ennobled many of his illegitimate sons and empowered many of his military cohorts with aristocratic titles and rewarded them with land.

The result was a weakening of the monarchy in favor of an increasingly voracious group of nobles, whose private agendas conflicted with those of the king. Valdemar's son, Eric IV (1216–50), also known as Eric Ploughpenny, argued with church bishops and with his brothers over royal prerogatives, and was assassinated by his younger brother, Duke Abel of Schleswig, who proclaimed himself king of Denmark in 1250.

Civil wars ensued, and three of the four successive kings were killed in battle. Eric VI (1274–1319) also waged wars with

- **1992** Denmark votes against the Maastricht Treaty, which establishes the framework for the European Economic Union.
- **1993** Denmark votes to support the Maastricht Treaty and then presides over the European Union for the first half of the year.
- **1996** Copenhagen is designated the "Cultural Capital of Europe;" the "Copenhagen

'96" festival attracts artists and performers from all over the world, with more than 25,000 performances staged.
- **1998** By a narrow margin, Denmark votes to enlarge its ties with the European Union.
- **2000** Danes vote not to join the Eurozone; Øresund Bridge links the island of Zealand with Sweden.

- **2004** Crown Prince Frederik takes a bride, HRH Crown Princess Mary.
- **2005–06** Muhammad cartoons published in Denmark set off worldwide protests in the Muslim world.

Norway and Sweden, which led to Denmark's debilitation and the mortgaging of large parcels of the kingdom to pay for unsuccessful military campaigns.

Between 1332 and 1340, Denmark had no king and was ruled by an uneasy coalition of nobles. Valdemar IV Atterdag (1320–75) retained his grip on the Danish throne only by signing the peace treaty of Stralsund in 1370 with the towns of the Hanseatic League (a federation of free towns in northern Germany and adjoining countries formed around 1241 for economic advancement and mutual protection). Its enactment did a lot to improve the fortunes of the city-states of the Hanseatic League, as it granted them enviable commercial privileges. The resulting prosperity of the Hanseatic League led to architectural enhancements, whose effects were visible all around the Baltic.

A UNITED SCANDINAVIA

Valdemar IV died in 1375, leaving Denmark without a male heir. Finally, Olaf (1375–87), the infant son of Valdemar's daughter Margrethe through her marriage with King Haakon VI Magnusson (1339–80) of Norway, came to the throne. (Through a complicated chain of bloodlines, the infant Olaf was the nominal heir to all of Norway, Denmark, and Sweden.)

During Olaf's infancy, Margrethe ruled the country as regent. When both her husband, Haakon, and 12-year-old Olaf died, she was acknowledged as queen of Norway and Denmark. A patroness of the arts and a savvy administrator of the national treasury, she was eventually granted wide political leeway in Sweden.

Although the three nations had already been combined under the stewardship of Margrethe, they were merged into a united Scandinavia in 1397 as The Union of Kalmar. One of the largest political

unions since the collapse of the Roman Empire, it extended from Iceland and the fledging communities in Greenland as far east as the western coast of Finland. It included the entire Danish archipelago as well as the Faroe, Shetland, and Orkney islands.

Acknowledging her advanced age and the need for a male figurehead at the reigns of power, Margrethe arranged for her nephew, Eric of Pomerania (1382–1459), to be crowned king of all three countries as Eric VII. Margrethe, however, firmly committed to the superiority of Denmark within the trio, continued to rule behind the scenes until her death in 1412. (A contemporary historian said of Margrethe's comportment at public events, "All the nobility of Denmark were seized by fear of the wisdom and strength of this lady.") Despite later attempts to expand the Scandinavian union to northeastern Germany, the concept of a united Scandinavia was never as far-reaching or powerful as it was under Margrethe. There were many 19th- and 20th-century visionaries who hoped in vain for the eventual unification of "the three separate nations of the Scandinavian north."

Margrethe's designated heir, Eric VII, was childless. He was dethroned in 1439 and replaced by his nephew Christopher of Bavaria. His reign lasted only about 9 years, after which Sweden pressed for autonomy. It elected Karl Knutson (Charles VIII) as its Stockholm-based king in 1471. Denmark and the relatively weak Norway shared King Christian I (1426–81). Although Christian I lost control of Sweden, he did gain sovereignty over Schleswig and Holstein, ancient territories to the south of modern-day Denmark. But it was a troubled and culturally ambiguous acquisition that would vex the patience of both Denmark and the German states for centuries, as its citizens waffled in their allegiances.

Throughout the rest of the 15th century, the Danish church accumulated great wealth, and the merchant class profited from increases in agricultural production. By around 1500, about 12,000 Danes were estimated to own their own farms; about 18,000 Danes operated farms on land leased by the Danish king, and some 30,000 Danes maintained lease lands belonging to either Danish nobles or the increasingly wealthy (tax-exempt) Catholic church. Denmark became an exporter of foodstuffs, especially beef and grain, and livestock, especially horses.

The early 15th century marked a fundamental change in the definition of nobility. Prior to that, any Dane could become a noble by contributing a fully equipped private army, invariably composed of feudal-style serfs and vassals, to the king's war efforts. In exchange for this, he would be granted an exemption from all taxes generated by his estates. After around 1400, however, only nobles who could prove at least three generations of aristocratic lineage could define themselves as noble, with all the attendant privileges that such a title implied. With no new blood coming into the pool of Danish aristocrats, the number of noble families decreased from 264 to 140 between 1450 and 1650. Shakespeare borrowed the names of two of those families, the Rosencrantz and the Guildenstern, for his drama about the mythical Danish prince, Hamlet.

The 16th century also saw changes in Danish religious practice as critiques of Catholicism began to gain currency across Europe. One of Denmark's most devoted Reformation-era theologians was Paul Helgesen, a staunch opponent of the corruption of Denmark's church. He was appointed to a position of academic prominence within the University of Copenhagen in 1519 and was a particularly vocal critic of the idea of buying salvation through the sale of indulgences.

Ironically, Martin Luther's break with the Catholic Church in 1521, from a base in nearby Germany, transformed the reputation of Paul Helgesen into something of an archconservative defender of Danish Catholicism.

THE 16TH CENTURY

Christian II (1481–1559) ascended the throne in 1513. Sympathetic to the common man during his regency over the throne of Norway, he was mistrusted by conservative nobles. Their distrust was exacerbated by his commitment to seeking financial and military advice from commoners. He went so far as to turn over control of the kingdom's finances to his mistress's mother, Sigbrit Villoms, the frugal and canny widow of a Dutch burgher. A former alchemist, who claimed to have a telepathic hold over the king, she contributed to a reign alternating between bouts of genius and bouts of blood-soaked madness. Despite the massacre of more than 600 Danish and Swedish nobles in the "bloodbath of Stockholm" in 1520 and other violent atrocities, many Renaissance-style reforms were activated under Christian II's reign, without which Denmark might have erupted into full-fledged revolution.

Christian II recaptured Sweden in 1520 but was defeated by the Swedish warrior-king Gustavus Vasa a year later. Christian was deposed in 1522, whereupon he fled to the Netherlands. In the spring of 1532, he returned to Denmark, where he was incarcerated until his death, first in Sønderborg Castle and then in Kalundborg castle.

His successor, Frederik I (1471–1533), signed a charter granting the nobility many privileges. Under his regime, the Franciscans, an order of Roman Catholic monks, were expelled from their conspicuously wealthy houses of worship, and Lutheran ministers were granted the freedom to roam throughout Denmark preaching. Upon Frederik's death, the Reformation took earnest hold within Denmark. Conflicts between Lutherans and Catholics erupted in a civil war, with Catholic power centered in Copenhagen and with Lutherans mainly based on the islands of Funen and Jutland. The war ended in 1536 with the surrender of Copenhagen. In the process, vast Catholic-owned estates were forfeited to the Danish crown.

The Danish Lutheran Church was founded in 1536 during the reign of Christian III (1534–59). Before the end of the 1570s, Protestantism was firmly entrenched within Denmark. A Danish church organized in accordance with German Lutheran models ousted virtually every trace of Catholicism. Disciples of Martin Luther were brought in to organize the new Reformed Church of Denmark, which soon took on patriotic and nationalistic overtones, as hymn books, liturgies, and sermons were eventually conducted exclusively in vernacular Danish. As for the monarchy, its finances were vastly improved at the end of the Reformation thanks to its confiscation of the vast wealth formerly controlled by the Catholic Church.

WARS WITH SWEDEN

Much of the 17th century in Denmark was consumed with an ongoing series of wars with its archenemy, Sweden. Despite that, the reign of the Danish king Christian IV (1577–1648) was one of relative prosperity. The Danes worked hard, investing time and money in the development of their "overseas territory," Norway. That territory's capital, Christiania (now known as Oslo), was named after their king.

Sweden was understandably concerned about Denmark's control of the entrance to the Baltic, the sea on which Sweden and many members of the Hanseatic League depended. Denmark, thanks to its control of the narrow straits near Copenhagen, its ownership of such Baltic islands as Ösel and Gotland, and, in the Atlantic, its control of Iceland and the Faroe Islands, could be accused of being far more imperial than its size, and present-day pacifism, would imply.

Denmark continued to meddle in German and English politics throughout the 1600s, notably in the Thirty Years' War that ripped apart the principalities of Germany.

Tensions between Denmark and Sweden also intensified during this period and were exacerbated by Sweden's emperor Charles V, who argued that Sweden held the right of succession to the Danish throne.

Sweden invaded Jutland and quickly defeated the Danes. Military scholars attribute the victory to Sweden's reliance on well-trained Swedish peasants who filled the ranks of the Swedish army. The Danes, in contrast, relied on paid, and less committed, mercenaries. By the Treaty of Christianople, Denmark was forced to cede to Sweden many of its former possessions, including scattered communities in Norway and the Baltic island of Gotland. Simultaneous with the loss of its territories in southern Sweden was the completion of two of Denmark's most-photographed castles: Frederiksborg in Hillerød and Rosenborg in Copenhagen, both finished under the regime of Christian IV.

Danish king Frederik III (1609–70) tried to regain the lost territories when Sweden went to war with Poland, but Charles X defeated him. Frederik ended up giving Sweden additional territory, including the island of Bornholm. Charles X attacked Denmark in an attempt to take control of the whole country, but this time Denmark won, regaining its lost territories. Sweden ended the war after the death of Charles X in 1660.

The Skane War (1675–79) was an ill-advised military campaign started by the Danish king Christian V (1646–99). Its outcome included Denmark's loss of Skane, a valuable territory in southern Sweden, which, because of its architectural appeal, is known today as Sweden's "château country." After the signing of the peace treaty that ended the war, Denmark managed to retain its claim on the island of Bornholm and on cities in northern Norway, such as Trondheim.

Frederik IV (1671–1730), Christian V's successor, resumed the war with Sweden in 1699. Named the Great Northern War, it raged, more or less inconclusively, from 1699 to 1730. Southern Sweden was not recovered, but part of Schleswig-Holstein (northern Germany) was ceded to Denmark by the German states.

During the 18th century, Denmark achieved many democratic reforms. Thanks to its navy and its seasoned core of merchant vessels, it also gained control of a group of islands in the West Indies (now the U.S. Virgin Islands) as well as the barren, snowy expanse of Greenland. Agriculture and trade prospered, and Copenhagen developed into a quietly prosperous but formidable guardian of the western entrance of the Baltic Sea.

THE 19TH CENTURY & THE NAPOLEONIC WARS

At the start of the Napoleonic wars, with France squarely opposed to most of the other nations of Europe, Denmark was engaged in a booming business of selling grain to both England and France. Despite the sweeping changes in the map of Europe engendered by Napoleon's military campaigns, Denmark strongly defended its right to remain neutral, and, as such, worked hard to ensure free passage of ships from other neutral nations within the Baltic.

This refusal to take sides, combined with the rich contracts that Danish merchants were able to acquire transporting supplies between hostile parties, infuriated England—the sworn enemy of Napoleon's France. In 1801, fearing that Denmark's formidable navy might be persuaded to cooperate with the French, England destroyed part of the Danish fleet in a battle at sea.

In 1807, as the threat of Napoleon's conquest of Europe became more and more of a reality, in one of the most arrogant acts of coercion in 19th-century history, England ordered the Danes to transfer their navy to British rule within 8 days or be bombarded. When the Danes refused, English warships opened fire on Copenhagen and destroyed the city's cathedral, its university, and hundreds of homes. England's treatment of Denmark forced the youthful king Frederik VI (1808–39) to ally Denmark with France and the policies of Napoleon. Later, after all of Napoleon's European allies abandoned him, Denmark remained loyal.

This led to a series of humiliating disasters for Denmark, especially when Napoleon was roundly defeated by an alliance of European countries in 1814. Because of England's embargoes on Denmark and the destruction of many Danish ships, Denmark lost control over its overseas colony of Norway, and its trade came to an almost complete standstill after the loss of its navy.

At a treaty that was signed at Kiel the same year, Denmark was forced to yield Norway to Sweden and Heligoland to England. The only remaining gems in Denmark's once-mighty empire included Greenland, Iceland, and the Faroe Islands.

Without a navy and crippled by huge debts and a loss of much of its prestige, Denmark sank into poverty. In 1813, the national treasury went bankrupt. Several years later, especially between 1818 and 1824, the price of grain virtually collapsed, which culminated in many farm failures and a massive exodus from Denmark to the New World. The country's precarious financial and military position also put a virtual end to any hope of liberal reforms.

Following the Napoleonic wars, the rulers Frederik VI and his successor, Christian VIII, formed very conservative governments. In 1848, as revolts and revolutions broke out across Europe, the Danes demanded a more liberal constitution. Representatives elected under a new constitution that was signed on June 5, 1849, tempered the absolute rule of the Danish monarchs.

The liberal reforms inaugurated in 1849 eventually applied to a smaller, more compact nation. In 1850, after a 2-year revolution, Schleswig-Holstein seceded from Denmark and allied itself with its German-speaking neighbor to the south, Prussia. After several years of indecisive referendums, military interventions, and the politicking of such European nations as Austria, Schleswig-Holstein was ceded to Prussia in 1866 under the Treaty of Prague.

On July 28, 1866, a new constitution was adopted, but it was more conservative than the earlier one (1849), and granted more power to those who paid the highest taxes—in other words, the landowners.

Throughout the rest of the 19th century, Denmark's conservatives struggled against reform-minded liberals. Conservatives pledged to build up trade incentives and military fortifications around Copenhagen. In the event of war, liberals argued, most of the Danish countryside would be sacrificed to the invaders, and only Copenhagen would be defended.

Members of the left favored social reforms, a downsizing of the Danish army, and an official allegiance to political neutrality. Despite opposition, a process of liberalization continued apace

with the changes wrought by the Industrial Revolution. In 1891, a system of old-age pensions was introduced; in 1892 came an early form of health insurance; and in 1899, funds were allocated for the acquisition of farmland by individuals who qualified for assistance from the Danish government.

WORLD WAR I & ECONOMIC CHAOS

When World War I broke out, Denmark found itself on a razor's edge and struggled to remain neutral, but its position astride the shipping lanes favored by both England and Germany made this especially perilous. On August 14, 1914, Germany laid mines in the sea channels of southern Denmark and then strongly implied that Denmark would be well advised to lay other mines in the channels leading toward Copenhagen. Fearing that if they didn't comply, Germany would lay the mines anyway and then commandeer parcels of Danish soil for installation of German naval bases, Denmark began laying mines.

Danish king Christian X had the unfortunate task of phoning his cousin, the king of England, about the situation. England agreed not to interpret Denmark's action as a direct act of hostility. Consequently, all the waters around Denmark were peppered with high-powered explosives, a situation that had a disastrous effect on Danish trade and the Danish treasury. Later, German U-boats sank at least 30% of Denmark's merchant fleet.

Eventually, through cooperation and joint commitments with Sweden and Norway, Denmark managed to retain its fragile hold on wartime neutrality, but at a high price in terms of unemployment, higher taxes, and endless neuroses and self-doubts.

Partly in reaction to the traumas of their untenable situation, the Danes signed a new constitution on June 5, 1915, establishing a two-chamber parliament and granting equal voting rights to men and women. In 1916, a law was passed that compelled industries to insure their workers against accidents. Also in 1916, a financially strapped Denmark concluded a treaty with the United States, selling the Danish West Indies (later known as the U.S. Virgin Islands) for $25 million.

In 1919, a land reform act resulted in the breakup of many large estates, with lands passing into the hands of greater numbers of farmers.

Because Germany was defeated in World War I, many people felt that all of Schleswig should be returned to Denmark and that the details should be hammered out during the Versailles Conference. But in an act that was later interpreted as remarkably callous, Denmark, because of its official neutrality during World War I, was not invited to the conference, despite the extreme losses its navy and merchant marine had suffered. Under pressure, the conventioneers eventually agreed to return North Schleswig, but not South Schleswig or Holstein, to Denmark.

A new treaty was drawn up between Iceland and Denmark in 1918. Although they functioned as separate, sovereign states, the two countries were united under one king, with Iceland under Denmark's protection. Danish ships were appointed as the official inspectors of Icelandic fisheries, and plans were laid for Iceland's eventual independence.

Denmark participated in the creation of the League of Nations and joined it in 1920. A crisis arose when Norway claimed jurisdiction over the territory of Greenland. However, in April 1933, the Permanent Court of International Justice granted Denmark sovereignty over Greenland, nullifying Norway's claim.

Although the Great Depression didn't begin in the United States until October 1929, Denmark was plunged into high levels of unemployment (30%) as early as 1926. Poor harvests and a 1926 tariff imposed on Danish grain by Germany, one of Denmark's largest trading partners, contributed to Denmark's fiscal woes. By 1932, a fiscal collapse of the Danish government seemed imminent. Fueled by the uncertainty, Danish branches of both the Fascist and the Nazi Parties were established by the mid-1930s, although they remained relatively small. Part of their lack of success derived from the Danish government's policy of forbidding the civilian use of any kind of uniform in public, with the exception of the Boy Scouts. As a result, no mass demonstrations in the style of what the Germans later developed into the Third Reich ever took place on Danish soil.

THE COMING OF HITLER & NAZI OCCUPATION

In May of 1939, Hitler asked Denmark to sign a nonaggression pact. Denmark accepted it; Norway and Sweden did not, and as such, any semblance of a united Scandinavian front collapsed. The pact specified that Denmark and Germany would not go to war with each other for 10 years, and that Denmark would not give aid or assistance to any nation with which Germany was at war. When war broke out in 1939, Denmark declared its neutrality. Denmark's ties with Iceland were severed, and the United States and Great Britain occupied Greenland and the Faroe Islands, respectively.

Despite the nonaggression pact, Nazi forces invaded and occupied Denmark in 1940. In 1943, Hitler sent General Hermann von Hanneken to impose martial law on Denmark and commandeered two Danish destroyers. Danish resistance continued against the German occupying forces, often in the form of sabotage of German-controlled industries and military installations. In many cases, Danish sailors scuttled their own ships to prevent them from falling under Nazi control. Danish Jews and homosexuals were arrested and sent to concentration camps beginning in 1942, but most, aided by the brave Danish people, were able to escape to Sweden. Danish civil servants tended to remain at their posts, as a means of ensuring an orderly administration of the country during terrible times.

In September 1944, many members of the Danish police, suspected (often correctly) of helping the Danish resistance, were imprisoned. The same year, a general strike among the Danes crippled Copenhagen, until the Germans accepted an uneasy compromise, and the Nazi troops became less visible in the capital.

On March 21, 1945, the Gestapo's headquarters (in what had been the Danish headquarters for Shell Oil) were demolished during an Allied air raid, sending most of the Gestapo's archives up in flames, much to the regret of later historians. Later, the Gestapo's Danish strongholds in Odense and Århus were also bombarded.

Beginning in February 1945, as the defeat of Germany appeared imminent, thousands of refugees from Germany poured across the border, seeking safety in Denmark. When Germany surrendered in 1945, British troops occupied most of Denmark. The island of Bornholm, however, was occupied by Soviet troops, who bombed parts of the island in a successful effort to dislodge the occupying Nazi forces. After the war, Denmark joined the United Nations.

POSTWAR DENMARK

After 1945, the Liberal Party under Knud Kristensen assumed control of Denmark. In 1947, Kristensen resigned. The Social Democratic Party, who governed under Frederik IX, then governed the country. The economy remained sluggish until 1948.

In 1949, Denmark joined NATO. In 1953, the Scandinavian Council was formed, composed of Denmark, Norway, Sweden, and Iceland; the council lasted until 1961. Also in 1953, Denmark adopted a new constitution, providing for a single-chamber parliament.

In 1972, Denmark became the sole Nordic member of the EEC. That same year, Queen Margrethe, born in 1940 (the year of the Nazi invasion), became queen of Denmark upon the death of her father, Frederik IX.

In 1982, Denmark seemed to abandon its long-cherished liberalism when it elected Poul Schluter, its first conservative prime minister since 1894. However, by 1989 Denmark was leading the world in the development of a liberal social agenda. It became the first NATO country to allow women to join frontline military units. Later, it became the first country to recognize marriages between partners of the same sex.

The early 1990s were dominated by Denmark's continuing debate over its role (or lack thereof) in the European Union. In 1992, Denmark rejected the Maastricht Treaty, which had established a framework for the European Economic Union. However, in a 1993 referendum Denmark reversed its position (by a close vote), voting to support the Maastricht Treaty and its own limited involvement in it. Denmark presided over the European Union for the first part of that year.

In 1993 Denmark also observed the 50th anniversary of the virtual overnight rescue of 8,000 of its Jewish citizens, who were smuggled out of the country in 1943 into neutral Sweden. That same year the Tivoli Gardens celebrated its 150th year, and *The Little Mermaid* statue, inspired by the famous character from H. C. Andersen's fairy tales, turned 80.

In 1996, Copenhagen was named the "Cultural Capital of Europe." Following in the footsteps of other European cities (including Athens, Florence, Paris, and Madrid), Copenhagen celebrated with a year of festivities. A massive campaign of restorations and new construction revitalized the city.

In May 1998, Denmark held a referendum on extending its ties and connections with the European Union. Danes, Greenlanders, and Faroese voted for enlargement of their position within EU. The margin was extremely narrow, indicating how divided Danes remain on this important issue.

Denmark had a royal wedding on May 14, 2004. His royal highness, Crown Prince Frederik, married Mary Elizabeth Donaldson. She is now HRH Crown Princess of Denmark. The wedding took place in the Copenhagen Cathedral. Copenhagen is now her address, but the Crown Princess of Denmark was born in the Australian state of Tasmania, the daughter of two educators.

When the Danish newspaper *Jyllands-Posten* in Autumn of 2005 published 12 editorial cartoons, it set off worldwide violence and protests in the Muslim world. Most of the cartoons depicted the Islamic prophet Muhammad, which is against Islamic law. Danish Prime Minister Anders Fogh Rasmussen called the controversy "Denmark's worst international crisis since World War II." Massive protests from Morocco to Indonesia led to violence. The protest also led to a boycott of Danish products in the Muslim world. Danish flags and effigies of the prime minister were burned.

3 Danish Cuisine: From *Smørrebrød* to *Rødgrød med Fløde*

Danish food is the best in Scandinavia—in fact, it's among the best in Europe.

Breakfast is usually big and hearty, just right for a day of sightseeing. It usually consists of homemade breads, Danish cheeses, and often a boiled egg or salami. In most establishments you can order bacon and eggs, two items that are well stocked here. However, you may prefer a simple continental breakfast of Danish *wienerbrød* (pastry) and coffee. The "Danish" is moist, airy, and rich.

The favorite dish at midday is the ubiquitous *smørrebrød* (open-faced sandwiches)—a national institution. Literally, this means "bread and butter," but the Danes stack this sandwich as if it were the Leaning Tower of Pisa—and then throw in a slice of curled cucumber and bits of parsley or perhaps sliced peaches or a mushroom for added color.

Two of these sandwiches can make a more-than-filling lunch. They're everywhere—from the grandest dining rooms to the lowliest pushcart. Many restaurants offer a wide selection; guests look over a checklist and then mark the ones they want. Some are made with sliced pork (perhaps a prune on top), roast beef with béarnaise sauce and crispy fried bits of onion, or liver paste adorned with an olive or cucumber slice and gelatin made with strong beef stock.

Smørrebrød is often served as an hors d'oeuvre. The most popular, most tempting, and usually most expensive of these delicacies is prepared with tiny Danish shrimp, on which a lemon slice and caviar often perch, perhaps even with fresh dill. The "ugly duckling" of the *smørrebrød* family is anything with a cold sunny-side-up egg on top of it.

For dinner, the Danes tend to keep farmers' hours: 6:30pm is common, although restaurants remain open much later. Many main-course dishes are familiar to North Americans, but they're prepared with a distinct flourish in

Denmark—for example, *lever med løg* (liver and fried onion), *bøf* (beef, in a thousand different ways), *lammesteg* (roast lamb), or that old reliable staple, *flæskesteg med rødkål* (roast pork with red cabbage).

Danish chefs are really noted for their fresh fish dishes. The tiny Danish shrimp, *rejer,* are splendid; herring and kippers are also greeted with much enthusiasm. Top-notch fish dishes include *rodspætte* (plaice), *laks* (salmon), *makrel* (mackerel), and *kogt torsk* (boiled cod).

Danish cheese may be consumed at any meal and then eaten again on a late-night *smørrebrød* at Tivoli. Danish bleu is already familiar to most people. For something softer and milder, try Havarti.

Danish specialties that are worth sampling include *frikadeller,* the Danish meatballs (prepared in various ways); a Danish omelet with a rasher of bacon covered with chopped chives and served in a skillet; and Danish hamburger patties topped with fried onions and coated with a rich brown gravy.

Two great desserts are Danish apple Charlotte, best when decorated with whipped cream, dried bread crumbs, and chopped almonds; and *rødgrød med fløde*—basically a jellied fruit-studded juice, served with thick cream.

As for drinks, Carlsberg and Tuborg beer are Denmark's national beverages. A bottle of Pilsener costs about half the price of a stronger export beer with the fancy label. Value-conscious Danes rely on the low-priced *fadøl* (draft beer); visitors on a modest budget might want to do the same.

You may gravitate more toward *akvavit* (schnapps), which comes from the city of Aalborg in northern Jutland. The Danes, who usually drink it at mealtime, follow it with a beer chaser. Made from a distilling process using potatoes, it should be served only icy cold.

For those with a daintier taste, the world-famous Danish liqueur, Cherry Herring, is a delightful drink; made from cherries, as the name implies, it can be consumed anytime except with meals.

Index

See also Accommodations index below.

ACCOMMODATIONS

FROMMER'S® COMPLETE TRAVEL GUIDES

Alaska
Amalfi Coast
American Southwest
Amsterdam
Argentina & Chile
Arizona
Atlanta
Australia
Austria
Bahamas
Barcelona
Beijing
Belgium, Holland & Luxembourg
Belize
Bermuda
Boston
Brazil
British Columbia & the Canadian Rockies
Brussels & Bruges
Budapest & the Best of Hungary
Buenos Aires
Calgary
California
Canada
Cancún, Cozumel & the Yucatán
Cape Cod, Nantucket & Martha's Vineyard
Caribbean
Caribbean Ports of Call
Carolinas & Georgia
Chicago
China
Colorado
Costa Rica
Croatia
Cuba
Denmark
Denver, Boulder & Colorado Springs
Edinburgh & Glasgow
England
Europe
Europe by Rail
Florence, Tuscany & Umbria

Florida
France
Germany
Greece
Greek Islands
Hawaii
Hong Kong
Honolulu, Waikiki & Oahu
India
Ireland
Israel
Italy
Jamaica
Japan
Kauai
Las Vegas
London
Los Angeles
Los Cabos & Baja
Madrid
Maine Coast
Maryland & Delaware
Maui
Mexico
Montana & Wyoming
Montréal & Québec City
Moscow & St. Petersburg
Munich & the Bavarian Alps
Nashville & Memphis
New England
Newfoundland & Labrador
New Mexico
New Orleans
New York City
New York State
New Zealand
Northern Italy
Norway
Nova Scotia, New Brunswick & Prince Edward Island
Oregon
Paris
Peru
Philadelphia & the Amish Country

Portugal
Prague & the Best of the Czech Republic
Provence & the Riviera
Puerto Rico
Rome
San Antonio & Austin
San Diego
San Francisco
Santa Fe, Taos & Albuquerque
Scandinavia
Scotland
Seattle
Seville, Granada & the Best of Andalusia
Shanghai
Sicily
Singapore & Malaysia
South Africa
South America
South Florida
South Pacific
Southeast Asia
Spain
Sweden
Switzerland
Tahiti & French Polynesia
Texas
Thailand
Tokyo
Toronto
Turkey
USA
Utah
Vancouver & Victoria
Vermont, New Hampshire & Maine
Vienna & the Danube Valley
Vietnam
Virgin Islands
Virginia
Walt Disney World® & Orlando
Washington, D.C.
Washington State

FROMMER'S® DAY BY DAY GUIDES

Amsterdam
Chicago
Florence & Tuscany

London
New York City
Paris

Rome
San Francisco
Venice

PAULINE FROMMER'S GUIDES! SEE MORE. SPEND LESS.

Hawaii

Italy

New York City

FROMMER'S® PORTABLE GUIDES

Acapulco, Ixtapa & Zihuatanejo
Amsterdam
Aruba
Australia's Great Barrier Reef
Bahamas
Big Island of Hawaii
Boston
California Wine Country
Cancún
Cayman Islands
Charleston
Chicago
Dominican Republic

Dublin
Florence
Las Vegas
Las Vegas for Non-Gamblers
London
Maui
Nantucket & Martha's Vineyard
New Orleans
New York City
Paris
Portland
Puerto Rico
Puerto Vallarta, Manzanillo & Guadalajara

Rio de Janeiro
San Diego
San Francisco
Savannah
St. Martin, Sint Maarten, Anguila & St. Bart's
Turks & Caicos
Vancouver
Venice
Virgin Islands
Washington, D.C.
Whistler

FROMMER'S® CRUISE GUIDES

Alaska Cruises & Ports of Call

Cruises & Ports of Call

European Cruises & Ports of Call

FROMMER'S® NATIONAL PARK GUIDES

Algonquin Provincial Park
Banff & Jasper
Grand Canyon

National Parks of the American West
Rocky Mountain
Yellowstone & Grand Teton

Yosemite and Sequoia & Kings
  Canyon
Zion & Bryce Canyon

FROMMER'S® MEMORABLE WALKS

London
New York

Paris
Rome

San Francisco

FROMMER'S® WITH KIDS GUIDES

Chicago
Hawaii
Las Vegas
London

National Parks
New York City
San Francisco

Toronto
Walt Disney World® & Orlando
Washington, D.C.

SUZY GERSHMAN'S BORN TO SHOP GUIDES

France
Hong Kong, Shanghai & Beijing
Italy

London
New York

Paris
San Francisco

FROMMER'S® IRREVERENT GUIDES

Amsterdam
Boston
Chicago
Las Vegas

London
Los Angeles
Manhattan
Paris

Rome
San Francisco
Walt Disney World®
Washington, D.C.

FROMMER'S® BEST-LOVED DRIVING TOURS

Austria
Britain
California
France

Germany
Ireland
Italy
New England

Northern Italy
Scotland
Spain
Tuscany & Umbria

THE UNOFFICIAL GUIDES®

Adventure Travel in Alaska
Beyond Disney
California with Kids
Central Italy
Chicago
Cruises
Disneyland®
England
Florida
Florida with Kids

Hawaii
Ireland
Las Vegas
London
Maui
Mexico's Best Beach Resorts
Mini Mickey
New Orleans
New York City

Paris
San Francisco
South Florida including Miami &
  the Keys
Walt Disney World®
Walt Disney World® for
  Grown-ups
Walt Disney World® with Kids
Washington, D.C.

SPECIAL-INTEREST TITLES

Athens Past & Present
Best Places to Raise Your Family
Cities Ranked & Rated
500 Places to Take Your Kids Before They Grow Up
Frommer's Best Day Trips from London
Frommer's Best RV & Tent Campgrounds
  in the U.S.A.

Frommer's Exploring America by RV
Frommer's NYC Free & Dirt Cheap
Frommer's Road Atlas Europe
Frommer's Road Atlas Ireland
Great Escapes From NYC Without Wheels
Retirement Places Rated

FROMMER'S® PHRASEFINDER DICTIONARY GUIDES

French

Italian

Spanish